ADVENTURE HEROES

Legendary Characters from Odysseus to James Bond

Jeff Rovin

Facts On File®

AN INFOBASE HOLDINGS COMPANY

Adventure Heroes: Legendary Characters from Odysseus to James Bond

Facts On File, Inc.
460 Park Avenue South
New York NY 10016

Library of Congress Cataloging-in-Publication Data

Rovin, Jeff.
    Adventure heroes : legendary characters from Odysseus to James
Bond / Jeff Rovin.
        p. cm.
    Includes bibliographical references and index.
    HC ISBN 0-8160-2881-8
    PB ISBN 0-8160-2886-9
    1. Heroes in mass media—Dictionaries. I. Title.
P96.H46R67 1994
700—dc20   93-46603

Jacket illustration by Vincent Di Fate
Text and jacket design by Robert Yaffe
Printed in the United States of America

VB KA 10 9 8 7 6 5 4 3 2 1
This book is printed on acid-free paper.

CONTENTS

INTRODUCTION

The first adventure hero was almost certainly the cave dweller who single-handedly slew a saber tooth tiger or saved the tribe from destruction. Told and retold, and painted on cave walls, these exploits were probably refined or expanded until they reached the level of local legend.

Many of civilization's earliest adventure heroes achieved their status thanks to a helpful poet, minstrel, or playwright. Though people such as Beowulf, Gilgamesh, and Jason may well have lived, their real-life deeds were but a shadow of the achievements song and lore have ascribed to them. And before long, the artists were doing away with the middleman, dipping into their own imaginations to create heroes who brought fire to earth, rid the world of demons, or placed the moon and stars in the sky. This book is a collection of the lives and outstanding deeds of such heroes—characters from the dawn of civilization to the present who were created to provide entertainment, hope, and examples of courage and dedication worth emulating.

This book does not include elaborately costumed superheroes or, with rare exception, men and women with supernatural or superscientific powers. We covered those characters in our previous *Encyclopedia of Superheroes.* Besides, isn't it something of an oxymoron to call a being with superpowers a hero? If you're faster than a speeding bullet and more powerful than a locomotive, where's the element of risk? When Hopalong Cassidy rides after an enemy and when Ellen Ripley hunts down aliens, they never know what will happen to their too-vulnerable flesh—but they go anyway. Now that's a hero!

In addition to eschewing superheroes and borderline characters such as Tarzan, Conan, Zorro, and Robin Hood (who were also included in the previous book), we've avoided historical figures whose real-life exploits loom as large or larger than their fictional ones. Though the deeds of heroes such as Davy Crockett, El Cid, King Arthur, and even Sheriff Buford Pusser have been popularized in films and literature—and we can recommend such films as *The Alamo, El Cid,* and *Excalibur* as shining examples of the genre—we still know and revere these characters primarily for their historical exploits. Conversely, the real-life Elfego Baca or Grizzly Adams won't be found in most history books—and both were

nothing like their TV and movie counterparts—so we've included their fictional sagas in this book.

We've also left out adventurers of questionable morality. The Greek hero Orion may have been a great hunter, but he was also a rapist. Paul Kersey, played by Charles Bronson in the *Death Wish* series, stalked the streets for muggers and drug dealers, but he also set himself above the law. Characters such as Charlton Heston's Taylor, from *Planet of the Apes,* is another man motivated by self-preservation, not heroism, and is not included. (Though he and his literary model, Ulysse Merou, are included in our next volume, *Robots, Spaceships, and Aliens.*)

Detectives also come in many shapes, sizes, and moral orientations. We have included the hard-bitten, action-prone, generally upright types such as Charlie Chan and Sherlock Holmes, but not those like Miss Marple who tend toward armchair crimebusting.

Which isn't to say that everyone in the book has to fall into the blood-and-guts category. You won't find a more daring hero than Dorothy Gale, who holds a special place in the adventure pantheon on our world and on Oz!

However, it is doubtful you will miss these figures and their ilk. There are well over 500 entries in this book, covering all of the great heroes of the West, war, science fiction, horror, mythology, folklore, literature, and fantasy. For fun, we've not only included the superstars from Odysseus to James Bond, but also a wide selection of obscure but interesting adventure heroes, such as Stick-Man the Barbarian and Admiral Fudge, who didn't make much of a splash when they appeared but deserve their place in history.

While we've made every effort to be complete, there are some dates that can only be guessed at (for example, the origins of mythological characters). Records for some early radio shows, old magazines, and even novelizations from 1960s TV shows are poor or, in some cases, nonexistent. Many fictional characters were considered disposable in their day, and it's discouraging how much information has been lost.

While we hope you find this book a useful reference tool, we also trust you'll enjoy skimming through the lives and deeds of some of the most extraordinary characters who never lived!

KEY TO FORMAT AND CODES

Entries are alphabetized by the first letter of each character's first name or, in many cases, by a better-known title (e.g., "Hunter" is under "H" and "Captain James T. Kirk" is under "C"). If you only know the hero's last name, please consult the index. Each entry breaks down in the following self-explanatory categories: the character's first appearance, biography, and comment. Note that abbreviations are alphabetized as if they were spelled out, for example "Mr." as "Mister." Cross-references appear in small capital letters throughout the text.

The codes beside the name of each adventure hero reveal the medium or media in which he or she appeared; these letters are organized chronologically.

In the codes below, be aware that "Literature" includes Big Little books—children's novels published by a variety of houses since the 1920s; that Toys includes both toys and games; and that Video Games includes both cartridge games for systems such as Nintendo and Sega and disc games for personal computers.

Codes:

C = Comic Book	O = Opera
CS = Comic Strip	R = Radio
F = Folklore	S = Stage
L = Literature	T = Toy
M = Mythology	TC = Trading Cards
MP = Motion Picture (theatrical)	TV = Television (series, specials, and TV movies)
	VG = Video or Computer Game

A

ACE DRUMMOND (CS, L, MP)

First Appearance: *Ace Drummond,* 1934, King Features Syndicate.

Biography: Ace is a pilot who, with his grumpy mechanic Jerry, flies around the world in search of jobs—and adventure.

Comment: The character was created by World War I flying aces Eddie Rickenbacker and artist Clayton Knight (a member of the Lafayette Escadrille). The strip lasted just over four years. However, that was long enough to spawn a Big Little Book, *Ace Drummond,* in 1935, and a 13-chapter movie serial, *Ace Drummond* (1936), in which the hero battles a criminal known as the Dragon—who is trying to prevent airline service from coming to Mongolia—and helps Peggy Trainor search for her missing father. John King played Drummond, Jean Rogers was Peggy, and Noah Beery, Jr., played Jerry. Lon Chaney, Jr., had a small part in the serial as a thug named Ivan.

ADMIRAL FUDGE (CS)

First Appearance: *The Explorigator,* May 1908, *The New York World.*

Biography: The young, bespectacled adventurer in a Napoleon outfit introduces himself with verse:

> Salute me now, and all kow-tow,
> for Admiral Fudge am I.
> I'm not so old, but none so bold
> have ever sailed the sky.
> I do not know just where we'll go
> on our aerial cruise.
> But never mind, we're sure to find
> material for the news.

With his youthful companions Detective Rubbersole, Maurice Mizzentop, Nicholas Nohooks, Grenadier Shift, Teddy Typewriter, and Ah Fergetitt, Fudge flies to the moon on his spectacular airship. There the adventurers meet the regal Man in the Moon, visit a moonbeam factory, and steal a beam at Fudge's behest;

they are tried, found guilty "in the 33rd degree," and Grenadier's prized hat is sentenced to be rehatched by the plaid hen. After leaving the court, the boys search for the hat, encounter large moon hens, go to the Moon-Queen's party, explore Catamarinktum Cave and battle the giant moon cats, take a ride on tame watermelons (big ones, with eyes and legs), and finally return to Earth.

Comment: The weekly strip was created by artist Harry Grant Dart, lasted 14 weeks, and was syndicated to other large newspapers by the *World.* Though derivative of LITTLE NEMO, *The Explorigator* was not without its own merits, not the least of which was its gorgeous artwork and a Lewis Carroll-like sense of absurd adventure. Throughout the strip's run, Fergetitt was also spelled Fergettit and Fergetit.

All of the strips were reprinted in black and white in *Nemo: The Classic Comics Library* #5, 1984.

ADMIRAL HARRIMAN NELSON (L, MP, C, TV)

First Appearance: *Voyage to the Bottom of the Sea,* 1961, Twentieth Century-Fox.

Biography: After retiring from the navy, Admiral Harriman Nelson spends the next four years teaching at the Naval Academy in Annapolis while working for the Bureau of Marine Exploration, where he supervises construction of the atomic submarine *Seaview.* He puts his own personal fortune into the vessel monies (from three generations of investment-banking Nelsons) as well as grants from various foundations. In his first chronicled adventure, Nelson uses the 400-foot-long *Seaview* to save the earth when the Van Allen Radiation Belt catches fire and warms the earth two degrees a day. Sailing out to the South Pacific with a crew commanded by Captain Lee Crane—the youngest submarine commander in U.S. history—he fires a nuclear missile into the belt, causing it to explode outward and eliminating the threat.

In future adventures Nelson—who is a widower—saves the world from tidal waves, discovers an underwater city, rescues San Francisco from a destructive Soviet satellite, is swallowed by a whale, and more.

Comment: The film was directed by Irwin Allen and starred Walter Pidgeon as Nelson, with Robert Sterling as Crane and Frankie Avalon as the number-three man on the *Seaview,* Lieutenant Colonel Chip Romano. In June, 1961, one month before the release of the film, Pyramid Books published Theodore Sturgeon's novelization of the screenplay by Irwin Allen and Charles Bennett.

In comic books, Dell published a movie adaptation in 1961 and Gold Key published 16 issues of *Voyage to the Bottom of the Sea* from 1964 to 1970.

On TV, Richard Basehart starred as Nelson in the hour-long series, which aired on ABC from September 1964 through September 1968. David Hedison costarred as Crane with Robert Dowdell as Chip Morton (not Romano).

AENEAS (M, L, MP)

First Appearance: *The Iliad* by Homer, circa 800 B.C. (see ODYSSEUS).

Biography: The son of Anchises, a member of the royal house of Troy, and the goddess Aphrodite, Aeneas was born on Mt. Ida and raised there by mountain nymphs until he was five. He is the husband of Creusa, the daughter of King Priam and Queen Hecuba of Troy, and the father of Ascanius (a.k.a. Iulus). Fighting against the Greeks during the Trojan War, he escapes the burning city after its fall, carrying his father on his back and leading his wife and son to Mt. Ida. (A second version has him fighting his way to safety, rather than simply leading his family out, while a third has him being permitted to leave by the Greeks.)

After a brief stay on the mountain of his birth, Aeneas rallies the remaining Trojans and leads them, in 20 ships, on a quest to find a new home and to found a new nation. Originally he sets out for Crete, thinking that that is what the god Apollo wishes; through a dream, he is informed by Apollo that he has misunderstood these instructions. Aeneas changes course and heads to what is now Sicily, where he establishes the colony that will one day become Rome.

En route, he is driven by a storm to North Africa, where he falls in love with Dido, the widowed queen of Carthage. She returns his love, but Jupiter orders Aeneas to move on; when he reluctantly does so, the queen takes her life. Leaving Africa, Aeneas and his friend Achates make their way to the underworld at the advice of the seer Sibyl to consult with Anchises, who shows his son the glorious future that lies ahead.

Journeying to the mouth of the Tiber, he reaches Latium, ruled by Latinus, a great-grandson of the god Saturn. Latinus wishes him to marry his daughter Lavinia, but King Turnus, of the nearby Rutulians, covets her himself. Turnus marches on Latium, whose citizens turn on Aeneas. With the help of a force of Etruscans, he defeats the Rutulians and slays Turnus, winning the hand of Lavinia.

After various battles and hardships, Aeneas and his followers found the city of Lavinium. There he and Lavinia begin the bloodline that will eventually found the city of Rome.

Comment: Despite his appearance in Homer's epic, Aeneas is best known as the hero of *The Aeneid* by the Roman poet Vergil. Composed of 12 books and left uncompleted when the poet died in 19 B.C., the poem was written at the behest of the Emperor Augustus.

In motion pictures, Steve Reeves starred as Aeneas in *The Last Glory of Troy* (1962). (Reeves also played Remus to Gordon Scott's Romulus in *Duel of the Titans,* 1961.) Another film, *Force of Trojans,* written by Greek scholar Beverley Cross, was slated to be shot by filmmaker Ray Harryhausen in 1983. Financing fell through, and the picture remains unmade.

AGENT KEN THURSTON (R, TV)

First Appearance: *The Man Called X,* 1944, ABC.

Biography: A government agent code-named X, Ken Thurston is initially stationed in Egypt, where he frequents the Cafe Tambourine, posing as a detective, aided by Pagan Zeldschmidt and traveling throughout Europe and the Middle East battling spies, smugglers, and ex-Nazis. Later (on TV), he gives up the detective cover as he roams the world battling Communists, rescuing captured scientists, locating microfilm and important dossiers, cracking a ring of lady spies, and the like.

Comment: The radio series aired until 1952 and starred Herbert Marshall, with Leon Belasco as Pagan. Barry Sullivan played the hero on the syndicated half-hour TV series, 39 episodes of which aired from 1956 to 1958. The TV adventures were based on actual government files.

ALADDIN (M, L, MP, C, TV)

First Appearance: "Aladdin, or the Wonderful Lamp" by Antoine Galland, 1704, *Mille et une nuits* (see COMMENT).

Biography: Poor, lazy, and stubborn Aladdin lives in China, the son of the tailor Mustapha. Even when Mustapha dies, the boy doesn't do much to help his widowed mother put food on the table. Visited one day by a "famous African magician" who claims to be his father's brother, Aladdin agrees to help him collect a magic lamp from a deep cave located behind a stone in a hill outside of the village. Descending into the twisting caverns, with a magic ring to protect him, Aladdin stuffs his pockets with jewels that he finds there; when he locates the lamp, his pockets are so thick and heavy that he can't get out. When he refuses to empty them, the magician shuts him in the cave. However, the magician neglected to take back the magic ring. Toying nervously with it, Aladdin accidentally invokes a genie, the Slave of the Ring, who frees him. (In some versions there is no ring; instead, Aladdin accidentally brushes the magic lamp as he wrings his hands in despair.) Back home, he shows his mother the lamp and she polishes it: Another genie appears, the Slave of the Lamp, who must do anything they ask of him. They demand a fine meal, served on golden plates, after which Aladdin asks for riches and a palace. His new social standing enables him to woo Badroulboudour (also spelled Bedr-el-Budr), the daughter of the Sultan, who—thanks to the genie's magic—has been prevented from consummating her marriage to her new husband, the son of the Vizier. The marriage is declared null and Aladdin weds her.

Back in Africa, the sorcerer hears about what has happened and, heading for China and disguising himself as a lamp-seller, walks the streets crying "New lamps for old!" The princess (or a servant, depending on the version) happily swaps the old lamp for a new one. After summoning the slave of the lamp, the magician has Aladdin's palace and the princess transported to Africa—without Aladdin. Aladdin sets off in pursuit, sneaks into the castle, and gives his bride a potion to slip to the magician. When he has fallen asleep, Aladdin slays him, claims the lamp, and has his palace and wife returned to China. However, the wizard has a brother who is, "if possible, more wicked and more cunning," and he follows Aladdin home. There, disguised as a holy woman, he is allowed to enter the palace. But the slave of the lamp alerts Aladdin as to his real identity, and the hero stabs the interloper through the heart.

Comment: Forms of the tale go back at least as far as A.D. 800 and appear in many cultures. For example, there is the Bohemian tale of Jenik, who saves a dog and cat from being slaughtered and is rewarded with an enchanted watch that enables him to court and marry a princess. But she steals it, builds a palace for herself in the middle of the sea, and it's up to the dog and cat to get the watch back. In an Albanian tale, a young hero obtains a magic stone, builds a palace, and wins a princess, only to have them all stolen.

Frances Brundage's illustration of the original Chinese *Aladdin,* whose mother lies prostrate after the genie appears. From an edition published in the 1930s.

The controversy over the authorship of the tale in its present form dates back to 1885, when explorer, scholar, and translator Sir Richard Francis Burton published his *Arabian Nights Entertainments,* which was a translation of original manuscripts. That Burton translated a bona-fide text from the Orient is unquestioned; the text still exists in the Bibliotheque Nationale in Paris. However, the text itself is from the early 1800s, and while it refers to an earlier Oriental manuscript from 1703, no copy of that 18th-century manuscript exists. Though Galland used various Syrian texts as the basis for his collection, it appears as if neither the tales of Aladdin nor ALI BABA were in them. Probably he had heard the tales told, then wrote them down and fleshed them out, and they became part of the Arabian Nights canon. Since Galland's work was translated back into Middle Eastern and Oriental languages, it's possible that what Burton was translating was itself an unattributed translation of Galland's story (most likely an Egyptian version printed in Cairo in 1835, which combined stories from several sources). In any case, in 1721 the story first appeared

Abdullah and *Aladdin* (right) prepare to escape from a Bagdad prison as their jailors play gin rummy. From *A Thousand and One Nights*. © Columbia Pictures.

in English in awful, unauthorized translations and condensations of Galland's work.

The first literate version in English was published by Elizabeth Newbery in 1791; however, her *The Oriental Moralist or the Beauties of the Arabian Nights Entertainments* was intended for children, and the character of Aladdin was cleaned up, made into a harder worker and a more honest lad. Anthologist Andrew Lang also cleaned the story up for his more juvenile collection of 1898.

In motion pictures, Aladdin has been portrayed by numerous actors in many different and loose versions of the tale, beginning with silent versions in 1898, 1899, 1900, 1906, 1917, 1922, and 1923. There were many others over the years, most notably a magnificently animated featurette *Popeye Meets Aladdin and His Wonderful Lamp* (1939) starring Popeye as Aladdin and Bluto as the Magician; *A Thousand and One Nights* (1945) starring Cornel Wilde as Aladdin (with a female genie and, wearing glasses, Phil Silvers as Aladdin's sidekick Abdullah); *1001 Arabian Nights* (1959), an animated feature with Mr. Magoo as Aladdin; *The Wonders of Aladdin* (1961) starring Donald O'Connor; and Walt Disney Productions' animated *Aladdin* (1992), which spawned a slew of books, magazines, and other memorabilia. (In truth, that film was based as much on Alexander Korda's epic 1940 film *The Thief of Bagdad* as it was on the Galland tale.)

The Lang tale was the basis for *Aladdin and His Lamp*, #516 of the Classics Illustrated Junior series (1954) and for *Aladdin* (*Dell Junior Treasury #2*, 1955). Disney has continued the adventures of their hero in *The Return of Aladdin* comic book, 1993.

On TV, the character is best remembered for the 1957 CBS broadcast starring Sal Mineo and Cyril Ritchard, with a score by Cole Porter (his last).

ALEXANDER MUNDY (TV)

First Appearance: *It Takes a Thief*, January 1968, ABC.

Biography: Alexander Mundy, a cat burglar, is caught by police officer Noah Bain and sent to San Jobel Prison. There he gets a proposition from Bain, who has gone to work for the Special Intelligence Agency: He can get out of jail if he agrees to work as a thief for the U.S. government. Mundy agrees, and when he isn't sneaking into embassies, hotel rooms, and offices, or romancing women at home and abroad, he's kept under house arrest.

After a year Mundy gets a new boss at SIA—Wallie

Robert Wagner as *Alexander Mundy*. © ABC TV, courtesy of Vic Ghidalia.

Powers. He is released from house arrest and gets an occasional partner—his father, Alister, a retired burglar who taught Alexander everything he knows. He also works from time to time with a cat burglar named Brown.

Comment: The hour-long series aired through September 1970 and starred Robert Wagner as Mundy, Malachi Throne as Bain, Fred Astaire as Alister, Edward Binns as Wallie, and Susan St. James as Brown. The series was originally going to be called *The Magnificent Thief*.

The series is unrelated to the 1960 British heist film *It Takes a Thief*.

ALI BABA (L, M, MP)

First Appearance: *Ali Baba and the Forty Thieves* by Antoine Galland, 1704, *Mille et une nuits* (see COMMENT).

Biography: In ancient Persia, poor brothers Cassim and Ali Baba are dealt different hands by fate: Cassim marries an heiress, while Ali Baba weds a woman "as poor as himself." Working as a woodcutter, Ali Baba and his three asses are out in the forest when a band of robbers rides toward him. Hiding in a tree, he watches as the 40 thieves stop by a steep rock. The captain touches it, says "Open Sesame," and the rock moves aside, revealing a cave. The thieves file through the small opening, each carrying bags of riches, and when the captain says, "Close Sesame," the rock slides shut. When they leave, Ali Baba climbs down, says the magic words, and enters a cave filled with "quantities of valuables, and large leather bags full of gold and silver." Taking some, he rushes home and tells his wife, who informs Cassim's wife. The news reaches Cassim, who rushes to the cave to see the riches for himself. The robbers enter the cave and find Cassim; they kill him and cut his body into four pieces, which they hang by the rock as a warning.

When Ali Baba goes looking for Cassim, he finds the body and brings it home. Fearing the robbers will come looking for the man who took the body—and their missing treasure—he pays a cobbler, Baba Mustapha, to sew Cassim back together, so they can say he died a natural death at home. Unfortunately, the cobbler tells what has happened and word reaches the thieves. They buy 19 mules and 38 large leather jars. (Three thieves have died.) The 37 thieves climb into the empty jars and, in the last, the Captain puts oil. Posing as an oil merchant, the Captain and his caravan head to the village.

Upon reaching Cassim's house (where Ali Baba is now staying), the captain asks for shelter for the night. He is welcomed in. However, when Cassim's slave girl,

Morgiana, goes to get oil for her lamp, she hears a voice from one of the jars and figures out what's afoot. After finding the jar full of oil, she boils it up and pours enough scalding oil into each jar to kill the occupant. The captain learns what has happened and flees.

The captain, determined to have his revenge, poses as a silk merchant, Cogia Houssain, befriends Ali Baba's son, and is invited for dinner. But Morgiana recognizes him and stabs him in the heart with a dagger. Ali Baba congratulates her for her "sagacity and readiness" and, in gratitude, frees her from servitude so she can marry his son (who is unnamed in the story). He also brings his son to the cave and gives all of the riches to the youmg couple.

Comment: See ALADDIN for controversial origin of the tale. Despite the fact that it's Ali Baba whose name is remembered, the real hero of the tale is Morgiana. When Sir Richard Francis Burton collected the tale, he used the title *The History of Ali Baba, and of the Forty Robbers Killed By One Slave*.

In his use of the word "sesame," Galland was referring to the oil-producing plant of the Middle East, and he apparently intended it as a cabalistic or endearing term. It is also apparent that he was inspired to do so (indeed, to write the tale itself) by a somewhat similar story several hundred years older than *Ali Baba*, *Simeli* (also known as *Semsi*) *Mountain*, which was later anthologized by the Grimm Brothers. However, some linguists suggest that Galland was simply having fun: Sesame was also a commonly used laxative.

There have been numerous film versions of the story, beginning with silents made in 1902, 1907, 1911, 1918, and others. Eddie Cantor starred in *Ali Baba Goes to Town* and Popeye top-billed in the featurette *Popeye the Sailor Meets Ali Baba's Forty Thieves,* both in 1937. However, the most famous film version was *Ali Baba and the Forty Thieves,* produced by Universal in 1943, directed by Arthur Lubin, and starring Jon Hall. Hall now becomes the heroic leader of the thieves, who hide in the oil jars to exact vengeance against a man who wronged Ali Baba years before. The film was remade (using a great deal of footage from the original) in 1965 as *The Sword of Ali Baba,* starring Peter Mann and Gavin MacLeod. Tony Curtis starred as *The Son of Ali Baba* in 1951.

ALIEN LEGION (C)

First Appearance: *Alien Legion* #1, 1984, Marvel Comics.

Biography: In the future, the galaxies of Thermor, Ophides, and Auron have formed the TOPHAN Galactic Union. Determined to maintain peace against Xenons—a generic term for any "hostile parties outside the Union"—the leaders have assembled mercenary troops known as the Alien Legion, whose task is primarily to halt any aggression on the Union frontiers. The Legion is eclectic, composed of representatives from many Union worlds, some of them professional soldiers, others criminals on the run, and still others artists, thrill-seekers, athletes, or scientists.

The adventures focus on the chronicles of the Legionnaires' crewmates: the serpentine Captain Sarigar of the planet Jentek, who is ruled by logic rather than emotion; Lieutenant Torie Montroc II, a human from the planet Aret and a man "of superb mental and physical conditioning"; Jugger Grimrod, a green humanoid from the planet Thrax and apparently a criminal; the apelike Durge, a wrestler from the planet Pleuron; Meico, a four-armed physician from Cho-Ad; and Torqa Dun, a materialistic, glory-seeking human from Denal. All are bipeds, save for Sarigar. All the Legionnaires wear black body suits with silver armor and carry Hel-guns, high energy laser guns. Grimrod also makes an explosive mix called black powder puddin'. Their shuttle crafts travel between star systems by warping (twisting the fabric of space.)

Comment: The characters starred in 20 issues of their own magazine (to 1987); returned for a second series that ran 18 issues (1987–90); appeared in a three-issue series called *Alien Legion: On the Edge* (1990–91); came back for two issues of *Alien Legion: Tennants of Hell* (1991); starred in *Marvel Graphic Novel #25*; and returned for the limited series *Alien Legion: One Planet At a Time* in 1993. They were created by artists Carl Potts and Frank Cirocco, and writer Alan Zelentz.

ALLAN QUATERMAIN   (L, MP, C)

First Appearance: *King Solomon's Mines* by Henry Rider Haggard, 1885, Cassell.

Biography: Born in 1817, Allan is an English gentleman who prefers adventure to leisure and becomes "a poor traveling trader and hunter." After a run of bad luck, he agrees to join a party sponsored by Sir Henry Curtis and Captain John Good. In his first chronicled adventure, he penetrates deep into the African jungle in search of the legendary diamond mines of King Solomon. Though they find them and return to England rich men, Allan cannot sit still and enjoy his wealth; after publishing a history of the journey, he sets out on further adventures. (See COMMENT.)

Allan, who is "universally respected in Natal," is known as Macumazahn by the natives (He-Who-Keeps-His-Eyes-Open). His honor is impeccable, and he will kill a man only in self-defense, which he has done many times.

Hans is Quatermain's devoted, clever, and cynical servant. His frequent nemesis is Zikali, a witch doctor also known as the Thing-That-Never-Should-Have-Been-Born. Quatermain has a son named Harry.

Comment: Author Haggard spent many years in Africa as a government official. He followed *King Solomon's Mines* with *Allan Quatermain* (1887), in which the author kills his hero in a remote lost city. But the outcry from readers was such that Haggard was forced to bring Quatermain back in a series of "prequels," most of them novels and most costarring Hans. These were *Marie* (1912), *Allan's Wife* (1889), *Child of Storm* (1913), *Maiwa's Revenge* (1888), *The Holy Flower* (1915), *Heu-Heu (or, The Monster)* (1924), *She and Allan* (1921) (bringing together Haggard's two most popular characters, She being the immortal Ayesha), *Treasure of the Lake* (1926), *The Ivory Child* (1916), *Finished* (1917), *The Ancient Allan* (1920), and *Allan and the Ice Gods* (1927) (coplotted by Haggard's close friend, Rudyard Kipling).

In motion pictures, *King Solomon's Mines* was filmed in 1937 starring Cedric Hardwicke as Allan with Roland Young and Paul Robeson; in 1950 starring Stewart Granger as Allan with Deborah Kerr and Richard Carlson; and in 1985 with Richard Chamberlain and Sharon Stone. *Allan Quatermain* was filmed as *King Solomon's Treasure* in 1977 starring John Colicos, David McCallum, and Patrick Macnee; and as *Allan Quatermain and the Lost City of Gold* in 1987, once again with Chamberlain and Stone. Quatermain does not die in these tales. George Montgomery played the part in *Watusi*, a 1959 sequel to *King Solomon's Mines*.

In comic books, the character appeared in an Dell movie adaptation in 1950 and in a *Classics Illustrated* version of *King Solomon's Mines* the following year.

AMANDA KING   (TV)

First Appearance: *Scarecrow and Mrs. King*, October 1983, CBS.

Biography: Amanda King, a newly-divorced suburban Washington, D.C., housewife, lives with her two sons, Philip and Jamie, and her mother, Dotty West. Waiting at the train station one day, Amanda is handed a parcel by a mysterious man, who subsequently vanishes. The package contains important secrets, and the somebody turns out to be Lee Stetson, code-named Scarecrow, who works for a government spy group known as the Agency. Mrs. King becomes embroiled in a plot against Russian spies. She loves the adventure and proves so good at it that she goes to work for the International Federal Film Company, the Agency's cover, trains to be an agent, and becomes Lee's partner. Both report to the Agency head, Dr. Smyth, and work closely with smart-mouthed agent Francine Desmond. T.P. Aquinas is Lee's trusted informant.

Amanda has her ups and downs over the years. At one point, fed up with her low salary, she quits and joins a security firm—which, as it turns out, is a front for mercenaries intending to kidnap an African leader. Another time, she's convinced that Lee has sold out to work for a notorious gunrunner; then the Agency becomes convinced that they *both* have sold out, thanks to an elaborate KGB sting operation.

Despite their personal ups and downs as well, Amanda and Lee marry after three and a half seasons.

Comment: The hour-long series aired through September 1987 and starred Kate Jackson (one of CHARLIE'S ANGELS) as Amanda, Bruce Boxleitner as Stetson, Beverly Garland as Dotty, Martha Smith as Francine, Myron Natwick as Smyth, Raleigh Bond as Aquinas, and Paul Stout and Greg Morton as Philip and Jamie.

AMOS BURKE (TV)

First Appearance: "Who Killed Julia Greer," *The Dick Powell Show,* September 1961, NBC.

Biography: A natty millionaire who is also the chief of detectives in Los Angeles, Amos Burke lives in a mansion, is driven to crime scenes (usually murders) in his Rolls-Royce by his chauffeur, Henry, and invariably has a gorgeous young lady on his arm. He's also a brilliant, hard-nosed detective, not afraid to get his hands bloody. His aides on the force include Detective Tim Tilson (who usually takes the beatings), Detective Sergeant Lester Hart, and Sergeant Ames.

Burke's skills come to the attention of the U.S. government, and, when last seen, he had become a globe-trotting secret agent, battling spies, smugglers, and saboteurs and reporting to a figure known only as The Man.

Comment: Powell himself played the part on the debut mystery of his hour-long series. Two years later Gene Barry took over the role on *Burke's Law,* an hour-long series that aired through January 1966. In September 1965 the series title was changed to *Amos Burke—Secret Agent.* Leon Lontoc played Henry, Gary Conway was Tilson, Regis Toomey played Hart, and Eileen O'Neill was Ames. In the final season, Carl Benton Reid was The Man.

A new made-for-TV movie, starring Barry, aired in 1994 and spawned a series.

ANGEL O'DAY (C)

First Appearance: *Showcase* #77, 1968, DC Comics.

Biography: It isn't known what Angel O'Day's father did for a living, but one of his closest friends was Charlie Chum, a famed sleuth, who gave Angel her schooling in detection. It also is not known how the beautiful platinum blonde met Sam Simeon, an extremely intelligent ape and aspiring cartoonist, or how she learned ape language (though it *is* similar to our own—"Yukkubinkle" is "You could've been killed!"). In any case, unable to make ends meet with his art, Sam teams with Angel and they open the O'Day and Simeon Detective Agency, which is based in New York City. In addition to her impressive deductive skills, Angel is a marksman and formidable martial artist.

Comment: The characters went on to star in six issues of *Angel and the Ape* (1968–69) and were revived for a four-issue run in 1991.

ANGUS MACGYVER (TV)

First Appearance: *MacGyver,* September 1985, ABC.

Biography: A former Special Forces agent, MacGyver now works for the Phoenix Foundation, a group of intellectuals and philanthropists committed to ridding the world of evil and assisting the endangered, whether it's a group of scientists trapped in an underground lab, pilots plane-wrecked in the Himalayas, victims of a high-tech Caribbean dictator, government agents trying to retrieve World War II gold lost in Alaska, a 15-year-old rocket scientist being hunted by black marketeers, kids tackling a crack gang, or a young girl with a drinking problem. A scientific genius, MacGyver is able to turn ordinary objects into useful tools, from a paper clip (to short a missile), to a chocolate bar (to plug an acid leak).

MacGyver's superior is Peter Thornton, director of Field Operations. His girlfriend is Nikki Carpenter.

Comment: The hour-long series aired for seven seasons and starred Richard Dean Anderson as MacGyver, Dana Elcar as Thornton, and Elyssa Davalos as Nikki.

ANTHRO (C)

First Appearance: *Showcase* #74, 1968, DC Comics.

Biography: The prehistoric Cro-Magnon teenager lives with his family: his (unnamed) mother; his Neanderthal father, Neahn, chief of the Bear Tribe; his (unnamed) maternal grandmother; and his younger brother, lame Lart. When we first meet Anthro, his father is teaching him how to hunt mastodon and create cave paintings. But Anthro comes up with his own way of doing things, and there is a strong generational gap between loutish father and clever son.

The first appearance of *Anthro*. © DC Comics.

Anthro's girlfriend is the lovely Embra, daughter of Chief Tugg of a nearby tribe. The rivals of these neohumans are the Cannibals, who are vicious "submen."

Anthro is adept with the spear but prefers nonviolence and intellectual solutions to combat.

Comment: After his single *Showcase* appearance, Anthro was given his own magazine, which lasted for six issues. The characters, created by artist/writer Howie Post, spoke colloquial English; the witty *Anthro* was intended to be a metaphor for the antiestablishment youth of the 1960s.

See also KONG.

APRIL DANCER   (TV, L, C)

First Appearance: *The Girl from U.N.C.L.E.,* September 1966, NBC.

Biography: An operative for the United Network Command for Law and Enforcement (see NAPOLEON SOLO AND ILLYA KURYAKIN), April Dancer is teamed with flip, mod English agent Mark Slate, a crack shot who has recently been transferred from U.N.C.L.E.'s London office. Together the two fight international crime and the nefarious doings of the organization THRUSH as well as T.O.R.C.H. (The Order of Reich Crusade Hierarchy). Both agents report to Mr. Alexander Waverly.

April was trained in ballet and loves classical music. Among her tools and weapons are a communications pen that reaches Mr. Waverly's desk from anywhere in the world, a headband with pearls made of explosive X-757, a charm bracelet with a powerful clown flashlight, and more.

Comment: The series aired through August 1967. Though Mary Ann Mobley played April in the series pilot, Stefanie Powers got the part in the series. Noel Harrison was Mark and Leo G. Carroll played Waverly. Slate had originally appeared on *The Man from U.N.C.L.E.*

There were two novels, both by Michael Avallone: *The Birds of a Feather Affair* and *The Blazing Affair,* both 1967.

Gold Key published five issues of the *The Girl from U.N.C.L.E.* comic book in 1967.

THE AQUANAUTS   (TV, C)

First Appearance: *The Aquanauts,* September 1960, CBS.

Biography: Drake Andrews and Larry Lahr are salvage divers who are based in Santa Monica and work off the Southern California coast. From the deck of their boat the *Scuba Doo,* they hunt for treasure, wrecks, missing divers, and the like. Eventually Drake decides to rejoin the navy and Larry teams with Mike Madison. They open an aquatic supply and sporting goods shop, the Happy Duck, in Malibu and have adventures with smugglers, kidnapers, stranded sportsmen, and the like, more often above the waves than below.

Comment: The title of the show was changed to *Malibu Run* when Mike Madison came along. Jeremy Slate was Larry, Keith Larsen (who had to give up the show because the underwater scenes gave him nosebleeds) played Drake, and Ron Ely was Mike. The hour-long series aired through September 1961.

In May/July 1961 Dell published one issue of *The Aquanauts* comic book as #1197 of their *4-Color* series.

ATARI FORCE   (C)

First Appearance: *Atari Force* #1, 1982, DC Comics.

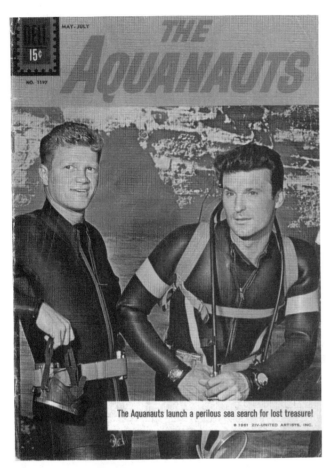

Larry Lahr, left, and Drake Andrews: *The Aquanauts*. © Ziv-United Artists.

Biography: By the year 2005, war—which began on October 18, 1998—has depopulated the world and left civilization in something of a shambles. Famine is rampant. Fortunately, the Atari Technology and Research Institute, headquartered in Northcal (and including what used to be NASA and the National Academy of Science), is seeking to solve humankind's hunger problem via Project Multiverse, "an attempt to [locate] inhabitable worlds among the infinity of alternate realities existing in other dimensions." The search is conducted onboard the dimension-spanning vessel *Scanner One*. Heading up the search are former NASA moon pilot Commander Martin Champion; Security Officer Li San O'Rourke, who was raised in war-torn Ireland by an Irish father and a Chinese mother and was a UN lieutenant and paratrooper in the war; Flight Engineer Mohandas Singh, born in poverty in India, who later became a ward of an Englishman, Professor Stanley Miles; Ship's doctor Lucas Orion, a former UN peace-keeping force medic; and Executive Officer and crackerjack pilot Lydia Perez. The result of their many

adventures is the establishment of a new and healthy society on New Earth—though it costs the life of Perez, who had married Commander Champion.

A quarter-century passes and the evil Dark Destroyer sets out to conquer the Multiverse. The original Atari Force returns to active duty, joined by Martin's son Christopher, alias Tempest, who can travel through the Multiverse without a ship; psychic and mercenary Erin Bia O'Rourke-Singh, daughter of Li San and Monahdas, also known as Dart; the towering alien Babe of the Eggites and his friend Taz; Tukla Oly, a.k.a. Pakrat, a Merkian outlaw; and Morphea, a psychiatrist from Canopia. Also part of the new team is Martin's ratlike pet Hukka.

The original Atari Force dress in red and white bodysuits with the Atari logo on the chest. The humans on the second Force wear variations on the costume; the nonhumans wear whatever they want.

Comment: The union of the then-hot Atari video games and DC came about when both companies were owned by Warner Communications. (Atari has since been sold.) The comic books were initially five digest-

The rare, first digest-size issue of *Atari Force*. From the left: Singh, Perez, Champion, Li San, and Lucas. © Atari, Inc.

size, 48-page magazines packaged with certain game cartridges for the second-generation Atari 2600 unit—number one with Defender, number two in Berzerk, number three in Star Raiders, number four in Phoenix, and number five in Galaxian. Later they got their own regular-size comic book that lasted 20 issues. The characters were created by writers Gerry Conway and Roy Thomas.

THE A-TEAM   (TV, C)

First Appearance: *The A-Team,* January 1983, NBC.

Biography: In 1972, four days after the end of the war in Vietnam, a crack commando team is accused of robbing the Bank of Hanoi. Tried by the U.S. government and imprisoned in a maximum security prison, they escape and become soldiers of fortune, based in Los Angeles and surviving one step ahead of the military men on their tail—Colonel Lynch and then Colonel Roderick Decker.

The members of this highly skilled squad are Colonel John "Hannibal" Smith, the leader and a master of disguises; Lieutenant Templeton Peck, a.k.a. "Faceman," a smooth-talking pretty boy; Captain H.M. "Howling Mad" Murdock, a pilot who may or may not be insane (but, in any case, acts it convincingly); and Sergeant Bosco "B.A." Baracus, a mechanic with awesome physical strength—and a fear of flying, particularly with H.M. (The B.A. stands for Bad Attitude, though were it not for the strictures of network TV, it surely would have meant something else.) They are joined in their exploits by reporter Amy Allen for a while, then by gun-toting Tawnia Baker. (Both women last only one season each.) In addition to the armed-to-the-hubcaps van in which they travel, the team is lucky that B.A. can build weapons out of almost anything he finds (i.e., a washing machine into a machine gun!).

After several years on the run, the team is caught by General Hunt Stockwell, who recruits them as deep-undercover government operatives. They are joined by a new member: "Dishpan" Frankie Sanchez, a master special effects artist who helps rig explosions and various illusions.

Comment: The hour-long series went off the air in June 1987. George Peppard played Hannibal, Mr. T was B.A.—and complete with his 35 pounds of gold necklaces and catch phrase "I pity the fool . . ."—Dirk Benedict was Faceman (after Tim Dunigan played him in the pilot episode), Dwight Schultz was H.M., Melinda Culrea was Amy, Maria Heasley was Tawnia, William Lucking played Lynch, Lance LeGault was

Decker, Robert Vaughn costarred as Stockwell, and Eddie Velez was Dishpan.

Marvel Comics published three issues of an A-Team comic book in 1984.

Although there was never an A-Team cartoon series, there was a *Mr. T* show that ran on NBC from 1983 to 1986, in which Mr. T played himself coaching a team of young gymnasts who compete around the world—and capture criminals while they're at it.

THE AVENGERS   (TV, C, L, S, R)

First Appearance: *The Avengers,* January 1961, ABC (Britain).

Biography: John Steed is an undercover agent who works for the mysterious One-Ten (who, implictly, is

John Steed of *The Avengers.* © EMI Film Distributors, Ltd.

employed by *both* the British espionage unit, MI5, and counterespionage MI6). A cultured man, Steed is fond of his Bentley, fine clothes (especially bowlers), food, wine, horses, antiques, and women, and is skilled at fencing, archery, croquet, and polo. He has been trained to withstand torture and brainwashing, and is an expert at forgery and the use of explosives and poison.

On the trail of drug dealers, he teams with a doctor, David Keel, who is seeking to avenge the murder of his fiancee by the gang; after the criminals are apprehended, the two remain a team. When Keel drops out of the sleuthing business, in steps Catherine Gale. A Ph.D. in anthropology, she was widowed in a Mau Mau raid and works for the British Museum until One-Ten hires her to join them. She accepts only because she wants to see justice done on behalf of crime victims. A master at judo, she is far more of a humanitarian than the cold, cavalier Steed.

When Gale retires, Steed teams with beautiful brunette jet-setter Emma Peel, the hip, witty young widow of pilot Peter Peel and the daughter of a shipping magnate. Skilled in a form of karate, she lives in a rooftop penthouse and finds herself and Steed battling fiends more incredible than Cathy Gale *ever* fought, from insane scientists trying to conquer the world to huge human-eating plants and killer robots.

In time, trainee Agent 69, Tara King, joins the duo; when Peter Peel is found alive in the jungles of the Amazon, Emma retires to be with him and Tara takes over as Steed's partner. Their union is short-lived. After years out of the public eye, Steed returns with two new partners: Purdey and Mike Gambit. Their relationship, too, is brief.

Comment: There were 161 hour-long episodes, all of which starred Patrick Macnee as Steed. Ian Hendry costarred as Keel; Honor Blackman came on as Cathy Gale for the second season, then left after three years to pursue other projects. After a few days' shooting, Elizabeth Shepherd was dismissed as Mrs. Peel (she was a fine actress, but lacked the necessary humor), and Diana Rigg took her place. When Rigg arrived, the shows were shot on film for the first time, rather than tape; this slicker look (plus the science fiction plots) helped the show find a home in the U.S., airing on ABC from March 1966 until September 1969. Tara King was introduced at the end of 1968, played by Linda Thorson. Tara lasted a single season, after which the show went off the air.

Macnee returned for *The New Avengers,* which ran for a season in England in 1976 (and on CBS in 1978-79). Joanna Lumley was Purdey and Gareth Hunt played Mike Gambit.

A stage production ran for two weeks in England in the summer of 1971, starring Simon Oates as Steed and Sue Lloyd as his new partner, Hannah Wild; a series of radio dramas aired in South Africa in the winter of 1972, starring Donald Monat as Steed and Dianne Appleby as Peel, based on episodes of the TV series.

Twelve novels were published based on the original series; noted science fiction author Keith Laumer wrote three of them expressly for the U.S. market, and Norman Daniels penned another two. These were all original stories. *The New Avengers* spawned six novels that were published in England and were based on episodes of the show.

Several comic books were published in England during the 1960s. Gold Key published one comic book in the U.S. in 1968; Eclipse published three issues of *Steed and Mrs. Peel* in 1990–91.

Though an *Avengers* theatrical film was talked about, it never got off the ground.

B

BANYON (TV)

First Appearance: *Banyon*, March 1971, NBC TV movie.

Biography: Mile C. Banyon is a Los Angeles private eye in the late 1930s. Two-fisted but incorruptible, he is not to proud to take any legal job for a $20-a-day fee. He often crosses paths (and swords) with Lieutenant Pete McNeil of the LAPD. Because Peggy Revere's secretarial school is located in the same building as Banyon's office, he gets—free of charge—a different secretary every week. He is in love with nightclub singer Abby Graham, though he refuses to commit to marriage.

Comment: The telefilm was a pilot for the hour-long *Banyon* series, which aired on NBC from September 1972 to January 1973. Robert Forster starred as Banyon, Joan Blondell was Peggy, Richard Jaeckel was McNeil (replacing Darren McGavin who played the part in the movie), and Julie Gregg played Abby.

Forster also starred in ABC's short-lived (September–December 1974) *Nakia*, about modern-day New Mexico Deputy Sheriff Nakia Parker.

BARBARELLA (CS, MP)

First Appearance: *Barbarella*, *V Magazine*, 1962.

Biography: A sex-loving blond astronaut of the 40th century, Barbarella hops from planet to planet wearing as little clothing as possible. The shapely heroine packs a ray gun, and, when she isn't battling monsters or nemeses like the Black Queen and the evil hunter Strikno—or adventuring with her friends the blind angel Pygar or fellow astronaut Dildano—she's sleeping with all the handsome men she meets (and even featureless robots, such as the apologetic Diktor, whose movements, she feels, are "a bit mechanical").

Comment: The character was created by Jean-Claude Forest; her adventures were collected in book form in 1964 (released in the U.S. two years later). Her print adventures ended for good in 1970. Roger Vadim directed Jane Fonda in the film *Barbarella* (1969). In that cult favorite the president of Earth sends astronaut Barbarella to find the evil Duran Duran, who has stolen a powerful new weapon, the Positronic Ray.

The success of the strip inspired other sexy comic strip heroines, most notably Scarth, the promiscuous space heroine who appeared in British newspapers from 1969 to 1972; Jodelle, a red-headed spy in ancient (and decadent) Rome; and Phoebe Zeit-Geist, a young American who is abducted from a party and has adventures (and suffered countless indignities) at the hands of Nazis, Communists, and others. Her adventures appeared in *Evergreen Review* in 1966.

See also MODESTY BLAISE.

BARETTA (TV)

First Appearance: *Baretta*, January 1975, ABC.

Biography: A streetwise Los Angeles police officer with the 53rd Precinct, Detective Tony Baretta is an orphan, the son of poor but hardworking Italian immigrants. An expert with disguises, he infiltrates gangs and criminal organizations and takes cases too dirty (drugs, prostitution, racketeers) or dangerous (city corruption, motorcycle thugs, mobsters) for anyone else to tackle. He lives in a basement apartment in a ramshackle hotel, the King Edward, where his only friends are his pet cockatoo Fred and retired officer Billy Truman. His chief informant is a pimp named Rooster; his first superior on the force was Inspector Shiller, followed by Lieutenant Hal Brubaker.

Comment: *Baretta* was actually inspired by the series *Toma*, which aired on ABC from October 1973 to September 1974, and starred Tony Musante as the real-life Newark, New Jersey Detective David Toma. When Musante quit—he didn't like the rush of doing a weekly series—Robert Blake was hired to replace him. However, the series had been only a moderate success in the ratings, and rather than hamstring Blake, he and the producers decided to make changes in the show—starting with the name of the main character.

Dana Elcar starred as Shiller (who appeared in the first season only), Edward Grover was Brubaker (from

Jane Fonda as *Barbarella*. © Paramount Pictures.

the second season on), Tom Ewell was Truman, and Michael D. Roberts was Rooster. The hour-long series lasted until June 1978.

Blake also starred as a gumshoe in the 1981 made-for-TV movie/pilot *The Big Black Pill,* which was later retitled *Joe Dancer,* after his L.A.-based character. Though the series failed to sell, it inspired two pilot-sequels: *The Monkey Mission* (1981) and *Murder 1, Dancer 0* (1983).

BARNABY JONES (TV)

First Appearance: *Barnaby Jones,* January 1973, CBS.

Biography: Following a long career as a private eye, the milk-drinking Barnaby turns his Los Angeles-based business over to his son Hal. But one of Hal's first cases is also his last: When he's murdered, Barnaby ends his retirement to find his killer (with the help of Frank Cannon). The elderly sleuth remains on the job, usually working for insurance companies, helped in, and occasionally out, of the office by Hal's widow, Betty. Later his young cousin, aspiring lawyer Jedediah Romano Jones, joins Barnaby to find out who killed his own father; he ends up joining the firm (to do the kinds of chases and take the physical abuse the producers

couldn't very well heap on the older sleuth). Barnaby's police department contacts are Lieutenant Joe Taylor, then Lieutenant John Biddle.

In addition to his office, Barnaby maintains a fully equipped home crime laboratory: Deduction, not violence, is the key to Barnaby's success as a crimefighter.

Comment: The hour-long series ran through September 1980. Buddy Ebsen starred as Barnaby, Lee Meriwether was Betty, and Mark Shera was J.R. (1976–80). Vince Howard was Taylor (1973 only), and John Carter was Biddle (1974–80).

BARNES (MP)

First Appearance: *Burn 'Em Up Barnes,* 1921, Affiliated.

Biography: Fascinated with cars since he was a boy, Barnes—whose rich father frowns on racing—runs away from home, lives the life of a hobo, lands a job at a track, and becomes one of the foremost racers in the country. When a friend dies in a crackup at the track, Barnes quits to raise his kid brother. With young Marjorie Temple, Barnes founds an auto transport business for hauling people or freight. But Marjorie has inherited land that, unknown to her, is rich with oil. Evil promoter Drummond wants to bankrupt her and force her to sell the land cheap. However, he's unable to do so thanks to Barnes's knack for winning races, earning money as a Hollywood stunt pilot, and surviving the succession of attempts Drummond makes on his life. In the end, Marjorie keeps her business, her land—and Barnes.

Barnes's adopted son is Bobbie, the kid brother of a friend who lost his life in a race.

Comment: This serial was remade in 1934, playing down the rich-kid angle; these mark the only screen appearances of Barnes (who had no first name in the films), one of the few race-car driver adventure heroes.

Credits are unavailable for the original film. In the remake, Jack Mulhall was Barnes, Lola Lane was Marjorie, and Jason Robards played Drummond. The 12-chapter serial was directed by Colbert Clark and Armand Schaefer. The serial was later edited into a feature film.

BARNEY BAXTER (CS, C)

First Appearance: "Barney Baxter," December 17, 1936, King Features Syndicate (see COMMENT).

Biography: A young, eager, freckle-faced pilot, Barney Baxter will go anywhere at any time in search of adventure, whether it's to battle spies, kidnapers, run-of-the-mill crooks, or rebels in foreign lands. His sidekick is Gopher Gus, a whiskered, pipe-smoking, big-eared prospector whom he meets in Alaska in an early escapade. During World War II, the pair joins the RAF; when the U.S. enters the war, the men jump to the air force. They serve primarily in the Pacific, bombing Tokyo as well as Japanese outposts. After the war the men were briefly involved with the up-and-coming field of space travel.

Comment: The strip was created by Frank Miller; a year before it had been introduced in a single newspaper in Denver, in a less polished form. Miller remained with "Barney Baxter" until 1942, at which time Robert Naylor took over. Miller returned in 1948 and the strip lasted until January 1950.

There were a handful of Barney Baxter comic books over the years, beginning with David McKay's 1938 one-shot, five issues from Dell in 1942-43, and two issues from Argo in 1956.

BARNEY BLAKE (TV)

First Appearance: *Barney Blake, Police Reporter,* April 1948, NBC.

Biography: Assisted by his glamorous secretary Jennifer Allen, two-fisted reporter Barney Blake covers (and solves) murders, often crossing the local police who resent his interference.

Comment: Though he was off the air in July after only 13 half-hour episodes, Barney holds the distinction of being TV's first series sleuth. Gene O'Donnell starred as Barney, and Judy Parrish was Jennifer. The series aired live and grew out of a tradition of tough-reporter radio shows such as *Casey, Crime Photographer* (see FLASHGUN JACK CASEY), *The Adventures of Christopher Wells*—which was broadcast on CBS in 1947 and starred Les Damon—and *Hannibal Cobb,* which starred Santos Oretega as a detective who worked for *Look* magazine and whose adventures aired on ABC beginning in 1949.

THE BARON (L, TV)

First Appearance: *Meet the Baron* by Anthony Morton, 1937.

Biography: When he was a young man, John Mannering was an upstanding citizen by day and a jewel thief known as the Baron by night. After meeting and marrying beautiful young artist Lorna Fauntley, he decides to use his skills on behalf of the law. Now he's an antique dealer at the fashionable Quinns in Mayfair who helps Scotland Yard when they come calling. Though Superintendent Bristow doesn't entirely trust Mannering (especially when he has to recover the Crown Jewels), he *does* solve cases none of his detectives can crack.

Comment: The U.S. title of the original novel is *The Man in the Blue Mask.* He starred in 46 additional novels.

Mannering was played by Steve Forrest on *The Baron,* an hour-long TV series that aired on ABC from January to July 1966. This time Mannering is an American who owns a string of antique shops in London, Paris, and Washington, D.C. But that's just a front for his real work—serving as a tough, two-fisted operative for British Intelligence. Typically, he works on cases involving art, smuggling, sabotage, murder, and the like. He reports to John Alexander Templeton-Green; his fellow agent is Cordelia Winfield, and his aide is David Marlowe. Colin Gordon was Templeton-Green, Sue Lloyd was Winfield, and Paul Ferris was Marlowe. The Baron's name was explained not by his immaculate clothing and manners, but by the fact that his family were ranching barons in Texas.

Anthony Morton is a pseudonym for author John Creasey.

BARON MUNCHAUSEN (L, MP)

First Appearance: *Baron Munchausen's Narrative of His Marvelous Travels and Campaigns in*

Russia by Rudolf Erich Raspe, 1785 (see COMMENT), Smith.

Biography: As he is riding through deep snow in Russia, the German Baron Munchausen (also spelled Munchhausen) ties his horse to a tree stump and takes a nap; when he wakes, he sees the horse dangling from the top of a church steeple, the snow having melted. Munchausen finds himself in a graveyard and sets out on foot, encountering a frozen horn that, when it thaws, plays by itself. He shoots a stag with a cherry stone and, later, finds a cherry tree growing from its forehead. He also encounters another horse that, when cut in two, is sewn up and made whole; and, stumbling into the middle of the Russian/Turkish war, he ends a fierce battle by riding a Russian cannonball into the enemy camp. In later adventures he journeys to the moon and meets Cyrano de Bergerac and Jules Verne, takes a ride on a mythical roc, and vacations inside a whale. According to some of the tales, the more active he is, the younger the Baron becomes.

The Baron is typically pictured as tall and slender, with a goatee, moustache, and peruke.

Comment: Raspe based his character on an actual figure, the braggart Baron Karl Friedrich Hieronymous von Munchausen (1720–97), who fought in the war between the Russians and the Turks and embroidered his reminiscences mightily. The first book was published anonymously, and additional tales were added by other writers over the years. The expanded volume of his outrageous tales was called *Gulliver Revisited;* the third, *The Vice of Lying Properly Exposed.* Before long the name Baron Munchausen had become synonymous with inflated tales of adventuring.

Silent films featuring the Baron were made in 1909 (two), 1911, and 1914. An animated short was made in 1948, and feature films were made in 1943 (*Baron Munchhausen* starring Hans Albers), 1961 (the Czechoslovakian *The Fabulous Baron Munchausen* starring Milos Kopecky), and 1989 (*The Adventures of Baron Munchausen* starring John Neville and directed by Terry Gilliam). Gilliam and Charles McKeown novelized the film.

BAT LASH (C)

First Appearance: *Showcase* #76, 1968, DC Comics.

Biography: Bartholomew Aloysius Lash lives on a farm with parents, Lemuel and Martha Lash, and siblings Thomas, William, and Melissa in the late 1800s. When his parents are cheated out of their home and forced to live in a shack, Bat seeks justice; he finds, instead, corruption and apathy. Forced to shoot a lawless deputy in self-defense, he returns to his family's shed only to find it burning, his parents dead. Hunted by the law for having killed the deputy, Bat takes his sister and girlfriend, Betsy, to a convent, then roams the Southwest one step ahead of the law, "destined always to be a fugitive." The friendly loner survives by gambling and by talking his way out of most scrapes—though when he has to fight, he's a quick draw and expert marksman.

Comment: Bat went on to star in seven issues of his own title and has popped up in other DC titles from time to time. The character's adventures were written by cartoonist Sergio Aragones (of *Mad* and *Groo* fame), and drawn by Nick Cardy.

BEANY BOY (TV, C)

First Appearance: *Time For Beany,* 1948, KTLA.

Biography: Young Beany Boy—who always wears overalls and his trademark propeller beanie—and his uncle, Captain Horatio K. Huffenpuff, sail the seas onboard the *Leakin' Lena,* always in the company of the big "seasick sea serpent" Cecil. At first only Beany can see Cecil; later the sea serpent reveals himself to the Captain. Their recurring foe is Dishonest John, though others include the Phantom of the Horse Opera, Tearalong the Dotted Lion, Jack the Knife, William Shakespeare Wolf, and many others.

Comment: The characters were created by former Warner Brothers animator Bob Clampett and debuted as puppets on a 15-minute serialized adventure-with-comedy program in Los Angeles in 1948, with Beany's voice provided by Daws Butler (later to become Huckleberry Hound and Yogi Bear, among countless others), and comedian Stan Freberg as the Captain and Clampett as Cecil. The show was syndicated nationwide from 1950 to 1955 and became a popular cartoon series that ran on ABC from 1962 to 1968; 76 half-hour adventures were produced. Jim McGeorge provided the voice for Beany and Captain Huffenpuff; Irv Shoemaker was Cecil and Dishonest John. The characters were revived in 1988 for a short-lived ABC cartoon series; only nine adventures were produced, with Mark Hildreth as Beany, Billy West as Cecil, and Jim McGeorge as Huffenpuff.

Dell published seven issues of *4-Color* starring Beany and Cecil from 1952 to 1955; the characters appeared in five issues of their own Dell title from 1962 to 1963.

BEAU GESTE (L, S, MP)

First Appearance: *Beau Geste* by Percival Christopher Wren, 1924.

Biography: Major Henri de Beaujolais and his men

enter the fort at Zinderneuf in the Sahara and find everyone dead, no trace of the Touareg enemies. On one body he sees an envelope addressed to the chief of police of Scotland Yard and is marked "Confession. Important. Urgent." Henri arranges a meeting with George Lawrence, First Class District Officer of His Majesty's Civil Service, to delve into the matter.

The twin Geste brothers, Michael and Digby, and their younger brother John, are orphans who live at Brandon Abbey with their aunt, Lady Patricia Rivers Brandon, and go to preparatory school; from earliest youth, Michael is known as "Beau" due to "his remarkable physical beauty, mental brilliance, and general distinction." Hiding inside a suit of armor one day, Beau sees his aunt sell the family heirloom, the Blue Water diamond, to an agent of a maharajah in order to keep the abbey and its surrounding lands. She has a fake made to fool her husband, Sir Hector. However, Beau is worried he'll find out, so he steals the fake and runs off to join the French Foreign Legion. Digby and John follow in turn, something the three have wanted to do since they first began playing military games as children.

The three end up in a marching unit of the 19th Army Corps, training under Lieutenant Debussy and Captain Renouf at Sidi-bel-Abbes before Michael and John are sent to the fort at Zenderneuf, Digby to Tokotu. Renouf commits suicide after a month in the "dreadful oven of a place," Debussy takes sick and dies, and the sadistic Sergeant-Major Lejaune—a miserable creature who would just as soon shoot one of his men as kill a scorpion—becomes the new commandant. Before long, Schwartz and several other soldiers plot to murder him and desert the fort. Out of "loyalty to duty," the Geste brothers reluctantly side with the hated Lejaune and help put down the "beastly conspiracy." Unimpressed by their devotion, Lejaune has undertaken a dastardly plot of his own: He plans to steal the Blue Water, unaware that it's a fake.

Before the officer can act, however, the Arabs attack. As the men fall, they are propped against the walls to make the enemy think that the fort is better manned than it is—and to afford the soldiers shields from which to fire behind. Michael is fatally wounded defending a weakened wall, and Lejaune goes over to search his corpse. He finds a sealed confession and Blue Water just as John arrives. The outraged John goes to stab the officer with his bayonet but hesitates; Lejaune raises his revolver to shoot John. Luckily, Beau is not quite dead and manages to grab the officer's foot and trip him. John plunges the blade in Lejaune's heart, ironically becoming the "ultimate" mutineer. Shortly after, a relief force arrives from Tokotu. Digby and John are reunited, and the two desert in order to get

back to the abbey with a letter Michael has written to his aunt. Meanwhile, the rest of the soldiers, led by Major Henri de Beaujolais, enter the fort and find the confession, which has been left behind. After ascertaining what has happened, Henri heads to Brandon Abbey with George Lawrence to brief Lady Patricia.

Taking a circuitous route home, Digby is shot in the head by an Arab, leaving only John left alive. Eventually he makes it home as well and presents his aunt with Beau's apology for having acted as he did to protect her honor. Ironically, Sir Hector had died of cholera soon after the theft of the fake Blue Water, and Lady Patricia no longer needs it.

Comment: Wren wrote other tales about the French Foreign Legion, including *Beau Sabreur* (1926) and *Beau Ideal* (1928), though none were as popular as *Beau Geste.* It was turned into a stage play in 1925 and was brought to the screen for the first time the following year, with Ronald Colman as Beau, Neil Hamilton as Digby, and Ralph Forbes was John (who returns to the abbey, essentially taking the place of George Lawrence). This film, like those that follow, adhere rather faithfully to the original story (though Lejaune becomes Sergeant Markoff).

The second and best-known screen adaptation was made in 1939 and starred Gary Cooper as Beau, Ray Milland as John, and Robert Preston as Digby (Donald O'Connor played Beau at age 12); a third version, in 1966, featured Guy Stockwell as Beau with Doug McClure and Telly Savalas. Marty Feldman starred as Digby with Michael York as Beau in the 1977 comedy *The Last Remake of Beau Geste.*

BEOWULF   (L, C)

First Appearance: Early eighth century A.D., anonymous.

Biography: Descended from Cain, the amphibious monster Grendel hates hearing the paeans to God sung at the great hall Heorot. Lumbering to the hall, it kills 30 men and, for 12 years, refuses to make peace with the leader Hrothgar. Learning of his plight, the mighty Beowulf, son of Ecgtheow and the nephew of King Hygelac of nearby West Gothland, takes 15 men and sails to the kingdom. Beowulf has already slain at least nine other monsters and vows to add Grendel to the list. When the monster comes, Beowulf grapples with "the pernicious spoiler." Never having faced anyone so powerful, Grendel tries to flee. But the hero holds him back as other men slash at the monster, finally yanking its arm from its socket. Mortally wounded, the creature flees to its den, where it perishes.

Beowulf hangs Grendel's claw near the ceiling of the hall, but his joy is short-lived: The next night

Grendel's more ferocious mother arrives, killing people and reclaiming her son's arm. Beowulf tracks the monster down to a pool; he dives into the water and swims down for nearly a day. When he reaches bottom, the monster carries him to her lair, where they fight. Beowulf's sword proves too flimsy to cut off her head but, fortunately, his corselet is able to fend off the dagger she tries to plunge in his chest. He spots a giant sword, grabs it, and stabs the monster in the throat, killing her.

Beowulf returns home and Hygelac presents him with a great sword that had belonged to the noble Hrethel. The two go to war together, in Freisland, where Hygelac is slain. The king's wife, Hygd, has little confidence in the ability of her son Heardred to rule and offers Beowulf the throne. He refuses, agreeing to advise Heardred instead. Beowulf becomes King of the Geats only when the prince is killed in battle. Apparently he rules well and contentment is widespread. Fifty years after his legendary encounter with the Grendel family, Beowulf fights his last monster, a fire-breathing dragon that has been terrorizing his realm. During the fight, Beowulf is bitten in the throat. Young Wiglaf, a kinsman, quickly attacks the monster, and, while the beast is distracted, Beowulf stabs it with his dagger. However, the creature's venom has poisoned Beowulf, who dies shortly thereafter. He is burned on a huge funeral pyre, with 12 of his thanes riding round singing his praises.

Comment: Scholars do not agree on the date of the events recounted in the poem. Some say the sixth century A.D., which is when Hygelac is thought to have lived; others say it's set in the eighth century and is a metaphor for that era's struggle between Christianity and paganism. The poem, which is 3,182 lines long and incomplete, is believed to have been composed in Mercia or Northumbria.

Author John Gardner took the monster's point of view in his novel *Grendel* (1971). In this retelling of the tale, the monster is intelligent and sensitive, hating the fact that it lives "in the shadow, stinking of dead men, murdered children, martyred cows."

From 1975 to 1976, DC published six issues of a *Beowulf* comic book, only very loosely inspired by the poem. In 1984 First Comics did a far more faithful adaptation in #1 of the *First Comics Graphics Novel* series.

BIFF BAKER (TV)

First Appearance: *Biff Baker U.S.A.,* November 1952, CBS.

Biography: Posing as a successful importer, secret agent Biff travels the world with his wife, Louise, ostensibly looking for bargains but really looking for Communist spies and saboteurs. The blustery Biff never shies from a scrap, and never avoids a bit of espionage that might help his government.

Comment: The half-hour series lasted until March 1953, and was indicative of TV's search for "different" kinds of heroes; the crime reporters and traditional gumshoes were already becoming overexposed, and westerns were regarded as kiddie fare. Unfortunately, the Cold War thrills of *Biff Baker U.S.A.* weren't the answer. Alan Hale, Jr. *(Gilligan's Island)* starred, with Louise Baker as Randy.

BIFF BANNON (C)

First Appearance: *Speed Comics* #1, 1939, Alfred Harvey (Harvey Publications).

Biography: He may not be a hero on a par with John Paul Jones and Admiral David Farragut, but U.S. Marine Biff Bannon repeatedly does his part for his nation, whether it's battling Nazi spies or searching for buried treasure in the South Seas. Big, dumb, and powerful, but as honest as they come, Private Bannon's greatest ambition is to become an admiral.

Comment: Art Helfant's character appeared regularly throughout the magazine's 44-issue run. *Speed Comics* was the home to several adventure heroes, most notably the Three Aces—commercial pilots Crash, Cork, and the Baron, the "Devil Dogs of the

Biff Bannon tackles a Nazi spy who's trying to steal a secret new compass. © Harvey Publications.

Air"—and Speed Taylor, "famous freshman athlete" of Clayton College, who gets into sundry adventures on and off campus with his friend Tubby.

BILBO and FRODO BAGGINS (L, TV, MP, C)

First Appearance: *The Hobbit* by J.R.R. Tolkien, 1937, Allen & Unwin.

Biography: Bilbo is a Hobbit, one of the dwarfish humans who inhabit Middle-earth. Hobbits average three feet tall, are sharp-eyed, nimble, and good with tools; they are also "inclined to be fat" and dress in bright clothes, though they wear no shoes since their feet have tough, leathery soles. Hobbits smoke pipes and tend to be brown-haired.

Born September 22, 2890, in the Third Age (a period delineated by the first and second falls of the evil wizard Sauron), Bilbo lives in Bag End, Hobbiton, a village in the Shire, a pleasant region in the land of Eriador. In his greatest escapade, which begins in 2941, Bilbo joins the benevolent wizard Gandalf, the Dwarf Thorin, and 12 others in their quest to steal the One Ring, the greatest of the Rings of Power forged by Sauron. Bilbo, the group's appointed thief, recovers the One Ring and also helps to obtain the vast treasure of the dragon Smaug. Returning to the Shire, he gives his chain mail to a museum, hangs his sword Sting over the fireplace, and dwells there for 60 years in great contentment. Upon the death of Drogo and Primula (Brandybuck) Baggins in a boating mishap in 2980, Bilbo adopts their son Frodo, his cousin, who was born in 2968 and shares Bilbo's birthday. In 3001 Bilbo throws a Farewell Feast for himself on his "eleventy-first" birthday, then heads to Rivendell, leaving the Ring and his other possessions to Frodo. Bilbo stays in the distant valley for two decades, writing poetry and studying, before partaking in the Last Riding of the Keepers of the Rings, a majestic journey over the Sea, in 3021. In 3018 the Nazgul, nine servants of Sauron, arrive in search of the Ring. Frodo flees to Rivendell, where he offers to go on the Quest of Mount Doom—a journey to the Crack of Doom in the Sammath Naur chambers located high in the core of Orodruin, a volcanic mountain in Mordor, Sauron's realm. He is joined by the human warrior Aragorn and the emaciated Hobbit Gollum. After an incredible (and long) journey, Frodo reaches his goal but decides not to destroy the One Ring; Gollum changes his mind by biting off Frodo's ring finger, falling with it into the Crack of Doom. After the mission, Frodo briefly becomes mayor of the town of Michel Delving in the Shire (3019–20). However, his body and soul have been battered by his adventures and he can't find peace. Thus, after leaving his belongings to his servant Sam Gamgee, he joins the one-way journey known as the Last Riding.

Comment: Tolkien also wrote about his Hobbits in *The Fellowship of the Ring* (1954), *The Two Towers* (1955), and *The Return of the King* (1956), known collectively as *The Lord of the Rings.* They are also featured in *The Silmarillion* (1977).

On TV, an animated film of *The Hobbit* aired in 1977 with Orson Bean as Bilbo; Bean did Frodo in *The Return of the King,* which aired in 1980. In motion pictures, the characters were seen in the 1978 animated feature *Lord of the Rings.* The film was adapted into "fotonovel" book form. In 1989–90 Eclipse published a three-issue comic book adaptation of *The Hobbit.*

BILLY JACK (MP)

First Appearance: *Born Losers,* 1967, American International.

Biography: Billy Jack is a halfbreed and martial arts (hapkido) master who, in his first (and least known) adventure, helps a young woman, Vicky Barrington, escape the clutches of a biker gang led by the ruthless Danny Carmody.

After serving as a Green Beret in Vietnam, Billy Jack returns to his reservation in Arizona only to find that the nearby town of Wallich has become corrupted by the powerful Posner, who not only discriminates against the Indians and tries to steal their horses, but is out to destroy Jean Roberts' Freedom School, which takes in needy children of all races. Billy respects Jean's pacifism—for a time. After an Indian is beaten up by Bernard, Posner's son, Billy Jack attacks the attacker, then tackles a mob that tries to subdue him. Later Bernard rapes Jean and Billy Jack goes after him again. Bernard shoots the hero, who kills him with his bare hands. When Mike, the local deputy, tries to kill the wounded Billy, Billy takes him out as well. Hiding in a church, Billy is convinced by Jean to surrender and stand trial: He agrees, and is saluted by the kids as he's taken away to jail.

The saga of Billy Jack picks up at his trial and then in a sojourn in Washington where he cleans up corruption in the Senate.

Comment: Tom Laughlin starred as Billy Jack, Elizabeth James was Vicky, and Jeremy Slate was Danny in the original film. In *Billy Jack,* Laughlin was back with Bert Greed as Posner and Delores Taylor (Laughlin's wife) as Roberts. T.C. Frank (Laughlin) directed. The sequel, *The Trial of Billy Jack,* was released in 1974; *Billy Jack Goes to Washington* (1977) received no theatrical release.

BILLY WEST (L)

First Appearance: "Billy West's Cowboy Band" by Cleve Endicott, 1927, *Wild West Weekly*.

Biography: A onetime miner and cowhand, Billy is now the "courageous young owner of the Circle J Ranch," a man who will not tolerate injustice. Supremely skilled at shooting, riding, and wrestling, Billy rides the chestnut stallion Danger into adventures against rustlers, outlaws, Indians, and gunslingers. He is assisted by young cowboy Joe Scott and older, former miner and military scout Buck Foster.

Comment: Billy West's adventures began just as those of YOUNG WILD WEST came to an end. There are hints, in the stories, that Billy is Wild's son. His adventures continued into the late 1930s.

THE BISHOP (R)

First Appearance: *The Bishop and the Gargoyle,* 1936, Blue Network.

Biography: With an academic interest in crime, a well-to-do man known only as the Bishop agrees to serve on the parole board of Sing Sing prison. When a convict known only as the Gargoyle is freed, the Bishop asks him to become his partner in crimefighting. With no other prospects, the Gargoyle agrees, traveling the low road, going out in the field and getting beaten up, while the Bishop sits in his study analyzing clues.

Comment: Richard Gordon starred as the Bishop, Milton Herman (then Ken Lynch) played the Gargoyle.

THE BLACK PIRATE (C)

First Appearance: *Sensation Comics* #1, 1942, DC Comics.

Biography: In 1558 England and Spain are at war. To safeguard English interests at sea, nobleman Jon Valor puts together a band of loyal men who prowl the waters as pirates. At a waterfront tavern in the port of Buena Dista, he meets a young lass, Donna Bonita ("Bonnie"), who sails with him until she's kidnaped by Spaniards. It seems the spunky lass is the ward of King Phillip of Spain and has run away from her betrothed, the king's wicked son Don Carlos. Naturally, Valor attempts to rescue her and is captured; wily Bonnie goes to see him in prison with Father Fernando in tow, and the two are wed. Rather than widow his ward, Phillip frees Valor, who agrees not to prey on Spanish ships as long as Spain recognizes the laws of the seas. Alas, the truce is short-lived, and the couple returns to England with their young son, Justin.

Years later Justin joins his father at sea and is lost,

The first appearance of *The Black Pirate* © DC Comics.

presumed dead. The senior Valor retires, though he returns to the sea when King Charles asks him to put an end to a pirate band that's been attacking British ships. Valor learns that his son is not only alive and well but has become a Puritan and is leading the pirates to raise money for Puritans who wish to go to the New World. Justin is allowed to head for America, after which Valor hangs up his skull-and-crossbones yet again.

Originally the pirate dresses in an orange shirt, green tights, orange and green shorts, and black boots. Later he adds a black hood and cape with different-colored clothing.

Comment: The Black Pirate's last appearance was in *Sensation* #51, 1946. As drawn by Sheldon Moldoff, the Pirate was a deadringer for Douglas Fairbanks, Sr.

BLACKSTAR (TV, T)

First Appearance: *Blackstar,* September 12, 1981, CBS.

Biography: An astronaut, John Blackstar is aboard his

gamma ray-propelled shuttle when he's pulled through a black hole to the planet Zagar in a parallel universe. There he is befriended by the lovely Mara, Princess of the Secret Power, and the dwarflike Trobits King Balkar and Gossamer, who can fly thanks to his big ears. (Less-endowed Trobits fly in the balloonlike Wind Machine.) With his friends at his side and the enchanted Star Sword in his hand, Blackstar mounts his flying dragon horse Warlock and fights the evil Overlord, the Wizard King, who dwells in his Ice Castle in the misty Shadowlands. Other foes include the equally evil Neptul, Lord of Aquaria, the wizard Kadray, the Leopard Man Tongo, and the Vampire Man Gargo.

The bare-chested Blackstar wears a red cape, fur boots, and loincloth.

Comment: There were 13 half-hour adventures in the series, which aired over and over through August 1983. The series was produced by Filmation; George DiCenzo provided the voice of Blackstar.

Galoob launched a toy line in 1983, but it was too late to save the series.

BLAZE BARTON   (C)

First Appearance: *Hit Comics* #1, 1940, Quality Comics Group.

Biography: The year: 50,017 A.D. The problem: The earth is spiraling ever closer to the sun and, according to Professor Solis, "in three years . . . life will disappear because of the terrific heat!" Blaze Barton is both an associate of the professor and a friend of his daughter Betty. (It isn't clear which relationship came first.) He helps the scientist construct a "great, heat-proof city," in which select men and women are invited to live. Everyone else on Earth dies, cities crumble, and Blaze and Betty don "heat helmets" to see what's left. They discover that "core creatures" from inside the earth, "accustomed to great heat," have crawled forth to live on the surface. War erupts between the two races, with Blaze the greatest hero of the human race.

Comment: Blaze appeared in the first 13 issues of *Hit Comics*. Other adventure heroes who appeared in the pages of the magazine include X-5, Secret Agent; Jack and Jill, Super Sleuths, clones of Nick and Nora Charles; Bob and Swabb, sailors Bob Masters and Swab Decker of the USS *Scarab*; and Casey Jones, the railroad engineer who's "never been a fraction of a minute late," despite battling crooks and natural disasters.

THE BLUE COATS   (C)

First Appearance: *Les Tuniques Bleues,* 1972.
Biography: A unit in the Union Army during the Civil War, the Blue Coats consist of the strict Captain Stark, the even stricter Lieutenant Lovelace, the somewhat hapless, red-headed Sergeant Chesterfield, and the equally inept, diminutive Corporal Blutch, the grumbling Private O'Brien, and others. All report back to the grumpy General Alexander. In addition to fighting the Confederates at Bull Run and elsewhere, the soldiers are concerned with protecting ammunition trains, battling Indians, interrupting enemy supply and gold lines, and even dealing with a testy Arab to obtain camels for long marches.

Comment: Though lighthearted, the French strip is historically accurate and superbly written. The characters were created by artist Louis Salverius and writer Raoul Cauvin, and continue to this day with art by Willy Lambil, who took over after the sixth adventure; 34 albums of adventures have been published to date, though none in the U.S.

BOBBY THATCHER   (CS)

First Appearance: *Bobby Thatcher,* March 1927, McClure Syndicate.

Biography: Bobby Thatcher is a 15-year-old boy who lives with his aunt, Ida Baxter, and his sister, Hattie, and gets into adventures involving crooks, bullies, missing treasure, and the like in Jonesboro, in the U.S. heartland. His cronies include his girlfriends, Lulu Bowers and Marge Hall, and other boys, Ulysses "Tubby" Butler, Elmer Bowers, and Peewee Nimmo.

Later Bobby falls in with the grizzled sailor Hurricane Bill and helps him battle the wicked Captain Bottlejohn.

Comment: The strip was created by artist George Storm. He retired from the strip in 1937, and it was discontinued a year later.

Storm created *Bobby Thatcher* after the disappointing failure of *Phil Hardy,* which began in November 1925 and is generally credited as having been the first adventure strip. *Phil Hardy,* cocreated with writer Edwin Alger, Jr. (a pseudonym for J.J. Williams), featured a lad of 15 as a modern-day seagoing hero who enjoys adventures around the world battling the likes of Captain Eli Bent, Baldy Scott, and Ghost Hansen. His closest friend among the rugged crew is ship's cook Jason Royle. Unfortunately, the rough, vivid, bloody strip lasted only until September 1926.

BOMBA   (L, MP, C)

First Appearance: *Bomba the Jungle Boy; or, the Old Naturalist's Secret* by Roy Rockwood, 1926, Cupples and Leon.

Biography: Bomba knows little about his past. His

Johnny Sheffield, right, looking a little long in the tooth in one of the last *Bomba* films, *Safari Drums.* © Allied Artists.

parents were "Bartow" and "Laura," and he was somehow separated from them in the Amazon jungle when he was quite young. Befriended by the wild animals, he lives among them for years until a naturalist named Casson discovers him. When Casson loses his memory in an accident, Bomba cares for the old man, and the two become close friends. Throughout his adventures involving hunters, wild animals, anthropologists, headhunters, explorers, and the like, Bomba is assisted by "his monkey friends and by Polulu, the great puma, whom he befriended in his cub days." The jungle boy, who runs with "deerlike leaps," is an expert with the knife and bow and arrow.

Comment: Rockwood (a house name for several authors) followed his first novel with *Bomba the Jungle Boy at the Moving Mountain, Bomba the Jungle Boy at the Giant Cataract, Bomba the Jungle Boy on Jaguar Island, Bomba the Jungle Boy in the Abandoned City,* and others, published two each year

through 1930. The character is also well-known from 11 feature films that starred Johnny Sheffield, who had played Tarzan's son Boy in several of the Tarzan films. The films in which the elephant-riding hero appeared were *Bomba, the Jungle Boy* (1949), *Bomba on Panther Island* (1949), *The Lost Volcano* (1950), *The Hidden City* (1950; a.k.a. *Bomba and the Hidden City*), *The Elephant Stampede* (1951; a.k.a. *Bomba and the Elephant Stampede*), *African Treasure* (1952), *Bomba and the Jungle Girl* (1952), *Safari Drums* (1953), *The Golden Idol* (1954), *Killer Leopard* (1954), and *Lord of the Jungle* (1955).

DC published seven issues of *Bomba the Jungle Boy* from 1967 to 1968. Early issues featured rare comic book art by the late science fiction illustrator Leo Summers.

An identical character was Jungle Boy, who starred in his own half-hour TV series in 1958. Filmed in Kenya, the syndicated show starred 14-year-old Michael Carr Hartley as Boy, the sole survivor of a plane crash, who has learned to survive in the jungle. Ronald Adam played the "Casson" character, Dr. Laurence.

BOMBER BURNS (C)

First Appearance: *Victory Comics,* 1941, Hillman Publications.

Biography: When the Germans shoot down American stunt flier Jack "Bomber" Burns, who is attached to the RAF, he decides to make some changes in the way he does battle. The hero gets hold of a P-38 and hides out in the Scottish Highlands, where he customizes the plane with "special superchargers," a dozen machine guns, a cannon, and even "a flame-thrower from an Aussie armored car." He also decides to use "only incendiary bullets," and—not surprisingly, given his last name—calls his plane the *Firebrand.* To complement the plane, Burns designs a red uniform with yellow goggles and even creates "calling cards dipped in phosphorous! When they dry out, they'll catch fire!"

Comment: Bomber Burns appeared in all four issues of the title, which starred the superhero the Conqueror, the war hero Sergeant Flagg, and other tales starring "The Fighting Forces of Uncle Sam in Deadly Combat!"

BOSTON BLACKIE (L, MP, R, TV)

First Appearance: "The Price of Principle" by Jack Boyle, 1914, *The American Magazine.*

Biography: Blackie is a former convict and ex-opium user who is one of the bravest and best safe crackers in the world. However, he is far from a common criminal. He does not view himself as "a criminal but a combatant." A university graduate and a gentleman who is devoted to his wife, Mary—his "best loved pal and sole confidant"—Blackie robs because he believes society is corrupt, and takes what he feels others should not have. He gives this to others, those whom the "Divine Spirit" moves him to help—for example, children who lost everything during the San Francisco earthquake. Another time he breaks off safe cracking to comfort a little boy whose parents have left him alone. He holds his honor, "the rigid mandates" of his conscience, "more sacred than life itself." Even Deputy Warden Martin Sherwood, after a long chase, refuses to bring Blackie in when the safe cracker declines to shoot him in cold blood. "The man I wanted to take back to prison is not here," he observes.

Blackie is "gray-haired, stern-faced, laconic, and efficient." His fingers are sandpapered until the blood shows "redly below the skin" to make them more sensitive. He is based in San Francisco; "Boston Blackie" is simply a name the narrator (Boyle himself) has chosen to conceal his "real" identity.

Comment: The next three tales also appeared in *The American Magazine:* "The Story About Dad Morgan," "Death Cell Visions," and "A Thief's Daughter." *Redbook* (then, *The Red Book*) magazine began publishing others in 1917, including two of the most famous: "Boston Blackie's Mary" and "The Baby and the Burglar." Blackie moved to *Cosmopolitan* two years later; the 28 stories were changed slightly to form the chapters of a novel, and were published in book form by H.K. Fly as *Boston Blackie* in 1919.

The character is best known through his appearances in film, on radio, and on TV.

In motion pictures, Blackie's career began in the silents, with Bert Lytell playing him in *Boston Blackie's Little Pal* (1918) and *Blackie's Redemption* (1919), Lionel Barrymore in *The Face in the Fog* (1922), David Powell in *Missing Millions* (1922), William Russell in *Boston Blackie* (1923), Forrest Stanley in *Through the Dark* (1924), and Raymond Glenn in *The Return of Boston Blackie* (1927). The character wasn't seen again until 1941, when Chester Morris played Blackie as a do-gooder who operated outside the law to track down stolen goods, battle counterfeiters and killers, find missing persons, and the like, frequently running afoul of Inspector Faraday (Richard Lane). When he wasn't reforming bad guys, he was practicing magic, a hobby of his that also helped him in several situations. The 14 Morris films were *Meet Boston Blackie* (1941), *Confessions of Boston Blackie* (1941), *Alias Boston Blackie* (1942), *Boston Blackie Goes Hollywood* (1942), *After Midnight With Boston Blackie* (1943), *The Chance of a Lifetime* (1943), *One Mysterious Night* (1944), *Boston Blackie Booked on Suspicion* (1945), *Boston Blackie's Rendezvous* (1945), *A Close Call for Boston Blackie* (1946), *The Phantom Thief* (1946), *Boston Blackie and the Law* (1946), *Trapped by Boston Blackie* (1948), and *Boston Blackie's Chinese Venture* (1949).

On radio from 1945 to 1950, Blackie was devoted to helping the impoverished or trying to convince crooks to turn over a new leaf. As the announcer put it before each episode, he was an "enemy to those who make him an enemy; friend to those who have no friends." Chester Morris was the first to play the role, after which Richard Kollmar took over for two years; Lesley Woods, then Jan Miner, was Mary.

On TV, Kent Taylor played the part in 58 half-hour episodes, which were syndicated beginning in 1951. Blackie was now based in Los Angeles, with Mary as his girlfriend; he even had a dog, Whitey. Lois Collier was Mary, with Frank Orth as Faraday.

THE BOY COMMANDOS (C)

First Appearance: *Detective Comics* #64, 1942, DC Comics.

Biography: During World War II four orphaned boys take to hanging around an American unit stationed in Great Britain: French boy Andrew Chavard; pudgy local kid Alfy Twidgett; Dutch boy Jan Haasan; and an American nicknamed Brooklyn. (His real name is unknown.) Captain Rip Carter organizes the lads into a fighting unit known as the Boy Commandos, forcing them to go through military training *and* school. Their *raison d'être*, as explained by Brooklyn, is "We're out ta get Hitler and his mob cuz dere ain't room fer both of us, see?" and they proceed to wreak havoc on the Axis in both Europe and Japan. After the war Jan goes to live with relatives on a farm in Holland while the other boys return to the U.S. with Carter, battling such foes as Diamond Hand or Crazy Quilt (the "artist in villainy"), solving mysteries under the sea, helping such celebrities as Dale Evans or Cleveland Indians pitcher Bob Feller, or girdling the globe in the Atomobile. When Alfy returns to England to go to college, young cowboy Tex joins the team; after Andrew returns to France where relatives have been located, bright young Percy Clearweather takes his place. The last member to join is Wolf, their dog mascot.

Comment: The characters were created by writer Joe Simon and artist Jack Kirby, and remained in *Detective Comics* through #83; they appeared in *Worlds Finest Comics* from #8 to #41 and had their own title, which lasted 36 issues, from 1942 to 1949.

The team also created the Boy Explorers, who starred in just two issues of their own Harvey Comics publication in 1946. They were orphans Mister Zero, Gashouse, Smiley, and Gadget, and they roamed the seas with Yankee clipper seaman Commodore Sinbad. (See also THE NEWSBOY LEGION.)

THE BRAVADOS (C)

First Appearance: *Wild Western Action* #3, 1971, Skywald Publishing.

Biography: The Bravados are ex-rancher and ex-soldier Joshua Reno; the "freewheeling" Jefferson Drumm; the "big, gentle Black man" Gideon, a former Civil War corporal and hired gun who is searching for the sadistic Confederate major, Jonas Payne; a mute Indian known as Charade; and a woman called Hellion. It is never revealed how and why they got together; with the exception of Gideon, they're all "a bunch of rag-tag losers who haven't got anywhere else to go."

On the engine, clockwise from the top, are *The Bravados:* Charade, Hellion, Joshua Reno, Jefferson Drumm, and Gideon. © Skywald Publishing.

In any case, the group rides around the West circa 1870, righting wrongs.

Comment: The characters were created by writer Len Wein and editor Sol Brodsky. The Bravados starred in the last issue of *Wild Western Action,* then went on to star in one issue of their own title. Both titles featured reprints of western adventures that had appeared elsewhere: the Durango Kid and his sidekick Muley Pike; drifter Billy Nevada; Bat Masterson; and Swift Arrow, a cowboy who was called Straight Arrow when the stories were first published. Skywald (for Brodsky and backer Israel Waldman) also published several other western titles. *Blazing Six-Guns* featured new stories of the Sundance Kid (also by Wein) and reprints of Wyatt Earp and Doc Holliday; *The Sundance Kid* got his own magazine, which also offered reprints of Swift Arrow, the Durango Kid, Billy the Kid, the Indian Red Hawk, and the one-of-a-kind Bowie-Knife Ben; and *Butch Cassidy,* with new stories plus reprints of Maverick (no relation to the TV series, though his foes the Pillowcase Gang would have fit nicely in the tongue-in-cheek show) and hero Whip Wilson.

BRENDA STARR   (CS, L, MP, C)

First Appearance: *Brenda Starr,* June 30, 1940, Chicago Tribune-New York News Syndicate.

Biography: A bold, flame-haired reporter for *The Flash,* Brenda travels the world in search of news and invariably becomes part of the story she's covering. Always dressed at the height of fashion, whether she's working at her desk or parachuting from a plane, she is constantly torn between the lure of adventure and the desire to settle down.

The desire is fueled by the fact that for over two decades, Brenda is courted by the mysterious, handsome, ultra-wealthy Basil St. John of Sun Valley, who wears an eye patch and sends her black orchids from his mountain retreat but refuses to wed her because his family suffers from insanity and he's afraid he'll pass that on. He finally relents in 1976, and the two were wed. Before that Brenda was briefly pursued by the aggressive Larry Nickels, editor of *The Cloud.*

Brenda's supporting cast includes her boss, the grumpy, bug-eyed editor Livwright; her close friend, fellow reporter and beret-wearing Hank O'Hair; Daphne, the city editor's spoiled, bumbling niece; copy boy Pesky; and Brenda's overweight cousin from Pinhook, Indiana, Abretha Breeze, daughter of Uncle Frank and Aunt Emmy. The nosy Abretha and her little dog, Tornado, are frequent crashers at the Starr pad.

Comment: The character was created by Dalia (Dale) Messick and appeared in a Sunday page only until a daily strip debuted in October 1945. She was named after Brenda Frazier, a famed debutante of the day. (Starr, of course, came from "star reporter.")

Today the strip is handled by Ramona Fradon and Mary Schmich.

In motion pictures, Brenda was played by Joan Woodbury in the 13-chapter serial *Brenda Starr, Reporter* (1945), directed by Wallace W. Fox, in which she learns the location of stolen money that is being sought by the mob; by Jill St. John in the made-for-TV movie *Brenda Starr* (1976), directed by Mel Stuart, in which she gets tangled up with a voodoo cult in Brazil; and by Brooke Shields in the theatrical film *Brenda Starr* (filmed in 1986, released in 1992), in which Brenda wants to quit the newspaper—until she's drawn into several new adventures.

Brenda has also starred in her own comic book—Four Star published 12 issues from 1947 to 1949, Charlton published two in 1955, and Dell issued one in 1963. She appeared in one Big Little Book, *Brenda Starr and the Masked Impostor* (1940).

BRET MAVERICK   (TV, C, MP)

First Appearance: *Maverick,* September 1957, ABC.

Biography: Dressed in black with a paisley vest, lazy young Bret Maverick is a cardsharp and a coward who roams the West of the early 1870s, towns with such names as Apocalypse and Oblivion (which should have tipped him off), trying to win money, woo women, and keep enemies at bay not with gunplay but with wisecracks and bootlicking. (Meeting a woman gambler in the third episode, "According to Hoyle," proves a *real* challenge.) When a shootout is unavoidable, it's usually Bret's more serious and marginally braver brother, Bart, who handles the chores—though he, too, prefers flight to fight wherever possible. Later, atypical cousin Beauregard Maverick hits the trail, a Texan who fought bravely in the Civil War, spent time in England, and has returned to the U.S. intent on increasing his wealth (and adding notches to his gun, if need be). Bret's other brother Brent is introduced shortly after. The Maverick brothers are all the sons of cantankerous widower Beauregard "Pappy" Maverick (who, in one episode, is intent on marrying an 18-year-old beauty).

A new member of the clan, Ben Maverick, appears years later. Bret's slick, dapper cousin is a Harvard dropout. The Maverick blood flows thickly in his veins, and he pursues a life of gambling while avoiding both work and confrontations. He roams Idaho and environs with his lover, Nell McGarrahan, his neck regularly being saved by Marshal Edge Troy.

When last seen (in *Bret Maverick*), Bret is living in the Arizona Territory, in the town of Sweetwater, in the 1880s. This more mature, more settled Bret owns the Lazy Ace ranch and is co-owner of the Red Ox Saloon, partnered with ex-sheriff Tom Guthrie.

Comment: The hour-long series aired through July 1962. Often crossing over into satire—as in the *Bonanza* spoof in which Bart has an adventure with rancher Joe Wheelwright (Jim Backus) and his sons Moose, Henry, and Small Paul of the Subrosa Ranch—the series was one of the most popular westerns in an era filled with them. Star James Garner (who played both Bret and Pappy) left in 1960 after the studio refused to give him a better contract. Beau was introduced in 1960, played by Roger Moore, and left the following year, replaced by Brent, who was played by Robert Colbert. Jack Kelly starred as Bart throughout the run of the series. *Young Maverick* debuted on CBS in November 1979 (following a TV movie/pilot the year before, *The New Maverick*) starring Charles Frank, but was gone by January 1980. Susan Blanchard costarred as Nell, John Dehner as Troy. Garner and Kelly guest-starred in the pilot in which they meet their kin on the trail. Garner returned to prime time in *Bret Maverick,* which aired on NBC from December 1981 to August 1982, with reruns airing during the summer of 1990.

In comic books, the character appeared in six issues of Dell's *4-Color* series from 1958 to 1959, after which he was given his own title that lasted from #7 to #19, 1959 to 1962.

In the 1994 motion picture *Maverick,* Mel Gibson starred with Richard Donner directing from a William Goldman script.

BRICK BRADFORD   (CS, L, MP, C)

First Appearance: *Brick Bradford,* August 21, 1933, Central Press Association.

Biography: As a boy growing up in Kentucky, Brick was fond of "fishing, swimming, shooting marbles," and exploring the hills and forests. It's no wonder that he grew up to be a two-fisted pilot and adventurer who goes where no hero has gone before. After rescuing scientist Kalla Kopak from a plane wreck, the two use the scientist's Shrinking Sphere to travel inside the atomic structure of a penny, fighting germs and finding subatomic civilizations; other adventures have Brick traveling through space aboard his rocket, journeying to the center of the earth, and moving through time via the Time Top. His sidekick in many of these adventures is brash Bucko O'Brien; his girlfriend (and frequent stowaway) is June Salisbury.

Brick dresses in a riding boots and breeches and a white short-sleeved shirt with a bold orange "B" in a circle on the chest.

Comment: The character was created by artist Clarence Gray and writer William Ritt. It was later taken over by King Features.

The hero's only Big Little Book was *Brick Bradford with Brocco the Modern Buccaneer* (1938).

In motion pictures, Brick was played by Kane Richmond in the 15-chapter *Brick Bradford* (1947), directed by Spencer Bennet. Hired by the United Nations to protect a new "anti-guided missile," Brick becomes involved with Laydron, a gang leader determined to get the missile and kidnap its inventor, Dr. Tymak. Thanks to his "crystal door" invention, Tymak ends up on the moon instead, where he's held by Lunarians who are trying to overthrow their corrupt leaders. After helping them and rescuing Tymak, Brick gets lost in time thanks to the Time Top. Naturally, he makes it back to the present in time to thwart Laydron.

John Merton was Tymak and Charles Quigley played Laydron.

Brick was costarred in a number of comic books and also starred in four issues of his own title, published by Standard from 1948 to 1949.

BRIGADIER GENERAL FRANK SAVAGE (L, MP, TV, C)

First Appearance: *Twelve O'Clock High,* 1949, Twentieth Century-Fox (see COMMENT).

Biography: After arriving in England to replace the war-weary Colonel Davenport, the American Frank Savage serves with the 918th Bomb Group of the U.S. Eighth Air Force, leading air raids against Germany and enemy positions throughout Europe. Initially the men dislike the strict Savage, but they relent when they realize that his concern is for their safety; ultimately, worrying about the men leads to a nervous breakdown, which results in Savage being relieved of his command.

He reports to Major General Wiley Crowe; Major Harvey Stovall is his adjutant.

Comment: The film starred Gregory Peck and was directed by Henry King. An hour-long ABC TV series began airing in September 1964, starring Robert Lansing, and has Savage actually flying on the bombing missions with his men. But Lansing was unhappy with the show (it was moved to an earlier hour, with the emphasis on adventure rather than characterization), and Savage perishes after being shot down.

Upon Savage's death, his command is assumed by Captain Joe Gallagher, who quickly rises to the rank of colonel—despite Savage having told him in the show's first episode, "You are a disgrace to the uniform that I hate to share with you. I hate you more than a Nazi because you're supposed to be on our side!" (Gallagher, the son of a three-star general, was arrogant and expected preferential treatment.)

Gallagher matures quickly, taking part in as many bombing missions as possible. He reports to Brigadier General Ed Britt, played by Andrew Duggan. The series lasted until January 1967.

Dell published two issues of a *Twelve O'Clock High* comic book in 1965.

The character of Savage was inspired by the real-life exploits of Major General Frank A. Armstrong; the film was based loosely on the book of the same name by Beirne Lay, Jr., and Sy Bartlett.

BRUCE GENTRY   (CS, MP, C)

First Appearance: *Bruce Gentry,* March 25, 1945, Robert Hall Syndicate.

Biography: Initially Bruce Gentry is one of a small group of pilots who establish a small cargo and passenger airline in South America, serving hitherto neglected areas of the continent. Bruce, the most experience flier, frequently flies "shotgun" with other planes of their small fleet, keeping an eye out for unscrupulous rivals.

After two years the hero works less and less with the company and becomes a hemispheric do-gooder, battling criminals and spies of all kinds.

Comment: The strip was created by Ray Bailey, who had been an assistant to Milton Caniff. (See STEVE CANYON.) The strip lasted seven years.

In films, the character appeared in the 15-chapter *Bruce Gentry—Daredevil of the Skies* (1949). Tom Neal starred as Gentry, who is hot on the trail of a spy known as the Recorder, who has developed a flying disc that can be sent to destroy targets as small as a car or as large as the Panama Canal. Spencer Bennet and Thomas Carr directed.

Gentry was the star of his own Better Publications comic book, which lasted eight issues from 1948 to 1949.

BUCK ROGERS   (L, CS, R, C, MP, TV, T)

First Appearance: "Armageddon 2419 A.D." by Philip Francis Nowlan, 1928, *Amazing Stories*.

Biography: Born in 1898, five-foot 11-inch Anthony Rogers fights in the skies over France as a Pursuit Pilot for 18 months. After the war he returns to the U.S. and becomes a surveyor. On December 15, 1927, while working for the American Radioactive Gas Corporation, he's exploring an abandoned coal mine near the Wyoming Valley just outside of Pittsburgh, Pennsylvania, when he's trapped by a cave-in. After passing out due to the lack of air and put into hibernation by "the rapid accumulation of the radioactive gases," he awakes 492 years later when the strata shifts, admitting fresh air. Wandering from the mine, he meets air patrol scout Wilma Deering and learns that while he slept the Soviets and Chinese banded together to conquer Europe. After that the Chinese defeated their erstwhile allies and conquered the United States. Rogers joins Wilma and her Wyoming Gang, one of the many gangs of resistance fighters that are busy waging the Second War for Independence against the evil Mongolian Han Airlords.

The scouts are divided into groups known as Jumpers, whose inertron belts enable them to take great jumps, and floaters, whose inertron blocks with rocket motors allow them to fly. All carry "rocket guns," which fire projectiles that are either "solid or explosive," and communicate over hundreds of miles by

Gil Gerard as *Buck Rogers,* with Erin Gray as Wilma. © Universal Pictures.

Ultrophone, which operates on "ultronic ethereal vibrations." In addition to these, Dr. Huer is constantly inventing new tools and weapons, such as the psychic restriction ray, the molecular expansor, the teleradioscope, radiovision transmitters, and a mechanical mole for burrowing inside the earth.

Comment: The original novelette was followed by a sequel, "The Airlords of Han," which appeared in *Amazing Stories* the following year and concluded with the overthrow of the Asian empire. The two stories were knit together into a novel, *Armageddon 2419 A.D.*, which enjoyed modest success. However, the tale came to the attention of the John Dille Company, a newspaper syndicate, which hired Nowlan to develop a comic strip based on the character. Nolan came up with a shorter, punchier name than Anthony—Buck—and the comic strip *Buck Rogers 2429 A.D.* was published on January 7, 1929, featuring art by Dick Calkins. The title was changed each year to keep events exactly 500 years in the future; eventually it was simply called *Buck Rogers in the 25th Century.* The strip ran until 1968 and was enormously popular, featuring jet packs, blasters, and spaceships, which brought science fiction into the modern era . . . and into the home of every kid in America.

The success of the strip launched the *Buck Rogers in the 25th Century* radio show, which aired from 1931 to 1939 and starred Matt Crowly, then Curtis Arnall, Carl Frank, and John Larkin as Buck, with Adele Ronson as Wilma. The show's listeners were able to join Buck and his freedom fighters by becoming "Solar Scouts."

In comic books, *Buck Rogers* (1933), a one-shot Kelloggs Corn Flakes giveway, reprinted the newspaper strips and was one of the first comic books ever published. Famous Funnies published six issues of *Buck Rogers* from 1940 to 1943, also reprinted the comic strips, as did the nine issues published by Toby Press in 1951. Gold Key published new material in a 1964 one-shot, after which they served up 14 issues based on the TV series (1979 to 1982).

The popularity of the character also spawned a 12-episode movie serial *Buck Rogers* (1939), in which major changes were made in the story. This time Buck and his young friend, Buddy Wade, are piloting a dirigible that crashes into a mountain in the Arctic. Nirvano gas in their gondola puts the two to sleep for 500 years, after which the heroes are found, taken to the rebels' Hidden City, and end up journeying to Saturn and enlisting the aliens' aid in the war against Killer Kane. Buster Crabbe was Buck, Jackie Moran was Buddy, and Constance Moore played Wilma. The serial was edited into two feature films, *Planet Outlaws* (1953) and *Destination Saturn* (1965).

From April 1950 to January 1951, a half-hour show starring Kem Dibbs and then Robert Pastene aired on ABC, in which Buck goes to sleep in a cave behind Niagara Falls and wakes up in A.D. 2430. The series introduced a Martian villain, Black Barney Wade.

A TV film, *Buck Rogers in the 25th Century,* starring Gil Gerard, was released theatrically first in 1979 and introduced a TV series that ran from 1979 to 1981. In this new incarnation, William "Buck" Rogers is the only passenger on a 1987 Ranger III deep-space shuttle flight that carries him through a cloud of meteoric gases that put him to sleep. When he wakes, he returns to earth 500 years in the future. There he meets Wilma (Erin Gray), plus a new sidekick, a robot named Twiki (Frank Silla, voice by Mel Blanc). In the second and final season, he is joined by the birdlike warrior Hawk (Thom Christopher) of the planet Throm. A new comic strip was introduced based on the TV show, but it expired shortly after the series did.

Two new novels, *Mordred* by John Eric Holmes (1980) and *Warrior's Blood* by Richard S. McEnroe (1981), continued Nowlan's tale, in which Marshal Anthony Rogers is now the leader of the U.S. government and must stave off a return of the Han conquerors. Addison E. Steele wrote two novels based on

scripts for the upcoming TV series: *Buck Rogers in the 25th Century* (1978) and *Buck Rogers #2: That Man on Beta* (1979).

In addition to countless action figures, board games, and toy ray guns, the hero has starred in video games such as *Buck Rogers: Planet of Zoom.*

BUCK RYAN (CS, C)

First Appearance: "Buck Ryan," March 22, 1937, *The Daily Mirror,* England.

Biography: A young, two-fisted British sleuth, brown-haired Buck and his teenage assistant, Slipper, get into dark, violent adventures involving murder, kidnaping, salmon smuggling, the S.S., and oddball criminals such as the acid-scarred woman Twilight. Not long after Buck reforms criminal Zola Andersen, the gorgeous blonde replaces Slipper at Buck's side. Though romance develops, the two never wed; indeed, Zola is eventually replaced by Twilight, who turns over a new leaf.

Buck works closely with Scotland Yard's Inspector Page.

Comment: The British strip was created by artist Jack Monk and writer Don Freeman, and ran until July 1962. Atlas Publications published a successful comic book in England, *Buck Ryan Detective.*

BUCKY BIZARRE (C)

First Appearance: *Bizarre Adventures* #28, 1981, Marvel Comics.

Biography: The bald, bespectacled, black-clad hero with his winged-Mercury helmet travels through time

Bucky Bizarre rescues a fair lady from a vampire. © Marvel Comics.

in a rinky-dink airplanelike craft that frequently malfunctions. Nothing is known about Bucky Bizarre's life other than that he has friends in the Paleolithic Age. Bucky moves in and out of the time stream, helping a sludge monster avoid hate-filled kids in the 1950s, saving a woman from a vampire in Victorian London, and even going back to a time before creation, waiting in darkness, and finally shouting "When the hell is someone gonna ask 'Let there be light'?"—and causing light to appear. His favorite expression is "Good gravity!"

Comment: The comedic character appeared through #33 in two- or three-page adventures, and was created by writer Steve Skeates and artist Steve Smallwood.

BULLDOG DRUMMOND (L, S, MP, R, TV)

First Appearance: *Bulldog Drummond* by H.C. McNeile (a.k.a. "Sapper"), 1920.

Biography: At the end of World War I, Captain Hugh Drummond finds himself restless and unfulfilled. A passionate patriot who once belonged to the Communist-hating Black Gang, the powerful six-footer devotes his life to battling the enemies of England, typically Germans, Russians, or the megalo-maniacal Carl Peterson who, in one adventure, tries to orchestrate strikes that will cause Britain to fall, and, in another, plans to rule the world through the use of a toxic poison. (When Peterson perishes, his mistress tries to avenge him by abducting Drummond's wife, Phyllis.)

Drummond believes in fairness and has ill-concealed contempt for those—including the police—who permit laws to stop them from apprehending wrongdoers. His contact with Scotland Yard is Colonel Neilson. He is also assisted, on occasion, by his valet, Tenny, and his high-born friend, Algie.

Drummond is an excellent boxer and marksman. The hero's nickname derives from both his tenacity and imposing physical presence, especially his deep-set eyes and flattened nose, the latter the result of a heavyweight boxing match in his last year of high school.

Comment: McNeile wrote nine other Drummond novels: *The Black Gang* (1922), *Bulldog Drummond's Third Round* (1925; *The Third Round* in England), *The Final Count* (1926), *The Female of the Species* (1928), *Temple Tower* (1929), *Bulldog Drummond Returns* (1932), *Bulldog Drummond Strikes Back* (1933; *Knockout* in England), *Bulldog Drummond at Bay* (1935), and *Challenge* (1937). After the author's death, friend Gerard Fairlie contin-

ued the series, writing *Bulldog Drummond on Dartmoor* (1938), *Bulldog Drummond Attacks* (1939), *Captain Bulldog Drummond* (1945), *Bulldog Drummond Stands Fast* (1947), *Hands Off Bulldog Drummond* (1949), *Calling Bulldog Drummond* (1951), and *The Return of the Black Gang* (1954).

On stage, the character first appeared in *Bulldog Drummond* on Broadway and on the London stage in 1921.

The character has had a long career in motion pictures: Carlyle Blackwell starred in the silent *Bulldog Drummond* (1922); Jack Buchanan played the part in *The Third Round* (1925); Ronald Colman was the hero in *Bulldog Drummond* (1929) and *Bulldog Drummond Strikes Back* (1934); Kenneth MacKenna had the role in *Temple Tower* (1930); and Ray Milland was the ex-soldier in *Bulldog Drummond Escapes* (1937). John Howard made the part his in seven films: *Bulldog Drummond Comes Back* (1937), *Bulldog Drummond's Revenge* (1937), *Bulldog Drummond's Peril* (1938), *Bulldog Drummond in Africa* (1938), *Arrest Bulldog Drummond!* (1938), *Bulldog Drummond's Secret Police* (1939), and *Bulldog Drummond's Bride* (1939). Ron Randell played the part in *Bulldog Drummond at Bay* and *Bulldog Drummond Strikes Back* (both 1947), and Tom Conway starred in *The Challenge* and *Thirteen Lead Soldiers* (both 1948). Walter Pidgeon played Bulldog in *Calling Bulldog Drummond* (1951), and Richard Johnson made the last two films (to date): *Deadlier than the Male* (1967) and *Some Girls Do* (1971). In 1934 British comedian Jack Hulbert starred in *Bulldog Jack,* a fumbler who must take the place of the ill Drummond.

On radio, *Bulldog Drummond* debuted on Mutual in 1941 and, over the years, starred George Coulouris, Santos Ortega, and Ned Wever *(sic)* as Drummond, with Luis Van Rooten and then Rod Hendrickson as Denny. A Bulldog Drummond TV series was produced by the BBC and starred Robert Beatty.

BUTCH CASSIDY AND THE SUN DANCE KIDS (TV)

First Appearance: *Butch Cassidy and the Sun Dance Kids,* September 1973, NBC.

Biography: The U.S. government has the answer to getting access to other countries: They'll enlist a touring rock group as spies. Enter World Wide Talent agency's Butch Cassidy and the Sun Dance Kids, consisting of lead singer Butch, Merilee, Harvey, Stephanie, and their dog-mascot Elvis. The group's boss is Mr. Socrates, and their adventures put them on the trail of counterfeiters, send them to Hong Kong, take them on the *Orient Express,* lead them to a haunted castle, and more.

Comment: There were only 13 half-hour episodes of this Hanna-Barbera series. The voice of Harvey was provided by former Monkees drummer/singer Mickey Dolenz; Chip Hand was the voice of Butch; Judi Strangis was Merilee; Tina Holland was Stephanie; and dependable Hanna-Barbera star Frank Welker was Elvis. John Stephenson was Mr. Socrates.

BUZ SAWYER (CS, L, C)

First Appearance: *Buz Sawyer,* November 2, 1943, King Features.

Biography: An all-American fresh from flight training, naval Lieutenant (JG) Buz Sawyer is stationed on the aircraft carrier *Tippecanoe,* from which he wages war on the Japanese, ably assisted by his gunner Roscoe Sweeney. Back home, Buz's girlfriend, Christy Jameson, waits for him—though seemingly in vain. After Buz is mustered out in October 1946, he be-comes embroiled in a tragic adventure. Hanging out in New York with fellow war pilot Chili Harrison, Buz is blamed when his new fiancee, Tot Winter, is pushed to her death from a skyscraper. The search for her real killer (who turns out to be the tiger owned by a female gang boss) sends Buz on an adventure that takes him around the world, battling Russians, pirates, and even the guardians of Hitler himself, who is alive and well and hiding in Africa. When the matter is resolved, Buz spends time as a private investigator and government troubleshooter, eventually marrying Christy. He returns to flying on occasion, battling spies, killers, and once a flock of geese released from a plane he's pursuing. Sweeney reappears occasionally; he and his sister Lucille work the family farm.

Comment: The character was created by Roy Crane. Buz appeared in one Big Little Book, *Buz Sawyer and Bomber 13,* in 1946; Standard Comics published three issues of the *Buz Sawyer* comic book from 1948 to 1949.

See also CAPTAIN EASY.

C

CAGNEY AND LACEY (TV)

First Appearance: *Cagney and Lacey,* October 1981, CBS.

Biography: Detectives Chris Cagney and Mary Beth Lacey of New York's 14th Precinct are as different as they could be: Cagney is unmarried, career-oriented, and somewhat emotionally unstable; Mary Beth is wed to Harvey Lacey, and has two sons, Harvey, Jr. and Michael, and a daughter, April, and is relatively well adjusted. Reporting to Lieutenant Bert Samuels, the two battle traditional crime—a car theft ring, a cop killer, a stalker, hotel murder, and so on—as well as sexism and other social problems in stories that involve the date rape of Cagney, her relationship with fellow cop and junkie Sergeant Dory McKenna, her struggle to overcome alcoholism, and more.

Chris's father, Charlie, appears now and then on the series. Other members of the force include Detectives Mark Petrie and Victor Isbecki and Desk Sergeant Ronald Coleman.

Comment: The original TV movie starred Loretta Swit as Cagney and Tyne Daly as Lacey, and had them solving the murder of a Jewish diamond merchant. When it was a hit, the network commissioned an hour-long series, which began airing in March 1982, starring Daly; Meg Foster replaced Swit, who was working on another project. Reaction to Foster was negative—despite having the most alluring eyes on TV, she was regarded as "too hard" by executives— and when the series returned in the fall, Foster had been replaced by Sharon Gless. The series continued to air until August 1988. In 1994, Gless and Daly returned in a series of made-for-TV movies featuring the characters.

Al Waxman was Samuels, John Karlen was Harvey, Dick O'Neill played Charlie, Martin Kove was Isbecki, Carl Lumbly was Petrie, and Harvey Atkin was Coleman.

The series was cocreated by Barney Rosensweig, Barbara Corday, and Barbara Avedon in 1974. It took them seven years to convince a network that the concept of realistic female cops could work.

CAPITAN TRUENO (C, L)

First Appearance: *Capitan Trueno* #1, June 1956.

Biography: A hero in the late 15th century, Capitan Trueno (Captain Thunder) is a wealthy knight and a superb warrior who dedicates his life to upholding the rights of humankind and battling despotism and monsters around the world. His two companions are Crispin, his squire, and the towering Goliath.

Comment: The Spanish character was created by artist Ambros and writer Victor Alcazar. The hero also appeared in the weekly magazine *Pulgarcito* for 232 issues. His adventures ended across the board in March 1968. Several novels were also written, though these have never appeared in English.

CAP KENNEDY (L)

First Appearance: *Galaxy of the Lost* by Gregory Kern, 1973, DAW Books.

Biography: In the future, only constant vigilance can guarantee the stability of the near-Utopian society that exists on Earth and on many of the thousand worlds of the civilized galaxy. To this end, the World Government establishes the Mobile Aid Laboratories and Construction Authorities, a group of technicians and soldiers who roam Earth and space, keeping the peace and sniffing out trouble of all kinds. At the forefront of MALCA is an elite force of Free Acting Terran Envoys. These agents of FATE are chartered to "investigate privately, to probe without alarming, to stop trouble before it could grow too big" and necessitate the involvement of MALCA itself.

Captain "Cap" Kennedy is the best of FATE's agents. Tall and muscular, curt and at times rude, the young hero is a superb hand-to-hand fighter and a crack shot with the paralyzing Dione pistol. Cap's dark hair is worn short; he is romantically unattached.

Comment: Kern is pseudonym for author E.C. Tubb. DAW published 15 other Cap Kennedy novels from 1973 to 1975: *Slave Ship from Sergan, Monster of Metelaze, Enemy Within the Skull, Jewel of Jarben,*

Seetee Alert, The Gholan Gate, The Eater of Worlds, Earth Enslaved, Planet of Dread, Spawn of Laban, The Genetic Buccaneer, A World Aflame, The Ghosts of Epidoris, Mimics of Dephene, and *Beyond the Galactic Lens.*

CAPTAIN ADAM TROY (TV)

First Appearance: *Adventures in Paradise,* October 1959, ABC.

Biography: A pipe-smoking Korean War veteran, Adam Troy is the captain of the schooner *Tiki,* which he sails around the South Pacific, carrying people and cargo from island to island or as far as Asia, becoming involved with smugglers, kidnapers, runaways, and anyone else in trouble. At first, it was only Troy and his Chinese-American partner, Oliver Lee, onboard. Then he took on a first mate, Clay Baker; when Baker retires to manage the Bali Miki hotel—which Troy often visits—he was replaced by Chris Parker. Toward the end of Troy's seagoing days, Inspector Bouchard frequently asks him to help out on cases in distant ports.

Comment: The show ran through April 1962 and starred six-foot-five acting newcomer Gardner McKay as Troy. Weaver Levy played Lee, James Holden was Clay, Guy Stockwell was Parker, and Marcel Hillaire was Inspector Bouchard. Although renowned author James Michener created the series, he had little to do with it once it was sold. As a result, as McKay correctly summed things up, there was little for other actors to do "but say hello, get arrested, and say goodbye."

CAPT. ARGO (TC)

First Appearance: *Jets*Rockets*Spacemen,* 1951, Bowman Gum, Inc.

Biography: Argo is the coleader of the 6X52, a spaceship 250 feet long, made of "rare lunar metals" and powered by an atomic motor. His second-in-command is Dr. Zara, a telepath. The vessel is launched from the rocket center in Manhattan by the Solar League, which protects "the sky lanes from the pirates of the planetoids and the hostile hooligans of outer space." First stop: a space station, and then it's on to the moon to check on a United Nations observatory. After killing some Mantis Men, the crew heads to Mercury, fighting Giant Mercurian steam frogs before traveling to Mars, Venus (where they huddle with King Vulcor), the watery Planet Ex (where they meet King Aquon and Prince Frost), Saturn, Saturn's moon Titan (whose occupants wear "Robin Hood costumes"), Jupiter's moon Ganymede, Jupiter, the planetoid belt, and then back to Earth.

After a brief layover, the crew heads for the Sirius Star System in the 500-foot-long 6X53. There they have adventures among the many races on the planet Kroto.

Comment: There were 108 cards in this vintage series; a second set, numbered 109 to 144, was prepared but never issued. WTW Productions reissued the original cards in 1985.

Argo, of course, was the name of the ship that carried the Greek hero JASON on his quest for the Golden Fleece.

CAPTAIN BLOOD (L, MP)

First Appearance: *Captain Blood: His Odyssey* by Rafael Sabatini, 1922, Houghton-Mifflin.

Biography: Born in 1652, the son of an Irish doctor, Peter Blood reluctantly follows in his footsteps, acquiring his medical degree at the age of 20 from Dublin's Trinity College. Three months later his father dies and Peter, driven by "a roving strain derived from his Somersetshire mother," decides to see some of the world. Adept with a sword, he becomes a soldier, taking the sea and serving under the Dutch Admiral de Ruyter against the French. Little is known of this period in his life, other than the fact that he spends two years in a Spanish prison, becoming fluent in Castilian, and then some time in France, becoming fluent in French. In January 1685 he shows up in England and settles in Bridgewater to practice medicine. Six months later Blood is accidentally caught up in the Monmouth Rebellion when he is asked to treat a man wounded at the Battle of Sedgmoor. A party of dragoons spots him helping the rebel and Blood is arrested, tried, and sentenced to death. This sentence is commuted, however, when officials realize that the thousands of rebels would be more valuable sold as slaves. Blood and his friend Jeremy Pitt are sold in Barbados, where it's discovered that he's a doctor and he's put to work healing the sick.

Granted "a certain liberty of action" in and around Bridgetown, Blood and a score of his comrades are able to steal aboard the Spanish ship *Cinco Llagas,* which has come to raid the English settlement: After overpowering the ten guards, he steals the vessel and sails away to help the oppressed and punish the wicked. He is pursued by the English Captain Easterling.

Blood is "a tall, spare man" with a swarthy face and eyes that are "startlingly blue, level, and penetrating." He wears a shoulder-length "heavy black periwig" and speaks in "a pleasant voice whose metallic quality [is] softened by a drawling Irish accent."

Comment: The seafaring sequels to the original

novel are *Captain Blood Returns* (1930) and *The Fortunes of Captain Blood* (1936). In the first, he searches for the treasure of Morgan the Pirate and matches wits with the lovely and treacherous Madame de Coulevain; in the second, he foils the nefarious Lady Court while trying to save the life of the beleaguered young Dona Isabel.

In motion pictures, a silent *Captain Blood* was produced in 1923 starring J. Warren Kerrigan. However, Errol Flynn made the part his in the 1935 version (Flynn's first swashbuckler), which was a faithful adaptation of the first novel. In 1935 Louis Hayward starred in what was virtually a remake of the 1935 film, *The Fortunes of Captain Blood,* while Flynn's son Sean played the part in the 1962 film *The Son of Captain Blood,* which was also part sequel, part remake.

Sabatini is also the author of SCARAMOUCHE and THE SEA HAWK and *The Black Swan,* the saga of the buccaneer Charles de Bernis who sails to a distant isle to rescue his beloved Priscilla Harradine from the wicked pirate Tom Leach. (After defeating him, Charles says blithely, "Leach may have been a swordsman to pirates; to a swordsman he was just a pirate.") Tyrone Power starred in the film version of *The Black Swan,* though here he was called Jamie Waring and his nemesis was Captain Billy Leech (George Sanders).

CAPTAIN COMPASS (C)

First Appearance: *Star Spangled Comics* #83, 1948, DC Comics.

Biography: A former private eye, dashing Mark Compass roams the seven seas in his capacity as an investigator for the Penny Steamship Lines. A capable frogman as well as an able captain, he frequently commands the line's vessels in order to sniff out saboteurs, smugglers, and other lowlifes. When he isn't traveling, he's headquartered in a spacious cabin aboard the SS *Nautilus.*

Comment: This character appeared in *Star Spangled Comics* through #130. Despite his longevity, he was never pictured on the cover of the anthology title, losing out to Robin (of Batman and Robin), TOMAHAWK, and DR. THIRTEEN.

CAPTAIN EASY (CS, L, C)

First Appearance: *Wash Tubbs,* February 6, 1929, NEA Syndicate.

Biography: Born somewhere in the South, young, rugged William Lee is framed for a crime he did not commit. Running off, he becomes a soldier of fortune named Captain Easy. Caught up in a revolution in a Central European nation in 1929, "the great American swashbuckler" meets fellow adventurer Wash Tubbs (see COMMENT), who becomes his partner.

Comment: The characters were created by Roy Crane (see BUZ SAWYER); Leslie Turner took over for him in June 1943. When he retired in 1970, he was succeeded by artist Bill Crooks and writer Jim Lawrence. *Wash Tubbs* began as *Washington Tubbs II* on April 24, 1924. (The title was shortened exactly two years later.) Short, bespectacled George Washington Tubbs II works for a rural food market, Crabtree Emporium, and begins his own life of adventure when he boards a ship christened the *Sieve* and finds himself caught up in a South Seas search for lost treasure. After finding it and becoming wealthy, he gets caught up in a mystery in the western town of Cozy Gulch, where he meets up with sidekick Gozy Gallup. The two share adventures in the circus, in Mexico, and against the evil Bull Dawson before Easy joins the team and replaces Gozy, who marries and settles down.

Captain Easy got his own Sunday strip on July 30, 1933, which chronicled his adventures before he met Tubbs; Tubbs continued in the daily strip, which had been renamed *Captain Easy* in 1932.

Easy appeared in three Big Little Books: *Captain Easy, Soldier of Fortune* (1934), *Wash Tubbs and Captain Easy Hunting for Whales* (1938), and *Captain Easy, Behind Enemy Lines* (1943). He also starred in *Captain Easy & Wash Tubbs* in the second issue of *Famous Comics Cartoon Books* in 1934, in 17 issues of his own comic book from 1939 to 1949, and in a one-shot in 1956. Most of the covers featured him punching out a villain or two while a young woman looked on admiringly.

CAPTAIN GALLANT (TV, C)

First Appearance: *Captain Gallant of the Foreign Legion,* February 1955, syndicated.

Biography: Captain Michael Gallant is the commander of the North African division of the Foreign Legion. Among those serving with him in the desert outpost (for an unspecified foreign power) are Cuffy Sanders, an orphan of a Legionnaire who has become Gallant's ward; Sergeant Du Val; and Private Fuzzy Knight. The heroes chase down camel rustlers, calm rivalries between Arab tribes, and sniff out smugglers and gun-runners.

Comment: Buster Crabbe played Gallant, and his real-life son Cullen played Cuffy in the half-hour series. Actor Al "Fuzzy" Knight was himself, more or less, and Gilles Queant was Du Val; real members of the French Foreign Legion were extras. The series was shot on location in the Sahara desert during the first season;

when war erupted in Algeria, they moved to Libya and northern Italy. Sixty-five episodes were shot by producer Harry Saltzman (later the coproducer of the JAMES BOND films); reruns were syndicated under the title *Foreign Legionnaire.*

Charlton Comics published four issues of a Captain Gallant comic book from 1955 to 1956.

A year after his Gallant stint, Crabbe shot a pilot about frogmen entitled *Davy Jones.* The show failed to find a sponsor or network.

CAPT. HAZZARD (L)

First Appearance: *Capt. Hazzard* #1, 1938, Ace Magazines.

Biography: Blind as a child, Hazzard develops his other senses to perfection, including limited telepathy—the ability to send his thoughts across many miles. When an operation restores his eyesight, Hazzard dedicates his life to helping others. An "ace adventurer, conqueror of fear, master of modern science," he sets up a laboratory on Long Island and takes on a pair of aides: bald mathematician Washington MacGowan and not-too-bright cowboy Jake Cole who is, nonetheless, a crack shot and superb with the lasso.

After rescuing lovely young Mary Parker from a fire, Hazzard learns of the evil Phoenix who, based in Honduras, plans to use the power of the nearby Omoxotl volcano to conquer the world. Flying south, Hazzard and his men battle Phoenix's servants, the Python Men, and barely escape with their lives when the volcano explodes.

Comment: This was the character's only appearance. The adventure, "Python Men of Lost City," was written by Chester Hawks and was obviously inspired by the success of Street & Smith's *Doc Savage* magazine.

CAPTAIN JAMES T. KIRK (TV, L, C, MP)

First Appearance: *Star Trek,* September 1966, NBC.

Biography: James Tiberius Kirk will be born to George and Winona Kirk on a farm in Council Bluffs, Iowa, on March 22, 2233, at least a year after the birth of his brother George Samuel Kirk (called Sam). As a young boy, Jim is a fan of HORATIO HORNBLOWER novels, is fascinated by his Uncle Harry's tales of the family's pioneer ancestors, and is a great admirer of Abraham Lincoln. Sam becomes a biologist, but Jim's sense of adventure drives him to enter Starfleet Academy, the California-based training center for the officers, scientists, and crew members who fly the starships of the United Federation of Planets. Jim scores very high on his entrance exams and proves himself to be both

serious and daring; the latter nearly gets him tossed from the Academy—twice. The first time is when he dares to romance Ruth, the daughter of an admiral. The second time involves the *Kobayashi Maru,* a no-win exam designed to help commanders deal with the prospect of defeat. Rather than accept defeat, Kirk goes into the computer, changes the program, and wins. He is commended for his initiative.

Kirk graduates in 2254, a lieutenant (serial number SC-937-0176-CEC), and is assigned to the starship *Farragut* under Captain Garrovick. At 29 Kirk makes captain, the youngest officer ever to do so. He's given command of the starship *Enterprise,* succeeding Captain Christopher Pike; his five-year mission is to "seek out new life and new civilizations and boldly go where no man has gone before" (in films, "no one has gone before"). Serving with him are the Vulcan-human hybrid Science Officer Mr. Spock, who is three years older and supremely logical; Chief Medical Officer Dr. Leonard H. "Bones" McCoy; Chief Engineer Montgomery Scott; Helm Officer Hikaru Sulu; Communications Officer Uhura; and Nurse Christine Chapel. Ensign Pavel Chekov later joins Sulu at the helm.

Kirk guides the 430 crew members of the *Enterprise* through dozens of adventures, after which he is promoted to admiral and, in 2268, becomes Starfleet chief of operations. He returns to active duty and a refitted *Enterprise* three years later to battle the malevolent space menace V'Ger, after which Kirk accepts a teaching position with Starfleet Academy and settles into an apartment in San Francisco, circa 2277. The return of an old enemy, Khan Noonien Singh, forces Kirk into the saddle yet again. Spock dies in the course of defeating the villain, and Kirk becomes a fugitive for commandeering the *Enterprise* in an effort to bring Spock's remains to Vulcan and, he hopes, restore him to life. He succeeds, and serves with distinction for the remainder of his days.

Kirk's love life has largely been one of heartbreak. Not only does the relationship with Ruth get him into trouble, but shortly after he makes captain he meets Dr. Carol Marcus, a Starfleet geneticist. They live together for three months, and a son, David, is the result. Kirk and his boy are estranged for over 20 years; when Kirk finally gets to know his son, the boy dies on Genesis Planet during a confrontation with a landing party of enemy Klingons. After the union with Carol, Kirk loses his memory on an unnamed planet and is briefly married to the priestess Miramanee, who is stoned to death. On a trip back in time, to 1930s America, he falls deeply in love with pacifist Edith Keeler. Unfortunately, Spock discovers that she is doomed to die and, to avoid changing history, Kirk must allow her to be hit by a car.

Kirk's brother, Sam, and sister-in-law, Aurelan, die when monstrous parasites attack them on the planet Deneva. Only their son, Peter, survives.

Among Kirk's many citations and awards are the Palm Leaf of Axanar Peace Mission; Medal of Honor; Starfleet Citation for Conspicuous Gallantry; Grankite Order of Tactics, Class of Excellence; Prantares Ribbon of Commendation, First and Second Class; Karagite Order of Heroism; and more. With the exception of Garth of Izar, Kirk is considered the finest military leader in the galaxy.

Comment: There were 79 hour-long episodes in the original series, which aired through September 1969. William Shatner starred as Kirk, Leonard Nimoy was Spock, DeForest Kelley was McCoy, George Takei was Sulu, Nichelle Nichols was Uhura, James Doohan was Scott, Majel Barrett was Chapel, and Walter Koenig was Chekov. The series was created by Gene Roddenberry.

The original adventures were adapted as short stories by famed science fiction author James Blish and were collected in *Star Trek* through *Star Trek 11; Star Trek 12* was completed by J.A. Lawrence after Blish's death. They were published from 1967 to 1977. Blish also wrote an original novel, *Spock Must Die*, published in 1970. Twelve episodes were also published in "Fotonovel" form from 1977 to 1978.

The characters returned to TV in the animated series *Star Trek*. The Filmation series aired on NBC from September 1973 to August 1975; a total of 22 half-hour episodes were produced. The voices were provided by the actors from the TV series. (Chekov was not used in the show.) Author Alan Dean Foster wrote short stories based on the animated episodes; these were collected in the books *Star Trek Log One* through *Star Trek Log Nine* beginning in 1974.

The characters were transported to the big screen in 1979 with *Star Trek: The Motion Picture*. The subsequent films in the series (which cover the years of Kirk's admiralship and demotion to captain) are *Star Trek II: The Wrath of Khan* (1982), *Star Trek III: The Search for Spock* (1984), *Star Trek IV: The Voyage Home* (1986), *Star Trek V: The Final Frontier* (1989), and *Star Trek VI: The Undiscovered Country* (1991). All of the movies have been adapted in novel form, the first by Gene Roddenberry, the second through fourth by Vonda N. McIntyre, the fifth and sixth by J.M. Dillard. The first film also appeared in paperback in "photostory" form.

The characters have been featured in over 70 *Star Trek* novels, which continue to be published on a regular basis. The early titles include *Death's Angel* by Kathleen Sky, *Devil World* by Gordon Eklund, *The Fate of the Phoenix* by Sondra Marshak and Myrna Culbreath, *Mudd's Angels* by J.A. Lawrence, *Perry's*

Planet by Jack C. Haldeman II, *Planet of Judgment* by Joe Haldeman, *The Price of the Phoenix* by Marshak and Culbreath, *Spock, Messiah!* by Theodore R. Cogswell and Charles A. Spano, Jr., *The Starless World* by Gordon Eklund, *Trek to Madworld* by Stephen Goldin, *Vulcan!* by Sky, *World Without End* by Joe Haldeman, *The Entropy Effect* by Vonda N. McIntyre, *The Prometheus Design* by Marshak and Culbreath, *The Covenant of the Crown* by Howard Weinstein, and *Enterprise the First Adventure* by McIntyre. There have also been collections of short stories in the *Star Trek: The New Voyages* series.

In comic books, Gold Key published 61 issues from 1967 to 1979, along with various specials and one-shots. Marvel published 18 issues from 1980 to 1982, after which DC took the title and published 56 issues from 1984 to 1988; they revived the title in 1989, and it is still being published. Marvel published an adaptation of the first film; DC has published adaptations of the third, fourth, fifth, and sixth films.

See also CAPTAIN JEAN-LUC PICARD.

CAPTAIN JEAN-LUC PICARD   (TV, L, C, MP)

First Appearance: *Star Trek: The Next Generation*, October 1987, syndication.

Biography: Born in 2305 in Labarre, France, to Maurice and Yvette Picard, Jean-Luc is admitted to Starfleet Academy when he is 18. There he becomes the only freshman who has ever won the Academy marathon. At some point after graduation, he is stabbed in the chest in a fight with a trio of Nausicaans and has to have a bionic heart implant. After graduating as the class valedictorian in 2327, he is given command, six years later, of the USS *Stargazer*. In 2355, he loses the ship in an altercation with a Ferengi spaceship and is court-martialed; acquitted, he ultimately assumes command of the *Enterprise*, the starship's fifth incarnation. The *Enterprise* is now much larger than it was, with a crew that numbers over 2,000.

Unlike "go-get-'em" Kirk, the self-disciplined Picard is a very private, paternal figure. He prefers diplomacy to battle, peace to confrontation, and cares deeply about the people around him. He is an amateur archaeologist, and a great lover of music. His catch phrases when giving an order are "Make it so" and "Engage."

Picard's officers are Commander William Riker; the Betazoid-human hybrid Counselor Deanna Troi; helmsman (later, Chief Engineer) Lt. Geordi La Forge; Klingon head of security Lt. Worf; Dr. Beverly Crusher; and Lt. Commander Data, an android.

Picard's only known relatives beside his parents

Maurice and Yvette are his aunt Adele, a brother Robert who lives in France, a sister-in-law Marie (Robert's wife), and a nephew, René. His one great love was Jenice, whom he had foolishly let slip away.

Comment: The hour-long series, set 78 years after the original show, aired its last episode on May 23, 1994. Patrick Stewart starred as Picard, with Jonathan Frakes as Riker, LeVar Burton as La Forge, Michael Dorn as Worf, Marina Sirtis as Troi, Gates McFadden as Crusher, and Brent Spiner as Data.

Beginning with an adaptation of the two-hour TV movie debut, *Encounter at Farpoint* by David Gerrold, Pocket Books has published over 40 novels inspired by the series. DC Comics published a six-issue series based on the show in 1988, then began a series of all-new adventures in 1989. The comic book continues to be published.

A motion picture, *Star Trek: Generations,* featuring actors from the original *Star Trek* and the crew of *Star Trek: The Next Generation,* was released in the fall of 1994.

See also CAPTAIN JAMES T. KIRK.

CAPTAIN JOHN BRADDOCK (TV)

First Appearance: *Racket Squad,* 1950, syndicated.

Biography: Captain Braddock is a dogged investigator for San Francisco's Racket Squad, which, according to the weekly narration, protects the public from "bunco squads, business protection associations, and similar sources all over the country . . . carefully worked-out frauds by which confidence men take more money each year from the American public than all the bank robbers and thugs with their violence." Among the victims he helps are a businessman being hounded by a loan shark, a soldier who's been duped by a "friendship club," and people bilked by a used car company that sells lemons.

Comment: After a year in syndication, the series was picked up by CBS, which produced new half-hour episodes. *Racket Squad* continued to air through September 1953. Veteran serial star Reed Hadley played Braddock.

The stories were based on actual cases in big-city police files.

CAPTAIN JOHN HERRICK (TV)

First Appearance: *Waterfront,* February 1954, syndicated.

Biography: Herrick is the captain of the tugboat *Cheryl Ann,* which he operates in the San Pedro harbor, assisted by his son Carl, Tip Hubbard, and Willi

Slocum. The crew's path is constantly crossed by smugglers, thieves, killers, kidnapers, saboteurs, escaped convicts, and others who come and go via the sea. Jim is married to May; the two have a son, Jim, a detective who invariably involves dad in his cases.

Comment: There were 78 episodes of the half-hour series. Preston Foster starred as John, with Lois Moran as May, Harry Lauter as Jim, Douglas Dick as Carl, Pinky Tomlin as Tip, and Willie Best as Willie.

The series was created by Ben Fox and shot on location in the Los Angeles harbor. (Foster once joked that because of all the scenes of boats moving in and out, "I appear in maybe a third of the footage in each show.")

CAPTAIN JOHN REISMAN   (L, MP, C, TV)

First Appearance: *The Dirty Dozen* by E.M. Nathanson, 1965, Random House.

Biography: It's February 1944 and the Allies decide to attack the Chateau de la Vilaine in Rennes, France, on the night of June 5–6, shortly before D-Day. The chateau is a recreation spot for high-ranking officers of the German Seventh Army, and the attack is designed to throw the German high command into chaos. Because the mission is deemed exceedingly dangerous, General Worden of the Judge Advocate General's office decides it should be undertaken by men who have nothing to lose—condemned men who, if they partake in this "Project Amnesty," may have their sentences commuted if they return alive.

Whiskey-drinking Captain John Reisman, the Chicago-born son of a German-Jewish father and Italian immigrant mother, is a five-year veteran and a loner who is transferred from Secret Intelligence to Special Operations; he goes from partaking in dangerous missions to training others for dangerous missions. He isn't happy about that, nor about his first job, which is to select, train, and lead the Project Amnesty team, nicknamed the Dirty Dozen.

He and his aide, Sergeant Claude Bowren, choose men from England's Marston-Tyne prison: Victor Franko, Calvin Ezra Smith, Glenn Gilpin, Roscoe K. Lever, Napoleon White, Luis Jimenez, Samson Posey, Vernon L. Pinkley, Archer Maggot, Myron Odell, Kendall T. Sawyer, and Joseph Wladislaw. The training is intensive and successful, the attack slightly less so, though the men perform heroically and achieve most of their goals.

Odell, Lever, Smith, Gilpin, and Franko are killed; Bowren, White, and Jimenez are wounded; Posey, Sawyer, Wladislaw, Pinkley, Maggot, Jimenez, White, and Reisman are missing in action, apparently found and looked after by French partisans.

Comment: Lee Marvin played Reisman (now a major) in the 1967 film version of the novel, with Charles Bronson as Wladislaw, Jim Brown as Robert T. Jefferson, Telly Savalas as Archer J. Maggott, John Cassavettes as Franko, Trini Lopez as J. Pedro Jimenez, Clint Walker as Posey, Tom Busby as Milo Vladek, Colin Maitland as Seth K. Sawyer, Ben Carruthers as Gilpin, Stuart Cooper as Lever, Al Mancini as Tassos R. Bravos, and Donald Sutherland as Pinkley. Robert Ryan was Colonel Everett Dasher, who trained the men for the parachute jump, Richard Jaeckel played Sergeant Bowren, and Ernest Borgnine was General Worden. Only Reisman and Wladislaw survive, making it back to England, though both are wounded. No one associated with the film remembers why the name changes were made.

Dell published a comic book adaptation of the original film in October 1967.

Marvin also starred in the film's made-for-TV sequel, *The Dirty Dozen: The Next Mission* (1985), in which he and a new Dozen become involved in a plot to kill Hitler. Non-Marvin made-for-TV sequels are *The Dirty Dozen: The Deadly Mission* (1987), which stars Ernest Borgnine as General Worden and Telly Savalas a new mission leader rescuing scientists who are captives of the Nazis; and *The Dirty Dozen: The Fatal Mission* (1988), which reteams Borgnine and Savalas as they fight Nazis on the *Orient Express.* This film introduced the first female member of the team, played by Heather Thomas.

A Fox TV series followed, the hour-long show airing from April to July 1988. Ben Murphy starred as Lieutenant Danko, a Reisman clone; his team included ex-actor Johnny Farrell (John Bradley), strategist Janosz Feke (Jon Tenney), explosives expert Jean Lebec (John DiAquino), forger Dylan Leeds (John Slattery), and powerful brothers Vern and Roy Beauboff (Mike Jolly and Glenn Withrow). The men reported to Master Sergeant Cutter (Barry Cullison) and Major General Worth (Frank Marth).

CAPTAIN KEITH MALLORY   (L, MP)

First Appearance: *The Guns of Navarone* by Alistair MacLean, 1956, Curtis Publishing.

Biography: Before World War II Keith Mallory was New Zealand's greatest mountaineer, a "human fly, the climber of the unclimbable." During the war, as Captain Mallory of the Long Range Desert Group, the Greek-speaking soldier operates on Crete until he's called upon to lead an attack against an iron fortress on Navarone, off the coast of Turkey. His mission: scale an "impossible precipice" and destroy the 210 mm guns that are menacing Allied ships. In addition to Mallory, the party is comprised of Corporal Dusty Miller of California, "a genius with explosives"; the Greek army Colonel Andrea, a big man and an expert with the knife; Lieutenant Andy Stevens, RNVR, who was an Alpinist, fluent in Greek, and can drive the boat that is to bring them to Navarone; and Petty Officer Telegraphist Casey Brown, who will maintain communications with home base.

After succeeding in destroying the guns, Mallory and Miller are asked to lead a mission to free a partisan army trapped in the mountains of Yugoslavia. Andrea joins them, as does a trio of marine commandos: pilot Sergeant Reynolds, electrics and explosives master Sergeant Groves, and radio operator Sergeant Saunders.

Comment: MacLean's sequel, *Force 10 From Navarone,* was published in 1968. New Zealand's Mallory was played by American Gregory Peck in the 1961 film *The Guns of Navarone,* while the American Miller was played by Englishman David Niven. Anthony Quinn was Andrea and Stanley Baker played Brown. Mallory was played by Robert Shaw in the 1978 film *Force 10 From Navarone,* fighting on a team which included Franco Nero as Lescovar and Harrison Ford as Barnsby.

CAPTAIN KRONOS   (MP, C)

First Appearance: *Kronos,* 1973, Hammer Films (see COMMENT).

Biography: In the early 19th century, Captain Kronos goes off to fight in a war, leaving behind his mother and young sister. When he returns—having become a master swordsman under Barloff of the Imperial Guard—his sister greets him with a kiss . . . "a vampire's kiss." She breaks the skin but doesn't infect him, and Kronos is forced to kill both her and their mother. Teamed with Professor Heironymous Grost, and armed with a rapier and a samurai sword, he resolves to hunt down and slay vampires wherever he finds them. Not long thereafter, in the village of Durward, England, a young girl is slain by a vampire. Kronos is summoned from the "eastern mountains" by his friend Dr. Marcus, with whom he served in the war, and he confronts and slays the vampiric Hagan, dead Lord of Durward.

Comment: The character was created by writer/director Brian Clemens; the film starred Horst Janson as Kronos, John Cater (*sic*) as Professor Grost, and John Carson as Marcus. It was released in the U.S. in 1974 as *Captain Kronos: Vampire Hunter.*

A new comic book adventure pitting Kronos against the vampire Balderstein in Landstadt (Bavaria) was serialized over several issues of *The House of Hammer*

Magazine beginning with #1 in 1976; a complete comic book adaptation of the film was published in *Halls of Horror* Magazine #20 in 1978.

CAPTAIN MAC WINGATE (L)

First Appearance: *Mission Code: Symbol* by Bryan Swift, 1981, Jove Books (see COMMENT).

Biography: Born in 1913, Peter Magnussen Wingate is the son of a German-Norwegian farmer and a woman whose father was an Ojibway who had fought against General Custer. Raised in Sawyer County, Wisconsin, Mac was always a self-reliant outdoorsman and a crack shot. After studying engineering at the University of Wisconsin, he went to work at a mining camp in Brazil, where he honed his expertise in explosives. He enlisted when the Japanese bombed Pearl Harbor and ended up in North Africa. There his "talents for explosives and survival" and his fluent German win him a commission as a special agent, sent throughout the European theater and answering directly to Franklin Roosevelt and Winston Churchill. Armed with a Sten gun and frequently working in civilian dress, Captain Wingate is "solidly built" with dark hair and eyes and high cheekbones.

Comment: Bryan Swift was a house name for numerous authors, including Ric Meyers. Eleven other Mac Wingate novels were published from 1981 to 1982, including *Mission Code: King's Pawn, Mission Code: Minotaur, Mission Code: Granite Island, Mission Code: Springboard, Mission Code: Snow Queen, Mission Code: Acropolis, Mission Code: Volcano,* and *Mission Code: Track and Destroy.*

CAPTAIN N (TV, C)

First Appearance: *Captain N: The Game Master,* September 1989, syndicated.

Biography: Kevin Keene is your typical, young, teenage video game nut who is drawn into his TV and finds himself in Videoland. There he becomes the heroic Captain N (for Nintendo) and keeps the wicked Mother Brain and her army of video ne'er-do-wells from overthrowing the lovely young Princess Lana. Helping N are his devoted pooch Duke and the video game superstars Mega Man and the winged Kid Icarus.

Comment: Though the hero himself wasn't based on any of the Nintendo video games, his companions and foes were. There were only 13 half-hour episodes of the DIC Enterprises series. Matt Hill was the voice of Captain N.

Valiant Comics published six issues of a *Captain N: The Game Master* comic book from 1990 to 1991.

See also MARIO.

CAPTAIN STEVE BURTON (TV, L, C)

First Appearance: *Land of the Giants,* September 1968, ABC.

Biography: Steve Burton, the commander of the space plane *Spindrift,* is on Los Angeles to London flight #612 in 1983 when it accidentally passes through a cloudlike space warp. When it emerges, it's on an earth-type world where the flora and fauna—including humans—are 12 times the size of Earth people. Because the ship is damaged by the storm, the earth people are unable to leave.

Burton's copilot is Dan Erickson, and Betty Hamilton is the stewardess. Onboard are engineer/magnate Mark Wilson, glamour girl Valerie Scott, Commander Alexander Fitzhugh (no one is quite sure why this gruff, mysterious fellow was aboard), and 14-year-old Barry Lockridge and his dog, Chipper. Searching for the earthlings is the alien giant Inspector Kobrick of the S.I.B., a security and intelligence bureau.

Dashing in his red uniform, the rugged Burton helps keep his comrades alive, works to repair the ship, and prevents them from fighting among themselves under stressful, dangerous circumstances that include being captured by a child to use in a doll house, clearing a homeless giant of a crime he didn't commit, escaping from a giant gypsy who wants to sell the little people to a circus, and summoning a giant doctor to operate on Barry when he's stricken with appendicitis.

Comment: Gary Conway was Burton, Don Marshall was Dan, Heather Young played Betty, Don Matheson was Wilson, Deanna Lund was Valerie, Kurt Kasznar was Fitzhugh, and Stefan Arngrim was Barry. There were 51 episodes of the hour-long series, which was created and produced by Irwin Allen and aired through September 1970.

From 1968 to 1969, Pyramid published three novels based on the series, all of them written by Murray Leinster: *Land of the Giants, The Hot Spot,* and *Unknown Danger.*

Gold Key Comics published five issues of *Land of the Giants* from 1968 to 1969.

CAPTAIN THUNDER (C)

First Appearance: *Jungle Comics* #1, 1940, Fiction House.

Biography: Though his term of enlistment has ended, brash, brave, British Captain Terry Thunder reinlists and is named the leader of the Congo Lancers. A two-fisted lot that includes Kerrigan, Doyle, and Red, the "toughest men in the regiment," the Lancers are sent to man the remote Yambezi outpost, "deep in the African jungles," where the bulk of their adventures involves action against the slave trade. Though he often catches villains red-handed, he always returns them to civilization to stand trial rather than punishing them at the fort.

Comment: The strip, created and drawn by Art Peters, appeared regularly throughout the run of *Jungle Comics,* which lasted 163 issues. Other adventure heroes who appeared in the pages of *Jungle Comics* included Fantomah, Daughter of the Pharoahs; Wambi the Jungle Boy who "speaks the langauge of the jungle beasts" and is accompanied on adventures by his best friend, Tawn the elephant; Camilla, Queen of the Lost Empire, who is descended from "Norsemen who went [to Africa] during the Crusades"; Buck, Slim, and Rex, the White Hunters of the African Safari; and Zomba, Jungle Fighter, a white man who maintains peace between the tribes.

See also KÄANGA.

CAPTAIN TOM RYNNING (TV)

First Appearance: *26 Men,* October 1957, syndicated.

Biography: In 1901 the Arizona Territorial Legislature establishes a force of state troopers consisting of 20 privates, four sergeants, a lieutenant, and a captain—a total of 26 men, which is all they can afford. Under the command of Captain Tom Rynning, the heroes roam the state, from the cities to the plains, chasing renegades of all kinds. Rynning's right hand man is new recruit, Ranger Clint Travis.

Comment: Seventy-eight episodes of the half-hour series aired through 1959 and starred veteran serial actor Tris Coffin as Rynning, with Kelo Henderson as Travis. The series was filmed on location.

The series was inspired by the success of *Tales of the Texas Rangers.*

See also RANGER JACE PEARSON.

CAPTAIN VENTURE (C)

First Appearance: *Space Family Robinson* #6, 1963, Western Publishing.

Biography: "Sometime after 2000 A.D." Captain Rex Venture and his copilot, Lieutenant Scotty Mackay, are exploring the star system Beta 52 in the Milky Way Galaxy. As they probe Plantis, the third world from the star, their ship 95711 is struck by a meteorite and crashes in the sea. After surfacing in an underground cavern, they find a junglelike world inhabited by giant monsters and a race of outcast humans at war with superadvanced people, all of whom communicate telepathically. Armed with laser pistols and levitation belts, the heroes run afoul of the advanced humans—the Kroppies—and fall in with the scientist Rompol, whose radical ideas (i.e., that there's life on other worlds) made him and his followers outcasts.

Comment: After being serialized in *Space Family Robinson* for several years, the hero was given his own title, *Captain Venture and the Land Beneath the Sea,* which lasted two issues in 1968–69. Western frequently published a few issues of adventure titles, such as *Fantastic Voyages of Sindbad* (one issue in 1965 and one in 1967), *John Carter of Mars* (three issues in 1964) and *Freedom Agent,* featuring John Steele of NATO (one issue in 1963). Western's plan was to publish additional issues if sales warranted—though by the time reports arrived and a new issue was released, the momentum was gone.

CAPTAIN VICTORY (C)

First Appearance: *Captain Victory and the Galactic Rangers* #1, 1981, Pacific Comics.

From left to right: Tarin, Orca, Major Klavus, and *Captain Victory.* © Jack Kirby.

Biography: Far out in space in our own era, Captain Victory leads the Galactic Rangers through the galaxy, upholding the law. His chief foe is the nefarious Lightning Lady and her invading hordes of humanoid Insectons, who turn peaceful and green planets into dead, rocky hives; Victory is the survivor of one world that suffered such a fate. His first chronicled adventure leads him to Tallant IV, which has been converted into a hive and must be destroyed. Then it's off to Earth, where a new hive has begun.

Victory's body has been cloned so that if he's ever killed—which, frequently, he is—his memory can be transferred to a new body. His executive officer is Major Klavus of Antares; other key Rangers are the lizardlike Orca from Epsilon Eridani; Tarin, the lionlike Alpha Centaurian; Mister Mind, a living computer; and Lovaleen, an intelligent spore from Ursa Minor. Victory's ship, the *Tiger,* is equipped with star engines that can achieve light speeds and the World-Killer, a bomb capable of destroying a planet. The Rangers themselves carry Baby-H Bazookas, which fire computer-guided hydrogen bombs; magnetic mine throwers; sun guns that create "a small supernova"; and the gang jazzler, which paralyzes enemies via neuron waves.

Comment: The characters were created by artist/writer Jack Kirby; the magazine lasted 13 issues.

CAPTAIN WINGS (C)

First Appearance: *Wings Comics* #16, 1941, Fiction House.

Biography: Captain Boggs of the air force is a desk soldier, ordering other fliers into the sky to fight the Japanese. Frustrated by his relative inactivity and by the ill-concealed disdain of the men who go out and *do* the fighting, Boggs climbs into a P-51 Mustang—painted like a giant eagle, with black wings, white wingtips, a black fuselage, and a white nose—and wages his own part-time, one-man war as Captain Wings. Eventually he stops returning to his Boggs identity and becomes Captain Wings full time, battling such foes as Colonel Kamikaze, the Radar Rocketeers, and the Sky Octopus. After the war he stars in "supersonic thrillers," fighting Communists, saboteurs, UFOs, and other Cold War enemies.

Comment: Captain Wings starred in every issue of *Wings Comics* until #116, then appeared in a few other adventures until the comic's demise with #124. *Wings Comics* was the home to a number of adventure heroes.

See also "SUICIDE" SMITH.

CARL DENHAM (L, MP, C)

First Appearance: *King Kong* by Delos W. Lovelace, 1932, Grosset & Dunlap (see COMMENT).

Biography: Sometime around 1931, Norwegian sea captain Nils Helstrom sells moviemaker Carl Denham a map of Skull Island in the Indian Ocean, west of Sumatra, a map he had drawn based on the description of the last survivor of a canoeful of natives that had been blown out to sea. Denham has been making wildlife features in exotic jungles. Now, in 1932, he has decided to go to Skull Island—but not to shoot the flora and fauna. He's decided, for the first time, to put an actress in one of his films because "The public, bless 'em, must have a pretty face to look at." After hiring Captain Englehorn and his ship, the *Venture,* Denham waits in the Hoboken docks for a theatrical agent, Weston, to get him an actress. When Weston refuses to let a woman go on such an insane voyage, Denham goes to the Bowery, finds a down-and-out young beauty named Ann Darrow, and gets her to join the voyage; en route, first mate Jack Driscoll falls in love with her. At Skull Island, the natives kidnap Ann and turn her over as a bride to their god Kong, a 50-foot-tall ape. Driscoll, Denham, and several crew members chase the gorilla into the thick jungle, where they are attacked by a stegosaurus, an apatosaurus, and finally by Kong himself. Only Driscoll and Denham survive. The former manages to rescue Ann from Kong's cave, and when the giant ape comes after her, Denham fells him with gas bombs. He has the surviving crew members build a raft and float the ape back to New York.

Kong is displayed, in chains, in a theater but breaks free when he thinks first-night photographers are attacking Ann. Jack rushes her away but Kong finds them, reclaims his bride, and carries her to the top of the Empire State Building. He's shot down by a squadron of navy biplanes; while Jack comforts Ann on top of the skyscraper, Denham stands beside the fallen Kong. When a police captain comments that the airplanes got him, Denham says sadly, "Oh, no. It wasn't the airplanes. It was beauty killed the beast."

The damage caused by Kong sparks countless lawsuits and forces Denham to go into hiding at Mrs. Hudson's boarding house. With the help of a sympathetic process server, Denham gets to the *Venture* and Englehorn sets sail. The two men carry cargo in the China Sea for several months. Stopping at a Malayan port, Dakang, Denham meets singer Hilda Peterson, whose father runs the ramshackle Peterson's Circus. They also meet Helstrom who, after accidentally murdering the elder Peterson, concocts a story about an ancient treasure on Skull Island. The three men set sail at once, with Hilda stowing away. When the crew learns where they're headed, they mutiny and put the four adrift with Charley, the cook. On Skull Island, they meet the kindly 12-foot-tall Son of Kong, whom Denham and Hilda free from quicksand. After several run-ins with dinosaurs, Denham and Hilda find the treasure—just as an earthquake rocks the island. Englehorn, Hilda, and Charley get their rowboat; Helstrom is eaten by a sea monster; and Son of Kong saves Denham from drowning as the island sinks. Unfortunately, Kong's foot is caught and he goes down with the island as he places Denham in the rowboat. The survivors are rescued by a passing ship, and, rich now, Denham and Hilda make wedding plans.

Denham is approximately 30 years old, dresses all in white, and is as smooth as he is brash and brave. He

Hilda Peterson, *Carl Denham,* and the Son of Kong. © Turner Broadcasting.

usually operates his own camera, since he worries that any other cameraman might run scared and miss a great shot.

Comment: Although the book was published before the release of the film in 1933—and differs in numerous details from the film—the novel was based on the screenplay. It was published in hardcover and, in 1933, was serialized in *Mystery* magazine. The original story was conceived by producer Merian C. Cooper and mystery writer Edgar Wallace.

Robert Armstrong starred as Denham in both films; Bruce Cabot was Driscoll, Fay Wray played Ann, Helen Mack was Hilda, Frank Reicher was Englehorn, and John Marston was Helstrom. *Son of Kong* was released in 1933.

Carl Denham did not appear in any other sequels or remakes of the films. According to Philip Jose Farmer's 1973 short story "After Kong Fell," Denham serves a year in jail before being paroled, after which he's murdered by a witch doctor who is angry because the showman had stolen his god.

Gold Key published a comic book adaptation of the novel in 1968, in which the ship is the *Wanderer* and Denham is pictured as a man of about 50.

CARSON NAPIER (L, C)

First Appearance: *Pirates of Venus* by Edgar Rice Burroughs, 1932, *Argosy* magazine.

Biography: The son of a British army officer and a woman from Virginia, Carson was born in India and tutored by Chand Kabi, a Hindu aide to his father. The elderly man taught Carson telepathy, though it works only with those who are in "psychological harmony" with him. (Author Burroughs happens to be such a man, and is thus able to "receive" Napier's accounts of his life and adventures.) He is 11 when his father dies and his mother brings him to the U.S., where they live in Virginia for three years with her grandfather, Judge John Carson. When the judge dies, the Napiers move to Southern California, where John is educated at Claremont College, becoming highly proficient in boxing, swimming, wrestling, and fencing. He graduates and, losing his desire to live when his mother dies, becomes a stunt pilot for the movies. But Carson finds Southern California boring, and he decides to use some of the wealth he inherited from the judge to build a rocket and travel to Mars. A year later the 27-year-old blasts off alone from Guadalupe Island off the coast of Mexico. However, he forgets to take into account the gravitational pull of the moon and is thrown off course, hurled instead to Venus. He parachutes to the surface before his "torpedo" crashes, and falls in with humans in the rebellion-torn country of

Vepaja. Called Amtor by the natives, Venus is a world of barbarism, monsters, superscience, and the beauteous Princess Duare, whom Carson eventually weds.

Napier has many adventures on Amtor, battling the living dead raised by the evil Skor, rescuing Duare's father Mintep from the Prison of Death in Amlot, countering the threat of the evil Mephis, a Hitleresque dictator, and finding out whether the magician Morgas is really turning humans into zaldars (alien cows).

Comment: Carson Napier's adventures were recounted in the novels *Lost on Venus* (1933) and *Carson of Venus* (1938) and in the short stories "Captured on Venus," "The Fire Goddess," "The Living Dead," and "War on Venus"—which were published in 1941–42 and revised as the novel *Escape on Venus* (1946). "The Wizard of Venus" was written in 1941 and collected in the book *Tales of Three Planets* (1964) and, later, in a slim paperback called *The Wizard of Venus.* Only a few pages exist of "A Venus Story," which Burroughs began in December 1941 in Hawaii; it went unfinished due to the Japanese attack on Pearl Harbor.

In comics, the character starred in a backup feature in DC's *Korak* from #46 to #56 from 1972 to 1974.

CARTER PRIMUS   (TV, L, C)

First Appearance: *Primus,* 1971, syndicated.

Biography: Based on their "floating home and sea lab," *Orca*—which incorporates design aspects of a hydrofoil and hovercraft—oceanographer Carter Primus is an underwater troubleshooter-for-hire who travels the world as needed, working for individuals (searching for missing persons or sunken treasure) or the government (testing new equipment or exploring uncharted areas under the waves). In addition to a sea sled, which he uses for local hops, Primus boards his minisubmarine *Pegasus* for deep voyages and sends the robot explorer *Big Kate* to handle dangerous jobs. His assistant is Toni Hayden, and his sidekick is Charlie Kingman.

Comment: Ivan Tors (*Flipper*) produced 26 half-hour adventures starring Robert Brown as Primus, Will Kuluva as Charlie, and Eva Renzi as Toni.

Bantam published a novel, *Primus,* by Bradford Street in 1971, and Charlton Comics published seven issues of a *Primus* comic book in 1972.

See also MIKE NELSON.

THE CARTWRIGHTS   (TV, C, L)

First Appearance: *Bonanza,* September 1959, NBC.

Biography: The Cartwright family lives on the Pon-

Carter Primus on the cover of his second Charlton Comic book. © Metromedia Producers Corporation.

derosa Ranch (named for the ponderosa pines that grow there), a 1,000-square mile spread outside of Virginia City, Nevada, in the days after the discovery of the Comstock Lode (1859). Widower Ben Cartwright is the patriarch of the clan, which consists of three sons, each of whom had a different mother: eldest son Adam, born in New England, is the son of Elizabeth who died of natural causes; big, good-natured Eric ("Hoss"), is the son of the Scandinavian Inger, who was slain by Indians ("hoss" means "good luck" in Norwegian); and small, hot-blooded Little Joe is the son of Marie, of New Orleans, who died when she fell off a horse. Their cook is Hop Sing; Sheriff Roy Coffee frequently calls on the Cartwrights for help with desperadoes. Regular ranch hands over the years include Candy, Dusty Rhoades, Jamie Hunter, and Griff King.

The men deal with the usual rustlers, outlaws, and lowlifes that come their way, as well as social ills.

Regardless of the problem, they prefer to settle disputes with talk rather than with gunplay.

Comment: The hour-long series aired through January 1973, making it the second-longest-running western in TV history (behind *Gunsmoke*; see MATT DILLON). Lorne Greene starred as Ben, Michael Landon was Little Joe, Dan Blocker was Hoss, Pernell Roberts played Adam, Victor Sen Yung was Hop Sing, and Ray Teal was Coffee. Roberts left the series in 1965, and Blocker died in 1972.

The series aired as *Ponderosa* in reruns and syndication.

Lorne Green went on to play *Commander Adama* as well as a Ben Cartwright-type fire batallion chief, Joe Rorchek, in the ABC series *Code Red,* which aired from September 1981 to September 1982. Julie Adams was Ann Rorchek, Andrew Stevens was Ted Rorchek, and Sam J. Jones was Chris Rorchek on the show.

In 1988 director William F. Claxton (who had worked on the original series) helmed the TV movie *Bonanza: The Next Generation,* the pilot for a new series. Ben has died, and his sailor brother (John Ireland) heads out to the Ponderosa to run it. He sells drilling rights to some shady operators, and it's up to several Cartwright nephews—including Little Joe's son, played by Michael Landon, Jr.—to ride to the rescue. Lorne Greene's daughter Gillian costarred.

Dell, then Gold Key, published 37 issues of the *Bonanza* comic book from 1960 to 1979.

In 1993 a new series of *Bonanza* novels was published, which thus far include *Pioneer Spirit, Ponderosa Empire, The High-Steel Hazard, Journey of the Horse,* and *The Money Hole.*

CASEY RUGGLES   (CS)

First Appearance: *Casey Ruggles,* May 22, 1949, United Features.

Biography: An army sergeant stationed in Fremont, California, at the onset of the Gold Rush, Casey Ruggles is returning east to collect his fiancee, Chris, when he falls for Lilli, the daughter of pirate Jean Lafitte, and ends up alone as he returns west to prospect. There he becomes embroiled in adventures involving other prospectors, Spanish landowners who have been there for centuries, Indians (including Kit Fox, a young brave) who have been there centuries longer, Chinese being forced into slavery, and more. Unfortunately for Casey, he spends more time hunting down the corrupt than he does prospecting—for, as he observes, "The law and the courts are being well paid to keep their noses *out.*"

Comment: The strip was created by artist Warren Tufts and lasted until September 5, 1954. It is arguably

the finest and toughest western strip of all time, with adult themes (sex was not avoided) and graphic action, torture, rape, and the like. Not surprisingly, Tufts was frequently at odds with the syndicate about the strip's contents, and his justified intransigence contributed to its demise.

See also LANCE SAINT-LORNE.

CASTOR AND POLLUX   (M, MP)

First Appearance: Greek mythology, circa 1500 B.C.

Biography: When Zeus, the king of the gods, visited Leda in the shape of a swan, he did so on the same night that she was with her husband, Tyndareus. Thus, by Zeus, she was the mother of Pollux and the famous Helen (of Troy), and by Tyndareus she was the mother of Castor and Clytemnestra. Castor and Pollux are twins, and they grow up loving each other dearly. Castor becomes renowned for his ability to tame and ride horses (his mount is a white horse named Xanthu), while Pollux becomes a famous boxer (his steed is a white horse named Cyllarus). They rescue Helen from Athens when she is abducted by the hero THESEUS, after which they join the voyage of the Argonauts. (See JASON.) During the journey Pollux boxes Anycus, king of the Bebryces, and hits him so hard he kills him; Pollux and Castor help battle the man of bronze Talos; and both found the city Dioscurias in Colchis. Later, in a battle with their cousins Idas and Lynceus, Castor is killed by Idas; Pollux, who is immortal, slays Lynceus, after which an angry Zeus kills Idas with a bolt of lightning. Sick with grief, Pollux pleads with Zeus to let him die so he can join his brother. Zeus does so, and honors the twins with stars in the sky. (According to a different version of the tale, the twins were allowed to spend alternating days in Hades and on Mt. Olympus.)

Roman mythology also honors the duo: It's said that they occasionally appeared on the field of battle, astride their magnificent horses, encouraging the Romans to victory.

In art, the heroes are typically pictured with ovoid helmets with one or more stars on top; they usually carry spears.

Comment: The stars that bear the heroes' names are part of the constellation Gemini. The heroes are seen fleetingly in the film *Jason and the Argonauts* (1963).

CAVE CARSON   (C)

First Appearance: *Brave and the Bold* #31, 1960, DC Comics.

Biography: Calvin "Cave" Carson is a lifelong spelunker who works as a lab technician with E. Borsten

From left to right: Johnny Blake, Christie Madison, *Cave Carson*, Bulldozer Smith (with Lena on his shoulder), and Dr. Damion, leader of the underground settlement Xanadu. Illustration by the wonderful comics artist Lee Elias. © DC Comics.

and Sons, a research firm. One of their undertakings is the Mighty Mole project, a car that can dig through the earth with a thermo-ray and allow access to deep-buried ore. Tired of being lab bound, Cave builds his own Mighty Mole at home and becomes the "king of the underground cave explorers," the foremost expert on the world beneath the surface of the earth. Helping him is a team consisting of powerful but "loyal ex-convict . . . strongman and expert on tunnels," Bulldozer Smith (who speaks a "private language" with his pet lemur Lena, which becomes the team's mascot); "beautiful girl geologist" Christie Madison; and "devil-may-care" Johnny Blake, who is Cave's rival for Christie's love. The group gets about in the Mighty Mole, which looks like a big, blue Buick and "can climb, swim, or dive," in addition to being equipped with a rock-melting thermo-ray. They also get around in the "Ground Effect" Saucer, which runs on compressed air and is useful for traveling on jagged terrain. The Mighty Mole is stocked with traditional firearms (the team *has* found hostile creatures inside the earth), sizzling magnesium guns, pickaxes, TNT, an electric jack for lifting heavy rocks, "special underwater suits," asbestos suits, and an antimagnetic switch to escape magnetism the Mole might encounter.

In their last chronicled adventure, the team prevented a band of Nazis from completing a time machine to bring Hitler into the present. Carson is now a member of the Forgotten Heroes.

The team members—including Lena—wear red boots and jackets with white collars, and white trousers and gloves.

Comment: The characters appeared in three issues of *Brave and the Bold,* then moved to *Showcase* for three appearances. Their origin was retold in *Secret Origins* #43.

See also RIP HUNTER.

CENTURIONS (TV, C)

First Appearance: *The Centurions,* 1985, syndicated.

Biography: In the 21st century, the evil Doctor Elias Terror—a diplomat with diplomatic immunity—sends his Doom Drones out to conquer the world. To combat him, the World Council turns the space station Skyvault over to scientist Crystal Kane, who brings together three men to form the core of the mighty Centurions. Oceanographer Max Ray is in charge of forces defending the seas, soldier Jake Rockwell patrols the land, and astronaut Ace McCloud looks after the skies. Each is "beamed" from Skyvault to trouble spots on earth, armed with an awesome arsenal of weapons that lock around their bodies when they utter "Powerxtreme!" These include Ace's Skyknight flying suit, Max's Depth Charger underwater gear (complete with torpedoes), and Jake's Fire-force uniform with a built-in plasma-shell-firing laser cannon.

Comment: There were 56 adventures in the animated Ruby-Spears series; most were a half-hour, a few were an hour. TV star Vince Edwards was the voice of Jake, Neil Ross was Ace, Pat Fraley was Max, and Diane Pershing was Crystal.

DC Comics published four issues of a *Centurions* comic book in 1987.

CHALLENGERS OF THE UNKNOWN (C, L)

First Appearance: *Showcase* #6, 1957, DC Comics.

Biography: The group has a long and and convoluted history. When they first begin, the team consists of four men who, surviving a plane crash, feel they're

The Challengers of the Unknown: The cover copy says it all! © DC Comics.

destined to challenge death in its many guises. The lineup consists of humorless leader and jet pilot Ace Morgan, a Korean War veteran, military tactician, and astronaut candidate; Red Ryan, a quick-tempered daredevil, acrobat, and mountain climber; glib muscleman Rocky Davis, a former Olympic wrestler; and Professor Haley, a scientist-archaeologist-linguist-electrician-deepsea-diver and so on. Based in a building in an unspecified city before moving to spacious headquarters in Challenger Mountain in the Rockies—and briefly abandoning this for underwater headquarters—the group takes on dangerous or unusual jobs around the world: testing new equipment; investigating phenomena; battling mad scientists, robots, aliens, despots, and other menaces; and even rescuing Henry Kissinger from the Bermuda Triangle.

June Walker joins them in their second adventure; since she already has a full-time job overseeing a team of government scientists, she is made an "honorary" Challenger. By her fifth appearance, she has gone from being black-haired to blonde, and her name is now June Robbins (apparently because "The Phantom" comic strip had a June Walker). Eventually she joins the Challengers full time. This is considered to be the "official" Challengers lineup (subsequent members come and go and are not regarded as canonical): Gaylord Clayburn, Tino Ryan, and Corinna Stark. Wealthy Clayburn retires after one adventure ("This job's *dangerous!*"), then returns several years later as a permanent member—his name now spelled Clayburne. Implicitly the Challengers take him back because they need the money. Rock star Tino joins when he and the group mistakenly believe that his older brother, Red, has been killed in an explosion; he appears in just a few issues. Ditto Corinna Stark, a student of the occult and a romantic interest for both Red and Rocky. Also making the odd appearance is the group's mascot, the space creature Cosmo.

Initially the heroes pack traditional firearms and travel by jet; in the middle 1960s, at the height of the James Bond craze, they begin using more and more gadgets, such as their flying Gallopin' Gizmo that can separate into four separate aircraft and fires energy blasts, X-ray beams, and more. Originally the Challengers wear red shirts and boots, brown or blue trousers, and yellow gloves; by their third appearance, the uniforms are solid purple. In #43 they change to sleeveless yellow body suits with red shoulders and boots and an hourglass symbol on the left breast. The next costumes, introduced in #70, are reminiscent of the purple suits; finally, in *Super Team Family* #8, they don pinkish body suits with white boots, gloves, and belt, a vertical yellow band down the left breast, with the hourglass symbol inside.

Comment: After starring in four issues of *Showcase,* the Challengers were given their own magazine, which lasted 87 issues, 18 of which were drawn by comics legend Jack Kirby. The characters were also featured in *Super DC Giant, Super Team Family,* and most notably in DC's long-lived *Adventure Comics* (beginning with #493). The characters' origin was retold in *Secret Origins* #12. Dell published the novel *Challengers of the Unknown* by Ron Goulart in 1977, in which the government hires the heroes to investigate an alien discovered in a remote lake.

CHANDU THE MAGICIAN   (R, MP)

First Appearance: *Chandu the Magician,* 1931 (see COMMENT).

Biography: Dr. Frank Chandler, a.k.a. Chandu, is an American secret agent who studies under a Hindu yogi and learns various mystic and occult skills to use in his fight against cultists, saboteurs, and criminals of all kinds.

Comment: The character was created by Harry A. Earnshaw, Vera Oldham, and R.R. Morgan, and first appeared as a children's radio serial heard only on the West Coast in 1931. Gayne Whitman starred. Executives at Fox thought the character had movie potential and brought him to the screen in *Chandu the Magician* in 1932, with Edmund Lowe in the title role. Bela Lugosi costarred as the evil Egyptian Roxor, who intended to use his death ray to conquer the world. Fox planned a series of films, but the failure of the first one caused those plans to be shelved. However, producer Sol Lesser saw potential in the character and made the 12-chapter serial *The Return of Chandu* in 1934, this time with Lugosi as the hero (and with native village sets borrowed from *King Kong*). In 1935 the serial was abridged as two separate feature films: *The Return of Chandu* and *Chandu on the Magic Isle.*

Chandu recieved a national radio audience in a series that was heard over ABC starting in 1949. Jason Robards, Sr., was the first radio Chandu, followed by Gayne Whitman, Howard Hoffman, and Tom Collins.

CHANOC (C, MP)

First Appearance: *Chanoc,* 1959, Publicaciones Herrerias (Mexico).

Biography: Chanoc is a fisherman who lives in the village of Ixtac. However, he has an inquiring mind and has become a self-taught oceanographer, ichthyologist, and zoologist. He is also at the peak of physical perfection and, with his old but powerful and energetic friend Tsekub, has adventures on the sea and on the land. His particular crusades are protecting the environment and wildlife, and keeping small villages (and, at times, small nations) from falling prey to smugglers, thiefs, and would-be despots.

Comment: The character was created by artist Angel Jose Mora and writer Martin de Lucenay, and is one of the most popular characters in Mexican comic book history. The hero was featured in eight motion pictures and remains a popular character.

CHARLIE CHAN (L, MP, R, CS, C, TV)

First Appearance: *The House Without a Key* by Earl Derr Biggers, 1925.

Biography: A detective sergeant of the Honolulu Police Department (he later makes inspector), Charlie Chan is a Chinese-Hawaiian who lives on Punchbowl Hill with his wife and 11 children. A student of philosophy—particularly Chinese—the genial Chan is fond of quoting aphorisms ("Mind like parachute— only function when open"). Though he speaks in broken English, he is well educated, incredibly astute, and never fails to crack a case. A portly man, he nontheless moves with surprising delicacy and is extremely gracious. His hair is black and cut short, his flesh is ivory-colored, and his eyes are very dark. He is assisted on his cases by his Oriental-looking but otherwise fully westernized "Number One Son" who handles whatever fisticuffs are needed for his pacifistic father.

Comment: Biggers based his character on the real-life Honolulu detective Chang Apana. The rest of the Biggers Chan novels are *Chinese Parrot* (1926), *Behind That Curtain* (1928), *Black Camel* (1929), *Charlie Chan Carries On* (1930), and *Keeper of the Keys* (1932). A non-Biggers novel, *Charlie Chan Returns,* was written by Dennis Lynds and published in 1974.

In movies, Chan was first featured in the 1926 screen adaptation of *The House Without a Key* from Pathe. It was followed by *The Chinese Parrot* (1928) and *Behind That Curtain* (1931), each with a different star. The character didn't really click onscreen until the Swedish-born Warner Oland took over the part in *Charlie Chan Carries On* (1931), which he followed

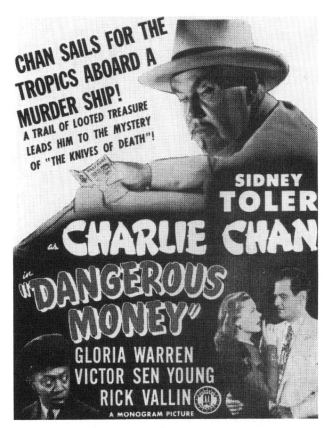

Original newspaper advertising art for a *Charlie Chan* film.

with *The Black Camel* (1931), *Chalie Chan's Chance* (1932), *Charlie Chan's Greatest Case* (1933), *Charlie Chan's Courage* (1934), *Charlie Chan in London* (1934), *Charlie Chan in Paris* (1935)—which introduced Key Luke as Lee, the Number One Son—*Charlie Chan in Egypt* (1935), *Charlie Chan in Shanghai* (1935), *Charlie Chan's Secret* (1936), *Charlie Chan at the Circus* (1936), *Charlie Chan at the Race Track* (1936), *Charlie Chan at the Opera* (1936), *Charlie Chan at the Olympics* (1937), *Charlie Chan on Broadway* (1937), and *Charlie Chan at Monte Carlo* (1938).

Missouri-born Sidney Toler took over the role next (with Victor Sen Yung as his Number Two Son, Jimmy) in *Charlie Chan in Honolulu* (1938), *Charlie Chan in Reno* (1939), *Charlie Chan at Treasure Island* (1939), *Charlie Chan in the City of Darkness* (1939), *Charlie Chan in Panama* (1940), *Charlie Chan's Murder Cruise* (1940), *Charlie Chan at the Wax Museum* (1940), *Murder Over New York* (1940), *Dead Men Tell* (1941), *Charlie Chan in Rio* (1941), *Castle in the Desert* (1942), *Charlie Chan in the Secret Service* (1944)—in which he now works for the FBI—*The Chinese Cat* (1944), *Charlie Chan in Black Magic* (1944), *The Jade Mask* (1945), *The Scarlet Clue* (1945), *The Shanghai Cobra* (1945), *The Red Dragon* (1945), *Dark Alibi* (1946), *Shadows Over Chinatown* (1946), *Dangerous Money* (1946), and *The Trap* (1946).

Toler died and the role passed to Roland Winters, who starred in *The Chinese Ring* (1947), *Docks of New Orleans* (1948), *The Shanghai Chest* (1948), *The Golden Eye* (1948), *The Feathered Serpent* (1948), and *Sky Dragon* (1949).

On radio, Chan made his debut on the Blue network in 1932 with Walter Connolly as Chan; he was succeeded by Ed Begley and Santos Ortega.

The *Charlie Chan* comic strip was created by Alfred Andriola and ran from October 1938 to March 1942.

In comic books, Chan has appeared as a supporting feature in a number of different titles. His own starring magazines were *The Adventures of Charlie Chan,* nine issues of which were published by Prize (to #5) and Charlton from 1948 to 1956. Dell published two issues of *Charlie Chan* in 1965–66.

On TV, J. Carrol Naish played Chan and James Hong was his Number One Son (Barry) in a half-hour show that was syndicated in 1958. A cartoon series, *The Amazing Chan and the Chan Clan,* aired on CBS from September 1972 to September 1974. Sixteen half-hour adventures were produced featuring Charlie solving adventures with his large family (Henry, Alan, Stanley, Suzie, Mimi, Anne, Tom, Flip, Nancy, and Scooter Chan). Keye Luke was the voice of Charlie; Jodie Foster was Anne Chan.

Ross Martin played the sleuth in the TV movie *Happiness Is a Warm Clue,* which was shot in 1970, aired in England in 1973, but wasn't shown on U.S. TV until 1979 as *The Return of Charlie Chan.*

The character's most recent incarnation was in the film *Charlie Chan and the Curse of the Dragon Queen* (1981), starring Peter Ustinov. Richard Hatch appeared as his half-Jewish, half-Oriental grandson Lee Chan Jr. The film was novelized by Michael Avallone.

CHARLIE'S ANGELS (TV)

First Appearance: *Charlie's Angels,* September 1976, ABC.

Biography: Former showgirl Sabrina Duncan, athletic Jill Munroe, and multilingual college graduate Kelly Garrett are all highly trained police officers who are disgusted with their boring, dead-end jobs on the force. Thus, they are delighted when contacted by John Bosley, who asks if they want to go to work for the Los Angeles branch of the Charles Townsend Detective Agency, which is staffed by female detectives, a.k.a. "Angels." The organization is run by super-wealthy Charlie Townsend, who is never seen but relays his instructions to John by phone. Yearning for a challenge and some excitement, the women agree to work for the agency.

After just one year of adventuring, Jill leaves the team and is replaced by her policewoman sister, Kris. After three years, Sabrina retires and is replaced by San Francisco police officer Tiffany Welles, the daughter of a Connecticut police chief. Welles lasts only one year, and is herself replaced by ex-model and narc Julie Rogers.

Over the years the women travel the world, posing as reporters, military recruits, nurses, insurance investigators, and even roller-derby entrants—anything it took to infiltrate operations and collect evidence.

Comment: The TV film was directed by John Llewellyn Moxie and spawned a series that aired from September 1976 to August 1981. Kate Jackson was Sabrina, Farrah Fawcett was Jill, Jaclyn Smith was Kelly, Cheryl Ladd was Kris, Shelley Hack was Tiffany, and Tanya Roberts was Julie. David Doyle played John and John Forsythe was the voice of Charlie.

Fawcett had left the show in an effort to become a film star by cashing in on her pin-up fame. She made six guest appearances on the show during the second season to avert a lawsuit for allegedly breaching her contract with the producers.

CHESTER GUMP (CS, C, R, L)

First Appearance: *The Gumps,* February 12, 1917, Chicago Tribune-New York News Syndicate.

Biography: Chester is about seven years old, the son of Andrew and Minerva Gump. His unnamed older sister is in college, and an older brother is in the navy. A wealthy uncle, Bim, lives in Australia. The Gumps own a dog named Buck and a cat named Hope.

Chester is a rogue who enjoys getting into trouble or adventure, whichever happens to be most convenient. His father frequently threatens to whip him with his razor strop (though Chester is usually canny enough to trick him out of it), and he has a post of honor in the yard of their suburban home: Each time he gets into a fight or lies, he hammers a nail into it. Naturally, the post resembles a porcupine. Many of Chester's later adventures take him around the world at his uncle's side or on his own.

Comment: The characters were created by artist Sidney Smith, with considerable input from newspaper owner Captain Joseph Medill Patterson; when the strip became a runaway hit, Smith signed the first $1 million contract in comic strip history, receiving $100,000 a year for ten years. The same day he signed a new $150,000 a year contract, he was killed in a car crash. The strip was continued by Gus Edson and ran through October 1959.

Eight early "comic" books reprinting the comic strips were published from 1918 to 1931; Dell published six *The Gumps* comic books from 1945 to 1947.

On the radio, a local show was aired over Chicago's WGN beginning in 1932 and starring Charles Flynn, Jr., as Chester; when it went to the CBS network in 1934 for a lengthy run, Jackie Kelk played Chester, with Wilmer Walter as Andy and Agnes Moorehead as Min.

Chester was the hero of several Big Little Book adventures: *Chester Gump at Silver Creek Ranch* (1933), *Chester Gump Finds the Hidden Treasure* (1934), *Chester Gump in the City of Gold* (1935), and *Chester Gump in the Pole to Pole Flight* (1937).

CHEYENNE BODIE (TV, C)

First Appearance: *Warner Brothers Presents,* 1955, ABC (see COMMENT).

Biography: Cheyenne Bodie is a taciturn, powerfully-built six-foot five-inch drifter who roams the West after the Civil War. At first he works as an army scout, accompanied by a mapmaker named Smitty. Together they rescue a young woman from Indians, track down stolen cattle, intervene in a war between prospectors and Indians, save a town from an outlaw gang that's taken over, and the like. Later Cheyenne becomes, in turn, a deputy, a ranch foreman, a guide, a guard, an undercover operative for the military, a scout for George A. Custer just before the Little Big Horn massacre (although this warps the internal time frame somewhat, occurring roughly a decade after the first episode), and other odd jobs, as long as they're legal.

Comment: After previewing as one of the three rotating series on *Warner Brothers Presents* for a season, *Cheyenne* was given its own hour-long ABC series, which lasted until 1963. There were 109 episodes in all. The show was very loosely based on the Warner Brothers film of the same name made in 1947 starring Dennis Morgan as gambler James Wylie trying to bring in outlaw Ed Landers. Clint Walker played Bodie on the TV series; L.Q. Jones was Smitty for the first season only.

During a dispute over money in 1958, Walker (and Bodie) were temporarily replaced on the series by Ty Hardin as Bronco Layne, a former Confederate captain who roamed the West just as Cheynne did. When Walker returned later that year, Hardin's character was spun off on his own series, *Bronco,* which aired from September 1958 to August 1962. For its last two seasons *Bronco* alternated with *Cheyenne* on what was now called *The Cheyenne Show.* A third show, *Sugarfoot,* was also made part of that umbrella title, making its debut in 1957. *Sugarfoot* was the story of Tom "Sugarfoot" Brewster, a law student who headed west in search of excitement. Will Hutchins played the part.

Dell published 25 issues of a *Cheyenne* comic book from 1956 to 1962. They also published six *Sugarfoot* comics as part of their *4-Color* series during 1958 to 1961. Poor *Bronco* never made it.

CHEYENNE KID (C)

First Appearance: *Wild Frontier* #7, 1957, Charlton Comics.

Biography: An orphan raised among the Cheyenne Indians, the Kid becomes a scout under Colonel Mackenzie, based at the fort in Sour Springs. During this time he is one of the few men trusted by both the army and the Indians, and he does his best to try to smooth over differences between the two and keep exploiters from using or abusing the Indians. After several years he becomes a scout and guide for hire, using his special knowledge of Indian ways to keep the West safe for *all* peoples. Though the Indians don't approve of him helping whites, especially soldiers, he is not afraid to complain to the authorities on their behalf, and they give him the name "Beloved Enemy." The only exception are the ruthless Kiowas, "his sworn enemies."

The Cheyenne Kid. © Charlton Comics.

The Kid dresses in a blue jacket and hat, with white trousers and a yellow bandana. He is an expert shot with his .45 Colt.

Comment: *Wild Frontier* became *Cheyenne Kid* with #8 and lasted till #99 (1973). Two issues were reprinted in 1978. Charlton Comics had one of the most successful lines of western comic books, publishing fictional adventures of historical characters in titles such as *Texas Rangers in Action, Frontier Marshal Wyatt Earp,* and *Billy the Kid,* and fiction heroes such as *Gunmaster and Bullet, the Gun Boy. Kid Montana* (a.k.a. *Montana Kid*) was a heroic "legend in the west."

CHIEF DAN MATTHEWS (TV)

First Appearance: *Highway Patrol,* September 1955, syndicated.

Biography: As the announcer says at the start of every episode, "Whenever the laws of any state are broken, a duly authorized organization swings into

aciton. It may be called the state police, state troopers, militia, the rangers, or the highway patrol. These are the stories of the men whose training, skill, and courage have enforced and preserved our state laws."

Actually, it was primarily the story of one man, gruff, burly Dan Matthews, who works for the highway patrol of an unnamed western state and chases down thieves, kidnapers, killers, smugglers, and other criminals.

Comment: Broderick Crawford played the part in the 156 half-hour episodes of the series. He was the only regular on the series. *Highway Patrol* was loosely inspired by the radio series of the same name, which starred Michael Fitzmaurice as State Trooper Corporal Steve Taylor, with John McGovern as his partner.

The success of the TV series inspired the syndicated *State Trooper,* starring Rod Cameron as Nevada State Trooper Rod Blake. The half-hour show debuted in 1957 and lasted just one season.

Crawford also starred in *King of Diamonds,* about John King, who was chief of security for the diamond industry. The syndicated series aired from 1961 to 1962.

CHINA SMITH (TV)

First Appearance: *China Smith,* June 1952, syndicated.

Biography: Based in a bar in Singapore, China Smith is a two-fisted detective and sometime mercenary who has been known to operate from time to time on the wrong side of the law. Smith roams the Orient tracking down missing persons, smugglers, gamblers who owe him money, or agents of a nefarious troublemaker named Shira, also known as the Empress. His frequent ally/nemesis is British Inspector Hobson.

Smith's nickname comes from his locale, not his nationality; the detective is Irish-American.

Comment: Dan Duryea played Smith, Douglas Dumbrille was Hobson, and Myrna Dell was Shira. Fifty-two half-hour episodes were produced, the second half of those syndicated as *The New Adventures of China Smith.* The entire package was rerun, in syndication, as *The Affairs of China Smith.*

CHIP OF THE FLYING U (L)

First Appearance: *Chip of the Flying U* by B.M. Bower, 1904, *Popular* Magazine.

Biography: Chip is actually Claude Bennett, a Montana cowhand who got his nickname due to a passion for potato chips. Astride the horse Silver, the square-chinned, straight-ahead, cigarette-smoking Chip is quick with his fists, not his guns, and usually turns them on land grabbers, rustlers, thieves, and coyotes. He's also a magnificent painter and is the calm, well-organized young man you want to have on a cattle drive. Chip is married to Dr. Della Whitmore, daughter of Old Man Whitmore, the ranch owner; they have a young son called "the Kid." Della is not only a physician but a crack shot as well, and does the shooting Chip is reluctant to do. Also on the ranch are cook Patsy, foreman Shorty, and hands Cal Emmett, fat Slim, Happy Jack, and Jack Bates.

A frequent foe is Dunk Wittaker, former coowner of the Flying U who tries to claim the ranch from time to time through various underhanded means. Eventually Wittaker gives up and leaves the territory.

Comment: B.M. Bower was a pseudonym for prolific author Bertha Sinclair-Cowan. Dozens of Flying U stories were published in *Popular, Argosy,* and other magazines. They were collected in book form in *Chip of the Flying U* (1906), *The Lonesome Trail* (1909), *The Happy Family* (1910), *Flying U Ranch* (1914), *The Flying U's Last Stand* (1915), *Rodeo* (1929), *Dark Horse* (1931), and *The Flying U Strikes* (1934).

CHRISTIE LOVE (TV)

First Appearance: *Get Christie Love,* September 1974, ABC (see COMMENT).

Biography: A hip, sexy, black officer with the Special Investigations Division of the Los Angeles Police Department, Christie Love works undercover with sidekick Sergeant Pete Gallagher, getting the goods on rapists, pimps, pushers, corrupt landlords, and other big-city predators. Both report to Lieutenant Matt Reardon and, later, Captain Arthur P. Ryan. Quick with a wisecrack, Love tends to call everyone she meets "Sugar."

Comment: The hour-long series lasted until July 1975. Former *Rowan and Martin's Laugh-In* star Teresa Graves played Love, with Charlies Cioffi as Reardon, Jack Kelly as Ryan, and Michael Pataki as Gallagher.

The series was inspired by a book called *The Ledger,* the exploits of white police officer Christie Opara. It was written by real-life police officer Dorothy Uhnak and was previously the basis for the made-for-TV movie *The Bait* (1973) starring Donna Mills (as Tracy Fleming). Writer George Kirgo was responsible for changing Christie Opara into Christie Love.

CHUCK WHITE (C)

First Appearance: *Treasure Chest of Fun & Fact* #1, 1946, George A. Pflaum (later, T. S. Denison).

Biography: A student at St. John's Boy's School in Steeltown, Chuck White is a star athlete on Father Carroll's various teams, and, when he attends St. Mark's College, he is also a star football and basketball player. After being sidelined by a football injury, White becomes a reporter for *The Steeltown News,* eventually becoming a foreign correspondent and getting involved with spies, insurrectionists, corrupt rulers, Communists, and other dangerous sorts. When he returns to the States and marries (1966), his young cousin Charlie "Chuck" White takes center stage.

Comment: The comic book was distributed primarily through parochial schools and lasted until July 1972. White was in almost every issue until the last two years when he appeared in alternating issues.

THE CISCO KID (L, MP, R, TV, C, CS)

First Appearance: "The Caballero's Way" by O. Henry, 1904, *McClure's* Magazine.

Biography: In his first appearance, the Kid is no hero at all: He's a 25-year-old who has killed six men in fair fights and murdered twice as many ("mostly Mexicans") because he likes "to see them kick." He roams the area around the Rio Grande and has thus far eluded capture because he can fire "five-sixths of a second sooner than any sheriff or ranger" and because his speckled roan horse (unnamed) knows "every cowpath . . . from San Antonio to Matamoras."

Captain Duval, of Company X near Laredo, is charged with the Kid's capture, and sends Lieutenant Sandridge to get him. He heads to the home of young Tonia Perez, with whom the Kid is in love; smitten with Sandridge, she agrees to betray Cisco. But Cisco learns of her plan and, in his own devious way, works it so that Sandridge guns Tonia down, thinking it's the outlaw.

In films the hero undergoes a change. He's now a turn-of-the-century Mexican do-gooder who rides the West on his horse Diablo, is dressed in a natty black outfit, captures outlaws, and woos women—whom he usually rescues. His devoted sidekick, Pancho—who does not appear in the original story)—rides the horse Loco. Though the Kid is an expert marksman, he usually aims for an adversary's hand.

Comment: Cisco's career in other media began with the film *In Old Arizona* in 1929, starring Warner Baxter—who won the Best Actor Oscar (the second ever awarded) for his performance. He played the part again in *The Arizona Kid* (1930), *The Cisco Kid* (1931), and *The Return of the Cisco Kid* (1939). Cesar Romero took over the role with *The Cisco Kid and the Lady* (1939), and followed it with *Viva Cisco Kid* (1940), *Lucky Cisco Kid* (1940), *The Gay Caballero* (1940), *Romance of the Rio Grande* (1940), and

Ride on Vaquero (1941). Gilbert Roland briefly took the role, after which Duncan Renaldo played the part in *The Cisco Kid Returns* (1945). Former serial star Renaldo also played the part in the popular TV series with Leo Carrillo as Pancho. There were 156 half-hour episodes produced between 1950 and 1956 by Ziv Television; the syndicated series was one of the first to be filmed in color.

On radio, the Cisco Kid was first broadcast over Mutual in 1943. Jackson Beck, then Jack Mather, played the part; Pancho was played by Louis Sorin, Harry Lang, and finally by Mel Blanc.

Dell published 41 issues of *The Cisco Kid* from 1950 to 1958. *The Cisco Kid* comic strip began on January 15, 1951, drawn by Jose-Luis Salinas and written by Rod Reed. It ended in 1968.

CLAY CULHANE (TV)

First Appearance: *Black Saddle,* January 1959, NBC.

Biography: Clay Culhane and his brothers are gunslingers; but when all save Clay are slain in a gunfight, he decides to change professions. After studying law, he becomes an attorney and rides throughout the New Mexico Territory after the Civil War, helping people settle their problems with the law instead of with the gun. He is pursued by Marshal Gib Scott, who doesn't believe Clay has turned over a new leaf—and wants to be there to nab him when he goes for his guns again.

When he isn't roaming the plains, Clay is based in the Marathon Hotel in Latigo; the proprietor is his friend (and more?), widow Nora Travers.

Comment: This literate, half-hour series debuted toward the end of the "adult western" craze (e.g., MATT DILLON) that had begun in 1955. As a result, it lasted only until September 1960—not as long as it deserved. *Black Saddle* starred Peter Breck as Clay, Russell Johnson as Scott, and Anna Lisa as Nora.

"CLIFF" CORNWALL (C)

First Appearance: *Flash Comics* #1, 1940, DC Comics.

Biography: Cornwall is a special FBI agent whose duties are "many and varied" but whose most important job "is to guard against sabotage and espionage activities." In his first mission, the red-headed hero is seconded to the army to investigate the disappearance of airplanes over Alaska. There he meets Lys Valliere, the daughter of one of the missing pilots, who joins him on the adventure. ("Say," says Cliff when he learns she can fly and operate a machine gun, "I could love you for that.") When the "international" elements

"Cliff" Cornwall and Lys wrap up their first adventure. © DC Comics.

behind the abductions are sniffed out and eliminated, the army asks to have Cornwall assigned to them permanently, with Lys as his sidekick. Cliff is a nickname; the hero's real name is not known.

Comment: The character was created by Sheldon Moldoff and appeared in the first 17 issues of *Flash Comics.*

CLUTCH CARGO (TV)

First Appearance: *Clutch Cargo,* March 1959, syndicated.

Biography: Clutch Cargo is a young, rugged author who pilots himself around the world, from Africa to the Arctic, looking for adventure. His companions are Swampy, the young boy Spinner, and the dog Paddlefoot. Their most tenacious foe is the wicked Colonel Bascom B. Bamshot.

Comment: The character was created by cartoonist Clark Haas; Richard Cotting was Clutch, Hal Smith was Swampy, and Margaret Kerry was Spinner.

The adventures were serials told in five-minute segments and were undistinguished except for the use of Synchro-Vox. This process superimposed human mouths over cartoon faces, so that the actors' own lips moved in synch with the dialogue. Apart from that, animation was extremely limited. Fifty-two separate adventures were produced by Cambria Productions through 1960. The studio also produced the much less successful *Captain Fathom* in 1965, the adventures of a submarine captain, and SPACE ANGEL.

COLONEL EDWARD McCAULEY (TV, L, C)

First Appearance: *Men Into Space,* September 1959, CBS.

Biography: U.S. Air Force Colonel Edward McCauley leaves his wife, Mary, and son, Peter, behind and commands the first flight to the moon. The first attempt to reach our satellite is aborted after the second stage malfunctions in space; the next try is successful, though a crewman is killed in the landing. In subsequent adventures McCauley supervises the construction of a space station; is faced with a crewman who suffers a heart attack on the moon (he'll die if he doesn't get to Earth, yet the G-forces of blast off will kill him); must capture a runawary nuclear-powered rocket; faces a moonquake; is stranded on an asteroid that has been rigged to explode; deals with sexual "tensions" as the first woman goes to the moon; and, in his last chronicled exploit, after many other adventures on the moon, leads an expedition to Mars.

Comment: The half-hour series aired through September 1960. William Lundigan starred as McCauley, with Joyce Taylor as Mary. (Angie Dickinson played the role in the pilot.) The show received the full cooperation of the Defense Department, making it as accurate as possible; it also borrowed heavily from the designs of renowned space artist Chesley Bonestell.

Author Murray Leinster wrote a novel, *Men Into Space* (1960), inspired by the TV series.

Dell published one issue of a *Men Into Space* comic book in 1960 as #1083 in their *4-Color* line.

COLONEL EDWARD STRAKER (TV, L)

First Appearance: *UFO,* September 1972, syndicated.

Biography: In the future (1980, then), UFOs and their green-skinned, humanoid occupants are discovered spying on our world. To spy back—and fight back, as necessary—the leading governments of Earth set up SHADO, Supreme Headquarters, Alien Defense Organization, and put U.S. Air Force Colonel Edward Straker in charge. As a soldier and astrophysicist with two years of lunar research at MIT, he is perfect for the job. SHADO is headquartered inside the Harlington-Straker Studios ten miles outside of London, where the white-haired Straker poses as a movie producer. His number-two man is Colonel Alec Freeman, Lieutenant Gay Ellis is in command of SHADO's moon base, and Captain Peter Karlin is the pilot of the X-ray ship *Seagull.* The computer satellite SID—Space Intruder Detector—helps keep track of alien comings and goings.

Comment: Ed Bishop starred as Straker in the hour-long series; George Sewel was Freeman; Gabrielle Drake played Ellis; and Peter Gordeno was Karlin. Twenty-six episodes were produced in England in 1970 by Gerry and Sylvia Anderson. (See COMMANDER JOHN KOENIG.)

Two *UFO* novels by Robert Miall were published by Warner Books in 1973—*Flesh Hunters* and *Sporting Blood.*

COL. MARCH (L, TV)

First Appearance: *Department of Queer Complaints* by Carter Dickson, 1940, William Morrow and Company.

Biography: The "large, amiable" pipe-smoking March is a former military officer who is put in charge of the Department of Queer Complaints (informally known as the Crazy House), located in room D-3 of Scotland Yard. The unflappable March is assisted by Inspector Roberts, with whom he served in the military. Though both men are able to defend themselves, they usually catch criminals off guard, making violence unnecessary. Together they solve cases that range from the odd (a blue pig terrorizing Stepney), to the seemingly impossible (a new Invisible Man—actually, mirrors cleverly positioned to conceal a criminal's presence in a room), to the strange throat-slitting of a man in a room where there wasn't a knife, sword, or even a pin to be found.

March has sandy hair and a mustache, a "mottled face," and "keen blue eyes."

Comment: *Department of Queer Complaints* is a collection of seven stories about March; a second volume, *The Men Who Explained Miracles,* was published in 1963 and contained two stories. The character was based on a friend of the author's, Major C.J.C. Street. Carter Dickson is a pseudonym of John Dickson Carr.

On TV, Boris Karloff starred in *Col. March of Scotland Yard,* 26 half-hour episodes that were produced in England in 1954 and shown in syndication in the U.S. Karloff's March wears a patch over his left eye.

Carr also created popular mystery heroes Henri

Bencolin and Dr. Gideon Fell and, as Dickson, wrote 24 mysteries about Sir Henry Merrivale, an expert at solving "locked room" mysteries.

COLONEL STEVE ZODIAC   (TV, C)

First Appearance: *Fireball XL-5,* October 1963, syndicated.

Biography: In the 21st century, Colonel Steve Zodiac and his copilot, Space Doctor Venus of the World Space Patrol, fly their 300-foot-long spaceship *Fireball XL-5* through the galaxy. Their mission: to defend Space City from the likes of Mr. and Mrs. Superspy and the Briggs Brothers. Lending the heroes a hand are Robert the Robot and Professor Matthew Matic.

The nose of the missile-shaped craft can be launched as a separate vehicle, *Fireball Junior.* Both vehicles can fire missiles.

Comment: The half-hour series continued to show first-run episodes through September 1965.

The characters were brought to life through "Supermarionation," a marionette technique developed by producers Sylvia and Gerry Anderson. In addition to very thin (.005 inches) strings to move the limbs, solenoid cells were used to control the eyes, lids, and mouth. *Supercar* was the first show to utilize the process, following the adventures of Mike Mercury and the title vehicle, which could travel "under the ocean . . . or high in the sky . . . it travels anywhere." Accompanying him are Dr. Beeker, Mike's young ward Jimmy, and their mascot Mitch, a monkey. *Fireball XL-5* was the second of these shows, followed by the syndicated *Stingray* in 1965, which recounted the adventures of World Aquanaut Security Patrol hero Troy Tempest and his submarine *Stingray; Thunderbirds* in 1966, the saga of International Rescue, a Pacific-based five-ship land/sea/space rescue team run by Jeff Tracy and his son Scott; and *Captain Scarlet and the Mysterons* in 1967, in which Mars and Earth go to war, with Captain Blue as the heroic agent of Spectrum.

Gold Key published one issue of the *Steve Zodiac and the Fireball XL-5* comic book in 1964.

COLT SEAVERS   (TV)

First Appearance: *The Fall Guy,* November 1981, ABC.

Biography: A Hollywood stuntman who earns $5,000 a day when he works, Colt Seavers supplements his income by working as a bounty hunter, capturing bail jumpers for money. Among his more unusual prey are Elizabeth "Mad Dog" McClosky, a roller-derby queen; Frank Dial, an oil company security chief who uses petrodollars to fund an illegal intelligence operation; and a gang that's hiding gold in stunt cars and extracting it when the wrecked cars are melted down. Between assignments, Colt helps those in need, such as a friend whose brother is being hunted by the mob; the manager of a women's wrestling team who's being threatened if he doesn't throw a match; homeless friend Ozzie and his imaginary friend Harold, who has a habit of witnessing crimes; and even Roy Rogers, whose movie is ruined by a gang of car rustlers.

Colt is assisted by his fumbling cousin Howie Munson and fellow stunt artist Jody Banks. Naturally, Colt and Jody get to use many of the stunts in real life that they used in the movies. Different bondswomen give Colt his assignments over the years: Samantha "Big Jack" Jack, Terri Michaels, and Pearl Sperling.

Comment: Lee Majors starred in the hour-long series, which aired until May 1986. There were 111 episodes in all. Douglas Barr played Howie and Heather Thomas was Jody. Jo Ann Pflug was Big Jack, Markie Post played Terri, and Nedra Volz was Pearl.

COMANCHE   (CS)

First Appearance: *Comanche,* 1971, *Tintin* (Belgium).

Biography: Comanche is a raven-haired, strong-willed young woman whose parents have left her the cattle ranch Triple-Six in Greenstone Falls, Wyoming. There Comanche, her red-haired foreman Red Dust, his young and admiring helper Clem, the black hand Toby, and the old, grizzled, white-bearded hand Ten Gallons fight rustlers, murderers, robbers, Indians, and others who pass through and cause trouble.

Comment: The strip, which continues to this day, was created by writer Michel Regnier ("Greg") and artist Hermann Huppen.

COMMANDER ADAMA   (TV, L, C, MP)

First Appearance: *Battlestar Galactica* by Glen A. Larson and Robert Thurston, 1978, Berkley Books (see COMMENT).

Biography: In a distant galaxy, humans known as Colonials have established 12 known colonies: Caprica, Gemoni, Canceria, Piscon, Sagitara, Leo, Libra, Aquaria, Virgon, Aeriana, Tarua, and Scorpio—and a rumored, long-lost 13th colony, Earth. For 1,000 (Earth) years the Colonials have also been defending themselves against an aggressive race of lizardlike creatures known as Cylons, who fight via powerful, robotic proxies. Pretending to want peace, the Cylons ask to meet the Colonial leaders, President Adar and the Council of 12, to sign a treaty. However, Commander

Adama of the Colonial Fleet's flagship mile-long battlestar, *Galactica*, doesn't trust them. When the Cylons betray the Colonials and attack their fleet, most of the Colonials are killed, including Adama's 51-year-old wife, Ila, and his Viper-pilot son, Zac; under Adama's leadership, the survivors board airbuses, tramp steamers, shuttlers, and anything that flies to follow Adama and the *Galactica* in search of Earth. Along the way they are dogged by the Cylons, who are still bent upon their destruction.

A former military man who rose through the Colonial Fleet from ensign, putting down uprisings and the like, Adama is assisted by an able crew that includes his daughter Athena, Lieutenant Starbuck, second-in-command Colonel Tigh, and Lieutenant Boomer. Adama's son is the dashing Captain Apollo, who becomes the stepfather of young Boxey when he weds the boy's mother Serina onboard the *Galactica*.

After roaming through space for 30 years, the "ragtag fleet" of 221 ships finally reaches Earth. However, the Cylons have found our world as well and are planning to destroy it. Captain Troy (who was the child Boxey in the original series) and Lieutenant Dillon go to the Pacific Institute of Technology to help Earth secretly prepare for the encounter.

Comment: Though the novel predated the debut of the three-hour pilot episode in September 1978, it was based on the TV film and is not considered the genesis of the series. There were another 19 one-hour episodes and a two-hour episode.

Lorne Greene starred as Adama; other cast members included Richard Hatch as Apollo, Maren Jensen as Athena, Dirk Benedict as Starbuck, Noah Hathaway as Boxey, Terry Carter as Tigh, and Herbert Jefferson, Jr., as Boomer. The original aired from September 1978 to August 1979, after which it was retooled as *Galactica 1980*, which aired from January to August 1980. In that series Kent McCord played Troy and Barry Van Dyke was Dillon. There were ten hour-long episodes.

The original series was edited into 12 two-hour-long TV movies, which were shown in syndication: the first film, plus *Lost Planet of the Gods, Guns on Ice Planet Zero, The Phantom in Space, Space Prison, Space Casanova, Curse of the Cylons, The Living Legend, War of the Gods, Greetings from Earth, Murder in Space*, and the inevitable *Experiment in Terra*.

After its TV debut, the original film was also released theatrically, in theater-rattling Sensurround; a second feature, *Mission Galactica: The Cylon Attack*, was cobbled together from the episodes "Living Legend" and "Fire in Space." It was shown without the subwoofer effects.

Marvel Comics published 23 issues of *Battlestar Galactica* from 1979 to 1981.

In addition to their tie-in with the pilot episode, Berkley published a series of novels based on episodes of the original series: Larson and Thurston wrote *The Cylon Death Machine, The Tombs of Kobol*, and *The Young Warriors;* Larson and Michael Resnick wrote *Galactica Discovers Earth* (based on *Galactica 1980*); and Larson and Nicholas Yermakov wrote *The Living Legend*. A photostory of the original film was published by Berkley, while Ace published a paperback edition of the first three issues of the Marvel comic book.

COMMANDER BENJAMIN SISKO
(TV, L, C)

First Appearance: *Star Trek: Deep Space Nine,* September 1992, syndicated.

Biography: In the 24th century, as Lieutenant commander of the USS *Saratoga*, Benjamin Sisko intercepts and battles an alien Borg ship at Wolf 359, a confrontation that costs the life of his wife, Jennifer. His nine-year-old son, Jake, survives. Sisko is reassigned to Mars, overseeing the construction of new ships for Starfleet, of which he's an officer. But the work is unrewarding and Jake doesn't like Mars, so Sisko is given command of Deep Space Nine, a former Cardassian mining base in orbit around the planet Bajor near the galaxy's first stable wormhole. With some 300 permanent residents, Deep Space Nine consists of a central core and habitat ring, which includes docking ports, living quarters, and the Promenade with shops for intergalactic commerce.

Sisko is a serious, taciturn man whose level tone and impassive face often make him difficult to read. On the positive side, he's supernaturally calm in the face of most emergencies.

Sisko's security chief is Odo, a shape-shifter and the last of his kind. Odo typically assumes Bajoran form when he's out and about; in his normal shape, he's a gelatinous mass. Other members of Sisko's command team include: the tough Major Kira Nerys, a Bajoran and a former terrorist; Chief Operations Officer Miles O'Brien, who is married to schoolteacher Keiko; Science Officer Jadzia Dax, an alien Trill who wears successive bodies over time; and Dr. Julian Bashir, a specialist in multispecies medicine. Most notable among the permanent residents is Quark, a Ferengi barkeep who is a likable gambler and thief, and the unofficial "community leader" of the Promenade.

Comment: Avery Brooks stars as Sisko and Rene Auberjonois is Odo. Nana Visitor is Kira, Colm Meaney is O'Brien, Armin Shimerman is Quark, Terry Farrell is Dax, and Siddig El Fadil is Bashir.

The characters have also appeared in original novels, including *Emissary* by J.M. Dillard (based on the pilot episode) and *The Siege* by Peter David (an original novel).

Dark Horse Comics began publishing a *Star Trek: Deep Space Nine* comic book in 1992.

COMMANDER BUZZ CORRY (TV, C)

First Appearance: *Space Patrol,* September 1950, ABC.

Biography: The United Planets is the governing body of the 30th century. Armed with paralyzer ray guns, the crew of the spaceship *Terra* flies throughout the universe keeping the peace, commanded by the intrepid Buzz Corry. Reporting to Major Robbie Robertson—Security Chief of the Universe—and Secretary General Karlyle of the United Planets, Buzz Corry is assisted by Cadet Happy and Miss Tonga, a former criminal who has joined the forces of good. Corry's girlfriend is Carol, the secretary general's daughter; his foremost enemies are Mr. Proteus and Prince Baccarratti, a.k.a. the Black Falcon. The space heroes wear sleek uniforms with insignias on their chests; Corry's is a lightning bolt.

Incidentally, no one is killed in the future. Once wrongdoers have been paralyzed, scientists remove their evil tendencies using the Brainograph, turning them into happy, productive citizens. "Smokin' rockets!" is a common expression of the future.

Comment: *Space Patrol* promised "high adventure in the wild reaches of space . . . missions of daring in the name of interplanetary justice." The show was created by Mike Moser and began as a 15-minute daily series; for the first few episodes the character was known as Commander Kit Corry. The series switched to a weekly half-hour after a year and remained on the air through February 1955. Ed Kemmer starred, Norman Jolley played the secretary general, Virginia Hewitt was Carol, and Nina Bara was Tonga. Marvin Miller was Proteus and Bella Kovacs was Baccarratti. Ziff-Davis published two issues of a *Space Patrol* comic book in 1952.

COMMANDER JOHN KOENIG (TV, C, L)

First Appearance: *Space: 1999,* September 1975, Syndicated.

Biography: The American astronaut holds doctorates in extraterrestrial biology, space propulsion systems, and organic chemistry. On September, 13, 1999, the cool, determined 35-year-old arrives at the 311-person strong Moonbase Alpha to take command. Shortly after taking his post, stored nuclear waste from Earth explodes, causing the moon to leave its orbit and fly through space. Journeying through the cosmos, the space pioneers encounter a black hole, find themselves headed straight toward the planet Astheria (whose queen, Arra, *wants* them to collide), meet the immortal alien Balor, are perplexed when an Alphan suddenly becomes a Cro-Magnon man, and so on.

The base is equipped with Eagles—utility spaceships that travel around the moon and through space—while base security forces pack stun guns. Other Alphans include Koenig's lover, Dr. Helena Russell; Koenig's mentor, Professor Victor Bergman, who established the base; chief astronaut First Lieutenant Alan Carter; and the shape-changing science officer Maya from the planet Psychon.

Comment: There were 48 episodes of the hour-long series, which was created by Gerry and Sylvia Anderson (of the marionette series *Thunderbirds, Fireball XL-5,* and others). Martin Landau starred as Koenig, Barbara Bain was Dr. Russell, Barry Morse was Bergman (first season only), Nick Tate was Carter, and Catherine Schell was Maya (second season only).

From 1975 to 1976, Charlton Comics published six issues of a *Space: 1999* comic book and eight issues of a magazine with comic strips and feature articles.

A total of 16 novels were written, based on scripts from the series: *Breakaway, Moon Odyssey, The Space Guardians, Collision Course, Lunar Attack, Astral Quest, Alien Seed, Android Planet, Rogue Planet,* and *Phoenix of Megarion,* written by E.C. Tubb or John Rankine and published in 1975 to 1976; *Planet of Peril, Mind-Breaks of Space, The Space Jackers, The Psychomorph, The Time Fighters,* and *The Edge of the Infinite,* written by Michael Butterworth and published in 1977.

COMMISSIONER STEWART MCMILLAN (TV)

First Appearance: *Once Upon a Dead Man,* September 1971, NBC.

Biography: McMillan is a former criminal lawyer who is asked by the mayor of San Francisco to become commissioner of police. Though he'd rather be in a courtroom, McMillan accepts the appointment. His wife, Sally, is an inquisitive soul who usually pokes into cases in which her husband is involved (a stolen sarcophagus, in the original TV movie), stumbles onto a body or crime, and ends up on the run or abducted.

After that, McMillan must leave his paperwork behind and rescue her, assisted by the devoted but none-too-bright Sergeant Charles Enright. In one of their best teamings, an earthquake reveals a skeleton in the wall of the McMillan home. After several years Sally's luck runs out and she dies in a plane crash. Enright is promoted to lieutenant and McMillan's new aide is Sergeant Steve DiMaggio. The commissioner's secretary is Maggie.

The MacMillans' housekeeper is Mildred. When Sally dies, Mildred leaves and is replaced by her sister, Agatha.

Comment: The made-for-TV movie launched the series *McMillan and Wife,* which aired as part of the *NBC* (later, *NBC Sunday*) *Mystery Movie,* rotating with *Columbo* and *McCloud* (see LT. COLUMBO and SAM MCCLOUD). It aired through August 1977. Rock Hudson was McMillan, Susan Saint James played Sally, Nancy Walker was Mildred, John Schuck was Enright, Richard Gilliland was DiMaggio, Martha Raye was Agatha, and Gloria Stroock was Maggie. After Saint James and Walker left, the series continued for one season, known as *McMillan.*

THE CONTINENTAL OP (L)

First Appearance: "The Tenth Clew" by Dashiel Hammett, 1923, *Black Mask.*
Biography: The "Op" has no other name. Overweight and 40, he is nonetheless the "toughest, hardest, strongest, fastest, sharpest, biggest, wisest, meanest" detective in the West. An operative for the Continental Detective Agency of San Francisco, he is equally quick (and effective) with a gun or with his pummeling fists and is fiercely loyal to his clients and to "the Old Man" who runs the agency. During his long career, the Op has battled burglars, killers, a town rotten with corrupt politicians whom he cleverly pits against each other, and even supernatural forces, always triumphing. In one of his most striking escapades (the novelette "The Gutting of Couffignal," collected in *The Return of the Continental Op*), he single-handedly protects an island of wealthy inhabitants from a small army of machine-gun-toting thieves.

The Op usually wears a nondescript overcoat and hat, carries a case of business cards that he's picked up "by one means or another," and introduces himself as whatever person or profession suits the moment. He has no sense of humor; clever people annoy him almost as much as criminals.

Comment: The first novel featuring the Op, *Red Harvest,* was serialized in *Black Mask* in 1927–28 and published in book form in 1929. The other books featuring the character are *The Dain Curse* (1929),

the novelette "$106,000 Blood Money" (1943), and eight collections of short stories: *The Continental Op* and *The Return of the Continental Op* (both 1945), *Hammett Homicides* (1946; four Op stories), *Dead Yellow Women* (1947; four stories), *Nightmare Town* (1948; two stories), *The Creeping Siamese* (1950; three stories), *Woman in the Dark* (1952; three stories), and *A Man Named Thin* (1962; one story).

The Op was one of the earliest and best of the "hard-boiled" detectives, establishing the mold used by Hammett himself and others in the future. The character was based on one of Hammett's coworkers at Pinkerton's Detective Agency, Assistant Superintendent James Wright.

See also NICK AND NORA CHARLES; SAM SPADE.

COOL MCCOOL (TV)

First Appearance: *Cool McCool,* September 1966, NBC.
Biography: The son of famed detective Harry McCool, Cool is an inept secret agent who nonetheless manages to solve all of his cases. He chases criminals in his souped-up Coolmobile, reports to his boss Number One, and has a sort-of romance with One's secretary, Friday.

Harry himself continues to be a force in upholding the law, despite the clumsiness of his own two sidekicks, police officers Tom and Dick. The men report to the sergeant and battle the likes of Big Benny, Mighty Morris, and the Green Dragon.

Cool's foes include the Owl, the Rattle, the Pussycat (who unites the nation's birds into a powerful crime syndicate), Hurricane Harry, and the Jack-in-the-Box.
Comment: The series ran until the summer of 1969. Cool was created by Bob Kane, the creator of Batman; Kane says, "It was a parody of the spy films and TV shows that were popular in the mid-'60s," though the series obviously drew its heaviest inspiration from *Get Smart.* (See MAXWELL SMART.) Cool's voice was provided by Bob McFadden. There were 38 Cool adventures, each eight minutes long; 19 Harry McCool cartoons were produced.

Bob McFadden was the voice of both Cool and Harry.

CORSAIR (C)

First Appearance: *X-Men* #107, 1977, Marvel Comics.
Biography: In the later 1950s air force test pilot Major Christopher Summers is flying his wife, Katherine Anne, and their sons, Scott and Alex, back from Alaska in his DeHaviland Mosquito when an alien

spaceship blasts them from the sky to keep its presence here a secret. Katherine has time to put a parachute on Scott, who holds onto Alex and bails out; Scott later becomes the superhero Cyclops, while Alex becomes Havok. Meanwhile, his parents don't die—they're teleported onto the extraterrestrial vessel, which hails from the Shi'ar Imperial Throneworld. The Summerses are separated and Christopher imprisoned; he breaks free in time to prevent Emperor D'ken from raping Katherine Anne. Unfortunately, he can't prevent the vengeful ruler from murdering her, after which Christopher is sent to the slave pits, where he meets the the froglike Ch'od, the cyborg Raza, and the humanoid skunk Hepzibah. (That's his nickname for her; her real name is unpronounceable. They later become lovers.) Escaping, they steal a starship that they christen the *Starjammer* and use to prey on Shi'ar starships. They are later joined by Earth superhero Binary and the dragonflylike physician Sikorsky, and help depose D'ken. Unfortunately, his benevolent replacement, his sister Lilandra Neramani, is herself ousted and joins the Starjammers.

In his new identity as the swashbuckling Corsair, Christopher makes it a policy never to hurt innocent beings they encounter on their raids. Corsair dresses in a red and black body suit with red boots and gloves, and carries a sword and blaster.

Comment: The origin of the Starjammers was told in *X-Men* #156; the characters have appeared in various Marvel titles over the years.

COTTON CARVER (C)

First Appearance: *Adventure Comics* #35, 1939, DC Comics.

Biography: A "world adventurer," Cotton Carver, a young man in riding breeches, travels around the world in search of "danger in many and varied shapes and forms," and even journeys inside the earth, where he helps establish peace between the kingdoms of King Marl and the pirate queen Deela of Barlunda.

Comment: The character's adventures were written by Gardner Fox, one of the best and most prolific writers in comic book history; Fox's contribution here was not characterization but exotic locales and stories. The character lasted until #59.

CRAIG KENNEDY (L, MP, S, TV)

First Appearance: *The Silent Bullet* by Arthur B. Reeve, 1912, Eveleigh Nash.

Biography: A professor at New York's Columbia University, Kennedy is a chemist and inventor who works as a consultant on criminal cases and uses a variety of innovative scientific devices and techniques to solve crimes. He also uses a gun, his fists, and various clever disguises when need be. Among the equipment he pioneers are polygraphs and a seismograph that can detect footsteps.

Kennedy works closely with Inspector Barney O'Connor of the NYPD and is a devotee of the opera. Reporter Walter Jameson is his faithful friend, assistant, and roommate.

Comment: *The Silent Bullet* is a collection of short stories, which includes "The Steel Door," "The Black Hand," and "The Artificial Paradise." There were 11 other short story collections as well as 14 novels: *Gold of the Gods* (1915), *The Exploits of Elaine* (1915), *The Ear in the Wall* (1916), *The Romance of Elaine* (1916), *The Triumph of Elaine* (1916), *The Adventuress* (1917), *The Soul Scar* (1919), *The Film Mystery* (1921), *Atavar* (1924), *The Radio Detective* (1926), *Pandora* (1926), *The Kidnap Club* (1932), *The Clutching Hand* (1934), and *The Stars Scream Murder* (1936).

The character also appeared in a number of motion pictures, beginning with the serial *The Exploits of Elaine* (1915; see ELAINE DODGE). Arnold Daly played the part in this film as well as in its sequels, made the same year: *The New Exploits of Elaine* and *The Romance of Elaine*. In 1919 Herbert Rawlinson starred in *The Carter Case* (a.k.a. *The Craig Kennedy Serial*), and in 1926 the sleuth returned in *The Radio Detective* starring Jack Daughterty. The hero's first and only talking film was the 15-chapter serial *The Clutching Hand* (1936), starring Jack Mulhall as Craig. *The Clutching Hand* has also been produced on the stage.

On TV, Donald Woods played the part in the short-lived syndicated half-hour series *Craig Kennedy, Criminologist*, which aired in 1952.

THE CREATURE COMMANDOES (C)

First Appearance: *Weird War Tales* #93, 1980, DC Comics.

Biography: In 1942, under U.S. Army Intelligence Lieutenant Matthew Shrieve, all of the branches of the military as well as various civilian groups labor over Project M (as in "monster"), which "researched . . . the symbols of fright and horror that all men seem to share regardless of social and cultural conditioning . . . and then . . . set about scientifically re-creating them!" They recruit 4F Oklahoma farm boy Warren Griffith, who suffers from lycanthropy (werewolfism), which they make even more extreme; they make a speechless, yellow-skinned giant of Marine Private Elliot "Lucky" Taylor, who stepped on a mine; and they offer orphaned, streetwise Sergeant Vincent Velcro a

The Creature Commandoes in action. © DC Comics.

choice of 30 years of hard labor for losing his temper and crippling a superior officer, or six months of injections with a chemical derived from vampire bat blood. The result? They become the Creature Commandoes. However, there are drawbacks. Velcro—who can become a bat—must drink blood to survive and doesn't care whether it comes from friend or foe, animal or human; and Griffith changes back to a boy "uncontrollably." Later they're joined by Dr. Myrna Rhodes, who is accidentally exposed to chemical vapors that turn her hair to snakes. Her team name, of course, is Dr. Medusa. Unlike the monster of Greek mythology, her hair doesn't turn people to stone; it just repulses them. When she isn't in action, Dr. Medusa wears a turban.

When last seen, the Creature Commandoes are flying a test rocket that carries them into space—and an unknown fate.

Comment: The characters starred in the title until it was discontinued with #124.

CRIME DOCTOR (R, MP)

First Appearance: *Crime Doctor,* 1940, CBS.

Biography: Because he's been hit on the head, Benjamin Ordway remembers nothing about his past. He goes on to become the foremost criminal psychiatrist and medical detective in the nation, serving as the head of the local parole board and invariably tracking down clues to help or put away all kinds of deranged criminals. Unfortunately, the biggest psychological problem Dr. Ordway faces is when he denies a criminal parole and, out of spite, the convict tells the doctor that he was once a gang leader. When Ordway is struck on the head again, not only does he remember his sordid past, but he recalls where he's stashed the money from a payroll robbery. Happily, all is forgiven when he returns it.

Ordway works closely with District Attorney Miller and Inspector Ross.

Comment: The character was created by writer Max Marcin. On the radio, Ordway was played by Ray Collins, then by House Jameson, Everett Sloane, and John McIntire. Columbia Pictures made ten films about the hero (now named Robert Ordway), all of them starring Warner Baxter: *Crime Doctor* (1943), *Crime Doctor's Strangest Case* (1943), *Shadows in the Night* (1944), *Crime Doctor's Courage* (1945), *Crime Doctor's Warning* (1945), *Crime Doctor's Man Hunt* (1946), *Just Before Dawn* (1946), *The Millerson Case* (1947), *Crime Doctor's Gamble* (1947), and *Crime Doctor's Diary* (1949).

CROCKETT and TUBBS (TV)

First Appearance: *Miami Vice,* September 1984, NBC.

Biography: James "Sonny" Crockett and Ricardo Tubbs are Miami vice detectives who couldn't be more unalike—except in their desire to see justice done. Tubbs is an ex-New York police officer who goes to Florida to find the drug dealer who killed his brother. Crockett is a smooth native Floridian who lives with his pet alligator Elvis on a 40-foot sloop named *St. Vitus' Dance.* Crockett has already lost a partner, so the two team to bring down the Colombian drug lord, after which Tubbs remains in Miami. They travel around in Sonny's black Ferrari Spider (later, a Testarossa), using the undercover identities of Sonny Burnett and Rico Cooper to sniff out pushers, smugglers, assassins, racketeers, pimps, gamblers, and other perpetrators of vice. They report to Lieutenant Castillo and work frequently with Detectives Gina Navarro Calabrese and Trudy Joplin.

Don Johnson as *Crockett* and Philip Michael Thomas as *Tubbs* of *Miami Vice.* © National Broadcasting Co.

Sonny has two ex-wives; his first, Caroline, is the mother of his young son.

Comment: The hour-long series aired until July 1989 and starred Don Johnson as Crockett, Philip Michael Thomas as Tubbs, Edward James Olmos as Castillo, Saundra Santiago as Calabrese, and Olivia Brown as Joplin. Lee Iacocca once appeared as Park Commissioner Lido, and G. Gordon Liddy guested as the untrustworthy Captain Real Estate.

Johnson's "look"—pastel sports jacket and T-shirt, no socks, facial stubble—started a fashion trend.

The characters are played live by various stunt actors on the Universal Studios tours in Hollywood and Florida.

Another Miami-based series was *Miami Undercover,* a half-hour show syndicated in 1961. It starred Lee Bowman as Jeff Thompson, an investigator who worked for the Miami Hotel Owners Association. Fighter Rocky Graziano costarred as his assistant, Rocky.

CRUSADER (TV)

First Appearance: *Crusader,* October 1955, CBS.
Biography: A freelance writer, Matt Anders travels the world—ostensibly on assignments, but actually using fist or gun to fight Red spies or help those who are suppressed by and/or are trying to overthrow Communist regimes. Matt's motives are more than simply altruistic: When Poland fell to the Communists, his mother was captured, sent to prison, and died there.
Comment: Brian Keith starred in this series, which ran until December 1956. Coming at the height of the "Red Menace" years, this show was perhaps the most fervently anti-Communist. It is no coincidence

that a title was chosen with the letters USA in the middle.

CUCHULAIN (F)

First Appearance: Irish folklore, circa A.D. 1000.
Biography: At her wedding Dechtire, the sister of Conchobar, the king of Ulster, drinks wine in which the sun god Lugh has concealed himself as a fly. Lugh spirits her away; a year later she returns to Conchobar's castle, Emain Macha, with her newborn son, Setanta. A most forgiving fellow, her former fiance, Sualtim, still takes her as his bride.

At the age of seven, Setanta kills a ferocious dog owned by the smith Culain; the owner is grief-stricken, and not only does Setanta promise to find him a new hound, but he agrees to guard the smith's house until he does. Thus, the boy becomes known as Cuchulain, the hound of Culain. Shortly thereafter, Cuchulain does his first bit of soldiering, killing three enemy champions who have attacked Ulster.

Cuchulain's friends seek out a bride for him (for their own good, since their own women long for the hero), and he weds Emer, daughter of King Forgall, after first defeating the warrior woman Scatbach to prove himself worthy. By this time Cuchulain is one of the 12 warriors of the Red Branch, protectors of Conchobar. To settle who is the strongest, the three top warriors—Cuchulain, Conall, and Laery—battle a giant known as the Terror, who lives within a lake. Only Cuchulain agrees to the fight, and he succeeds in decapitating the fiend. Cuchulain's other major foe is the evil Briccriu, whose life is devoted to stirring unrest among the members of the Red Branch. He stirs jealousy among the wives of the heroes, causes the soldiers to quarrel among one another, and remains a thorn in Cuchulain's side for his entire life.

That life turns out to be a short one. After successfully defending Ulster against the forces of Queen Maeve of Connacht, he is stabbed by the spear of a longtime enemy, Lugaid. The weakened hero is then beheaded by his foe—though even in death Cuchulain triumphs, his falling sword severing Lugaid's right hand. Upon learning of her husband's death, Emer dies of grief and the two are buried together. It is said that Cuchulain drives his chariot through the hills to this day, singing songs of combat.
Comment: The legend appears to have been pieced together from earlier tales, dating to at least some 500 years earlier.

CUTTER (C, L)

First Appearance: *Elfquest,* 1977, *Fantasy Quarterly* #1.

Biography: Ages ago slender, elegant, magically powered, pointy-eared aliens land on the Paleolithic earth. Frightened cave dwellers attack and slaughter most of the newcomers; those who survive flee into the woods, where they make their home. "Through countless generations" evolving humans battle the elves, who are championed by the warrior Cutter and his Wolfriders. Though his real name is Tam, the elves call him Cutter due to the power in his sword arm. And while he is "artless, frank hearted, wild as a beast of prey . . . the blood of ten chiefs flows in his veins." Like all elves, the Wolfriders possess limited telepathic powers called "sending."

When the humans burn the woods to destroy the elves, Cutter leads his people to the caverns of the trolls of King Greymung, through a desert, to another elfin village. There, among these Sun Folk, he meets the lovely Leetah, becomes her mate, and they parent the twins Ember, a tomboy, and the mystically powered Suntop. After a battle with wandering humans, Cutter decides to find all other elves on Earth and unite them to battle their common foe.

Other elves include Cutter's right-hand elf Skywise, the red-haired tracker Redlance, his "lift-mate" Nightfall, the mighty Treestump, the archer Strongbow, stealthy One-Eye, and Scouter.

Cutter's wolf is named Nightrunner.

Comment: The characters were created by artist Wendy Pini and her husband, Richard. After the first and only issue of *Fantasy Quarterly,* the Pinis founded WaRP Graphics and published *Elfquest* on their own. The magazine was a success, and in August 1985 Marvel Comics began reprinting the issues as part of their Epic line. The adventures have also been collected in a series of trade paperbacks, which began with *Elfquest Book 1* from Starblaze in 1981.

Marvel Comics published thirty-two issues of *Elfquest* from 1985 to 1988.

An *Elfquest* novel, written by Wendy and Richard Pini, was published by Playboy Paperbacks in 1982.

D

DAGAR THE INVINCIBLE (C)

First Appearance: *Tales of Sword and Sorcery, Dagar the Invincible* #1, 1972, Western Publishing.

Biography: In a time "between the end of the Stone Age and the beginnings of Babylon," Dagar is orphaned when his parents are killed in the Great Wars. He lives with his grandfather Ando, both of whom watch helplessly as the entire nation of Tulgonia is massacred by the legions of the mysterious Scorpio. Once a mighty warrior, Ando trains Dagar in secret, and, when the old man dies, Dagar becomes a mercenary, "fighting only for pay . . . for I bear *no* love for mankind." In time, he rescues the lovely maiden Graylin from being used in a sacrificial rite, and she becomes his companion and lover. Dagar rides the black steed Kasa, Graylin the white horse Tarnu. In addition to his broadsword, the hero carries a mace.

Comment: The title lasted 19 issues (the last was a reprint) and is unrelated to the Fox Features Syndicate hero from 1948–49, Dagar, Desert Hawk. The newer Dagar was created by writer Don Glut, who also created Western's *Tragg and the Sky Gods,* the von Danikenesque saga of the origin of humankind, as scientists from the planet Yargon mutate apes into the humans Tragg and his mate, Lorn. The title lasted nine issues. Both Dagar and Tragg also appeared in several of Western's anthology comic books.

DAN DARE (CS, R)

First Appearance: *Eagle* #1, 1950, Hulton Press.

Biography: Born on February 5, 1967, in Manchester, England, Daniel MacGregor Dare was educated at Rossall, Cambridge, and Harvard and became a Class 3 Space Pilot by the age of 20. At 28 he took a Planetary Exploration Course on the moon and, two years later, made chief pilot of the Space Fleet. Colonel Dare's hobbies include fencing, painting, riding, and cricket.

His sidekick is Spaceman Class 1 Albert Fitzwilliam Digby; other characters include Captain Henry Brennan Hogan of Houston, Texas; Professor Jocelyn Mabel Peabody, a botanist and nutritionist; Major Pierre Au-gust Lafayette of Dijon, a mathematician and cook; Junior Cadets "Flamer" Spry and Steve Valiant; Space Fleet Controller Sir Hubert Guest, who is based in the organization's London skyscraper headquarters; and Commander Lex O'Malley, whose combination boat/submarine the *Poseidon* helps the heroes get around on Earth. The adventurers' arsenal is stocked with various spaceships—from two-seaters to big interplanetary cruisers—as well as helicars for short hops and two-rider whirlibird helicopter platforms for hovering or tough-to-reach spots. Weapons include disintegrator guns of various sizes and power, and gadgets such as the vocalon, which translates foreign or alien tongues.

Dare's greatest challenges over the years include preventing the evil, green superbrain Mekon from conquering Venus and stopping the cruel Phants from Phantos in their effort to dominate the peaceful world Cryptos.

Comment: The character was created by artist/writer Frank Hampson (with an art assist by Don Harley), who left the strip in 1959. Dan Dare was originally going to be a detective, Dorothy Dare, and then a spacefaring priest. Hampson says, "I wanted to give hope for the future, to show that rockets and science in general could reveal new worlds, new opportunities." *Dan Dare* continued as the first- and second-page feature in *Eagle* until 1966, when it went to one page. It remained in *Eagle* until the title folded in 1969, then shifted to *Lion and Eagle,* though these were reprints of a sort, the original adventures redrawn by new artists. The strip died for good after two years. During its long run, however, it spawned a daily radio adventure that originated at Radio Luxembourg, the fan magazine *Astral,* and a great deal of merchandizing. Early adventures were reprinted in book form in 1979 by the Netherlands-based Dragon's Dream.

See also LANCE O'CASEY.

DAN DUNN (CS, C, L)

First Appearance: *Dan Dunn, Secret Operative 48,* October 16, 1933, Publishers' Syndicate (see COMMENT).

Biography: A two-fisted agent with the secret service, Dunn battles assassins, spies, smugglers, drug dealers, counterfeiters, and other enemies of the American way of life. He is assisted by his pet "wolf dog" Wolf, an orphan girl named Babs, and a chubby assistant named Irwin Higgs.

Comment: The character was created by Norman Marsh, who remained with the strip until 1942. Paul Pinson and then Alfred Andriola continued the strip for its final year.

To coincide with his newspaper debut, Dan appeared in a black-and-white one-shot comic book, *Detective Dan, Secret Operative 48,* published by Humor Publishing Company. Over the years he also appeared as a backup strip in a number of other titles.

The hero also appeared in a series of Big Little Books: *Dan Dunn Secret Operative 48* (1934), *Dan Dunn on the Trail of the Counterfeiters* (1936), *Dan Dunn Secret Operative 48 and the Crime Master* (1937), *Dan Dunn Secret Operative 48 and the Underworld Gorillas* (1937), *Dan Dunn Secret Operative 48 on the Trail of Wu Fang* and *Dan Dunn Secret Operative 48 and the Border Smugglers* (both 1938), and *Dan Dunn Secret Operative 48 and the Dope Ring* (1940). Dunn was also featured in two issues of his own pulp magazine in 1936.

After military service Marsh went to work for rival King Features and created the nearly identical strip *Hunter Keene,* which lasted exactly one year, from April 1946 to 1947. He followed that with the ill-fated pioneer strip *Danny Hale.*

DAREDEVILS OF THE RED CIRCLE (MP)

First Appearance: *Daredevils of the Red Circle,* 1939, Republic Pictures.

Biography: After escaping from prison, James Crowell, prisoner 39013, goes after his former partner, millionaire Horace Granville, who turned him in for embezzling. Upon abducting Granville, the convict takes his place, intending to destroy his gas and oil investments, utilities operations, and, as a lark, his Granville Amusement Pier. The Daredevils are a trio of athletic college kids—high diver Gene Townley, strongman Tiny Dawson, and nimble escape artist Burt Knowles—who perform stunts in a Granville side show (wearing sleeveless T-shirts with a red circle in the center, hence the name). Before the Daredevils' act Crowell's men substitute gas for water in Gene's tank. When the ensuing fire results in the death of little Sammy, Gene's kid brother, the Daredevils resolve to bring the perpetrator in, assisted by Blanche, the

The poster for episode one of *Daredevils of the Red Circle.* Gene and Blanche are on the left, Tiny and Burt are on the right. © Republic Pictures.

granddaughter of the real Granville, and Tuffy, Sammy's dog. After surviving a tunnel flood, a mine flood, a sabotaged gamma ray machine, and other traps, the acrobatic heroes triumph when 39013's thugs inadvertently place their unconscious boss in a car rigged with a bomb to destroy Blanche. It's not a pretty victory for the Daredevils, but Sammy is avenged.

Comment: Charles Quigley was Gene, Herman Brix (arguably the best movie Tarzan) was Tiny, legendary stuntman Dave Sharpe played Burt, Carole Landis was Blanche, Charles Middleton played 39103, and Miles Mander was the real Granville. The 12-chapter serial was directed by William Witney and John English.

D'ARTAGNAN   (L, MP, C)

First Appearance: *Les Trois Mousquetairs* by Alexandre Dumas, 1844.

Biography: D'Artagnan is a young Gascon in France of 1625. At 18 he sets out on his aged yellow pony, with three crowns in his pocket and a letter of introduction from his father to M. de Treville, an old neighbor and now captain of the King's Musketeers, whom d'Artagnan is determined to join. Upon reaching Paris, the lad is told by de Treville that he must first attend the Royal Military Academy and then spend two years in a lesser regiment. De Treville agrees to help him get into the academy and, thrilled, d'Artagnan leaves—only to offend, by accident, Musketeers Athos, Porthos, and Aramis in turn. He agrees to duel them in succession, but the first engagement is interrupted by the arrival of five guards of the power-hungry Cardinal Richelieu. They engage the Musketeers in battle (ironically, for having been brawling), and D'Artagnan, bravely helping the Musketeers, earns their respect and friendship.

After settling into a modest apartment and acquiring a down-and-out valet, Planchet, d'Artagnan learns that Constance, the wife of his landlord, M. Bonacieux, has been kidnaped by the cardinal's men; as the queen's seamstress, Constance has overheard secrets that might prove useful in the clergyman's efforts to usurp power. D'Artagnan sets off to rescue Mme. Bonacieux, and, when she's safe, she entrusts the youth with an important mission. The queen has been having an affair with England's Duke of Buckingham and, as a token of her affection, had given him 12 diamond studs; upon learning of this, the troublemaking cardinal has persuaded the king to ask that his wife wear them at a ball. D'Artagnan sets off with the other three Musketeers—who become waylaid—journeys to England, and retrieves the studs in time. With that threat ended, he must deal with the cardinal's henchwoman, Milady de Winter, who seeks vengeance against the Musketeers and Constance. Though the treacherous Milady poisons Constance and slays the Duke of Buckingham, she is eventually executed for her crimes—and d'Artagnan receives a lieutenant's commission in the Musketeers.

The hero has a long face, high cheekbones, a hooked nose, and "open and intelligent" eyes.

Comment: All of the characters are based on actual people, though d'Artagnan is closest of all: He is modeled after Chares de Baatz d'Artagnan (1623–73), on whose memoirs much of the novel is based.

Dumas wrote two sequels to the original tale, *Vingt Ans Apres (Twenty Years After)* (1845) and *Le Vicomte de Bragelonne (The Viscount of Bragelonne)* (1848 and 1850). In the former d'Artagnan and Porthos are still guardsmen when foes of Cardinal Mazarin attempt to overthrow him and the king in an uprising known as the Fronde (1648–52). Aramis,

who had entered a monastery, and Athos, a country gentleman, come out of retirement to join in the excitement. The next volume focuses on the efforts of Aramis, now Bishop of Vannes, to gain even more power. The second half of the novel, *Le Masque de Fer,* is often published separately as *The Man in the Iron Mask,* about a conspiracy to substitute the eponymous man for his royal brother.

There have been many film versions of *The Three Musketeers*—two silent versions (1921 and 1922), followed by others in 1935 with Walter Abel as the hero, in 1939 with Don Ameche, in 1948 with Gene Kelly, and Richard Lester's 1974 version with Michael York. York repeated the role in *The Four Musketeers* (1975) and in *The Return of the Musketeers* (1989), the latter based on *Twenty Years After.* Chris O'Donnell played the part in the 1993 *The Three Musketeers.* Other films inspired by the novel or its sequels are *The Iron Mask* (1929), *The Man in the Iron Mask* (1939), *Milady and the Musketeers* (1951), *Sword of D'Artagnan* (1952), *Lady in the Iron Mask* (1952), *The Knights of the Queen* (1954), *Zorro and the Three Musketeers* (1963), *Revenge of the Musketeers* (1964), and *The Fifth Musketeers* (1979), which was based on *The Man in the Iron Mask.*

There have been a number of comic book versions of the story, the best known being the *Classics Illustrated* editions: *The Three Musketeers* inaugurated the popular series (1941), with *Twenty Years After* published six years after (#41). The first tale was also told in Marvel Classic Comics #12 (1976).

DAVID CHASE (TV)

First Appearance: *Front Page Detective,* July 1951, Dumont Network.

Biography: David Chase is a newspaper columnist who covers crime, typically murders, and ends up solving them. He can't be bought by those who perpetrated the crimes, though they always try. His girlfriend is a fashion designer.

Comment: Edmond Lowe (see CHANDU THE MAGICIAN) played Chase. The half-hour series was filmed in Los Angeles and lasted through November 1953. The show was obviously inspired by radio's *Front Page Farrell,* which aired over Mutual beginning in 1941 and starred Richard Widmark (followed by Carleton Young and Staats Cotsworth) as David Farrell.

DAVID INNES (L, C, MP)

First Appearance: *At the Earth's Core* by Edgar Rice Burroughs, April 4–25, 1914, *All-Story Weekly.*

Biography: David Innes is born in Connecticut in 1883, the son of a wealthy mine owner. David's father dies when the boy is 19, and for six months he oversees the mining operations. However, the gray-eyed youth becomes fascinated by an invention of an acquaintance, aged and eccentric scientist Abner Perry—the Iron Mole, an earth-burrowing vehicle. Innes joins him on his journey into the earth, and, 500 miles down, they penetrate the hollow interior. Lit by an internal sun, this Stone Age land, known as Pellucidar, is populated by apelike as well as modern humans, by dinosaurs and prehistoric mammals, and by intelligent, telepathic, human-eating rhamphorhynchuses known as Mahars. There is no night and time is relative; a busy person's hour quite possibly is a listless person's day. (In one of his last adventures, although he should be 56, the *very* busy Innes is still in his 20s.)

After ten years in Pellucidar, during which time he weds Dian the Beautiful, Innes uses the Mole to return to the surface for books and tools. Innes emerges in the Sahara desert, collects what he needs and returns, organizes the construction of a navy to help rid Pellucidar of Mahars and other enemies, and rescues Dian from the evil warlord Hooja (and, later, from a runaway balloon designed by Perry). Innes's sometimes companion is Raja, a wolf-dog whose life he saves.

Another Pellucidarian adventurer is Innes's friend, the young chieftain Tanar, who leads the battle against the piratical Korsars.

David communicates details of his adventures by radio to his surface-dwelling friend, Jason Gridley.

Comment: The character's further adventures were chronicled by Burroughs in *Pellucidar* (1915), *Tanar of Pellucidar* (1929), *Tarzan at the Earth's Core* (serialized 1929–30), *Land of Terror* (1944), and the short stories "The Return to Pellucidar," "Men of the Bronze Age," "Tiger Girl" (all 1942), and the posthumously published "Savage Pellucidar" (1963), collected in book form as *Savage Pellucidar* (1963). John Eric Holmes continued the saga with the novel *Mahars of Pellucidar* (1976), published by Ace Books, and its unpublished sequel, *Red Axe of Pellucidar.*

In comic books, the character starred in Hawley Publications *Hi-Spot* Comics #2 in 1940, and in the first seven issues of DC's *Weird Worlds* from 1972 to 1973.

In motion pictures Innes was played by Doug McClure in director Kevin Connor's 1976 film *At the Earth's Core.*

DAVID VINCENT (TV, L, C)

First Appearance: *The Invaders,* January 1967, ABC.

Biography: "How does a nightmare begin?" David Vincent, the California architect-partner of Al Landers, finds out at 4:20 in the morning. Driving home from a business meeting, exhausted, he pulls up to Bud's Diner, hoping to get some coffee, only to find the diner shuttered. Deciding to catch some sleep, he witnesses the landing of a flying saucer and hurries to tell the local sheriff. The lawman doesn't believe him, especially when Bud's Diner has had its name changed to Kelly's Diner and two young newlyweds, the John Brandons, say they were camped there all night and saw nothing. Later, Vincent pays the Brandons a visit, and John begins to glow red, his "acclamation" period to human form wearing off. The Invader beats Vincent to a pulp and leaves him in his wrecked car so the authorities will think he had an accident. When he *still* insists there are aliens among us, an old lady Invader at the hospital waits until David is released, then tries to burn his house down. Confiding in Kathy Adams, a widow who runs a nearby hotel, Vincent learns that she too is an Invader. Kathy explains that they are from a dying world and have chosen to conquer Earth because its inhabitants will be easy to conquer and its environment is suitable. (According to the first novel, the aliens have spent "a thousand millennia" in the saucers, searching for a suitable world. Though our sun is relatively dim, Earth is still livable.)

Vincent gives up his work and his swinging bachelor life and devotes his energies to preventing the invasion from another world. In time, he discovers that a fleet of saucers is in orbit around Earth, and that many Invaders are already among us, infiltrating business and government. For a time, Vincent fights alone against these aliens, who pack rayguns and lack emotions (except for the mutation Vikki, who falls in love with Vincent and is killed by the aliens). Over the course of his adventures, he protects an important Earth scientist, drives the aliens away from a nuclear test site in another, learns that they've infiltrated a public school in another, fights an alien weather-control device, saves his brother and pregnant wife from a kidnap attempt, undermines an alien evangelist, and thwarts an alien plan to assassinate all of the world's leaders, among other exploits.

Eventually, David links up with a team of seven other allies, informally known as the Believers and headed by electronics magnate Edgar Scoville.

Comment: Roy Thinnes starred as Vincent, with Kent Smith as Scoville. In the first episode, James Daly guest-starred as Landers, Diane Baker as Kathy. There were 43 episodes of the hour-long series, which aired until September 1968. It was created by Larry Cohen. The pilot episode was 90 minutes, cut to one hour for broadcast; that original film is rarely screened.

Pyramid published three novels based on the series: *The Invaders* by Keith Laumer, *Enemies from Beyond* by Laumer, and *Army of the Undead* by Rafe Bernard, all 1967. According to these, Vincent lives in the sumptuous Columbia Towers in Alexandria, Virginia. A Big Little Book, *Alien Missile Threat* by Paul S. Newman, was published in 1967.

Gold Key Comics published four issues of *The Invaders* from 1967 to 1968.

See also MIKE DONOVAN.

DAX THE WARRIOR (C)

First Appearance: Eerie #39, 1972, Warren Publishing.

Biography: Dax is a famed mercenary of an unspecified barbaric age, a fighter in his middle 20s "who has lived through a thousand battles." Equally skilled with sword or bow and arrow, Dax is a tragic wayfarer who is doomed to travel the land on his stallion Staxion (until he's swallowed by quicksand) in search of elusive happiness. The woman he loves is snatched by Death whom he must fight in a foredoomed effort to recover her. When the chessmaster of the universe

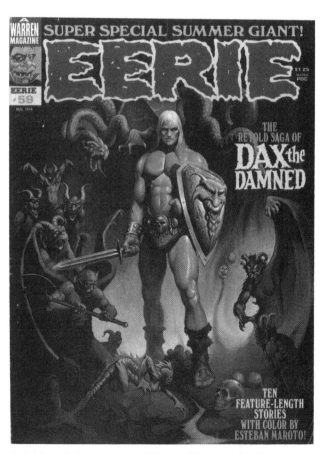

Artist Ken Kelly's portrait of *Dax*. © Warren Publishing.

challenges him to a game using people from the barbarian's past as pieces, his ineptitude at a thinking game causes their death. Even when he becomes lord of the enchanted land of Bahalle Knar—home of the beautiful Crenae, the guardians of the springs—he discovers that peace and routine can be boring, and leaves. Dax does not enjoy battle, but fights on so he can continue to know the "joys of life. Eating after a long hunger. Drinking away a deep thirst. Sleeping. Loving." In his last adventure Dax receives a sword thrust to the spine and is paralyzed; abandoned even by Death, he is left to lie there, damned to recall his sad adventures over and over.

At some point in his brooding career, he meets the time-traveling Bishop Dane (see THE ROOK), and the two share an adventure.

Comment: The interesting but often obtuse strip was created, written, and drawn by Spanish artist Esteban Maroto, and appeared regularly in *Eerie* until #52. Ten of the stories were reprinted in #59, rewritten in a more colloquial style by Budd Lewis. The Dane adventure appeared in *Eerie* #120.

DEAD END KIDS (S, MP, R)

First Appearance: *Dead End* by Sidney Kingsley, October 28, 1935.

Biography: Originally the kids are delinquent slum boys Angel, Dippy, Milt, Spit (the leader), T.B., and Tommy. They live on a dead-end street in a slum that Gimpty, a crippled architect, wants to raze. For several years they remain juvenile delinquents—until they get turned around, graduate from military school, and turn into young detectives (also known as the Little Tough Guys) when they help Tommy's father beat a bum jail rap. After that Tommy becomes a mailman and the boys help him defeat gangsters. The kids move to California to work on a farm and protect it from interlopers, become cropdusting pilots, take on the mob when their fathers are killed in a shootout, tackle hijackers, and so on. Most of their triumphs come through dogged determination and courage rather than great deductive skill.

Several of the same characters resurfaced with name changes: Muggs McGinnis, Glimpy Williams, and Danny were now the East Side Kids, involved in more comedic adventures with haunted houses, racehorses, boxers, spies, and Bela Lugosi (twice). Two of them returned as Slip Mahoney and Horace DeBussy "Sach" Jones, better known as the Bowery Boys, alternating in comedic and dramatic adventures.

Comment: *Dead End* (with Humphrey Bogart) was filmed in 1937, and first brought the Dead End Kids to the screen, played by the actors who had starred on Broadway: Gabriel Dell (T.B.), Leo Gorcey (Spit;

No longer the *Dead End Kids* but the East Side Kids: Bobby Jordan tries to free Leo Gorcey (left) and Huntz Hall from Bela Lugosi. © Monogram Pictures.

though Charles Duncan had created the part on stage, Gorcey replaced him early in the show's run), Billy Halop (Tommy), Huntz Hall (Dippy), Bobby Jordan (Angel), and Bernard Punsley (Milt). The characters' names were changed when they were sent to reform

school under tough superintendent Mark Braden (Humphrey Bogart) in their second film, *Crime School* (1938). Now they were Bugs Burke (Dell), Fats Papadopolo (Punsley), Spike Hawkins (Gorcey), Goofy (Hall), and Frankie Warren (Halop). Their names changed again when they fell in with gangster Rocky Sullivan (James Cagney) and began to reform in their third film, *Angels With Dirty Faces* (1938). This time they were Soapy (Halop), Swing (Jordan), Bim (Gorcey), Hunky (Punsley), Pasty (Dell), and Crab (Hall).

In *They Made Me a Criminal* (1939), the original Dead End Kids were back and working on a ranch—which, with the help of boxer Johnnie (John Garfield), they keep from being foreclosed. Their reformation continues in *Hell's Kitchen* (1939), *Angels Wash Their Faces* (1939), and *On Dress Parade* (1939), in which the military school transformation is complete. The films in which they appear as solo stars are *Little Tough Guy* (1938), *Call a Messenger* (1939), *You're Not So Tough* (1940), *Give Us Wings* (1940), *Hit the Road* (1941), *Mob Town* (1941), *Tough As They Come* (1942), *Mug Town* (1943), and *Keep 'Em Slugging* (1943).

The East Side Kids—with Gorcey as Muggs, Hall as Glimpy, and Jordan as Danny—were featured in 22 films from 1940 to 1945. The Bowery Boys—with Gorcey as Slip and Hall as Sach—were featured in 48 films between 1946 and 1958.

Several of the actors also starred in a trio of serials based on the *Junior G-Men* radio show: Halop was Billy Barton, Hall was Gyp, Dell was Terry, and Punsley was Lug in the 12-chapter *Junior G-Men* (1940), searching for kidnaped military and scientific leaders; Halop was Billy Adams, Hall was Toby Nelson, Dell was Bilge, and Punsley was Butch in the 12-chapter *Sea Raiders* (1941), battling saboteurs; and Halop was "Ace" Holden, Hall was "Bolts" Larson, Dell was "Stick" Munsey, and Punsley was "Greaseball" Plunkett in the 13-chapter *Junior G-Men of the Air* (1942), fighting spies in the Order of the Black Dragonfly.

DEREK FLINT (MP)

First Appearance: *Our Man Flint,* 1966, Twentieth Century-Fox.

Biography: During some past war—presumably, Korea—Derek Flint worked under Lloyd C. Cramden, who found him arrogant and not a team player—though that didn't stop Flint from earning three field promotions in one month and winning the Medal of Honor. The two parted ways, Cramden going on to become the head of Z.O.W.I.E. (Zonal Organization World Intelligence Espionage), and Flint an agent. Now the Galaxy Group is threatening to take over the world via weather control. Teams of agents have failed to stop them, and Cramden goes to see Flint in his ritzy New York apartment. Flint agrees to help and, tracking the masterminds and their scientists to Galaxy Island, destroys them and their equipment.

In his second chronicled adventure, Flint tackles a renegade U.S. military officer, General Carter, who replaces the president with a double, then attempts to reach a U.S. space platform in a ship armed with nuclear missiles, in an effort to take over the world. Flint is able to board the spaceship just before takeoff, tie Carter up, and exit into space just before the capsule blows up. He seeks sanctuary on a Russian spaceship (occupied entirely by female cosmonauts) until he can be rescued.

The extremely wealthy Flint is a martial arts and fencing master, a chemist, gourmand, tightrope walker, and frogman. He teaches ballet in Moscow, pilots his own Learjet, and is a practitioner of Zen; to relax, he stops his heart for up to three hours (a little "hammer" emerges from his watch to tap him awake). He is known to speak Japanese, French, Italian, Russian, and dolphin (a cetacean, Eric, lives in his apartment pool), has between three and five live-in girlfriends at any given time, and is a master of disguise and a published author. His butler is a highly trained German shepherd named Caesar.

On the job, Flint's primary piece of equipment is a cigarette lighter that has 82 functions—"eighty-three, if you wish to light a cigar." His watch serves as a magnifying glass, hypnotic device, and cardiogram; his belt buckle emits a sonic beam able to shatter various substances; and he also carries a pen microscope and a minigrapnel.

Comment: The second film, *In Like Flint,* was released the following year. Both were wonderful parodies of the spy genre. James Coburn starred as Flint in both films, with Lee J. Cobb as Cramden. Daniel Mann directed the first film, Gordon Douglas the second.

DEREK SCHRECK (C)

First Appearance: *Eerie* #53, 1974, Warren Publishing.

Biography: Derek Schreck is a newspaper reporter when, in the near future, Chinese and U.S. bases on the moon go to war. Radiation rains down on the earth, causing a plague that drives most of the world murderously mad. Only 8 percent of the world's population remains normal: whether it's a "higher resistance to the radiation [or] odd metabolism," no one knows, since order quickly falls before the mobs of white-eyed, cannibalistic "werewolves." When Schreck's wife, Paula, finally succumbs to the "moon-

Bright Eyes and *Derek Schreck* survey the carnage wreaked by the latter. © Warren Publishing.

taint" one night and goes mad, she severs his right hand with a meat cleaver before running into the night; he cauterizes the wound in the fireplace and, fleeing the house, is found by a scientist, a woman he nicknames Bright Eyes. She fits his stump with a magnetic metal cup, to which he can attach utensils, tools, weapons, or even a robot hand with limited mobility. While Bright Eyes works to perfect an antidote she's discovered, Schreck protects the asylum that serves as their base. However, a lunatic sniper gets through and picks off Bright Eyes in the last adventure. Though Schreck finds a new friend, lovely Debra James, he realizes they will not be Adam and Eve and that humankind is doomed. After decades of slashing and blasting away at werewolves, Schreck is captured and imprisoned in Bathory Castle, where he meets HUNTER. Schreck manages to kill the present-day leader of the mutants, Ofphal, and the rest of the monsters go into hiding.

Comment: *Schrecken* means "terror" in German. The character was created by writer Doug Moench, inspired (uncredited) by both the Richard Matheson novel *I Am Legend* and the film *Night of the Living Dead.* Art was handled in most stories by Vincente Alcazar; the series lasted until issue #57, though the hero guest-starred in *Eerie* #130, in a story starring the vampire Vampirella.

Schreck was spelled Shreck in issue #55.

DETECTIVE LIEUTENANT MIKE STONE (TV)

First Appearance: *The Streets of San Francisco,* September 1972, ABC (see COMMENT).

Biography: When we first meet Mike Stone he is a 23-year veteran of the San Francisco police force, working with the Bureau of Inspectors Division and attempting to solve the murder of a young girl. A widower with a daughter in college, Stone himself is only a high school graduate who learned everything he knows in the streets. He lives for his work, battling crime and corruption throughout the Bay area. For several years Stone is partnered with an eager young college graduate, Assistant Inspector (later, Inspector) Steve Keller, who could have become a lawyer but preferred to help people "on a different level." Inspector Dan Robbins takes his place when Keller leaves the force to become a teacher.

Years later Keller is murdered and now-Captain Stone returns to the streets to hunt down his killer.

Comment: The original two-hour TV movie was very loosely based on Carolyn Weston's novel *Poor, Poor Ophelia.* It served as the pilot for the hour-long TV series, which aired until June 1977. Karl Malden starred as Stone, Michael Douglas was Keller, and Richard Hatch was Robbins, who was seen in the last season only. The series was shot on location.

Stone's return to action occurred in the 1992 TV movie *Back to the Streets of San Francisco,* starring Malden and directed by Mel Damski.

DETECTIVE SGT. JOE KELLER (L)

First Appearance: *The Smack Man* by Nelson DeMille, 1974, Manor Books.

Biography: Keller works in the homicide department, 21st Precinct. The cynical, world-weary "old-line cop" relies on instinct rather than evidence to bust crooks, rapists, and killers. He doesn't hesitate to act on his hunches using the .38 Police Special he wears in an ankle holster for his left hand and/or the Ruger .357 Magnum tucked in a shoulder holster for his right hand.

The green-eyed Keller dresses in a "disreputable trench coat," has a fondness for cheap cigars and cheap bar liquor, and lives on the fifth floor of a cheap brownstone on West 88th Street. He has no social life to speak of and has been known to patronize prostitutes.

Comment: DeMille wrote three other Keller novels: *The Cannibal, Night of the Phoenix,* and *Death Squad.* After churning out these pulpish paperback thrillers for Manor Books, DeMille went on to become

MANOR BOOKS 12313 ★ $1.25

KELLER
Nelson DeMille

DEATH SQUAD

BRUTALLY AUTHENTIC!
The police Death Squad upset Keller.
It wasn't the murders he minded—
it was the competition.

Detective Sgt. Joe Keller cleans up the New York subways.
© Manor Books.

one of the top-selling authors of the 1980s and 1990s with novels like *The Charm School* and *The Gold Coast.*

DETECTIVE SGT. RICK HUNTER (TV)

First Appearance: *Hunter,* September 1984, NBC.

Biography: Armed with a Magnum named Simon ("Simon says," he tells crooks when giving them an order), Los Angeles Police Department's tough, unorthodox Rick Hunter works in homicide, assisted by his partner, Detective Sergeant Dee Dee McCall. He also gets help from morgue employee Carlos and the streetwise Arnold "Sporty" James. Hunter reports to a number of different superiors over the years, most notably Captain Charlie Devane. His rival is the sycophantic Sergeant Bernie Terwilliger.

After six years Hunter is moved to the Metro Division, where he helps keep peace in the city (e.g., battling corruption or investigating the slaying of immigrants). Dee Dee retires to get married, and Hunter is teamed with former beat cop Officer Joanne Molenski, who is killed after a few months. When he shifts to Metro Hunter gets a girlfriend, divorcee Chris, a sergeant on the force.

Comment: The hour-long series aired until August 1991 and starred Fred Dryer as Hunter, Stepfanie Kramer as McCall, Richard Beauchamp as Carlos, Garrett Morris as Sporty, James Whitmore as Bernie, Charles Hallahan as Devane, Lauren Lane as Chris, and Darlanne Fluegel as Joanne.

The character is unrelated to the Hunter, star of an eponymous TV series that aired from July 1953 to December 1954 on CBS, then NBC. Barry Nelson, then Keith Larsen, starred as Bart Adams, a wealthy businessman and master of disguise, who furthers the cause of capitalism by battling Communists and other enemies of the American way.

DETECTIVE STEVE CARELLA (L, MP, TV)

First Appearance: *Cop Hater* by Ed McBain, 1956, Morrow.

Biography: Stephen Louis Carella is a detective with the 87th Precinct, located on the metropolitan island of Isola (i.e., Manhattan). A slow, methodical, tough, effective police officer who carries a .38 and believes that caution never hurts, he deals with a variety of criminal types and cases, from the mastermind the Heckler, to a gang war, to a glitzy world of fashion models and drug dealers, to murders committed during a sizzling summer heat wave. Carella reports to Lieutenant Peter Byrnes.

There are 16 detectives assigned to the 87th Precinct. Other members of Carella's squad include Desk Sergeant Dave Murchison, newly appointed Detective Bert Kling, Detective Brown, Detective "Cotton" Hawes—a transplanted Southerner—Detective Meyer Meyer, black detective David Foster, and clerk Alf Miscolo.

Carella is a big man, muscular rather than meaty. He has short brown hair and downward-slanting brown eyes that give him an "Oriental appearance." His shoulders are wide, hips narrow, and hands big. He is married to the lovely Theodora "Teddy" Franklin, a deaf mute.

Comment: There are 43 novels and a collection of

short stories about the 87th Precinct, all of them vividly re-creating the details of minute-by-minute police work. The most recent is *Mischief,* published by Morrow in 1993. McBain is a pseudonym for Evan Hunter, who was inspired to create the police setting by the success of the radio series *Dragnet.* (See SGT. JOE FRIDAY.) He used Isola instead of New York so the NYPD wouldn't have "to verify every detail of the procedure in the books."

In motion pictures, there have been several films about the 87th Precinct. Robert Loggia starred in *Cop Hater* (1958), in which the character's surname is Carelli; Kent Smith starred in *The Mugger* (1958); and Burt Reynolds starred in *Fuzz* (1972), which moved the setting to Boston. Toshiro Mifune starred in the Japanese film *High and Low* (1963), which was based on the 87th Precinct novel *King's Ransom,* and Jean-Louis Trintignant starred in *Without Apparent Motive* (1972), which transplanted *Ten Plus One* to Europe.

The characters came to NBC TV in the hour-long *87th Precinct,* which aired from September 1961 to September 1962. Robert Lansing starred as Carella, Ron Harper was Kling, Norman Fell was Meyer, and Gena Rowlands played Teddy.

DETECTIVE STEVE MCGARRETT (TV)

First Appearance: *Hawaii Five-O,* September 1968, CBS.

Biography: Based in the Iolani Palace in Honolulu, Steve McGarrett heads up the Hawaiian State Police and answers directly to Governor Philip Grey. The Five-O unit specializes in battling statewide criminal doings as well as fighting underworld leaders such as the infamous Red Chinese villain Wo Fat, a recurring villain. The tough, taciturn McGarrett is ably assisted by Detective Danny "Dan-O" Williams, Detective Chin Ho Kelly, and Detective Kono, among others. His secretaries, over the years, are May, Jenny Sherman, and Luana.

Little is revealed about McGarrett's private life, other than that he's a bachelor and has a passion for sailing.

Comment: Hawaii Five-O was created by Leonard Freeman. Jack Lord starred as McGarrett, James MacArthur was Danny, Kam Fong was Kelly, Zulu played Kalakaua, and Richard Denning was Grey. (In the show's pilot, which aired in September 1968, Dan-O was played by Tim O'Kelly and the governor was Lew Ayres.) Khigh Dhiegh starred as Wo Fat. The hour-long series aired through April 1980. The series was known as *McGarrett* when it aired as an element of the *CBS Late Night* show.

Detective Steve McGarrett at work. © Leonard Freeman Productions.

DICKIE DARE (CS)

First Appearance: *Dickie Dare,* July 1933, Associated Press Newsfeatures.

Biography: Dickie Dare is originally a young boy with an active imagination; whenever he reads a book that captures his fancy, he imagines his way into it. Accompanied by his dog Wags, he first joins Robin Hood on his adventures, followed by visits with Long John Silver and Robinson Crusoe. After nearly a year of these flights of fancy, Dickie meets up with adventurer Dan Flynn, on whose yacht he travels the world battling spies, despots, smugglers, and pirates.

Comment: The character was created by Milton Caniff and was a prototype for his later *Terry and the Pirates.* (See TERRY LEE.) Coulton Waugh took over the strip in October 1934, when Caniff moved on to *Terry and the Pirates,* and remained with it for a decade; his future wife, Mabel Odin Burvik, was Dickie's chronicler for the next 14 years.

DICK TRACY (CS, L, C, R, MP, TV)

First Appearance: *Dick Tracy,* October 4, 1931, Chicago Tribune-New York News Syndicate.

Biography: No sooner has Dick Tracy arrived at the Trueheart home to dine with his fiancee, Tess, than burglars break in, shoot her father Emil Trueheart, steal the delicatessen receipts (he didn't trust banks after the crash), knock out Tracy, and kidnap Tess. Tracy hasn't had much luck in business ventures, but now he finds his calling: Joining the plainclothes squad (and donning his characteristic yellow fedora), the lantern-jawed hero helps the police find the criminals and rescue Tess. Reporting to Chief Brandon, Tracy tackles various "normal" criminals, such as Boris Arson and Shirtsleeve Kelton, before he meets Frank Redrum, the Blank, in 1937. This begins his regular run-ins with the most extraordinary rogues' gallery in history, which includes supervillains such as Prune-face, the Brow, the Mole, Little Face Finny, B.B. Eyes, Mumbles, B.O. Pleny, Breathless Mahoney, Flattop, 88 Keys, the midget Jerome Trohs, and others.

Tracy adopts the waif Junior Tracy; he and Tess finally marry in 1949 and have a daughter, Bonny Braids, who, coincidentally, is also abducted. Helping Tracy in his war against crime are Pat Patton, Sam Catchem, and the policewoman Lizz. Equally at home in the field or in the crime lab, Tracy uses various crime-busting tools, the most famous of which is his two-way wrist radio, introduced in 1946. A recent improvement on the radio is "a voice-activated ultra-compact disc with millions of bits of information ready for immediate call-up."

For the record, in his first quarter-century, Dick Tracy endured 27 separate bullet wounds.

Comment: Created by Chester Gould, the strip was originally going to be called *Plainclothes Tracy;* editor James Patterson bought it but suggested the name change. The strip appeared for two Sundays before the debut of the popular daily strip on October 12. The strip continues to this day, drawn by Dick Locher; until March 1993 it was written by noted mystery author Max Allan Collins.

The character has also had great success in other media. In comic books Dick Tracy was featured in various one-shot titles from 1933 to 1948, in various Dell one-shots from 1939 to 1948, and in 145 issues of his own title from 1948 to 1961, which were published by Dell until 1949 and by Harvey thereafter. Blackthorne published 24 issues of a Dick Tracy comic book from 1984 to 1989 as well as 99 issues of a Dick Tracy monthly/weekly title from 1986 to 1989 and various other titles and specials. Disney adapted their film as a three-part comic book in 1990.

The *Dick Tracy* radio series was first broadcast on Mutual in 1935 and ran for just over ten years. The part was played by various actors including Ned Wever, Matt Crowley, and Barry Thomson; actress Mercedes McCambridge did some of her first acting on the series. There were four movie serials: *Dick Tracy* (1937), *Dick Tracy Returns* (1938), *Dick Tracy's G-Men* (1939), and *Dick Tracy vs. Crime, Inc.* (1941). Ralph Byrd played the title role in all. A series of feature films followed: *Dick Tracy, Detective* (1945) and *Dick Tracy vs. Cueball* (1946), both of

Ralph Byrd as *Dick Tracy.* © Republic Pictures.

which starred Morgan Conway, and *Dick Tracy Meets Gruesome* (1947)—with Boris Karloff as the evil Gruesome—and *Dick Tracy's Dilemma* (1947), both starring Byrd. Byrd went on to play the part in the 1950–51 ABC TV series and in syndication the following year, until his death. The syndicated half-hour cartoon show *The Adventures of Dick Tracy* debuted in 1961, produced by UPA. New sidekicks were introduced in the semicomedic series: Hemlock Holmes, Heap O'Calory, Go Go Gomez, Jo Jitsu, and the Retouchables. There were 130 five-minute adventures in all. In 1990 Warren Beatty starred as *Dick Tracy* in a big-budget Disney film that he also directed. Dick Tracy has had an unsuccessful history in prose; in addition to a novelization of the film, there was a rather juvenile novel, *Dick Tracy,* written by William Johnston in 1970, published by Tempo Books.

From 1932 to 1948 30 Big Little novels were published for children.

DINO-RIDERS   (T, TV, C)

First Appearance: Dino-Riders, 1988, Tyco Toys.

Biography: In 65 million B.C., the humanoid survivors of a distant planet have come to Earth, pursued by the evil Rulons. The survivors tame the indigenous life they find here—the dinosaurs—and, using their advanced technology, build elaborate saddles and weapons attachments. They use this powerful cavalry to battle the Rulons.

Among the known Dino-Riders are Questar, Mind-Zei, and Aries, who ride a diplodocus that's been turned into a "walking fortress" complete with cluster rockets and laser tail guns; Gunnar and Magnus who ride their laser-cannon equipped torosaurus (which doubles as a battering ram); Sky, who sits atop his deinonychus and fires supersonic rockets; Turret and his battering-ram, laser-cannon armed styracosaurus; Llahd, who fires heat-seeking missiles from a perch slung below a pterodactyl; and Yungstar, who shoots laser-sting projectiles from the back of a quetzal-coatlus. Catching on, the Rulons train their *own* dinosaur force: Antor with a deinonychus; Rasp on a pteranodon; Mako on a monoclonius; Sting on an ankylosaurus; Hammerhead and Side-winder on a triceratops; and Krulos, Bitor, and Cobrus on a tyrannosaurus.

Comment: The dinosaurs became extinct around this time; presumably, the aliens had something to do with that. Implicit in the "legend" is that the refugees became gods or modern humans. Tyco also produced a half-hour animated videocassette that recounted the legend of the Dino-Riders.

On TV, eleven cartoons aired on the *Marvel Action Universe* series, which debuted in syndication in October, 1988.

Marvel also published three issues of a *Dino-Riders* comic book in 1989.

DIRK THE DARING (VG, TV)

First Appearance: *Dragon's Lair*, July 1982, Cinematronics.

Biography: King Ethelred's daughter, Princess Daphne, is the prisoner of the ferocious dragon Singe, and only the brave, sword-swinging Dirk the Daring has a chance of rescuing her. During his quest the noble but somewhat clumsy hero must fight his way through 42 separate rooms of the dragon's lair, chambers and tunnels that house the likes of the Robot Knight, the Flaming Sword, the Giant Chicken Foot, the Mudmen, the fierce Lizard King, the Magical Orb, the Sorcerer's Laboratory, along with various bats, skulls, slime, goblins, tilting floors, pits of fire, retracting bridges, and much more.

Comment: The original arcade video game was an animated cartoon stored on a laser disc, which allowed almost immediate access to whatever choice the player made; a successful player could get all the way through in six minutes! The technology for the game was developed by Rick Dyer of Advanced Microcomputer Systems and animated by Don Bluth Productions.

The hero returned to the videogame fold in 1991 in the arcade game *Dragon's Lair II: Time Warp.*

A cartoon series inspired by the first video game, but less effectively animated by Ruby-Spears, fleshed out the kingdom and presented Sir Dirk (and his bloodhoundlike horse Bertram) with a companion, Sir Timothy, and foes such as the Phantom Knight or the witch Sevilla. In an effort to imitate the "choice" aspect of the video game, the series showed what would happen if Dirk did something wrong—and then what happens when he makes the right choice. There were 13 half-hour adventures in all; the ABC series ran from September 1984 until the following April. Bob Sarlatte provided the voice of Dirk, Ellen Gerstell was Daphne, and Fred Travalena was King Ethelred.

Dragon's Lair has also been adapted for various home video game systems using traditional computer graphics. In the popular Nintendo version, the hero must rescue Daphne from the evil wizard Mordroc, whose dragon Singe is watching over her.

A second Bluth-animated video game, *Space Ace*, failed to catch on. In it, the hero Dexter pursues the blue alien Borf, who has run off with the Space Ace's girlfriend.

DI 13 (C)

First Appearance: *DI 13*, 1947, *Pilipino Komiks* #1.

Biography: "DI" stands for Detective Bureau of Investigation, and 13 ("Trese") is one of its foremost agents. Smart, confident, and handsome, the sleuth is equally adept with fists, pistol, or knife. He tackles criminals of all kinds in the Philippines as well as, on occasion, international agents bent on sabotage.

The hero's longtime girlfriend is Sally. Notwithstanding, he has many other romantic liaisons over the years.

Comment: The character was created by writer Damy Velasquez and artist Jesse Santos, and lasted for 14 years. The detective is not to be confused with the comic book hero Captain Richard Anthony, a.k.a. Secret Agent D-13, who appeared in *Mystery Men Comics* beginning in 1939. He, in turn, should not be mixed up with Q-13, a secret agent who appeared in *Super-Mystery Comics*, or, for that matter, Z-2 of *Crash Comics*, X-10 of *Silver Streak Comics*, M-11 of *Prize Comics*, F-4 of Air Intelligence in *Wings Comics*, or K-7 of *Miracle Comics*. All of these characters appeared in the early 1940s.

DR. GRAVES (C)

First Appearance: *Ghostly Tales* #55, 1966, Charlton Comics.

Biography: Dr. M.T. Graves—who lives, at least part of the time, in Greenwich Village—is a "supernaturalist" who has traveled the world investigating eerie phenomena. A wealthy man, he does "not often accept

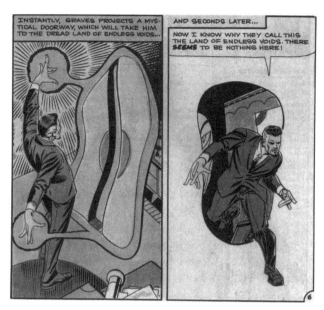

Steve Ditko's magnificent artwork gave class to many of *Dr. Graves*'s adventures. © Charlton Comics.

commissions," but will do so if the case is sufficiently intriguing, or if the person is "female, young, helpless . . . and very, very pretty." A man of many talents, Graves is able, for example, to translate hieroglyphics and can sense the approach of evil. He has also been known to retire to his library, "find the proper incantations," and send his spirit from our astral plane to another.

The distinguished, goateed, pipe-smoking Graves appears in a number of adventures, but more often than not tells the stories "of the dozens of cases I couldn't solve . . . the ones that got away."

Comment: Dr. Graves's own magazine, *The Many Ghosts of Dr. Graves,* debuted the following year and lasted 74 issues. Another Charlton "host" is Colonel Whiteshroud, the far-famed "monster hunter" who tells stories from Ghost Manor. Though he usually wears a safari outfit and carries a handgun and rifle, we never see the narrator in action—only recounting tales involving other victims of ghosts, monsters, or the supernatural. Whiteshroud appeared in *Monster Hunters,* which lasted 20 issues from 1975 to 1979.

DR. MARSH TRACY (MP, TV, C)

First Appearance: *Clarence the Cross-Eyed Lion,* 1965.

Biography: Dr. Tracy and his daughter, Paula, live in Africa, where they work as veterinarians and conservationists. They become involved in adventures with District Officer Hedley, a British game warden, who frequently requires assistance with animals, hunters,

natives, and others. The Tracys are helped by American Jack Dane and a native named Mike. Later a young orphan, Jenny Jones, joins the team. Providing cuddly comic relief are Clarence and a chimpanzee named Judy.

Comment: The film was the source of an hour-long TV series, *Daktari* (meaning "doctor" in Swahili), which aired on CBS from January 1966 to January 1969 and starred—as did the film—Marshall Thompson, with Cheryl Miller as Paula. Erin Moran *(Happy Days)* played Jenny. Both projects were shot at Africa, U.S.A., producer Ivan Tors's 500-animal ranch outside of Los Angeles, where Clarence was raised.

Dell published four issues of a *Daktari* comic book from 1967 to 1969.

A similar Ivan Tors project was the series *Cowboy in Africa,* which aired from September 1967 to September 1968 and featured Chuck Connors as Jim Sinclair, an American rodeo rider who relocates to Kenya to help manage animals on a sprawling game ranch. The series was inspired by the film *Africa—Texas Style* (1967), which starred Hugh O'Brian as Sinclair.

DR. RICHARD KIMBLE (TV, MP)

First Appearance: *The Fugitive,* September 1963, ABC.

Biography: Upon returning from work one day, Dr. Richard Kimble arrives home to find his wife, Helen, dead and a one-armed man leaving the scene of the crime. Arrested and convicted, Kimble is sentenced to die. While Kimble is being taken to jail by Lieutenant Philip Gerard, their train derails and the lieutenant is knocked out; Kimble escapes and, while he crisscrosses the country in search of the killer, the dogged Gerard crisscrosses the country in search of him. During his long flight, Kimble takes various jobs, helps those in need, and occasionally visits his married sister, Donna Taft.

Eventually Kimble learns that the one-armed man has been arrested in Los Angeles, and he turns himself in. When the killer escapes, however, Kimble convinces Gerard to let him go after him. The two meet in an abandoned amusement park, where they fight atop a water tower. As the one-armed man is about to kill Kimble, he confesses to the killing; moments later Gerard shoots him from below. Even though the one-armed man falls to his death, the lieutenant realizes that justice has been miscarried and Kimble is innocent.

Comment: The hour-long series went off the air in August 1967. David Janssen starred as Dr. Kimble, with Barry Morse as Lieutenant Gerard and Bill Raisch as

Fred Johnson. Jacqueline Scott was Donna, and Diane Brewster played Helen (seen in the opening credits). William Conrad narrated.

In the 1993 film *The Fugitive*, Harrison Ford stars as Kimble. In this retelling of the tale, Chicago-based Dr. Kimble stumbles onto a drug company scam being run by his colleagues. He is targeted for death, with the one-armed security officer as the hitman, but Kimble's wife is slain instead; tried and sentenced, Kimble escapes from the prison bus when it's hit by a train. Gerard—who did not know Kimble before this point—is called in and gives chase. Though he is on the run (and at one point, on the leap, jumping hundreds of feet from a conduit into a river), the film's Kimble risks his own safety to give medical attention to a wounded police officer and a sick child.

As in the series, Kimble finds the one-armed man, whom he captures on a subway and handcuffs to a pole. He does not kill him, but rushes off to a medical convention to expose the corrupt physician and thereby prove his innocence. The film was directed by Andrew Davis and costarred Tommy Lee Jones as Gerard.

DR. SAM BECKETT   (TV, C, L)

First Appearance: *Quantum Leap*, March 1989, NBC.
Biography: Sam Beckett was born in 1953, the son of dairy farmers John and Thelma Beckett of Elk Ridge, Indiana. His sister's name is Kate, his brother Tom. An MIT graduate with an IQ of 267, Beckett is also a varsity basketball star, an acrophobic, and an expert in hieroglyphics. Thanks to a flawed experiment, Beckett has been sent on a journey through time, making regular "leaps" into the bodies of strangers. Several rules govern his journeys: He can go back only as far as his own birth; he can alter only small events, not major historical ones; and though he (and the camera) sees him as Beckett, everyone else sees him as the person into whom he's leapt. He is accompanied through time by the holographic image of an "Observer," navy Admiral Al Calavicci, who interfaces with a computer named Ziggy to provide Beckett with information. This often proves useful, as Beckett arrives in each time, place, and person with no knowledge about any of them. Only Beckett, dogs, and children can see Al.

Over time Beckett is a black man in the pre-Civil Rights South, a sexually harassed secretary, a globetrotter, a blind pianist, a pregnant teenager, and others. In two of his most interesting excursions, Beckett leaps into Al's body as the navy flyboy is about to go on trial for the rape and murder of his commander's wife; and Sam returns to the present while Al leaps into the body of a World War II POW.

Beckett was briefly engaged to Donna Eleese.
Comment: The hour-long series was created by Donald P. Bellisario and went off the air in May 1993, after nearly 100 episodes. Scott Bakula played Beckett and Dean Stockwell was Al.

Innovation began publishing a *Quantum Leap* comic book in 1991 and discontinued it in November, 1993. Ace has published Ashley McConnell's novels *Quantum Leap: The Novel* (1993), *Too Close for Comfort* (1993), and *The Wall* (1994).

DOCTOR SPEKTOR   (C)

First Appearance: *The Occult Files of Doctor Spektor* #1, 1973, Western Publishing.
Biography: Based in the sprawling Spektor Manor, hidden deep in the country, Adam Spektor and his Indian secretary, Lakota Rainflower, are both students and foes of the occult. They have battled the mummy Ra-Ka-Tep, the vampire Baron Tibor, the Frankenstein Monster, Mr. Hyde, Kareena the witch, Simbar the lion-man, and the powerful Dark Gods and their king Neffron, who have lived on Earth since before the coming of humans, "exist as mere shadows" today, and plot to find servants so they can "dominate the world of mortals." The elegant Spektor—who drives around in his Bentley—occasionally works with psychic Elliott Kane and with Police Inspector Frank Sinke.
Comment: There were 25 issues of Doctor Spektor's own title (the last one was a reprint); the hero also made guest appearances in other Western titles, such as *Gold Key Spotlight*, *Mystery Comics Digest*, and *Spine Tingling Tales*.

DR. THIRTEEN   (C)

First Appearance: *Star Spangled Comics* #122, 1951, DC Comics.
Biography: Descended from a line of scientists and inventors who were branded as witches by superstitious people, Dr. Terrence Thirteen has never believed in the supernatural—even though many of his ancestors died prematurely from a supposed curse. After his father's unexpected death in a car crash, Dr. Thirteen shuts up the family mansion, Doomsbury Hall, moves to the city, and goes into business as the Ghost Breaker, debunking curses, voodoo, specters, an ancient Egyptian queen, a demon-hound, the Phantom of the Paris Opera, and even plant people known as the Human Orchids. His wife, Marie, helps him in his work, which takes them both around the world.
Comment: The character lasted until #130—

featured on the cover of each issue—when *Star Spangled Comics* changed to *Star Spangled War Stories.* He has been featured on occasion in other DC titles.

DOCTOR WHO (TV, MP, C, L)

First Appearance: *Doctor Who,* November 1963, BBC.

Biography: For untold centuries, a race of super-intelligent beings known as the Time Lords of the planet Gallifrey have studied all of space and time via devices known as the TARDIS (Time and Relative Dimensions in Space), devices that blend, chameleonlike, with their surroundings so the Time Lords can watch without being seen themselves. It has always been the practice of the Time Lords to observe and learn but never to interfere. However, one Time Lord is horrified by the war and evil he encounters and refuses to remain inactive. The brilliant, inquisitive, and compassionate Time Lord steals a TARDIS and flees—unaware that the device was in for repairs. Not only does it become "locked" in the first likeness it assumes—that of a modern-day British police call box (a tiny exterior that conceals a larger, more spacious interior)—but the Time Lord never knows where or when the faulty device is going to leave him.

But, gamely, the renegade Time Lord, $d^3 \Sigma x^2$—Doctor Who to us—travels through time and space helping the needy and defeating countless foes, foremost among them the robotic Cybermen and the mutated metal-encased Kaleds known as Daleks. His willingness to fight evil is due to his devotion to good, though he *does* have an edge: Time Lords possess the ability to transform their old bodies into new ones when natural causes do them in (and when old actors need to be replaced by new ones). They also can survive being murdered if an alternate body (a Watcher) is nearby, ready to merge with the slain one.

In his earliest adventures, Doctor Who travels with his granddaughter Susan, though no reference is ever made to a wife or other family. After a dangerous confrontation with the evil Cybermen, Who collapses and becomes the second Doctor Who with a personality change, losing some of his inherent crankiness and gaining a more whimsical nature. His second companion is a Scotsman named Jamie McCrimmon, a soldier and piper whom he picked up in 1746.

Eventually the Time Lords find Who, take him back to Gallifrey, and put him on trial for interfering with the fates of other races. He is found guilty and returned to the 20th century with his memory erased. Still a super-scientific genius, however, and still in possession of the faulty TARDIS, he becomes a consultant to UNIT—the United Nations Intelligence Taskforce—

and helps battle spies, megalomaniacs, mad scientists, aliens, and other ne'er-do-wells. He does all of this in his third incarnation, his previous face being too well-known for him to work as a secretive government agent. In this guise he is more foppish and courtly than ever and, with new companion, UNIT's Jo Grant, gets around more in his roadster Bessie than in his TARDIS.

After defeating the renegade Time Lord known as the Master, Who is allowed to return to his former lifestyle. After a run-in with the Giant Spiders of Metebelis Three, he gains his fourth likeness, which incorporates traits from the previous three lives and adds a new one, a fondness for scarves ranging from 14 to 20 feet long. Among his companions in this phase of his life are the robot dog K-9 and the lady Time Lord Romana. He becomes the fifth Doctor when the Master causes his body to be crushed—his new companion is the Australian airline hostess Tegan Jovanka. He is transformed into the sixth after being infected by spectrox toxaemia, contracted on Androzani Minor from eating raw spectrox, an elixir prepared using bat guano; he becomes the seventh when the TARDIS crash-lands on the planet Lakertya and he is forced to regenerate.

Doctor Who looks human, but he isn't. He has one heart on either side of his chest (each beats ten times a minute), his blood pressure is 70/70, his body temperature is 60 degrees, and he requires one-third as much oxygen as the average human. He is over 750 Earth-years old.

Comment: On TV, Dr. Who has been played by William Hartnell, Patrick Troughton, Jon Pertwee, Tom Baker, Peter Davison, Colin Baker, and Sylvester McCoy. To help guarantee international box office, star Peter Cushing played the part in two theatrical films, *Doctor Who and the Daleks* (1965) and *Daleks—Invasion Earth 2150 A.D.* (1966).

Doctor Who made his British comic book debut in 1965, appearing in *TV Comic,* drawn by the popular Neville Main, and then in *TV Century 21* and *TV Action.* In October, 1979, the *Doctor Who Weekly* began publication, a black and white magazine drawn by Dave Gibbons. Color muddied up Gibbons' work when Doctor Who's adventures with the Iron Legion and then the City of the Cursed were published in the U.S. in *Marvel Premiere* #57–#60 (1980). Marvel began a regular *Doctor Who* title in 1984, reprinting Gibbons' stories; it lasted 23 issues (to 1986).

Over 40 novels, adaptations of the TV scripts, have been published in England by various authors, beginning in 1974. Five years later Pinnacle Books began issuing these in the U.S., with *Doctor Who and the Day of the Daleks* by Terrance Dicks, followed by *Doctor Who and the Doomsday Weapon* by Malcolm

Hulke, *Doctor Who and the Dinosaur Invasion* by Hulke, *Doctor Who and the Genesis of the Daleks* by Dicks, *Doctor Who and the Revenge of the Cybermen* by Dicks, *Doctor Who and the Loch Ness Monster* by Dicks, *Doctor Who and the Talons of Weng-Chiang* by Dicks, *Doctor Who and the Masque of Mandragora* by Philip Hinchcliffe, *Doctor Who and the Android Invasion* by Dicks, and *Doctor Who and the Seeds of Doom* by Hinchcliffe.

THE DOLL SQUAD (MP)

First Appearance: *The Doll Squad,* 1973, Gemini Films.

Biography: When America's space program is sabotaged, CIA director Victor Connelly contacts freelance operative Sabrina Kincaid to help the agency find out why. Sabrina and two of her Doll Squad members—martial artist Carol and pathologist Cherisse—investigate but are waylaid by the sadistic Munson. Only Sabrina escapes, eventually tying Munson to former CIA operative Eamon O'Reilly. She brings together the rest of her team, in their skin-tight leotards: Sharon O'Connor, Elizabeth White, "Cat," and Lavelle Sumara. After tracking O'Reilly to his desert stronghold, they learn his diabolical plan: If the world doesn't submit to his rule, he will cause an all-new bubonic plague. While the Doll Squad takes out the guards and sets explosives to destroy the lair, Sabrina confronts O'Reilly and kills him with a handy sword.

Comment: Francine York starred as Sabrina, with Leigh Christian as Sharon, Sherri Vernon as Cat, Judy McConnell as Elizabeth, Tura Satana as Lavelle, Carol Terry as Carol, and Bret Zeller as Cherisse. Anthony Eisley was Connelly and Michael Ansara was O'Reilly. The film was directed by Ted V. Mikels. *The Doll Squad* was reissued in 1980 as *Hustler Squad.* Though *The Return of the Doll Squad* was planned—pitting the heroines against a rogue Doll Squad—it was never made.

The film predated TV's CHARLIE'S ANGELS which also boasted a leader named Sabrina.

DON WINSLOW (CS, L, R, MP, C)

First Appearance: *Don Winslow of the Navy,* March 5, 1934, Bell Syndicate.

Biography: Working for Admiral Colby of naval intelligence and assisted by Lieutenant Red Pennington, Commander Don Winslow travels the world battling enemies of America, in particular the spy master Scorpion, who runs a spy ring. During World War II the heroes tackle Axis spies, both abroad and at home. Don is engaged to Mercedes Colby, daughter of the admiral.

Comment: The hero was created by Lieutenant Commander Frank V. Martinek, who had originally intended to write a series of Winslow novels to interest young men in joining the navy. When Secretary of the Navy Frank Knox got wind of the enterprise, he contacted a friend at the Bell Syndicate and Don Winslow became a comic strip hero instead, written by Martinek and drawn by Lieutenant Leon A. Beroth and Carl Hammond. When Hammond was drafted during the war, Ed Moore, then Al Levin replaced him. The strip lasted until July 30, 1955.

The strip was an instant success, and Martinek went ahead and finished the novels he'd plotted; six of them were published between 1935 and 1940. These were also adapted by Martinek as Big Little book novels: *Don Winslow, U.S.N. Lieutenant Commander* (1935), *Don Winslow of the Navy vs. the Scorpion Gang* (1938), *Don Winslow of the Navy and the Great War Plot* (1940), *Don Winslow Navy Intelligence Ace* (1942), *Don Winslow of the Navy and the Secret Enemy Base* (1943), and *Don Winslow and the Giant Girl Spy* (1946).

On radio, the character was heard over the Blue network beginning in 1937; it originated from Chicago with Bob Guilbert, then Raymond Edward Johnson, in the lead.

In film, the character headlined a pair of movie serials: *Don Winslow of the Navy* (1942) and *Don Winslow of the Coast Guard* (1943), both starring Don Terry and pitting the hero against the Scorpion.

Don Winslow was a supporting character in a number of comic books, but also starred in his own title, *Don Winslow of the Navy:* 69 issues were published by Fawcett (later, Charlton) from 1943 to 1955.

DOROTHY GALE (L, S, MP, C)

First Appearance: *The Wonderful Wizard of Oz* by L. Frank Baum, 1900, Hill Publishing.

Biography: Dorothy Gale, an orphan, lives on "the great Kansas prairies" with farmers Uncle Henry and Aunt Em. Her only known companion is a small black dog, Toto. When the prairie is hit by a cyclone, Dorothy and Toto aren't able to reach the storm cellar in time; the house is lifted and flies through the air for several hours, until it is set down "very gently—for a cyclone" in the middle of beautiful countryside. Dorothy is greeted by short people named Munchkins, who thank her for having killed the oppressive Witch of the East by dropping her house on her. The good Witch of the North, a friend of the Munchkins, arrives at once and presents Dorothy with the dead Witch's

An original illustration of *Dorothy Gale* from 1910 by John R. Neill.

silver shoes, which are said to be magic. Dorothy, desperate to get back home to Kansas, asks her advice on how to do so. The Witch tells her to follow the yellow brick road to the City of Emeralds to ask for the help of the great Wizard of Oz.

After putting on her only other dress and locking the door of the house, Dorothy departs; along the way, she is joined by a Scarecrow who wants to ask the Wizard for a brain, a Tin Woodman who yearns for a heart, and a Cowardly Lion who wants courage. After crossing the Deadly Poppy Field and having an adventure among the Field Mice, the quartet reaches Oz. Unfortunately, the Wizard won't honor their requests until they kill the wicked Witch of the West. Though they succeed—Dorothy drenches her with water as they argue about the silver shoes—Oz turns out to be a mortal man and a fraud. Still, in undertaking their great adventure, Dorothy's companions have found brains, love, and courage. As for the little girl, the Wizard agrees to fly her back to Kansas by balloon. But as they're about to leave, Toto chases a cat and, before Dorothy can catch him, the Wizard departs. Saddened, she goes to the King of the Winged Monkeys, whose minions used to work for the Witch, but he can't do anything for her because his kind "don't belong" in Kansas. However, Dorothy learns that Glinda, the powerful Witch of the South, might help her. After

surviving a journey through the forest of the Fighting Trees, Dainty China Country, and the land of the short, fat Quadlings, Dorothy reaches Glinda's castle and learns that she'll return home if she clicks her heels together three times. So doing, she is spun through the air and finds herself in the field beside the new farmhouse Uncle Henry has built.

Comment: The novel was originally going to be called *The Emerald City,* but Baum changed his mind because it was considered unlucky to publish a book with a jewel in the title.

Dorothy did not figure in the second novel, *The Land of Oz* (1904), which was about young Tip, who flees from the witch Mombi in the company of Jack Pumpkinhead and the wooden Saw-Horse, and makes his way to the Emerald City.

Dorothy returns in *Ozma of Oz* (1907). When Henry goes to Australia to visit some relatives, Dorothy joins him. But a storm sweeps her overboard, and, clutching a chicken coop, she bobs back to Oz, where she and the talking Yellow Hen Billina help Princess Ozma save the royal family from the wicked Nome King.

In *Dorothy and the Wizard of Oz* (1908), Dorothy and her cat Eureka are swallowed by an earthquake as they visit California. They meet the Wizard there as well, and, together, they try to get back to Oz. In *The Road to Oz* (1909), Dorothy and Toto get lost while helping a hobo, the Shaggy Man, find his way and end up in Oz, where they have adventures with Polychrome, daughter of the Rainbow, as they head to Ozma's birthday celebration. In *The Emerald City of Oz* (1910), Dorothy—now Princess Dorothy of Oz—goes to Oz with her uncle and aunt to battle the Nome King.

After this tale, Dorothy has mostly supporting roles in *The Patchwork Girl of Oz* (1913), in which Scraps, the eponymous heroine, helps the Munchkin boy Ojo save his Unc Nunkie, who has been turned to marble; *Tik-Tok of Oz* (1914), which pits Betsy Bobbin, Hank the Mule, and the Shaggy Man against the Nome King and Queen Ann of Oogaboo; *The Scarecrow of Oz* (1915), the story of Cap'n Bill and Trot help the Scarecrow battle King Krewl; *Tinkitink in Oz* (1916), which pits Prince Inga of Pingaree, King Rinkitink, and Bilbil the goat against the Nome King; *The Lost Princess of Oz* (1917), which sends Dorothy and the Wizard on an epic search for Ozma; *The Tin Woodman of Oz* (1918), a tale of the Scarecrow and Woot the Wanderer helping the Tin Woodman find his lost love Nimmi Amee; *The Magic of Oz* (1919), a tale of magic gone awry as an ex-Nome King and a Munchkin, Kiki Aru, turn the people of the Emerald City into beasts; and *Glinda of Oz* (1920), the story of Dorothy and Ozma's efforts to prevent war between the Skeezers and the Flatheads.

Following Baum's death, 19 other Oz novels were written by Ruth Plumly Thompson.

Dorothy and her friends first appeared onstage in 1902, in a musical revue-style show written by Baum. It ran in Chicago, on Broadway, and toured for several years. The characters were back in the 1975 Broadway musical *The Wiz,* which starred Stephanie Mills and an all-black cast.

There were several silent film versions: *The Wizard of Oz* (1908, 1910, and 1924; the latter starred Dorothy Dwan as Dorothy with Oliver Hardy as the Tin Man); *Dorothy and the Scarecrow in Oz* (1910), *The Land of Oz* (1910), *His Majesty the Scarecrow of Oz* (1914), *The Magic Cloak of Oz* (1914), *The Patchwork Girl of Oz* (1914), and *The Ragged Girl of Oz* (1919). The most famous film version starred Judy Garland (with Ray Bolger, Jack Haley, Bert Lahr, Frank Morgan, Billie Burke, and Margret Hamilton) and was released in 1939, directed by Victor Fleming. Garland's daughter Liza Minnelli provided the voice of Dorothy in the animated feature *Journey Back to Oz* (1964), Diana Ross starred in the 1978 film of *The Wiz* directed by Sidney Lumet, and Fairuza Balk was Dorothy in Disney's *Return to Oz* (1985), directed by Walter Murch. Joan D. Vinge wrote the Ballantine novel based on the screenplay.

Both *Classics Illustrated Jr.* and *Dell Junior Treasury* adapted the original novel in comic book form in the early 1950s. Dell's *4-Color* title offered one issue of *Tales of the Wizard of Oz* in 1962, Marvel published its one-shot adaptation of the 1939 film, *MGM's Marvelous Wizard of Oz,* in 1975, and *First Comics Graphic Novel* published *The Secret Island of Oz* and *The Ice King of Oz* in the middle 1980s. DC published a bizarre three-issue series *The Oz-Wonderland Wars* in 1986.

DRAY PRESCOT (L, T)

First Appearance: *Transit to Scorpio* by Alan Burt Akers, 1972, DAW Books.

Biography: Dray Prescot is a sailor in Nelson's Navy who is transported to Kregen—a world orbiting the twin suns of Antares in the constellation Scorpio—by the superhuman Savanti nal Aphrasöe (Savanti of the Swinging City). From these mighty mortals, he is handed over to the godlike Everoinye (Star Lords), who dispatch Prescot to help the island empire of Vallia achieve a manifest destiny by first resisting the imperial designs of the empire of Hamal and its Empress Thyllis. He succeeds, and, in time, his heroism raises him to Emperor of Vallia, Lord of Strombor,

Krozair of Zy, and finally Warlord of Kregen when he defeats the piratical Shanks from the southlands and the magic of the witch Csitra. He is wed to the Empress Delia and the father of Jaidur, who is himself a king, and the Princess Dayra. Among Dray's many companions are the bold Pompino, captain of the seagoing vessel *Tuscurs Maiden,* and the fabulous Seg Segutorio, a.k.a. Seg the Bowman.

Dray stands "above" medium height, has brown hair and "level brown eyes," and "enormously broad shoulders." He is honest, courageous, and "moves like a savage hunting cat."

Comment: The novels are grouped in the successive Delian Cycle, the Havilfar Cycle, the Krozair Cycle, the Vallian Cycle, etc. In addition to the 37 novels (to date) by Akers (pseudonym for Kenneth Bulmer), the hero is featured in the role-playing Beneath Two Suns by Mayfair Games.

DRIFT MARLO (C, CS)

First Appearance: *Drift Marlo* #1, 1962, Dell Publishing.

Biography: A "space detective," Drift Marlo works for the Strategic Aerospace Division of the Strategic

The splash page of *Drift Marlo*'s one and only adventure. © Dell Publishing.

Air Command (SAD), helping to oversee security for the Pacific Coast Rocket Base. The young, red-headed hero works closely with Dr. Hugo Barcus, head of the missile program, and has been with SAD for at least a year, though probably longer.

In his most famous adventure, Drift prevents the Peace-Maker missile from being sabotaged by its creator, Dr. Fowler, who's concerned about the dangers of offensive weapons in space.

Drift lives on the base and dates Barcus's secretary, Claire.

Comment: There was only one issue of the title, which is too bad—the story raised important issues, and the comic book was accurate and generally educational in its presentation of space hardware and NASA operations.

Drift resurfaced as a comic strip hero in 1967, turned into a space detective by the team of artist Tom Cooke and writer Phil Evans, investigating mysteries onboard U.S. spacecraft, on the moon, and in spaceships of unknown origin. The strip ran for just over five years.

DUDLEY DO-RIGHT (TV, C)

First Appearance: *The Bullwinkle Show,* September 1961, NBC.

Biography: Based in the Canadian Rockies, Dudley Do-Right is a fumbling but well-meaning corporal in the Royal Canadian Mounted Police who, despite his ineptitude (and his allergy to marigolds), always gets his man. Dressed in a red uniform and hat (as is his nameless horse), Corporal Do-Right regularly battles the evil, green-skinned Snidely Whiplash, "the most wanted man in Canada" and a former snake-oil salesman, who is described as being "eight jumps ahead of Dudley Do-Right." Snidely is assisted in his crimes by the timid Homer.

When he isn't out hunting Snidely, Dudley woos the "fickle but beautiful" redhead Nell, daughter of post commander, Inspector Ray K. Fenwick. Both men report to Colonel Crimcrammer.

The adventures cover the late 19th century through the early 20th century (Dudley trains for the 1904 decathlon, a year the event wasn't held), though anachronisms abound. (For instance, the outpost has a TV.)

In one adventure, it is suggested that the characters aren't real but are merely actors Acne Pitz and Clot Ballew re-creating the adventures of Dudley and Snidely for the viewers.

Comment: The character remained a five-minute segment of *The Bullwinkle Show* until the prime-time series went off the air in September 1962. After that

the character was seen on his own program, *Dudley Do-Right and His Friends,* which was aired on ABC from April 1969 to September 1970 and featured episodes originally run on Bullwinkle's program. There were 38 adventures in all, with Bill Scott as the voice of Dudley, June Foray as Nell, Paul Frees as Fenwick (and the narrator), and Hans Conreid as Snidely.

Charlton published seven issues of a Dudley Do-Right comic book from 1970 to 1971.

THE DUKES (TV)

First Appearance: *The Dukes of Hazzard,* January 1979, CBS.

Biography: Hazzard County can be found "east of the Mississippi and south of the Ohio," though exactly where is never revealed. It's run by the corrupt politician Jefferson Davis "Boss" Hogg and his puppet enforcer and brother-in-law, the inept Sheriff Roscoe P. Coltrane. Giving both men a hard time are a pair of self-appointed do-gooders, cousins Luke Duke and Bo Duke. At the wheel of their customized Dodge Charger, General Lee, the young men lead the law on wild car chases as they help the downtrodden or just try to give Hogg and Roscoe a tough time. Sometimes they're gainfully employed (e.g., driving the county's only taxi and, of course, picking up a pair of fugitives) or are bona-fide crimebusters (rescuing Loretta Lynn from kidnapers and cousin Daisy Duke from the rotten Beaudry clan). When they're not tooling around, the men help their uncle Jesse Duke and the stunning Daisy back on the farm, which Hogg and the sheriff regularly try to repossess.

Eventually the two leave Hazzard County to race on the NASCAR circuit (they'd once got involved with a crooked NASCAR driver on the show), and their cousins Coy and Vance return after being away for six years. Failing to make a name for themselves, Luke and Bo return and, after a brief period, Coy and Vance resume their travels.

Comment: The hour-long series aired until August 1985. Tom Wopat starred as Luke, John Schneider was Bo, Catherine Bach played Daisy, Denver Pyle was Jesse, Byron Cherry was Coy, Christopher Mayer was Vance, James Best was the sheriff, and Sorrell Booke played Hogg. The actors also provided the voices for the half-hour cartoon series *The Dukes.* Twenty episodes aired on CBS from 1982 to 1984.

Luke and Bo "left" in 1982 because Wopat and Schneider had a contract dispute with the producers. When it was settled in February 1983, they returned, and, by the fall, their replacements were gone.

E

EAGLE (C)

First Appearance: *The Rook* #12, 1981, Warren Publishing.

Biography: Eagle is the war chief of the Crow Indians who lives in the Wyoming Territory circa 1870. The Crows' only enemies are the vicious Blackfeet; Eagle and his people are at peace with the "blue eyes," the white settlers from the East. Indeed, Eagle—who speaks English—has been known to ride to their rescue when they are attacked by Blackfeet. Eagle and his people enjoy stealing the horses of rival tribes, though he resists the urging of his vicious tribesman Mad Dog to raid white parties as well.

Comment: The strip, written and drawn by John Severin, appeared in the last three issues of *The Rook.*

EARL DUMAREST (L)

First Appearance: *The Winds of Gath* by E.C. Tubb, 1967, Ace Books.

Biography: At some future time, Earl Dumarest is born on a world that is all but deserted. When he's still just a young boy, he stows away on a tramp freighter in order to find a more exciting place to live. But

Eagle lectures a Blackfeet rival. © Warren Publishing.

questions nag at him about his home world. Were his people colonists or, as rumors suggest, did they flee from terra (i.e., from "terror")? As an adult, he desires to return to his native world, "that mythical place from which a thousand colonized planets had originated." But most don't believe the planet exists, and those who do have no idea where it is or why Earl's people left. Determined to find Earth and understand the mystery, Earl begins at the center of the galaxy and hops from star to star, surviving adventures on various planets as he collects clues. For a time he pursues his quest as captain of the spaceship *Erce.*

His nemeses are the Cyclan, a network of emotionless human beings who are determined to capture Earl and obtain the secret of the body-switching formula that is his alone—and that will enable them to rule the universe. They know the location of Earth, but keep it a secret: It's their headquarters, a place where the brains of loyal Cyclan are removed from their bodies, preserved, and cybernetically joined to a powerful, organic computer.

Comment: Tubb has written many novels about his spacefarer. To date, theses are *Derai, Toyman, Kalin, The Jester at Scar, Lallia, Technos, Veruchia, Mayenne, Jondelle, Zenya, Eloise, Eye of the Zodiac, Jack of Swords, Spectrum of a Forgotten Sun, Heaven of Darkness, Prison of Night, Incident on Ath, The Quillian Sector, Web of Sand, Iduna's Universe, The Terra Data, World of Promise, Nectar of Heaven, The Terridae, The Coming Event, Earth Is Heaven, Melome, Angado, Symbol of Terra,* and *The Temple of Truth.*

See also Tubb's CAP KENNEDY.

ELAINE DODGE (MP, L)

First Appearance: *The Exploits of Elaine,* 1914, Pathe.

Biography: Taylor Dodge is the president of the Consolidated Insurance Company. When he is mysteriously murdered, his daughter Elaine sets out to find his killer, a fiend known only as the Clutching Hand.

Assisting her is inventor/detective CRAIG KENNEDY, who has the latest scientific gadgets at his disposal—such as a miniature torch, a camera triggered by footfalls, an early lie detector, and an electrical resuscitator to revive the newly dead—and helps rescue Elaine from many tight spots. These include being injected with the hypnotic drug scapolarium, being fed arsenic, being bound and gagged and left to drown as the tides begin to rise, being imprisoned in a sewer, and others. Eventually the Hand is revealed to be Perry Bennett, Dodge's lawyer.

No sooner is that crime solved than Elaine and Craig meet up with an accomplice of the Clutching Hand: The Oriental fiend Wu Fang, who is searching for the fortune the Hand left behind and also wants to destroy Elaine and Craig. There are more traps—Elaine is hypnotized and nearly burned alive, while Craig is infected with a deadly disease—before Craig and Wu Fang fight each other on a dock, fall into the bay, and Wu Fang is consumed by sharks.

Craig survives (though that isn't revealed until the third serial) and, with the help of Elaine, goes searching for the mysterious saboteur Mr. X, who wants to obtain a new torpedo Craig invented and mine all of the harbors in the United States. The duo survive paralyzing gas, an exploding bridge, and X's henchman before the fiend and his submarine are sunk.

Comment: Pearl White starred in the first hugely successful 14-chapter serial and its sequels, both made in 1915—the ten-chapter *The New Exploits of Elaine* and the 12-chapter *The Romance of Elaine.* All of the serials later became novels by Arthur B. Reeve. Reeve also wrote the novel *The Triumph of Elaine* (1916). Arnold Daly was Craig in all three and the distinguished Lionel Barrymore was Mr. X. Louis Gasnier. George B. Seitz directed the first serial, Seitz the last two.

See also PAULINE.

ELFEGO BACA (TV)

First Appearance: "The Nine Lives of Elfego Baca," *Walt Disney Presents,* October 1958, ABC.

Biography: According to the theme song, "The legend is that, like el gato the cat, nine lives has Elfego Baca." The mustachioed Mexican/American lawyer and sheriff is based in Tombstone, Arizona, and comes close to losing several of those lives in every adventure, as he doesn't hesitate to use fists or guns to uphold the law or defend the innocent.

Comment: The miniseries was serialized in hour-long parts over six nonsuccessive weeks the first season. The chapters were "The Nine Lives of Elfego Baca," "Four Down and Five Lives to Go," "Lawman or Gunman,"

"Law and Order, Inc.," "Attorney at Law," and "The Griswold Murder." Several of these episodes were edited into features and shown theatrically abroad. Elfego returned in the 1959–60 season with the four-part *Elfego Baca and the Mustangers,* the chapters of which were "Move Along, Mustangers," "Mustang Man, Mustang Maid," "Friendly Enemies at Law," and "Gus Tomlin Is Dead." Robert Loggia played the part, which was loosely based on the real-life exploits of "the man they couldn't kill"; James Dunn costarred as his senior law partner. Disney also serialized the adventures of the historical Swamp Fox (Francis Marion, played by Leslie Nielsen), frontiersman Andy Burnett (Jerome Courtland), and Texas ranger John Slaughter (Tom Tryon). All of these were efforts to duplicate the success Disney had had airing the adventures of Davy Crockett, starring Fess Parker, beginning in December 1954 with "Davy Crockett, Indian Fighter" and including "Davy Crockett Goes to Congress," "Davy Crockett at the Alamo" (Walt Disney killed his hero before he appreciated the depth of the craze, then had to do flashbacks), "Davy Crockett's Keelboat Race," and "Davy Crockett and the River Pirates."

Dell published six issues of *Walt Disney Presents* from 1959–1961. The comic book featured the adventures of Elfego Baca, Texas John Slaughter, and other Disney TV characters.

Robert Loggia as *Elfego Baca.* © Walt Disney Productions, courtesy of Bill Latham.

ELLEN RIPLEY (MP, L, C)

First Appearance: *Alien,* 1979, Twentieth Century-Fox.

Biography: Ripley is a warrant officer onboard the *Nostromo,* a deep-space tug owned by the Company. Also onboard are Captain Dallas, navigator Lambert, engineers Brett and Parker, Executive Officer Kane, Science Officer Ash (an android), and Jones the cat. Responding to an SOS from a nearby world, Acheron, they discover a derelict spaceship; Kane finds eggs inside, and, when one hatches, he is attacked by a facehugger. Through his mouth, the crablike monster impregnates him with an Alien seed. Days later, onboard the *Nostromo,* the Alien erupts from his chest and, having assumed the general attributes of its host, grows into an eight-foot-tall black, bipedal carnivore with concentrated acid blood. The crew soon discovers that, unknown to all but Ash, it was no coincidence that the ship picked up the SOS: The Company wanted the Alien for its bioweapons division. Eventually all are torn to bits by the Alien, and only Ripley and the cat are left alive. After climbing into a spacesuit, the warrant officer is able to open the hatch of the ship and the Alien is sucked into space.

Ripley and Jones go into hibernation and are found 57 years later by a deep-space salvage team. Back on Earth, Ripley is told that her daughter, Amanda, whom she had left as a child, has grown old and died. Meanwhile, to her horror, she also learns that Acheron has been colonized and that contact with the colony has been lost. Since she's the only one who has ever fought the Aliens, now-Lieutenant Ripley joins a contingent of 11 U.S. Colonial Marines sent to find out what happened to the colonists. They find that other Aliens have been produced and that only one colonist has survived, a 12-year-old girl named Newt Jorden. The Aliens attack the marines, and after Ripley uses a flamethrower to destroy a queen Alien's hive, she, Newt, android Bishop, and marine Corporal Hicks manage to escape in the ship *Sulaco.* The queen Alien also gets aboard, but Ripley climbs into an exoskeletonlike Power Loader and beats her out into the vacuum of space. The quartet go into suspended animation.

Sometime later, the *Sulaco*'s 337 model EEV pod crash-lands on Fiorina ("Fury") 161, a backwater, Class C prison planet whose 25 cons are "all scum." All but Ripley perish in the crash. Upon reanimating Bishop's remains and accessing the ship's computer, she learns that an electrical fire onboard the *Sulaco* had caused the pod to jettison, and that a facehugger was aboard the pod. It escapes, face-hugs a dog, and a quadrupedal Alien is now killing the prisoners and guards—though it refuses to attack Ripley. Wondering why, she takes a neuro-scan and learns that she was impregnated on the pod and is carrying a queen. Ripley uses her "immunity" to get close to the Alien in the prison world's leadworks. Though the creature survives having molten metal poured over it, Ripley quickly drenches it with water and the hot/cold combination causes it to explode. A Company Medivac Rescue Team arrives then and wants to operate on Ripley to remove the Alien embryo. But she knows they'll use it for their own wicked purposes and choses, instead, to leap to her death in the furnace, taking what may or may not be the last Alien spawn with her.

Ripley held an ICC commercial flight officer's license, number NOC 14472.

Comment: The characters were created by writers Dan O'Bannon and Ron Shussett. Ripley was played by Sigourney Weaver in the first film and in its sequels *Aliens* (1986) and *Alien 3* (1992).

All of the films have been novelized by Alan Dean Foster, and a new series of novels featuring different protagonists has also been published.

Heavy Metal magazine published a comic book adaptation of the film by writer Archie Goodwin and artist Walt Simonson; the series was also published in book form.

Dark Horse Comics published a six-issue adaptation of the second film and also spun off a new series of comic books featuring the monsters and new human adversaries. The titles include *Aliens vs. Predator* (four issues in 1990), *Aliens: Earth War* (four issues in 1990), and *Aliens: Genocide* (four issues in 1991–92).

ELLERY QUEEN (L, MP, R, C, TV)

First Appearance: *The Roman Hat Mystery* by Ellery Queen, 1929, Frederick A. Stokes Company.

Biography: Ellery was born in 1905, the son of famed New York Inspector Richard Queen. A writer who collects rare books, he works in Hollywood for a time before returning to New York to work as a private eye. Because of his father's connections and reputation, Ellery is permitted to examine crime scenes that might otherwise be off-limits to him. He briefly leaves Ellery Queen, Inc., during World War II to write movie scripts for the army and, later, to work without pay for a mayoral task force trying to find a murderer.

Despite his extraordinary deductive abilities, Queen is rather absentminded. He lives in an apartment on West 87th Street and enjoys spending weekends and holidays in Wrightsville, Connecticut. Tall and slender, with a fondness for tweeds, the handsome Ellery has had numerous romantic relationships over the years, most notably with Hollywood reporter Paula Paris and with his devoted secretary, Nikki Porter.

Comment: "Author" Queen is actually writers/cousins Frederic Dannay and Manfred B. Lee, who wrote the first novel to try to win a $7,500 mystery writing prize sponsored by *McClure's* magazine. They won, but the magazine went under before they were paid or the story was published. It went out as a book instead. Dannay and Lee used the Queen name as both character and author, feeling readers would remember the author if they saw his name in the story as well. The men wrote a total of 33 Queen novels through 1971 and another seven short stories. The early, best-known novels are *The French Powder Mystery* (1930), *The Dutch Shoe Mystery* (1931), *The Greek Coffin Mystery* (1932), *The Egyptian Cross Mystery* (1932), *The American Gun Mystery* (1933), *The Siamese Twin Mystery* (1933), *The Chinese Orange Mystery* (1934), and *The Spanish Cape Mystery* (1935).

There were nine Ellery Queen motion pictures, none of them especially good, beginning with *The Spanish Cape Mystery* (1935) starring Donald Cook and *The Mandarin Mystery* (1937) starring Eddie Quillan. Both were low-budget, miscast affairs. Even worse was Ralph Bellamy as a fumbling Queen in his films *Ellery Queen, Master Detective* (1940), *Ellery Queen's Penthouse Mystery, Ellery Queen and the Perfect Crime,* and *Ellery Queen and the Murder Ring,* all in 1941. William Gargan was only a slight improvement, top-lining *Close Call for Ellery Queen, Desperate Chance for Ellery Queen,* and *Enemy Agents Meet Ellery Queen,* all in 1942. Peter Lawford made a good detective in the 1971 TV movie *Ellery Queen: Don't Look Behind You,* but the best of the movie Queens was Jim Hutton, whose TV movie *Ellery Queen* (1975) was the pilot for his short-lived series.

On radio, the character settled in for a nine-year run on CBS in 1939, played, in succession, by Hugh Marlowe, Larry Dobkin, Carleton Young, and Sidney Smith.

In comic books, Queen headlined his own four-issue Superior Comics title in 1949, in two issues of a Ziff-Davis magazine in 1952, and in three issues of Dell's *4-Color* from 1961–1962.

On TV, *The Adventures of Ellery Queen* aired on DuMont from October 1950 to December 1951, before moving to ABC, where the half-hour series aired until December 1952. Richard Hart starred on the DuMont show, Lee Bowman on ABC. The show returned as an hour-long NBC series from September 1958 to August 1959 with George Nader, then Lee Philips in the title role (as *The Further Adventures of Ellery Queen*), then came back to NBC again from September 1975 to September 1976, with Jim Hutton in the part.

In 1941, Mercury Press began publishing the enormously successful *Ellery Queen's Mystery Magazine,* which printed short stories by other authors. It continues to this day, published by Dell Magazines.

In 1932, authors Dannay and Lee took the pseudonym Barnaby Ross and wrote a series of mysteries featuring the moderately popular sleuth, retired Shakespearean actor Drury Lane.

ENEMY ACE (C)

First Appearance: *Our Army At War* #151, 1965, DC Comics.

Biography: Baron Hans Von Hammer, "The Hammer of Hell," grows up in his family's ancestral castle. From a sense of duty, not a love of war, he enlists in flight school at the outbreak of World War I and becomes a

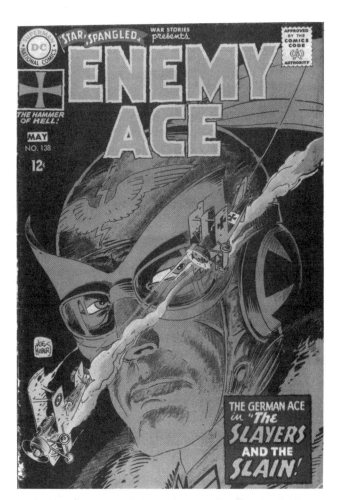

One of Joe Kubert's evocative covers featuring *Enemy Ace.*
© DC Comics.

fighter pilot, patrolling the "killer skies" in his Fokker DR-1 triplane. His sense of honor is such that he rarely fails to salute adversaries who have fallen before his twin Spandaus, and he refuses to attack wounded or unarmed foes. Even so, he has shot down over 70 aircraft. Set in 1918, his adventures invariably have an ironic aspect that underscores the madness of war—for example, shot down over France and wounded, he runs from a search party and is constantly being fed or tended to by relatives of those he knows he has shot down.

He is the Rittmeister of Jagdstaffel 17; his valet at the field is Schulz. In addition to flying, Von Hammer is a fine fencer—he received the scar on his left cheek during a duel—and has been schooled in martial arts. He enjoys hunting and invariably meets up with a gray wolf who becomes his companion for the day.

Comment: The character appeared in three issues of *Our Army At War,* flew solo in *Showcase* #57–#58, was featured in *Star Spangled War Stories* from #138 to #161, and had his own one-shot reprint title in 1990. Joe Kubert's art was always exquisite, and the stories by creator/writer Bob Kanigher were well written.

Another DC World War I ace was Balloon Buster, a.k.a. Steven Henry Savage, Jr., who was raised in Wyoming, dresses like a cowboy, and has frequently tangled with Von Hammer. He first appeared in *All-American Men of War* #112.

THE EQUALIZER (TV)

First Appearance: *The Equalizer,* September 1985, CBS.

Biography: An operative for a government spy agency, Robert McCall (known as the Equalizer) quits because he doesn't like the bureaucracy and immorality. Deciding to go into business for himself, he sets up shop in Manhattan, advertising his services in the newspaper and helping those in need. ("Got a problem? Odds against you? Call the Equalizer." The number is 212-555-4200.) In his new role, he takes on stalkers, drug dealers, killers, and even freelances for his old agency, reporting to a man known only as Control.

McCall's assistant is Mickey Kostmayer; his friend and former agent is Pete O'Phelan, owner of a cafe where McCall hangs out.

Divorced, McCall is trying very much to make up for all the years he was away by getting to know his 18-year-old son Scott, who studies music at the High School of the Performing Arts in New York.

Comment: Edward Woodward starred in the hour-long series, which ran through September 1989. Rob-

ert Lansing was Control, William Zabka was Scott, and Keith Szarabajka was Mickey.

ERIC JOHN STARK (L)

First Appearance: "Queen of the Martian Catacombs" by Leigh Brackett, 1949, *Planet Stories.*

Biography: Eons ago, the solar system's worlds were seeded by aliens, referred to as "some parent human stock." Now the worlds have evolved their own governments, banded together as part of the Milky Way's Galactic Union. Stark is born of human parents on Mercury. After they die, he is raised by Mercurian natives and goes by the name N'Chaka; in time, he is discovered by Simon Ashton of the Earth Police Control, who raises him.

Noble and honorable, Stark nonetheless becomes a wanted man for running guns to rebels who are revolting against the oppressive Terro-Venusian Metals. Found by Ashton, Stark is offered amnesty if he'll go to Mars to help battle a barbarian chief named Kynon, who is mounting a holy war. Stark agrees to go and is joined by other wanted criminals: Themis of Mercury, Knighton and Walsh of Earth, Luhar of Venus, and Arrod of Jupiter's moon Callisto. After Kynon is defeated, Stark is given a great and sacred talisman by his dying comrade, the Martian Camar; the hero agrees to undertake the arduous journey to return the mystic lens to the city from which it was stolen long ago.

Upon leaving the solar system for his next adventure, Stark journeys to the planet Skaith after Ashton disappears. Stark succeeds in rescuing him, destroying the powerful and violent Wandsmen in the process; after slaying the king-dog Flay, he becomes the leader of the nine fierce, white Northhounds. But his reign is short because he's betrayed by the evil Antarean Penkawr-Che, and in his third and final adventure on Skaith, the hero must find a way to leave the dying world orbiting the Ginger Star. With the help of Ashton and the Union, he succeeds.

Stark is tall and lean, with black hair and pale eyes.

Comment: The short story was expanded into the novel *Secret of Sinharat* in 1964 and published by Ace Books; the second story was "Black Amazon of Mars" (1951), originally published in *Planet Stories* and revised as the novel *People of the Talisman* (1964). Brackett followed these with *The Book of Skaith* Stark trilogy: *The Ginger Star* (1974), *The Hounds of Skaith* (1974), and *The Reavers of Skaith* (1976), after which the first two novels were reissued in one volume as *Outlaw of Mars.*

Brackett also wrote the first draft of the screenplay for *The Empire Strikes Back* (see HAN SOLO) as well as many other books and short stories. She was married to author Edmond Hamilton. (See MORGAN CHANE.)

EXPLORERS OF THE UNKNOWN (C)

First Appearance: *Archie Giant Series* #587, 1988, Archie Publications.

Biography: Red Andrews is a former CIA agent who turns soldier-of-fortune. Eventually he writes an autobiography entitled *Explorer of the Unknown,* which is sold to the movies. While the film is in production, a giant prop robot goes on a rampage in Riverdale. While Red tries to stop it with a lasso, pilot and mechanic Wheels Cooper flies overhead in her souped-up helicopter. She uses a hook to yank off the robot's head, but even that doesn't stop it. Nor is the film's demolitions expert, Nitro Mantle, able to bring it down with an explosion. Gizmo Doiley's scientific know-how is of no help, but daredevil cyclist Squint Jones is able to slow it down with dynamite, after which martial artist Angel Lodge finishes it off with a karate kick.

Realizing they make a terrific team, the specialists—along with mighty Spike, a stuntman from the film—cut a deal with beautiful CIA agent Blaze Blossom: In exchange for federal aid to build a headquarters in Explorer Mountain and various equipment, they'll help their country when danger strikes. The heroes go about their normal lives until the small beepers they carry tell them they're needed. The group is later joined by F/X Clayton, a master of special effects.

Among their tools are the supersonic VTOL jetcraft, a hydrofoil sub, a power suit that boosts Spike's strength, instant airbags to cushion falls from great heights, F/X's fiber optic cloak of invisibility, rocket belts, and Nitro's vest buttons that "interact to form a small blast." The group's most resilient foe is mad inventor Myron Pepperdinkle.

Comment: The characters—based on the long-running Archie Comics roster—appeared in two issues of *Archie Giant Series* before being given their own magazine in 1990. It lasted six issues.

F

FAFHRD (L, C)

First Appearance: "Two Sought Adventure" by Fritz Leiber, 1939, *Unknown* magazine.

Biography: Standing nearly seven feet tall and possessed of a "limber-looking ranginess," the red-headed Fafhrd is the son of Mor (his mother) and of Nalgron the Legend-Breaker. He lives on Nehwon, a barbaric world located in a different dimension, and hails from the Cold Waste north of the Eight Cities and the Trollstep Mountains. Though he sleeps "in his mother's tent" until he's 18, the strong youth finally leaves the Snow Clan, a "huge longsword" in his hand. Early on he falls in with the Gray Mouser, a man of "childlike stature, gray garb," and a mouse-skin hood. The two great swordsmen, both good-natured and generally kind-hearted men, have incredible adventures together, searching for treasure, trying to steal the valuable eye of an idol, and performing various services for their sometime employers, the wizards Sheelba of the Eyeless Face and Ningauble of the Seven Eyes.

Comment: The characters' many short story and novella-length adventures have been collected in the books *Two Sought Adventure* (1957; expanded in 1970 as *Swords Against Death), The Swords of Lankhmar* (1968, an expanded version of the short story "Scylla's Daughter" published in *Fantastic* in 1961), *Swords in the Mist* (1968), *Swords Against Wizardry* (1968), and *Swords and Deviltry* (1970), which contains the earliest stories, chronologically, including the tale of how the heroes met. Leiber's later short stories about the characters, including "The Curse of the Smalls and the Stars," were featured in anthologies such as *Heroic Visions* in 1983. *The Knight and Knave of Swords,* published in 1988, was only the second hardcover edition devoted solely to the characters and contains "The Curse of the Smalls and the Stars," the short story "Sea Magic," the novelette "The Mer She," and the novel *The Mouser Goes Below.*

The characters starred in five issues of DC's *Sword of Sorcery* comic book in 1973 and in four issues of their own Marvel comic book from 1990 to 1991.

THE FALCON (L, MP, R, TV)

First Appearance: "Gay Falcon" by Michael Arlen, 1940.

Biography: Gay Stanhope Falcon is a tall, slender, swarthy, hard-boiled sleuth with riveting eyes and dark, graying hair. He is a former soldier, war correspondent, and airplane salesman who turns private investigator. In his first adventure, he finds missing jewelry for an insurance company, gems on which claims have already been paid. An excellent swimmer, dancer, hunter, and fisherman, the twice-divorced Falcon also goes by a pair of aliases: Colonel Rock and Spencer Pott.

Comment: The character made only one appearance in literature, but it was enough to launch a long multimedia career. In movies, he was Gay Lawrence, played debonair rather than tough by George Sanders in *The Gay Falcon* (1940), a loose adaptation of the original story; *A Date with the Falcon* (1941), in which he is hired to rescue the missing inventor of an artificial diamond; *The Falcon Takes Over* (1942), sending him on a search for an old girlfriend and pitting him against a killer; and *The Falcon's Brother* (1942), pitting him and his brother Tom (Tom Conway, Sanders's real-life brother) against Nazis and ending with the death of the Falcon. (Sanders was tired of the part.) Conway continued to star as Tom Falcon in *The Falcon Strikes Back* (1943), *The Falcon in Danger* (1943), *The Falcon and the Co-Eds* (1943), *The Falcon Out West* (1944), *The Falcon in Mexico* (1944), *The Falcon in Hollywood* (1944), *The Falcon in San Francisco* (1945), *The Falcon's Alibi* (1946), and *The Falcon's Adventure* (1946). John Calvert took over the part in *The Devil's Cargo* (1948), *Appointment with Murder* (1948), and *Search for Danger* (1949). Though Calvert's character was called the Falcon, his real name was Michael Waring.

It was Michael Waring Falcon who appeared on radio and TV as well. He began his four-year radio run on Mutual in 1945, played, in succession, by James Meighan, Les Damon, Berry Kroeger, Les Tremayne, and George Petrie. On TV, Charles McGraw played the hero—now an American agent—in the half-hour series that was syndicated in 1955 and lasted a single season.

THE FATMAN (TV)

First Appearance: *Jake and the Fatman,* September 1987, CBS.

Biography: Jason Lochinvar "Fatman" McCabe is a one-time police officer who becomes the Los Angeles district attorney. The Fatman puts criminals in prison with the help of his private investigator Jake Styles, a flashy young man with expensive tastes who frequently goes undercover, as everything from a gunrunner to a dope dealer, to collect evidence. (He also, on occasion, proves that a person who has been accused of a crime isn't guilty, as when a private eye friend is accused of murder.) Fatman's other aides are Assistant D.A. Derek Mitchell and his secretary, Gertrude.

Growing tired of Southern California, he moves to Hawaii (1989) and goes to work as an investigator for the local prosecuting attorney. Jake and Derek go with him, and, within a few months, the Fatman has been named the new prosecuting attorney. There Lizabeth Berkeley-Smythe works as his secretary. His stint as the Honolulu prosecutor lasts just a year: The Fatman leaves when the mayor of Los Angeles asks him to return and look into reports of rampant corruption in the D.A.'s office. After completing the task, the Fatman takes over as D.A., with Derek once again as his assistant and Jake still doing his legwork.

Fatman's dearest friend is his pet bulldog Max, which he bought from the pound for $12.50.

Comment: The hour-long series ran five seasons and starred William Conrad as the Fatman, Joe Penny as Jake, Alan Campbell as Derek, Lu Leonard as Gertrude, and Olga Russell as Lizabeth.

The character is unrelated to the original Fatman. (See NICK AND NORA CHARLES.)

FEARLESS FOSDICK (CS, C, TV)

First Appearance: *Li'l Abner,* November 22, 1942, United Features Syndicate.

Biography: Dressed in black with a flat bowler on his head and a gold star over his heart, Fosdick is the hero and favorite comic strip character of hillbilly Li'l Abner. In his first adventure, Fosdick is lashed to explosives and left to die. Since the last part of the page has been torn away, Abner puts himself in the same situation to see how Fosdick might have escaped. He blows up. Later Abner learns that Fosdick was suffering from a nightmare and simply woke up.

In the character's second and subsequent adventures, he battles bizarre villains such as Stone-Face, Bomb-Face, Rattop, Sydney the Parrot, and (Julius) Anyface. ("Eek!" cries the woman. "That fire extinguisher is stealing my mink!" Fosdick replies, "That's *Anyface!* He gave himself away!! Why would a fire extinguisher want a mink?") Though Fosdick is frequently shot—indeed, at times perforated—he is never stopped by these "flesh wounds." (Though he does complain in one strip, "Could you close the window? There's a *draft* blowing through me.")

Fosdick's chief weapons are his nightstick and revolver; he's a crack shot, able to hit most targets even when he's looking elsewhere. When his gun is stolen—as in "The Case of the Poisoned Beans"—he falls back on the bow and arrow. Fosdick lives in a small New York apartment and reports to the hard-driving Chief. Though an avowed woman-hater, the square-jawed hero is engaged to red-headed Prudence Pimpleton. His preferred grooming product is Wildroot Cream-Oil.

Comment: The character was a parody of DICK TRACY and appeared in a strip-within-a-strip in Al Capp's *Li'l Abner.* Originally intended as a one-shot gimmick, Fosdick proved popular and returned in May 1943, then again in June 1944 and regularly thereafter. The strip was "drawn" by Lester Gooch.

Fosdick appeared in several issues of Abner's comic book from Harvey Publications, numbers 68 and 95 being full-length Fosdick issues.

He also starred in a short-lived puppet show that aired on NBC from June to September 1952.

Capp also sent up STEVE CANYON with his *Steve Cantor* strip by Milton Goniff (i.e., "Thief") in 1957. Tired of working for Capp (he's annoyed that he's "still as ragged an' iggorant as th' day he dreew mah fust breath!!") Cantor agrees to serve as a bodyguard for the colonel during his dangerous pursuit of the evil Jewel Brynner. ("The only bald girl spy in the Orient.") He quits after three weeks when he discovers that pork chops are difficult to come by in the Orient.

THE FIGHTIN' 5 (C)

First Appearance: *The Fightin' 5* #28, 1964, Charlton Comics.

Biography: Thanks to a fortune left to him by his grandfather, U.S. army special forces man Hank Hennessey is able to pull together and underwrite a band of superpatriots who work with the government to uncover enemy or gangland plots. The team dresses in blue uniforms with red berets and, in addition to Hennessey (FF4), consists of, Irv "the Nerve" Haganah (FF2), Granite Gallero (FF3), Frenchy the Fox (FF1), and Tom-Tom (FF5). When Hank loses his left eye and becomes a "desk soldier," he's replaced in the field by Sonya. The Fightin' 5 is headquartered in Hank's lavish

New York town house, which is equipped with "special labs, an armory containing every type of modern weapon," and other facilities. The team gets about on a yacht-size power boat capable of reaching 95 knots and in a mach-four jet equipped with air-to-air missiles, spy cameras, and an electronic shield. Each member carries a small radio with which he or she can contact headquarters.

Comment: The characters were created by editor Dick Giordano and writer Joe Gill. The first issue simply continued the numbering of the discontinued Charlton title *Space War.* It was discontinued with #41, after which the team appeared as a backup feature in all five issues of the comic book *The Peacemaker.* Eight *Fightin' 5* reprint issues were published from 1981 to 1982.

FIGHTING DEVIL DOGS (MP)

First Appearance: *Fighting Devil Dogs,* 1938, Republic Pictures.

The Fightin' 5. Art by Dick Giordano. © Charlton Comics.

Biography: In a tropical nation, U.S. Marine lieutenants Tom Grayson and Frank Corby are part of a force protecting the locals from rebels and outlaws. When a mysterious electrical bolt kills all the marines but Tom and Frank, they are assigned to find out who sent it and how. Aided by a group of scientists that includes Tom's father, Colonel Grayson, the heroes and their team of marines known as the Fighting Devil Dogs discover that a black-clad scientist known as the Lightning is behind the "artifical thunderbolt": Soaring through the skies in his fantastic plane, the *Wing,* he is able to fire lightning at any target. One of his next attacks is against several scientists, killing the senior Grayson. Eventually Tom and the Devil Dogs track the Lightning to his lair, discover that he is Warfield, a member of their scientific team, and blast the *Wing* from the skies using a ray created by science team member Crenshaw.

Comment: Lee Powell starred as Grayson, with Herman Brix as Corby and Sam Flint as Colonel Grayson. Hugh Sothern was Warfield. The 12-chapter serial was directed by William Witney, John English, and Robert Beche. In 1966 the serial was edited into the feature film *The Torpedo of Doom.*

FINIEOUS FINGERS (CS)

First Appearance: *Finieous Fingers and Friends,* October 3, 1976, *Dragon* magazine #3.

Biography: A thief in a Middle Ages where magic is real, Finieous works for the Guild-Master and is determined to become a Master Thief. Despite his chosen profession, he is "kind, soft-hearted, and concerned about doing things for the benefit of everyone." The long-haired, dagger-carrying adventurer is courageous but accident prone; though he can climb sheer walls, chances are good the wall will fall with him on it. If he battles a dragon and asks someone for a hand, the odds are good he'll be given a severed hand.

His companions are the warriors Fred and Charly; the adventurers occasionally cross paths with Eric the Paladin, one of the greatest (and dumbest) fighting men of all time. Though he has a wife and twins at home, Finieous is never with them.

Comment: The full-page, very humorous strip was created by J.D. Webster and appears monthly; it went to color in *Dragon* #12. Collected adventures appeared in *The Finieous Treasury,* published by TSR Hobbies, Inc., in 1981.

FIREHAIR (C)

First Appearance: *Showcase* #85, 1969, DC Comics.

Joe Kubert's *Firehair.* © DC Comics.

Biography: Circa 1815, only a red-headed infant survives a Blackfeet Indian attack on a wagon train in the Great Western Plains. Chief Grey Cloud prevents the savage Little Crow from slaying the boy and takes him to raise as his own. In a foredoomed effort to overcome prejudice within the tribe, young Firehair must "do more than his contemporaries . . . outwrestle, outrun, and outshoot [with a bow and arrow] any of the boys his own age." As a young man, he ventures into his first "white" town and is nearly strung up; spurned or hated by people of all races, the buckskin-clad adventurer leaves the tribe and his girlfriend Evening Star, learns English at a settlement, and sets out to "find a place for myself where I will not be shunned by Indian and white alike." Though he ventures west and has adventures in and around the Grand Canyon, he never finds the peace he seeks.

Comment: The character starred in three issues of *Showcase,* all of which were superbly drawn by Joe Kubert. An earlier, much sillier Firehair starred in 11 issues of Fiction House's *Firehair Comics* from 1948 to 1952. This one was a red-haired heroine in a green dress, the "White Queen of the Redskin Range," the "Warrior-Maid of the Wild Dakotas," who was adopted by the Sioux and was equally adept at slaying enemies of her people with a bow or blazing six-guns, or killing a bear with a knife or a wolf with a tomahawk.

FLASH GORDON (CS, R, L, MP, C, TV)

First Appearance: *Flash Gordon,* January 7, 1934, King Features Syndicate.

Biography: A new planet is on a collision course with Earth, but Dr. Hans Zarkov has a plot to avert catastrophe. Meanwhile, an eastbound transcontinental airplane is knocked from the sky by a chunk of the approaching planet. The two passengers—lovely Dale Arden and handsome, blond Flash Gordon, "Yale graduate and world renowned polo player"—parachute to safety, land near Zarkov's laboratory, and are ushered into his rocketship at gunpoint when Zarkov assumes they are spies. They crash-land on the approaching world, Mongo, and are taken prisoner by the minions of Ming the Merciless, the self-proclaimed Emperor of the Universe, whose people "possess none of the human traits of kindness, mercy or pity." Flash escapes and, with the help of Prince Thun of the Lion Men, Prince Barin of Arboria, and King Vultan of the Hawkmen, saves the earth and wages ongoing war against Ming. Except for the occasional superscientific device, such as an acetylene ray, Flash typically uses his fists, swords, lances, and so on, to fight enemies. (Indeed, though set in space, the strip is closer in look and feel to PRINCE VALIANT than to BUCK ROGERS, whose success it was trying to match.)

Following Ming's defeat (1941), Flash, Dale, and Zarkov return to Earth only to go back to Mongo to fight the new despot, Brazor. Eventually Flash, Dale, and Zarkov become agents of World Space Control, intergalactic law officers. Onboard a starcruiser that is now capable of traveling through subspace, they battle the Aphrods of the Death Planet, return to Mongo to fight Queen Undina of Mongo's Water World, find themselves in the Trojan War due to a malfunctioning Time-Hopper, and more. With computers, laser beams, and supersleek hardware, the strip becomes just another space opera. Flash is also a member of the *Defenders of the Earth.*

Comment: The character was created by artist Alex Raymond, who wrote the early adventures until Don Moore was hired late in 1934. Raymond drew the gorgeous Sunday pages while his assistant, Austin Briggs, handled the art on the daily strip. When Raymond left the Sunday page in 1944, Briggs took it until 1948; he was followed by Mac Raboy, who stayed until 1967, followed by Dan Barry. The daily strip was canceled in 1944 but revived in 1951 during the nuclear age science fiction renaissance, handled by Barry and a succession of artists.

When the original story was retold in the strip in 1975, new details were added: Zarkov's observatory was in the Rocky Mountains; Flash was also a quarterback, fencing champion, and gymnast; and the runaway Mongo was first spotted by Professor Decachek; and Flash was airborne to skydive for charity, accompanied by journalist Arden.

Mutual's *Flash Gordon* radio series debuted in 1935, starring Gale Gordon as Flash, followed by James Meighan. The series lasted into the middle 1940s.

The first Flash novel was *Flash Gordon in the Caverns of Mongo,* published in 1936 and credited to Raymond. Fourteen Big Little Book adventures were published between 1935 and 1948. New Flash Gordon novels were written by Con Steffanson or Carson Bingham and published by Avon: *The Lion Men of Mongo, The Plague of Sound, The Space Circus, The Time Trap of Ming XIII, The Witch Queen of Mongo,* all in 1974, and *The War of the Cybernauts* (1975).

Others were issued by Tempo Books beginning in 1980, to tie in with the big-budget film; the titles, which do not have author credit, are *Massacre in the 22nd Century, War of the Citadels, Crisis on Citadel II,* and *Forces from the Federation.*

In movies, Buster Crabbe played Flash, Charles Middleton was Ming, and Frank Shannon was Zarkov in three serials: the 13-chapter *Flash Gordon* (1936), directed by Frederick Stephani with Jean Rogers as Dale; the 15-chapter *Flash Gordon's Trip to Mars* (1938), directed by Ford Beebe and Robert Hill, again with Rogers; and the 12-chapter *Flash Gordon Conquers the Universe* (1940), directed by Beebe and Ray Taylor, with Carol Hughes as Dale. These were later edited into the respective feature films *Rocket Ship* (a.k.a. *Spaceship to the Unknown, Space Soldiers,* and

Sam J. Jones and Melody Anderson's plane loses altitude in the 1980 film *Flash Gordon.* © King Features Syndicate.

Atomic Rocketship), *Mars Attacks the World* (a.k.a. *Deadly Ray from Mars*), and *Purple Death From Outer Space* (a.k.a. *Peril from the Planet Mongo* and *Space Soldiers Conquer the Universe*). When George Lucas was unable to obtain the rights to the characters, he made *Star Wars* instead (1977). King Features played catch-up by licensing the rights to Dino DeLaurentiis, who made *Flash Gordon* (1980) starring Sam J. Jones as Flash, Melody Anderson as Dale, Max von Sydow as Ming, and Topol as Zarkov. The film, directed by Mike Hodges, has Flash as a quarterback for the New York Jets and Dale as a reporter. The film was a flop, though it has found an audience on video and television.

Flash has had numerous comic book incarnations, with runs from Dell (eight issues from 1943 to 1953), Harvey (four issues from 1950 to 1951), Gold Key (one issue, 1967), and a longer run that lasted 37 issues and was spread over three publishers: King, Charlton, and Gold Key/Whitman from 1966 to 1982. DC failed to click with their heavily promoted *Flash Gordon* title, which lasted nine issues from 1988 to 1989. The character has also been the hero of numerous video games.

On TV, Flash was played with success by Steve Holland in the syndicated, half-hour 1953 series. Irene Champlin was Dale and Joe Nash was Dr. Alexis Zarkov. The 39 episodes were shot in Germany. In 1979 Filmation produced 16 half-hour cartoons featuring Bob Ridgely as Flash; the series aired on NBC until 1980.

Flash's most recent incarnation has been as the member of a team known as *The Defenders of the Earth,* which was King Features' attempt to get some mileage out of its heroes The Phantom, Mandrake the Magician, and Flash. In the year 2015, the heroes are brought together to battle Ming in 65 animated adventures that were syndicated on TV in 1985. The series introduced Jedda, the telekinetic 17-year-old daughter of Flash and the Empress of Cerebra. Marvel published five issues of their *Defenders of the Earth* title in 1987.

If Flash is only a nickname, the character's "real" first name has never been given.

FLASHGUN JACK CASEY (L, MP, R, TV)

First Appearance: "Return Engagement" by George Harmon Coxe, March 1934, *Black Mask* magazine.

Biography: A sergeant with the Allied Expeditionary Forces in France during World War I, by World War II Jack is too old (around 35)—and suffers from a bad knee—to serve. This frustrates him enormously, and he takes out his anger on criminals—whom he was already predisposed to hate. Despite the knee problem and his hard-drinking ways, the six-foot one-inch Casey is trim and muscular, and gets plenty of scoops for his paper, the *Boston Globe*; frequently he gets the photo *and* the criminal who perpetrated the crime. Despite the fact that he's the highest-paid photographer in town, he thinks nothing about quitting and joining the *Express* when one of his photographs is censored.

Casey is a bachelor who lives in a Marlborough Street brownstone. His assistant is Tom Wade, who worships him; his editor, McGrath, and his police department enemies—Lieutenant Logan and Sergeant Manahan—don't much care for him.

Comment: In addition to the dozens of short stories, there are six Casey books (some of which were serialized in *Black Mask*): *Silent Are the Dead* (1942), *Murder for Two* (1943), *Flash-Casey, Detective* (a short story collection, 1946), *Error of Judgment* (1961), and *Deadly Image* (1964).

There were also a pair of films: *Women Are Trouble* (1936) starring Stuart Erwin, in which his editor is kidnaped; and *Here's Flash Casey* (1937) starring Eric Linden, in which he's the assistant to the paper's chief photographer and inadvertently becomes involved with blackmailers.

The character is perhaps best known, however, because of his radio and TV series, *Casey, Crime Photographer,* which debuted on CBS in 1946 and ran until 1955. The setting is now New York and, working for the *Morning Express,* Casey spends most of his time at the Blue Note Cafe, where he listens to jazz and chats with bartender Ethelbert while waiting for news or clues. His girlfriend is fellow reporter Ann Williams, and his frequent nemesis/ally is Captain Logan of the NYPD. The series starred Staats Cotsworth as Casey and a succession of actresses as Ann, including Betty Furness. John Gibson was Ethelbert, and Jackson Beck, then Bernard Lenrow, was Logan. Art Carney was a supporting character on the show.

Casey came to TV from April 1951 to June 1952 in a half-hour series called *Crime Photographer.* Richard Carlyle was Casey for two months, after which Darren McGavin took over. Jan Miner (the fifth and last radio Ann) played Ann; John Gibson, then Cliff Hall, was Ethelbert; and Donald McClelland was Logan. The series added cub reporter Jack Lipman to the team, played by Archie Smith.

Creator Coxe also chronicled the popular adventures of more refined and educated (and patient) Boston photographer Kent Murdock of the *Boston Courier-Herald.*

FLASHMAN (L, MP)

First Appearance: *Tom Brown's Schooldays* by Thomas Hughes, 1857, Macmillan (see COMMENT).

Biography: In the 1830s, Tom Brown, the son of a country squire, goes to Rugby for his education. There he and his friend Harry "Scud" East are tormented by a bully named Harry Flashman, who insists that younger boys work for him; those who refuse are punished. (Tom is nearly cooked in a fire.) Ultimately Tom and East turn on their tormentor and beat him up; not only does he never lay "a finger on either of them again," but the 17-year-old is expelled from Rugby in 1839 for drunkenness. An inauspicious beginning for a future hero!

In 1965, in a Leicestershire saleroom, Mr. Paget Morrison obtains oilskin packets containing the "Flashman papers," accounts of the man's adventures after 1839. He doles them out to author George MacDonald Fraser, who recounts Flashman's life in a series of novels. After joining the military, the former bully quickly rises to the rank of lieutenant as he fights in the first Afghan War of 1842, coming away with a devoted wife named Elspeth (whom he later rescues from savages in Borneo). Later exploits place him in the middle of the Crimean War in the middle 1850s, involve him in the China War of 1860, embroil him in the Sioux wars of 1876 (where he meets Custer, Wild Bill Hickok, and other historical figures), and even team him with SHERLOCK HOLMES in 1894. Through it all, Sir Harry remains "immoral and unscrupulous," better at "taking cover and squealing for mercy" than riding into battle . . . but always coming through in a pinch and ending up on the winning side.

Comment: Although Flashman first appeared in the Hughes novel, his reemergence as a hero came in the Fraser novels, which began appearing in 1969. The titles jump about chronologically; in order of issue, they are *Flashman, Royal Flash, Flash for Freedom!, Flash at the Charge, Flashman in the Great Game, Flashman's Lady, Flashman and the Redskins, Flashman and the Dragon,* and *Flashman and the Mountain of Light.*

In 1975 Malcolm McDowell starred in director Richard Lester's film *Royal Flash,* in which the hero must impersonate a Prussian nobleman. Fraser wrote the script.

FLETCH (L, MP)

First Appearance: *Fletch* by Gregory McDonald, 1974, Avon Books.

Biography: Los Angeles-based Irwin Maurice Fletcher is an undercover reporter for the *News-Tri-bune;* utterly lacking respect for authority, he constantly ticks off editor-in-chief Frank Jaffe as well as his coworkers, including cooking writer Clara Snow, society editor Amelia Shurcliffe, and religion editor Clifton Wolf. Despite his annoying sarcasm, Fletch is a crackerjack reporter who is equally at home investigating drug dealers, millionaires, murderers, and even the real reasons why his father, Walter, abandoned him and his mother, Josie, when Fletch was born.

In time, Fletch goes to work for Global Cable News, bums around, takes a job as a press secretary for presidential candidate Governor Caxton Wheeler, then visits Brazil where he becomes involved in an attempted murder—his.

When he isn't wearing some sort of disguise, Fletch's preferred attire—even in the office—is faded jeans and a T-shirt, with no shoes. The pot-smoking journalist drives an MG and, for most of his chronicled career, lives on the seventh floor of a building that has "everything but design."

Fletch is in his "mid-twenties," twice divorced, and way behind on his alimony to ex-wives Barbara Ralton and Linda Haines. Though they left him because of his infidelity (he would sleep with five or six different women a week)—and, in Linda's case, because he threw her cat out the seventh-floor window—both women still love him.

Comment: The other novels in the series are *Confess, Fletch* (1976), *Fletch's Fortune* (1978), *Fletch and the Widow Bradley* (1981), *Fletch's Moxie* (1982), *Fletch and the Man Who* (1983), *Carioca Fletch* (1984), *Fletch Won* (1985; chronologically, the first novel), and *Fletch, Too* (1986).

Chevy Chase played the detective in a pair of motion pictures: *Fletch* (1985) and *Fletch Lives* (1989).

McDonald introduced Boston Police Detective Francis Xavier Flynn in *Confess, Fletch,* and spun him off in a series of novels: *Flynn* (1977), *The Buck Passes Flynn* (1981), and *Flynn's In* (1984). Unlike the irreverent, itinerant Fletch, Flynn is a devoted family man fond of tweeds.

FLEXOR (T)

First Appearance: Flex-a-Tron, 1986, S&T Sales.

Biography: The heir apparent to the throne of the planet Flexidia, Flexor has been living in exile ever since the evil viceroy Varyk slew his father, the king. Despite the fact that Varyk is aided by a trio of powerful warriors, Vipen, Devilor, and Herr Bone, the brave Flexor is determined to claim his birthright. To do this, he must buy an army, which means reaching the vault to the Princess Treasure of Flexidia: Only he knows the code, which was given to him by his father. Helping Flexor in his efforts is his bold friend Zorn.

Comment: The line of fully posable action figures achieved only moderate success.

FLINT BAKER (C)

First Appearance: *Planet Comics* #1, 1940, Fiction House.

Biography: A space pioneer with his own ship at some unspecified time in the future, Flint Baker is regularly accompanied by his reporter friend Mimi. In the first adventure, they enter unexplored space by passing Pluto and, traveling at "ten miles per second," swiftly reach another star, where they battle the militaristic denizens of the planet Grango. The hero always becomes embroiled in alien conflicts (witness such titles as "Slave Planet," "Space War," "Renegade Queen of Mars," and "Revolt of the Robots"). Not surprisingly, it isn't long before Flint is being referred to not just as a "space scout" but as a "space soldier."

Comment: The character appeared regularly in *Planet Comics* through its 73-issue run. Many other space heroes were introduced in the comic's pages, including the Tarzan-like Auro, Lord of Jupiter; Fero, Planet Detective ("The one man who can thwart the evil doings of vampires and werewolves, that have invaded the Earth from Pluto"); Space Admiral Curry ("Admiral," says the Universal president when heat is being siphoned from the sun, "you are placed in full

Flint Baker gets an ultimatum from the evil Gargonians in his first chronicled adventure. © Caplin-Iger Co. Ltd.

charge of the universe during this emergency." To which the humble Curry replies, "Thank you, sir!"); Lieutenant Buzz Crandall of the Space Patrol who, with his sidekick Sandra Curan, explores "strange new worlds"; Spurt Hammond, "American pilot of an interplanetary transport rocket"; Captain Nelson Cole of the Solar Force"; Gale Allen of the Girls' Space Patrol; Planet Payson; Crash Parker; Reef Ryan—Explorer; Hunt Bowman of the Lost World; Star Pirate, Robin Hood of the Spaceways; Mysta of the Moon, a space heroine; and others.

Interestingly, though many of these characters appeared in the same issue, no attempt was made to integrate the story lines or have one future agree with another.

THE FLYIN' FOOL (C)

First Appearance: *Joe Palooka* #7, 1946, Harvey Publications.

Biography: After being wrongly court-martialed and discharged from the marines, red-headed, lighthearted pilot Lieutenant Chickie Ricks and his friend and mechanic Sergeant Gooch decide to become charter pilots, and land a job flying "seeds" from T'sao San, near Tibet. Unaware that they're really transporting opium, the duo is forced down by Chinese revolutionaries led by the dashing Maylene. Convinced that the pair has been duped, Maylene allows them to continue on their journey, with her soldiers onboard instead of drugs. After the drug dealers are dispatched, the trio have other adventures together. Chickie is eventually cleared of the false charges, and he returns to the United States for a handful of adventures at home.

Comment: The character appeared in *Joe Palooka* through issue #25. It's unrelated to the *Airboy Comics* adventures of Link Thorne, the Flying Fool, who, with the help of his secretary Wing-Ding, ran an air charter service in and around Shanghai, competing with ruthless Riot O'Hara and his airline.

FRANK CANNON (TV)

First Appearance: *Cannon,* March 1971, CBS.

Biography: On the heavy side thanks to his love of food, former police officer, now detective Cannon lets his Lincoln Continental handle the action as he chases kidnapers, extortionists, killers, and others through the streets of Los Angeles. His fee is equally "heavy," though Cannon has been known to take cases for little or no remuneration when the cause is just.

In his first and most famous adventure, Cannon is hired by Diana Langston, an old girlfriend, to find out

Frank Cannon on the job. © CBS.

who killed her husband. In the process, he becomes caught in a web of small-town corruption.

Comment: The original TV movie spawned an hour-long series that aired from September 1971 through September 1976 and starred William Conrad as Cannon. There were no other regulars.

FRANK MERRIWELL   (L, MP, CS, R, C)

First Appearance: *Frank Merriwell,* by Burt L. Standish, 1896, *Tip Top Weekly.*

Biography: When we first meet orphan Frank Merriwell, he's wearing knee pants and a cap and taking care of a ruffian—just what you'd expect from a teetotaling, nonsmoking, baseball, football, and basketball star at Fardale, a top prep and military school. Graduating from Fardale, he goes to Yale, where he equals his earlier successes in sports (even when he's kidnaped to keep him out of the big game) until his guardian mismanages his money. Frank goes broke, drops out of school, and goes to work for a railroad.

He manages to earn his fortune back and, with his brother Dick—an electrical engineer—he founds the Merriwell Company, which has extensive mining and ranching interests.

During the course of his professional career, Frank—who speaks fluent Spanish—travels the world, where he overcomes bandits, wild animals (holding off a big, mad dog with a pocket knife), dictators, forces of nature (tidal waves, avalanches, quicksand), and the like. Frank and Dick bring many of these dangers upon themselves; as the magazine itself once explained it, "They are both clean-cut, vigorous fellows who dare to do right no matter what the consequences."

Ultimately, Frank marries his longtime girlfriend, Inza Burrage, and they have a son, Frank Jr., and a daughter.

Comment: Over 1,000 Merriwell stories were published in *Tip Top Weekly* (later, *New Tip Top Weekly, Tip Top Semi-Monthly,* and *Wide Awake Magazine;* Junior debuted in *Sports Story Magazine* in 1927 and remained there a year before moving on to *Fame and Fortune Magazine* (to 1929) and *Top Notch* (to 1930). Both appeared in numerous novels, the sagas of Frank Jr. continuing into the early 1940s, albeit with decreasing popularity. An effort to spark new interest in the series by featuring Frank Jr.'s sister in the novel *Mister Frank Merriwell* (1941) failed.

Senior was the star of a 12-chapter serial, *The Adventures of Frank Merriwell* (1936), starring Don Briggs. Set during his Fardale days, it involves Frank and girlfriend Elsie Belwood (Jean Rogers) in an adventure involving a deserted mine and $30,000 in gold nuggets. Cliff Smith directed the Universal film. There were no others; the character's time had passed, as evidenced by a short-lived comic strip, a single Big Little Book, *Frank Merriwell at Yale* (1935), and the quick failure of a radio series that debuted on NBC in 1946 and promised to return listeners to "an exciting past . . . a romantic past. The era of the horse and carriage . . . and free-for-all football games."

Charlton Comics failed to revive the character with its four-issue run of *Frank Merriwell at Yale* from 1955 to 1956.

FRIDAY FOSTER   (CS, MP)

First Appearance: "Friday Foster," January 18, 1970, New York News-Chicago Tribune Syndicate.

Biography: Friday Foster is a cool, professional, somewhat naive, beautiful, ghetto-raised young black woman who comes to New York to make her mark on photojournalism. Working as a freelancer for newspapers and photo agencies, she travels the world getting embroiled in dangerous political, racial, and criminal situations. When she's not snapping her photos, she's usually fending off the advances of each "good-looking soul brother" who assumes she can't live without him.

Comment: The strip was created by writer Jim Lawrence and artist Jorge Longaron; in 1974, shortly before the strip expired, artist Gray Morrow replaced Longaron. It was the first comic strip to star a black woman as an adventure hero.

Pam Grier played the heroine in the 1975 theatrical film, trying to undermine a scheme to assassinate black politicians.

G

THE GALAXY RANGERS (TV)

First Appearance: *The Adventures of the Galaxy Rangers,* September 15, 1986, syndicated.

Biography: In the year 2086, alien emissaries Waldo Zeptic of Andor and Zozo of Kirin come to Earth and ask the World Federation for help in battling the space outlaws that have been preying on their worlds. The Federation agrees to help and forms BETA, the Bureau of Extra-Terrestrial Affairs, which, in turn, assembles the Galaxy Rangers, comprised of heroic Zachary Fox, Doc Hartford, Niko, and Goose.

Comment: Sixty-three half-hour adventures were produced in all, at a time when westerns were expected to make a comeback; the combination of horse and space opera failed to click with viewers. Jerry Orbach provided the voice of Zachary Fox, Hubert Kelly was Doc Hartford, Laura Dean was Niko, and Doug Preis was Goose.

One year later Filmation tried to come up with a western/science fiction combination that would work better than *The Galaxy Rangers.* They produced 55 half-hour episodes of *Bravestarr,* a syndicated series about a lawman on the planet New Texas. It, too, failed to catch on, as did the feature-length film released in 1988, *Bravestarr, The Movie,* in which he battles recurring foe Tex-Hex. In 1987 World Events Productions also got into the western/science fiction act, producing 50 episodes of *Saber Rider and the Star Sheriffs* for syndication, the saga of space cowboys who defend the galactic frontier against the evil Outriders.

GEORGE OF THE JUNGLE (TV, C)

First Appearance: *George of the Jungle,* September 1967, ABC.

Biography: Nothing is known about the origin of this sort-of great jungle hero who lives in the Umbweebwee Valley of Africa. Though he's dumb as a rock and barely articulate, George is incredibly strong—and lucky—and manages to defeat foes that range from evil developers and hunters, to unruly natives. The loin-clothed muscleman has a nasty habit of colliding with a tree every time he goes swinging on a handy vine. George lives in a treehouse with his mates Stella and Ursula, whom he is never able to tell apart. Also inhabiting the house are the intelligent gorilla Ape, who speaks like Ronald Colman, and the elephant Shep—whom George thinks is simply a "big, gray, peanut-loving doggie." George receives information from distant regions of the jungle thanks to the Tuki-Tuki bird, who never says anything other than "Ah-ah, ee-ee, tuki-tuki."

Comment: Only 16 shows were produced, each of which had one seven-minute George of the Jungle cartoon, another of the fowl superhero Super Chicken, and a third featuring the race car driver Tom Slick. The cartoons were created by Jay Ward Productions, the studio responsible for Rocky and Bullwinkle, and were way too sophisticated for their Saturday morning slot. The show departed in September 1970.

Bill Scott provided the voice of George, June Foray was Stella and Ursula, and Paul Frees was Ape.

George also starred in two issues of a Gold Key comic book published in 1968–69.

GEORGE SMILEY (L, MP, TV)

First Appearance: *Call for the Dead* by John le Carre, 1962, Alfred A. Knopf.

Biography: George Smiley, the former Oxford scholar (German poetry) graces the halls of academia only when he isn't doing something for the country he loves—working as a lethal operative for British Intelligence. His duties are varied, ranging from fieldwork to vetting new recruits. He reports to a chief known as Control; when Control launches "a private war against the Czechs," he is replaced by Percy Alleline. Smiley briefly retires from the "Circus," drawing a pension and selling off rare books in his collection, but returns to find a mole.

Smiley is "short, podgy *(sic),* and . . . middle-aged"; his legs are "short, his gait anything but agile, his dress costly, ill-fitting." His ordinary appearance, of course, is among his greatest weapons.

His adventures involve finding out who really killed a British government official whom everyone else believes committed suicide *(Call for the Dead)*, investigating the death of a schoolteacher's wife in the snooty Carne School *(A Murder of Quality)*, sniffing out a mole in British Intelligence *(Tinker, Tailor, Soldier, Spy)* and rebuilding the shattered institution *(The Honorable Schoolboy)*, and battling his longtime enemy, Karla of Moscow Centre *(Smiley's People)*, who eluded him in the previous tale.

Smiley is married to the beautiful Lady Ann Sercomb, who leaves him for other men from time to time. They have no children.

Comment: Le Carre's other Smiley novels were published in 1962, 1974, 1977, and 1980. Le Carre is a pseudonym for David John Moore Cornwall.

In motion pictures, James Mason starred in *The Deadly Affair* (1967), based on *Call for the Dead*, in which Smiley is called Charles Dobbs. The story is otherwise faithful to the novel.

On TV, Alec Guinness played Smiley in the PBS series *Tinker, Tailor, Soldier, Spy* (1981) and returned in the sequel *Smiley's People.*

G-FORCE   (TV, C)

First Appearance: *Gatchaman*, 1972, Tasunko Productions.

Biography: At some unspecified time in the future, the evil Zoltar of the planet Spectra turns his megalomaniacal eye on the Milky Way. All that stands in his way is the G-Force, a team comprised of earthbound leader Mark Venture and spacefaring warriors Jason (whose utility belt contains all sorts of handy gadgets), Tiny (a big man who wears an owllike uniform), Princess, and Keyop. The heroes patrol the galaxy onboard their ship the *Phoenix,* while Mark remains at the team's home base, Center Neptune, an underwater facility whose main ingress and egress are Decoy Island. The team is regularly assisted by the computerized robot 7-Zark-7.

Comment: The Japanese *Gatchaman* series came to the U.S. in October 1978 and was syndicated as *Battle of the Planets;* there were 80 half-hour adventures in all. Casey Kasem provided the voice for Mark Venture, Ronnie Schell was Jason, Alan Young was Keyop and 7-Zark-7, Keye Luke portrayed Zoltar, Janet Waldo was Princess, and Alan Dinehart spoke for Tiny. Gold Key/Whitman published ten issues of a *Battle of the Planets* comic book from 1979 to 1980.

GHITA OF ALIZARR   (C)

First Appearance: *1984* #7, 1979, Warren Publishing.

Biography: Ten thousand years before the birth of Jesus, Alizarr is the capital of the Khalian empire and the sacred city of the goddess Tammuz. Born in the streets, the bisexual blonde Ghita is a pickpocket and whore who becomes the woman of King Runthar of Urd, after which she becomes a favorite of King Khalia—even though she herself prefers the company of the court wizard Thenef, a charlatan and her childhood friend and co-pickpocket. Peace and prosperity reign until the Troll hordes attack from Nergal; King Khalia perishes, Alizarr falls, and, armed with the sword of the legendary warrior Khan-Dagon—which she refers to as "the great penis of annihilation"—Ghita leaves the palace, taking along Thenef and the devoted half troll Dahib. After becoming a fierce warrior, she finds and beheads the Troll leader Nergon and liberates Alizarr, ruling as part of a triumvirate that includes Thenef and Dahib. But she tires of the quiet life and sets out to restore Runthar to his throne, which has been seized by the four-armed sorcerer Rahmuz. She succeeds in killing Rahmuz by severing his arms.

Comment: Ghita was written and drawn by longtime comic book artist Frank Thorne. While drawing Marvel's *Red Sonja* comic book, Thorne had "felt there were a lot of unexplored possibilities" in the areas of characterization and eroticism, and the delightful *Ghita* was the result. Laced with humor, sex, and bloodshed—as well as Thorne's splendid art and writing—*Ghita* ran in all but five issues of *1984,* lasting until #29. (The magazine became *1994* with #11.) Two Ghita collections were published in trade paperback by Catalan Communications.

GILGAMESH   (F)

First Appearance: Babylonian folklore, circa 2000 B.C.

Biography: A great warrior and the ruler of Erech, a kingdom in southern Babylonia, Gilgamesh was created by the goddess Aruru. He becomes so intent on building a wall around Erech that his exhausted people beseech Aruru, "Shape now a rival to oppose him, so that the men of Erech may have rest"; even his queen, Ninsun, thinks he's too severe. Aruru makes Enkidu, a shaggy giant, from clay, and their battle is so violent that it shakes the buildings of the realm. Though Gilgamesh is victorious, he develops a deep respect for Enkidu and the two become dear friends.

Determined to slay the monster Humbaba, Gilgamesh next sets out with Enkidu. The latter is

THE WOMAN'S MIND BECOMES A BLAZING THEATER OF *NIGHTMARES* AS GHITA AND HER COMRADES ARE *REUNITED* IN *BATTLE* AGAINST A SQUEALING HORDE OF *DEVIL IMPS!*

Ghita lays into her foes, with Dahib to the left and Thenef to the right. © Frank Thorne.

severely wounded, and only the help of the sun-god Shamash allows them to prevail. Meanwhile Ishtar, the queen of the gods, falls in love with Gilgamesh and asks to become his queen; when he spurns her, she has Anu, king of the gods, send a mighty bull against him. Five hundred warriors die before Gilgamesh and Enkidu slay it. But Enkidu takes ill and dies shortly thereafter (most probably at the whim of the goddess of love and war, Ishtar), and Gilgamesh undertakes a dangerous and arduous journey to the mountain at earth's end, to ask his ancestor Utnapishtim if there is a way to conquer death. After much soul-searching, Utnapishtim reveals, "At the bottom of the underworld sea is a briar-plant. If you pluck it, it will pierce your hand, but hesitate not. It is the plant of life."

Binding stones to his feet, Gilgamesh journeys to the bottom of the sea and obtains the plant. However, not far from Erech, Gilgamesh stops to bathe and sets the plant aside; a serpent eats it (and, hence, can shed old skin for new), leaving Gilgamesh in despair. After brooding for some time, the king goes to Arallu, the underworld, to try to rescue Enkidu. But the powers of Allatu, the god of the dead, are too strong, and Gilgamesh barely makes it back to the surface with his life. Humbling himself before the earth god Enlil, the moon god Sin, and the water god Ea, he is permitted a visit from Enkidu's ghost. The two embrace, after which Gilgamesh asks his old friend a single question: Do human actions in life affect their status in death? Yes, says Enkidu, the brave are treated with the greatest honor. Satisfied that his friend is comfortable and that a glorious afterlife awaits him as well, Gilgamesh bids Enkidu a final farewell.

Comment: There was a real King Gilgamesh of Erech, though nothing is known of his historical feats. The earliest account of the fictional hero is on 12 tablets that were found in the ruins of Nineveh, from the library of Assurbanipal.

GORDON FIFE (CS)

First Appearance: *Gordon Fife and the Boy King,* October 1935, *The Brooklyn Eagle.*

Biography: An American soldier-of-fortune, Gordon Fife finds himself in Kovnia, in Central Europe, where he and his sidekick Ali, a Hindu, become the protectors of the young King Nicholas and his sister, Princess Caroline (who, to no one's surprise, becomes Gordon's girlfriend). His adversaries are the ruthless Prince Karl of Livonia, who covets Novinia, and a criminal group called the Markala, both of which are constantly launching ingenious coup and assassination attempts.

Comment: The strip was created by writer Bob Moore and artist John Hales. After 14 months, Carl Pfeufer took over the art chores. Renamed *Gordon Soldier of Fortune* after several months, the strip lasted until July 1941.

GRIMJACK (C)

First Appearance: *Starslayer* #10, 1983, Pacific Comics.

Biography: John Gaunt owns Munden's, a small bar in the pan-dimensional city of Cynosure, where the multiverse meets and reality is "relative to where you're standing; it can change sometimes from block to block." But owning Munden's is only his pleasure. His real job is to sally forth as a soldier-of-fortune named Grimjack who, for 500 creds a day, will "bust people out of prison, hunt down vampires, fight alien gods—all the *fun* jobs people are too *squeamish* or too *polite* to do." His long, black hair streaked with white, he wears a blue beret and cloak, a red bandana, and carries a sword and several pistols. Grimjack has a strong moral code and won't take advantage of a foe.

Comment: The character was created by writer John Ostrander and artist Timothy Truman. Grimjack remained a backup feature in *Starslayer* through #17, though he met the main character in the next issue; First Comics gave the mercenary his own title in 1984 and it lasted 80 issues—a remarkable run for an "independent" company.

GRIZZLY ADAMS (MP, TV, L)

First Appearance: *The Life and Times of Grizzly Adams,* 1976.

Biography: In the late 1800s, city dweller James Adams is accused of a crime he did not commit. Fleeing to the mountains of the Northwest, he builds a shack and becomes an early environmentalist, fishing but never hunting, and wearing clothes made of cloth,

Timothy Truman's definitive portrait of *Grimjack.* © First Comics.

not leather. He also rescues a bear cub from a ledge; the animal, whom he calls Ben, grows up to become his staunch ally. Adams is befriended by another wilderness man, Mad Jack, and by the Indian Nakuma, both of whom call him "Grizzly" because of his imposing figure and full beard.

Grizzly is an altruistic man who not only helps animals, wounded or motherless, but also the lost or ill who pass through his domain.

Comment: Former animal trainer Dan Haggerty starred in the film and in the hour-long TV series, which aired on NBC from February 1977 to July 1978. Denver Pyle played Jack (who narrated Adams's adventures) and Don Shanks was Nakuma. Ben was played by a female bear named Bozo. An ongoing series of young adult novels by Thomas L. Tedrow features Grizzly and his nephew from Boston, Kodiak Jack.

The real-life Grizzly Adams was born in 1812 and

became a mountain man after going bankrupt. He was not, however, a hero, having left his wife and children so he could prowl the Sierra Nevadas. He eventually opened a zoo and toured with P.T. Barnum.

GUNGA DIN (L, MP)

First Appearance: "Gunga Din" by Rudyard Kipling, 1892.

Biography: A "regimental *bhisti*" (water carrier) for a British Indian regiment in the time of Queen Victoria, Gunga Din carries a goatskin bag and wears a "twisty rag" of a uniform. He stays close to the regiment during battle and bandages the wounded, even if bullets are "kickin' dust-spots" around him. If the man run low on bullets, he will fetch the ammunition mules.

When the narrator is wounded, Din rushes to his side, "plugs" him up, and drags him to safety—just before a bullet cuts Din down. The narrator survives, observing that, despite the water carrier's low social status, "You're a better man than I am, Gunga Din!"

Comment: "Gunga Din" was published in *Barrack-Room Ballads,* a collection of poems celebrating British soldiers in the far-flung empire. Despite its imperialist subject matter, Kipling wrote the poem to honor the *bhisti,* the natives who worked with the British soldiers.

The film versions of "Gunga Din" have been based in part on the poem and in part on Kipling's tale *Soldiers Three* (1890), about the adventures of soldiers Learoyd, Mulvaney, and Ortheris. In the 1939 adventure classic, the Thuggee murder cult is on the rampage. Led by Gunga Din (Sam Jaffe), Sergeants Cutter (Cary Grant), MacChesney (Victor McLaglen), and Ballantine (Douglas Fairbanks, Jr.) find the Thuggee guru (Eduardo Ciannelli) in a temple of gold. Taken prisoner, the soldiers are unable to warn the rest of the regiment that they're riding into a trap. Fortunately, Din makes it to the top of the temple and blows the bugle to warn them—though he is killed by gunfire.

Soldiers Three was filmed, Din-less, in 1951, with Stewart Granger, David Niven, Robert Newton, and Walter Pidgeon loose in 19th-century India. In *Sergeants 3* (1962), the action was shifted to the American West with Frank Sinatra, Dean Martin, and Peter Lawford as the rollicking soldiers, and Sammy Davis, Jr., as the Din character.

THE GUNSMITH (L)

First Appearance: *Macklin's Women* by J.R. Roberts, 1984, Jove Books.

Biography: Clint Adams is "the finest man with a shootin' iron" and an expert at pistol-whipping men "without scrambling their brains." A lawman for ten years in the days following the Civil War, he decides to become a bounty hunter, less for the reward money than for the chance to hunt down wrongdoers. Known as the Gunsmith, he travels around "every state and territory in the West," often becoming involved in larger matters than just capturing the men he's after, including oppressed settlers, women in need, feuding ranchers, and the like.

The Gunsmith is dark-haired and clean-shaven, with a long scar on his left cheek. He wears a Stetson and rides a black gelding, Duke, who lets no one else ride him.

Comment: As of this writing, there have been over 120 Gunsmith novels. Some of the titles provide a short, accurate summary of the hero's escapades: *Killer Grizzly, The Nevada Timber War, The Stagecoach Thieves, Grand Canyon Gold, Geronimo's Trail, The Oregon Strangler, Bullets and Ballots, The Ponderosa War, Wagon Train to Hell,* and *The Fast Draw League.*

See also LONGARM; SLOCUM.

H

HAGGARTH (C)

First Appearance: *Eerie* #118, 1981, Warren Publishing.

Biography: At some time in the past, Tunic warlords from the mountains are sent by the mad dwarf-king Thall to raid the lowlands, intent on conquest. Haggarth is one such invader; mortally wounded in battle, he is found by a passing peddler, Mathias de Mossa, who has been caring for a young woodcutter recently blinded by the Tunics. Mathias takes both men to the witch Arnia, who removes Haggarth's head, boils off the flesh, and fuses the "mask" over the woodcutter's face. With the prowess of the warrior and the strength of the woodcutter, and "possessing the knowledge of each," the "new" Haggarth—dead and, thus, immortal—goes to work defending the rights and property of the lowlanders. He eventually finds and slays Thall, thus ending the war. However, his personal war is not yet over: Riding to the Mystic Lands, he seeks "both reason and purpose for his conflicting and confusing dual natures." Along the way he battles Amazons, monsters, and other fantastic foes.

Comment: The adventures were written and drawn by creator Victor de la Fuente, and appeared in *Eerie* through #134.

See also HAXTUR.

HAIRBREADTH HARRY (CS, MP)

First Appearance: "Hairbreadth Harry, the Boy Hero," 1906, *The Philadelphia Press*.

Biography: Harry is actually Harold Hollingsworth, a teenage adventurer (who grows more or less in "real time" as the strip progresses). Harry is enamored with Belinda Blinks, who has a nasty habit of continually falling into the hands of the evil, mustachioed Rudolph Rassendale, who carries her to the far corners of the earth, from mountains to seas to razor-sharp buzz saws, only to have the dogged Harry rescue her—often via dangerous and incredible means.

Comment: After several months in just one newspaper, the strip was picked up by the McClure Syndicate and, in 1923, by the Philadelphia Ledger Syndicate. The strip was created by Charles William Kahles and, at his death in 1931, passed to F.O. Alexander. It ended in 1939. Six short, silent motion pictures were produced in the middle 1920s.

A similar strip, *Desperate Desmond*, was created by others to cash in on the success of Kahles's strip.

HAN SOLO (MP, L, C, CS, R, TV)

First Appearance: *Star Wars*, 1978, Twentieth Century-Fox (see COMMENT).

Biography: A wise-cracking rogue in his middle 30s, Han attended the Imperial (Military) Academy and graduated at the top of his class. However, he was framed for a crime he didn't commit and was banned from serving in the military. After taking a succession of odd jobs, he became a smuggler. During one job, he meets the towering, 200-year-old Chewbacca, a shaggy Wookie of the planet Kashyyyk. The two become partners, soaring through the universe aboard Solo's hyperspace tramp freighter *Millennium Falcon*, which he won from former soldier-of-fortune Lando Calrissian in a high-stakes game of sabacc.

Despite his criminal background, Solo has a good and brave heart. In his first chronicled adventure, he has recently had to jettison a cargo of spice owned by Jabba the Hutt and, desperate for money, agrees to help transport wanted young rebel Luke Skywalker and his mentor, Obi-Wan Kenobi. This brings him into contact with rebel leader Princess Leia Organa and her comrades, whom he helps to destroy the Death Star of the cruel emperor (Palpatine).

In his second adventure, he is still with Princess Leia and Luke, this time helping to defend the rebel base on the ice planet Hoth. Fleeing the forces of the empire, and the evil Darth Vader in particular, they seek refuge on the planet Bespin, where Lando is now the Baron-Administrator of the gas-mining post. But Vader is there too and Han is captured, frozen in carbonite, and turned over to Jabba.

In his third adventure, Han is freed by Luke and

I SEEM TO BE PART OF **BOTH** MEN...POSSESSING THE **KNOWLEDGE** OF EACH...YET, BELONGING SOLELY TO THE WORLDS OF **NEITHER!**

I AM **COMPELLED** TO SEEK AND **SLAY SOMBRA**... HE WHO SENT THAT PART OF ME WHICH IS **TUNIC** RAIDER INTO THE LOWLANDS, TO **STEAL** AND **DIE** FOR HIM!

The introspective *Haggarth.* © Warren Publishing.

joins the rebels in a final, all-out assault on the Galactic Empire. They destroy the new Death Star, the emperor is killed by Vader (who, ironically, is Luke's father and defends him when the emperor attempts to kill him), and Han and Leia end up together.

Han is a crack shot with a blaster and other guns. A wisecracking cynic who trusts no one but Chewbacca (until he meets Luke and Leia), Han enjoys courting danger and living on the edge.

Comment: Harrison Ford played the part in *Star Wars* and its sequels, *The Empire Strikes Back* (1980) and *Return of the Jedi* (1983). Though the film came out after the novel, the book was based on the screenplay.

In addition to the novelizations of the films—by creator George Lucas, Donald Glut, and James Kahn, respectively—there have been a number of *Star Wars* novels, namely: *Splinter of the Mind's Eye* (1978) by Alan Dean Foster; *Han Solo at Stars' End* (1979), *Han Solo's Revenge* (1979), and *Han Solo and the Lost Legacy* (1980) by Brian Daley; *Lando Calrissian and the Mindharp of Sharu, Lando Calrissian and the Flamewind of Oseon,* and *Lando Calrissian and the Starcave of ThonBoka,* all 1983 by L. Neil Smith; and the ongoing Timothy Zahn series, *Heir to the Empire, Dark Force Rising, The Last Command,* and others.

Marvel Comics adapted all three films and also published a *Star Wars* comic book that ran 107 issues, from 1977 to 1986. Han also appeared occasionally in Marvel's *Droids* comic book, eight issues of which appeared from 1986 to 1987. Dark Horse published a six-issue *Star Wars: Dark Empire* comic book in 1992.

A *Star Wars* comic strip drawn by Al Williamson and written by Archie Goodwin was syndicated from 1980 to 1984.

National Public Radio broadcast a 13-part, six-and-one-half-hour adaptation, an "expanded edition" of the film in 1977, followed by a ten-part adaptation of *The Empire Strikes Back* in 1980.

On TV, many of the characters appeared in *The Star Wars Holiday Special,* which aired on CBS in 1979, and in the made-for-TV movies *The Ewok Adventure* (1984) and *Ewoks: The Battle for Endor* (1985), both on ABC. Thirteen animated *Droids* adventures aired in 1985, and 26 episodes of *Ewoks* the following year.

See also Harrison Ford's character INDIANA JONES.

HARDCASTLE and MCCORMICK
(TV)

First Appearance: *Hardcastle & McCormick,* September 1983, ABC.

Biography: After 30 years, 65-year-old retired Judge Milton G. Hardcastle has had it with criminals using

Hairbreadth Harry attacks Rudolph (with top hat) and rescues Belinda.

loopholes and other legal tactics to walk out of courtrooms, free. Deciding to do something about it, he agrees to help washed-up young race car driver Mark "Skid" McCormick walk away from a (false) charge of auto theft, provided the kid joins him as a vigilante, meting out justice to criminals who have been able to beat the rap. Skid agrees, and the two use their contacts in the police force, in the halls of justice, and on the streets to find evidence that will put known criminals behind bars. Their police force contacts are Lieutenant Michael Delaney and, later, Lieutenant Frank Harper.

The duo rides around in a red sportscar (license: DE JUDGE); they are based in Hardcastle's mansion, which is run for a time by housekeeper Sarah Wicks. The Judge's one "vice" is poker.

Comment: The hour-long series aired through July 1986 and starred Brian Keith as Hardcastle and Daniel Hugh-Kelly as McCormick. John Hancock was Delaney (until 1985) and Joe Santos was Harper (1985–86).

THE HARDY BOYS (L, TV, C)

First Appearance: *The Tower Treasure* by Franklin W. Dixon, 1927, Grosset & Dunlap.

Biography: Forty-year-old Fenton Hardy is a world-famous detective who, having left the New York police force, now lives with his wife, Laura, and sons, Frank and Joe, in Bayport, a town on Barmet Bay, three miles inland from the Atlantic Coast. Frank is 18, with straight black hair, brown eyes, and a strong but "good-humored expression." Joe is a year younger, equally good-natured, but with blond locks and blue eyes. They all live in an old stone house on the corner of High and Elm. The boys attend Bayport High and tool around town and to neighboring Willowville or Duckworth on their motorcycles, often running errands for Fenton (delivering legal papers or picking up packages) or visiting their plump farmboy friend Chet Morton, and more often than not becoming involved in one of their father's investigations or a mystery of their own. The lads also get around in their boat, *Sleuth,* and travel with their father onboard his plane.

Frank's girlfriend is Callie Shaw; Joe is sweet on Chet's younger sister Iola.

Comment: Dixon was a house name. The characters were created by Edward L. Stratemeyer, head of the syndicate that published their adventures and author of the first nine stories. Daughter Harriet S. Adams cowrote others and oversaw those she didn't write. *The Tower Treasure* was followed by 57 other titles in the original series. Another 62 have been published, to date, by new writers working under the Dixon byline; to this day the boys are teenagers. They also costarred in a novel that teamed them with TOM SWIFT: *Time Bomb.*

On TV, Walt Disney produced the 20-chapter *Mystery of the Applegate Treasure,* an adaptation of the first novel, which aired on *The Mickey Mouse Club* beginning in October 1956. The following year, in September, the 15-chapter *Mystery of Ghost Farm* aired. Both adventures starred Tim Considine as Frank and Tommy Kirk as Joe, who played the brothers as 15 and 14. The boys returned to TV in an animated series in September 1969, with Byron Kane as the voice of Frank and Dallas McKennon as Joe. The half-hour Filmation series had the boys as rock-and-roll singers traveling the world and solving crimes wherever they performed. The show aired until September 1971 and spawned both a short-lived group that recorded under the name and a Gold Key comic book that lasted four issues from 1970 to 1971. The other members of their troupe are beautiful Wanda Kay Breckenridge, clumsy Chubby, and Pete.

In January 1977 a new live-action show, *The Hardy Boys Mysteries,* premiered on ABC. Parker Stevenson was the now-18-year-old Frank, Shaun Cassidy was 16-year-old Joe, and Edmund Gilbert played Fenton. The hour-long episodes aired until August 1979.

HARRISON DESTRY   (L, MP, R, S, TV)

First Appearance: *Twelve Peers* by Max Brand, 1930, *Western Story Magazine.*

Biography: A roguish and cheerful cowboy, Harrison Destry's happy-go-lucky ways change when he's framed for a train robbery. Unfortunately, the jury of his peers is stocked with men he'd beaten in fights or athletic accomplishments, and he's found guilty. After six years in jail, Destry returns, seething with rage but pretending to be timid and rehabilitated. Not only does he nail the real thief (whom he thought was his best friend) and punish the crooked jurors, but he wins the hand of Charlotte, the rancher's daughter.

Comment: The novel was first published in book form in 1930 as *Destry Rides Again.* When it was first brought to the screen in 1932, starring Tom Mix, the character became known as Tom Destry; he would remain Tom in all future films. The film was retitled *Justice Rides Again* when the second film version was released (in 1939); this one starred James Stewart and introduced a new love interest in the person of barroom belle Frenchy, who was played by Marlene Dietrich. The film introduced the classic song "See What the Boys in the Back Room Will Have." Audie Murphy and Marie Blanchard were Tom and Frenchy in the 1955 film version. A role-reversal film called *Frenchie* was released in 1951, starring Shelley Winters as the avenging angel and Joel McCrea as her love interest.

Destry Rides Again was performed on CBS radio in February 1941, starring Henry Fonda and Paulette Goddard.

On Broadway, Andy Griffith played Tom, with Dolores Gray as Frenchy, in the musical *Destry Rides Again,* which ran 473 performances in 1957.

John Gavin played the part on the hour-long TV series that aired on ABC from February to September 1964. Though the show lasted only 13 episodes, at least Destry got his original first name back as the son of lawman Tom Destry. This time Harrison is a sheriff who is framed for embezzlement and roams the West trying to find the rats who framed him. Along the way he helps others in need, talking his way out of trouble more often than fighting.

HARRY CALLAHAN   (MP, L)

First Appearance: *Dirty Harry,* 1971, Warner Brothers.

Biography: "Dirty" Harry Callahan is a tough, inscrutable inspector with the San Francisco Police Department, Homicide Division. He carries a .44 Magnum and likes to be in the thick of things, where he can be most effective. Usually he is given difficult assignments no one else will take.

Little is known of Harry's early years. He did not go to college and joined the force in 1961. His wife was killed by a drunken driver in 1970; even before her death, however, he tended to spend day and night on the job. He has won the Police Benevolent Association target shooting contest every year except 1967, when he was unable to enter due to a splintered finger he suffered while subduing an acid freak. Harry loathes the police bureaucracy and believes in the rights of the victim above all. His views first came to the attention of the media and brought disciplinary action down upon him in 1970, when he shot a man in the Filmore district for "intent" to rape. (Harry caught the naked knife-wielder chasing a woman into an alley.)

In his first chronicled adventure, Harry is assigned to track down Scorpio, a madman who vows to shoot a person every day until the city pays him $100,000. (The amount doubles when he has to ask a second time.) Harry reluctantly accepts a partner, Chico Gonzalez, who is wounded during a shootout with Scorpio and thus joins the list of Harry casualties; his previous partner was gut-shot, and the one before that was killed. After Scorpio hijacks a busload of children, Harry intercepts the killer; taunting him to go for his gun with his catch phrase "Do you feel lucky, punk?" Callahan blows the madman away with his .44 Magnum—"the most powerful handgun in the world"— and, disgusted with the hypocrisy of the American legal system, throws away his badge.

In his second adventure, Harry—somehow still on the force—traces a series of murders to a police vigilante squad commanded by Detective Lieutenant Neil Briggs; in his third adventure, assisted by his first female partner, Kate Moore, Harry chases down terrorists in San Francisco. In his fourth escapade, Captain Briggs and Chief Jannings put him on the trail of a woman, Jennifer Spencer, who's killing the men who raped her and her sister years before at a carnival;

during the course of his investigation, he dares a criminal to "make my day" by shooting a hostage, so Harry can blast him. And in his fifth chronicled case, he chases down a killer who's got a long list of people he's planning to murder—including Callahan. He also has one of his rare romances in the last adventure, with newswoman Samantha Walker.

Harry's badge number is 2211. His favorite eatery is Burger Den where, individualist that he is, he orders hot dogs for lunch and dinner.

Harry's nickname is Dirty Harry, though no one is quite sure why. In the first film, three suggestions are put forth: he gets all the dirty jobs; he is a voyeur; and he "always gets the shit end of the stick." In the second film, his new partner, Inspector Early Smith, suggests a fourth reason as he sits down in Harry's litter-filled Chevy.

Comment: Clint Eastwood starred as Harry in four more films: *Magnum Force* (1973), *The Enforcer* (1976), *Sudden Impact* (1983), and *The Dead Pool* (1988). In the first film, Harry Guardino costarred as Lieutenant Al Bressler, with Andy Robinson as Scorpio and Reni Santoni and Chico. Hal Holbrook was Briggs in the second film, and Tyne Daly was Kate in the third. In the fourth film, Sondra Locke was Jennifer, Bradford Dillman played Briggs, and Pat Hingle was Jannings; Liam Neeson was the lunatic filmmaker Peter Swan in the fifth film, with Patricia Clarkson as Samantha.

The characters were created by Harry Julian Fink and Rita M. Fink. The first film was directed by Don Siegel and Eastwood himself directed *Sudden Impact.* The films have all been novelized.

HARRY ORWELL   (TV)

First Appearance: *Smile, Jenny, You're Dead,* March 1974, ABC.

Biography: Harry Orwell is a former marine and a police officer who is shot in the back while on the job. Since the bullet is too close to his spine to be removed and can shift at any moment and leave him paralyzed, Harry is retired with a pension. Living in an oceanfront house in San Diego and renovating a boat called the *Answer,* he becomes bored with inactivity and supplements his income by working as a private eye—but only when a case intrigues him, or if the woman asking him to become involved is beautiful enough. Because his car rarely works, Harry usually gets around by bus. (This is particularly true after Harry's mechanic is killed in a blast meant for the detective.)

His neighbor in San Diego is a lovely young woman named Sue (who is kidnaped in one episode), and his nemesis on the San Diego Police Force is Lieutenant Manuel Quinlan. When Manny is shot dead in the line of duty (February 1975), Harry moves to Santa Monica and crosses swords with Lieutenant K.C. Trench. Santa Monica also provides him with a pair of occasional assistants—amateur sleuths Dr. Fong and Lester Hodges.

Comment: The original TV movie served as a pilot for the series, *Harry-O.* It had Harry (David Janssen) looking into the murder of a friend's son-in-law and falling for his widow, who is the prime suspect in the killing. Jodie Foster costarred. The regular hour-long series began in September 1974 and aired through August 1976. It starred Janssen as Harry, Henry Darrow as Quinlan, Anthony Zerbe as Trench, Keye Luke as Fang, and Les Lannom as Hodges. Farrah Fawcett appeared as Sue.

Janssen also starred in *O'Hara, U.S. Treasury,* an hour-long series that aired on CBS from 1971 to 1972. Jim O'Hara's job put him at the disposal of the Secret Service, the Internal Revenue Service Intelligence, Alcohol, Tobacco, and Firearms Division, the Customs Bureau, and other government agencies.

HARRY PALMER   (L, MP)

First Appearance: *The Ipcress File* by Len Deighton, 1962, Simon & Schuster.

Biography: The lazy, sarcastic character who is fond of "dawdling" (and who is unnamed in the novels) worked for British Military Intelligence for nearly three years. When he leaves, he goes to work as a civilian for "the smallest and the most important of the Intelligence units" (a group so thorough at covering their employees' tracks that any newspapers containing photos of them—for example, winning a grade school math prize in 1939—are removed from library and newspaper files). He reports to Dalby, who poses as the head of a detective bureau; Dalby's assistant is Alice.

The spy's first mission: to find out why biochemists are disappearing. The trail takes him from London, to Beirut, back to London, to Tokwe Atoll in the Pacific; what he discovers is a complex brainwashing program known as Operation Ipcress (Induction of Psycho-neuroses by Conditioned Reflex with Stress), which Dalby is behind for his own gain.

His second chronicled adventure involves a sunken sub; his third (and arguably most exciting) has him helping to arrange for the defection of a Russian spy; his fourth pits him against a Communist-hating Texas billionaire who plans his own invasion of the Soviet Union; his fifth has him being used to get fake secrets to the Soviets; and his last finds him turned over to the Strategic War Games in London, where someone is playing mind games with him.

The spy carries an assortment of business cards that identify him as Bertram Loess, Assessor and Valuer, Brian Serck, Inter News Press Agency, and the like. One character in the first novel calls him Harry, hence the name "Harry Palmer."

Comment: The other novels are *Horse Under Water* (1963), *Funeral in Berlin* (1964), *Billion Dollar Brain* (1966), *Expensive Place to Die* (1967), and *Spy Story* (1974). Three of these have been made into motion pictures, which gave the spy his name: *The Ipcress File* (1965), *Funeral in Berlin* (1966), and *Billion Dollar Brain* (1967). Michael Caine starred as Palmer in all of them. In the films, Palmer is a black marketeer who, when he is exposed, agrees to work as a government spy.

THE HAWK   (1) (C)

First Appearance: *Jumbo Comics* #1, 1938, Fiction House.

Biography: The Hawk, a former galley slave, and his Hawks of the Seas prowl the ocean preying on ships that have or deal in slaves. As he explains his mission, "We don't fight for money, we fight for the freedom of weak slaves and for the love of adventure." A master of disguise, he signals his men by shouting "Crooowooo!" and is constantly outwitting the law in the person of the king's officer, Captain Marrystone. Among the Hawks he is closest to are Fluth and Sagua, an American Indian, who attacks enemies with bow and arrow.

Comment: The Hawk appeared in almost every one of *Jumbo Comics'* 167 issues and was created and drawn by Willis Rensie (Will Eisner). Other adventure heroes who appeared in its pages included the heroic Wilton of the West (some of the first comic book art by Jack Kirby); the crime-busting Inspector Dayton; ZX-5, a top spy whose first exploits pit him against the Nazi-like Transovania (after the war, the hero becomes a private investigator); wilderness scout Tom Sherrill; the jungle queen Sheena (who eventually became so popular she dominated the magazine); adventurer and foe of the underworld Spencer Steel; Long Bow the Indian boy; the airborne War Aces; and the starborne Space Scouts.

THE HAWK   (2) (R)

First Appearance: *The Sparrow and the Hawk,* 1945, CBS.

Biography: During World War II, Spencer Mallory rose to the rank of Lieutenant colonel in the Army Air Corps. Now that the war is over, he works as a freelance aviator, training his young nephew Barney Mallory to fly. Nicknamed the Hawk and the Sparrow,

Sagua and *The Hawk* discuss strategy. © Caplin-Iger Co. Ltd.

respectively, the two get into adventures with missing persons, smugglers, spies, and the like.

Comment: The series aired for three years and starred Michael Fitzmaurice as the Hawk and Donald Buka as the Sparrow. The show was a sequel, of sorts, to CBS's wartime drama *Sky Blazers,* which was first broadcast in 1939.

HAXTUR   (C)

First Appearance: *Trinca,* May 1971 (Spain).

Biography: A late-20th-century mercenary who was slain in a "stinking South American jungle," the bearded Haxtur recalls being wounded, plunging into darkness, dying, and waking in a barbaric afterlife. Because he was corrupt in life, he must spend his time doing good deeds, "condemned to die . . . again and again" until he atones for all of his mortal sins. Carrying a sword and wearing a loincloth, he roams this world where monsters and tyrants dwell, helping the downtrodden in realms such as the Humidlands, the Slow Deathland (a land of radiation), the Outworld, and others. Eventually he is slain in battle and freed from his living hell.

Comment: The hero's 14 adventures were written and drawn by creator Victor de la Fuente and appeared in the U.S. in *Eerie* magazine beginning with #111, 1980, and lasting through #117. It moved to *1984* magazine for two issues (#10 and 11).

See also HAGGARTH.

HECTOR HEATHCOTE (MP, TV, C)

First Appearance: "The Minute and One-Half Man," July 1959.

Biography: A young scientist, Hector Heathcote invents a time machine with which he intends to study the Revolutionary War and other historic events. When he gets into the past, however, it turns out these events would not have occurred without his heroic participation. Among his brave deeds are helping George Washington cross the Delaware (he built the boat), Paul Revere make his famous ride (who do you think looked after the horse?), get the Liberty Bell to Philadelphia, coinvent the telephone and airplane, strike gold in the Klondike, blaze trails with Daniel Boone, and the like. He also has a few fictitious adventures, such as a visit to Untidy Gulch in the 1870s, where he stops Black Bart Bromide and his band of outlaws.

Hector's companion on his journeys is his dog Winston.

Comment: Fifteen theatrical short subjects were produced between 1959 and 1963; another four were made in 1970–71. The character got his own TV series, *The Hector Heathcote Show,* which aired on NBC from October 1963 until September 1965. Twenty additional short cartoons were produced for the series, which also showed the theatrical cartoons.

John Myhers was the voice of Hector in all his adventures.

Gold Key published one issue of a *Hector Heathcote* comic book in 1964.

HIAWATHA (L, C, MP)

First Appearance: "The Song of Hiawatha" by Henry Wadsworth Longfellow, 1855.

Biography: An Ojibway Indian, the son of Wenonah and the West Wind, Mudjekeewis, Hiawatha lives "By the shores of Gitche Gumee/By the shining Big-Sea-Water" (Lake Superior). After Hiawatha is born, his mother dies, deserted by her "false and faithless" mate. Raised by his grandmother Nokomis, the daughter of the Moon, the hero becomes a great hunter, collects wisdom from the elderly, and learns "all manly arts and labors." He can run so fast that an arrow he shoots will fall "behind him," and he can launch ten arrows upward in turn, the last being fired "ere the first to earth had fallen." From Nokomis, he obtains magic deerskin mittens that allow him to smash rocks and magic deerskin moccasins that permit him to cover a mile with every stride.

Thus equipped, with eagle feathers on his head, his ash-wood bow in his hand, and oaken arrows, he sets out to find Mudjekeewis, his father, and avenge his mother. They meet, and after chatting about Hiawatha's brothers Wabun, the East-Wind, Shawondasee, the South-Wind, and Kabibonokka, the North-Wind, Hiawatha attacks. Mudjekeewis flees, and Hiawatha chases him for three days, to the very portals of the Sunset. There Mudjekeewis reveals that he cannot be slain but has simply been testing his son to determine his courage. He tells Hiawatha to return home, clean the earth of evil and woe, and when he dies he will share the kingdom of his father, who will make him ruler of the Northwest-Wind, Keewaydin.

Hiawatha leaves, his anger gone, and pauses in the land of the Dacotahs. There he meets an arrow-maker's daughter, Minnehaha, "Laughing Water," who will eventually become his bride. Upon returning home, he fasts for wisdom and strength and battles the evil tempter Mondamin. Hiawatha's defeat of Mondamin causes corn to grow on the land and become the food of his people.

In time, Hiawatha marries Minnehaha and becomes the leader of his tribe, seeing them through famine and preaching peace and brotherhood with the white settlers. After Minnehaha is felled by Ahkosewin, "Fever," and perishes, Hiawatha leaves his people, departing to the west "to the regions . . . of the Northwest-Wind . . . to the land of the Hereafter."

Hiawatha's best friends among the tribe members are the powerful Kwasind and the singer Chibiabos.

Comment: Longfellow was influenced by the epic *Kalevala* (see WAINAMOINEN) and by the writings of American ethnologist and explorer Henry Rowe Schoolcraft. In particular, the author was impressed by stories of the great Algonquian warrior Manabozho, the grandson of Nokomis. Indeed, Longfellow intended to write about Manabozho, but changed his mind because he felt Schoolcraft had tainted the subject with his "huge ill-digested" writing. Among Manabozho's great deeds were stealing fire from the Old Man to give to his people.

As *The Song of Hiawatha*, the poem was adapted in comic book form by *Classics Illustrated*, #57 in 1949. It was filmed in 1952 as *Hiawatha* starring Vincent Edwards.

HONDO LANE (L, MP, TV)

First Appearance: *Hondo* by Louis L'Amour, 1953, Bantam Books.

Biography: "A big man, wide-shouldered," with a "lean, hard-boned face," Hondo Lane is also a champion bronc rider, an expert gunman, and a former soldier. He lives with the Apaches for five years and had an Indian wife, Destarte; when she dies, he rides dispatch and works as a scout for General Crook in southeastern Arizona.

When Hondo has his horse shot from under him by renegade Apaches, he and his dog Sam wander onto the ranch of Angie Low and her six-year-old son, Johnny; Angie's husband, Ed, is gone, ostensibly to get protection from soldiers, but actually he has grown tired of hard work and has wandered off to play cards. When Hondo leaves on one of Angie's horses, Apaches led by Chief Vittoro and "subchief" Silva arrive at the ranch. Silva kills Sam (the dog) with a lance through the gut. Johnny shoots Silva, wounding him; Vittoro admires the boy's bravery and leaves them in peace.

Sometime later, Hondo finds Ed at the army post. The latter, convinced that Hondo is a horse thief, tries to sneak up on him in a gully one night; Hondo guns him down. Immediately thereafter, though, Hondo is captured by Silva and several Apaches. Vittoro orders that instead of being tortured, Hondo must fight Silva; though Hondo is victorious, he spares the subchief's life. Returning to the Lowe ranch, Hondo witnesses Vittoro being slain by soldiers and Silva (now the chief) leading an attack on the ranch. After killing the new chief with a lance through the gut—which is how Silva killed Sam—Hondo takes Angie and Johnny to the ranch he owns in California.

Comment: Famed western author L'Amour also wrote stories about HOPALONG CASSIDY.

In motion pictures, John Wayne starred as Hondo in the 1953 film. The story is the same, with the exception that when Hondo kills Ed, he doesn't know who he is until he finds a photo of Johnny on his body.

On TV, the character was played by Ralph Taeger in an hour-long series that aired from September to December 1967. In this version, Hondo is once again a former Confederate Cavalry captain who lives among the Apaches after the war. When his Indian bride is murdered by soldiers, Hondo and Sam go to work for the army out of Fort Lowell, roaming the Arizona Territory and trying to stop feuds among the Indians, army, and settlers. At the same time, he battles claim jumpers, land grabbers, outlaws, gunslingers, and other ne'er-do-wells. He reports to Captain Richards and occasionally works with scout Buffalo Baker (a minor character in the novel). His ladyfriend is still a husbandless mother, here called Angie Dow.

HONEY WEST (L, TV, C)

First Appearance: *Gun for Honey* by G.G. Fickling, 1958, Doubleday.

Biography: A private eye in her late 20s, the blonde, tough, but feminine Honey West is a graduate of Long Beach City College and lives in Long Beach. She became a detective in order to find the killers of her private eye father; she enjoyed the work and, after that case was closed, stayed on the job. She works closely with her friend Lieutenant Mark Storm of the Long Beach Sheriff's Office—a man who wants her to give up sleuthing and become his wife.

Honey stands five foot five, weighs 120 pounds, and is in excellent physical shape. Readers (and villains) get to see that shape a great deal as, for one reason or another, Honey removes all or some of her clothing during every adventure.

Comment: G.G. Fickling is actually Gloria and Forrest E. Fickling. There were ten other Honey West novels, including *Honey in the Flesh* (1959), *Blood and Honey* (1961), and *Hurricane Honey* (1964).

On TV, Honey was played by Anne Francis in the hour-long series that aired on ABC from September 1965 to September 1966. (She was introduced on an April 1965 episode of *Burke's Law;* see AMOS BURKE.) In this version she takes over her late father's detective agency and works with his partner, Sam Bolt (John Ericson), who is essentially the same as Mark. This Honey is a martial arts expert and carries a small arsenal in and out of her alligator handbag, including a .38, a pearl-handled derringer, an exploding compact, a gas mask garter belt, tear-gas earrings, a bug in the shape of an olive (for spying during those intimate cocktail moments), and lipstick that is actually a radio transmitter. She has a pet ocelot named Bruce, a fussy Aunt Meg (Irene Hervey), and travels around in a fully equipped van that says H.W. Bolt & Co., TV Service.

In comic books, Gold Key published one issue of *Honey West* in 1966.

A motion picture is in the works as of this writing.

HOPALONG CASSIDY (L, MP, C, TV, R)

First Appearance: by Clarence E. Mulford, *Outing* Magazine, 1906.

Biography: Lean, big-shouldered, red-headed William "Hopalong" Cassidy got his nickname when he was helping Sheriff Harris of Albuquerque and took a bullet in the right thigh, thus giving him a limp (which was ignored in the film versions). When we first meet the 23-year-old, he's wearing dirty clothing, a faded bandana, and his twin Colt .45s—which he uses, ambidextrously, with incredible speed and accuracy. He also packs a .50-caliber Army Sharps, smokes cigars and hand-rolled cigarettes, chews tobacco, drinks beer and whiskey, swears, and plays cards.

After getting a job at the Bar 20 Ranch, which is located 50 miles south of the Texas/New Mexico border, adjoining the C 80 spread, Hopalong learns everything he needs to know about ranching from the kindly foreman Buck Peters. There he and his best friend, Red Connors, are often forced to rely on their guns or fists, not because they are "lawless, nor drunken, shooting bullies, but 'naturally peaceable,' rubbing elbows with men who were not." Along with fellow hands Lanky Smith, Billy Williams, Skinny Thompson, Pete Wilson, and teen Johnny Nelson, they fight rustlers such as Tamale Jose and Slippery Trendley, battle Indians, take on such gunfighters as Tex Ewalt (who's annoyed at how Hopalong has killed some four dozen of his men to date), and even go prospecting and fight claim jumpers.

Hopalong dies in 1911 at the age of 60, causes unknown—though, implicitly, ill health and not violence was responsible.

Hoppy is considerably different in films. This "new" hero is a rancher, though he spends most of the time riding his horse Topper and hunting down lawbreakers. Dressed entirely in black, he doesn't drink, smoke, or curse. He also doesn't limp after the first film, and doesn't have much to do with women (a subordinate leading man usually serves this purpose). He's too busy being a hero to be a lover. And though he rides and punches hard, he doesn't use his guns unless absolutely necessary—and only then to shoot the gun from someone's hand.

Comment: Clarence E. Mulford, who lived in Brooklyn, wrote about Hoppy, the Bar 20, and its people for 20 years, most of the tales running some 2,000 to 3,000 words. The earliest collection of these stories was in the book *Bar 20* (1907). Much later, inspired by the success of the TV series, Thrilling published *Hopalong Cassidy's Western Magazine* from 1950 to 1951. It included, among other stories, four new Hoppy novels penned by Louis L'Amour (writing as Tex Burns): *The Riders of the High Rock, The Rustlers of West Fork, The Trail to Seven Pines,* and *Troubleshooter.*

Despite his success on the printed page, it is through his films and TV shows—all of them starring William Boyd—that the character is best known. A former oil-field worker and night watchman, Boyd broke into films as an extra, then went on to star in 66 Hopalong Cassidy films through 1948—a record for an actor with one character. The best of these were *Hop-A-Long Cassidy* (1935; hyphenated for the first and only time), *The Eagle's Brood* (1935), *Bar 20 Rides Again* (1935), *Hopalong Cassidy Returns* (1936), *Hopalong Cassidy Rides Again* (1937), *The Texas Trail* (1937), *Rustler's Valley* (1937), *Borderland* (1937), *Cassidy of Bar 20* (1938), *In Old Mexico* (1938), *Hoppy Serves a Writ* (1943; arguably the strongest and best known in the series), *Riders of the*

Deadline (1943), *False Colors* (1943), *Forty Thieves* (1944), *The Devil's Playground* (1946), *Marauders* (1947), and *The Dead Don't Dream* (1948).

In comic books, Fawcett published 85 issues of *Hopalong Cassidy* from 1943 to 1954, DC taking over and continuing to #135 in 1959.

The character came to NBC TV in June of 1949 and remained on the network until December 1951; it went into syndication and aired until 1954. The series consisted of the feature films cut into half-hour and hour segments (with new material filmed when needed); 52 all-new episodes were filmed just for TV in 1951–52. (Boyd himself owned the TV rights to the character and made the fortune that had eluded him in his film career.) Edgar Buchanan played Red Connors.

The character came to radio the same year he debuted on TV, with Boyd as Hoppy and his frequent film costar, Andy Clyde, appearing as his sidekick Arizona. The series was heard over the Mutual.

Incidentally, author Mulford found Boyd's interpretation "an absolutely ludicrous character."

HOP HARRIGAN (C, R, MP)

First Appearance: *All-American Comics* #1, 1939, DC Comics.

Biography: Colonel A. Harrigan is an early aviator whose wife, Maria, takes their daughter Mariana—but not their son, Hop—and returns to Colombia. The grieving colonel is subsequently lost on a flight, leaving their son Hop (a nickname; his real name is unknown) in the care of abusive farmer Silas Crass. After teaching himself to fly his father's old biplane, Hop runs—or rather, flies—away from his guardian. No sooner has he departed than he saves mechanic Ikky Tinker (a.k.a. Tank Tinker), whose parachute has become tangled in a plane; Hop and Ikky become fast friends. The grateful pilot of Ikky's plane, Prop Wash, gets Hop a job at the airfield and becomes his new guardian, and the three go on to form the All-American Aviation Company, building airplanes for the military and for private buyers. Hop soon meets and falls in love with a young woman named Gerry. During World War II, Hop—now known as "America's Ace of the Airways"—and his friends join the U.S. Army Air Corps, fighting under Wash (now a major) in the Pacific and South America. On one adventure in the South American jungle, he finds an orphan named Hippity, who is an expert at throwing the bola; the boy accompanies him on several adventures, at one point bringing down a Nazi plane. ("You ruined *my* chance to be a hero," Hop complains. "Oh, well! I can't help lovin' that pan!").

Comment: The character was created by Jon L. Blummer and appeared through issue #99; his Guardian Angel phase was #25 to #28.

Hop went to the radio airwaves in 1942, airing on ABC. In this somewhat different incarnation, he's a heroic World War II pilot who served in Europe and, after VE Day, in the Pacific. After the war, Hop and his mechanic and former gunner, Tank Tinker, open a small airport and flight school. During the course of their adventures, they fight spies and smugglers, fly rescue missions, test new kinds of aircraft, engage in races, and find time for romance—Hop with young Gail Nolan. Chester Stratton, then Albert Aley, starred as Hop; Mitzi Gold was Gail and Kenny Lynch, then Jackson Beck, was Tank.

The 15-chapter serial *Hop Harrigan* was released in 1946, directed by Derwin Abrahams and starring William Blakewell as Hop, Jennifer Holt as Gail, and Sumner Getchella as Tank. Their foe is the mysterious Chief Pilot, who abducts a scientist who has discovered a new source of power.

Other adventure heroes who appeared in the pages of *All-American Comics* include marine, army, and navy heroes Red, White, and Blue; Wiley of West Point; and the mystical Sargon the Sorcerer, whose power derives from the ancient Ruby of Life.

HORATIO HORNBLOWER   (L, MP)

First Appearance: *Beat to Quarters* by C.S. Forester, 1937, Michael Joseph.
Biography: Born on July 4, 1776, Horatio Hornblower is the son of a doctor and something of a Greek scholar when, in January 1794, he opts to become a sailor of the Channel Fleet onboard the Royal Navy's *Justinian* under Captain Keene. Thin, "above middle height," dark-eyed, and pale, Hornblower is ignorant of the ways of the sea. He learns quickly, though, as the ship escorts vessels of the West India Company around the world. Hornblower then transfers to the frigate *Indefatigable* under Captain Pellew. The ship becomes embroiled in the ongoing war with the French, and the young midshipman distinguishes himself in battle. Eventually he is assigned to the HMS *Renown* as a lieutenant and sent on a mission to the West Indies, where he suppresses a mutiny by Spanish prisoners. On subsequent missions he serves on the *Retribution,* then the *Hotspur,* spying on the French as Napoleon prepares to invade England, and then battling him on the Baltic Sea.

Throughout over a quarter century of service, Hornblower works his way up the ranks to become one of the most distinguished naval officers in English history. "Horry" is married to schoolteacher Maria Ellen Mason, the daughter of his landlady at Highbury Street when he's ashore.

Comment: The Hornblower sequels and prequels cover the years 1794 to 1823 and were written and published out of chronological sequence. In order of publication (with numerical chronology indicated following the date), the books are: *Beat to Quarters* (#5; known as *The Happy Return* in England); *Ship of the Line* (1938, #6); *Flying Colours* (1938, #7); *Commodore Hornblower* (1945, #8); *Lord Hornblower* (1946, #9); *Mr. Midshipman Hornblower* (1950, #1); *Lieutenant Hornblower* (1952, #2); *Hornblower and the Atropos* (1953, #4); *Admiral Hornblower in the West Indies* (1958, #10); *Hornblower and the Hotspur* (1962, #3); and *Hornblower During the Crisis* (#11), which was published following the author's death in 1966. Forester also wrote the novel *African Queen,* which was the basis for the classic film.

Gregory Peck was miscast as the hero in director Raoul Walsh's otherwise colorful 1951 film *Captain Horatio Hornblower.*

Horatio, incidentally, was not inspired by Nelson, but by Hamlet.

HUNTER   (C)

First Appearance: *Eerie* #52, 1973, Warren Publishing.
Biography: In 2001, war erupts and the adversaries fling N-Bombs at each other; radiation causes many humans to become mutants, called Demons "by the superstitious remnants of mankind." The Demons are green or copper-skinned, with lizardlike tails and the ability to project "a lethal lash of thought-waves" that can explode human minds. After 50 years of an uncomfortable truce between the races, the Demons Wars erupt, with the Demons clearly at an advantage. Centuries pass. After suffering defeat, a Demon army commanded by Ofphal retreats to the farmhouse of humans James and Elizabeth Hunter. They slay James and rape his wife, who ultimately gives birth to a half-breed who is human save for his copper-colored skin and slit-gold eyes.

When the "mottled pox" takes his mother, 15-year-old Demian Hunter joins America's elite Attack Force as an Alpha-Class scout—determined to exterminate Demons. Working as a loner, Hunter is garbed in a red body suit with a yellow stripe down the arms and legs; the suit contains alarms that "tingle" when an enemy is approaching from behind. He wears a helmet equipped with night-vision goggles and carries a staff that can be used for clubbing or to fire an "electrosurge" of half a million volts. Though Hunter dies in hand-to-hand combat with Ofphal—stabbed in the chest by the Demon—the evil general is slain by a crossbow bolt fired by the hero DERECK SCHRECK and the remaining Demons go into hiding, thus ending the wars.

Twenty years pass and a medieval society of humans develops. In 2394 young Karas—who, as a babe, was saved by Hunter—is out for a ride on his steed Goldflax when he finds a man who claims to have been wounded by Demons. Karas discovers that a new race of mutant Goblins known as the Ouphe has been created by a scientist named Yaust. Karas's guardian, the magician Mandragora, gives him the helmet of the old Hunter, and he sallies forth as Hunter II. He is joined by Exterminator Two, a robot with a human brain. Upon reaching Yaust's fortress, Hunter II learns that Yaust is a good guy who created *his* Goblins to stop the mutant Trolls of the megalomaniacal Mandragora. When Hunter II slays the wizard, the threat ends and his job is through—but only for a decade.

Karas builds himself a castle—Castle Demian, named for his hero—and makes himself a benevolent lord. As his betrothed, Lady Ragan, approaches the castle, she is kidnaped; Karas sets out after her, accompanied by Exterminator Two, and finds that Mandragora survived and is plotting anew to rule the world. Pushed into a yawning lava pit, the wizard dies—this time, for good.

Comment: The characters were created by artist Paul Neary and editor Bill DuBay—fans of *The Exorcist,* as evidenced by the names of the characters. The first Hunter appeared in seven adventures; he died in *Eerie* #57. Hunter II first appeared in *Eerie* #67 in 1975; he, too, starred in seven tales, then returned in #101 for the final showdown with Mandragora.

The Exterminator itself had been featured in its own series, which began in *Eerie* #60 and the introduction of Exterminator One, a robot with the brain of Peter Orwell. Its job in the overpopulated world of 2014 was to kill imperfect humans. Exterminator Two, which had tank treads instead of feet, was first introduced in that series in #64.

There was also, briefly, a playful Hunter 3—a boy, Max Hallibut, who made himself a costume and battled evil frogs. He appeared in *Eerie* #87.

The original Hunter saga was reprinted in its entirety in *Eerie* #69.

I

ILYA MUROMETZ (F, MP, C)

First Appearance: Russian folklore, 11th century A.D.

Biography: For the first 30 years of his life, Ilya, son of Ivan of Murom, lay utterly paralyzed in his cottage. However, Jesus and two apostles heal him one day, telling him that his strength will be needed to defend Christian Russia from the heathens. After mounting his horse Cloudfall, he encounters the giant Svyatogor, who carries his wife around in a crystal casket. After falling in love with Ilya, she drugs her husband and forces Ilya to sleep with her (lest she tell the giant that Ilya was rude to her). The next day the conscience-striken hero confesses to Svyatogor, who kills his wife and sets out with his newfound friend. Soon the two come upon a giant coffin. Svyatogor hands Ilya his sword and lies down inside, to see if it is intended for him: It is indeed, for they can't raise the lid once it's shut, and Svyatogor smothers.

Setting out alone, Ilya finds the city of Chernigov besieged by 120,000 Tatar warriors. After pulling an oak tree from the ground, the hero rides into the warriors, slaying them all. Riding on, he captures Nightingale the Robber, a bird that breathes flame, which he presents to Prince Vladimir of Kiev. The prince honors Ilya, and the two fight side by side to protect the realm against another force of Tatars led by the ruthless warlord Kalin. Ultimately, however, victory goes to the Russians' heads, and they boast that if they could get to heaven, even the angels could not stand against them. To punish them, God causes two Tatars to rise for every one they kill, and the Russians are defeated. However, Ilya and Cloudfall are turned to stone, and remain so to this day.

Comment: The character was played by Boris Andreyev in the Soviet-made *Ilya Murometz* (1956), which was released in the United States as *The Sword and the Dragon* in 1960. In this colorful and spectacular film, Ilya is healed, captures the Wind Demon, and defends the realm of Prince Vanda from the invading Tugar hordes of Chief Kalin, whose three-headed, fire-breathing dragon Ilya also slays.

Dell published a one-issue comic book adaptation of the film in 1960.

IMPOSSIBLE MISSIONS FORCE (TV, C, L)

First Appearance: *Mission: Impossible,* September 1966, CBS.

Biography: The Impossible Missions Force is a team of highly skilled government agents who hold other jobs until summoned by their leader Daniel Briggs (replaced after one year by James Phelps) to pull off a job. Briggs/Phelps gets his instructions from a tape recorder, which also includes a file on the dictator, rebel, or criminal they are to undermine. Before self-destructing, the tape always warns the listener, "As always, should you or any member of your I.M. Force be caught or killed, the secretary will disavow any knowledge of your actions."

Briggs/Phelps invariably chooses the same group of people (plus the occasional guest star): master-of-disguise Rollin Hand (later replaced by master-of-disguise Paris, then by "Doug"); cool, beautiful Cinnamon Carter (replaced by Dana Lambert, then Lisa Casey and Mimi Davis); electronics and mechanical genius Barney Collier; and strongman Willie Armitage. The Force typically works sting operations, creating complex scenarios that trap or expose their prey.

Years later, after his successor is slain, Phelps returns to lead a new I.M.F. Now he gets his instructions on laser disc, which provides both audio and video but still self-destructs five seconds after shutting down. The members of the new team are master-of-disguise Nicholas Black; strongman Max Harte; sexy Casey Randall (later Shannon Reed); and electronics expert Grant Collier, son of Barney. Former operatives Barney and Lisa return in separate episodes, the former being rescued from a Turkish jail, the latter from a team of assassins.

Comment: The hour-long series aired until September 1973 and starred Steven Hill as Briggs, Peter Graves as Phelps, Barbara Bain as Cinnamon, Martin

Landau as Rollin, Greg Morris as Barney, Peter Lupus as Willie, Leonard Nimoy as Paris, Lesley Ann Warren as Dana, Sam Elliott as Doug, Lynda Day George as Lisa, and Barbara Anderson as Mimi. Reportedly, Hill left after one season because he was an Orthodox Jew and unable to shoot late Fridays or Saturdays.

The revived series aired from October 1988 to June 1990, and starred Graves along with Thaao Penghis as Nicholas, Antony Hamilton as Max, Phil Morris (son of Greg) as Grant, Terry Markwell as Casey, and Jane Badler as Shannon. In both versions of the show, Bob Johnson was the voice on the tape/disc.

Dell published five issues of a *Mission: Impossible* comic book from 1967 to 1968. John Tiger wrote the *Mission: Impossible* novel, published in 1966.

INCH HIGH PRIVATE EYE (TV)

First Appearance: *Inch High Private Eye,* September 1973, NBC.

Biography: Despite the fact that he's only 1/12th of a foot tall, the trench-coated Inch High is one of the most successful detectives of the Finkerton Detective Agency, using disguises and gadgets rather than any kind of deductive skill to apprehend evildoers. The dull-witted Inch High is assisted by his niece, Lori, by her Gomer Pyle-like boyfriend, Gator, and by his St. Bernard, Braveheart. The sleuth travels about hiding in Braveheart's fur; the keg strapped to the dog's neck contains the hero's many costumes and crimefighting tools. If the group has to travel a great distance, they take the Hushmobile, which is parked in an unused freight elevator.

Among the more exotic foes of the World's Biggest Little Detective are the Doll Maker, Super Flea, the Cat Burglars, Spumoni, and the Music Maestro.

Comment: Hanna-Barbera produced 13 episodes of the half-hour series, which featured Lennie Weinrib as the voice of Inch High, Kathi Gori as Lori, Bob Lutell as Gator, and Don Messick as Braveheart. The series went off the air in August 1974.

INDIANA JONES (MP, L, C, TV)

First Appearance: *Raiders of the Lost Ark,* 1980, Paramount.

Biography: Born in 1899 or 1900, the son of Henry Jones—professor of medieval literature at George-town University—Indiana Jones grows up with a passion for history and mystery and decides, at a young age, to become an archaeologist. He works at a jazz club to pay his way through the University of Chicago, rooming with future lawman Eliot Ness and aspiring writer Ernest Hemingway, graduates in 1920, ends up on a dig in Greece in 1922, and has a series of adventures around the world. His most famous escapades have him crossing swords with the Frenchman Belloq in Saudi Arabia in 1934 and then again in a search for the Ark of the Covenant in 1936; battling the evil Mola Ram at the Temple of Doom in Mayapore, Asia; and searching for the Holy Grail with his father.

The love of Indy's life was young Marion Raven-wood, whose father, Abner, was a mentor. Marion was infatuated with Indy but he left her, in 1928, promising to return—something he doesn't do until he needs her help in his search for the Ark, eight years later. Though old feelings are rekindled, ultimately they go their separate ways. Indy is also fond of Willie Scott, a cabaret singer, among many other women.

Indy teaches archaeology at Marshall College in Connecticut. In class, he's reserved and even shy; when he's out adventuring, he's confident and swaggering, armed with a ten-foot bullwhip and a pistol (he's a crack shot) and wearing a leather jacket and trademark fedora. Though Indy is an accomplished pilot, he often travels with the more experienced flier Jock Lindsey. And though Indy is virtually fearless, he does have an aversion to snakes.

Comment: Directors George Lucas and Philip Kaufman created the character, drawing heavily on the pulp magazine adventures of Doc Savage and on the movie serials featuring Zorro (especially *Son of Zorro* and *Zorro's Fighting Legion*).

The character was featured in two other theatrical films: *Indiana Jones and the Temple of Doom* (1984) and *Indiana Jones and the Last Crusade* (1989). All starred Harrison Ford as Indy and were directed by Steven Spielberg. The last film also starred River Phoenix as the teenage Indy and Sean Connery as his father, Harry.

On TV, *The Young Indiana Jones Chronicles* aired from 1991 to 1993 on ABC, starring Sean Patrick Flanery as the teenage Indy, Cory Carrier as the younger Indy, and George Rose as old Indy. In 1994–95, Lucas produced four made-for-TV "Young Indiana Jones" movies, which aired on the Family Channel and starred Flannery. The first was *Young Indiana Jones and the Hollywood Follies.*

In literature, all three films were novelized, and there have also been four series of novels. The earliest are the "Find Your Own Adventure" novels, *Indiana Jones and the Curse of Horror Island* and *Indiana Jones and the Lost Treasure of Sheba.* The second are based on the exploits of the adult Indy: *Indiana Jones and the Peril at Delphi, Indiana Jones and the Dance of the Giants, Indiana Jones and the Seven Veils, Indiana Jones and the Genesis Deluge, Indiana Jones and the Unicorn's Legacy,* and *Indiana Jones and the Interior World.* All were were written by Rob MacGregor and published in 1991–92. That series was continued by Martin Caidin in 1993 with the publication of *Indiana Jones and the Sky Pirates.*

A third series was based on episodes of *The Young Indiana Jones Chronicles: The Mummy's Curse, Field of Death, Safari Sleuth, The Secret Peace, Trek of Doom,* and *Revolution!* A fourth series was based on the Young Indiana Jones character, though the stories were originals: *Plantation Treasure, Tomb of Terror, Circle of Death, Secret City, Princess of Peril, Gypsy Revenge, Ghostly Riders,* and *Curse of the Ruby Cross.* Various writers wrote these last two series.

Marvel Comics published adaptations of all three movies as well as a title containing all-new stories, *The Further Adventures of Indiana Jones.* Thirty-four issues were published from 1983 to 1986. In 1991 Dark Horse published a four-issue comic book *Indiana Jones and the Fate of Atlantis.*

Dark Horse also published a six-issue series called *Thunder in the Orient* in 1993.

INSPECTOR LEWIS ERSKINE (TV)

First Appearance: *The F.B.I.,* September 1965, ABC.

Biography: Little is known about Lewis Erskine's private life. He has a young adult daughter, Barbara, whose boyfriend is Agent Jim Rhodes. Erskine is a man of integrity and dogged determination with no sense of humor. His preferred attire is a gray suit, and he's equally at home in a car chase (always in a Ford, which sponsored the show), doing photographic surveillance, or shooting an enemy of the country (always in the shoulder). In addition to Rhodes, the agents who help Erskine track down Communists, dissidents, terrorists, kidnapers, and other criminals are Tom Colby and Chris Daniels. Erskine's superior is Assistant Director Arthur Ward.

Comment: Efrem Zimbalist, Jr., starred as Erskine, and Philip Abbott was Ward throughout the hour-long show's run. Lynn Loring played Barbara, who appeared only in the first season—there was no room for family in this hunt-'em-down series. Her agent-boyfriend, played by Stephen Brooks, lasted just two seasons. Colby was played by William Reynolds and lasted the longest, from 1967 to 1973, while Daniels, played by Shelly Novak, appeared in only the last two seasons. *The F.B.I.* went off the air in September 1974. The series was based on actual cases and was authorized by then-Federal Bureau of Investigation director J. Edgar Hoover.

From October 1981 to August 1982 Mike Connors starred as Ben Slater, a 20-year veteran on ABC's hour-long *Today's F.B.I.*

THE IRON ACE (C)

First Appearance: *Air Fighters Comics* #2, 1942, Hillman Publications.

Biography: According to an ancient legend, "Centuries ago . . . an Iron Ace fought side by side with Charlemagne." The warrior's heroism was such that, "at his death, Charlemagne predicted that this Iron Ace would live again . . . as the champion of freedom." Cut to World War II—RAF flier Captain Britain is shot down over occupied France and takes refuge in the castle of Dr. LaFarge, leader of a resistance group. Unfortunately, enemy soldiers have followed Britain; while he hides behind a case containing the Iron Ace's armor, the Nazis shoot LaFarge for having helped the downed pilot. After sneaking the armor on, Britain charges the Germans with his broadsword, their bullets bouncing ineffectively from his silvery-blue attire. Then, fitting an airplane with armor that resembles his own, the hero takes to the skies, slicing enemy planes in two with his heavily shielded aircraft.

Comment: *Air Fighters Comics* became *Airboy Comics* with #23; Sky Wolf continued in the title until 1947.

See also SKY WOLF.

IRONWOLF (C)

First Appearance: *Weird Worlds* #8, 1973, DC Comics.

Biography: In the 61st century, Lord Ironwolf of Illium—a member planet of the Empire Galaktika—owns forests filled with trees whose antigravity wood is used in the manufacture of starships. When Empress Erika Klein-Hernandez requests that Ironwolf let aliens have the wood, he refuses, concerned that the ships they construct will be used against them. Branded as a traitor and outlaw, Ironwolf takes to his ship, the *Limerick Rake,* destroys the trees, and becomes an outlaw who battles the Empress and her vampiric Blood Legion. Ironwolf's companion and first mate is Shebaba O'Neal, a former freedom fighter who wants to replace the Empire with a democratic form of government.

Dressed in thigh-high boots, a blue shirt and trousers, red cape, and tartanlike sash and tam, Ironwolf is equally adept with the sword or his "old-fashioned gun," a .357 Magnum.

Comment: *Weird Worlds* was created to showcase JOHN CARTER of Mars. When DC's license expired, editor/writer Denny O'Neil and artist Howie Chaykin created Ironwolf. The magazine was canceled with #10 due to a paper shortage; Ironwolf later appeared in a one-shot title (1986). Given the similarities between the comic book and *Star Wars* (see HAN SOLO), it isn't surprising that Chaykin was hired to draw Marvel's *Star Wars* comic book.

IVANHOE (L, C, MP, TV)

First Appearance: *Ivanhoe* by Sir Walter Scott, 1819.

Biography: In the closing years of the 12th century, in the days of the Norman King Richard, Wilfred of Ivanhoe, the son of Cedric of Rotherwood, a Saxon, is in love with the Lady Rowena, the ward of his father and a descendant of the ninth-century Saxon King Alfred. Cedric views a marriage between Rowena and the Saxon noble Athelstane of Coningsburgh as a means of gaining back the English throne for the Saxons. Furious with his son for posing a threat to his plan, Cedric orders him out of the house. Wilfred goes to the court of King Richard, learns "tricks of horsemanship," and joins him as a trusted member of the king's inner circle. Meanwhile, with the support of rebellious Norman nobles, Richard's brother John plots to usurp the throne in the king's absence.

To foil John, Richard returns to England with Ivanhoe, who is disguised behind a laced helmet he never removes, as the Disinherited Knight. Partaking in a tournament at Ashby de la Zouch, Ivanhoe defeats all of John's knights, including the powerful knights Sir Brian de Bois-Guilbert and Sir Reginald Front-de-Boeuf. After refusing to remove his helmet, Ivanhoe is unmasked and lanced, in the chest, by marshals of the field.

Ivanhoe's triumph in the tournament deepens John's fear about the way the Saxons begin to "rise in spirit and courage." Thus, he approves a plan that results in the abduction of Athelstane, Cedric, Rowena, the Jews Rebecca and Isaac of York, and the wounded and helpless Ivanhoe, all of whom are held at Front-de-Boeuf's castle of Torquilstone. A plan is also made to wed John's ally Sir Maurice de Bracy to Rowena, to further weaken any Saxon claims. Rebecca is given to Bois-Guilbert as a handmaiden, and he falls in love with her; she, however, loves Ivanhoe, whom she nurses to health—though not quickly enough to help him join an army of Saxons, led by the famous Locksley (Robin Hood) and Richard (disguised as the Black Knight), attack and burn the castle. Ivanhoe is set free, however, carried to safety by Richard himself. Front-de-Boeuf perishes in the flames and Rebecca is spirited away by Bois-Guilbert, taken to the Preceptory of Templestowe where, to her savior's horror, she is charged by the wicked Grand Master of the Temple and his tribunal with being a witch. She demands a trial by combat, and the still-weak Ivanhoe insists upon being her champion; Sir Brian is named to fight against him. Ivanhoe unseats Sir Brian with but a touch of his lance; the knight dies "a victim to the violence of his own contending passions." Rebecca is released and leaves England with her father. Cedric is impressed enough with Richard to forgive Ivanhoe and permit him to wed Rowena.

The 25-year-old Ivanhoe has "well-formed yet sunburnt features . . . amidst a profusion of short fair hair."

Comment: Author William Makepeace Thackeray wrote a comical sequel to the tale, *Rebecca and Rowena* (1850), in which Ivanhoe is bored with the frankly dull Rowena. Just before she dies, he promises her he will never marry a Jewess. Inevitably, he ends up with the very exciting Jewish woman Rebecca, who converts to Christianity and becomes his wife. Readers of Scott have always suspected that Ivanhoe would have been happier with Rebecca in any case.

Ivanhoe was the second of the *Classics Illustrated* comic books and was published in 1941; a movie adaptation was the last issue of *Fawcett Movie Comics,* #22 in 1952, and Dell published one issue of *Ivanhoe* in 1963.

In motion pictures, Robert Taylor was miscast in the 1952 film *Ivanhoe,* which costarred Elizabeth Taylor as Rebecca.

On TV, Roger Moore played the character in 1958 for a single season in the syndicated half-hour *Ivanhoe;* Eric Flynn (son of Errol) starred in the ten-part adaptation that aired on the syndicated *Family Classics Theater* in 1972. Anthony Andrews played the part in a 1982 made-for-TV movie, *Ivanhoe.*

J

JACK (AND THE BEANSTALK)   (F, L, MP, C, TV, S)

First Appearance: English folklore, date unknown.

Biography: Young Jack and his widowed mother live in a small cottage in the woods. Because they are poor, Jack's mother reluctantly tells him to sell his cow to the butcher; instead of money, however, Jack accepts magic beans. He plants them outside the house (some versions have his mother throwing them away in disgust), and by the following morning they've become a cloud-piercing beanstalk. Climbing it, Jack discovers a land of sheep, beautiful meadows, and an immense castle. He also learns that the realm, which borders Fairyland, was once ruled by a kindly knight and his family. One day a giant (known as Thunderel in some tellings) came and slew the knight, though he spared the knight's wife and three-month-old son. Jack realizes that he himself is that son, and vows to avenge his father.

Hiding in the castle, Jack is nearly discovered when the giant comes to dinner grumbling "Fe, fi, fo, fum. I smell the blood of an Englishman. Be he alive or be he dead, I'll grind his bones to make my bread." But his one-eyed giantess wife serves him dinner and, after eating, the giant falls asleep. While he sleeps, Jack steals a hen that lays golden eggs, a harp with a diamond frame and golden strings, and other treasure. As he runs toward the beanstalk to bring the booty to his mother, the harp decides it doesn't want to go and shouts for help. The giant wakes and gives chase down the beanstalk; Jack reaches the ground first and cuts the beanstalk down, causing the giant to fall and break his neck. Just then a fairy appears, revealing that she had disguised herself as a butcher to test Jack's courage. Now that he's proven himself, she places Jack and his mother in a peacock-drawn chariot and flies them to the giant's castle, where he becomes the benevolent new ruler. As for the poor giantess, she slips down a flight of stairs and breaks her neck as well.

Comment: Some historians consider this Jack to be the same as the heroic JACK, THE GIANT-KILLER. Moreover, the beanstalk appears in the legends of many nations, such as the Norse tree Yggdrasil, which supports the universe. The giant is the equivalent of Zeus, Odin, and other father figures; the treasures, in one form or another, are the rain (riches), the sun (golden eggs), and the wind (the harp). The beanstalk was also the inspiration for the Indian rope trick.

Anthologist Andrew Lang wrote what is considered by many to be the definitive version of the tale, which was published in his *Red Fairy Book* (1890).

In motion pictures, silent short subjects were produced in 1902, 1903, 1912, 1913, 1917, and 1924; cartoon shorts were produced in 1931 and 1933. One segment in the Walt Disney feature *Fun and Fancy Free* (1947) was *Mickey and the Beanstalk,* in which Mickey, Donald, and Goofy go up the beanstalk; the cartoon has also been shown as a separate featurette. Abbott and Costello starred in *Jack and the Beanstalk* in 1952, with Costello as Jack and Buddy Baer as the giant; an animated short, done with silhouette figures, was produced in 1954. An animated short, *Woody and the Beanstalk,* starring Woody Woodpecker, was made in 1966.

In comic books, the traditional tale was told in *Classics Illustrated Junior* #507, 1954.

On TV, Gene Kelly produced and costarred in the 1967 Emmy-winning production *Jack and the Beanstalk.*

On stage, the character was seen in the musical *Into the Woods* by Stephen Sondheim, which premiered in 1987.

JACK ARMSTRONG   (R, L, MP, C)

First Appearance: *Jack Armstrong, the All-American Boy,* 1933, CBS.

Biography: A student at Hudson High in Hudson, U.S.A., (Rah Rah Boola Boola) team captain and top-student Jack Armstrong gets into trouble with his best friend Billy Fairchild—who wants to be just like perfect Jack—and Billy's sister Betty, his girlfriend. These early adventures involve football and basketball games and off-the-court romance and intrigue, often involving crooks who stole the ticket money, test answers snatched from under lock and key, thugs trying to fix the big game, and the like. Jack also has problems with jealous tough Monte Duval, who is constantly trying to frame the hero so *he* can be big man on campus. His sister Gwendolyn is also devious.

When these adventures become redundant, along comes Billy and Betty's uncle Jim, who runs an airplane factory, used to be a captain in army intelligence, and owns an amphibious plane, *The Silver Albatross.* The heroes travel the world with Jim. Many adventures occur in the Hollow World located deep inside the planet. (Jack is rarely at school during this period though, presumably, he was given leave or independent study because of his excellent academic record.)

Throughout his early adventures, Jack seeks peace and happiness for the whole world. After the outbreak of World War II, he urges listeners to be brave and turn the Axis powers into fertilizer.

Eventually graduating, Jack becomes the chief investigator of the Scientific Bureau of Investigation, assisted by Billy and working with Vic Hardy.

Comment: The daily, half-hour series was created by Robert Hardy Andrews and originated in Chicago. It aired until 1950, during which time Jack was played by St. John Terrell (1933), Jim (brother of Don) Ameche (1933–38), Stanley Harris (1938–39), Charles Flynn (1939–43), Michael Rye (1943–44), and Flynn again (1944–50). Playing Billy over the years were Murray McLean, John Gannon, Roland Butterfield, Milton Guion, and Dick York. Noted fantasy author Talbot Mundy was one of the show's scripters.

The series became *Armstrong of the S.B.I.* from 1950 to 1951, with Charles Flynn as the hero. Three 30-minute adventures aired each week, heard over ABC. Dick York was Billy and Ken Griffen, then Carlton Kadell, played Vic.

Jack also starred in a pair of Big Little books: *Jack Armstrong and the Ivory Treasure* (1937) and *Jack Armstrong and the Mystery of the Iron Key* (1939).

In 1947, Wallace Fox directed John Hart in *Jack Armstrong,* a 15-chapter serial. Pierre Watkin was Jim Fairfield, Rosemary La Planche was Betty, and Joe Brown was Billy.

The Parents Institute published 13 issues of a Jack Armstrong comic book from 1947 to 1949. Given the name value of the character, it's surprising that Jack never made the transition to TV.

JACK, DOC, AND REGGIE (R, MP, TV)

First Appearance: *I Love a Mystery,* January 1939, NBC.

Biography: Americans Jack Packard, Doc Long, and Englishman Reggie York fight on behalf of the Chinese during their struggles with Japan and are thought dead after the Japanese bombing of Shanghai. However, they end up in an Oriental prison and, after escaping, agree to get together at New Year's Eve in a bar in San Francisco. There the self-described "Three Comrades" opt to stay together as the A-1 Detective Agency, whose motto is "No job too tough, no mystery too baffling." While their secretaries Jerri Booker and Mary Kay Brown hold down the fort, the heroes travel the nation and solve crimes using their specialties: Jack, his analytical mind (and passionate distrust of women); Texan Doc, his lock-picking ability (and passionate attraction to women); and Reggie, his great strength. Among their foes are ghosts, an ax murderer, smugglers, Indians, kidnapers of millionaires (and sometimes billionaires), a vampire, a magician and his werewolf accomplice, and more.

Jack also partakes in many adventures without his partners. In these he teams with United Nations agents Terry Burke, Swen, and Michael.

Comment: Jack was played, in turn, by Michael Raffetto, Russell Thorson, Jay Novello, and John McIntire. Doc was played by Barton Yarborough and Jim Boles. Reggie was Walter Paterson and Tony Randall. Gloria Blondell was Gerry. The series was created and written by Carlton E. Morse; Sibelius's "Valse Triste" was the famous theme song. The popular series originally aired for 15 minutes five days a week, went to a half hour once a week, then went back to a five-day-a-week schedule when it moved to CBS. It went off the air in December 1944; five years later Mutual started it up again as a five-day-a-week show that lasted until 1952 (the Thorson/Novello/McIntyre, Boles, Randall years).

In motion pictures, Henry Levin directed three films based on the characters: *I Love a Mystery* (1945), *The Devil's Mask* (1946), and *The Unknown* (1946). Jim Bannon played Jack and Barton Yarborough was Doc; there was no Reggie.

The made-for-TV movie *I Love a Mystery* aired in 1973 (it was made in 1967) starring Les Crane as Jack, David Hartman as Doc, and Hagan Beggs as Reggie. In this version the three are now based onboard a 727, which carries them around the world on assignments.

JACK, THE GIANT-KILLER (F, L, MP, C)

First Appearance: Welsh folklore, circa A.D. 600.
Biography: Jack is a young boy who lives in Cornwall

during the reign of King Arthur. During this time, the 18-foot-tall giant Cormoran dwells on nearby St. Michael's Mount and, for years, eats livestock and deprives the farmers of their livelihood. Fond of tales of knights and their deeds, Jack decides to be like his heroes and slay Cormoran. He sets forth, armed with a horn, a shovel, a pickax, armor, and a lantern. After digging a pit outside the giant's cave, Jack covers it over and blows the horn to wake the giant. Cormoran

stumbles forward and falls in; Jack kills him with a blow to the head.

Upon learning of Cormoran's death, the giant Blunderbore vows to get revenge if he ever gets his hands on Jack. Soon thereafter Jack happens to be passing through the wood where the giant lives in an enchanted castle. While Jack naps, Blunderbore captures him and locks him in a room in the castle. Blunderbore goes to fetch his brother, while Jack picks among the

Kerwin Mathews as *Jack, the Giant-Killer.* (Question: Why doesn't he, the princess, and their enchanted animal friends just crawl through the passageway?) © United Artists.

bones and objects in the room looking for some kind of weapon. He finds a long rope and, making a slip knot in either end, waits until the giants return: Jack drops the nooses over their heads, chokes them both, then slides down the rope and stabs each in the heart. He frees three women prisoners and allows them to keep the castle.

Continuing on his journey to Wales, Jack stops at a house and seeks hospitality. Naturally, a giant lives there and invites Jack in. After failing twice to kill the hero, the giant takes his own life. Departing—and now armed with a powerful Sword of Sharpness and an Invisible Coat (presumably taken from one of the previous giants)—Jack rescues a knight and his lady from another giant. After killing the brute with his sword, he learns that the monster has a brother and goes after him in the woods. Wearing his Invisible Coat, Jack swings at the giant's head but takes off only his nose; as the giant flails about with his club, Jack stabs him in the back.

After taking to the road once more, Jack comes to a hermit's hut at the foot of a mountain. The hermit informs Jack that a wizard who lives on top of the mountain has turned the duke's daughter into a deer and is holding her prisoner, guarded by the giant Galligantus. Donning his Coat, Jack climbs the mountain, slips past two fiery griffins, finds a magic trumpet, blows open the castle gates, and slays Galligantus. The sorcerer rides off on a whirlwind; when he leaves, the duke's daughter becomes a human once more and the castle vanishes "like smoke." Jack brings the giant's head to King Arthur, marries the duke's daughter, and lives the rest of his life "in joy and contentment."

Comment: The tales were apparently inspired by the adventures of a warrior who fought for Arthur, though nothing is known of the historical Jack. Some writers view him as a Welsh counterpart to the historical St. George, who lived in the third century A.D. and is famous for his slaying of the dragon. Anthologist Andrew Lang wrote the definitive version of the tale in his *Blue Fairy Book,* published in 1891. It was also collected in his omnibus *The Rainbow Fairy Book.*

The legend of Jack was filmed in 1962 as *Jack the Giant Killer* starring Kerwin Mathews. In the film, which derives from the Lang tale, the sorcerer Pendragon (Torin Thatcher) sends the giant Cormoran to kidnap the Princess Elaine (Judi Meredith). When farmer Jack rescues her, Pendragon sends demons to bring her to his uncharted island. Jack pursues them and saves her once again, destroying Pendragon, who has transformed himself into a harpy.

Dell published a comic book adaptation of the film

in 1962. In 1948 Woody Woodpecker was the hero in *Woody, the Giant Killer.*

JACK RYAN (L, MP)

First Appearance: *The Hunt for Red October* by Tom Clancy, 1984, the Naval Institute Press.

Biography: John Patrick Ryan is the son of Catherine Burke Ryan and Baltimore police officer Emmet William Ryan, both of whom were killed in a plane crash. He has a sister, is married to M.D. Catherine Muller Ryan, and is the father of John Jr. and Sally. After studying economics at Boston College and obtaining his doctorate in history from Georgetown University, Ryan joined the marines as a second lieutenant. A helicopter crash in Crete sidelined him, and to this day he hates flying. Following his truncated military service, Ryan uses his economic training to earn some $20 million on Wall Street. Tired of the rat race, he joins the Naval Academy faculty as a history teacher and writes a number of books, including *Fighting Sailor*—a biography of Admiral Halsey—and *Agents and Agencies,* about intelligence gathering. The latter work comes to the attention of the CIA, and the restless Ryan agrees to join them as an agent.

In his first chronicled adventure, Ryan is working as a liaison between the CIA and the British Secret Intelligence Service when he learns that Soviet Captain Marko Ramius wants to defect with his new magneto-hydrodynamic drive submarine, *Red October.* Only Ryan's intervention prevents the incident from becoming an international disaster. Ryan's second escapade tells of an earlier exploit, when he saves the Prince and Princess of Wales, and their son, from being kidnaped by terrorists.

His third adventure pits him against KGB intrigue during arms negotiations in Moscow, when he must protect Soviet army officer and CIA agent Colonel Mikhail Filitov; and in his fourth he is named deputy director of the CIA and inherits the CIA's illegal but effective antidrug operation in Colombia. In his fifth adventure, the increasingly pressured Ryan becomes embroiled in Middle Eastern politics—as well as a bout with alcoholism that puts a strain on his marriage. He resolves it by leaving government service—at least for now.

Ryan stands six foot one, is a superb marksman, and stays in shape by jogging.

Comment: Ryan is also featured in the novels *Patriot Games* (1987), *The Cardinal of the Kremlin* (1988), *Clear and Present Danger* (1989), and *The Sum of All Fears* (1991). He did not appear in the author's second novel, *Red Storm Rising* (1986). The character was played by Alec Baldwin in the 1990 movie, which costarred Sean Connery as Ramius. Harrison Ford took the part in the 1992 film *Patriot Games*.

JACK WANDER (C)

First Appearance: *Super Comics* #21, 1940, Dell Publishing.
Biography: Red-headed war correspondent Jack Wander is sent to Europe to cover the "great conflict between the nations" (not specifically named . . . yet). When his ship is sunk by a U-boat, Jack is taken prisoner, then liberated when the submarine is bombed by a British plane. Eventually reaching Europe, Jack sets up headquarters in England and, always looking "for something fit to print" that will satisfy his "great and avid public," covers battles, investigates spies, examines POW camps, and witnesses air raids from the ground and from the air. By this time the Germans are identified as such.

His best friend and confidant is George Melton.
Comment: The character was created by Ed Moore and appeared through the fall of 1941.

JAKE CUTTER (TV)

First Appearance: *Tales of the Gold Monkey,* September 1982, ABC.
Biography: In 1938 the Marivella Islands in the South Pacific are the base of spies such as the Dutch priest/German spy Reverend Willie Tenboom; the sinister Princess Koji, a trader and Japanese ally based at Matuka; and her Samurai military leader Todo. It's also the home of Jake Cutter, a former Flying Tigers ace whose Grumman Goose is the only means of flying from island to island. Cutter does more than shuttle passengers and cargo, though; he locates lost travelers, hidden treasure, stolen goods—and works to undermine the activities of Tenboom, Koji, and Todo.

Based at Bora Gora, the freewheeling, two-fisted Jake wears an aviator jacket and a holstered revolver. He smokes cigars and is assisted by his boozy mechanic Corky and the one-eyed terrier Jack, who wears a gold patch over the missing eye. (Jake anted up and lost the poor dog's jewel-bedecked glass eye while gambling.) He's also aided by the foppish Bon Chance Louis, a French official and the owner of the Monkey Bar where the locals hang out (and whose decor gave the show its title); and by singer Sarah Stickney White, who's not only Jake's on-again/off-again girlfriend but an American operative.
Comment: Stephen Collins starred as Jake, with Jeff MacKay as Corky, Caitlin O'Heaney as Sarah, Roddy McDowall as Bon Chance Louis, John Calvin as Tenboom, Marta Dubois as Koji, and John Fujioka as Todo. The hour-long series aired through July 1983.

JAMES BOND (L, TV, MP, CS, C, VG, T)

First Appearance: *Casino Royale* by Ian Fleming, 1953, Jonathan Cape, Ltd.
Biography: James Bond was born on November 11, 1924, the son of a Scottish father, Andrew, and a Swiss mother. Andrew worked for the Vickers Armaments Company, and the family spent a great deal of time on the continent, where young James learned to speak French and German. When he was 11, James's parents were killed in a climbing accident and the boy went to live with his spinster aunt, Charmian Bond. He entered Eton at the age of 12, got into unspecified (but deducible) trouble with a maid in the second semester, and was asked to leave; he transferred to Fettes, where he acquired renown as a lightweight boxer and saw to the establishment of a judo class.

Bond quit school when he was 17, though he subsequently took courses at the University of Geneva, where he also learned to ski. Claiming he was 19, Bond landed a job with the Ministry of Defense in 1941, working for the Special Branch of the Royal Naval Volunteer Reserves. A commander by the end of World War II, he was invited to join the secret service. After successfully executing two important assassinations, he was awarded the seventh Double-O number, which gave him legal license to kill but *only* in the line of duty. By 1954, 007 had been promoted to commander of the Order of St. Michael and St. George in recognition of his exceptional service.

The agent stands 183 centimeters (just over six feet), weighs 76 kilograms (just over 167 pounds), and has "dark, rather cruel good looks" as well as "a three-inch scar (on) the right cheek" (which he does not have in the films). His hair is black. Bond was briefly married to Countess Tracy di Vicenzo; he met the beautiful young woman when her father, powerful gangster Marc-Ange Draco, agreed to provide 007 vital information about his archenemy, Ernst Stavro Blofeld, if Bond would spend some time with the flighty Tracy. The two fell in love and wed; she was shot to death on their honeymoon by Blofeld after Bond thwarted his latest scheme to control the world.

Bond lives in a spacious ground-floor apartment off the King's Road in Chelsea. He has an elderly Scottish housekeeper named May; his hobbies are golf, gambling, luscious and exotic women, and cards. His favorite drink is a dry vodka martini, "shaken not stirred." His best friend is Bill Tanner, chief of staff to "M" (Admiral Sir Miles Messervy), the head of the secret service. He is also close to CIA operative,

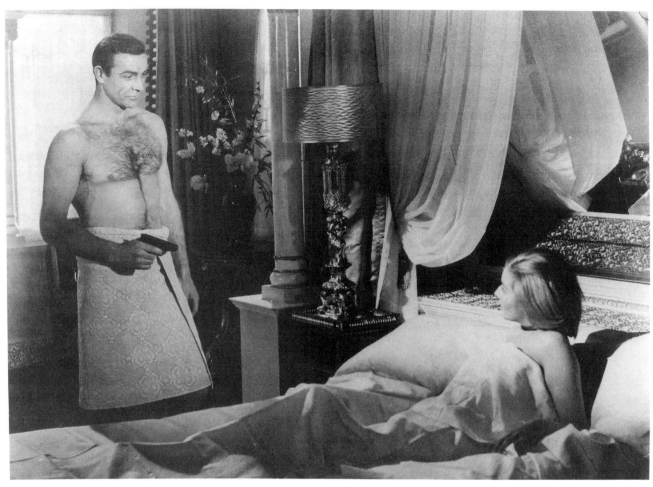

Sean Connery as *James Bond* in *From Russia With Love*. © Eon Productions, courtesy Jerry Juroe.

Texas-native Felix Leiter. Q supplies all of Bond's neat gadgets, from his teletype watch to the Lotus Esprit which transforms into a submarine.

Comment: Bond was created by author Ian Fleming (1908–1964), who wrote 14 books about the master spy: *Casino Royale, Live and Let Die* (1954), *Moonraker* (1955), *Diamonds Are Forever* (1956), *From Russia With Love* (1957), *Dr. No* (1958), *Goldfinger* (1959), *For Your Eyes Only* (1960)—which consisted of the short stories "From a View to a Kill," "For Your Eyes Only," "Quantum of Solace," "Risico," and "The Hildebrand Rarity"—*Thunderball* (1961), *The Spy Who Loved Me* (1962), *On Her Majesty's Secret Service* (1963), *You Only Live Twice* (1964), *The Man With the Golden Gun* (1965), and *Octopussy* (1966)—which contained the short stories "Octopussy," "The Living Daylights," and "The Property of a Lady." After Fleming's death, Kingsley Amis contributed one novel, *Colonel Sun* (1968), but the series wasn't continued in earnest until author John Gardner published *License Renewed* (1981). He has followed

it with *For Special Services* (1982), *Icebreaker* (1983), *Role of Honor* (1985), *Nobody Lives Forever* (1986), *No Deals, Mr. Bond* (1987), *Scorpius* (1988), *Never Send Flowers* (1993) and others, including the novelization of *Licence to Kill* (1989).

Bond's first nonprint incarnation was in a one-hour adaptation of *Casino Royale* for CBS's *Climax Mystery Theater* in 1954; Barry Nelson played Bond as an American, with Leiter as British. Peter Lorre starred as the villain Le Chifre. The character went from TV to the silver screen in 1962, with Sean Connery starring as what many consider to be the definitive Bond in *Dr. No.* He followed it with *From Russia With Love* (1963), *Goldfinger* (1964), *Thunderball* (1965), and *You Only Live Twice* (1967). Connery was replaced by George Lazenby in *On Her Majesty's Secret Service* (1969), returned for *Diamonds Are Forever* (1971), then turned over the mantle to Roger Moore. Moore starred in *Live and Let Die* (1973), *The Man With the Golden Gun* (1974), *The Spy Who Loved Me* (1977), *Moonraker* (1979), *For Your Eyes Only* (1981), *Oc-*

Roger Moore as *James Bond* and a reporter between takes during the shooting of the mountain-climbing sequence in *For Your Eyes Only.* © Danjaq S.A., courtesy Jerry Juroe.

topussy (1983), and *A View to a Kill* (1985). After Pierce Brosnan became unavailable due to a TV commitment, Timothy Dalton was cast and starred in *The Living Daylights* (1987) and *Licence to Kill* (1989). Two Bond films that are not considered part of the series—they weren't made by producers Harry Saltzman and/or Albert "Cubby" Broccoli—are the comedy *Casino Royale* (1967), starring David Niven, who must prevent nephew Woody Allen from shrinking anyone taller than he is, and *Never Say Never Again* (1983), a remake of *Thunderball* with Connery back in the Bond role.

A *James Bond* comic strip, mostly consisting of adaptations of the novels, was begun in the *London Daily Express* in 1957 and continued until 1963. It started up again in 1964, a mix of adaptations and new material, and lasted until 1977. Several collections of

these strips have been published in the U.S., starting in 1981 with *The Illustrated James Bond, 007,* which reprinted *Diamonds Are Forever, Dr. No,* and *From Russia With Love.*

In comic books, Bond starred in an adaptation of *Dr. No* that appeared in DC Comics' *Showcase #43* in 1962; Marvel Comics published a one-shot adaptation of *For Your Eyes Only;* First Comics published new adventures in a title that lasted from 1988 to 1989; Eclipse published a *Licence to Kill* adaptaion as well as the three-issue *James Bond: Permission to Die,* which was published from 1989 to 1991; and Dark Horse Comics published a three-issue *James Bond 007: Serpent's Tooth* in 1992.

A half-hour cartoon series, *James Bond Jr.,* about 007's nephew, went into syndication in September 1991. In 1992 Marvel published 12 issues of a comic book based on the series. In addition to the many toys based on the character, there have been a number of home video games.

JAMES T. WEST (TV, C)

First Appearance: *The Wild Wild West,* September 1965, CBS.

Biography: James T. West is an undercover operative who battles subversives, revolutionaries, master criminals, and other bigtime ne'er-do-wells in the American West. He reports directly to President Ulysses S. Grant and is assisted by fellow secret agent Artemus Gordon, a master of weaponry, accents, and disguises. West is popular with women and handy with a derringer (which can also fire a grapnel). Among his other weapons and tools are a sword hidden in his pool cue, a skeleton key behind his lapel, a two-part derringer in his boot heels, and smoke bombs hidden beneath his holster. The two men travel about in a private railroad car that has sleeping facilities, a kitchen, and is equipped with all of the tools, weapons, chemicals, and papers they might require for any task. If need be, they can exit quickly by a hatch in the fireplace.

Their recurring foe is Dr. Miguelito Loveless, a megalomaniac intent on world conquest.

Comment: The hour-long series aired until September 1970 and starred Robert Conrad as West and Ross Martin as Artemus Gordon; Michael Dunn appeared as Loveless. The series was created by Michael Garrison. The characters returned in the TV movies *The Wild Wild West Revisited* (1979), in which Loveless is cloning world leaders (his "$600 men"), and *More Wild Wild West* (1980), in which Jonathan Winters is looking to take over the West.

In comic books, Gold Key published seven issues of *The Wild Wild West* from 1966 to 1969, while Millennium Publications published four more from 1990 to 1991.

The character bears some similarities to Shotgun

James T. West (right) works undercover. © Viacom.

Slade, who was featured in the half-hour, syndicated *Shotgun Slade* from 1959 to 1961. Played by dashing Scott Brady, Slade was a detective who worked out West for the likes of Wells Fargo, miners, insurance companies, saloon owners, and ranchers. He spent nearly as much time romancing the ladies as he did hunting down wrongdoers.

JANDAR (L)

First Appearance: *Jandar of Callisto* by Lin Carter, 1972, Dell Publishing.

Biography: Born in Rio, the son of Scottish engineer Matthew Dark and a Danish mother (whose name is not provided), the yellow-haired, blue-eyed Jonathan Andrew Dark learns how to fight, handle a knife, and shoot while hanging out with his father's workers. A naturalized American, Dark spends three years at Yale and becomes captain of the fencing team. Unable to join the air force and serve in Vietnam due to "some technicality over my naturalization papers," the over six-footer goes to work as a pilot for the International Red Cross. Engine trouble forces his helicopter down over Cambodia in March 1969. Lost in the jungle, he comes upon the ancient city of Arangkôr, stumbles into a magic well, and, thanks to a mystic transporter beam therein, finds himself spirited to Callisto, the fifth moon of Jupiter. Called Thantor by the natives, the jungle world of Callisto is the home of barbaric races—some human, some not—monsters, and strange magic and science. Dark is called Jandar by the locals, and, after rescuing the Ku Thad warrior-princess Darloona of Shondakor from the evil Black Legion, he makes her his mate and thus becomes Prince of Shondakor.

Comment: The first Callisto novel was followed by *Black Legion of Callisto* (1972), *Sky Pirates of Callisto* (1973), *Mad Empress of Callisto* (1975), *Mind Wizard of Callisto* (1975), *Lankar of Callisto* (1975), *Yylana of Callisto* (1977), and *Renegade of Callisto* (1978). The character was inspired by JOHN CARTER and, indeed, Lin Carter dedicated the first book to author Edgar Rice Burroughs.

See also THONGOR.

JASON (M, MP, C)

First Appearance: Greek mythology, circa 1500 B.C.

Biography: Jason is the son of Alcimede and Aeson, the king of Iolcus (a.k.a. Jolco) in Thessaly. When Aeson's half brother Pelias murders the king and seizes the throne, young Jason is carried off to Mt. Pelion, where he is raised by the wise Chiron, the centaur who also reared Hercules. Jason remains with Chiron until he reaches the age of 20, at which time he returns to Iolcus to reclaim his throne. But Pelias has other ideas: He tells Jason to fetch him the Golden Fleece—the skin of a golden ram sacrificed to Zeus years before—which is kept in faraway Colchis. If the gods see fit to protect Jason, Pelias says he will give up the throne without a struggle.

Jason agrees and assembles a crew consisting of the demigod Hercules, Castor and Pollux, Orpheus, Theseus, Nestor, Peleus, and others. Their ship is the *Argo,* built by Argus (a.k.a. Argos), whose work is closely supervised by the goddess Athene, a daughter of Zeus—who wishes to see Jason triumph. The journey is long and arduous. Jason first encounters the Sirens, three women—Leukosia, Ligeia, and Parthenope (some accounts say there were only two, Aglaiophemi and Thelxiepeia)—whose beautiful song lures sailors to their deaths on the nearby reefs. (Athene's onboard priest, Butes, jumps overboard to reach them, but is rescued by the goddess Aphrodite.) Next he defeats the winged harpies who plague the seer Phineus; in gratitude, Phineus tells them how to pass through the Symplegades, the Clashing Islands. Once under way, the Argonauts lose Hercules when his dear friend Hylas dies, lured to his death in a well by a nymph. Hercules is so enraged that his fellow sailors refuse to let him back onboard and set sail without him.

Once through the Symplegades, the journey to Colchis is relatively uneventful. However, King Aetes will not just hand over the Fleece. Jason must first tame the wild bulls and kill the dragon that never sleeps, creatures that Zeus appointed to guard the Fleece since it was placed there. With the help of Aetes's daughter, the sorceress Medea, Jason succeeds in these two tasks, and also defeats the fully armed soldiers who arise when the dead dragon's teeth are sown in the ground.

Though Aetes goes back on his word, Jason takes the Fleece and flees with Medea, who has fallen in love with him. The witch delays her father and his soldiers by chopping up her half brother, Apsyrtos, and scattering his remains about the sea; Aetes pauses to collect and bury them. However, the Argonauts are so horrified by the deed that they insist on stopping at the island of the sorceress Circe to make a sacrifice and be purified. They also stop in Crete, where they are met by Talos—a bronze man who sits in fire, becomes superhot, and then embraces sailors. Medea saves the crew by imploring spirits of the underworld to guide Talos toward rocks, where he scrapes his ankle and bleeds to death.

Upon reaching Iolcus, Jason finds that Pelias has no intention of giving up the throne. Once again Medea intervenes—she tells Pelias that his youth will be restored if he bathes in a magic pot filled with boiling water. He agrees, she provides the pot, and Pelias boils to death. Jason has the throne, but the populace is so sickened by the witch that he and Medea are forced to leave the kingdom. They settle in Corinth where they're happy for several years, until Jason falls in love with Glacue, the daughter of King Creon. He leaves Medea and their two sons to marry her, and, in a rage, the witch sends Glauce a poisoned garment that burns her to death as soon as she dons it. Then Medea slits the throats of her sons, murders Creon, and burns his and Jason's palace to ashes. Medea climbs into a chariot drawn by winged dragons and laughs at Jason as she flies to her new home in Athens. (She weds King Aigeus, but is banished when she tries to kill his son Theseus. With nowhere else to go, she eventually returns to Colchis.)

Lost and grief-stricken, Jason goes back to the *Argo*. After falling asleep on its deck, he is crushed to death when a rotting mast falls on him. (Some accounts say he was murdered by an unspecified interloper.) Though there are no physical descriptions of Jason, it is believed that the story is based on a quest that did, in fact, take place.

Comment: The argosy of Jason has been recounted in a number of films, most notably *Hercules* (1957), *Giants of Thessaly* (1960), *Jason and the Argonauts* (1963), and *Medea* (1970). *Jason and the Argonauts* was adapted in comic book form by Dell in their *Movie Classics* title (1963).

JEAN ROGERS   (C)

First Appearance: "Just Imagine Jeanie," *Questar* #4, 1979, MW Communications.

Biography: During World War II, a scientist creates a formula that turns ordinary men into "demigod supersoldiers." Only one such superman is created before the scientist is slain by enemy agents. (Implicitly, the superman is the comic book hero Captain America, a.k.a. Steve Rogers.) After the war, he marries and fathers a daughter, Jean. But agents of unknown origin find him, murder his wife, and the hero vanishes. Jean is raised by relatives and becomes an accomplished athlete, attorney, author, and head of the Harvard Law School. Some time in the 1970s, agents discover the original supersoldier formula, determine that Jean was the most suitable subject on which to test it, and abduct her, taking her to Pittsburgh. But instead of turning her into a superhero, the serum puts her to sleep for a century. After awaking in the city of Pitz, she suffers from amnesia and sets about trying to learn what happened to her. In the meantime, she

enters and wins the World Beauty Contest, finds a good friend in Telenews reporter Dee, and gets into various adventures in the brave new world of the future.

Comment: Jean was created by science fiction fan Forrest Ackerman, who drew inspiration from the films *Metropolis* and *Just Imagine,* and the hero BUCK ROGERS. Ackerman wrote the first four of the six adventures; different artists worked on the strip.

J.E.B. STUART   (C)

First Appearance: *G.I. Combat* #87, 1959, DC Comics.

Biography: In 1942 the ghost of Alexander the Great orders the ghost of Confederate General James Ewell Brown Stuart to watch over the Stuart M3 tank commanded by Sergeant Jeb Stuart Smith in North Africa. At first, the general is furious, since Jeb and his crew are Yankees. But he's won over by their bravery and by the fact that young Jeb idolized the general as a kid. He becomes the advisor to the sergeant, tipping him off when he sees something in the near future that will be a menace to him. Except for those who are dying, Jeb is the only mortal able to see the guardian spirit; as a courtesy, the sergeant (later, lieutenant) flies the Stars and Bars over his tank.

In one adventure J.E.B. Stuart gets back into battle himself, battling the Nazi-summoned ghost of Alaric the Goth. If anything happens to his namesake during the war, the general will find himself in limbo as a "punishment" for not doing a good job.

Tanks come and go over the years (at last account, Stuart commands a Sherman), as do members of his crew. The original team is comprised of Corporal Arch Asher, the loader; Corporal Slim Stryker, the driver; and Private Rick Rawlins, the gunner. When Asher dies inside a burning Nazi tank—leading it away from his friends—he is replaced by Corporal Gus Gray, a 1936 Olympic star and former POW. When Stryker is killed in another blast, Sergeant Bill Craig takes his place, bringing along 30 years of military experience. Craig's son Eddie joins shortly thereafter, as a loader.

Comment: The characters continued to appear in *G.I. Combat* through most of its run, which lasted to #288. They were instrumental in the formation of THE LOSERS and have guest-starred in other DC war titles. *DC Special Blue Ribbon Digest* #12 consisted entirely of Haunted Tank reprints.

JEFF DILLON   (TV)

First Appearance: *Fame Is the Name of the Game,* November 1966, NBC (see COMMENT).

Biography: Beginning his journalistic career as a newsboy, tough, brash Jeff Dillon works his way up the ladder and becomes an investigative reporter for Glenn Howard's powerful *People* magazine. He is based in Los Angeles, where his first chronicled adventure is trying to find out which client was responsible for the murder of a call girl. After that, he becomes involved with other murders as well as abductions and robberies.

Also part of the Howard team is Dan Farrell, a retired FBI agent who is senior editor of *Crime.* His bailiwick is the mob.

Editorial assistant Peggy Maxwell works for Dillon, Farrell, and Howard.

Comment: The original TV movie was very loosely inspired by both Tiffany Thayer's novel *One Woman* and the 1949 Alan Ladd film *Chicago Deadline.* The success of the film inspired a regular 90-minute series, *The Name of the Game,* which aired on NBC from September 1968 to September 1971. Anthony Franciosa played Dillon in both the film and series, with Gene Barry as Howard (George Macready played the part in the movie), Robert Stack as Farrell (not in the movie), and Susan Saint James as Peggy ("introduced" in the movie).

JEFF HAWKE (CS)

First Appearance: *Jeff Hawke, Space Rider,* February 1954, *The Daily Express* (Great Britain).

Biography: Jeff Hawke is a squadron leader with the RAF, a test pilot who flies supersonic aircraft until he meets up with a flying saucer. Jeff's X.P.5 is outmaneuvered by the alien vessel, but as the experimental ship goes down, Jeff is saved by the tentacled extraterrestrials. They spirit him to a point beyond the moon and make him an offer: They will return him to Earth, with no recollection of the encounter, or he can help to make Earth a member world of the vast Galactic Federation. The choice is a simple one for Hawke, who elects to join the aliens and bring Earth rocketing into the space age. With the help of the aliens, and with a hand-picked partner, Commander "Mac" Maclean of Canada, he helps to build a space station for terrestrial families, explores remote worlds, and battles the evil Chalcedon, who seeks to overthrow the Overlord of the Galactic Federation.

Comment: The strip was created by writer Eric Souster and artist Sidney Jordan and ran until 1974.

The British have a rich history of space heroes, especially in comic books. Among them are Crash Carew, "Daredevil of the stratosphere," who, with his assistant Billy, pilot their spaceship the *Marlin* on many adventures in *Comic Adventures* in the early 1940s; Dane Jerrus, Agent One of the Interplanetary Solar Force, who, with his sidekick Chummy Brown, fight their way through space in *Super Duper Comics* of the late 1940s; Swift Morgan and his fiancee, Silver, who battle aliens and travel through time in the pages of *The Adventures of Swift Morgan* from 1948 to 1954; Sam English, Museum Rover, who, with his secretary Vel Burrows, travels from planet to planet in a backup feature in Swift Morgan's magazine; the 21st century's Rex Cosmo, Cosmic Scientist, who, with his aide Stella Vance, zooms through the pages of *Scoop Comics* in the late 1940s, battling the Martian Pirates, the Zombies of Pluto, and the like; Pat Peril, "the fearless fighter of the future," who flies the spaceship *Terra* through the pages of *Modern Comics* in the late 1940s; Ace Rogers, who commands the *Planet Plane* and stout fellows such as Mark Logran in the pages of *Comic Adventures* of the late 1940s (during the early 1940s, Ace had battled Axis agents aboard the submarine *Salvo*); Martin Power, Space Investigator, who guides his one-man ship through space in *Power Comics* of the early 1950s; Bradford Kane of the Galactic Patrol, who appeared in *Space Hero* comics in the early 1950s; Space Rover Pete of *Dynamic Thrills* in the early 1950s; Space Kingley of the Interplanetary Rangers, who had his own title in the early 1950s; Ace Hart, Space Squadron Commander, who appeared in *Lone Star Magazine* in the middle 1950s, along with his mascot Marmaduke, a chimpanzee; Jack Trent, Space Flyer, pilot of the spaceship *Starflash* and hero of *The Jet Comic* in the middle 1950s; Dick Barton, Special Agent, who flew through space in the pages of *Comet* in the middle 1950s; Captain Sciento, a bearded investigator who travels through the universe onboard the spaceship *Asteroid,* working the will of the United Interplanetary Organization in *Star-Rocket* and *All Action Comic* of the middle 1950s; Captain Valiant, ace of the Interplanetary Patrol, a space-police force that appeared in *Space Comics* of the middle 1950s; Pete Mangan of the Space Patrol, who appeared in his own title at the same time as Ace; Space Commander Kerry, who worked for the Interplanetary Special Service and also had his own title in the middle 1950s; Sparky Malone of the Special Assignment Group, who starred in *Space Commando* in the middle 1950s; Hal Starr of the Galactic Federation's Space Security Patrol, a feature in *Strange Worlds* in the middle 1950s; Thor Steel, chief of the Interplanetary Police in the 23rd century, whose adventures were chronicled in *Super-Sonic* in the middle 1950s; Rex Strong, Space Ace, who appeared in several different titles in the middle 1950s; and Space Ace, Guardian of the Future, who appeared in his own title in the early 1960s.

Jesse Bravo takes a break. © Alex Toth.

JESSE BRAVO (C)

First Appearance: *The Rook* #3, 1980, Warren Publishing.

Biography: A dead ringer for Errol Flynn, the two-fisted Jesse Bravo is an ex-navy pilot who spent time in Nevada and Alaska before becoming a movie stunt pilot. After earning enough money to buy a plane, he founds Bravo Air Charter Service in 1935. The endeavor is marginally successful, and Bravo still works in movies to pay the bills. His friend/mechanic/body-guard is the .45-packing Bumper.

Comment: The *Bravo for Adventure* strip was written and drawn by the inimitable Alex Toth, and appeared in a lengthy serialized adventure involving gamblers, Orion Pictures, and corrupt pilots.

JET DREAM AND HER STUNT-GIRL COUNTERSPIES (C)

First Appearance: *Jet Dream* #1, 1968, Gold Key Comics.

Biography: Jet Dream is the leader of a group of "acrobeauts" who work with government counterintelligence agent Martin Brown, protecting free people the world over. The other members of the team work their everyday jobs until they're needed: Cookie Jarr, an Olympic gymnast turned movie stunt actor; Petite, an actress who is tough as steel and is a connoisseur of wine, perfume, and cuisine; Ting-a-Ling, who works at the headquarters; and Marlene (profession unknown). When Jet signals them via radio earrings, they drop what they're doing and report by any means possible to her headquarters, an underground complex located "somewhere on the southern coast of California."

In their only chronicled adventure, the ladies pro-

tect a Central American freedom fighter who's been targeted for death.

All of the women are martial arts masters and pilots with their own private jets; their cars are equipped with TV spy cameras, smoke bombs, and other gadgets. Ting-a-Ling wears a ring camera to take candid shots.

Comment: Alas—there was only one issue of *Jet Dream*.

JET SCOTT (CS)

First Appearance: *Jet Scott,* September 1953, New York Tribune, Inc.

Biography: Jet Scott is an employee of the Pentagon's small, secret, Office of Scientifact, where he is on hand to oversee or safeguard the testing of atomic-age weapons, tracking down stolen plutonium, helping to dispose of deadly new chemicals safely, and, in one of his most dazzling exploits, commandeering a three-

Jet Dream, left, with Ting-a-Ling and Petite; Cookie Jarr is in the plane with Marlene behind her. © Gold Key Comics.

stage rocket in an effort to rescue a pilot stranded in a test plane 250 miles up.

Comment: The strip was created by artist Jerry Robinson and writer Sheldon Stark and lasted nearly two years.

JIM HARDIE (TV, C)

First Appearance: *Tales of Wells Fargo,* March 1957, NBC.

Biography: Jim Hardie is a special agent for Wells Fargo and handles chores as diverse as investigating holdups and retrieving stolen goods; riding shotgun on important shipments, helping passengers or employees who have been threatened, gone crooked, or are just having problems at home; and nipping robberies in the bud.

In his later years (the final season), Jim buys a ranch near San Francisco. When he isn't working as an agent, he is busy working as a rancher. His sidekick is Beau McCloud and his foreman is Jeb Gaine; the widow

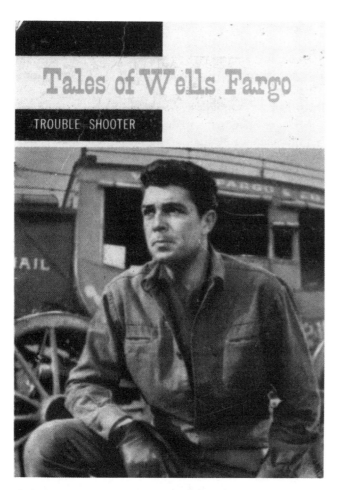

Dale Robertson as Jim Hardie in a rare Tales of Wells Fargo trading card from 1958. © Topps Chewing Gum.

Ovie lives on the adjoining spread, with her daughters Tina and Mary Gee.

Comment: The half-hour series aired through September 1961, then expanded to an hour until September 1962. Dale Robertson starred as Hardie, with Jack Ging as Beau, William Demarest as Gaine, Virginia Christine as Ovie, Lory Patrick as Tina, and Mary Jane Saunders as Mary Gee. Plans to have Hardie work at other Fargo offices around the world—beginning with Rome—were scrapped in favor of the ranch motif, much to star Robertson's chagrin.

Dell published seven issues of *Tales of Wells Fargo* under their *4-Color* banner from 1958 to 1961, and also in numbers 22 to 24 of their *Western Roundup* series.

JIMMIE ALLEN (R, L)

First Appearance: *The Air Adventures of Jimmie Allen,* NBC, 1933.

Biography: Originally Jimmie Allen is a pilot in training out of the National Airways terminal in Kansas City. However, World War I ace Speed Robertson takes him under his wing, and, in no time, Jimmie has gone from copilot to pilot. Together he and Speed have many adventures on his sleek plane, the *Blue Bird Special,* chasing spies and smugglers, engaging in races, searching for missing persons, and even fighting a mad scientist now and then, such as the insane Professor Proteus, who intends to drop poison gas on major American cities. Once in a while they actually manage to get some work done for National, their employer.

At the airfield, Flash is the pilot's trusted mechanic; Barbara Croft is Jimmie's girlfriend.

Comment: Murray McLean starred as Jimmie in the original adventures, which aired weekdays until 1936; after that, various local stations recreated the adventures for approximately 15 years, using the original scripts from the series as performed by new actors.

One Big Little Book, *Jimmie Allen in the Air Mail Robbery,* was published in 1936.

The character was created by Robert M. Burrtt and Willfred G. Moore, who also created SKY KING.

JIM ROCKFORD (TV)

First Appearance: *The Rockford Files,* March 1974, NBC.

Biography: Jim Rockford is a detective who once did time for a crime he didn't commit. When new evidence turned up and he was set free, Rockford decided to take on cases that appeared to be open and shut—and open them again. His ability to embarrass the police in this fashion earns him both the respect and wrath of Detective Dennis Becker, who is frequently and unhappily drawn into the cases. Rockford's father, Joseph "Rocky" Rockford, a retired truck driver, also lends a hand, as does Rockford's inamorata Beth Davenport, an attorney, and one of the few people who puts up with his abrasive personality. Rockford is frequently coming to the rescue of his former cellmate, Evelyn "Angel" Martin.

Rockford lives in a trailer on a beach in Los Angeles. (He says it's "cheap, tax-deductible, earthquake-proof, and when I get a case out of town, I take it with me.") When he needs to get around locally, the detective drives a gold Pontiac Firebird.

His fee is a hefty $200 a day.

Comment: James Garner starred as Rockford, Noah Beery, Jr., was Rocky, Joe Santos was Becker, Gretchen Corbett played Beth, and Stuart Margolin was Angel. Tom Selleck joined the cast in the show's last season as rival sleuth Lance White.

The series, created by Stephen J. Cannell, began as a TV movie and made its debut in September 1974. The hour-long episodes aired through July 1980.

Beginning in 1994, Garner returned as Rockford in the first of six, two-hour-long made-for-TV movies.

JOE MANNIX   (TV, L)

First Appearance: *Mannix,* September 1967, CBS.

Biography: Originally the Los Angeles-based Joe Mannix is an employee of Intertect, a detective agency that uses high-tech equipment to solve crimes. Reporting to Lou Wickersham, Joe Mannix forgoes the computers and relies on nothing more than his wits, fists, and gun. Indeed, Mannix is so independent that after a year he sets up his own agency in West Los Angeles, hiring secretary Peggy Fair—the widow of a murdered police officer. Over the years, Mannix works closely with Lieutenants Adam Tobias, Dan Ives, George Kramer, but especially Adam Tobias of the police department.

Comment: The hour-long series aired through August 1975. Mike Connors starred as Mannix, Gail Fisher was Peggy, Robert Reed was Tobias, Jack Ging was Ives, Larry Linville was Kramer, Ward Wood was Malcolm, and Joseph Campanella was Lou Wickersham.

Connors had previously starred in *Tightrope,* a half-hour series that aired on CBS from September 1959 to September 1960. In it he played an undercover agent named Nick (his last name was never revealed) who infiltrated and undermined organized crime.

Michael Avallone wrote a novel, *Mannix,* inspired by the series.

JOE PALOOKA   (CS, C, MP, L, R, TV)

First Appearance: "Joe Palooka," 1928, McNaught Syndicate.

Biography: A blond, naive, good-hearted country boy, Joe Palooka is a 207-pound boxing hero who, managed by Knobby Walsh, becomes heavyweight champion of the world, battling tough opponents in the ring and out, as he faces corrupt handlers, headline-seeking politicians, gamblers, and killers. Indeed, in one of his first adventures, Joe is accused of being part of a fix and, with no other options, joins the French Foreign Legion. During World War II, he enlists in the army and becomes the champ, defeating the navy's best man, 219.5-pound Tarpaulin Grumpopski. He also finds time to fight Nazis, punching them out on submarines and on the streets of Paris, and even shooting at Hitler. Defying military tradition, he reenlists during the Korean War and fights at Inchon, where he is wounded in the arm.

Joe has also battled a number of animals: He's boxed a bear, fought a bull, and wrestled with an alligator. In addition to boxing, Joe is an excellent swimmer, horseman, and ice skater. His close friends are Jerry Leemy, Smokey, the rotund Humphrey, and young Little Max, a mute.

Joe marries longtime Ann Howe in 1949, and they have two children, Joe, Jr. (Buddy), and Joannie.

Comment: The strip was created by Ham Fisher, who personally peddled it to newspapers while working as a salesman for McNaught. It went national two years later. Fisher took his life in 1956. Moe Leff was the artist briefly, then Tony Di Preta became the permanent new artist.

The first *Joe Palooka* comic book, published in 1933, was a one-shot reprint of newspaper strips. Publication Enterprises published four issues featuring new stories from 1942 to 1944; in 1945 Harvey Publications launched a 118-issue run that lasted until 1961.

In motion pictures, the character was played by Stu Erwin in the 1934 film *Palooka,* with Jimmy Durante as Knobby. The picture has also been shown as *Joe Palooka.* A series of short subjects was made during the 1940s.

Joe was the subject of one Big Little book, *Joe Palooka, The Heavyweight Boxing Champ* (1934).

On radio, the character was played, in turn, by Teddy Bergman, Norman Gottschalk, and Karl Swenson. The Chicago-based show aired during the 1930s.

On TV, the character was played by Joe Kirkwood, Jr., in the half-hour series that was syndicated for a single season in 1954.

Other boxing strips followed "Joe Palooka," including "Curley Kayoe" in 1945 and "Big Ben Bolt" in the

1950s to 1960s. In comic books, Boom Boom Brannigan was a protagonist in *Prize* comics in the late 1940s, battling Urko the gorilla in the ring as well as the Man with the Fighting Feet, overcoming a poisoned glove, and more.

JOHN CARTER (L, CS, C)

First Appearance: *Under the Moons of Mars* by Edgar Rice Burroughs, Feb.-July 1912, *The All-Story* Magazine.

Biography: John Carter was born in Virginia, exact date unrevealed. He fights the Sioux for several years, then joins the Confederate army at the outbreak of war and rises to the rank of captain. After the war, when Carter is "about 30," he and his friend Captain James K. Powell head west in search of gold. After discovering a mine in Arizona, they're attacked by Apaches; Powell dies, but Carter escapes to a cave. There he is mystically drawn to the planet Mars (which is called Barsoom by the natives), where he is captured by giant, four-armed, green Tharks. Because of the lesser gravity of Mars, Carter has great strength and is able to jump higher than the natives; he is also so adept with a sword that he is known as the greatest swordsman of two worlds. Carter manages to escape from the Tharks (who call him Dotar Sojat) with another human, the beautiful Princess Dejah Thoris of Helium, whom he eventually weds. They enjoy five Mars years together (nine Earth years), undergoing many adventures alongside Carter's closest friend, Tars Tarkas, a Thark, before Carter is inexplicably drawn back to Earth (called Jasoom by the Martians).

He is able to return to Mars again in March 1886, taken from his home on the banks of the Hudson, where he often raised his hands to the starlit skies.

Carter stands "a good two inches over six feet," and his features are "regular and clear-cut." His eyes are steel gray.

Carter and Dejah Thoris have a son, Carthoris, who is married to Thuvia, Princess of Ptarth; and a daughter, Tara, who is the wife of Gahan of Gathol and the mother of Llana.

Another earthman drawn to Mars is Ulysses Paxton, who is hit by a German shell while serving in France during World War I; moments later he's on Mars.

It is clear that Barsoom is actually the Mars of another time and/or dimension, though the physics of it all is never made clear.

Comment: The original novel was attributed to "Norman Bean," a misreading of the pseudonym Burroughs had selected: Normal Bean. It was first published in book form as *A Princess of Mars* in 1917. The next eight novels were published between 1913 and 1939.

In both magazine and book form, they were titled *The Gods of Mars; The Warlord of Mars; Thuvia, Maid of Mars; The Chessmen of Mars; The Master Mind of Mars* (which introduces Paxton); *A Fighting Man of Mars; Swords of Mars;* and *Synthetic Men of Mars.* Four short stories were published in *Amazing* in 1941: "The City of Mummies," "Black Pirates of Barsoom," "Yellow Men of Mars," and "Invisible Men of Mars"; these were collected in book form as *Llana of Gathol.* The novellas "John Carter and the Giant of Mars" and "Skeleton Men of Jupiter" were published in *Amazing* in 1941 and 1943, respectively; they were published in book form as *John Carter of Mars* in 1964.

Edgar Rice Burroughs's son, John Coleman Burroughs, created a comic strip that was published in 1941–42. It was reprinted in 1970 in paperback by the House of Greystoke.

In comic books, John Carter starred in four issues of Dell's *4-Color* magazine in 1952–53; these were reprinted by Gold Key in three issues of *John Carter of Mars* in 1964. This time he is fighting in a 20th century war when he is swept to Mars. DC published new comics featuring John Carter in *Tarzan* #207–#209 in 1972, and in the first seven issues of *Weird Worlds* (1972–73). Marvel Comics published 28 issues of *John Carter, Warlord of Mars* from 1977 to 1979, with three annuals.

In the late 1960s Leigh Brackett wrote a screenplay for an unproduced film; in 1991 Bob Gale wrote one for Cinergi. Though $5 million was spent on preproduction, the film was canceled when the budget was projected at $80 million.

See also CARSON NAPIER; DAVID INNES.

JOHN DRAKE (TV, C)

First Appearance: *Danger Man,* 1961, BBC (Great Britain).

Biography: One of the world's greatest security agents and womanizers, John Drake works under the auspices of NATO. The suave, two-fisted Drake travels around the world, selling his services only to governments. Later he goes to work for the British government as a spy, still traveling the world, posing as an Arab, a sportsman, a soldier, an aspiring Russian spy, or any other identity that will help him "preserve world peace and promote brotherhood" among the nations of the world.

Though Drake dislikes guns ("ugly, oily things"), he uses them when he has to. He also carries a typewriter loaded with gadgets, including a camera, tape recorder, and an electric shaver.

Comment: The half-hour *Danger Man* aired in the U.S., on CBS, from April to September 1961. Drake resurfaced as a spy on *Secret Agent,* an hour-long show that aired on the BBC in 1964 and on CBS from April 1965 to September 1966. Patrick McGoohan played the part in both shows.

Implicitly, the character is the same as McGoohan's Number 6, a spy who resigns from the secret service and is gassed unconscious in his London flat. When he wakes, he's in a pastoral place called the Village, whose masters (British? Communist? Both?) keep him on a short leash, demanding to know why he resigned. The character's efforts to resist and escape were the heart of the 17 hour-long episodes of *The Prisoner,* which aired on CBS from June 1968 to September 1969.

Dell published one issue of *Danger Man* as part of their *4-Color* series (#1231) in 1961, and Gold Key published two issues of a *Secret Agent* comic book, one in 1966 and one in 1968.

JOHN HENRY   (F, MP)

First Appearance: American folklore, 1872, author unknown.

Biography: Weighing 33 pounds at birth (some sources say 44) and learning to sing songs that same day, the powerful John Henry picks up his father's 12-pound hammer, leaves home before midnight, and goes to work for the Chesapeake and Ohio Railroad in West Virginia for $4 a day plus room and board. His job is to hammer long steel rods into rock, making openings into which nitroglycerin can be poured to blast a path for the track layers. He also meets and weds Polly Ann, to whom he is devoted.

When a salesman offers foreman Captain Tommy a steam drill to drive in the rods, Henry tells Tommy that no machine can do a job better than a man—and he sets out to prove it. A contest is held at the Big Bend Tunnel pitting Henry and two 20-pound hammers against the steam drill. The race lasts for nine hours, with Henry stopping just once an hour to drink water from Polly Ann's dipper. Henry wins by three holes, though the strain proves too great for him and his heart bursts. After kissing one of his hammers and then his wife, Henry expires. The steel-driving man is buried in a hillside, a hammer in each hand, a steel rod across his chest, and a shovel at his head and feet.

Comment: There was a real-life John Henry, a strong, proud black laborer who worked for the C. & O. Railroad. According to scant historical records, he may well have met and defeated a mechanical drill.

In motion pictures, Henry was the subject of George Pal's 1946 Puppetoon *John Henry and the*

Inky Poo. In it Henry is 12 feet tall and has muscles of steel. His voice was provided by actor Rex Ingram.

JOHN LAW   (C)

First Appearance: *Smash Comics* #3, 1939, Quality Comics.

Biography: A product of the slums of Crossroad City's Lower East Side, John Law is the son of a widower, a washed-up boxer and part-time crook. After accidentally killing his close friend Officer Serf during a robbery, the elder Law blows his own brains out. Young John goes to work as a junior clerk in the D.A.'s office, eventually joins the Crossroad police department—losing his left eye in the line of duty—and becomes a crack detective, a man who is "strong, decent, and believes in the rules he defends."

Law reports to Chief Bunyan and is frequently assisted by shoeshine boy Nubbin Butts (who is himself helped by his pet puppy Tiger) and by Sergeant O'Cork.

The proposed cover for the never-published magazine featuring *John Law.* © Will Eisner.

Comment: The character was created by artist Will Eisner and appeared in just ten issues. Eclipse published a one-shot *John Law Detective* in 1983, featuring stories drawn in 1948 for a proposed Nubbin magazine but never published in their original form. (They were revised and used in Eisner's superhero strip "The Spirit.")

Smash Comics also featured the adventure heroes Wings Wendall and police office Rookie Rankin.

JOHNNY CYPHER (TV)

First Appearance: *Johnny Cypher in Dimension Zero,* 1967, syndicated.

Biography: A young scientific genius, Johnny Cypher invents a time/space machine and, together with his young friend Zena, uses it to fight evil through the ages and in other dimensions. Among his foes are Captain Krool, Dr. Flood, the Mothmen, Mr. Mist, the powerful Rhom, and many others.

Comment: There were 130 six-minute films in all. Paul Hecht was the voice of Johnny, with Corinne Orr as Zena.

JOHNNY DYNAMITE (C)

First Appearance: *Dynamite* #3, 1953, Comic Media.

Biography: A "wild man from Chicago," Johnny Dynamite is a crack shot with a hair-trigger temper and a motto: "Never trust a dame." The one time he forgets his code, it costs him his right eye (#4)—thus making him the "one-eyed private eye." Johnny's early cases involve run-of-the-mill gangsters, but he later tackles Communists and enemy agents.

Comment: The magazine became *Johnny Dynamite* with #10 (under the Charlton Comics banner), changed its name to *Foreign Intrigues* with #13 (with Johnny Dynamite as a feature), and made a final switch (sans Johnny) to *Battlefield Action* with #16. Pete Morisi handled the early art for the strip.

JOHNNY HAZARD (CS)

First Appearance: *Johnny Hazard,* June 1944, King Features Syndicate.

Biography: After escaping from a German POW camp, U.S. pilot Johnny Hazard punches his way to Allied territory onboard a stolen bomber and is reassigned to the Pacific, where the end of the war is not yet in sight. There he kills Japanese soldiers, spies, and saboteurs on the land, sea, and especially in the air until the end of the war, after which he becomes a commercial aviator and then heads up a privately held airline, finding adventure wherever he travels. With the rise in tensions between the U.S. and the Iron Curtain countries, and then the war in Korea, Johnny becomes a secret agent, once again traveling around the world in search of information, hostages, defectors, and captured agents. In these latter adventures, he is occasionally accompanied by navigator Gabby Gillespie and a journalist named Snap. When the war ends, Johnny returns to aviation, becoming an investigator for the airline companies, after which he becomes a secret agent for the globe-spanning organization WING, a pro-democracy group. He reports to Mr. Alpha and flies around the world in an atom-powered jet.

Comment: The strip was created by artist Frank Robbins.

JOHNNY PERIL (C)

First Appearance: *Comic Cavalcade* #22, 1947, DC Comics.

Biography: Nothing in the annals of Johnny Peril's adventures reveals anything about his past. He is, at various times, a "master adventurer," reporter, and private eye. In each guise, however, he looks into bizarre mysteries (typically, with a new female companion each time), investigations that have taken him from the jungles of Africa to the Himalayas, from haunted houses to the moon. Johnny—who is equally adept with wits and fists—carries a knife in his pocket and usually packs a handgun.

Comment: Johnny appeared sporadically in *Comic Cavalcade,* in *Danger Trail* in 1951 and, in the 1980s, in *Tales of the Unexpected.*

JOHNNY RINGO (TV)

First Appearance: *Johnny Ringo,* October 1959, CBS.

Biography: A gunfighter, Johnny Ringo decides he's had enough of operating on the wrong side of the law. After signing on as sheriff of Velardi, Arizona, he keeps the peace with his remarkable seven-shooter and the aide of his deputy, Cully. Ringo's girlfriend is Laura Thomas, daughter of the owner of the town's general store.

Comment: The half-hour series aired until September 1960. Don Durant starred as Ringo, Karen Sharpe was Laura, and Mark Goddard (of *Lost in Space*) was Cully. The series was inspired by the late 19th century life and career of a historic outlaw turned lawman named Johnny Ringo.

Johnny Peril investigates a haunted house in an adventure from 1952. © DC Comics.

JOHNNY THUNDER (C)

First Appearance: *All-American Comics* #100, 1948, DC Comics.

Biography: John Tane is the son of William Tane, the sheriff of Mesa City in the late 1800s. (Though not indicated in the text, Mesa City is clearly located in Arizona.) On her deathbed, John's (unnamed) mother makes him promise to become a schoolteacher, someone who fights crime with education, not gunplay. He promises, even though his father has taught him to be a crack shot. When the sheriff asks the bespectacled John to become his deputy, the young man declines, earning his father's contempt ("So yuh won't give up this woman's work 'stead o' helpin' me keep law an' order?"). However, he secretly helps the sheriff by blacking his hair with makeup, donning flashy blue trousers with a yellow stripe down the side and a buckskin shirt (which he'd ordered for a costume ball), mounting the white stallion Black Lightnin'—so-called because of the jagged mark on its forehead—and fighting crime as Johnny Thunder, a name inspired by a fortuitous thunderclap. Not only does Black Lightnin' come when Johnny whistles, but the clever horse has been taught to untie ropes. Thanks to them, Mesa City is what outlaw Raze Ruin calls "Th' only law west o' the Pecos."

Meanwhile, in Tombstone, Arizona, a man named Walker is cheated of his claim in a gold mine and dies disconsolate. To strike back at all corrupt men who manage to beat the system, his daughter Jeanne dons a white suit and mask, dyes her blond hair red, and robs criminals to pay back their victims. Dubbed a "Madame .44" by Wyatt Earp, the female Robin Hood eventually settles in Mesa City, working as a photographer by day and crimefighter by night. Eventually she and Johnny Thunder team to stop the villain Silk Black. After learning one another's identities when rain washes the color from their hair, the two fall in love, marry, and have two children, Charles and Rebecca.

Toward the end of his adventures, the schoolteacher is also assisted by the Indian Swift Deer.

Comment: *All-American Comics* became *All-American Westerns* with #103; Johnny Thunder continued with the title through #126. Swift Deer was introduced in #113. The great Alex Toth drew Johnny's early adventures; when the character appeared in *All Star Western*, beginning with #67, Gil Kane handled the art. The character appeared in most issues of *All Star Western* until its demise with #119.

JOHNNY YUMA (TV, C, L)

First Appearance: *The Rebel*, October 1959, ABC.

Biography: Johnny Yuma is a former Confederate

soldier who took the defeat of the South hard (he was present at Appomattox, in the room with Grand and Lee) and roams through the West in search of inner peace. Along the way, he does odd jobs and becomes involved in various legal and ethical issues. An aspiring writer, he keeps track of events and his feelings in a journal.

Johnny is equally at home with his six-shooter and his famous scattergun, a sawed-off double-barrel shotgun.

Comment: The series switched to NBC in June 1962; reruns continued to air until September. A total of 76 half-hour episodes were produced. Nick Adams starred as Yuma; Johnny Cash sang the popular theme song. When originally conceived (by Adams, director Irvin Kershner, and producer Andrew J. Fenady), the series was going to be called *Young Johnny Yuma.*

Dell published four issues of *The Rebel* as part of its *4-Color* series: numbers 1076, 1138, 1207, and 1262, from 1959 to 1961. The series spawned a novel, *Rebel of Broken Wheel,* by Dean Owen (1960).

A similar series was *The Loner,* which aired on CBS from September 1965 to April 1966. The half-hour series was created by Rod Serling and starred Lloyd Bridges as William Colton, an ex-Union officer who roams the West becoming involved in various legal and ethical issues.

JOHN RAMBO (L, MP, TV, C)

First Appearance: *First Blood* by David Morrell, 1972, M. Evans and Company.

Biography: Rambo, who works in a garage, enlists before he can be drafted and trains in a Special Forces school under Captain Sam Trautman. He becomes a killing machine, is briefly a POW, wins the Medal of Honor, and returns home. He suffers a nervous breakdown, and, though unwilling to go back to a garage, he is poorly equipped for any other work. On the outskirts of Madison, Kentucky, the long-haired, bearded veteran is escorted from town by redneck Chief of Police Wilfred Logan Teasle. Told not to return, Rambo thinks, "I won't have somebody decide that for me," and returns. Teasle arrests him (Rambo is satisfied just *thinking* about the damage he could do to the officer), but when Officer Galt tries to shave him, Rambo has a flashback to when he was tortured with a razor. He makes a break, killing Galt and heading into the mountains. His plan is to make for Mexico—living on a beach is all he wants.

Meanwhile, Teasle organizes volunteers into a search party and they go after Rambo. The ex-soldier picks off the men one by one, careful not to kill Teasle

. . . yet. The National Guard is called in, as is Captain Trautman, after 13 men are killed. Trautman, privately cheering for his boy, helps the law close in on Rambo—though Rambo surprises even Trautman by making his way back to town. He begins blowing up buildings, then steals a police car, ignoring Trautman's pleas over the radio to surrender. After crashing into one of Teasle's roadblocks, Rambo runs into the night, with Teasle in pursuit. The two exchange fire; Rambo is hit in the chest, Teasle in the gut. Rambo runs off to a shed, where Trautman shoots him in the head with a shotgun; Teasle dies when Trautman returns, oddly unsatisfied that the warrior has died.

Comment: The character has no first name in the original novel, only in the films.

Sylvester Stallone starred as Rambo in the film *First Blood* (1982), which followed the book faithfully except that in the end Rambo surrenders to Trautman (Richard Crenna) and the authorities. Brian Dennehy costarred as Teasle. This Rambo holds the Congressional Medal of Honor, five Purple Hearts, two Silver Stars, four Bronze Stars, two Soldier's Crosses, and four Vietnamese Crosses of Gallantry.

In the sequel, *Rambo: First Blood Part II* (1985)—written by Stallone and James Cameron—the hero is plucked from prison by Trautman, then parachuted into Southeast Asia to find out if POWs are still being held there. However, the CIA Special Operations officer who organized the reconnaissance mission, Murdock (Charles Napier), doesn't want Rambo to succeed, since it would indicate the government's carelessness in having abandoned countless soldiers in Vietnam. Naturally, with the help of Communist-hating Co Phuong Bao (Julia Nickson), Rambo not only lives but finds POWs and exceeds his orders, freeing the POWs and bringing them home.

David Morrell wrote the novelization of the second film, pointing out in an author's note, "In my novel *First Blood,* Rambo died. In the films, he lives."

In *Rambo III* (1988), Trautman is captured by Russians in Afghanistan, and Rambo goes in with freedom fighters to get him out. Needless to say, he succeeds.

On TV, the character was seen in the animated series *Rambo,* which changed the concept somewhat: Rambo is now the leader of the Force of Freedom team, which battles the evil organization S.A.V.A.G.E. *Rambo* debuted in syndication in September 1985, with Neil Ross as the voice of Rambo and Alan Oppenheimer as Trautman. Other members of the team included Kat, Turbo, and Nomad. There were 65 cartoons in all.

In comic books, the character was featured in *Blackthorne 3-D Series* #49, *Rambo in 3-D,* in 1986.

JOHN RIDD (L, MP, C)

First Appearance: *Lorna Doone, A Romance of Exmoor* by R.D. Blackmore, 1869.

Biography: In 17th-century Exmoor, at the time of Monmouth's Rebellion (when a duke tried to wrest the throne from King James II), the outlaw clan, the Doone, terrorize the countryside, killing and robbing. One such victim is the farmer Ridd, whose 12-year-old son, John, survives with the help of a sympathetic Doone girl, Lorna. John is smitten with her. Growing older—not to mention extremely tall and powerful—John falls in with the highwayman Tom Faggus, who marries John's sister Annie. He also resolves to find Lorna and save her from her family. When the rebellion erupts, John encounters the irredeemably wicked Carver Doone, from whom he snatches Lorna during a blizzard. Most of the Doones are destroyed, and, not long after, John discovers that Lorna isn't really a Doone but is an heiress who had been kidnaped by the clan from her nobleman father. The two are wed, but Carver shows up at the ceremony and shoots Lorna as she stands at the altar. John kills him, Lorna survives, and the hero finds himself, at last, in a state of bliss.

Comment: Blackmore based the characters of Ridd and Faggus on historical figures.

In motion pictures, the story was filmed in 1935 starring John Loder and Margaret Lockwood, and in 1951 with Richard Greene and Barbara Hale. In comic books, the tale was part of the *Classics Illustrated* series, #32, published in 1946.

JOHN SHAFT (MP, TV)

First Appearance: *Shaft*, 1971, MGM.

Biography: A streetwise private investigator, John Shaft is as cool and tough as they come, willing to throw men from skyscraper windows if he doesn't get what he wants. In his first chronicled adventure, Shaft must find the kidnaped daughter of Harlem mobster Bumpy Jonas. In his second adventure, he looks into the murder of a friend and finds himself hunted by the mob. In his third escapade, he heads to Africa to battle slavers. Shaft gets an occasional assist from Lieutenant Vic Androzzy.

In his later (TV) adventures, Shaft searches for the murderer of a lawyer friend, the people who beat up his ex-girlfriend Diana Richie, the white men who disguise themselves as blacks and kidnap a banker's wife, and a desperate arsonist, among others. On television, he is frequently helped by his friend Lieutenant Al Rossi of the New York Police Department.

Comment: Richard Roundtree played Shaft in the original film and in its sequels, *Shaft's Big Score* (1972) and *Shaft in Africa* (1973). He also played the part in the TV series, which was one of the rotating segments of *The New CBS Tuesday Night Movies*. Seven 90-minute episodes aired between October 1973 and August 1974; Shaft was sanitized and much less dangerous than he was in the films.

The seminal black action hero was created by Ernest Tidyman.

JONAH HEX (C)

First Appearance: *All-Star Western Tales* #10, 1972, DC Comics.

Biography: Born in 1838, Jonah is the son of drunk Woodson Hex and his wife, Virginia, who eventually leaves her husband and takes up with salesman Preston W. Dazzleby. Woodson and Jonah head west in search of gold, where his father swaps the 13-year-old to Apache Indians in exchange for animal skins. Two years later the boy saves the chief from a wildcat and goes from being a whipping boy to a surrogate son.

However, the chief's real son, Noh-Tante, hates Hex; during a raid on a white camp, he knocks the 16-year-old out and reports him killed. After falling in with a trapper, Hex becomes a buffalo hunter for the army, then a cavalry scout. He is engaged to marry young Cassie Wainwright, daughter of his commanding officer, Colonel Marcus Wainwright, but she's murdered by Comanches. When the Civil War begins, Hex joins the Confederate Army and becomes a cavalry lieutenant. But it bothers him to fight *for* slavery, and he surrenders to Union soldiers at Fort Charlotte, which inadvertently leads to the murder of most of his soldiers. After the war, ostracized by former friends and foes alike, he returns to the Apache camp and is forced to slay Noh-Tante in a showdown; loathed now even by his only family, Hex has the "Mark of the Demon" branded on the right side of his face with a heated knife, and he becomes an itinerant, mean bounty hunter. He wears a matched set of ivory-handled Colt .44 frontier pistols and is one of the fastest guns in the West. His only friend during this time is a gray wolf named Ironjaws, who dies saving his master from his enemies. Hex enjoys a brief period of happiness when he meets and weds the Chinese woman Mei Ling and gives up gunplay. They have a son (unnamed in the chronicles), but for one reason or another Hex is constantly forced to resort to using his guns, and Mei leaves him. Hex returns to bounty hunting.

Then, in 1875, he finds himself in Seattle in the year 2050, brought there by scientist Reinhold Borsten. Eight years before, Borsten had invented a time machine, sent someone into the future, learned that there would be a nuclear catastrophe in 2042, and hopped

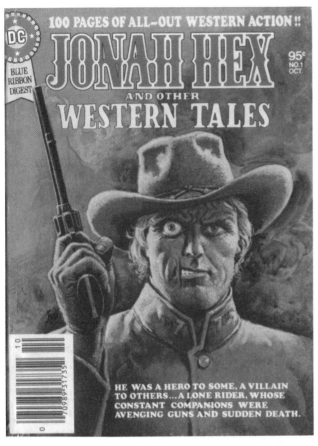

Jonah Hex, painted by Luis Dominguez. © DC Comics.

ahead five years so he could set himself up as dictator of a new society. However, the future world is already ruled by the evil Conglomerate, which rules thanks to its ability to clean radiation-poisoned water. Hex becomes a loner once again.

At some point in the future, Hex manages to return to the past (it is never revealed how), and in 1899 meets a Cheyenne woman, Tall Bird, who becomes his common-law wife. In 1904 Hex is shot to death by bank robber George Barrow. The body is stolen by Lew Wheeler, who has Hex stuffed and put on display as part of his Wild West Revue. The body eventually becomes an exhibit at New York's Westworld Amusement Park and is purchased in a bankruptcy sale in 1987 by Wyoming's Frontier City. Thieves hired by a wild west collector try to steal it and are shot dead, apparently by Hex; at last account, the aged Tall Bird sues to reclaim Hex's remains, in order to give her husband a traditional Cheyenne funeral.

Comment: The character was created by editor Joe Orlando and writer John Albano, though Michael Fleisher wrote most of the adventures and came up with the bulk of the mythos. *All-Star Western Tales*— this was the second incarnation of the Golden Age

title, and began the numbering again with #1— became *Weird Western Tales* with #12, and Jonah continued in the title. He got his own magazine, *Jonah Hex,* in 1977; it ran for 92 issues. A second title, *Hex,* starring the future-Hex, ran for 18 issues. The hero also starred in three issues of *DC Blue Ribbon Digest* (#1–#3); the body-theft story appeared in *Secret Origins* #21.

In 1993 DC published a new five-issue series about Hex's western days as well as a one-shot comic book, *Two-Gun Mojo,* in which Hex battles zombies.

JONATHAN and JENNIFER HART (TV)

First Appearance: *Hart to Hart,* 1979, ABC.
Biography: After a friend dies at a health spa, the romantic, jet-setting Jonathan and Jennifer Hart resolve to find out whodunit. Encouraged by their success, the Harts continue to solve crimes, dashing from Beverly Hills to places around the world onboard their private jet: overhearing murder plans on Maui; attending an elusive billionaire's party where someone is murdered after seeing the host; helping a friend who's been accused of counterfeiting wine; and even staging Jonathan's death after a murder attempt so he can go undercover and find out who wants him dead. They are aided by their crusty valet Max and even, on occasion, by their dog Freeway.

Industrialist Jonathan makes millions from his Hart Industries, though he's rarely in the office; Jennifer is a freelance writer, whose work sometimes gets her into trouble.
Comment: The made-for-TV movie was directed by Tom Mankiewicz and spawned an hour-long TV series, which aired from August 1979 to July 1984. Robert Wagner was Jonathan, Stephanie Powers played Jennifer, and Lionel Stander was Max. A TV-movie *Home Is Where the Hart Is* aired in February, 1994 on NBC.

JONNY QUEST (TV, C)

First Appearance: *The Adventures of Jonny Quest,* September 1964, ABC.
Biography: Jonny is an 11-year-old, blond boy, the son of red-bearded scientist/explorer Dr. Benton Quest, "one of the three top scientists in the world." With his tutor/bodyguard Roger "Race" Bannon, an Indian lad named Hadji who has been adopted by Dr. Quest, and bulldog Bandit, Jonny gets into adventures around the globe, encountering Egyptian curses, Lizardmen, pygmies, killer robots, pirates, Tree People, extraterrestrials, the evil Dr. Zin (on several occasions), and more. The dead Mrs. Quest is never men-

tioned, though the presence of Bannon—who was assigned to the boy by the government agency Intelligence I—suggests she was the victim of a plot against Dr. Quest. The only other known relatives are Dr. Quest's grandfather, Quinton Quest, who once invented a time machine.

When they're not traveling, the team is based on balmy Palm Key Island.

Comment: The series aired in prime time through September 1965, with reruns of the 26 half-hour adventures shown on CBS from September 1967 to September 1970; on ABC from September 1971 to September 1972, and then on NBC from September 1979 to September 1981. A new syndicated series debuted with 13 new half-hour episodes in September, 1987, part of *The Funtastic World of Hanna-Barbera.*

The voices in the original and second series were Tim Matheson/Scott Menville (Jonny), John Stephenson/Don Messick (Benton), Danny Bravo/Rob Paulson (Hadji), and Don Messick (Bandit).

In comic books, Jonny appeared in one issue of a Gold Key title (1964), 31 issues of a Comico title (1986–1988), two issues of Comico's *Jonny Quest Special* (1988), and three issues of Comico's *Jonny Quest Classics* (1987).

The characters were originally designed by Doug Wildey, the great comics artist.

A feature-length animated film, *Jonny's Golden Quest,* debuted in April 1993 on the cable USA Network.

JOSH RANDALL (TV, C, MP)

First Appearance: *Trackdown,* March 1958, CBS.
Biography: During the late 1860s, the taciturn Josh Randall works as a bounty hunter, wandering from town to town picking up assignments and wanted posters. Unlike most bounty hunters, though, he isn't motivated as much by pay as by the desire to see justice done. Or by charity—in one episode he accepts two bits from a kid to track down Santa Claus. In other adventures he hunts down a man who uses an elephant to chase people from their homes, which he proceeds to rob; he finds a wanted woman and, convinced of her innocence, helps her to prove it; and knows that a wanted poster for Colonel J.J. Sykes, his former commander, is a fake, and he sets out to reach Sykes before anyone else does. In one episode he falls in love with a captive, Susan, and finds his affection for her undermining his sense of duty.

Randall carries what he calls his "mare's laig": a .44-70 sawed-off carbine that fires like a handgun but is more accurate because of the greater length of the barrel.

For one year Josh works with an eager sidekick named Jason Nichols, a deputy sheriff.

Comment: The series spawned by the pilot was *Wanted: Dead or Alive,* which aired on CBS from September 1958 to March 1961, 94 half-hour episodes in all. Steve McQueen played Randall, and Wright King was Jason (in 1960 only).

Dell published two *Wanted: Dead or Alive* comics as part of its *4-Color* series.

In 1987 Rutger Hauer starred as Josh's grandson Nick Randall in the theatrical film *Wanted: Dead or Alive.* Upholding the family tradition, Nick goes to work for the CIA hunting down an Arab terrorist.

Trackdown, a series about Texas Ranger Hoby Gilman, starred Robert Culp and aired from October 1957 to September 1959.

JUDGE COLT (C)

First Appearance: *Judge Colt* #1, 1969, Western Publishing.
Biography: In the early 1870s, in Missouri, young Maria Colt is slain, "an innocent bystander in a bank robbery." Her husband, Mark Colt, a former Civil War major, spends five years searching for her killer—without success. Then Washington sends him to the Oklahoma territory, to "ride the circuit" where the current judge, Carver, is old and scared of local outlaws. Colt has no such fear, handing down death sentences from the bench and, when necessary, dealing in fists and having shootouts outside the courtroom. Colt's one weakness: After gunplay, the expert marksman always shakes uncontrollably, a (mercifully) delayed reaction to fear. Even Colt doesn't know whether he's trying to bring justice to the West or seek revenge for his wife's death.

Comment: There were four issues of *Judge Colt,* published under Western's Gold Key banner.

JUNGLE JIM (CS, MP, R, L, C, TV)

First Appearance: *Jungle Jim,* January 7, 1934, King Features Syndicate.
Biography: "Jungle" Jim Bradley is an explorer from the U.S. who roams Africa, the Middle East, and even India and Tibet, becoming embroiled in tribal wars and battling slavers, poachers, pirates, smugglers, and criminals of every sort, often landing him in nasty spots (i.e., buried chin deep in sand, covered with molasses, and waiting for "fierce jungle ants" to swarm over him.) He is accompanied by his girlfriend, Joan, and the native Kolu; after a year, Joan decides to go back to the States ("I love you [but] you were born for a life of adventure and I would only spoil it for you by

Grant Withers as the original screen *Jungle Jim.* © Universal Pictures.

imposing on you longer . . . ") Jim is joined by the more exotic Lil de Vrille, a.k.a. Shanghai Lil, whom he plucks from a life of disrepute to make her his friend and companion.

Comment: The character was created by artist Alex Raymond *(Flash Gordon).* Austin Briggs took over the strip in 1944, then Paul Norris took over in 1948; it expired in 1954.

Part of Jim's latter-day longevity as a comic strip was due to the popularity of the Jungle Jim films. The first was a 12-chapter serial, *Jungle Jim,* made in 1937 and starring Grant Withers as Jim, Betty Jane Rhodes as Joan, Evelyn Brent as Lil (the two ladies together for the first time), and Al Duvall as Kolu.

More successful were the feature films starring Johnny Weissmuller, fresh from 16 years as the movies' Tarzan. The entries in this series were *Jungle Jim* (1948), *The Lost Tribe* (1949), *Captive Girl* (1950), *Mark of the Gorilla* (1950), *Pygmy Island* (1950), *Fury of the Congo* (1951), *Jungle Manhunt* (1951), *Jungle Jim in the Forbidden Land* (1952), *Voodoo Tiger* (1952), *Savage Mutiny* (1953), *Valley of the Headhunters* (1953), *Killer Ape* (1953), and

Jungle Man-Eaters (1954). Three other films were made—*Cannibal Attack* (1954), *Jungle Moon Men* (1955), and *Devil Goddess* (1955)—and, though the Jungle Jim name was no longer used (why pay for a license when all they needed was Weissmuller?), the character was the same. Future Superman George Reeves costarred in *Jungle Jim.*

On the radio, Matt Crowly played Jim, Juano Hernandez was Kolu, and Franc Hale was Lil.

Two Big Little Books featured the hero: *Jungle Jim* (1936) and *Jungle Jim and the Vampire Woman* (1937).

Jim starred in David McKay's *Ace Comics,* beginning with #1 in 1937; he starred in his own title for Standard, which lasted ten issues from 1949 to 1951; in eight issues of his own Dell title, from 1953 to 1959; in a King Features one-shot published in 1967; and in eight Charlton issues from 1969 to 1970.

A half-hour TV series, starring Weissmuller, was syndicated in 1955; Martin Huston costarred as his son Skipper, and Norman Fredric was his aide Kassim (Fredric later became Dean Fredericks, star of STEVE CANYON). Tamba the chimp was also featured.

K

KÄANGA (C)

First Appearance: *Jungle Comics* #1, 1940, Fiction House.

Biography: As a boy, Käanga (his real name is unknown) is orphaned when his father and other members of his (exploration?) party are attacked and killed by natives in the Congo. The boy runs off and, found by a "strange man," is taken to his village and raised among his people, the ape-men. Soon Käanga forgets "white man's ways and talk" and, dressed in a leopard-skin loincloth, "strong as the elephant, swift as the cheetah, bold as the lion," the blond hero fights injustice in the heart of the Congo, assisted by the ape-men. As an adult, he rescues beautiful explorer Ann Mason from slave trader Bill Blacton. The two spend weeks together, during which time Käanga relearns English and falls in love with the woman. Eventually she becomes his mate and dons an outfit fashion-coordinated with Käanga's. During the course of his long career, Käanga battles foes ranging from jungle witch doctors, to dinosaurs, to Nazis.

Comment: Clearly inspired by Edgar Rice Burroughs's Tarzan, Käanga appeared in all 163 issues of *Jungle Comics* (see CAPTAIN THUNDER) and also starred in 20 issues of his own title from 1949 to 1954.

KAMANDI (C)

First Appearance: *Kamandi* #1, 1972, DC Comics.

Biography: The Great Disaster—"a natural catastrophe of cyclopean dimensions"—causes an end to civilization as we know it. Human beings survive, but animals such as apes (who are evil and hunger for conquest), lions (who are benevolent), tigers, dogs, gophers, dolphins, and others mutate into equally intelligent bipeds. As a result, beasts are the masters and humans are hunted. The only humans who prosper are the mutants, who retain a knowledge of science and have the ability to use radiation in their bodies to become "steel-hard humanoids." (It is unclear from whence the radiation comes, as the authors take pains to point out that the disaster was "not an atomic war.")

This is the world of Earth A.D. (After Disaster). Dressed in blue cutoffs and boots, armed with his wits and a hand gun, the teenager Kamandi, "The Last Boy on Earth," inhabits what was once the United States. Though he is not a mutant, one of his good friends is mutant Ben Boxer, who frequently helps him get out of scrapes. Later in the series he is accompanied on his adventures by the superintelligent dog Dr. Canus; Pyra, an energy being from another galaxy; and his

The first appearance of *Käanga*. © Caplin-Iger Co. Ltd.

138

Kamandi prepares to pull a David and Goliath on the brutish Chaaku. Art by Jack Kirby. © DC Comics.

girlfriend, Spirit, who, thanks to "racial memories of the caterpillar people" with whom she once lived, can spin webs.

Comment: The series—heavily inspired by the *Planet of the Apes* film series—was created by artist/writer Jack Kirby and lasted 59 issues. In one of the most inane undertakings in comics history, DC "remade" its universe in 1985–86 with the 12-issue *Crisis on Infinite Earths* series. In it, "extraneous" dimensions, characters, and future histories were eliminated. Thus, the future in which Kamandi exists never happened. Instead, the individual who would have become Kamandi becomes TOMMY TOMORROW.

Or so it seems. In 1993 DC published a six-issue mini series called *Kamandi: At Earth's End,* in which it's revealed that the artificial intelligence known as Machine Mother, which has nurtured Kamandi since the age of seven, sends him on a mission of vengeance: to find and destroy the force that created what is now being referred to as the Second Apocalypse.

KARATE KOMMANDOS (TV, C)

First Appearance: *Chuck Norris and the Karate Kommandos,* September 1986, syndicated.

Biography: The evil Cult of the Klaw is an international terrorist organization that movie star and martial arts expert Chuck Norris is determined to destroy. To this end, he helps the government design the antiterrorist Supercruiser, which looks like an ordinary trailer but contains state-of-the-art weapons and defense systems.

To help him in his battle, Norris has created the Karate Kommandos, a team consisting of Kemo, Reed and his twin sister Pepper, mighty sumo wrestler Tabe, schoolboy Too Much, and Chuck's dog Wolf.

Comment: The Ruby-Spears series failed to find a market in syndication and was canceled after only five half-hour episodes had been produced. Chuck Norris provided his own voice; Keye Luke was Kemo; Robert Ito was Tabe; Mona Marshall was Too Much; Sam Fontana was Reed; and Kathy Garver was Pepper.

In 1987 Marvel Comics published three issues of a tie-in comic book as part of their juvenile Star Comics line. The title was distinguished by the work of veteran artist Steve Ditko.

KELLY ROBINSON and ALEXANDER SCOTT (TV, C)

First Appearance: *I Spy,* September 1965, NBC.

Biography: Kelly Robinson and Alexander Scott ("Scotty") are secret agents for the American SSA (secret service agency) who pose as a tennis champion and his trainer, respectively. These covers allow them to travel around the world on assignment, battling spies, recovering secrets, helping defectors, and the like.

Kelly is, in fact, a former Princeton law student and two-time Davis Cup team member; Scotty is a Temple University graduate, Rhodes scholar, and linguist. Both are extremely fit and have a sense of humor, the latter enabling them to get through some of the more dangerous jobs they tackle.

Comment: Robert Culp starred as Kelly and Bill Cosby was Scotty. The hour-long series aired through September 1968.

In the 1994 *I Spy* made-for-TV movie *Return to I Spy,* which reunited Culp and Cosby, we learn that Scott has a son, Bennett, and Kelly has daughter, Nicole (George Newbern and Salli Richardson). The two kids work as spies, end up getting caught in Vienna, and it's the two fathers to the rescue.

Gold Key published six *I Spy* comics from 1966 to 1968.

Kemo and Reed work out while Tabe pigs out. From the *Karate Kommandos.* © Ruby-Spears Entertainment.

I Spy was the first prime-time drama in which a black actor had a starring role; Cosby won three consecutive Best Actor Emmy awards for his work.

KERRY DRAKE (CS, C)

First Appearance: *Kerry Drake,* October 1, 1943, Publisher's Syndicate.

Biography: Originally an assistant district attorney, and later the chief of investigation for the D.A.'s office, Kerry Drake is a determined sleuth who refuses to make deals with lawbreakers; he feels that if they commit a crime, they should pay. During his career he battles routine criminals from crooks to dope dealers as well as such colorful rogues as diamond thief Kid Gloves, the obese Meatball, the sexy Vixen, the sexier Pussycat, Bottleneck, Angel-Puss, Mr. Goliath, Dr. Zero, Stitches, No Face, and the squinting Shuteye. Kerry is frequently aided by his wife, Mindy, to whom he is devoted (and whom he often ends up rescuing).

When his wife is slain on a case, Kerry briefly retires, then returns to action as a rookie police officer. He later marries the widow of a police officer and becomes the father of quadruplets. In these later adventures, he's assisted (and for all intents and purposes replaced) by his kid brother Lefty Drake, as beatniks and hippies cause trouble in the city.

The pipe-smoking, blond (later, white-haired) Kerry prefers fists to guns ("Drop the gun, Torso . . .

or I'll snap this wing like a pencil!"), though he has been known to fell adversaries with handy items, such as a spilled box of roulette balls. He is rarely without his trench coat and fedora. Kerry's secretary is Sandy Burns.

Comment: The strip was created by Alfred Andriola, who was a veteran of CHARLIE CHAN and DAN DUNN; it is quite reminiscent of the earlier DICK TRACY.

Kerry Drake starred in 33 issues of *Kerry Drake Detective Cases* (the last two issues were *Kerry Drake Racket Buster*), published by Harvey Comics from 1944 to 1952, and in two issues of his own Argo Publications comic book in 1956.

KID COLT (C)

First Appearance: *Kid Colt, Hero of the West* #1, 1948, Marvel Comics.

Biography: In the middle 1800s, Blaine Colt is the son of Daniel Colt, owner of the Flying-C Ranch outside of Abilene, Wyoming. Blaine realizes that he's too fast and accurate with Colt .45s ever to wear one. "You know my temper," he tells ranch hand Gabby. "I'm scared of hurtin' someone." However, when his father is killed in a gunfight with Lash Larribee—after refusing to subscribe to Larribee's protection racket— Blaine seeks revenge. He guns Lash down, then makes the mistake of fleeing, "instead," according to the legend, "of staying to stand trial! Since then, he has

One of the nuttier villains encountered by *Kid Colt:* The Invisible Gunman, whose gun and metal-banded hat are controlled by ventriloquist Doctor Danger using a "powerful magnet." © Marvel Comics.

spent his life trying to atone for his mistake!" He also tries to avoid any town with a sheriff, since he'd be a prize at the end of any lawman's rope. He roams the West astride his horse Steel, fighting some of the more bizarre nemeses, including the Fat Man, the Robin Hood Raider, the Invisible Gunman, and Iron Mask. The Kid always wears blue jeans and scarf, a red shirt, a white Stetson, yellow gloves, and a black-and-white calfhide vest.

Comment: The title became *Kid Colt Outlaw* with #3 and ran a remarkable 229 issues. Other Marvel western heroes who had short runs over the years include Matt Slade, Gunfighter (a.k.a. Kid Slade); the Western Kid, who fought crime with his dog Lightning and his horse Whirlwind; "timid" Lance Temple, alias the Outlaw Kid; the Ringo Kid, implicitly a government agent cleaning up the West; and Caleb Hammer, a Clint Eastwood "Man With No Name" takeoff.

KILLRAVEN (C)

First Appearance: *Amazing Adventures* #18, 1973, Marvel Comics.

Biography: The son of Maureen and Joshua Raven, New Yorker Jonathan is one year old when Martians invade the earth on June 29, 2001. Exactly a century before, the aliens had tried to invade and failed, felled by terrestrial bacteria; since then they've developed an immunity and, after neutralizing Earth's nuclear power sources, successfully conquer the planet. With her husband dead, Maureen hides with Jonathan and his brother, Joshua; she is slain and her children taken away. Jonathan is trained to be a gladiator known as Killraven, while Joshua becomes an Exterminator—a willing helper of the Martians and one who is surgically remade into Deathraven, a werewolf who can control other wolves.

But Jonathan gets his surgical remaking as well, thanks to Whitman, a human who has been brainwashed into servitude (a Keeper)—though not as entirely as the Martians think. In his laboratory, he gives Jonathan the ability to transfer his mind into Martian bodies; gives him injections that heighten his physical abilities; and implants in his mind the collected knowledge of human history, culture, and science so that it will never be eradicated.

In 2014, after four years of gladitorial combat in

From the left: Old Skull, M'Shulla, and *Killraven,* in their final appearance. Art by Craig Russell. © Marvel Comics.

New York, Killraven flees from Martian captivity and becomes the leader of a band of freedom fighters known as Freemen, a group that also includes the former gladiators Old Skull (a.k.a. Bald Eagle), M'Shulla Scott, and scientist Carmilla Frost. Over the next six years, Killraven, the "Warrior of the Worlds," travels the country waging an increasingly successful battle against the Martians; he is determined not only to chase them off Earth (to "win back humanity's right to destroy itself") but to go to Mars and destroy them there.

In addition to the abilities given to him by Whitman, Killraven carries a long sword and a blaster.

Comment: The series is a "sequel" to H.G. Wells's 1898 novel *War of the Worlds.* The characters remained in *Amazing Adventures* until the magazine's demise with #39.

KING FARADAY (C)

First Appearance: *Danger Trail* #1, 1950, DC Comics.

Biography: Code-named I-Spy, King Faraday was hired by the U.S. government after a distinguished record in the military (the details of which were never revealed). Dressed in a trench coat and packing a handgun, the white-haired Faraday travels the world from Trinidad, to Thailand, to under the sea, watching out for American interests; he has the tacit approval of the government to do whatever is necessary to protect those interests.

Comment: The character's name was inspired by the expression "King for a Day." He appeared in the first four issues of *Danger Trail;* the magazine of "worldwide adventures in mystery and intrigue" lasted five issues. Faraday also starred in *Showcase* #50–#51, issues entitled *I-Spy* (before the TV series of the same name).

The hero returned in 1993 in DC's revival of *Danger Trail,* working for the CIA and reporting to SARGE STEEL. He is now fluent in many languages, adept with prosthetics to change his appearance, and armed with everything from night-vision goggles, to a collapsible tungsten/aluminum alloy vaulting pole, to curare powder that is "instantly narcoleptic."

KING PETER (L, TV)

First Appearance: *The Lion, The Witch and the Wardrobe* by C.S. Lewis, 1950.

Biography: During World War II, English children Peter, Susan, Lucy, and Edmund are sent to the country to live with an old professor and his housekeeper, Mrs. Macready. While poking around inside a wardrobe cabinet, Lucy finds herself in a forest where she meets a mythical faun, Tumnus, who tells her she's in the land of Narnia ruled by the evil White Witch. She returns to the wardrobe and then comes back with Edmund; they meet the White Witch, who calls herself the Queen of Narnia and denies that she is evil. The children go back home, confused, and this time return with their two elder siblings. Their confusion turns to sadness when they learn that Tumnus has been arrested for treason and that the witch has used her Deep Magic to lock Narnia in a perpetual winter. After Edmund is captured by the queen, Peter arms himself with a sword and encounters the heroic lion Aslan, who shows him the mighty castle Cair Paravel, in which he predicts Peter, "the firstborn . . . will be High King over all the rest." After killing a monstrous wolf that tries to kill the girls, Peter is dubbed Sir Peter Fenris-Bane by Aslan and then sets out with a small army to liberate Narnia. Helped by Aslan's knowledge of magic deeper than the witch's, magic that goes back to "the darkness before Time," the lion is able to return from death and Peter is able to reach the witch's side. The two fight, Peter's sword against the witch's stone knife; witnessing the lopsided battle, Aslan throws himself at the witch, Edmund smashes her wand, and together the three destroy the fiend. The children all become kings and queens, Peter growing into "a tall and deep chested man and a great warrior" known as King Peter the Magnificent; Edmund becoming King Edmund the Just; Susan being called Queen Susan the Gentle; and Lucy being dubbed Queen Lucy the Valiant. They rule well and wisely for years until they return to the wardrobe . . . and are back in the house, children once more.

But they return to Narnia for other adventures. In the second, they arrive thousands of years in the future and help to conquer the Telmarines and restore a young ruler, Prince Caspian, to his throne; in the third, Edmund, Lucy, their mean cousin Eustace, and King Caspian go sailing to the End of the World; in the fourth, a more mature Eustace helps to save the captured Prince Rilian from the Emerald Witch; in the fifth—set during the reign of King Peter—a prince and a horse help to protect Narnia from invasion; in the sixth, we learn how Aslan created Narnia and its inhabitants by song and taught them to speak; and in the seventh, Aslan helps Narnia move forward into a greater plane of existence.

Comment: The other volumes in the seven-book *Chronicles of Narnia* series are *Prince Caspian: The Return to Narnia* (1951), *The Voyage of the "Dawn Treader"* (1952), *The Silver Chair* (1953), *The Horse and his Boy* (1954), *The Magician's Nephew* (1955), and *The Last Battle* (1956).

On TV, the characters were seen in *The Lion, The Witch and the Wardrobe,* a one-hour animated film that aired on CBS in 1979. Reg Williams was the voice of Peter; Stephen Thorne was Aslan.

Author Lewis intended for Aslan to be a Christ figure and for his tales to retell the major events in the chronicles of Christianity.

KNIGHT ARDENT (C)

First Appearance: *Chevalier Ardent,* 1966, *Tintin.*

Biography: During the Middle Ages, brave, powerful Ardent inherits the manor Rougecogne. However, it is seized by local brigands who want to keep the land and its castle for themselves. Ardent is forced to take his inheritance back from the interlopers, who are impressed by his valor; they agree to stay on as lords and manage the sprawling estate while the warrior becomes a knight in the court of King Arthus. There he courts Arthus's daughter Gwendoline, while putting down rebellions, bringing corrupt lords to justice, and even making a pilgrimage to the Middle East, looking for the "Holy Grail" of this saga, the Lady of the Sands.

Comment: The strip was created by Francois Craenhals; several collections of Knight Ardent adventures have appeared in Belgium. Craenhals had previously created the similar strip *Druka,* in 1948, which appeared for four months in the weekly magazine *Le Soir Illustre.* He also drew IVANHOE, which appeared in TINTIN in 1953.

KONG (C)

First Appearance: *Kong the Untamed* #1, 1975, DC Comics.

Biography: In prehistoric times, the Cro-Magnon Kong is born to the woman Attu, a member of the tribe of the one-eyed Chief Trog. When a shaman predicts that the "whelp" may one day challenge his authority—he has yellow hair and was born during the full moon, just like a once-great warrior named Kong—Trog banishes the woman and her boy. The two manage to survive for years—during which time Kong discovers how to make fire—until Trog finds and kills Attu while her son is out searching for medicinal herbs. After vowing to slay Trog one day, Kong saves the life of the Beast Man (Neanderthal) Gurat, who becomes his fast friend and companion. The two enter a hidden valley, where they find dinosaurs and various other tribes, including pterodactyl-riding warriors. Fortunately, all of the tribes of prehistoric Earth—indeed, all the Cro-Magnons and Neanderthals—speak

Kong, as interpreted by Berni Wrightson, who drew the first two covers. © DC Comics.

the same language. It isn't known whether Kong ever does kill Trog.

Comment: *Kong the Untamed* lasted for five issues and was created by editor Joe Orlando and writer Jack Oleck. The adventures were initially more serious than DC's previous cave hero, ANTHRO; they became preposterous when the heroes entered the valley at the end of issue #3.

KROMAG THE KILLER (C)

First Appearance: *Thrilling Adventure Stories* #1, 1975, Seaboard Periodicals.

Biography: Kromag is the leader of a small Cro-Magnon tribe that roams the woods and plains of what is now France. Blond, possessing rudimentary speech, and equally adept with a spear or club, Kromag is not only a great hunter but he's also unusually intelligent; for example, he is one of the first of his race to connect

Kromag battles a prehistoric serpent. © Seaboard Periodicals.

falling leaves to "the season of the white death," which he prepares for by stockpiling food. The other members of the tribe are Kromag's mate, Nean, their young son, Bekmin, Kromag's younger sister, Lin, their kid brother, Dubok, and his mate, Sherne. All dress in skimpy loincloths. Kromag also takes in the orphaned wolf cubs Ceeb and Uth, who become loyal hunting companions.

Comment: The character was created by artist Jack Sparling; the stories were written by Gabriel Levy. Kromag appeared in both issues of *Thrilling Adventure Stories.* Third and fourth adventures were drawn but never published.

KWAI CHANG CAINE (TV, L)

First Appearance: *Kung Fu,* February 1972, ABC.
Biography: Born in China in the middle 1800s to American/Chinese parents, Kwai Chang Caine is raised in a Shaolin temple after his parents are slain by a warlord. The blind Master Po, Master Kan, and other monks teach him mysticism and pacificism, though he is also schooled in the martial art of Kung Fu—just in case ideas and words fail him. He studies to become a priest, and is informed he can leave only when he is able to snatch a pebble from Master Kan's palm before his hand can close around it.

When Caine reaches adulthood, tragedy strikes. Master Po accidentally bumps into a guard of the emperor's nephew, and the blind man is murdered for the affront. Caine slays the royal nephew and flees to America in the 1870s. There, after landing work on the railroad and narrowly escaping bounty hunters, he flees again and works on a ranch, helps a blind man build a church while searching for his grandfather Henry Caine, helps a girl who has been raped by a soldier, and then begins an ongoing search for his half brother while both bounty hunters and Chinese agents search for him. His cousin Margit McLean eventually becomes Caine's occasional companion.

Though the fate of Caine is unknown, his grandson lives in a modern-day metropolitan Chinatown with his own son, an undercover police officer whom he'd thought was dead.

Comment: The TV movie spawned an hour-long series that aired from October 1972 until June 1975; there were 60 episodes in addition to the original 90-minute pilot and a two-hour episode. The show starred David Carradine as the adult Caine, Radames Pera as young Caine (a.k.a. "Grasshopper"), Keye Luke as Po, and Philip Ahn as Kan. Season Hubley was Margit. It is unclear how much actor/Kung Fu master Bruce Lee was involved with the creation of the show, but he was rumored to have come up with the idea as a vehicle for himself.

Howard Lee wrote a series of Kung Fu paperback novels in 1972–1973.

Caine returned in the made-for-TV *Kung Fu: The Movie* (1986), battling opium dealers in California of the 1880s; Bruce Lee's son, Brandon, had one of his earliest roles as a nemesis of Caine's here.

The television series was revived in January 1993 as *Kung Fu: The Legend Continues* with Carradine and Chris Potter. Though the setting is not named, the show was filmed in Toronto.

L

LANCE O'CASEY (C)

First Appearance: *Whiz Comics* #2, 1940, Fawcett Publications.

Biography: A "swashbuckling sailor of fortune," the red-haired Lance O'Casey plies the South Seas onboard his vessel *The Brian Boru* (later, *The Starfish*), battling cruel natives, pirates, smugglers, and the like. He is always accompanied by his monkey first mate, Mister Hogan; after several adventures, he picks up a sidekick, Cap'n Dan, who is later replaced by young Mike.

Comment: The character was created by Bob Kingett and had a healthy run in *Whiz Comics,* though he was overshadowed by the popularity of Captain Marvel, who also debuted in that issue. Lance also starred in his own title, which lasted just four issues, from 1946 to 1948. Other adventure characters who debuted in in *Whiz Comics* #2 and lasted only a few

Lance O'Casey and Mister Hogan assist wounded Skipper Jones, whose trading post has been attacked by natives. © Fawcett Publications.

issues at most were DAN DARE, the "ace private detective" who shuttles around the U.S. on his private plane; and Scoop Smith, "crack newshawk" of the *News,* who breaks stories with the aid of his stuttering photographer Blimp Black.

In 1940 Fawcett also launched *Master Comics* and *Slam Bang Comics. Master Comics* introduced such adventure heroes as Shipwreck Roberts, a diver for hire; Streak Sloan, who worked for a newsreel; Frontier Marshal; and Rick O'Shay, a world adventurer. *Slam Bang Comics* gave us cowboy Lucky Lawton; time traveler Mark Swift; sea hero Hurricane Hanson; the Jungle King; and magazine editor Jim Dolan.

LANCE SAINT-LORNE (CS)

First Appearance: *Lance,* June 1955, Warren Tufts Enterprises.

Biography: Second Lieutenant Lance Saint-Lorne serves with the 1st Dragoons, based at Fort Leavenworth, Kansas, in the 1840s. Armed with a heavy cavalry saber but also adept with firearms, the ruggedly handsome, usually well-groomed Lance battles the Sioux and other Indians, reporting to Colonel Dodge. During his many adventures—including run-ins with Kit Carson and being stranded in the desert without horse or supplies—Lance's companions are Sergeant Blaze and Big Fallon. Lance eventually makes colonel.

For a while Lance is pursued by the lovely Indian Many Robes, who falls in love with him after nursing an arrow wound. Instead, he marries the beauteous trader Valle Dufrain.

Comment: Creator Tufts syndicated the strip himself, at the height of the TV western fad, hoping it would be adapted for television. It wasn't, and barely hung on to enough newspapers to survive five years. The strip remains noteworthy for the splendor of the art—which often flirted with photorealism—and the creator's memorable, true-to-life characterizations. Like PRINCE VALIANT, there were no word balloons; the text was in boxes below or above each panel.

See also CASEY RUGGLES.

LARIAT SAM (TV)

First Appearance: *The Captain Kangaroo Show,* September 10, 1962, CBS-TV.

Biography: Lariat Sam is a heroic but easygoing cowboy who is averse to violence and doesn't carry a gun. Riding the range on Tippytoes, a talking "Wonder Horse" who's fond of reading poetry and wears a derby, Sam always manages to talk or run his way out of trouble. His perennial foe is Badlands Meeney.

Comment: Thirteen "Adventures of Lariat Sam" were produced over three years, each of them comprised of three short chapters and written for young children. The shows were later syndicated. Dayton Allen provided the voices of both Sam and Tippytoes.

LEMUEL GULLIVER (L, MP, C, TV)

First Appearance: *Gulliver's Travels* by Jonathan Swift, 1726.

Biography: Lemuel Gulliver was born in Nottinghamshire, the third of five sons. When he's 14, he attends Emanuel College in Cambridge for three years, apprentices with London surgeon James Bates for another four, and attends Leyden University (in Holland) for two years and seven months, to complete his medical training. He also studies mathematics and navigation, intending to travel; with Bates's help, he is named surgeon of the *Swallow,* serving for three and a half years. Upon returning to London, he takes rooms in the Jewish quarter of London, sets up a practice, and marries Mary Burton. But his practice fails, and Gulliver returns to the sea for several voyages lasting six years. Upon his return, he settles in a house on Feter Lane, then in Wapping, where he opens another practice, hoping to draw sailors. That, too, fails after three years, and he goes back to the sea, setting sail from Bristol on May 4, 1699, onboard the *Antelope,* bound for the South Seas.

On November 5 a storm drives the ship against a rock and it goes down; Gulliver ends up on the shore of an island southwest of Sumatra. After walking "near half a mile," he lies down and goes to sleep on the grass. When he wakes, he finds that he's been tied down by the inhabitants of the island, the Lilliputians, who are 1/12th his size. After eventually convincing the emperor of his peaceful intentions, Gulliver is released. Called *Quinbus Flestrin*—Great Man Mountain—he learns that Lilliput is at war with Blefescu, a kingdom across the channel, because they break their eggs at different ends. Gulliver stops the war by destroying Blefescu's fleet. He is praised as a hero, but when he puts out a fire at court by urinating on it, the emperor decides to have him blinded. Fed up with Lilliput, Gulliver finds a "prodigious vessel" in Blefescu and goes out to sea on September 24, 1701. Two days later he's rescued by an English merchantman.

He reacquaints himself with his wife, his son Johnny—named after a well-liked uncle—and daughter Betty. Two months afterward, on June 20, 1702, he returns to the sea, this time headed for Surat onboard the *Adventure.* A year later he joins a dozen men in a longboat and heads for an island off the west coast of North America to look for water. Gulliver's fellows desert him when a giant farmer appears; taken in by the farmer and entrusted to his daughter, Glumdalclitch, Gulliver learns that he is in pacifistic Brobdingnag, where the inhabitants are 12 times the size of humans. The hero has terrifying encounters with a huge frog, a monkey, a spaniel, and giant breasts (women enjoy placing him on their nipples) before the box in which he's kept is spirited away by an eagle and dropped in the ocean. He is rescued by an English ship and returns to his family.

Once more his stay is brief. On August 5, 1706, he sails onboard the *Hopewell,* which is boarded by pirates the following April. Gulliver is set adrift in a canoe and after five days reaches the island of Laputa, whose inhabitants incline their heads to the right or left, one eye pointed inward and the other upward. Moreover, they can fly their island about and exact tribute from other lands by blocking the sunlight. Gulliver is dropped off on the continent of Balnibari, a land whose inhabitants walk fast, look wild, dress in rags, and are so concerned with knowledge and the future that they let the present fall to ruin. From there he makes his way to Japan, Amsterdam, and then England, arriving home on April 10, 1710.

On September 7 he assumes the captaincy of another ship, also called the *Adventure,* and after a series of misfortunes finds his crew in mutiny. He is put ashore in parts unknown on May 9, 1711. It turns out to be another island, this one inhabited by savage humans named Yahoos and intelligent, cultured horses called Houyhnhnms. He remains among these creatures for nearly three years (even though the Houyhnhnms are indignant when they learn that people ride horses in England), after which he sails off on a canoe. He lands at Hew Holland, hoping to settle there, but is wounded in the knee by a native arrow; fortunately, a Portuguese ship happens by, and he is taken aboard. From Lisbon, he sails for home. But his homecoming is not a happy one: Memories of the foul Yahoos are ripe in his memory, and he can't even bear to have his wife or children touch him. Conversely, he buys two horses and spends at least four hours a day with them in the stable.

Comment: Though the specific targets of Swift's satire will not mean much to nonhistory and nonliterary scholars, the work retains its biting prose and tone. The author, a founder of the icon-puncturing Scriblerus Club, apparently began working on the novel in 1720.

In motion pictures, the first three versions of the tale were short subjects. Special effects pioneer George Melies made a silent short in 1902, *Le Voyage de Gulliver a Lillput et ches les Geants;* French filmmakers Albert Mourlan and Raymond Villette created an animated puppet film, *Gulliver in Lilliput,* in 1923; and Walt Disney produced an animated short, *Gulliver Mickey,* in 1934. *Gulliver's Travels* (1939) by the Fleischer Studios *(Betty Boop, Popeye)* was the second animated feature film and was released just after *Snow White and the Seven Dwarfs.* Special effects artist Ray Harryhausen worked his magic on *The Three Worlds of Gulliver* (1959), which sent the hero to Lilliput and Brobdingnag and starred Kerwin Mathews. The Japanese company Toei produced *Gulliver's Travels Beyond the Moon* (1965; released in the U.S. 1966), in which a young boy is knocked out and imagines himself traveling with Gulliver to the planet Hope. Richard Harris was among the few live actors in an otherwise animated feature film *Gulliver's Travels* (1977).

In comic books, #16 of *Classics Illustrated* (1943) was an adaptation of the novel. Dell published an adaptation of *The Three Worlds of Gulliver* as part of their *4-Color* series (#1158) in 1960 and, from 1965 to 1966, unrelated to the film, published three issues of *Gulliver's Travels.*

On TV, Ross Martin provided the voice of Gulliver in an animated special that was part of *CBS Famous Classic Tales* and aired in November 1980. There were also 17 adventures of *The Adventures of Gulliver,* which debuted in September 1968, on the series *The Banana Splits and Friends.* After finding a treasure map that belonged to his missing father, Thomas, Gary Gulliver and his dog Tagg set sail to find him. A storm blows him to Lilliput, where the people are six inches tall and ruled by King Pomp. Upon learning that his father is on the island, Gary, Tagg, and several Lilliputians go searching for him, dogged by the wicked treasure hunter Captain Leech. Jerry Dexter provided Gary's voice.

LEW ARCHER   (L, MP, TV)

First Appearance: *The Moving Target* by Ross MacDonald, 1949, Alfred A. Knopf.

Biography: Born on June 2, 1914, Lew Archer becomes a member of the Long Beach, California, police department in 1935. But the department is corrupt and he quits to become a private eye, circa 1940. After a spell with military intelligence during World War II, working primarily in the U.S., he returns to Southern California and resumes his practice, "peeping on flea-bag hotel rooms, untying marital knots, blackmailing blackmailers out of business." He often flashes his Special Deputy badge from the war to get cooperation from people who don't bother to examine it too closely.

In his first adventure, he's hired by a wealthy family to find the missing head of the household. Subsequent cases involve mostly divorces and murders, investigations that sometimes lead to fisticuffs, car chases, and gunplay—occasionally with the police. In one of his most famous adventures *(The Chill),* he searches for Alex Kincaid's new bride, Dolly, who has run away; Archer's quest involves him in a complex web of murder and bizarre family members.

Lew's wife, Sue, divorced him because she didn't like the people with whom he's forced to associate. Despite the sleeze factor inherent in his work, Lew is a cultured man who enjoys classical music and literature, and is up on flora and bird species. He is particularly fond of the Japanese artist Kuniyoshi. However, he's also a cynic who feels there's nothing wrong with most people that "a prefrontal lobotomy wouldn't fix," and he has a particularly low tolerance for any "fool in an official job," especially stupid police officers.

As for his weaknesses and faults, Archer drinks highballs with "plenty of soda" and likes betting on the horses at Santa Anita. He drives a convertible.

Comment: The other Lew Archer novels include *The Drowning Pool* (1950), *The Way Some People Die* (1951), *The Ivory Grin* (1952), *Find a Victim* (1954), *The Name Is Archer* (1955; short stories), *The Barbarous Coast* (1956), *The Doomsters* (1958), *The Galton Case* (1959), *The Wycherly Woman* (1961), *The Zebra-Striped Hearse* (1962), *The Chill* (1964), *The Far Side of the Dollar* (1965), *Black Money* (1966), *The Instant Enemy* (1968), *Archer in Hollywood* (1968; a collection of three novels), *The Goodbye Look* (1969), *Archer at Large* (1970), *The Underground Man* (1971), *Sleeping Beauty* (1973), *Blue City* (1974), *Archer in Jeopardy* (1979), and *Lew Archer Private Investigator* (1988). MacDonald was a pseudonym of Kenneth Millar.

In the movies, Paul Newman played the character in *Harper* (1966), a faithful adaptation of *The Moving Target,* and again in *The Drowning Pool* (1975). The character's name in these was Lew Harper, because Newman had had his greatest successes with movies that began with "H" (*The Hustler* and *Hud*).

On TV, *The Underground Man* was filmed as a TV movie in 1974, in which the detective looks for the kidnaped son of an ex-girlfriend and stumbles on a series of murders. Peter Graves was sadly miscast as Archer. Brian Keith starred in *Archer* in the hour-long series, which aired on NBC from January to March 1975. He, too, was the wrong man for the part.

LT. BLUEBERRY (CS)

First Appearance: "Fort Navajo," 1963, *Pilote* magazine (France).

Biography: Not long after the Civil War, Mike Donovan is framed for murder and flees from justice. He changes his name and, as Mike S. Blueberry, serves as a lieutenant with the 17th U.S. Cavalry Regiment at Fort Navajo, New Mexico. At the onset of his adventures, Blueberry spends most of his time protecting the laborers working on the transcontinental railway. Afterward, he moves on to fighting Indians and chasing down gunrunners, bandits, and renegade Mexicans with his men (or just as often on his own, looking more and more grizzled). He also does some prospecting and goes searching for a mythical mine in Arizona.

His friend and constant companion is whiskey-chugging Jimmy McClure. Blueberry enjoys whiskey, but his major weakness is gambling.

Lieutenant Blueberry is as proficient with his fists as he is with all forms of firearms.

Comment: Blueberry proved to be such a popular attraction in the initial story that he was given his own strip. The character was created by writer Jean-Michel Charlier and artist Jean Giraud.

LT. COLUMBO (S, TV)

First Appearance: *Prescription: Murder* by Richard Levinson and William Link, 1961.

Biography: Rumpled, seemingly dullwitted and incompetent, the scrupulously polite Lieutenant Columbo (he has no first name) is actually a sharp police lieutenant who always knows (or suspects) exactly what's going on, and skillfully maneuvers murderers, thieves, and other criminals into a corner. (As actor Peter Falk puts it, "He likes to save his best shot for last. Columbo's got a terrific sense of timing.") In his first escapade, he is confronted with Doc Fleming, who is convinced he has committed the perfect murder of his wife. In his second chronicled case, he is faced with lawyer Leslie Williams, who has killed her husband.

Columbo is rarely without his wrinkled old raincoat and a cigar. He drives a battered old wreck.

Columbo's wife is Kate and they have a young daughter, Jenny. (Mrs. Columbo is a part-time journalist for a newspaper called *The Valley Advocate,* who

Peter Falk, left, as *Lt. Columbo,* with guest star Patrick McGoohan. © CBS TV.

often becomes involved with murder mysteries of her own.)

Comment: Thomas Mitchell played the part in the Broadway play, which inspired a 1968 made for TV film version starring Peter Falk. Gene Barry was Fleming. The sequel, *Ransom for a Dead Man,* starred Falk with Lee Grant as Williams. Richard Irving directed both films.

A *Columbo* TV series followed, beginning with "Murder by the Book," in which a best-selling author murders his collaborator. It aired as part of the *NBC* (later, *NBC Sunday*) *Mystery Movie* lineup with *McCloud, Hec Ramsey,* and *McMillan and Wife.* (See SAM MCCLOUD and COMMISSIONER STEWART MCMILLAN.) The regularly scheduled series went off the air in September, 1977, but Falk returned to making occasional Columbo TV movies in 1989.

Bing Crosby was originally offered the part in the TV series and turned it down.

The Columbo character himself was inspired by police inspector Porfiri Petrovich in Dostoevski's *Crime and Punishment* (1866).

Mrs. Columbo was the heroine of her own TV series that began airing in February 1979 under the title *Mrs.*

Columbo. Over the next few months it was changed to *Kate Columbo, Kate the Detective* (with all references to Columbo gone; she was now Kate Callahan and had a police force contact, Sergeant Mike Varrick), and then *Kate Loves a Mystery.* It was off the air by December. Kate Mulgrew played Kate, Lili Haydn was Jenny, and Don Stroud was Varrick.

LT. FRANK DREBIN (TV, MP)

First Appearance: *Police Squad,* March 1982, ABC.

Biography: A detective in a "large American city," the white-haired, deadpan, incredibly inept Lieutenant Frank Drebin works with Captain Ed Hocken and always manages to beat killers, crooked fight promotors, protection racketeers, terrorists, and the like—though just barely. He often goes undercover (posing as a key store owner, boxing trainer, etc.), getting tips from shoeshine boy Johnny the Snitch as well as useless assistance from police scientist Ted Olson.

Comment: The half-hour TV series aired through September 1982; reruns were shown on CBS from July to September 1991. Leslie Nielsen starred as Drebin, Alan North was Hocken, Ed Williams was Olson, and William Duell was Johnny. Nielsen also played the character in the motion pictures *The Naked Gun: From the Files of Police Squad!* (1988), in which he prevents the assassination of the queen, *The Naked Gun 2 1/2: The Smell of Fear* (1991), in which he breaks an energy conspiracy, and *Naked Gun 33¹/₃: The Final Insult* (1994). The characters were created by David and Jerry Zucker and Jim Abrahams (producers of *Airplane!*).

Nielsen also played big-city Deputy Police Chief Sam Danforth in *The Protectors,* a ("serious") hour-long series that aired on NBC from September 1969 to September 1970 (one of the three series airing under the blanket title of *The Bold Ones,* the others being *The New Doctors* and *The Lawyers*).

LT. GULLIVAR JONES (L, C)

First Appearance: *Lt. Gullivar Jones: His Vacation* by Edwin L. Arnold, 1905, S.C. Brown, Langham & Co.

Biography: Cleveland native Gullivar Jones is a lieutenant in the U.S. Navy who is overlooked for a promotion—one that would have enabled him to woo his beloved Polly. While on leave in New York, he helps a stranger to the hospital, where the man dies; Jones takes the fellow's carpet, which is all he was carrying, feeling it would "do nicely for the messroom on the *Carolina.*" But, frustrated with his superiors, Jones

wishes aloud he were on Mars and, in a flash, the carpet—now revealed to be magical—carries him there. Jones finds Mars a barbaric world, and, armed with sword and spear and befriended by Prince Hath of Hither, he protects the gorgeous Princess Heru from the forces of Thither. Ultimately cornered by enemies, Jones determines that Heru is safe and uses the carpet to return to New York. There the carpet disappears forever and Jones goes back to Polly, whom he weds.

Comment: Arnold's novel was published only in London until 1964, when Ace Books released a paperback edition entitled *Gulliver of Mars.* Curiously, the character's name and all references to the original novel in the preface are misspelled as "Gulliver." Despite similarities, the novel does not seem to have been the inspiration for JOHN CARTER.

New adventures featuring the character were published in Marvel Comics' *Creatures on the Loose* title, numbers 16 to 21, from 1972 to 1973.

LT. THEO KOJAK (TV, CS)

First Appearance: *The Marcus-Nelson Murders,* March 1973, CBS.

Biography: Theo Kojak is a brash, streetwise New York City police veteran, who works at the 13th Precinct in Manhattan South and reports to his longtime friend and former partner, Chief of Detectives Frank McNeil. Frank was promoted because he's better at playing politics than his outspoken friend. Kojak's associates are Detective Stavros and Lieutenant Bobby Crocker.

In time, Kojak makes inspector, assisted by Detectives Winston Blake and Paco Montana, and his secretary, Pamela.

Kojak is rarely without his trademark lollipop (which he started sucking to quit smoking) or his catch phrase, "Who loves ya, baby?"

Comment: The first TV film, about a ghetto kid wrongly accused of murder, was directed by Joseph Sargent, based on the real-life New York Wylie-Hoffert murders in 1963. It spawned the hour-long *Kojak* TV series, which aired from October 1973 to April 1978 on CBS and itself spawned a 1985 TV film, *Kojak: The Belarus File,* which pits Kojak against Nazi spies; *Kojak: The Price of Justice* (1987), in which Kojak investigates a woman who's accused of killing her two sons; and a new *Kojak* series, which aired on ABC from November 1989 to January 1990.

Telly Savalas starred as Kojak, Dan Frazer was McNeil, George Demosthenes Savalas was Stavros, and Kevin Dobson was Crocker. In the second series, Andre Braugher was Blake, Kario Salem was Paco, and Candace Savalas was Pamela.

Telly Savalas, left, as *Kojak*. © CBS TV, courtesy of Telly Savalas.

The British publication *TV Comic* ran a Kojak strip in the 1970s and gave him a sidekick called the Kicktail Kid.

LINK (VG, TV, C)

First Appearance: *The Legend of Zelda*, 1985, Nintendo.

Biography: In the long-ago Age of Chaos, in the land of Hyrule, peace was maintained by a wondrous, mystic triangle known as Triforce. Alas, the evil Ganon and his minions steal Triforce and also abduct the beloved Princess Zelda. Fifteen-year-old Link sets forth to find the eight scattered pieces of Triforce, rescue Zelda, and defeat Ganon, the King of Evil, and his many monsters, such as the centipede Lanmola, the wizard Wizzrobe, the arrow-shooting Molblins, and many others. He succeeds with the aid of his sword as well as other arms he finds along the way, such as bombs, rafts, ladders, keys, and Hearts, which boost his inherent life force.

But the peace brought by his victory is short-lived. In his second adventure, "many seasons" later, Link discovers that there's more to the Triforce than he has recovered. There are three kinds of force: Power, Wisdom, and Courage. Courage is missing. To obtain it—and to wake Zelda, who has fallen into a deep sleep—Link must fight his way to the Great Palace in the Valley of Death and defeat his own shadow.

Link succeeds, but his job is not yet done. Before very long, the mighty sorcerer Agahnim conquers Hyrule and kidnaps several maidens, including Zelda. Not only must Link defeat the wizard, he must do so before Agahnim can open a doorway to the Dark World, which will give him access to all the powers of evil.

In his last adventure to date, Link must make his way through seven dangerous dungeons in order to face the evil, all-powerful Wind Fish.

Comment: The game, which was first released in Japan, was introduced in the U.S. in 1986, playable on the Nintendo Entertainment System. It was followed by *Zelda II: The Adventure of Link* and by *The Legend of Zelda: A Link to the Past,* created for the Super Nintendo system. In the summer of 1993, Nintendo released *The Legend of Zelda: Link's Awakening* for the Game Boy system.

In 1989 DIC Enterprises launched a syndicated, half-hour *The Legend of Zelda* animated series; only 13 episodes were produced. Jonathan Potts was the voice of Link and Cyndy Preston was Zelda. There were also four issues of a Valiant comic book, *The Legend of Zelda,* published in 1990.

Many sword and sorcery games have been manufactured for the Nintendo Entertainment System. These, and the adventure heroes who star in them, include *Deadly Towers,* in which the young Prince Myer of the kingdom of Willner must prevent the sorcerer Rubas from invading; *Ghosts 'N Goblins,* in which the knight Arthur must save his beloved princess from the devil himself; *Karnov,* in which circus strongman Jinborov Karnovski must track down the dragon Ryu, who has stolen the Treasure of Babylon from the small town of Creamina; *Solomon's Key,* in which the wizard Dana must find the magic key to destroy the demons that have invaded the fairy kingdom of Lyrac; *Gauntlet,* in which four heroes—Thyra the Valkyrie, Thor the Warrior, Merlin the Wizard, and Questor the Elf—must recover the Sacred Orb from Morak and restore peace to Rendar; *Milon's Secret Castle,* in which the eponymous hero rescues Queen Eliza of Hudson from the Evil Warlord; *Rygar,* in which Rygar of Algosu seeks to destroy the wicked Ligar, who has come to Argool, deposed the Indora gods, and stolen the Door to Peace; *Hydlide,* in which a Fairyland knight known only as Jim must save Princess Ann from the demon Boralis; *Final Fantasy,* in which the Light Warriors of Coneria set out to defeat

Link, the heroic youth of a series of video games. ©
Nintendo of America.

LION-O (TV, T, C)

First Appearance: *ThunderCats,* January 1985,
syndicated.

Biography: When the planet Thundera slips from its
orbit and is destroyed, the native ThunderCats—humanoid cats—board starships and migrate to a distant
galaxy. While the ThunderCats lie in suspended animation as the decades pass, the ship is looked after by
the faithful Jaga, who dies shortly before the ship
finishes its journey of many light-years to the Thunder-
Cats' new home: Third Earth. Thereafter, the spirit of
Jaga occasionally appears to Lion-o, the hereditary
leader of the ThunderCats. Unfortunately, Third Earth
is the home of the evil Mumm-Ra and his mutant
armies, and he wants what Lion-o has—the Sword of
Omens, a powerful weapon with the Eye of Thundera
set in its hilt. Whoever possesses this blade has "sight
beyond sight, for the eye enables you to see dangers
that lie in wait before you face them." When thrown,
the sword returns to its owner. Thus, instead of finding
peace on their new world, it's constant war for Lion-o
and his fellow ThunderCats—Cheetara, Wilykat, Wilykit, Panthro, Snarf, Tygra, and Lynxana. The heroes
frequently travel in the heavily armed Thunder-tank,
with drill blades that can dig through the ground.

Comment: Sixty-five half-hour adventures were produced by Rankin-Bass, featuring Larry Kenney as the
voice of Lion-o. LJN toys produced a popular series of
action figures, and Marvel Comics published 24 issues
of a *ThunderCats* comic book.

LITTLE NEMO (CS, S, MP, VG)

First Appearance: *Little Nemo in Slumberland,*
October 15, 1905, *New York Herald.*

Biography: Nemo is a young (about four- or five-
year-old) child who visits Slumberland when he goes
to bed each night. There, dressed in his white night-
shirt, he explores the many wonders of the dream
world, from Jack Frost's Palace of Ice, to the Candy
Islands, to the deck of a pirate ship where he's held for
$100 million ransom. He is accompanied at various
times by his dog Slivers, the cigar-smoking green dwarf
Flip, the cannibal Impy, the mad Dr. Pill, and the
daughter of King Morpheus: Known only as the Princess, she is roughly the same age as Nemo and has been
yearning for a playmate.

Each adventure ends with Nemo waking, his "papa"
chastising him for sleeping too late or his "mama"
threatening to spank him for throwing the covers off
during the night. Nemo is often awakened by something related to what he was dreaming—for example,
he's called for breakfast when he's about to be served

the wicked knight Garland, reclaim the Orbs of
Power, and save Princess Sara; and *Wizards & War-
riors,* in which the knight Kuros unsheaths the mighty
Brightsword and takes on the malevolent wizard
Malkil, who has taken the princess to his stronghold
in Elrond.

There are also many games for the rival Sega and
Genesis systems, including *Forgotten Worlds,* in
which the Nameless One on future Earth (now known
as the Dust World) must rid it of alien conquerors;
Ghouls 'N Ghosts, in which Sir Arthur must battle Loki,
the Prince of Darkness; *Golden Axe,* in which three
heroes—the Amazon Tyris-Flare, the dwarf Gilius
Thunderhead, and the barbarian Axe-Battler—must
save the kingdom of Yuria from Death Adder; *The Last
Battle,* a post-World War III saga in which the martial
arts master Aarzak must battle Garokk, ruler of the
Ultimate Savage Land; *Mystic Defender,* in which a
nameless hero must prevent the surpassingly evil
Zareth from conquering the earth (and rescue the
beauteous Alexandra); and many more.

The ThunderCats, from the left: Cheetara and Wilykit, Panthro, Tuska warrior, *Lion-o,* Snarf, Hachiman, Tygra and Wilykat, and the Snowman of Hook Mountain. © LJN Toys Ltd.

at a cannibal banquet, or splashed with a pan of water while he's drowing at sea.

Comment: The strip was created by the brilliant Winsor McCay, whose comic strip art remains a high point of design and rendering. It ran in the *Herald* until April 1911, after which McCay continued it for the Hearst newspapers under the title *The Land of Wonderful Dreams.* It ended in July 1914. In 1908 it was the subject of a stage musical with music by Victor Herbert, and a year later McCay turned it into an animated cartoon short.

A feature-length film, *Little Nemo: Adventures in Slumberland,* was released in 1992. In it Nemo is whisked to Slumberland where he tries to rescue the King of Slumberland, who has been abducted by the King of Nightmares. The plot is the same in the Nintendo video game, *The Dream Master.*

LITTLE ORPHAN ANNIE (CS, L, R, C, S, MP)

First Appearance: "Little Orphan Annie," August 5, 1924, Chicago Tribune-New York News Syndicate.

Biography: A curly redhead with blank eyes, "little chatterbox" Annie was born on February 29, 1920, and was left, as an infant, at the door of a home for orphans run by the strict Miss Asthma. Picked on by the other kids and by Asthma, she learns to survive by her wits and fists. At first, her only friend is her doll, Emily Marie. Later (January 1925), she saves an airedale/collie puppy from a group of toughs. She names the dog Sandy (its vocabulary consists of "Arf!" and "Arf! Arf!") and, though she can't keep him, he rescues her when she's kidnaped by a band of Gypsies. They become comrades in adventure from then on. When Annie is adopted by wealthy Mr. and Mrs. Oliver Warbucks, the woman finds the precocious Annie rather crude and doesn't particularly enjoy having her around—even after Annie scares off a burglar by impersonating a police whistle. But the bald Oliver, a munitions tycoon, international businessman, and one of the richest men in the world, loves the lass and insists that she call him "Daddy." Annie attends school, where she's unafraid to stand up to such girl gangs as the Valentines. When they try to rob her at knifepoint, she beats one of the girls up, steals the knife, and says, "One more step and I'll open you so wide th' sun'll tan yer insides!" (Quite a change from "The sun'll come out tomorrow"!).

Annie quickly emulates Daddy's work ethic and takes a job as a newsboy, packing a horseshoe in her pocket and socking any boy who hassles her; she then takes a job waitressing at a diner. A suspicious-looking customer leads her to her first big adventure, involving a robbery on a train. After she helps bring in the culprits, Annie has other adventures involving the escaped murderer Silverfish, the wealthy Pinchpenny who attempts to take over Cosmic City, ghosts in the attic of the bizarre Mr. Ninety, leprechauns in a cemetery, the wicked J. Gordon Slugg who tries to steal the secret of the Warbucks-controlled substance Eonite, the corrupt politicians who seek to bankrupt Warbucks, and more.

In the early months, Annie was fond of alliterative exclamations such as "Leapin' Limburger!" and "Sufferin' Scissorbills!" By 1925 she finally settled on "Leapin' Lizards" as her favorite. Annie plays a mean harmonica and almost always dresses in a red skirt and a red blouse with white collar and sleeves and a white belt. Her frequent companions are her father's Asian associates the Asp and the towering Punjab. Later, in a battle with spies, Annie acquires another companion—the monkey Elwood, who is not only a pickpocket but knows how to use a hand grenade.

Comment: The strip was created by Harold Gray, though it was Captain Joseph Patterson of the *News* who suggested changing Gray's original character, a boy named Otto, into a girl. Tex Blaisdell took over the strip in 1968, when Gray died; today it is drawn by Leonard Starr. Mrs. Warbucks was phased out early on.

Orphan Annie was the star of 17 Big Little Book adventures published from 1933 to 1948, including *Little Orphan Annie and the Big Train Robbery* (1934), *Little Orphan Annie and the Ghost Gang* (1935), *Little Orphan Annie and the Ancient Treasure of Am* (1939), *Little Orphan Annie and the Haunted Mansion* (1941), *Little Orphan Annie and Her Junior Commandos* (1943), *Little Orphan Annie and the Gooneyville Mystery* (1947), and *Little Orphan Annie in the Thieves' Den* (1948).

On radio, Annie had a somewhat different life from in the comic strips. The "little chatterbox . . . with pretty auburn locks" lived with characters that had been supporting players in the strip in 1925, farmers Mr. and Mrs. Silo of Simmons Corners; her boyfriend was Joe Corntassle. Daddy Warbucks was a mentor but was not center stage. Shirley Bell, then Janice Gilbert, played Annie; the series debuted on the Blue Network in 1931.

The first *Little Orphan Annie* comic book was a one-shot published by David McKay in 1937. Dell published seven titles as part of their *4-Color* series from 1941 to 1948; other one-shot comic books, mostly comic strip reprints, have been published over the years.

On stage, the musical *Annie* had its Broadway debut in 1977, with Andrea MacArdle in the part, and ran for 2,377 performances. A sequel, *Annie II,* died on the road with Lauren Gaffney in the title role; it was completely revamped as *Annie Warbucks* and opened off-Broadway in July 1993.

In motion pictures, Annie was played by Aileen Quinn in the 1982 adaptation of the Broadway musical. Albert Finney played Warbucks. Marvel Comics published a two-issue adaptation of the film that same year.

There have been many parodies over the years, from *Playboy*'s "Little Annie Fanny" strip to "Little Orphan Amphetamine" of the underground comics.

LITTLE WISE GUYS   (C)

First Appearance: *Daredevil Comics* #13, 1942, Lev Gleason Publications.

Biography: While running away from an orphanage, young Meatball encounters tall, lanky orphan Scarecrow, who's also on the lam. Elsewhere, young Jock saves little Pee Wee from being beaten up; as fate would have it, the four kids meet in a barn. They agree to look out for one another—though it's the superhero Daredevil who saves them, later, when they're attacked by a bull. In one of the foursome's first challenges (#15) they're forced to defend themselves against the rowdy Steamrollers, another gang; while hiding from them in a freezing river, Meatball perishes. After the remaining Wise Guys trash their foes, one of the "good" Steamrollers, bald Curly, joins the team, and they work with Daredevil to battle Japanese soldiers, black marketeers, and other criminals. All of the kids carry boomerangs like their hero.

Comment: The characters were created by writer/artist Charles Biro, and took over *Daredevil Comics* from Daredevil with #70; they stayed there until the magazine was discontinued with #134 (1956).

Other action heroes that costarred in *Daredevil Comics* were the Pirate Prince, "Robin Hood of the Seas," and Dickie Dean, the boy inventor.

LOGAN   (L, MP, C, TV)

First Appearance: *Logan's Run* by Willam F. Nolan and George Clayton Johnson, 1967, Dial Press.

Biography: "Beyond the 21st century," most of the world's population is under 21. As a result, a "flower" is attached to one of their palms, glowing yellow until they're seven, blue to 14, then red to 21. When it goes black, they must submit to voluntary euthanasia at a Sleepshop; the "runners" who try to flee their fate are hunted down and killed by "Sandmen," police officers in black tunics. This neatly ordered world is run by the Thinker, a vast and all-powerful computer complex.

Logan is a Sandman in the Los Angeles area. He decides to "run" on his "lastday," and he and fellow runner Jessica flee the Sandman Francis and make their way to Florida's Cape Steinbeck. There the rebel leader Ballard puts them in a rocket and launches them to Argos, an abandoned space station near Mars, where humans live normal life spans.

In his second chronicled adventure, which begins ten years later, supply ships have stopped coming from Earth. As Argos dies, Logan, Jessica, their eight-year-old son, Jaq, and nine others leave for Earth to find out why. They learn that Sandmen had taken over the base, Ballard had sacrificed his life to destroy the Thinker, and civilization had fallen into ruin. Young and previously pampered "City People" had become "Wilderness People," and different tribes had sprung up, including slavers, mutants, motorcyclists, and others. Using his skills as a former Sandman and survivor, Logan organizes various groups into a new, nonviolent, and democratic society.

In Logan's third adventure, aliens in search of amusement spirit him to a parallel Earth similar to the cruel world of the Thinker he'd left behind. He triumphs here as well, in an adventure that takes place in "nontime," and is returned to his pregnant wife who didn't even know he was gone.

Comment: Nolan, who had created Logan four years before his first adventure saw print, was the sole author of the sequels *Logan's World* (1977) and *Logan's Search* (1980).

The character was played by Michael York in the 1976 film, with Jenny Agutter as Jessia. The film is set in the year 2274, when people live in domed cities and are slain on their 30th birthdays in a ceremony known as the Carousel. In this version Logan and Jessica run, and, though they're pursued by the Sandman Francis (Richard Jordan), they are able to overthrow the government and liberate humankind from early death. The film was directed by Michael Anderson.

In 1977 Marvel Comics published seven issues of *Logan's Run,* inspired by the film.

An hour-long TV series aired on CBS from September 1977 to January 1978, and starred Gregory Harrison as Logan and Heather Menzies as Jessica. Set in 2319, it teams Logan and Jessica with the robot Rem (Donald Moffat). As the trio flees the Sandman Francis (Randy Powell), they encounter different civilizations outside the dome.

THE LONE EAGLE (C)

First Appearance: *Thrilling Comics* #3, 1940, Better Publications.
Biography: Known only as the Eagle (even the ID he carries says Lone Eagle), this brave pilot flies his fighter around the world to fight Nazis and other enemies of democracy. When he isn't flying, the hero is terrific with his fists.

Comment: The Lone Eagle appeared through issue #55. During its 80-issue run, *Thrilling Comics* was the home to a number of adventure heroes, including Nickie Norton of the Secret Service; Hale of the Herald (with his assistant Vickie); Lucky Lawrence, Leatherneck; the Rio Kid; the immortal Buck Ranger, Cowboy Detective; the jungle heroine Princess Pantha; and the youthful World War II heroes, the Commando Cubs (one of whom was a black youth).

THE LONE WOLF (L, MP, R, TV)

First Appearance: *The Lone Wolf* by Louis Joseph Vance, 1914, *Munsey's Magazine.*
Biography: Born around 1888 and brought to France when he is five, Michael Troyon is raised in Paris, in a seedy hotel, and survives by robbing and lying. When he tries to steal from master thief Bourke, the Irish crook doesn't turn him in. Rather, he takes him under his wing and, in addition to giving him a new name, Michael Lanyard, and an academic education (he excels in math), he shows him the ropes, everything from the use of weapons to appraising and fencing jewels. Bourke also teaches the lad the "three cardinal principles of successful cracksmanship": being thoroughly familiar with the ground he's going to be on; coming and going quickly; and remaining friendless.

Based in a Paris flat, and frequently using the apartment of the drunken painter Solon as a hideout, Lanyard poses as an art connoisseur during the day and works as a burglar by night, frequently journeying to England and the U.S. for business—and crime. He is extremely successful in both pursuits until he breaks Bourke's third commandment. After falling in love with British secret service agent Lucy Shannon, Lanyard gives up his night job and the couple settles in New York—though not for long. They cross swords with the German spy Ekstrom and are forced to flee to Belgium. There Michael and Lucy have a son and daughter, though all but Michael are slain by Ekstrom when the Germans invade. Lanyard devotes himself to bringing the German in, and, as he chases Ekstrom through Europe and the United States, the hero gathers intelligence that proves invaluable to the Allies. Eventually he leads the German into a trap and Ekstrom is gunned down.

Back in New York, Lanyard befriends and works closely with Detective Crane of the NYPD, after which the Lone Wolf returns to Europe and goes to work with the British Secret Service, preventing the assassination

The Lone Eagle gets ready to teach a lesson to Nazi saboteurs. © Better Publications.

of the king and cabinet. Vacationing in Spain, he is framed for the theft of the jewels of wealthy widow Eve de Montalais, whom he weds after clearing himself of the crime. She dies shortly thereafter, and Lanyard becomes the manager of the New York office of the antique dealer Delibes of Paris. Much to his surprise, he discovers that his son, Maurice, is alive and has been earning his living as a cat burglar for nearly 20 years. The two are reunited, and Maurice marries a wealthy young woman and becomes a Lone Wolf fighting for justice just like his dad.

Lanyard is tall and slender, but exceptionally strong and a master of several forms of hand-to-hand combat. He has dark, longish hair, dark eyes, and a face of "extraordinary pallor." Lanyard speaks French, English, and German and has a passion for the gambling tables.

Comment: Vance wrote eight Lone Wolf adventures, which were published through 1934, the last of them posthumously. The sequels are *The False Faces* (1918), *Alias the Lone Wolf* (1921), *Red Masquerade* (1921), *The Lone Wolf Returns* (1923), *The Lone Wolf's Son (1931)*, *Encore the Lone Wolf* (1933), and *The Lone Wolf's Last Prowl*. In 1965 a previously unpublished tale, "The White Terror," set on a train, was published in *The Saint Mystery Magazine*.

The character was featured in a number of films that date back to the silents: *The Lone Wolf* (1917) starring Bert Lytell; *The False Faces* (1919) and *The Lone Wolf's Daughter* (1919), both starring Henry B. Walthall; and *The Lone Wolf* (1924) starring Jack Holt. Lytell returned for *The Lone Wolf Returns* (1926), *Alias the Lone Wolf* (1927), *The Lone Wolf's Daughter* (1929), and *Last of the Lone Wolf* (1930), after which Thomas Meighan starred in *Cheaters at Play* (1932). Melvyn Douglas took the part in *The Lone Wolf Returns* (1935), followed by Francis Lederer in *The Lone Wolf in Paris* (1938). Warren William took over the role for nine films: *The Lone Wolf Spy Hunt* (1939), *The Lone Wolf Strikes* (1940), *The Lone Wolf Meets a Lady* (1940), *The Lone Wolf Takes a Chance* (1941), *The Lone Wolf Keeps a Date* (1941), *Secrets of the Lone Wolf* (1941), *Counter-Espionage* (1942), *One Dangerous Night* (1943), and *Passport to Suez* (1943). Gerald Mohr took over the role for *The Notorious Lone Wolf* (1946), *The Lone Wolf in London* (1947), and *The Lone Wolf in Mexico* (1947), and Ron Randell starred in the last entry, *The Lone Wolf and His Lady* (1949).

Magazine Publishers Group began publishing the *Lone Wolf Detective Magazine* in 1939, featuring short stories of detectives who work alone.

The character had a short radio run in 1948. On TV, he was played by Louis Hayward in 1955 on a syndi-

cated half-hour series called *The Lone Wolf* when it first aired, then shown as *Streets of Danger* in reruns.

The *Lone Wolf* detective novels of 1974–75 are unrelated to the Vance tales. In the Mike Barry novels, former Vietnam vet and NYPD narcotics officer becomes a vengeful guerilla warrior attacking the international drug trade after dealers murder his fiancee, Marie Calvante. The novels in the series include *The Lone Wolf: Boston*, *The Lone Wolf: New York*, *The Lone Wolf: San Francisco*, *The Lone Wolf: Las Vegas*, and *The Lone Wolf: Havana Hit*.

LONGARM (L)

First Appearance: *Longarm* by Tabor Evans, 1978, Jove Books.

Biography: In the late 1800s, U.S. Deputy Marshal Custis Long, a.k.a. Longarm, works for Billy Vail, a Denver-based marshal attached to the Federal District Court. Vail sends the deputy on difficult assignments throughout the West, which he always manages to pull off. The thickly mustachioed hero rides a chestnut horse and carries a Winchester, a Colt .44, and a pocket knife. He is rarely without a cheroot.

Comment: Tabor Evans is a house name. As of this writing, there have been over 160 Longarm novels. The titles pretty well sum up the breadth of the hero's adventures: *Longarm and the Skull Canyon Gang*, *Longarm and the Crooked Railman*, *Longarm and the Indian Raiders*, *Longarm and the Crooked Marshal*, *Longarm and the Pawnee Kid*, *Longarm and the Lone Star Rustlers*, *Longarm and the Treacherous Trial*, *Longarm and the Nex Mexico Shoot-Out*, and *Longarm and the Denver Bustout*.

Jove also publishes the long-running (130 titles to date) *Lone Star* series by Wesley Ellis, the adventures of western sharpshooter/vigilante Jessica Starbuck and her American/Japanese companion, the martial arts master Ki.

See also THE GUNSMITH; SLOCUM.

LORD CUMULUS (S, C)

First Appearance: *Warp*, 1971, Organic Theater Company.

Biography: David Carson is a teller for the Central City Bank working for Mr. Bigelow and in love with his daughter, Mary Louise. But David has a secret: He had spent several years in an insane asylum because of headaches, strange voices, and bizarre nightmares that torture him. One afternoon the voices return and David is drawn to Fen-Ra, a "fortress city" in the fifth dimension. There, as Cumulus, he battles with his brother, Prince Chaos of the Fortress Rottwang. According to Cumulus's tutor Lugulbanda, who is "knowledge incarnate," if he fails to defeat Chaos, then "all that lives shall end—and that includes Earth." Lugulbanda turns Cumulus over to the care of the warrior woman Sargon, who teaches him how to wield an energy spear and to channel his own thoughts into powerful energy beams.

Thanks to their ability to become phantoms on Earth, Cumulus and Chaos do battle by entering the bodies of Carson and Marie Louise; Carson dies and Cumulus is forever stranded in the fifth dimension, where the battle with Chaos continues.

Comment: Written by Bury St. Edmund and Stuart Gordon, *Warp* was "the collective designation for three separate full-length plays" presented in Chicago from 1971 to 1972: *My Battlefield, My Body; Unleashed, Unchained* (later changed to *SlitherlusT* (*sic*), and *To Die . . . Alive. Warp (My Battlefield, My Body)* moved to the Ambassador Theater on Broadway and opened February 14, 1973, with John Heard as Cumulus and art direction by comics great Neal Adams; it closed after just three weeks. It returned to Chicago in 1979 and also played other cities with great success.

First Comics published 19 issues of a *Warp* comic book from 1983 to 1985, along with three *Warp*

specials. The early issues of the comic book were based loosely on the plays, drawn by Frank Brunner and written by Peter Gillis.

LORD PETER WIMSEY (L, MP, S, TV)

First Appearance: *Whose Body?* by Dorothy L. Sayers, 1923.

Biography: Peter Death Bredeon Wimsey was born in 1890, the younger son of Mortimer Gerald Bredon Wimsey, the 15th Duke of Denver, and the Dowager Duchess of Denver; his older brother is Gerald, his sister, Mary. Peter is schooled at Eton and Balliol College (Oxford), where he's a standout pianist, cricket player, and historian. He graduates first in his modern history class in 1912. Engaged to be married before going off to fight in World War I, he decides to postpone his nuptials lest he be killed or maimed; when he returns to London on leave in 1916, he learns that his betrothed has married another. The experience shatters Peter, who becomes a one-man army corps, not caring if he lives or dies as long as he takes Germans with him. He lives, of course, earning the Distinguished Service Cross—and suffering a nervous breakdown when his experiences finally catch up with him.

After his recovery, Captain Wimsey moves into a flat at 110 Piccadilly in London. There, in addition to his interest in music, history, and literature, the monocled scholar and adventurer satisfies his restless mind and body by pursuing criminology. In addition to solving crimes, he works as an emissary/agent for the British Foreign Office. With the outbreak of World War II, he once again goes to work for the government on dangerous missions abroad.

Wimsey's frequent assistant is the elderly Miss Climpson, who works from one of Wimsey's offices with other elderly aides. In 1935 he weds mystery writer Harriet Vane, whom he clears of murder *(Have His Carcase)*. They have three sons. Peter's valet is Bunter, who served with his boss in France. He is a superb chef and photographer.

Comment: The other novels are *Clouds of Witness* (1926), *The Dawson Pedigree* (1927; *Unnatural Death* in the U.S.), *The Unpleasantness at the Bellona Club* (1928), *Strong Poison* (1930), *The Five Red Herrings* (1931; *Suspicious Characters* in the U.S.), *Have His Carcase* (1932), *Murder Must Advertise* (1933), *The Nine Tailors* (1934), *Gaudy Night* (1935), and *Busman's Honeymoon* (1937). There are also several short story collections.

In motion pictures, Peter Haddon played Peter in

Lord Cumulus has a tough time obeying his ally Sargon in Neal Adams's art from *Warp*. © Organic Theater Company.

The Silent Passenger (1935) and Robert Montgomery starred as Wimsey in The Haunted Honeymoon (1940).

On stage, the character appeared in a play version of Busman's Honeymoon, which opened in London in 1936, and on which the novel was based.

Wimsey was featured in a series of BBC TV dramas beginning in 1973 and seen in the U.S. on PBS's Masterpiece Theatre and Mystery! Ian Carmichael starred.

THE LOSERS (C)

First Appearance: G.I. Combat #138, 1970, DC Comics.

Biography: The Losers are comprised of heroes who established sterling reputations in their own right as war heroes before forming a combat team.

Captain William Storm enters the navy as a lieutenant. When his boat, PT-47, is sunk by a Japanese submarine, only Storm survives—albeit, with the loss of his lower left leg. After recovering and being fitted with a wooden leg, he returns to duty. Though he distinguishes himself heroically, he never overcomes the psychological blow of having lost his crew and ship, and throws in his lot with other "failures"—the Losers. During a mission to Norway, he loses his right eye and also his memory; until the latter returns, he prowls the North Atlantic as a pirate, preying on Allies as well as "swastika bilge rats." While he is away the Losers replace him with a Norwegian resistance fighter, Ona.

No one but the Pentagon knows the real names of the World War II marine heroes Gunner and Sarge. Both men grew up in the streets of an unnamed U.S. city and spend the early part of the war in the Pacific, aided by the K-9 Corps dog Pooch. After a distinguished career, the two are transferred to the European theater to train recruits. When their first team is killed, the two join forces with Captain Storm and the other self-described failures.

Johnny Cloud—a.k.a. Flying Cloud—is the son of a Navajo chief, named after a cloud that looks like an Indian riding a horse. Cloud frequently sees this vision in the skies, even after he becomes an air force lieutenant during World War II. During one battle, Cloud and his P-47 take out a number of German aircraft, though he himself has to be saved by patrol leader Mack, who sacrifices his own life. Cloud succeeds him as the leader of the Happy Braves and eventually makes captain, enjoying many years of success against the enemy. But after a new pilot, Wyoming, is killed in Cloud's command, the distraught captain crashes. Though he survives, he blames himself for what happened and joins the Losers.

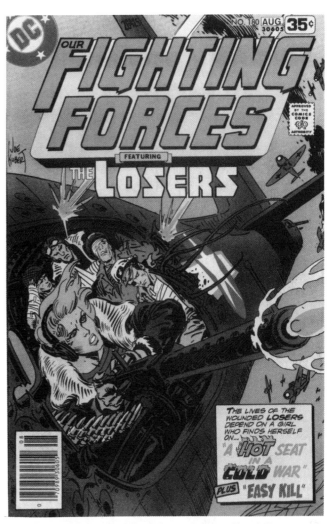

The Losers. From the left: Gunner, Johnny Cloud, Sarge, and Captain Storm look on as Ona fights for their lives. © DC Comics.

The Losers come together when Lieutenant JEB STUART happens to rescue them after their respective traumas. They successfully fight alongside Stuart on a mission, after which the High Command in London recommends that they stay together as "combat troubleshooters" known as the Losers. (Despite numerous triumphs, they *still* have a low estimation of themselves. When sent to a briefing at OSS headquarters, Sarge quips to Gunner, "Maybe the C.O. lost us shootin' crap.")

Comment: Gunner and Sarge first appeared in All-American Men of War #67, 1959, then moved to Our Fighting Forces #45 and remained until #94. Captain Storm first appeared in Capt. Storm #1, 1964, which ran for 18 issues. Johnny Cloud made his debut in All-American Men of War #82 in 1960 and remained until #115. The Losers moved from G.I. Combat to

Our Fighting Forces, where they appeared from #123 to the magazine's demise with #181 (1978).

LUCAS MCCAIN (TV, C)

First Appearance: *The Rifleman,* September 1958, ABC.

Biography: A rancher and a widower in North Fork, New Mexico, the strong, upright Lucas McCain is constantly faced with the problems of raising his 12-year-old son Mark, earning a living, and helping Marshal Micah Torrance when the going gets tough. And it often did, as the town was beset by rustlers, outlaws, gunslingers, drunks, and the like. After several years of macho, womanless doings, storekeeper Milly Scott comes to town, followed by wealthy, aggressive hotelier Lou Mallory.

The six-foot five-inch Lucas carries a customized .44 Winchester that cocks when he draws. The hero is able to get off a shot in three-tenths of a second.

Comment: The half-hour series aired through July 1963 and starred Chuck Connors as Lucas, Johnny Crawford as Mark, and Paul Fix as Torrance. Joan Taylor played Milly and Patricia Blair was Lou. Several episodes were directed by Sam Peckinpah, who went on to make a name for himself in the arena of gritty, bloody westerns.

Lucas McCain (right) and son Mark.

From 1958 to 1964, Dell (through #12) then Gold Key published a total of 20 issues of *The Rifleman* comic book.

LUCKY COYNE (C)

First Appearance: *Dynamic Comics* #1, 1941, Harry 'A' Chesler.

Biography: Lucky Coyne is a detective with a twist— he makes key decisions by flipping a coin. If the coin falls on heads, he goes ahead with something (takes a case, enters a dark room, etc.); tails, he does not. The private eye's "two-fisted pal" and assistant is Terry. Lucky usually dresses in a bright red business suit, is a crack shot, an impressive athlete, and possesses a "steel grip."

Comment: Lucky appeared throughout the 25-issue run of *Dynamic Comics.* Two adventures were reprinted in Israel Waldman's *Daring Adventures* in 1963–64.

LUCKY LUKE (CS, MP, TV)

First Appearance: 1946, *Almanach de Spirou* (Belgium).

Biography: With his white hat and jangling spurs, Lucky Luke roams the West in search of work (typically as a sheriff) and adventure. He finds a great deal of the latter, thanks to run-ins with horse thieves, card sharps, robbers, killers, and such towering figures as Billy the Kid, Jesse James, Black Bart, Judge Roy Bean, and the Daltons (cousins of the famous brothers)— Joe, William, Jack, and Averall, each one of whom is bigger and dumber than the other.

The cigarettes Luke constantly smokes are so strong their smoke kills circling flies; the liquor he drinks has

Lucky Luke sounds the charge astride Jolly Jumper. © Editions Dupuis.

Lucky Coyne and Terry. © Harry 'A' Chesler.

such high alcohol content that a match will cause it to explode. No wonder, as he puts it, "I'm a poor lonesome cowboy."

Luke's horse is the clever Jolly Jumper (he can beat his master at chess), and his dog is the craven dog Ran-tan-plan.

Comment: The character was created by Maurice de Bevere. His intial one-shot appearance proved so popular that so Lucky Luke became a regular in the weekly edition of *Spirou* in July 1947; the strip moved to *Pilote* in 1968.

Luke was initially a gentle send-up of western heroes. However, with the coming of writer Rene Goscinny in 1955, the strips became more serious without completely losing their parodic edge.

The hero has been seen in two feature-length animated cartoons: *Daisy Town* (1971) and *The Ballad of the Daltons* (1978).

Hanna-Barbera produced a two-hour made-for-TV animated feature in which the hero faced the Daltons; Luke's dog became Bushwack for the 1985 film. Bill Callaway provided the voice of Luke, Bob Ridgely was Jolly Jumper, and Peewee Herman was Bushwack.

LUCKY STARR (L)

First Appearance: *David Starr, Space Ranger* by Paul French, 1952, Doubleday and Co.

Biography: Lawrence Starr is a space ranger reporting to the ruling Council of Science. En route to Venus, where he and his wife, Barbara, are stationed, their ship is attacked and they are slaughtered by space pirates. The only survivor is their four-year-old son, David, whom they were able to set adrift in a space lifeboat. Lawrence's best friends, Chief of the Council Hector Conway and Section Director Augustus Henree, adopt the boy and raise him as their own. At the age of 29, David is ready to assume his role as a councilman and space ranger, defending the far-flung Terrestrial Empire (a.k.a. the Solar Confederation) aboard his vessel the *Shooting Starr*. In addition to the pirates, he battles Sirian invaders from 50 trillion miles away, "ghosts" on Mercury, and saboteurs seeking to poison Martian food sources, and defends his academy roommate, Lou Evans, against charges of treason.

Six feet tall, with brown eyes and a powerful, athletic build, David is a superintellect—the result, apparently, of having been exposed to solar radiation while he was onboard the lifeboat. He is nicknamed Lucky early in his career due to his uncanny ability to survive any calamity. His best friend is short, Mars-born fellow ranger John Bigman Jones.

Comment: Paul French was an early pseudonym for Isaac Asimov. The titles in the series are *Lucky Starr and the Pirates of the Asteroids* (1953), *Lucky Starr and the Oceans of Venus* (1954), *Lucky Starr and the Big Sun Mercury* (1956), *Lucky Starr and the Moons of Jupiter* (1957), and *Lucky Starr and the Rings of Saturn* (1958).

LUKE MALONE (C)

First Appearance: *Police Action* #1, 1975, Seaboard Periodicals.

Biography: Lieutenant Lucius Gabriel Malone, a.k.a. Manhunter, is a 15-year veteran of the San Francisco police force who gets kicked off when he mishandles a hostage crisis, one in which Mary, his wife of ten years, is killed. After drinking for a solid month and sleeping on the beach, Luke is found by his police friend Joe Wong, who talks sense to him—shortly before being shot dead. Wong's death brings Luke out of his depression: He gets his private investigator's license and sets out to find his friend's killer and start a new life. Unable to afford the rent in his new office, he relocates to Paddy's Pub, where Andy the bartender takes his calls.

Comment: The character was created by writer/artist Mike Ploog. There were only two issues of *Police Action,* and Malone appeared in both. The cofeature was "Lomax NYPD," which covered the adventures of Sam Lomax, a Korean War veteran and 15-year man with the New York Police Department. Third adventures for each character were created but never printed. In the third Luke Malone story, a beautiful young woman named Jill goes to work as his secretary.

M

MACK BOLAN (L, C)

First Appearance: *The Executioner* by Don Pendleton, 1969, Pinnacle Books.

Biography: During the war in Vietnam, Master Sergeant Mack Samuel Bolan is nicknamed the Executioner, a sniper with dozens of kills to his credit. But he's also known by the nickname Sergeant Mercy, because of the compassion he shows for wounded American soldiers and innocent Vietnamese civilians. While he's serving his second tour of duty, Bolan's mother, father, and sister are slain in the States. The hero returns home to bury them in Pittsfield, Massachusetts, and to inaugurate a new war—on the mob. As he begins to make headway against the Mafia, the government takes notice and offers him amnesty for his lawlessness if he'll take on a new target: the KGB. He agrees to help and becomes Colonel John Phoenix, at Stony Man Farm in Virginia with his crack Able Team and Phoenix Force. After his dearly beloved April Rose is killed by the Soviets, Bolan becomes a freelancer once more, though he and the government help each other out when the need arises. After the fall of the USSR, Bolan turns his formidable marksmanship on terrorists.

Bolan is tall, powerfully built, and dark-haired, with an intent "warrior's gaze."

Comment: Pinnacle published the first 38 Bolan adventures through 1979, after which Worldwide Library (under that imprint and Gold Eagle Books) published another 130 Executioner books (as of this writing) as well as a spinoff series featuring Able Team and Phoenix Force. Innovation briefly published *The Executioner* comic book in 1993.

Pendleton also created Ashton Ford, a psychic detective, for Warner Books, and Joe Copp, a two-fisted private eye, for Donald I. Fine Inc.

MAC TAVISH (C)

First Appearance: *Eerie* #95, 1978, Warren Publishing.

Biography: Maximillian Myron Mac Tavish is a brash red-haired youth who, at some unspecified future time, joins the Space Force. He becomes close friends with apelike Spider Andromeda of Alcimedon and they fight in sundry battles, from the Phobos Rebellion to struggles with the Ortouvian Gas Men and the Zorovian Zanies (who tried to dry them and slice them into beef jerky). The two spend six years fighting in the Aesthetics Wars, after which they part, Spider remaining a soldier and Mac becoming a famed "adventurer, startrotter, luminary-for-hire [and] hero supreme to trillions of people on thousands of worlds." For 15

Mac Tavish kicks some bolts while Spider Andromeda looks on. © Warren Publishing.

years the wise-cracking egomaniac (he charges for his autograph) flies about the universe in the *Sunfisher,* "the last and biggest of the neutronium-9 starships" and the only one equipped with "homicide drive." Also known as the Master of Zodiac V (where, apparently, he helped to foil a coup), Mac packs a talking lucite revolver that communicates with his belt computer and fires "everything from decibel salvos to nova blasts."

Mac's longtime girlfriend is Ida Lizer, actually a fantasy created by a virtual reality-like "service machine" on the planet Rara Avis. The machine was destroyed by a bomb in Mac's final adventure. Thanks to vials of the immortality serum polyprismite that he drinks in that last escapade, Mac will likely prowl the spaceways for a long time to come.

Comment: The character appeared in five issues of *Eerie* (ending in #111). The strip was created by writer Alabaster Redzone (Jim Stenstrum) and boasted his usual wit and clever plotting. The adventures were drawn by Pepe Moreno Casaures.

MADDIE HAYES and DAVID ADDISON (TV)

First Appearance: *Moonlighting,* March 1985, ABC.

Biography: When successful model Maddie Hayes discovers that her manager has stolen most of her fortune, Blue Moon Detective Agency of Los Angeles is one of her few remaining assets. She's prepared to sell the agency until detective Addison talks her out of it; she becomes a hands-on owner, working with her running, ducking, daring, less-bright employee and eventually falling in love with him. A pregnancy with Addison's child ends in a miscarriage; she also has relationships with successful young Sam Crawford and is briefly married to Walter Bishop.

The pair solve both usual and unusual cases. Two of the latter involve dream sequences. In one such dream the duo must find the solution to a 40-year-old murder case. In another Maddie and David appear as Kate and Petruchio in *Taming of the Shrew.*

David's brother is Richard, and his father is David Sr. Maddie's parents are Virginia and Alex. The agency's receptionist is Agnes Dipesto.

Comment: Bruce Willis starred as David, Cybill Shepherd was Maddie, and Allyce Beasley was Agnes. Mark Harmon guest-starred as Sam, Dennis Dugan was Walter, and Paul Sorvino was David Sr. The hour-long series aired through May 1989. The show was created by Glenn Gordon Caron.

MLLE. MARIE (C)

First Appearance: *Star Spangled War Stories* #84, 1959, DC Comics.

Biography: "Zey call me Mlle. Marie," our heroine says in a very early adventure, "ze battle doll! I fight for la belle France!" To the Nazis, she's the French Canary. To her American friends, she's a "beautiful babe . . . who carries a lipstick and a tommygun."

Raised on a farm in France, with her (unnamed) father and grandfather Andre, Marie and her father join the Resistance when Germany invades France during World War II. After her father dies, she is acknowledged to be the most dangerous resistance fighter of them all, especially by her archfoe Commander Von Ekt. Right before the liberation of France, Marie is shot by a Nazi spy, Roget, and falls into the St. Joan River. Reports are sketchy about her fate: Reportedly she is rescued and has a daughter, Julia, by a liaison with Alfred Pennyworth (none other than Batman's butler!).

Her characteristic wardrobe during the war is a yellow blouse, blue skirt, and red beret. In addition to fighting on land, Marie is a skilled "frog-girl."

Comment: The heroine appeared in solo adventures and in team-ups (as with the Haunted Tank) in *Star Spangled War Stories* and in other DC war titles through the 1970s.

MAD MAX (MP, L)

First Appearance: *Mad Max,* 1979, American International.

Biography: Five years from today, a war (implicitly nuclear) has reduced the world to a barbaric state dominated by warring gangs. In Australia, the Bronze (the police) are the only law. They include the taciturn, relentless Max and his partner, Jim Goose, who report to Fifi. When a chase leads to the death of cycle gang leader Nightrider, the remaining gang members target Max and Goose. Goose is captured alone and burned beyond recognition in his car; Max, deciding he's had enough, takes his wife, Jessie, and baby to her mother's seaside home. But the cyclists find them, killing the baby and fatally wounding Jessie. After donning his uniform, shouldering his sawed-off shotgun, and climbing back into his high-powered car, an Interceptor, Max (now "mad" with intent on revenge) finds and kills all of the gang members in turn. He then rides off alone.

In his second chronicled adventure, Max (now teamed with a dog) comes upon a small oil-producing settlement and agrees to drive a tanker through several hundred miles of biker territory in exchange for all of the gasoline he can carry. By the time of his third adventure, the world has virtually run out of gasoline and Max has been living a nomadic existence. After the camels that pull his vehicle are stolen, Max is left to die in the desert. When he reaches Aunty Entity's Bartertown—which is powered by methane gas produced by the defecation of pigs—he is sent into the Thunderdome arena to fight Aunty's champion, MasterBlaster, who is actually two creatures: Blaster, a giant in an iron mask, and Master, a dwarf who rides a harness on his shoulders. After defeating his foe (but refusing to kill him), Max is exiled and becomes the leader of orphaned children living in the desert.

Comment: Mel Gibson starred as Max in the cult favorite *Mad Max,* with Joanne Samuel as Jessie, Steve Bisley as Goose, and Roger Ward as Fiffi. Rocker Tina Turner was Aunty Entity. The Australian-made film, directed by George Miller (who cowrote it with James McCausland), was dubbed by American actors when released in the U.S. That remains a source of frustration to Mel Gibson fans, who don't quite get all of the star in his first major role.

Gibson also starred in, and Miller directed, the next two films, *Mad Max II* (known as *The Road Warrior* in the U.S.) in 1981 and *Mad Max Beyond Thunderdome* in 1985.

Joan D. Vinge novelized the third film, the only one to appear in book form.

MAGNUS, ROBOT FIGHTER (C)

First Appearance: *Magnus, Robot Fighter* #1, 1963, Western Publishing.

Biography: In the year A.D. 4000 , robots work alongside human beings. Sometimes these robots simply malfunction; other times they are sabotaged or even catch diseases from space robots. Whenever that happens and the pol-robs (police robots) can't handle it, the call goes out to Magnus, Robot Fighter. Not only is he an expert at hand-to-hand combat, but he's had a "robot speech receptor 1A" inserted in his skull so he can communicate with robots.

Unlike the rest of society, Magnus is antirobot, believing that humans have "grown *weak* by depending too much on robots."

Magnus is based in North Am, and flies around the world in his personal "sky cruiser." He wears a tight red T-shirt and matching shorts, with white boots and a black belt. He is equipped with a heat shield for surviving cold climates, and often carries a jet pack for flight and "anti-grav" units to move heavy objects. His girlfriend is Leeja Clane, the daughter of powerful Senator Clane.

Comment: Western published 46 issues of Magnus

Magnus, Robot Fighter, uses his patented "chop" on a renegade automaton. © Gold Key Comics.

under the Gold Key imprint, featuring exquisite art by Russ Manning. Valiant Comics revived the title in 1990, and it continues to this day.

The Gold Key titles featured a backup strip, *The Aliens,* which ran in the first 28 issues and had a one-issue title of its own. It chronicles the adventures of Captain Johner and his space crew, and his contact with a ship of alien beings. The two races institute an "exchange" program, with Commander Zarz and a pair of aliens joining Johner and his crew and two earthmen for sundry adventures.

MAJOR SETH ADAMS (TV, C)

First Appearance: *Wagon Train,* September 1957, NBC.

Biography: After the Civil War, a wagon train sets out from St. Joseph, Missouri, to California, led by the strong, no-nonsense Major Seth Adams. Adams leads the train through Indian territory, hazardous mountains, deserts, and other terrain, aided by scout Flint McCullough. The wagonmaster also lends a hand when members of the train have personal problems.

Other members of the train include Chris Hale, cook Charlie Wooster, assistant wagonmaster Bill Hawks, and scouts Duke Shannon and Cooper Smith.

Comment: The hour-long series moved to ABC in September, 1962, where it remained until September 1965; episodes were 90 minutes from 1963 to 1964. Ward Bond starred as Adams; when he died in 1960, John McIntire came aboard as Hale. Robert Horton played Flint, Frank McGrath was Charlie, and Terry Wilson was Hawks. When Horton left, Scott (Denny) Miller joined the cast as Shannon, and Robert Fuller signed up as Smith. The emphasis of the show, however, was on the guest stars, with the regulars playing mostly supporting roles to an eclectic mix of settlers, gamblers, preachers, bankers, prospectors, Europeans, deserters, and you-name-it. (One episode starred Bette Davis and served as a pilot for her unsold series *Madame's Place*.)

Reruns were aired under the title *Major Adams—Trailmaster*. The series was inspired by the 1950 film *Wagon Master*, which starred Ben Johnson, James Arness, and (of course) Ward Bond; the budget for the series was a then-record $100,000 an episode.

Dell published 13 *Wagon Train* comic books from 1958 to 1962, and Gold Key published four in 1964.

MAJOR SKY MASTERS   (CS)

First Appearance: *Sky Masters of the Space Force*, September 22, 1958, George Matthew Adams Service, Inc.

Biography: At some point in the near future, Sky Masters is the "most valuable" pilot in the U.S. space program. Based at Cape Hope, Hawaii, he solves mysteries on the Space Wheel in Earth orbit 4,000 miles up, investigates alien vessels, and helps other spacemen cope with professional and personal problems. Sky's girlfriend is Holly Martin, daughter of pioneer spaceman Colonel Martin; her brother, Danny, is a junior spaceman. General Hascomb is the commander of Cape Hope, and Dr. Royer is the chief space scientist.

Comment: The strip, which lasted just 18 months, was cocreated by comic book legends Jack Kirby and Wally Wood.

MARINE BOY   (TV)

First Appearance: *Kaitai Shonen Marine*, 1965 (Japan).

Biography: The son of oceanographer Dr. Mariner, who is the leader of an international peacekeeping force known as the Ocean Patrol, Marine Boy helps keep the seas clean and free of such criminals as Dr. Slime, Count Shark, and Captain Kidd. Dressed in a bulletproof wet suit and propeller boots, and armed with other gadgets, Marine Boy travels about in his P-1 submarine, working closely with his pet dolphin Splasher and crewmates Bulton and Piper. Whenever necessary, he can remain underwater indefinitely thanks to Oxygum—breathable air in gum form.

Comment: The series was syndicated in the U.S. beginning in 1966, with Corinne Orr as the voice of Marine Boy. There were 78 episodes in all.

MARIO   (VG, TV, C, MP, L)

First Appearance: *Donkey Kong*, 1981, Nintendo.

Biography: Little is known about the feisty, heroic man with the thick mustache, other than that he's an Italian carpenter (later, plumber) from Brooklyn, has a twin brother Luigi, and isn't afraid to face foes on this world or in other realms. Mario is heavyset because of his fondness for pasta, a passion his thinner brother does not share. Both brothers dress in blue overalls; Mario wears a red shirt and cap, Luigi green.

In *Donkey Kong*, Mario must rescue poor Pauline, who has been kidnaped by a big ape. He follows them up a building at a construction site, leaping crates, barrels, and other objects the gorilla throws at him. In *Donkey Kong, Jr.* (1982), Mario turns tables on the ape; it is up to the titular ape to rescue his pop from a cage in which Mario has placed him. In the third game, *Mario Bros.* (1983), Mario and Luigi (making his video game debut) are now plumbers and have to clean crabs, turtles, and other vermin from a sewer.

However, it was the fourth game that set the tone for most of what followed. In *Super Mario Bros.* (1985; the first created for home video gaming without an arcade counterpart), he is dropped in the middle of a complex fantasyland, the Mushroom Kingdom, where he must find and defeat the evil Bowser. This was followed by *Super Mario Bros. 2* (1988), in which he, Luigi, and Princess Toadstool make their way through the land of Sub-Con to defeat the wicked Wart. In *Super Mario Land* (1989, for Game Boy), he must pass through the Kingdom of Sarasaland—on foot, flying in his plane, or swimming in his submarine—to rescue Princess Daisy from Dragonzamasu. Next followed *Super Mario Bros. 3* (1990), in which Mario can become a raccoon Mario (swatting enemies with his tail), fly, or swim as he tackles Bowser and a variety of Koopas. This was followed by *Dr. Mario* (1990), in which he pitches medicine onto viruses, and *Super Mario World* (1991, for the Super NES), in which he rides a dinosaur named Yoshi as he seeks to destroy Bowser and his Koopa army yet again. Most recently he appeared in the racing game *Super Mario Kart*.

Power-ups that give Mario additional strength in his fantasyland games include: Starman, which, when caught, makes Mario invincible for a brief time; Fire Flower, which allows him to shoot fireballs; and Super Mushroom, which makes him giant. Lesser foes that dog his trail include the Piranha Flower, Lakitu, Hammer Brothers, Bullet Bill, Spiny, Pokey, Goomba, Shy Guy, Cobrat, Bob-Omb, Birdo, Rip Van Fish, Sledge Brother, Mouser, and Tryclyde.

Mario has also made cameo appearances in other games: *Punch-Out* (1984), *Wrecking Crew, Pinball, Tennis,* and *Golf* (all 1985), *Alleyway, Tennis,* and *Tetris* (all 1989 for Game Boy), *Golf* (1990, Game Boy), *NES Open Tournament Golf* (1991), and *F-1 Race* and *Qix* (1991, Game Boy).

Incidentally, it was Stanley the Bugman and not Mario who was the ape's nemesis in *Donkey Kong III*. By the time the game was released, Mario was too popular to costar with another big name!

Comment: Named after an employee at Nintendo's U.S. headquarters, Mario is the most successful video game character in history and is now the company's official mascot. He began his life in arcade games that later moved to home video gaming via such companies as Coleco and Nintendo; since *Super Mario Bros.,* the programs have been made for home video gaming.

In addition to the games, Mario has appeared in the syndicated *Super Mario Brothers Super Show,* which premiered in September 1989, with Lou Albano as the voice of Mario and Danny Wells as Luigi. DIC Enterprises produced 54 half-hour episodes. Prior to this, he costarred from 1983 to 1985 in CBS's *Saturday Supercade,* of which Donkey Kong was a part; in this show, Mario was a circus animal trainer who drove Donkey Kong around in a van. Ruby-Spears produced the series.

Valiant published a dozen issues of the *Super Mario Bros.* comic book from 1990 to 1992. The character also appeared in Valiant's *Nintendo Comics System* titles. Pocket Books also published a series of "choose-your-own-adventure" books for children in 1990.

Bob Hoskins played the hero (who now has a complete name—Mario Mario) in the 1993 motion picture *Super Mario Bros.* John Leguizamo costarred as Luigi Mario. Todd Strasser adapted the film as a novel.

There are numerous Mario-like heroes in the video game field, including Sammy Lightfoot, Bashful Buford, Sewer Sam, and many others.

MARK HAZZARD (C)

First Appearance: *Mark Hazzard: Merc* #1, 1986, Marvel Comics.

Biography: Mark Hazzard is a six-foot-four soldier who disappointed his parents, Margaret and Leonard (a general), when he dropped out of West Point to sign up for a tour of duty in Vietnam. One tour becomes three, as he distinguishes himself in a special operations group, always working "in the middle of the nastiest jobs." Today he lives in an apartment in the Gramercy Park section of New York City. A soldier-of-fortune who will go anywhere and fight for anyone if the cause (and price) is right, Mark is a student of war and strategy, has an awesome collection of firearms, and is so physically fit that he can catch a knife thrown in his direction. His partner is a New Zealander named Mal.

Mark is divorced from wife, Joan, who has since remarried, and he rarely sees son, Scott.

The fiery debut of *Mark Hazzard.* © Marvel Comics.

Comment: The character ran for 12 issues plus an annual; he was part of Marvel's ambitious "New Universe" line of more realistic, adult comic books that failed to find an audience and lasted only a year. Other titles in the series were the superhero comics *D.P. 7, Justice, Nightmask, Psi-Force, Kickers, Inc., Star Brand,* and *Spitfire and the Troubleshooters.*

MARK MERLIN (C)

First Appearance: *House of Secrets* #23, 1959, DC Comics.

Biography: A "far-famed supernatural sleuth," Mark Merlin and his assistant, Elsa, are based high atop Mystery Hill, in a mansion that boasts a sophisticated laboratory and a complete supernatural library. When strange events occur anywhere in the world, they board his private plane to get to the bottom of things.

Mark wears ordinary clothing, the pockets of which are usually stuffed with weapons he's picked up from various cultures, such as the antifire spheres of the

Mark Merlin and Elsa accidentally tying up a benevolent alien. © DC Comics.

Toltec Indians, the cat charm of the pharaohs that transfers his mind into his pet cat, Memakata, when his body is in danger, the magic eye that creates mass illusions, the antipotion that opens a doorway between our world and the supernatural dimension, and more.

Mark's recurring foe is Doctor-7, a mad scientist who uses technology to tap the evil powers of the supernatural.

Comment: The character appeared in *House of Secrets* until #73.

MARK SABER (TV)

First Appearance: *Mark Saber Mystery Theater,* October 1951, ABC.

Biography: Initially, the refined, intellectual Inspector Mark Saber is a British lawman who works for New York City's Homicide Squad, aided by the good-natured Sergeant Tim Maloney. The character disappears for several years. When next seen, he has finished a stint as chief inspector of Scotland Yard and is working as a private investigator based in London—having lost an arm somewhere along the way. Traveling throughout Europe, he battles smugglers, killers, blackmailers, kidnapers, and other criminals. His reluctant ally at Scotland Yard is Inspector Parker.

Comment: Tom Conway (the brother of George Sanders) starred as Saber from 1951 to 1954 with James Burke as Maloney; the half-hour show was retitled *Inspector Mark Saber—Homicide Squad* in 1952. Donald Gray took the part when the series returned to the air in 1955 as *The Vise;* it was changed to *Saber of London* in 1957 and lasted until 1960. Colin Tapley played Parker. The show was titled *Detective's Diary* in syndication. *Detective's Diary* also included reruns of *Man from Interpol,* which had aired from January to October 1960 on ABC. That series featured the exploits of international police officer Anthony Smith (Richard Wyler).

MARK TRAIL (CS, C)

First Appearance: *Mark Trail,* 1946, *The New York Post.*

Biography: Mark Trail is a rugged, pipe-smoking conservationist and expert on wildlife who uses mostly pacifistic means to protect our natural resources from fire, illegal hunters, overpopulation, natural disasters, and more. He also goes on safaris to protect species abroad. He is assisted by young college graduate Scotty and by his devoted St. Bernard, Andy. Mark spends what little spare time he has with his girlfriend, Cherry.

Comment: Ed Dodd's strip was syndicated to other papers over the next few months and, under the auspices of the newly created Post-Hall Syndicate, became extremely successful.

Standard, Pines, and Fawcett each published a *Mark Trail* comic book in 1955, 1958, and 1959 respectively.

M.A.R.S. PATROL   (C)

First Appearance: *Total War* #1, 1965, Gold Key Comics.

Biography: On July 4, at two in the morning, the northeastern coast of the United States is invaded by a nameless enemy—soldiers who look more or less the same and may or may not be of this planet. Moscow, Calcutta, Hong Kong, and other places around the world are also invaded. On a three-day pass in Atlantic City when the assault begins are the four members of the Marine Attack Rescue Service, a "new hush-hush

M.A.R.S. Patrol member Joe Striker torches the aliens as Lieutenant Adams (in beret) and Ken Hiro lend support. © Gold Key Comics.

Marine combat team": Lieutenant Cy Adams, the blond leader and a pilot; Sergeant Ken Hiro, a Japanese frogman; Sergeant Joe Striker, a master of communications and reconnaissance; and Corporal Russ Stacey, a bull of a demolitions and weapons expert. The team is quickly summoned back to their base—defeating the enemy along the way—and goes to war defending their country as new fronts open up in San Francisco and elsewhere. The men answer to General Kripps at the Pentagon.

In time, the marines discover that the invaders are *not* human, but are bald "alien beings from the infinite void of space." Moreover, after using conventional weapons for several encounters, the aliens suddenly demonstrate "the fantastic ability to materialize out of nowhere" and attack "with weapons beyond our imagination" (the result of a change in the creative force behind the magazine—see COMMENT). The humans seemed to be gaining, finally, when the title ended.

Comment: *Total War* became *M.A.R.S. Patrol* with the third issue; it lasted ten issues in all. Comics great Wally Wood created the series and drew the first three issues. When Mike Royer subsequently took over, the science fiction elements of the strip were emphasized, and the series became less chilling to kids reading the book in a Cold War world.

MARTIN KANE   (R, TV, C)

First Appearance: *Martin Kane, Private Eye,* 1949, Mutual.

Biography: When Martin Kane first appears on the sleuthing scene, he's a smart-aleck New York detective who works closely with the police, in the person of Lieutenant Bender. After a year (on radio and TV), he becomes a tougher, more calculating, more independent operator, crossing swords with a succession of officers: Captain Willis, Sergeant Ross, Captain Leonard, Captain Burke, and Lieutenant Grey.

Kane spends most of his time in the tobacco shop owned by Happy McMann. There is never any romance for the cigarette- and pipe-smoking Kane.

Some time later, Martin leaves New York and becomes a private eye based in London, with occasional forays to Paris.

Comment: On radio, William Gargan (a real-life private eye turned actor) played Kane and Walter Kinsella was Happy. The series debuted on TV later that year, in September 1949, and aired for a half-hour until June 1954. A succession of actors played the part, beginning with Gargan, then Lloyd Nolan (1951–52), Lee Tracy (1952–53), and Mark Stevens (1953–54). Kinsella was Happy throughout the entire run of the show, which aired live from New York.

The series was revived for syndication in 1958 as the European-based *The New Adventures of Martin Kane*, which was shot on film and brought Gargan back to the role.

Fox Features Syndicate published two issues of a *Martin Kane* comic book in 1950.

MATT DILLON   (R, TV, C, MP)

First Appearance: *Gunsmoke*, April 1952, CBS.

Biography: Matt Dillon, U.S. Marshal and Union Army veteran, is based in Dodge City, Kansas, in the 1870s, though his work also takes him to "far-flung cattle ranches and mines." A towering figure, he is incorruptible and quick with a gun. His deputy is Chester B. Goode; his friends are Dr. Galen "Doc" Adams and Kitty Russell, an "employee" (prostitute) at the Long Branch Saloon, with a heart as big as all of Kansas. Kitty and Matt may be romantically involved, though Matt is known to have fathered at least one child with another woman.

Comment: The character was first played, on the radio, by William Conrad; Parley Baer was Chester, Georgia Ellis was Kitty, and Howard McNear was Doc. It came to TV in September 1955, with James Arness as Dillon (John Wayne had turned the part down, but suggested the six-foot-seven Dillon, veteran of motion pictures such as *The Thing from Another World* and *Them!*), Dennis Weaver as Chester (until 1964), Amanda Blake as Kitty—she was no longer a prostitute but the saloon's owner—and Milburn Stone as Doc. When Weaver left, he was replaced by Deputy Festus Haggen, (Ken Curtis, another friend of Wayne's). Also introduced on TV were blacksmith Quint Asper (Burt Reynolds), gunsmith Newly O'Brien (Buck Taylor), and Sam the bartender (played by former Frankenstein monster Glenn Strange). When Blake left, she was replaced for one season by Miss Hannah (Fran Ryan). Director Sam Peckinpah was a veteran of the series.

Gunsmoke, one of the first adult westerns on TV, lasted an astonishing 20 years, going off the air in September, 1975. It was a half-hour program until September 1967 when the show was stretched to an hour until its demise. While the series was on the air, the half-hour shows were syndicated as *Marshal Dillon*.

Dell published 27 issues of a *Gunsmoke* comic book from 1956 to 1961; Gold Key published six more from 1969 to 1970.

There have been five TV movies starring Arness: *Gunsmoke: Return to Dodge* (1987), with the last appearance of Miss Kitty as she and Dillon rekindle their old relationship; *Gunsmoke: The Last Apache* (1990), costarring Michael Learned as the mother of a 21-year-old who is revealed to be Dillon's daughter (and who has to be rescued from Apaches); *Gunsmoke: To the Last Man* (1992), in which Dillon gets caught between two warring ranchers in the Pleasant Valley War; *Gunsmoke: The Long Ride* (1993), with Dillon searching for a lookalike who has robbed and killed; and *Gunsmoke: One Man's Justice* (1994), in which he teams with a boy whose mother is killed by outlaws—and reveals, for the first time, that it was the murder of his own father that prompted him to embark on a career as a lawman. By now, though Dillon himself admits he is "sick . . . of all the killing."

As for any relationship between Matt and Miss Kitty, actress Blake once said that the most physical contact they ever had "is when I fainted and Matt picked me up."

MATT GROVER   (C)

First Appearance: *The Crime Machine* #1, 1971, Skywald Publishing.

Biography: With his shoulder holster and big 1970s head of hair and sideburns, this NYPD detective is the spitting image of HARRY CALLAHAN. A crime historian as well as a crime fighter, Matt Grover considers criminals to be "human lice" and tells their sordid sagas so that law-abiding citizens can learn "the inner workings of . . . the crime machine." He's devoted to his mother, Rose, who lives alone in Queens; his father, Joe—a cop—died in the line of duty. Matt's girlfriend is his secretary, Janet Reynolds.

Comment: Matt narrated all of the stories that appeared in the two issues of the comic book *The Crime Machine*. Incredibly, he was called *Nat* Grover in the second issue. Matt was created by editor Sol Brodsky and was slated to star in his own color comic book if sales had warranted. They did not.

MATT HELM   (L, MP, TV)

First Appearance: *Death of a Citizen* by Donald Hamilton, 1960.

Biography: Raised on a Texas range and taught to use a .22 when he was still a child, Matthew Helm becomes a crack shot. During World War II, Helm (code-named "Eric") becomes a top U.S. spy and killer. Afterwards he marries, raises a family, and works as a freelance photographer—covering wildlife—and as a novelist, writing mostly westerns. But part of Helm is restless for the old life, and when his former boss "Mac" in Washington comes calling for his help in sniffing out and eliminating spies and collaborators, he's ready. His wife leaves him as Helm gets back into the spy game. (She remarries but they remain on good terms.)

Using photojournalism as his cover, Helm travels around the U.S. in a beat-up old pickup truck; he also travels to Europe and the South Pacific on assignment. In addition to ferreting out spies, Helm has helped to overthrow Communist dictators, searched for missing nuclear weapons, captured missing Nazis, carried top-secret plans, and even protected a leading scientist by marrying her.

Helm has an apartment in Washington and a small home in Santa Fe. However, whenever he's wounded or exhausted, he vacations in a government facility called the Ranch in Arizona. Since his divorce, he's had serious but short-lived relationships with Madeleine and Jo. He has a dog named Happy.

Comment: Other Helm novels are *The Wrecking Crew* (1960), *The Removers* (1961), *The Silencers* (1962), *Murderers' Row* (1962), *The Ambushers* (1963), *The Shadowers* (1964), *The Ravagers* (1964), *The Devastators* (1965), *The Betrayers* (1966), *The Menacers* (1968), *The Interlopers* (1969), *The Poisoners* (1971), *The Intriguers* (1973), *The Intimidators* (1974), *The Terminators* (1975), *The Retaliators* (1977), *The Terrorizers* (1978), *The Revengers* (1979), *The Annihilators* (1980), *The Infiltrators* (1981), *The Detonators* (1983), *The Vanishers* (1985), *The Demolishers* (1987), *The Frighteners* (1989), and *The Threateners* (1992).

Dean Martin played Helm in four motion pictures, *The Silencers* (1966), *Murderers' Row* (1966), *The Ambushers* (1967), and *The Wrecking Crew* (1968). In these, Helm is a photographer who shoots beautiful women and works for ICE: the Organization for Intelligence and Counter-Espionage. His assistant is Lovey Kravezit, played by Beverly Adams. Unfortunately, the filmmakers turned the serious hero into a smarmy, suave ladies' man.

In May 1975 Anthony Franciosa starred in the TV movie *Matt Helm*, in which Helm is now an agent who has become a Los Angeles-based private eye. In the film, he becomes involved with munitions smuggling while protecting an actress. The movie spawned an hour-long series starring Franciosa, which aired on ABC from September 1975 to January 1976. Laraine Stephens costarred as his attorney girlfriend Claire Kronski; Sergeant Hanrahan, his police contact, was played by Gene Evans.

MATT HOLBROOK (TV)

First Appearance: *The Detectives,* October 1959, ABC.

Biography: Stationed in an unnamed big city, Captain Matt Holbrook is a single-minded man who lives to capture killers, drug dealers, con artists, and other criminals. A widower, he has no social life to speak of (there's an abortive romance with police reporter Lisa Bonay), no sense of humor, and he demands a great deal from his trio of plainclothes detectives—tough Lieutenant John Russo, dashing Lieutenant James Conway, and veteran Lieutenant Otto Lindstrom. (Sergeant Chris Ballard replaces Conway after a year, and Sergeant Steve Nelson replaces Lindstrom for the final year.)

Comment: Robert Taylor played the character in the series, which aired for a half-hour until September 1961, then moved to NBC, where it ran for an hour until September 1962. Tige Andrews played Russo, Lee Farr was Conway, Russell Thorson was Lindstrom, Mark Goddard *(Lost in Space)* was Ballard, and future Batman Adam West came aboard in 1961 as Nelson. Taylor's real-life wife, Ursula Thiess, played Lisa. The series was renamed *Robert Taylor's Detectives* for the final season. Taylor is on record as having done the show solely for the money, and his monotonous performances show it.

MATT HOUSTON (TV)

First Appearance: *Matt Houston,* September 1982, ABC.

Biography: The son of a wealthy Texas oil man, Matlock Houston leaves the family ranch in the Lone Star State to oversee the family's offshore drilling operations in California. Since things are well under control there, Matt has time to enjoy his favorite pastime: detective work. Before long he ignores the oil business altogether in order to sleuth full time. Flying his helicopter or motoring around in his Excalibur or Mercedes 380SL convertible, he regularly solves cases with the help of his attorney, C.J. Parsons and her sophisticated computer "Baby." After two years Matt's famed detective uncle, Roy, comes out of retirement to lend a hand.

Typically, their clients are the rich and famous, such as the famous chef who is murdered in an orange Jell-O mold, though Matt and P.J. are also happy to try to clear an ex-cop framed for murder or stop a murdering robot. At first, Lieutenant Vince Novelli is an understanding ally; later, his replacement, Lieutenant Michael Hoyt, is considerably less friendly.

Matt's favorite food is Texas chili.

Comment: The hour-long show aired through July 1985. Lee Horsley starred as Houston, Pamela Hensley was Parsons, and Buddy Ebsen was Roy.

IF THAT *WALKING BOX* FOREMAN HAD GUNNED ME DOWN—WITH JIM AND CLAY AND LUTE IN JAIL—WITH RED AND ABE LAID UP, THERE'D BE ONLY MANUEL AND COOKIE TO STOP ANYONE FROM STEALING THE *DOGIRON* STEERS!

From the John Wayne swipe file—*Matt Savage.* © DC Comics.

MATT SAVAGE, TRAIL BOSS (C)

First Appearance: *Western Comics* #77, 1959, DC Comics.

Biography: A Union Army veteran (and John Wayne look-alike), Matt works as a miner after the Civil War, then drives cattle between Texas and Abilene, Kansas. Enjoying the work, he forms a drive of his own "in the Big Bend country of Texas," the 2,000-head herd handled by the Dogiron Crew: fellow veteran Clay Dixon, Confederate veteran Jim Grant, cook "Biscuits" Baker, and four others. Each drive presents its own dangers, "flood and drought—Indian attacks and thundering stampedes—and any number of untamed desperadoes." Fortunately, the Trail Boss is able to use his skills as a tracker, marksman, and two-fisted fighter to meet them.

Matt always dresses entirely in blue: jacket, trousers, bandana, and hat.

Comment: The strip and the title both ended with #85.

MAXWELL SMART (TV, C, L, MP)

First Appearance: *Get Smart,* September 1965, NBC.

Biography: Raised in a city (implicitly, Washington, D.C.), Maxwell Smart grows up idolizing a real-life spy, Agent 4, who works for the top-secret government agency, CONTROL. After serving in Korea, Corporal Smart attends college and, upon graduating, goes right to work for CONTROL (for $35,000 a year), as Agent 86. At CONTROL, he reports directly to the Chief (first name, Thaddeus); Max's partner (and eventually his wife) is the fetching Agent 99.

Max is equipped with a black shoe phone, the later model of which has steel tips for kicking and a heel-compartment containing concussion, smoke, and poison pellets. If it's out of order, Max can always fall back on his balloon phone or comb phone. If he's driving, he uses his steering wheel phone—carefully, though, since the wheel is a giant rotary dial. Other equipment includes: the inflato-girl for make-out use during stake-outs; the magic ear for hearing faraway conversations; the pen gun; the lighter gun; the Professor Peter Peckinpah mini-mauser; and absorbo pills to nullify the effects of alcohol. In Max's apartment, if he dials 117 on his phone, it will fire a bullet. At CONTROL headquarters, agents wishing to converse in utmost security use the cone of silence, which makes it impossible for even the speakers to hear one another. In the first year, Max's car is a red Sunbeam Tiger; after that, he drives a blue Karmen Ghia.

The other agents with whom Max works over the years are Larabee, the only person dumber than Max; the robot Hymie, who takes everything literally; Admiral Harold Harmon Hargrade, the former chief; and Agents 4, 8, 8½, 12, 13, 17, 18, 21, 23, 24, 25, 26, 27, 34, 38, 39, 41, 42, 43, 44, 46, 47, 48, 49, 51, 52, 53, 54, 73, 74, 77, 85, 91, 95, 198, 199, K-13 (the devoted dog Fang), and B17—a parrot. Agent 13 may have the toughest job of all, since Max typically finds him hiding in uncomfortable places that include a medicine cabinet, a cello case (in which he's squeezed upside-down), a penny-scale, a washing machine, a cigarette machine, a locker, and more. His replacement, Agent 44, has hidden in places ranging from a wood-burning stove (lit, of course) to a baby buggy. Max has also worked with the Israeli equivalent of CONTROL—YENTA, Your Espionage Network and Training Academy. (Neither CONTROL nor KAOS, described below, is an acronym.)

Though the 5-foot-9-inch Max is a fumbler, he doesn't realize it and invariably triumphs. Indeed, he wins the coveted Spy of the Year award in both 1965 and 1966, and KAOS—the evil, multinational spy group that is incorporated in Delaware for tax purposes—has a $500,000 price on his head. Smart's chief nemesis there is Conrad Siegfried, the vice president in charge of Public Relations and Terror. Smart's other foes include Mr. Big (a 3-foot-6-inch dwarf) and the Claw (or Craw, as the Oriental fiend pronounces it).

Max's four famous catch phrases are "Missed it by *that much,*" "Sorry about that, Chief," "And loving it," and "Would you believe . . .?"

Comment: The half-hour series was cocreated by Mel Brooks (who came up with the shoe phone) and Buck Henry (who created the cone of silence) and aired through September 1970. The show starred Don Adams as Smart, Barbara Feldon as 99, Edward Platt as the Chief, Robert Karvelas as Larabee, and Dick Gautier as Hymie.

Dell published eight issues of a *Get Smart* comic book from 1966 to 1967, and Tempo Books published a series of novels by William Johnston, beginning with *Get Smart!* and including *Get Smart Once Again, Missed It by That Much,* and others.

In addition to the TV series, Max appears in the film *The Nude Bomb* (1980) as a spy for PITS (the Provisional Intelligence Tactical Service). The tale of Nino Sebastiani's plans to destroy the world's clothing in order to force people into wearing his fashions was retitled *The Return of Maxwell Smart* when it was shown on TV. In the made-for-TV movie *Get Smart Again!* (1989) Max returns to CONTROL to battle KAOS once again. Adams returned for the film, along with Barbara Feldon, Dick Gautier, and Robert Karvelas. In the fall of 1994, the Fox network plans to air six episodes of a new *Get Smart,* with Don Adams and Barbara Feldon reprising their original roles. The original Chief was also back: Though actor Edward Platt has died, the Chief's still-active brain has been preserved in a tank.

MICHAEL KNIGHT (TV)

First Appearance: *Knight Rider,* September 1982, NBC.
Biography: When undercover police officer Michael Young is shot in the face, he is found and saved by dying millionaire William Knight. Knight pays for his plastic surgery, provides him with a new identity (Michael Knight), leaves him his fortune, and gives him a job: to fight crime with the help of an amazing car, the Knight Industries Two Thousand called KITT. The car (a Pontiac Trans-Am) is armed with smoke screens, flamethrowers, various sensors, and a voice; can reach speeds of 300 miles per hour and clear 50 feet with a running start; is heavily armored; automatically avoids collisions; and can be summoned via remote control.

Knight expires and Michael reports to his trusted lieutenant, Devon Miles, at Knight's estate, which is now called the Foundation for Law and Government. Among their foes over the years are gunrunners, street gangs, and even a criminal mastermind who is planning to steal a radioactive isotope. KITT's mechanics (depending on the season) are Bonnie Barstow, April Curtis, or Reginald Cornelius III ("RC3").

Comment: The series aired through August 1986 and starred David Hasselhoff as Knight, Edward Mulhare as Miles, William Daniels as the voice of KITT, Patricia McPherson as Bonnie, Rebecca Holden as April, and Peter Parros as RC3.

MICHAEL SHAYNE (L, MP, R, TV)

First Appearance: *Dividend on Death* by Brett Halliday, 1939, Henry Holt.
Biography: Six-foot-one-inch, handsome, red-headed Mike Shayne is a rugged, two-fisted, cognac- or brandy-drinking sleuth who works for the World-wide Agency in Manhattan in 1935. He moves to Miami sometime around 1939; when his wife, Phyllis, dies in 1943, he briefly relocates to New Orleans. Among his diverse cases are flushing out corrupt politicians in Washington, settling a violent coal miners' strike in Kentucky, pursuing drug dealers in Texas and Mexico, fleeing a crossbow-toting killer in the jungle (while trying to save Lucy, his secretary, from a gorilla!), serving as a temporary police chief, and rounding up the usual murderers, smugglers, kidnapers, and robbers.

He is assisted by his devoted and lovely secretary, Lucy Hamilton, and is a friend and frequent ally with Police Chief Will Gentry and *Miami Daily News* reporter Timothy Rourke.

Shayne has a small interest in the Miami Dolphins football franchise, his fee for solving a case for the team.

Comment: There are 67 Shayne novels in all as well as many more short stories, which appeared in the long-lived *Mike Shayne Mystery Magazine.* Brett Halliday is a pseudonym for David Dresser.

In motion pictures, Lloyd Nolan played the part in *Michael Shayne, Private Detective; Sleepers West; Dressed to Kill;* and *Blue, White and Perfect* (all 1941), and in *The Man Who Wouldn't Die, Just Off Broadway,* and *Time to Kill* (all 1942). Hugh Beaumont played the part in *Murder Is My Business, Larceny in Her Heart,* and *Blonde for a Day* (all 1946) and in *Three on a Ticket* and *Too Many Winners* (both 1947).

On radio, Jeff Chandler played the character in *Michael Shayne, Private Detective,* which aired briefly in 1944.

On TV, Richard Denning played the part in the hour-long NBC series that aired from September 1960 to September 1961. Jerry Paris was Rourke, Herbert Rudley was Will, Patricia Donahue, then Margie Regan played Lucy, and Gary Clarke costarred as Lucy's younger brother Will.

MIKE DONOVAN   (TV, C, L)

First Appearance: *V,* May 1983, NBC.

Biography: V stands for both Visitors and Victory. The Visitors are Sirians, thousands of lizardlike alien beings who disguise themselves with human skins and come to Earth, ostensibly as friends, but actually to conquer our world and eat its human inhabitants. Their plan is uncovered by TV newsman Mike Donovan, Dr. Julie Parrish, Ham Tyler, and Elias Taylor, who form a small group of resistance fighters to battle the aliens and their leader, Diana. Ultimately, the aliens are repulsed thanks to a lethal bacteria, but the setback is only temporary. Profit-motivated humans, especially industrialist Nathan Bates, help Diana reestablish a beachhead and continue the assault.

The resistance fighters are based in the Club Creole, and soon pick up other aides, including Willie, a renegade alien; Kyle, Nathan's patriotic son; and Robin, an Earth woman who had an affair with an alien and has given birth to a hybrid daughter, Elizabeth. In the end, the aliens and the Earth people make peace.

Comment: Marc Singer starred as Mike, Faye Grant was Parrish, Michael Ironside was Ham, Michael Wright was Elias, and Jane Badler was Diana in this show, which borrowed liberally from both Damon Knight's short story "To Serve Man" (1950) and H.G. Wells's novel *War of the Worlds* (1898).

See also DAVID VINCENT.

The first and second adventures were miniseries (four hours and six hours, respectively, the second broadcast in May 1984). A weekly, hour-long series aired on NBC from October 1984 to the following July.

DC published 18 issues of a *V* comic book from 1985 to 1986, while Pinnacle published a series of novels, including *V* by A.C. Crispin, *V: East Coast Crisis* by Howard Weinstein and A.C. Crispin, *V: The Pursuit of Diana* by Allen Wold, *V: The Chicago Conversion* by Geo. W. Proctor, *V: The Florida Project* by Tim Sullivan, and *V: Prisoners and Pawns* by Howard Weinstein.

MIKE HAMMER   (L, R, MP, TV)

First Appearance: *I, the Jury* by Mickey Spillane, 1947, E.P. Dutton.

Biography: A World War II veteran, Pacific Theater, Mike Hammer of Hammer Investigating Agency is the toughest dick ever to hit the streets of New York, quick to break limbs, kick groins, or shoot to wound or kill. If there are witnesses, he encourages their silence with terse admonitions, such as "Act like a clam or I'll open you up like one." He has no patience for the law, only justice, a trait in evidence in his first case, in which he

hunts the killer of Detective Jack Williams, the man who saved his life during the war. After Hammer shoots murderer Charlotte Manning (a jury would have bought her alibi, so he simply skips the trial), succeeding adventures find him searching for the killer of a streetwalker friend, sniffing out spies, looking for a missing container of radioactive material, hunting down a stolen gem collection, and seeking a Communist fiend named the Dragon, who has apparently killed his girlfriend/assistant Velda (who had "million-dollars legs" and carried a .32 automatic).

Hammer wears a tan trench coat, wears his hat pulled low, and carries a .38 revolver or a .45; he's a dead-on shot with both. Beer is his preferred beverage. He frequently works with Pat Chambers, the chief of homicide, who doesn't always approve of his methods.

Comment: The other Hammer novels are *Vengeance Is Mine!* (1950), *My Gun Is Quick* (1950), *The Big Kill* (1951), *One Lonely Night* (1951), *Kiss Me, Deadly* (1952), *The Girl Hunters* (1962), *The Snake* (1964), *The Twisted Thing* (1966), *The Body Lovers* (1967), and *Survival . . . Zero!* (1970). The most recent novel is *The Killing Man* (1989).

On radio, the character was heard on Mutual's *That Hammer Guy* in 1951–52. In motion pictures, Biff Elliot starred as Hammer in *I, the Jury* (1953), Ralph Meeker took the role in *Kiss Me Deadly* (1955), Robert Bray played the private eye in *My Gun Is Quick* (1957), Spillane himself starred in *The Girl Hunters* (1963), and Armand Assante starred in an update of *I, the Jury* (1982).

On TV, Darren McGavin starred as Hammer in a syndicated series that began airing in 1958. Seventy-eight half-hour episodes were shot; Velda was not seen on the show. In January 1984 Stacy Keach starred in *Mickey Spillane's Mike Hammer,* an hour-long series that aired until July 1985 and costarred Lindsay Bloom as Velda. After Keach was released from prison in England (he served six months for cocaine possession), he made the TV movie *The Return of Mickey Spillane's Mike Hammer* (1986), which has Hammer on the trail of a gang of Vietnam veterans who are abducting and selling children. That was followed by *The New Mike Hammer* in September 1986, which aired through July of the following year.

MIKE KOVAC   (TV)

First Appearance: *Man With a Camera,* October 1958, ABC.

Biography: After serving as a combat photographer during World War II, Mike Kovac becomes a freelancer. He occasionally works as a photojournalist and also takes pictures for the government, insurance companies, private investigators, and others. Most often, however, he's employed by Lieutenant Donovan of the New York Police Department, assignments that typically end up with him discovering and following up clues to crimes. Mike occasionally seeks assistance from his father, Anton.

Comment: The half-hour series aired until February 1960 and starred Charles Bronson as Mike, Ludwig Stossel as Anton, and James Flavin as Donovan.

MIKE NELSON (TV, C)

First Appearance: *Sea Hunt,* January 1958, syndicated.

Biography: Based on his boat the *Argonaut,* former navy frogman Mike Nelson is an undersea adventurer-for-hire, who will tackle any job as long as it's legal, from searching for sunken treasure, to testing new equipment, to stopping smugglers or criminals, to rescuing trapped divers (or even, in one episode, a pilot trapped in a submerged plane).

Comment: There were 156 half-hour episodes in the original *Sea Hunt,* which starred Lloyd Bridges as Nelson; he was the show's only regular. Incredibly, the three networks had turned the show down, feeling the subject had limited dramatic potential. Thus producer Ivan Tors was forced to go the ultimately more lucrative syndication route. Dell published 13 issues of a *Sea Hunt* comic book from 1958 to 1962.

A second *Sea Hunt* series, comprising 22 half-hour episodes, was syndicated in September 1987 and starred Ron Ely as Nelson. By this time, Mike is a widower who travels about on the boat *Sea Hunt,* which he hires out for charters, research, and other undertakings. With him on many of his adventures is his daughter Jennifer (played by Kimberly Sissons), a marine biology major.

MIKE NOMAD (CS)

First Appearance: *Steve Roper,* 1953, Field Newspaper Syndicate.

Biography: The son of Polish immigrants, the Nowaks, manly Mike Nomad—who Americanized the name—is a truck driver for the news magazine *Proof,* which is published by magnate Major McCoy. His close friend is blond, refined, pipe-smoking young photographer Steve Roper, who works for the periodical. Together they have many adventures—Mike tackling most of the rough-and-tumble dirty work. These escapades not only involve Steve's assignments and criminal elements that try to keep the magazine from the stands, but are brought to them by Crandall Mellon, a private investigator and the uncle of Steve's secretary, Honeydew Mellon.

Mike lives in a small apartment over a restaurant owned by Ma Jong.

Comment: The strip later became *Steve Roper & Mike Nomad.* It was originally called *Big Chief Wahoo* when it was launched in 1936 by artist Elmer Woggon and writer Allen Saunders. The setting was a modern-day Indian reservation and chronicled the comic adventures of the Chief, his medicine show friend the Great Gusto, and Wahoo's girlfriend, Minnie-Ha-Cha. The tone of the strip changed when Roper parachuted onto the reservation in the early 1950s. Not only does Ruper take over the strip with Wahoo as his sidekick, but Minnie-Ha-Cha falls for him.

MILO MORAI (L, T)

First Appearance: *The Coming of the Horseclans* by Robert Adams, 1975, Pinnacle Books.

Biography: It is the 27th century A.D., six centuries after a combination of World War III and subsequent natural disasters remade the face of the earth and reduced civilization to barbarism. New empires have arisen, along with a great and long-prophesied hero: Milo, who is immune to death by ordinary means. After two centuries of roaming the world, the 652-year-old Milo returns to his home, the high plains of what used to be the United States. There his mission is to join the tribe of the Horseclansmen and lead them back to their homeland and to glory. Ultimately becoming known as the Undying High Lord, Milo is able to communicate with his noble warhorse Steeltooth and huge prairie cats via telepathic Mindspeak.

His mate is Lady Mara of Pohtohmahs.

Comment: The first six Horseclans books—*The Swords of the Horseclans* (1977), *Revenge of the Horseclans* (1977), *A Cat of Silvery Hue* (1978), *The Savage Mountains* (1978), and *The Patrimony* (1978)—follow the adventures of Milo after his coming. Beginning with *Horseclans Odyssey,* author Adams tells of the hero's and Horseclans' earlier years, ultimately covering ten centuries. Subsequent titles are *The Death of a Legend, The Witch Goddess, Bili the Axe, Champion of the Last Battle, A Woman of the Horseclans, Horses of the North, A Man Called Milo Morai* (in which the hero tells of his earliest adventures in the first half of the 20th century), *The Memories of Milo Morai, Trumpets of War, Madman's Army,* and *The Clan of the Cats.* In addition to the novels, various authors contributed stories to the anthologies *Friends of the Horseclans* and *Friends of the Horseclans II.*

A role-playing *Horseclans* game was created by Steve Jackson Games.

Adams was also the author of the Castaways in Time series, in which a time storm sends Sebastian Foster and his five house guests back to the time of King Arthur.

MISSION IMPOSSIBLE   *See* IMPOSSIBLE
MISSIONS FORCE.

MR. AND MRS. NORTH   (L, S, MP, R, TV)

First Appearance: "The Norths Meet Murder" by Frances and Richard Lockridge, *The New Yorker,* 1940.

Biography: Jerry North, a Manhattan-based mystery publisher, is married to the restless, ditzy Pamela North, who, when she isn't caring for their cats (Martini, Gin, and Sherry among others) is busy investigating crimes, a hobby she acquires after finding a nude woman's body in a Greenwich Village bathtub. Her husband invariably becomes involved in her cases, mostly murders; assisting them (or vice versa) are Lieutenant Bill Weigand—who later makes captain on the strength of the many cases they've solved together—and Detective Sergeant Aloysius Clarence Mullins.

Tennis is the second-favorite hobby of the charming Norths.

Comment: The team was featured in 26 novels, many of them serialized in *The New Yorker*. The duo achieved success in other media as well.

On stage, they appeared in the Broadway play *Mr. and Mrs. North* in 1941, starring Peggy Conklin and Albert Hackett. The play was filmed in 1941 starring Gracie Allen and William Post, Jr. In both, the dithery Pam opens the liquor cabinet to get her husband a drink and finds a dead body within.

On radio, Alice Frost and Joseph Curtin starred in *Mr. and Mrs. North,* which debuted on NBC in 1942 and lasted most of the decade. Betty Jane Tyler co-starred as their helper, niece Susan; their driver, Mahatma McGloin, was played by Mandel Kramer.

On TV, Barbara Britton and Richard Denning starred in the half-hour-long series that aired on CBS from October 1952 to September 1953, then on NBC from January to July 1954.

MR. MOTO   (L, MP)

First Appearance: *No Hero* by John P. Marquand, 1935.

Biography: A slight man, polite and bespectacled, his black hair slicked back, I.O. Moto is an enormously effective Japanese agent; he is highly adept at judo, schooled in many languages, a fine navigator, and more. Speaking softly and sibilantly through his gold teeth, Moto looks after Japanese interests, which invariably means working for American interests, as his enemies tend to be Russian or Chinese.

Comment: The character appeared in the novels *Thank You, Mr. Moto* (1936), *Think Fast, Mr. Moto* (1937), *Mr. Moto Is So Sorry* (1938), *Last Laugh, Mr. Moto* (1942), and then *Stopover: Tokyo* (1957), which deal with a power struggle in postwar Japan. Obviously, during and immediately following World War II, the domestic demand for stories featuring heroic Japanese agents was nil.

Peter Lorre played the character in eight films, in which the character is less nationalistic than in the novels and a master of disguise. The films are *Think Fast, Mr. Moto* (1937), in which he chases diamond smugglers from San Francisco's Chinatown; *Thank You, Mr. Moto* (1937), about a search for the lost treasure of Genghis Khan; *Mr. Moto's Gamble* (1938), a film that teams Moto with Lee, the son of *Charlie Chan,* in the search for a boxer's killer (the film was planned as a Chan film, but was changed when actor Warner Oland died); *Mr. Moto Takes a Chance* (1938), pitting Moto and an American aviatrix against a megalomaniacal rajah; *Mysterious Mr. Moto* (1938), about the hero infiltrating a group of assassins; *Mr. Moto's Last Warning* (1939), in which he helps thwart a plot to sink the fleets of England and France; *Mr. Moto in Danger Island* (1939), the story of smugglers working from Puerto Rico; and *Mr. Moto Takes a Vacation* (1939), which finds him battling a thief who's after the priceless crown of the Queen of Sheba. Like the books, the films came to an end during the war. Indeed, when *Stopover: Tokyo* was filmed, the Moto character was cut entirely. The character's last screen appearance was in *The Return of Mr. Moto* (1965), starring Henry Silva as a Moto who is now a member of Interpol.

MODESTY BLAISE   (CS, MP, L, TV)

First Appearance: *The Evening Standard,* 1963 (London).

Biography: A shell-shocked war orphan with no recollection of her early childhood, our little heroine-to-be is put in a prison camp in Greece, escapes, and lands in a relocation camp in Persia. When she rescues an old man from a robber, she is taken in, named Modesty Blaise (the surname from Merlin, the magician's mentor), and works at a gambling establishment in Algeria. Her boss runs an international underworld syndicate,

"The Network," which the clever woman takes over. Soon thereafter, in Saigon, she meets soldier-of-fortune William ("Willie") Garvin, a streetwise fighter who becomes her partner and calls her "Princess." Moving to London and living it up with the fortune they've earned, the two are contacted by Sir Gerald Tarrant of the secret service, who needs their help with a case involving the underworld. Looking for some excitement, they accept and decide to remain Sir Gerald's agents, roaming the world on assignments, from infiltrating a call-girl operation in Florida, to battling drug dealers, to eluding headhunters in New Guinea.

Though Modesty is a skilled martial artist, she also carries an assortment of tools and weapons, including a handgun, a very compact grapnel, and the kongo—a hand-size wooden dumbbell that turns her fist into "iron."

Comment: The strip was created by writer Peter O'Donnell and artist Jim Holdaway. It was a hit almost from the start, spawning a film in 1966, directed by cult favorite Joseph Losey, and starring Monica Vitti with Terence Stamp as Willie and Harry Andrews as Sir Gerald. O'Donnell wrote a number of novels featuring the heroine. In *Modesty Blaise* (1965), she gives up crime to work for the British secret service; in *Sabre-Tooth* (1966), she battles a would-be world-conqueror; in *I, Lucifer* (1967), she takes on a bigtime terrorist; *A Taste for Death* (1969) pits her and Willie against the Sahara desert and a killer; and in *The Impossible Virgin* (1971), Willie is slain and Modesty avenges his death.

A TV pilot starring Ann Turkel was made in 1982 and aired in September of that year. It had Modesty looking into a Wall Street heist being handled by computers.

Modesty Blaise gets a workout. © Beaverbrook Newspaper Ltd.

THE MOD SQUAD (TV, C, L)

First Appearance: *The Mod Squad,* September 1968, ABC.

Biography: Julie Barnes is the daughter of a San Francisco prostitute who has run away to Los Angeles and is arrested for vagrancy. Linc Hayes is one of 13 children of ghetto parents who is arrested during the Watts riots. And Pete Cochran is a rebellious kid who is thrown out of the house by his Beverly Hills parents, steals a car, and is also arrested. The trio gets probation, but that isn't all: They are approached by Captain Adam Greer of the LAPD who wants them to form a "youth squad." They agree and go undercover, mingling with the young to catch the shake-down artists, drug dealers, kidnapers, and other *adults* who are taking advantage of them. (The three would never have ratted on their peers!)

In the first season, the trio drive a clunky station wagon named Woody; it goes off a cliff in the second season.

The cover of one of Dell's *Mod Squad* comic books. © Thomas-Spelling Productions.

Comment: The hour-long series stayed on the air until August 1973. Peggy Lipton was Julie, Clarence Williams III was Linc, Michael Cole played Pete, and Tige Andrews was Captain Greer. A made-for-TV movie, *The Return of the Mod Squad,* aired in 1979.

Dell published eight issues of a *Mod Squad* comic book from 1969 to 1971. There were also four uncredited novels with such hip titles as *The Sock-it-to-'em Murders* and *Spy-In.*

MORGAN CHANE (L)

First Appearance: *The Weapon from Beyond* by Edmond Hamilton, 1967, Ace Books.

Biography: When Earth people go to Varna to encourage trade, the mighty Varnans learn how to make starships and rocket through space, looting other worlds and becoming known as Starwolves. The son of David Chane from Earth (his mother's name is not known), the rugged, dark-haired Morgan Chane is a Varnan and, like all of his kind, is strong due to his giant world's enormous gravity: A stunner that would kill a human only weakens him, and he is able to endure G-forces that would crush a normal man. Though he is a Starwolf for a time, Chane objects to their violent, thieving ways and is exiled. Falling in with John Dilullo's interstellar mercenaries, he helps those in need, whether it's finding persons missing on hostile worlds or battling pirates and Starwolves.

Comment: Hamilton followed the first adventure with *The Closed Worlds* (1968) and *World of the Starwolves* (1968). The prolific science fiction author also created the enormously popular space hero Captain Future and wrote dozens of other stories as well. He was married to author Leigh Brackett. (See ERIC JOHN STARK.)

MOWGLI (L, MP, C, TV)

First Appearance: "In the Rukh" by Rudyard Kipling, 1893, *Many Inventions* magazine (see COMMENT).

Biography: In the jungles of Central India, near the Waingunga, the tiger Shere Khan attacks and drives off a party of human woodcutters, who leave behind "a naked brown baby who could just walk." The boy is found by Father Wolf of the Seeonee Wolf Pack, who brings him to his den to suckle at Mother Wolf with their own four cubs—angering Shere Khan, who wanted to eat him. Raksha, the Mother Wolf, names the new cub Mowgli (meaning "the Frog" and with the first syllable pronounced to rhyme with cow), and at a meeting of the Pack the boy's fate is debated. He is, after all, a man, and three times men have nearly killed Akela, the pack leader. The meeting is attended by wise council members Baloo the bear and Bagheera the black panther, who ask that the boy be allowed to live. Baloo agrees to teach him the Law of the Jungle, and Bagheera agrees to oversee his physical training. The panther also offers the wolf pack a token, a dead bull, to "buy" the boy's life. Akela agrees to let Mowgli stay—and much later, Mowgli must agree never to touch cattle as a tribute to the bull that helped save him.

Ten years later, Shere Khan still hopes to eat the boy, and orders old Akela to turn him over. But canny Mowgli has stolen fire from outside a human hut and drives Khan away with a burning branch. Mowgli leaves, then, to join a Man-Pack. Named Ohe Nathoo, he learns the language but never adapts and is cast out. He returns to the jungle until he is "nearly 17." When only Baloo and Bagheera remain among his old friends and family, the young man realizes it's time to leave for good. Bagheera brings down a young bull to close out the debt and, tearfully, Mowgli departs. In his later years, Mowgli goes to work for the Indian Forestry Department, looking after the families of the animals that reared him.

Other chronicled adventures, set while Mowgli was still in the jungle, tell of him being carried off by the Bandar-Log (Monkey People); how he and his friends survive a drought; the vengeance he wreaks on the hunter Buldeo who attempts to torture and kill his adoptive parents; an adventure with Kaa the python in which they journey to a ruined city where the wicked White Cobra guards a magnificent treasure; a battle between Mowgli, Kaa, and a pack of terrifying dhole (red dogs); and a final, sentimental tale in which Mowgli realizes that he no longer belongs among the animals but among men.

In his prime, Mowgli is "strong, tall, and beautiful, his long black hair sweeping over his shoulders." His only weapons are a knife and his powerful hands.

Comment: "In the Rukh" featured, briefly, Mowgli as an adult. Kipling decided, then, that it would be fun to spin yarns about Mowgli as a child, and wrote "Mowgli's Brothers", which was published in January 1894 in *St. Nicholas* (an American magazine; Kipling was living in Vermont at the time). He wrote other stories and, later that year, they were collected as *The Jungle Book. The Second Jungle Book* was published the following year. Not all of the stories in the two books featured Mowgli; those were first collected in 1933 as *All the Mowgli Stories.*

The stories and poems in the Jungle Books featuring Mowgli are "Mowgli's Brothers," "Kaa's Hunting," "Mowgli's Song," "How Fear Came," "Letting in the Jungle," "The King's Ankus," "Red Dog," and "The Spring Running."

In motion pictures, Sabu played the part in a lavish and generally faithful live-action adaptation in 1942, while the 1967 Walt Disney animated feature transformed Mowgli from a brave and wise hunter into a precocious, All-American kid.

Classics Illustrated published an adaptation of the Mowgli stories in 1951 as *The Jungle Book* (#83), while Gold Key published several Disney-related titles, including an adaptation of the cartoon and, in 1968, a one-shot called *King Louie and Mowgli.*

On TV, the character appeared in *The Jungle Book,* three animated films that aired in 1975–76. Only the last, *Mowgli's Brothers,* narrated by Roddy McDowall, featured Mowgli.

Baron Baden-Powell, founder of the Boy Scouts, established the Wolf Cub division in honor of his friend Kipling.

MS. TREE (C)

First Appearance: *Eclipse, The Magazine* #1, 1981, Eclipse Enterprises.

Biography: Ms. Michael Friday is a police officer who meets Mr. Michael Tree of Tree Investigations, Inc., when she gives him a ticket. He asks her out, and they discover they have differences (he fought in Vietnam and she fought against it) and similarities (both dropped out of law school due to lack of funds and became police officers). He convinces her to give up her beat and work for him as a private eye; after three years, they wed. Then, on their wedding night, the 34-year-old Mr. Tree is gunned down. Ms. Tree takes over the agency and, investigating her husband's death, learns that he had quit the force because his partner, Chick Steele, was in with the mob and that Tree was murdered by the mob because he was helping the assistant D.A. investigate police corruption. During the course of the investigation, she also learns that her husband had been married before, to Anne, and has a son, Mike, Jr.

Ms. Tree enters her fourth-floor apartment with care. . . . © Collins and Beatty.

After solving the case, the pistol-packing sleuth in a blue trench coat goes back to work, aided by her husband's ex-employees, investigators Dan Green and Roger Freemont and secretary Effie.

Comment: The character was created by writer Max Allan Collins and artist Terry Beatty, who based her look on the young Lana Turner. The team is also responsible for the DICK TRACY comic strip. Ms. Tree solved her husband's murder in the first six issues of *Eclipse, The Magazine,* though she has had a life beyond its pages, starring in *Ms. Tree's Thrilling Detective Adventures* (changed, simply, to *Ms. Tree* with #4), which lasted 50 issues from 1983 to 1989, and then in *Ms. Tree Quarterly,* which began in 1990.

N

NANCY DREW (L, MP, TV)

First Appearance: *The Secret of the Old Clock* by Carolyn Keene, 1930, Grosset & Dunlap.

Biography: Blond, blue-eyed, 18-year-old Nancy lives with her father, attorney Carson Drew, in River Heights. Nancy is a bright, inquisitive young woman who is constantly stumbling upon mysteries, missing treasure, suspicious persons, and crimes of all kind, which she invariably solves with the help of her friends, George Fayne and Bess Marvin, as well as an occasional assist from dad and from her boyfriend, Ned, who attends college outside of River Heights. Her rivals are jealous schoolmates Ada and Isabel Topham.

Mrs. Drew has been dead for "many years," and Hannah Gruen is the Drewses' housekeeper.

Comment: Keene was the pen name of the character's creator, Edward L. Stratemeyer, and his daughter, Harriet S. Adams. Stratemeyer penned the first three adventures, and Adams wrote the remainder of the original 56 tales. More recent stories—an additional 55 at last count—were written by various authors under the Keene byline.

In motion pictures, Nancy Drew was played by Bonita Granville in four films: *Nancy Drew, Detective* (1938); *Nancy Drew, Reporter; Nancy Drew, Trouble Shooter;* and *Nancy Drew and the Hidden Staircase* (all 1939).

On TV, Pamela Sue Martin played Nancy in *The Nancy Drew Mysteries,* an hour-long series that aired on ABC from February 1977 to January 1978. When the series was merged with *The Hardy Boys Mysteries* in the fall of 1978, Martin left and was replaced by Janet Louise Johnson. Nancy and *The Hardy Boys* continued to share adventures until August 1979.

Interestingly, Nancy's first adventure begins with her delivering legal papers for her father, the same way the first Hardy Boys story began.

NAPOLEON SOLO and ILLYA KURYAKIN (TV, L, C)

First Appearance: *The Man From U.N.C.L.E.*, September 1964, NBC.

Biography: Solo, Agent 11, is a suave American; Kuryakin, Agent Two, is a pensive Russian master of disguise. Both work for U.N.C.L.E.: United Network Command for Law and Enforcement, an organization devoted to battling international crime, would-be dictators, and the forces of THRUSH (Technological Hierarchy for the Removal of Undesirables and the Subjugation of Humanity). Though both agents are handy with fists and guns, Illya is more aggressive than Napoleon. He's also more resourceful—able, for example, to improvise a deadly slingshot using an ink bottle and the elastic from his underwear. He also plays a mean guitar, English horn, and sings. Napoleon's greatest skill is getting others to take risks while he monitors the action, pitching in only when it becomes necessary. Napoleon is also a crack helicopter pilot and drives a futuristic, gull-wing car.

U.N.C.L.E. is based in New York, somewhere in the east 40s, 50 feet underground, near the United Nations building (here, Council of Nations). The facility is equipped with seismic detectors, to prevent enemies from tunneling toward them. The U.S. headquarters are accessible through a "front": Del Floria's Tailor Shop. The tailor presses down his ironing machine, the agent twists a hanger, and a wall slides back. The agency is comprised of eight sections, several with overlapping responsibilities: Policy and Operations; Operations and Enforcement; Enforcement and Intelligence; Intelligence and Communications; Communications and Security; Security and Personnel; Propaganda and Finance; Camouflage and Deception. The agents report to Mr. Alexander Waverly, Agent One, a British operative who regrets being stuck behind a desk while they have all the fun. Waverly later acquires a secretary, Lisa Rogers.

U.N.C.L.E. agents carry customized P.38 automatics, with scopes, silencers, a shoulder stock, and other embellishments. Among their more exotic accoutrements are pen communicators that can reach headquarters from anywhere in the world, an exploding money clip, a distress transmitter, and Illya's drill, which he carries in the hollow heel of his shoe. One good tug on a lace gets it spinning.

Comment: The hour-long series aired through January 1968. Robert Vaughn starred as Solo, David McCallum was Kuryakin, Leo G. Carroll was Waverly, and Barbara Moore played Lisa. Solo and Kuryakin returned in the April 1983 TV movie *The Man From U.N.C.L.E.: The 15 Years Later Affair*, in which the evil Sepheran reopens THRUSH. We learn that during those 15 years, Solo has been running a computer firm while Illya has hit it big in the fashion biz, a neat revearsal of the talents they exhibited on the show. Episodes of the series have also been edited together as the movies *To Trap a Spy, The Spy with My Face, One Spy Too Many, One of Our Spies Is Missing, The Spy in the Green Hat, The Karate Killers, The Helicopter Spies*, and *How to Steal the World*.

Ironically, actors William Shatner and Leonard Nimoy appeared for the first time together on the show in "The Project Strigas Affair." The future *Star Trek* costars (see CAPTAIN JAMES T. KIRK) play hero and villain, respectively, as Shatner helps Solo and Kuryakin bring down a megalomaniacal diplomat. Before she played Agent 99 on *Get Smart* (see MAXWELL SMART), actress Barbara Feldon appeared in "The Never-Never Affair," playing Mandy Stevenson, Agent 23.

Ace Books published 23 novels: *The Thousand Coffins Affair* by Michael Avallone, *The Doomsday Affair* by Harry Whittington, *The Copehagen Affair* by John Oram, *The Dagger Affair* by David McDaniel, *The Mad Scientist Affair* by John T. Phillifent, *The Vampire Affair* by McDaniel, *The Radioactive Camel Affair* by Peter Leslie, *The Monster Wheel Affair* by McDaniel, *The Diving Dames Affair* by Leslie, *The Assassination Affair* by J. Hunter Holly, *The Invisibility Affair* by Thomas Stratton, *The Mind Twisters Affair* by Stratton, *The Rainbow Affair* by McDaniel, *The Cross of Gold Affair* by Fredric Davies, *The Utopia Affair* by McDaniels, *The Splintered Sunglasses Affair* by Leslie, *The Hollow Crown Affair* by McDaniels, *The Unfair Fare Affair* by Leslie, *The Power Cube Affair* by John T. Phillifent, *The Corfu Affair* by Phillifent, *The Thinking Machine Affair* by Joel Bernard, *The Stone Cold Dead in the Market Affair* by Oram, and *The Fingers in the Sky Affair* by Leslie.

A Big Little book, *The Calcutta Affair* by George S. Elrick, was published in 1967.

In comic books, Gold Key published 22 issues from 1965 to 1969, Entertainment Publishing put out 11 issues from 1987 to 1988, and Millennium Publications began publishing a new title in 1993.

The characters were cocreated by Ian Fleming, the creator of JAMES BOND, who had been asked to come

Napoleon Solo is flanked, on the left, by *Illya Kuryakin* and Mr. Waverly. © MGM.

up with a spy for TV. He came up with the tongue-in-cheek Solo, his ideas being heavily embellished by producer Norman Felton and especially by writer/producer Sam Rolfe. (See PALADIN.)

In 1960 star Robert Vaughn made a little-known TV pilot for producer Blake Edwards: *Boston Terrier*, in which he played a sleuthing dandy.

The success of the show inspired countless imitations, such as the 1970 film *The Man from O.R.G.Y.* starring Robert Walker.

A regular *Man from U.N.C.L.E.* short-story magazine was published in 1967.

NATHANIEL DUSK (C)

First Appearance: *Nathaniel Dusk* #1, 1984, DC Comics.

Biography: A World War I fighter pilot, Nathaniel Dusk returns to the U.S. and joins the police force, eventually quitting because of the corruption in the department. After opening his own private investigation agency, he falls in love with Joyce Gulino, whom he believes is a widow; she is, in fact, hiding out from her husband, mobster Joseph Costilino, who orders both Joyce and Dusk whacked. Dusk survives the hit, but Joyce does not; Costilino is killed by the hit man during a confrontation with Dusk, after which Dusk takes out the killer. He has since made sure that Joyce's children, Jennie and Anthony, are provided for.

In his only other recorded case, he is hired to look after wealthy Cranston Clement—and, when the man is murdered, to find his killer.

Comment: There were four issues of Dusk's first comic; he returned for four more issues *(Nathaniel Dusk II)* in 1985–86. All issues were drawn, superbly, by Gene Colan.

NATTY BUMPPO   (L, MP, C, TV)

First Appearance: *The Pioneers, or the Source of the Susquehanna* by James Fenimore Cooper, 1823.

Biography: In Glimmerglass (Lake Otsego, New York), between the years 1740 and 1745, Nathaniel "Natty" Bumppo, a.k.a. the Deerslayer, Hawkeye, or Leatherstocking, is just over 20 and "Christian, and white-born . . . and Christian-edicated [sic], too." A "reg'lar dealer in ven'son," he has lived among the Delaware Indians for ten years, though he and his friend "Hurry" Harry March stay together for mutual protection against their "adopted" people. Natty has never killed a man, cannot read, and isn't intellectual, though he has a very strict, knightlike code of honor.

Natty and Harry meet the trapper "Floating" Tom Hutter and his two daughters, Judith and Hetty, on their ark. Judith falls in love with the Deerslayer, who helps repulse an attack by Mingos. Natty kills one of them, though his treatment of the fatally wounded Indian earns him the respect of the Mingos and the name Hawkeye. Meanwhile, Tom and Harry are captured and Natty's close friend, the "noble, tall, handsome, and athletic" Delaware chief Chingachgook, "The Big Serpent," reaches the ark. Upon approaching the Mingo chief Rivenoak, Natty is able to swap chess pieces for the captives. But the Mingos still hold the maiden Hist, Chingachgook's beloved, and the two set out to rescue her. Natty is captured and tortured with rifle, fire, and tomahawk. After proving his courage and honor again, he is asked to join the tribe. He declines. Soldiers from a nearby garrison arrive and kill most of the Indians, though too late to save Tom and Hetty. Though Harry loves Judith, she literally begs the Deerslayer to marry her; he declines, Harry is jealous and leaves his friend, and the Deerslayer departs with Chingachgook and Hist.

The French and Indian War rages, with the Huron leader Magua united with the French. His activities have prevented young Alice and Cora Munro from joining their father, the British commander stationed at Lake Champlain in Fort William Henry. Working as a scout in 1757, Natty (also called *La Longue Carabine*, The Long Rifle, by the French) and Chingachgook help the women, aided by the chief's son Uncas, also known as the Last of the Mohicans. Uncas dies trying to save Cora, who is slain by Magua.

The war continues and the setting moves to the regions around Lake Ontario, as Natty becomes engaged to Mable Dunham. However, she is in love with Jasper Western, who, though accused of being a traitor, is ultimately acquitted—and Natty moves on. Years pass, and after settling in upstate New York, he watches with distress the coming of civilization. In particular, he is disturbed by the growth of the town of Templeton and its crimes against nature. Natty is prosecuted when he kills a deer for food out of season; meanwhile, the people of Templeton kill pigeons for sport and cut down trees and fish with impunity. Disgusted with their "wasty ways," the noble Natty heads west and forms a close bond with young Oliver Edwards and Major Effingham. Ironically, by blazing new trails, he helps to open the West for his enemies. In his old age, Natty, now a trapper moving about with his devoted dog Hector, encounters squatters, typified by the selfish and destructive Ishmael Bush and Paul Hover, who cut down cottonwood trees simply to make a camp, and shoot a buffalo each day to enjoy just the meat of the hump. In 1804, at just over the age of 70, Natty dies in the village of the Pawnee Loups, succumbing to "a gradual and mild decay of the physical powers." A figure symbolic of the world that has died with him, he is buried by his adopted son Hard-Heart "beneath the shade of some noble oaks," nurturing them with his death.

Natty stands "about six feet in his moccasins," with a slender frame that possesses "unusual agility, if not unusual strength." He usually carries a rifle and a hunting knife.

Comment: The four other novels in which the character appeared are *The Last of the Mohicans* (1826), *The Prairie* (1827), *The Pathfinder, or The Inland Sea* (1940), and *The Deerslayer* (1841), known collectively as the Leatherstocking Tales. In 1954 Allan Nevins abridged and combined the tales into a single volume, *The Leatherstocking Saga*.

Author Cooper was raised at the foot of Lake Otsego and knew the area and its history well, incorporating them into the novels. However, he says that Natty is a synthesis of "different individuals known to the writer in early life."

In motion pictures, *The Deerslayer* was filmed in 1957 and 1978 (for TV) starring Lex Barker and Steve

Forrest, respectively; *The Last of the Mohicans* was filmed in 1936 (with Randolph Scott), in 1977 (for TV with Forrest), and in 1992 (with Daniel Day-Lewis). *The Pathfinder* was filmed in 1952, starring George Montgomery.

In comic books, *Classics Illustrated* adapted *The Last of the Mohicans* (#4, 1942), *The Deerslayer* (#17, 1944), *The Pathfinder* (#22, 1944), and *The Pioneers* (#37, 1947).

On TV, in 1957, John Hart starred as Hawkeye, and Lon Chaney, Jr., as Chingachgook, in *Hawkeye,* a half-hour syndicated series that aired for just one season.

THE NEWSBOY LEGION (C)

First Appearance: *Star Spangled Comics* #7, 1942, DC Comics.

Biography: Big Words, Scrapper, Tommy, and Gabby are orphans struggling to survive in the Suicide Slum section of York City (or Metropolis, according to later texts). The kids sell newspapers to earn money, but finally decide to supplement their meager income by stripping cars for Freddie the Fence. They're eventually arrested by police officer Jim Harper, a.k.a. the superhero the Guardian, while stealing tools to build a clubhouse. Though the kids are sent before a judge, who is inclined to send them to reform school, Harper suggests that he take responsibility for them instead. The kids become the Newsboy Legion, with Tommy as their leader, publishing a local newspaper that reports on the superhero's activities, helping other kids in trouble—such as Silent Sam, who witnesses a crime—and also helping the Guardian fight wrongdoers.

Eventually the boys go to college and become scientists; their sons form a new Newsboy Legion, with the addition of a black youth, Flipper Dipper.

Comment: The characters were created by the legendary art/writing team of Jack Kirby and Joe Simon (creators of Captain America) and remained in *Star Spangled Comics* through #64; their sons were introduced in *Jimmy Olson* #133 (1971). The origin of the characters was retold in *Secret Origins* #49.

See also THE BOY COMMANDOS.

NIBSY THE NEWSBOY (CS)

First Appearance: "Nibsy the Newsboy in Funny Fairyland," *The New York World,* May 1906.

Biography: Nibsy is a lanky young teenager who wears a felt hat as he hawks newspapers (*The World,* of course) and becomes involved in exotic adventures. Each week, while working his Cherry Street corner, he is approached by a fairy of one kind or another who waves her wand and sends him "to the fairy realms." His adventures there are brief and busy. If he isn't besting an ogre or fleeing a dog turned into a giant by the wicked fairy Flirtissima, he's helping himself to royal treasure and getting booted from the kingdom; turning the king into a monkey and the fairy realm into a mini-Coney Island; or helping the queen lose weight by using a funhouse mirror that turns images into reality. (Unfortunately, she hadn't wanted to look *quite* so distorted.) At the end of each adventure, Nibsy returns to his streetcorner.

Whether the adventures are real or part of Nibsy's imagination is for the reader to decide.

Comment: The strip was created by George McManus and ran on Sundays through July 1906. McManus, who later created the classic *Bringing Up Father* strip, was one of the pioneers of comic strip art.

NICK CARTER (L, MP, R, TV, C)

First Appearance: "The Old Detective's Pupil; or, The Mysterious Crime of Madison Square" by John Russell Coryell, September 1886, *Street & Smith's New York Weekly.*

Biography: The son of Sim Carter is a young man who stands roughly 5 foot 4 inches and, trained by his father, is strong enough to "lift a horse with ease . . . while a heavy man is seated in the saddle." Nick's mind is also well developed, the youth having studied languages, art, physiology, and science. He hopes one day that he can use his skills to "aim for the right and for righting wrongs." Nick gets the chance sooner than he expects when his father is murdered. After solving that case, Nick becomes the New York-based "Master Detective," helping the needy or punishing the wicked. And when his great physical strength just isn't enough, he also has small guns up his sleeves, which a jerk of his arms spring-launches, fully cocked, into his hands. He often goes out in disguise, one of his favorite being Thomas Bolt, "Old Thunderbolt," a "shaggy and unkempt" country detective. In one case, Nick meets 14-year-old Nevada ranch hand Chickering Valentine, whom Nick takes back to New York and adopts. Before long, Chick is solving crimes alongside (as well as independent of) his father.

Both Nick and Chick are assisted by Patrick Murphy (whose name was inexplicably changed to Patsy Garvin later in the series), a bootblack who proves a terrific detective and fighter. Relatives Nellie and Warwick Carter also help out from time to time, as does restless and ambitious Ida Jones.

Nick is married to Ethel, who becomes Edith in later

stories (due to an editing error), but is eventually murdered in any case; he later proposes to Carma, an Amazon Queen, but nothing comes of that. His devoted butler for many years is Peter, who is ultimately replaced by Joseph, while his chauffeur is Danny Maloney.

Chick marries Bertha Mortimer, who is immediately slain. A second marriage, to Leila Loring, is more successful and results in a son, Trim Carter, who also assists the team.

Nick eventually retires and opens a detective school, which turns out many able young sleuths, then comes out of retirement. A new assistant joins the crew, detective student Ten-Ichi, a martial arts expert, as does a bloodhound, Pedro. Nick begins working closely with Conroy Conners of the U.S. Secret Service, hunting down spies, counterfeiters, smugglers, and other lowlifes. On several occasions Nick also battles the maniacal killer Dr. Jack Quartz, who not only vivisects women for fun, but runs a crime school on the side.

Comment: The character was created by publisher Ormand G. Smith, who outlined the story that Coryell wrote (under the house name "Nicholas Carter"). The original serial continued through December and proved so popular that it was quickly followed by "A Wall Street Haul; or, A Bold Stroke for a Fortune" (March–June 1887) and "Fighting Against Millions; or, The Detectives in the Jewel Caves of Kurm" (September 1888–January 1889). Writer Frederick Van Rensselaer Dey took over when *Nick Carter Library* magazine was launched in 1896. He wrote over 1,000 stories, with other writers contributing to the canon as well. Over the years, the title of the magazine was changed to *New Nick Carter Library, New Nick Carter Weekly, Nick Carter Weekly,* then back to *New Nick Carter Weekly,* and finally *Nick Carter Stories.* In 1915 it became *Detective Story Magazine,* with Carter remaining in its pages for three years. He returned for a spell from 1924 to 1927, then was relaunched in a new *Nick Carter Magazine,* which lasted from 1933 to 1936.

In 1964 book packager Lyle Kenyon Engel created a new series of Nick Carter novels for Award Books. Now, however, Nick is a superspy known as Killmaster; over 100 novels were produced for the series.

In the movies, Nick appeared in four silent, French-made serials and then in silent shorts starring Thomas Carrigan (1920) and then Edmund Lowe (1922). Carter next appeared in three elegant features starring Walter Pidgeon: *Nick Carter, Master Detective* (1939), *Phantom Raiders* (1940), and *Sky Murder* (1940). Lyle Talbot starred as his son in *Chick Carter, Detective,* a 15-chapter serial (1946). Eddie Constan-

tine starred as Carter in a pair of French films: *Nick Carter Va Tout Casser* (1963) and *Nick Carter et le Trefle Rouge* (1965), while Michal *(sic)* Docolomansky appeared as the hero in the Czech *Nick Carter in Prague* (a.k.a. *Dinner for Adele*) made in 1978.

On radio, *Nick Carter, Master Detective,* began airing on Mutual in 1943. Lon Clark starred as Nick. Chick also had his own radio show, with Billy Lipton, then Leon Janney, playing the young detective. It aired from 1943 to 1945, expiring shortly before the series that spawned it.

On TV, Robert Conrad starred in the 1972 movie *The Adventures of Nick Carter,* which was set in the early 1900s and was the (failed) pilot for a proposed series. That same year, a parody of the detective, also called *Nick Carter,* enjoyed some success as part of the Italian TV series *Gulp!* which also spawned a moderately successful comic *Nick Carter* comic book.

In American comic books, Nick was a backup feature in *The Shadow* from #1, 1940, to #101, 1949, appearing in most issues. In the early tales, he frequently battled saboteurs and spies. He also appeared in the first issue of *Army and Navy Stories* in 1941 and in several issues of *Doc Savage Comics* in 1943. Chick also appeared in many issues of *The Shadow,* often with his allies, the Inner Circle Gang, and serving a stint in the Air Cadets.

NICK and NORA CHARLES (L, MP, R, TV, S)

First Appearance: *The Thin Man* by Dashiell Hammett, 1934, Alfred A. Knopf, Inc.

Biography: Charalambides "Nick" Charles is a former gumshoe for the San Francisco-based Trans-American Detective Agency. After meeting and falling in love with 26-year-old millionairess Nora, the tall, slim Nick weds her and moves into her posh apartment at the Normandie in New York. Though he gives up womanizing (not drinking, though), he can't quite shake his sleuthing ways—especially when Julia Wolf, the secretary of an old friend, missing inventor Clyde Wynant, is found murdered. Nora encourages her husband to look into the matter, and, described by one police officer as "a woman with hair on her chest," she eagerly tags along on the search for the lanky, over-six-feet Wynant—the Thin Man.

Nora listens to Chaliapin; Nick is fond of speakeasies and a drink before breakfast. She's fun-loving; he's cynical.

The couple has a beloved Schnauzer, Asta (a wire fox terrier everywhere else but the original novel).

Comment: *The Thin Man* was the only literary exploit of the Charleses, who are better known to the general public through their appearances in other media.

In motion pictures, William Powell and Myrna Loy starred in six "Thin Man" films: *The Thin Man* (1934), *After the Thin Man* (1936), *Another Thin Man* (1939)—which introduced Nick, Jr.—*Shadow of the Thin Man* (1941), *The Thin Man Goes Home* (1944), and *Song of the Thin Man* (1947).

The Thin Man came to NBC radio in 1941 and ran for most of the decade, starring Claudia Morgan as Nora and a succession of Nicks: Lester Damon, Les Tremayne, Joseph Curtin, and David Gothard.

On TV, Peter Lawford starred as Nick, with Phyllis Kirk as Nora in the half-hour NBC series, 74 episodes of which aired from September 1957 to June 1959. Craig Stevens and Jo Ann Pflug starred in the TV movie *Nick and Nora* in 1975.

The musical *Nick & Nora*, starring Barry Bostwick and Joanna Gleason, had a brief run on Broadway in 1991.

Hammett also created the Fat Man especially for radio, the eponymous series airing over ABC in 1945. The Fat Man was actually Brad Runyan, a 237-pound sleuth who worked closely with Sergeant O'Hara of the police force. J. Scott Smart played the detective in the short-lived series.

See also THE CONTINENTAL OP; SAM SPADE.

NICK FURY (C)

First Appearance: *Sgt. Fury and His Howling Commandos* #1, 1963, Marvel Comics.

Biography: Nicholas Joseph Fury is the son of World War I pilot Jack Fury, who died in combat (his mother's name is not known) and the brother of Dawn and Jacob. Raised in the Hell's Kitchen section of Manhattan, Fury enlists in 1941, goes through basic training at Fort Dix, and serves as a sergeant in the European Theater, leading the famed Howling Commandos, which consist of Isador "Izzy" Cohen, Timothy Aloysius Cadwallader, Timothy "Dum Dum" Dugan, Gabriel Jones, Jonathan "Junior" Juniper (who perishes in combat), Eric Koenig, Dino Manelli, Percival Pinkerton, and "Rebel" Ralston. The team reports to Captain Samuel "Happy Sam" Sawyer. During one battle, a grenade shatters the bones around Fury's left eye, damaging the optic nerve. The injury ultimately causes him to lose most of his vision in that eye, and he dons an eyepatch. One exploit also results in his being given the experimental "Infinity Formula," annual doses of which have caused him to age more slowly than other men.

Fury served with the Howling Commandos in Korea, which earned him a promotion to second lieutenant; spy activities for France in Vietnam during the 1950s booted him up to colonel, after which he went to work for the CIA. After a number of years, he went to work for the newly formed international spy and espionage group S.H.I.E.L.D. (Supreme Headquarters International Espionage Law-enforcement Division). He has been its public director and occasional powerhouse operative ever since; Howling Commando Dum Dum serves with him. When he's in the field, Fury packs a .15-caliber needle gun, which fires explosive darts.

In addition to his skill with weapons, Fury was a heavyweight boxer in the army and holds a Tae Kwon Do black belt and a Jiu Jitsu brown belt.

Comment: *Sgt. Fury and His Howling Commandos* lasted 167 issues, ceasing publication in 1981. Concurrently, Fury was starring in the adventures of S.H.I.E.L.D. in *Strange Tales* from #135 to #168, beginning in 1965; the series was spun off in its own title, *Nick Fury, Agent of S.H.I.E.L.D.,* which lasted for 18 issues. After appearing in different titles over the years, the series was revived in its own magazine in 1989.

Another of Marvel's combat titles was the less successful *Capt. Savage and His Leatherneck Raiders,* which lasted 19 issues from 1968 to 1970. The group consisted of Captain Simon Savage, Sergeant Sam "Yakkety" Yates, Corporal Jacques Larocque, Private Jay Littlebear, Private Lee Baker, and Seaman Roy "Blarney" Stone. Marvel also failed with a third title, the derivative *Combat Kelly and His Deadly Dozen,* which lasted nine issues from 1972 to 1973. The comic takes place during World War II, as Kelly leads a group of twelve ex-cons on dangerous missions in Europe.

NIGHT FORCE (C)

First Appearance: *New Teen Titans* #21, 1982, DC Comics.

Biography: For years, Baron Winters has studied and battled the occult—just how *many* years is unclear, since he has said he's been an advisor to "emperors, warriors, and barbarians," claims to have known Merlin and to have fled Russia during the Revolution. He ran a fortune-telling booth at a carnival in the 1940s and today dwells in Wintersgate Manor, a mansion on a cul-de-sac in Georgetown, Washington, D.C. The mansion is a portal to other times and places, and though the baron cannot leave his home in our time period, he can go through the many doors that lead to other times.

The smug, aloof Winters protects our time from occult dangers. Though he himself rarely becomes involved in battle, he commands the Night Force, whose members come and go but whose core group includes scientist Donovan Caine, who loses his right arm and leg (and wife Marianne) in a battle with the occult; journalist Jack Gold of the *National Chronicle;* his wife, Vanessa Van Helsing, a psychic and great-granddaughter of Dracula's foe; and reformed convict Paul Brooks, who dies in the course of battle. Winters shares his home with his leopard, Merlin, and his ex-wife, Katina, and son, Gowon.

Comment: After their debut story, the Night Force got their own title, which lasted 14 issues. The characters—which were originally going to be called the Challengers, then the Dark Force—were created by artist Gene Colan and writer Marv Wolfman.

NIGHTMASTER (C)

First Appearance: *Showcase* #82, 1969, DC Comics.

Biography: A hot young rock singer with the band Electric, former slum kid Jim Rook and fiancee Janet Jones walk around the East Village after his gig at the Electric Band Aid. Impulsively entering a shop called Oblivion, Inc., they are whisked, by magic, to the kingdom of Myrra in another dimension. There King Zolto explains that Rook is a descendant of Nacht, wielder of the enchanted Sword of Night, who was sent to Earth 1,000 years before by the traitorous sorcerer Farben, leaving the Sword of Night embedded in a pillar. Since only someone of the family of Nacht can lift the sword, Zolto asks Rook to take it up and help overthrow the evil Warlocks who seek to conquer the kingdom. Rook agrees, and though he has never fought with a sword, it has a mind of its own and helps him in battle. Dressed in the traditional garb of a blue body suit and red cloak, Rook gets about astride a Zelk, a giant grasshopper. His aides are the albino guide Boz and the giant Tickeytarkapolis Troutrust.

After defeating the Warlocks, Rook and Janet return to Earth.

Comment: The character, created by writer Denny O'Neil, appeared in two issues of *Showcase.*

NYOKA (MP, C)

First Appearance: *Jungle Girl,* 1941, Republic.

Biography: Kindly Dr. Meredith moves to the African jungle not just to help cure sick natives but to avoid being confused with his criminal twin brother "Slick." He takes his young daughter, Nyoka, with him, and she grows up among the natives, learning their ways. When Slick shows up, searching for diamonds, he has Dr. Meredith abducted; fortunately, Nyoka escapes—

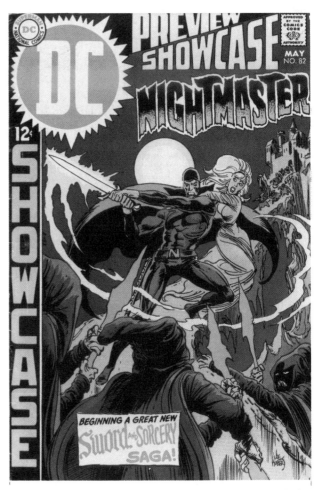

Janet hangs on as Jim Rook, *Nightmaster,* battles Warlocks. Art by Joe Kubert. © DC Comics.

wearing her sexy miniskirt and leopard-skin belt—and, teamed with aviators Jack Stanton and Curly Rogers and a small army of natives, foils Slick and his cohorts.

In her next adventure—still miniskirted but now wearing a leather belt—Nyoka is now the daughter of missing anthropologist Henry Gordon, for whom she is searching. Her quest takes her to the Middle East in the company of two archaeologists, who are looking for a lost treasure. The trio tangle with the evil Arab leader Vultura, who commands a cutthroat band of Bedouins and a powerful gorilla named Satan.

Comment: The first serial was 15 chapters, directed by William Witney and John English, and starred Frances Gifford as Nyoka. Kay Aldridge took the part in the second serial, the 15-chapter *Perils of Nyoka* (1942). It was directed by William Witney and costarred future TV Lone Ranger Clayton Moore as archaeologist Dr. Larry Grayson. The second serial has been edited into a feature film known as both *Nyoka and the Lost*

Secrets of Hippocrates and *Nyoka and the Tigermen.* The first serial was not featurized and is rarely seen.

Fawcett published 77 issues of a *Nyoka, the Jungle Girl* comic book from 1945 to 1953, and Charlton published nine issues from 1955 to 1957.

The character was inspired by author Edgar Rice Burrough's novel *The Jungle Girl,* which was originally published as *The Land of Hidden Men* in *Blue Book* Magazine in 1931 and in novel form a year later. In it, American doctor Gordon King becomes lost in the Cambodian jungle and finds a lost race of humans living in Pnom Dhek—including the titular Princess Fou-tan. He cures them of a mysterious disease (caused by eating too many mushrooms), helps stop a war between King Beng Kher and Lodidhapura, and ends up becoming a prince. Republic decided to use only the title and come up with their own story; Burroughs responded by removing his name from the project.

O

ODYSSEUS (L, MP, C)

First Appearance: *The Iliad* by Homer, circa 800 B.C. (see COMMENT).

Biography: Odysseus is the son of Laertes and Anticleia, the brother of Ctimene, the husband of Penelope, and the father of Telemachus. He apparently has other sisters, though their names are not revealed. His grandparents are Autolycus and Amphithee on his mother's side. On his father's side, only Arceisius is known.

During the Trojan War, waged between the Greek invaders and the defenders of Troy, Odysseus is one of the greatest of the Greek warriors, as well as one of the cleverest: After ten years of warfare, it is he who suggests constructing a hollow wooden horse and presenting it as a gift to the Trojans. Once the horse is inside the gates, the soldiers slip out, admit their comrades, and take Troy.

Intent upon returning home to his wife in Ithaca, Odysseus raids the land of the Ciconians, Trojan allies, then stops in Lotus-land, the home of the Lotus-Eaters; many of the men partake of the lotus and, forgetting about their homes, have to be carried back to the ship. After landing on the island of Polyphemus and the other Cyclopes—a race of giant beings with only one eye—the men are captured. Six are eaten before Odysseus is able to blind Polyphemus with a burning pole while he sleeps. This incurs the wrath of the giant's father, the sea god Poseidon. On their next stop, the isle of Aelous—King of the Winds—Odysseus is given unfavorable winds in a leather sack. Thinking there's treasure in it, his men open the bag and the ship is blown back to the island. Aeolus refuses to help again, and the hero sets out, only to be caught by the Laestrygonians, cannibals who consume most of the crew. Escaping, Odysseus and the survivors land on Aeaea, where the sorceress Circe turns his men into swine. The god Hermes gives Odysseus the herb moly to protect him, after which the hero compels Circe to restore his men.

Lost at sea, Odysseus descends into Hades to ask the ghost of Tiresias, a seer, for instructions on how to reach home. Passing, next, through the Straits of Messina and the murderous Scylla and Charybdis—respectively, a six-headed human-eating monster and a monster that creates devastating whirlpools by swallowing water—Odysseus loses six men. However, he sails past the Sirens without incident: Though their song is so sweet sailors forget everything else and die of starvation, Odysseus takes the precaution of putting wax in his men's ears. (He has himself lashed to the mast, however, so he can listen.)

With Ithaca in reach, the men stop on the island of Thrinacia and take cattle belonging to the sun god Helios. Their ship is sunk by a thunderbolt and Odysseus is the only one who survives, washing up on the shores of the island of Ogygia. There he is captured by the sea nymph Calypso, who offers him immortality if he will remain of his own free will. He refuses, and after seven years Zeus orders the nymph to set him free. But the hero's troubles are not over. He builds a raft, but Poseidon sends a storm to keep him from land; Odysseus is rescued from drowning by the sea goddess Leucothea. After landing on the island of Scheria, he is provided with a ship by King Alcinous and Queen Arete. (Angry at them for helping, Poseidon turns the ship to stone after Odysseus has left it.)

In Ithaca, Odysseus must find a way to rid his house of the 100 surly suitors who are trying, and failing, to win the hand of his devoted wife, Penelope. She has said that she will wed only he who can draw her husband's bow, knowing full well that only Odysseus can do so. Disguised as a beggar, the hero rests at the hut of the devoted swineherd Eumaeus, where he is recognized by his own faithful dog, Argus (who dies from excitement). After introducing himself to his son Telemachus, who was a babe when he left, Odysseus hides the suitors' weapons. With arrows and spears, Odysseus, Telemachus, and Eumaeus attack and slay the suitors, and Odysseus is finally reunited with his family; because he was able to draw the bow, Penelope knows the beggar is her husband. Only one task remains: to satisfy the suitors' angry families, who prepare to make war against the house of Odysseus. Fortunately, the goddess Athena, a friend of the hero's, steps in and calms the mourners. Though Odysseus is outraged that they would have dared to attack him, a thunderbolt tossed by Zeus calms him as well, and he rules the rest of his days in peace.

Comment: The hero is known as Ulysses to the Romans. Homer's epic—which, in spoken form, is surely somewhat older than its first written version—is based on historical fact: Archaeological excavations in Troy (in what is now Turkey) since 1988 suggest that, while details of the war and the odyssey itself will probably never be known, the non-fantasy events of 1300 B.C. generally appear to have happened as described by Homer.

The tales are each 24 books long and have been rewritten in prose form and retold many times. Most notably, the Roman poet Vergil recounted the tale in his epic poem *The Aenid.* (See AENEAS.)

In motion pictures, the silent *Ulysses and the Giant Polyphemus* was produced in 1905. Kirk Douglas played the hero in the 1955 film *Ulysses,* and the character also appeared in numerous sword-and-sandal epics of the 1960s: *Ulysses Against Hercules* (1961), *Ulysses Against the Son of Hercules* (1963), and *Hercules, Samson, and Ulysses* (1963). These continue the adventures of Homer's hero with more swordplay than literacy and more action than historical accuracy.

In comic books, *Classics Illustrated* adapted both *The Iliad* (#77, 1950) and *The Odyssey* as #81 (1951).

In addition to Odysseus, the other great hero of the saga is Achilles, son of Peleus (later, one of the Argonauts of *Jason*) and of the nereid Thetis. Dipped by his mother into the river Styx when he was a babe, Achilles was invulnerable to harm, save for the heel by which his mother held him. A mighty warrior and the slayer of the Trojan hero Hector—a noble and generous man—Achilles was slain by an arrow shot in his heel by Paris, Hector's younger brother. (By some accounts, it was the god Apollo disguised as Hector.) Odysseus meets Achilles again during his trip to the underworld.

OFFICER FRANK PONCHERELLO (TV)

First Appearance: *CHiPS,* September 1977, NBC.
Biography: CHiPS stands for the California Highway Patrol, and Officer Frank "Ponch" Poncherello and his partner Officer Jonathan Baker spend their time driving their Kawasaki motorcycles in and around Los Angeles, reporting (when they feel like it) to Sergeant Joe Getraer. When they aren't involved in high-speed chases, the officers are busy cracking auto theft rings, busting robbers disguised as tow truck operators,

helping a pilot who is forced to land on the freeway, chasing down poisoned baby food stolen from a delivery truck, dousing burning gasoline tankers, and the like.

Though both men are unmarried, the serious Baker yearns for a family, while the devil-may-care Ponch can't imagine ever settling down. Their choppers are looked after by mechanic Harlan.

Female highway patrol officers, a.k.a. "Chippies," are Officer Sindy Cahill, Officer Bonnie Clark, and Officer Kathy Linahan. Unlike their macho colleagues, they ride for the most part in patrol cars.

Comment: Reserve L.A. deputy sheriff Rick Rosner created the hour-long series, which ran through July 1983. Erik Estrada played Ponch, Larry Wilcox was Baker, Robert Pine was Getraer, Lou Wagner was Harlan, and Bruce Penhall (a real-life motorcycle racer) was Nelson.

OFFICER TOM HANSON (TV)

First Appearance: *21 Jump Street,* April 1987, Fox.
Biography: Along with Officers Doug Penhall, Judy Hoffs, and Harry Truman Ioki, Tom Hanson is an undercover member of the Los Angeles Police Department. Their job is to pass as students at local schools. Over the years they investigate killings and beatings, stop gang rivalries, break up a pornography ring disguised as a modeling agency, arrest dope pushers, straighten out teen prostitutes, and the like. The group's headquarters is a dilapidated chapel at 21 Jump Street.

When the original leader of the team, Captain Richard Jenko, is killed by a drunken driver, Captain Adam Fuller takes his place.

Hanson has a lengthy relationship with Jackie Garrett, who works for the D.A.; it ends with a major fight.

Comment: The pilot spawned a series that ran four seasons, three on the Fox network, the last in syndication. The pilot starred Jeff Yagher as Hanson; Johnny Depp played the role in the hour-long series. Peter DeLuise was Penhall, Holly Robinson was Hoffs, Dustin Nguyen was Ioki, Frederic Forest was Jenko, and Steven Williams was Fuller.

When Depp and Nguyen left the show at the end of its Fox run, they were replaced by Officers Anthony "Mac" McCann and Doug's younger brother, Joey, played by Michael Bendetti and Michael DeLuise.

OPERATOR NO. 5 (L)

First Appearance: *Operator No. 5,* #1, 1934, Popular Publications.

Biography: Jimmy Christopher, "America's undercover ace," is "the miracle man" of the secret service, helping the United States face countless threats from invaders and anarchists. In his first adventure, the White House blows up. Soon thereafter the so-called Purple Invasion occurs, spearheaded by European tyrant Maximilian I who is joined later by the Mongol leader, the Yellow Warlord. The saga ends with the enemy's defeat. Jimmy is assisted in his work by Tim Donovan, convict-turned-patriot Slips McGuire, and Chief of Intelligence Z-7.

The hero's father, John, was code named Q-6 and died in the line of duty; Jimmy's sister is Nan and his fiancee is Diane Elliott.

Comment: The stories were written by Curtis Steele (Frederick C. Davis and, later, Emile Tepperman); the magazine expired in 1939, after 48 issues.

P

PALADIN (TV, C, L)

First Appearance: *Have Gun, Will Travel,* September 1957, CBS.

Biography: After serving in the Civil War, West Point graduate Paladin decides he's had enough of the military. Heading west, he takes a room at the Hotel Carlton in San Francisco and becomes a gun for hire, traveling the West on behalf of clients. He will not work for criminals, however, and if he finds out his employers are corrupt, he'll hunt them down—for free. His only confidant is the hotel employee who brings him his messages; this is Hey Boy most of the time, though he is briefly replaced by Hey Girl.

Paladin is equally adept with a pistol, rifle, or military saber. His famous calling card shows a white chess knight and says, "Have Gun, Will Travel . . . Wire Paladin, San Francisco." The mustachioed hero likes fine clothing, fine food, and intelligent conversation. He can quote famous philosophers or hum the scores of great operas. He's a flashy dresser except when he's on the job, when he wears black.

Comment: The half-hour series aired through September 1963, 225 episodes in all. It was titled *Paladin* in syndication. Richard Boone starred as Paladin. Kam Tong was Hey Boy and Lisa Lu was Hey Girl; the latter appeared briefly during the 1960 season when Tong was offered a larger role in the short-lived *Mr. Garlund.*

The series was created by Herb Meadow and Sam Rolfe and was originally going to be set in modern-day New York. They changed it to a western setting when famous western star Randolph Scott expressed interest in doing it. When he dropped out, and Robert Taylor passed, Boone—a distant relative of Daniel Boone—came aboard.

Dell published 14 issues of the *Have Gun, Will Travel* comic book from 1958 to 1962. Dell also published a novel, *Have Gun Will Travel* by Noel Loomis.

In the series *Hec Ramsey,* Boone also starred as an aging lawman who reluctantly teams up with a college-educated cop, Chief Oliver Stamp (Rick Lenz).

The hour-long series aired from October 1972 to August 1974.

PANHANDLE PETE (CS)

First Appearance: *Panhandle Pete,* April 1904, *The New York World.*

Biography: Pete is a potbellied, stubble-faced hobo in ragged clothing whose travels take him around the world on adventures to the South Pole (he keeps the pole as a souvenir), to the jungle where he survives an encounter with cannibals, traveling via balloon and even rocket through mountains and deserts, and the like. At one point, he even bluffs his way to the throne of an African nation.

Pete's companions are the skinny hobo Cecil, a fat one who has no name but smokes a big, foul pipe, and a goat named Bill.

Comment: The strip was created by George McManus and ran for six and one-half years.

PAUL ATREIDES (L, MP, C)

First Appearance: "Dune World" by Frank Herbert, December 1963, *Analog* magazine.

Biography: The son of Duke Leto Atreides I and the Lady Jessica Harkonnen, Paul is born on the planet Caladan in the year 10175 (some 26,400 years hence). As a child, Paul is schooled in history, politics, military tactics, fencing, music, martial arts, and other disciplines. Key among these are "the mind-body lessons" his mother taught him, a way of achieving an expanded awareness. (As a member of the elite Bene Gesserit, the Lady Jessica is schooled in such metaphysical lore.) In 10190, the Padishah Emperor Shaddam IV appoints Leto to replace Jessica's father, Siridar-Baron Harkonnen, as the governor of Arrakis, the Dune World, a planet vital to the spice mining trade. Paul and Lady Jessica follow him there a year later. But the baron is not quite finished with Arrakis: He has the duke assassinated, forcing Paul and his pregnant mother to hide with the desert-dwelling natives, the

Fremen of Sietch Tabr. There Jessica gives birth to Paul's sister, Alia. Two years later, having learned to summon and ride the enormous sandworms, Paul leads the Fremen in revolt against the Padishah emperor and the Baron Harkonnen. His forces are victorious in the decisive Battle of Arrakeen, and thereafter Paul is referred to as Muad'Dib, Messiah. In an effort to make peace with his former adversaries, he weds Shaddam IV's daughter, Irulan Corrino. However, it is his concubine Chani Liet-Kynes, a Freman, who gives birth to his twins Leto and Chanima.

Meanwhile, Paul carries out the successful greening of Arrakis, turning it into a fertile, hospitable world. But an assassination attempt in 10205 leaves him blind, and, following the Fremen tradition that the blind be left in the desert, he goes there in self-imposed exile. Legend has it that he will return one day; indeed, some say they have seen him in the flesh or had visions in which he has warned of impending disaster. These sightings are uncorroborated.

Paul is skilled with the crysknife, a blade made from the tooth of a sandworm.

Comment: The original story was serialized through February 1964; it was published as the novel *Dune* in 1965. The sequels to the original novel are *Dune Messiah* (1969), *Children of Dune* (1976), *The God Emperor of Dune* (1981), *Heretics of Dune* (1984), and *Chapterhouse: Dune* (1985).

Kyle MacLachlan played the part in the 1984 film *Dune;* Marvel Comics published a three-issue adaptation of the film in 1985.

PAUL BUNYAN (F, MP)

First Appearance: Red River Lumber Company (Minnesota) advertising booklets, written by W.B. Laughead, 1870s.

Biography: A hero of the Great Lakes and Pacific Northwest, Paul is reported to have been born in Michigan, Minnesota, or the Canadian Woods, depending on which side is telling the tale. However, the records show that he was born in Maine. When he's three weeks old, the government tells his family to move because the babe rolls so much in his sleep that he knocks down four square miles of trees a night. They try placing him in a cradle in the ocean, but the waves he creates are so high they nearly drown Nova Scotia; it takes seven hours of constant bombardment from the British navy to wake him.

Paul is 20 feet tall by the time he leaves home at the age of one month, and, as befits his size and strength, he becomes a lumberjack. During his many years on the job—which begin in and around Niagara Falls, then five years in Michigan, then up to Wiscon-

sin—his companions are his wife (who isn't named in the stories); his son, Jean; his cook, Hot Biscuit Slim; bookkeeper Johnnie Inkslinger (who went through nine barrels of ink a day recording Paul's accomplishments); hunter Little Meery; singer Shanty Boy; tool-sharpener Febold Feboldson; and Paul's personal assistant, the Galloping Kid, a former cowboy. His pet and best friend is Babe, a blue ox whom he discovers as a calf frozen in the Great Lakes. (Some tales say Babe was born white but turned color in the winter of the blue snow.) Paul weighs more than the combined weight of all the fish that ever got away. Babe's friend is Benny, a little blue ox, who dies after swallowing a red-hot stove.

Among Paul's many accomplishments are digging the St. Lawrence River; thawing the lumberjacks' shadows when they froze to cabin walls during a very cold winter; training whales (with kindness) to haul logs; clearing North Dakota of trees; and much more. Frequently he saved the lives of lumberjacks when bad weather, drought, or famine threatened. It was the bursting of Paul's water tank that formed the Mississippi River.

Comment: Writer Laughead based his tales on legends he had heard at logging camps—though, ironically, the "folklore" he created is better known than the tales that spawned it thanks to the deft blend of heroism, tall tale telling, and humor. Other writers later write more tales of the hero, most notably Esther Shephard in 1924, who published stories such as "Paul Bunyan's Birth" and "The Round Drive," among others.

Walt Disney produced an animated featurette (17 minutes) about the hero in 1958.

In Pennsylvania, the legendary Tony Beaver was considered nearly as great as Paul Bunyan. It is likely that the older tales of this lumberjack became part of the Bunyan "legend." Indeed, the two met in one of Paul's many adventures.

PAULINE (MP, TV)

First Appearance: *The Perils of Pauline,* 1914, Pathe.

Biography: After inheriting a fortune, Pauline decides not to wed fiance Harry but to become a writer. To this end, she travels about, collecting plots and locales for her work, with Harry in pursuit. But the greedy Owen and his band want to get their hands on Pauline and her money. With the help of Harry—and the spirit of a mummy, of whom Pauline is the reincarnation—she survives Owen's attacks, Indians, rolling boulders, lions released at a wedding, a snake hidden in a basket of flowers, runaway trains and balloons, water rising in a mill with rats swimming toward her, and even poisoned candy that makes her want to drown herself. Eventually Pauline realizes she loves Harry more than writing and gives up her adventuring.

Comment: The first Pauline serial was a fat 20 chapters, directed by Louis Gasnier and Donald MacKenzie. The film was devoid of plot, characterization, and even competent cinematography. (It was shot in New Jersey.) Its success was due almost entirely to the charisma of 25-year-old star Pearl White, whose fame surpassed that of the formidable Mary Pickford. She went on to star as heroic *Elaine Dodge* in a trio of adventure serials and also made *Pearl of the Army* (1916), among others. However, it is the Pauline serial for which she will always be remembered. Paul Panzer costarred as Owen and Crane Wilbur was Harry.

The serial had little in common with the 1934 "remake" starring Evalyn Knapp—a tighter, 12-chapter adventure from Universal directed by Ray Taylor. This time Pauline Hargrave and her friend, engineer Robert Ward, must protect Pauline's scientist father, who has discovered a deadly new gas and is being pursued by Asian villains. In 1967 a made-for-TV film directed by Herbert Leonard, *The Perils of Pauline*, starred Pamela Austin being chased by the Russians, hunted by pygmies, pursued by a smitten ape, sought by a millionaire who wants to freeze her until his grandson grows up, and—worst of all—wooed by Pat Boone.

The title was also used in the 1947 film biography of Pearl White starring Betty Hutton.

The original film was parodied in a surprisingly more effective 1918 film *The Agonies of Agnes* starring Marie Dressler.

PECOS BILL (F, MP)

First Appearance: American folklore, circa 1850.
Biography: Bill was born in East Texas in the 1820s, to a pioneer woman who once killed 45 Indians with a broomhandle. Bill is weaned on moonshine and, as a baby, plays with bears and cougars. When Bill is a year old, his father decides to move the family west, where it's less crowded (another family had moved within 50 miles); as they're crossing the Pecos River, Bill falls from the wagon. Since he has 16 siblings, he isn't missed. Raised by coyotes, he learns their language and is able to run down a deer. When he's ten, a cowboy spots him killing a pairy of grizzly bears for breakfast. The cowpoke convinces Bill that he's human and takes him to town. Bill steals cows for food but makes up for it by killing gunslingers, skinning them and tanning their hides. When all of the bad men in Texas have been disposed of, Bill heads west in search of folks mean enough to kick fire from flint with their bare toes. He cleans up New Mexico and Arizona, and

also raises the colt Widow-Maker, to whom he feeds nitroglycerin and dynamite; Bill is the only person who can ride him. Bill's devoted hound is Norther.

Among his other feats are beating a ten-foot rattlesnake after first spotting him three bites; roping, riding, and taming a tornado (which, when it couldn't throw him, rained out from under him, creating the Grand Canyon and leaving Bill to ride home on a lightning bolt); roping and hauling down a friend who is stranded atop Pike's Peak; helping to build the S.P. Railroad; and helping the Kiowa Indians to find food.

Bill has many girlfriends, but falls in love with a famous rider named Slue-Foot Sue, whom he notices riding catfish down the Rio Grande. (They're bigger in Texas, of course.) On their wedding day, she insists on riding Widow-Maker: The horse throws her so high she has to duck her head to avoid the moon. When she finally comes down, she bounces for three days; Bill finally shoots her to keep her from starving. He never gets over her, despite many subsequent marriages. There are two accounts of Bill's death: One says that he drank strychnine after liquor lost its kick; another says that after spotting a Boston man dressed as a cowboy, he laughed himself to death.

Comment: The character is typically pictured as slender and blond, with a cigarette hanging from his lip.

Bill was featured in a segment of Walt Disney's animated feature *Make Mine Music* (1946); the segment, *Pecos Bill*, was also released separately as a featurette.

PEER GYNT (F, L, O, MP, S)

First Appearance: *Peer Gynt* by Henrik Ibsen, 1867 (see COMMENT).
Biography: The son of the late John Gynt, a peasant, and his widow, Aase, Peer is a "scurvy lout," a wayward, brawling, boastful youth who lives in the early 1800s in Gudbrandsdal, in the shadow of the mountains. His mother is frustrated that he won't do any more work than he has to, nor take a wife. At a wedding, he tries to make her happy by grabbing the bride, Ingrid, who loves him, and running into the hills; pursued by villagers, he releases her and runs through the peaks, where he meets the Woman in Green, daughter of the Mountain King, also known as the Troll King. Peer accompanies her to his castle, where he talks of marrying the Woman—until he angers her father with his impudence. The King orders his Trolls to tear Peer to bits and the lad flees, only to encounter Boyg, a giant, invisible Troll. He is saved by church bells in the distance, rung by young Solveig, a girl

whom Peer met at the wedding and who has fallen for him. Peer returns home.

Still a wanted outlaw for having abducted Ingrid, he builds himself a hut in the woods. Solveig comes to live with this man who discovers that "at worst I might be called a bungler, but certainly not an out-and-out-sinner." And realizing this, Gynt says he will endeavor to make amends henceforth, whenever he realizes that he has done wrong. After the death of his mother, Peer leaves Solveig behind, goes into business as a merchant, and settles in Morocco, shipping idols to China and slaves to North America. He soon ends the latter trade, though, when he realizes how "hateful" it is. Instead he begins trafficking in missionaries and Bibles (neutralizing the effect of the idols, he feels), though his business and his life seem doomed when his ship is stolen and he is stranded on a distant shore. After being taken in by Bedouins, he slowly makes his way to Cairo, where he is held for quite some time by Professor Begriffenfeldt, who runs an insane asylum there. Eventually making his way back to Norway by sea, Peer realizes how his life could have been better spent. He wanders about the countryside for a time, meeting people new and old, himself growing old. Finally facing his judge, the Button Moulder, Peer is to be melted in his casting ladle so he can become "food for worms." However, he is saved by the power of Solveig's love: He runs to the hut where she has waited for him all these years, and they are reunited.

Comment: The author drew upon existing characters to fashion his Peer, combining the real-life 18th century man Peer Gynt of Gudbrandsdal with fairy tales he found in Asbjornsen's *Norwegian Fairy Tales,* including one in which a more heroic but otherwise nondescript Peer battles a Troll. Ibsen also drew upon the fabled adventures of Grettir the Strong to fashion the protagonist and his heavily symbolic tale.

Composer Edvard Grieg created incidental music for the original production of Ibsen's drama (1876), which he later arranged into two suites. *Peer Gynt* Suite no. 1 consists of *Morning Mood, The Death of Aase, Anitra's Dance,* and *In the Hall of the Mountain King.* Suite no 2 is comprised of *Abduction of the Bride and Ingrid's Lament, Arabian Dance, Per Gynt's Home-Coming,* and *Solveig's Song.*

The composer Werner Egk wrote an opera based on Ibsen's play; it was first performed in 1938.

In film, there was a silent version produced in 1915, a German film produced in 1934, and an amateur production made in 1941 that starred a teenage Charlton Heston as Peer.

On stage, Ingmar Bergman staged the play in New York with Borje Ahlstedt as Peer.

The 17-year-old Charlton Heston stars in David Bradley's amateur version of *Peer Gynt.* Courtesy of David Bradley.

PENELOPE PITSTOP (TV, C)

First Appearance: *The Wacky Races,* September 1968, CBS.

Biography: Penelope Pitstop is a race car driver who travels the world in her quest to win the "World's Wackiest Racer" award. Initially, the Southern belle competes against the Ant Hill Mob, the Gruesome Twosome, Pat Pendig, the Red Max, Rufus Ruffcut, Saw-tooth, and the Slag Brothers; trying to spoil things for them all are the evil Dick Dastardly and his dog Muttley. Later, with the Ant Hill Mob as her guardians, Penelope goes off on her own adventures—with a name change for her car, from the Bulletproof Bomb to Chug-a-Boom.

Comment: There were 34 ten-minute Wacky Races adventures. Penelope got her own series, *The Perils of Penelope Pitstop,* in September 1969, on CBS. This spoof of the old "Perils of Pauline" serials (see PAULINE) featured the voices of Janet Waldo as Penelope, Paul Lynde as Sylvester Sneekly, and Mel Blanc and Paul Winchell in various supporting roles. Gary Owens (*Rowan and Martin's Laugh-In*) was the narrator.

Penelope Pitstop at the wheel of the Bulletproof Bomb. © Hanna-Barbera.

Seventeen half-hour episodes were produced; these were later included in the syndicated *Fun World of Hanna-Barbera* in 1977.

Penelope was also featured in the seven issues of *The Wacky Races* comic book, published by Gold Key from 1969 to 1972.

PERRY RHODAN (L, MP, C)

First Appearance: *Perry Rhodan* #1, 1961, Moewig-Verlag.

Biography: Major Perry Rhodan is an earthman, 35 years old and a test pilot for the U.S. Space Force. General Lesley Pounder gives him command of the spaceship *Stardust,* which is launched from the Nevada Fields on the first trip to the moon; also onboard are Captain Reginald Bull, Captain Clark G. Fletcher, and Lieutenant Eric Manoli. They crash-land on the moon, but find a ship occupied by tall, humanoid aliens led by the beautiful Thora and scientist Crest. The extraterrestrials explain that they hail from Arkon, a world in the remote Imperium, a sprawling galactic empire that is in its decline. They are traveling through space in search of a race that they can help to fulfill "the promise and potential that once was ours"; Rhodan convinces them that humankind may be that race.

Rhodan returns to Earth with the aliens. He lands in the Gobi Desert and, using Arkonide superscience, forms the Third Power, a military/political movement devoted to uniting the nations of Earth. His first move is to deactivate the world's nuclear missiles. Via hypnoschooling, Rhodan himself becomes a superscientific genius, averts an invasion of forces from the Arkonide Empire, defeats evil reptilian creatures known as the

Topides, and in countless adventures onboard the super battlecruiser *Stardust II* rises to the post of Peacelord of the Universe, head of what is now called the New Power. As such, he is in charge of the galactic peace corps, which is populated by humans and mutations who have supernormal powers.

In addition to the beautiful Thora and Crest, as well as the devoted Bell—who is his copilot and first officer—Rhodan's aides include mutant Tanaka Seiko whose brain "is sensitized to electro-magnetic waves," the teleporter Tako Kakuta, seer Wuriu Sengu, and Ralf Marten, an optics scientist. The ship's mascot is the "mouse-beaver" Pucky.

Comment: The series was created by Clark Darlton (real name: Walter Ernsting) and Karl Herbert Scheer, though other authors such as Kurt Mahr, Kurt Brand, H.G. Ewers, Hans Kneifel, and W.W. Shols have contributed to the series as well. Over 800 novels have appeared in Germany. In the U.S., Ace published reprints in paperback; in their heyday, they were appearing twice each month. Just over 100 of the novels were published, translated by Wendayne Ackerman. Crest was renamed Khrest and Bull was called Bell in these editions.

A motion picture, *Mission Stardust* (also known as *S.O.S. from Outer Space*) was produced in 1968. The Spanish/Italian/West German coproduction starred Lang Jeffries and generally followed the plot of the first novel. Directed by Primo Zeglio, it has largely been disowned by Rhodan fans.

A comic book based on the character, *Perry Rhodan im Bild (Perry Rhodan in Pictures),* began publication in Germany in 1968. It became *Perry* with number 27 and was translated for distribution throughout Europe.

PERSEUS (M, MP, L)

First Appearance: Greek mythology, circa 1300 B.C.

Biography: Perseus is the son of Zeus and the mortal Danae, the daughter of Acrisius, King of Argos. After learning from an oracle that his daughter's son will cause his death, the king has Danae and Perseus placed in a wooden box and tossed into the sea. But Zeus guides it to the Isle of Seriphos in the Aegean Sea, where they are found by the poor, honest fisherman Dictys and Perseus is raised by King Polydectes. The king falls in love with Danae, but sees her love for Perseus as an impediment. When the lad is grown, Polydectes sets him the deadly task of fetching him the head of Medusa, the snake-haired Gorgon whose direct gaze turns people to stone and can be viewed only in reflection.

Upon the advice of the gods Hermes and Athene, Perseus goes to visit the Graiae, the witch-like Gray Ladies. After stealing the one eye and tooth they share, he refuses to return them unless they give him magic items in their possession: winged sandals, the helmet of Hades for invisibility, and a large sack. Later Hermes provides him with a sharp, powerful sword and Athene gives him a mirror in which to view Medusa. Perseus flys to Oceanus, where Medusa lives with her Gorgon sisters, lops off her head, and heads back to Seriphos. En route, he stops in Ethiopia, where Princess Andromeda is chained to a rock and about to be sacrificed to a sea beast. Perseus flies down and kills the monster, marries Andromeda, and uses the Gorgon's head to calcify a jealous romantic rival, Andromeda's uncle Phineus. Back home, no one's fool, Perseus turns Polydectes and his supporters to stone and turns Atlas into a mountain when the giant refuses to let him rest in his garden of golden fruit. Then he returns his weapons to Hermes, who gives the sandals, sack, and helmet back to the Graiae. Perseus gives the head of Medusa to Athene, who places it in the center of her breastplate. Perseus sets the just fisherman Dictys on the throne of Seriphos.

During an athletic competition in Thessaly, Perseus accidentally strikes and kills his father, Acrisius, with a discus. The remainder of his life is devoted to constructive pursuits, building Persepolis and Mycenae in Argolis and fathering the daughter Gorgophone and the sons Perses, the father of the Persians; Alcaeus, father of Amphitryon; Sthenelus, whose son Eurystheus will impose the 12 labors on Heracles; and

Harry Hamlin as *Perseus* (kneeling) from *Clash of the Titans.* The Princess Andromeda is to the right; the mechanical owl Bubo is on his hand. © MGM, courtesy Ray Harryhausen.

Electryon, whose daughter Alcmene will become the mother of Heracles by a coupling with her grandfather, Zeus.

Comment: In motion pictures, Perseus was featured in the Italian-made *Perseus the Invincible,* released in the U.S. in 1962 as *Medusa vs. the Son of Hercules* and starring Richard Harrison. In 1981 Harry Hamlin played the part in *Clash of the Titans,* an English-made epic about Perseus's efforts to destroy Medusa and rescue the Princess Andromeda. The film was the basis for a novel by Alan Dean Foster, published in 1981.

PETER GUNN (TV)

First Appearance: *Peter Gunn,* September 1958, NBC.

Biography: A suave, tough, intelligent private eye who packs a snub-nosed revolver and a mean uppercut, Peter Gunn accepts big fees to help people get rid of trouble. Though he operates within the law, Gunn knows and uses people in every walk of life, from police officers to criminals. Once in a while he'll accept a case for free if someone truly needs his help and can't afford it.

Though he has comfortable digs at 351 Ellis Park Road in Los Angeles, Gunn can usually be found at the waterfront, in the jazz nightclub Mother's, listening to the singing of his girlfriend and helper Edie Hart. Gunn's friend and frequent ally is Lieutenant Jacoby.

Comment: The half-hour series moved to ABC in October 1960 and remained there until September 1961. Craig Stevens starred as Gunn, Lola Albright was Edie, and Herschel Bernardi played Jacoby. The series was created by Blake Edwards. Henry Mancini's pulsing, memorable theme song was a huge hit.

Edwards also directed two films based on the character. The first was a theatrical film, *Gunn,* in 1967, cowritten by Edwards and *The Exorcist* author William Peter Blatty. Stevens was here but Albright and Bernardi were missing, as the hero looks into the murder of a gangster and stumbles onto a protection racket. Laura Devon played Edie and Ed Asner was Jacoby. Edwards also helmed a TV movie in 1989 starring Peter Strauss as Gunn, Barbara Williams as Edie, and his own daughter, Jennifer Edwards, as Gunn's secretary. This time Gunn finds himself caught in a war between mobsters and bad cops.

In 1959 artist/writer Harvey Kurtzman did a clever send-up of Gunn in his comic book-style book *Harvey Kurtzman's Jungle Book.* In it, private eye Thelonius Violence hangs out in the jazz club Tasmanian Cellar, getting beaten up and waiting for clients.

PETER PAN (S, L, MP, C, TV)

First Appearance: *Peter Pan, or The Boy Who Wouldn't Grow Up* by Sir James Matthew Barrie, 1904.

Biography: Peter Pan is a motherless, magical boy who can fly; his companion is the fairy Tinker Bell, who appears as a light "no bigger than your fist" and whose "tinkles" only Peter can understand. They come to the London nursery of Wendy, John, and Michael Darling; Peter is startled when Mrs. Darling enters the room, and the dog Nana shuts the window on his shadow, snapping it off. Pan returns while the Darling parents are out, and Wendy sews his shadow back on. When Peter—the boy who refuses to grow up—learns that Wendy knows lots of stories, he teaches her and her brothers to fly—through a combination of fairy dust and thinking "lovely wonderful thoughts"—and brings them to his island home of Never Never Land. There they have many adventures with Indians, mermaids, wolves, Peter's friends the parentless Lost Boys, and especially pirates commanded by the evil Captain James Hook. At some time in the past, during a fight, Peter lopped off Hook's right hand and tossed it to a passing crocodile; the animal liked the taste so much he's been following Hook ever since.

Hook, who now wears a steel hook where the hand had been, abducts the children and, during a second and decisive battle with Pan, suffers a kick from the flying boy and lands in the crocodile's mouth. The children are saved and Peter takes them back to London. Years after this adventure, Peter returns to the nursery window. Wendy is grown now, but her daughter Jane accompanies the ageless Pan back to Never Never Land to help with spring cleaning. Years later Peter returns for Jane's daughter Margaret, and "thus it will go on, so long as children are gay and innocent and heartless."

Physically, Peter is "a lovely boy" who dresses in "skeleton leaves and the juices that ooze out of trees." He has all of his baby teeth, which shine like little pearls whenever he offers his triumphant "crowing." The lad is "a superb swordsman" whose nimble wrist compensates for his limited reach; his preferred blade is a long dagger. He lives in a spacious home under ground, where he can cut through the floor to fish, sits on "stout mushrooms," and warms himself before a large fireplace.

Comment: The play grew from Barrie's notion that he himself was a boy who wouldn't grow up. It was first performed in London in 1904 at the Duke of York's Theater, with Nina Boucicault as the star; it opened in New York at the Empire Theater the following year. In this original version, Never Never Land is called Neverland, and Hook escapes and becomes a Kensington Gardens schoolmaster. Barrie retold the story in novel form as *Peter and Wendy* (1911); today this novel is most often published as *Peter Pan*, and it contains much information that is not in the play (for example, Jane taking Wendy's place). Ironically, it has always been better known than the play, which wasn't published until 1928.

In addition to the original stage production, the character is perhaps best known through the musical *Peter Pan*, which debuted on Broadway in 1954 starring Mary Martin as Peter. The same production was aired on NBC the following year and, annually, for 17 years thereafter. The play has been popularly revived over the years, on Broadway with Sandy Duncan in 1972 and, in touring companies with athlete Cathy Rigby, actress Robin Taylor, actor B.D. Wong, and others.

In film, the character was first brought to the screen in the impressive *Peter Pan* (1924) starring Betty Bronson, and then as an animated Walt Disney feature in 1953 with the voice of Bobby Driscoll as Peter. In 1991 the property was updated, ham-fistedly, as *Hook,* with Robin Williams as an adult Peter returning to save his children from Captain Hook (played by Dustin Hoffman).

On TV, the character was seen in the short-lived animated series *Peter Pan and the Pirates,* a half-hour series that was syndicated in 1992.

In comic books, Peter Pan was seen in a number of Disney titles published by Dell: three issues in the *4-Color* series (numbers 442 [1953], 446 [1953], and 926 [1958]), *Movie Comics* in 1963, 1969, and 1983, respectively, reprinting the *4-Color* titles, *Dell Giants* featuring *Peter Pan's Treasure Chest* (1953), and *Walt Disney Showcase* #36 (1976). Western published one

Betty Bronson stars as the first movie *Peter Pan.*

issue of Disney's *The New Adventures of Peter Pan* in 1953, and Adventure Comics published two issues of the non-Disney *Peter Pan: The Return to Never-Never Land* in 1991. Marvel adapted *Hook* as a four-issue comic book series in 1992.

In Barrie's original draft of the play, Tinker Bell was called Tippy-Toe.

PHILEAS FOGG (L, MP, C, TV)

First Appearance: *Le Tour du Monde en Quatre-vingt Jours (Around the World in Eighty Days)* by Jules Verne, 1872, *Le Temps.*

Biography: The British Phileas Fogg and his French valet, Jean Passepartout, live at No. 7, Saville Row, Burlington Gardens. (Passepartout replaces James Forster, who had brought the finicky Fogg shaving water that was two degrees too cold.) "An enigmatic character" who is "exactitude personified," the bearded Fogg has no known friends or family. He is nonetheless a distinguished member of the London Reform Club, rich and giving money freely to worthwhile causes.

At the club, playing whist, Messrs. Fogg, Stuart, Fallentin, Sullivan, Flanagan, and Ralph discuss a recent bank robbery, the escape of the perpetrator, and how the world is shrinking. Prompted by an article in the *Daily Telegraph*, Fogg wagers £20,000 that he can go around the world in 80 days. The others put up £4,000 each (bonds are also traded on the stock exchange!) and, after collecting Passepartout, Fogg departs for Dover on Wednesday, October 2, 1872, at 8:45 P.M. Meanwhile, in part because of the amount of cash he is carrying, one detective Fix believes that Fogg is the bank robber attempting to flee the country and sets out after him.

Fogg goes from Paris to Turin to Brindisi to Suez in six and one-half uneventful days. From Egypt, he heads to Bombay—with Fix in pursuit—and arrives on the 20th. He crosses India by train and elephant, stopping to save a beautiful young woman, Aouda, from being burned at the stake as a sacrifice, then is arrested in Calcutta, thanks to Fix, for desecrating a pagoda by trespassing. Fix hopes, in the meantime, to obtain a warrant for Fogg's arrest for the robbery. But Fogg posts bail and he and Passepartout depart, heading by steamer to Singapore and then Hong Kong, and Fix follows. Fogg sails, next, to Shanghai to meet the San Francisco steamer; once in the U.S., they head to Chicago and then New York by rail and by sledge, moving through a snowstorm, across a rickety bridge, surviving an encounter with Sioux (Passepartout just barely)—all of which leaves Fogg 45 minutes late for the ship bound for Liverpool. Fortunately, he is able to book passage on a small ship to Queenstown,

Ireland, though they end up having to burn the ship piecemeal for steam. Fix, who has since joined the party, stays with them as they board a steamer for Liverpool. As soon as they arrive, Fix arrests Fogg, who sits in prison until Fix learns that the real thief has already been arrested. Freed, Fogg hires a train and speeds toward London only to arrive five minutes too late—or so he thinks. He had forgotten that he gained a day heading eastward. He realizes this in time to reach the club—with a second or so to spare.

Fogg wins his wager and marries Aouda.

Comment: The story was published as a novel the year after its newspaper serialization. In motion pictures, the novel was spectacularly filmed in 1956 starring David Niven as Fogg and Cantinflas as Passepartout. Michael Anderson directed.

In comic books, the novel was #69 in the *Classics Illustrated* series, first published in 1950. It was the seventh issue of Western's *A Golden Picture Classic* published in 1957; the film was also adapted that year, #784 of Dell's *4-Color* series.

On TV, an *Around the World in Eighty Days* animated series aired on NBC from September 1972 to September 1973 with Alistair Duncan and Ross Higgins as Fogg and Passepartout, respectively. The characters also appeared in the syndicated animated series *Around the World in Eighty Days* seen in 1973. The series follows the novel rather faithfully; 16 half-hour adventures were produced in Australia, with Alistair Duncan as Fogg and Ross Higgins as Passepartout.

Among his non-Vernesian adventures, the character also appeared in the motion picture *The Three Stooges Go Around the World in a Daze* (1963) and in Philip Jose Farmer's 1973 novel *The Other Log of Phileas Fogg*, in which he encounters aliens.

PHILIP MARLOWE (L, MP, R, TV)

First Appearance: *The Big Sleep* by Raymond Chandler, 1939.

Biography: A rarity among private eyes, Philip Marlowe is college educated, fond of literature, enjoys art by the old masters and classical music, and is extremely fond of chess. He opens his one-man agency to help people in need, as long as they are law-abiding. Marlowe himself will not break the law. He is not keen on gunplay or fisticuffs, though he can take a great deal of punishment. He has endured more than one beating rather than betray a trust or compromise his ideals.

Based in Los Angeles, Marlowe speaks fluent Spanish. He is 42 years old, tall, with a strong jaw, thin nose, and gray eyes. Though he eventually marries wealthy Linda Loring and lives in Palm Springs, he refuses to give up his detective work, feeling he must "be what I will be."

Perhaps Chandler said it best when he wrote that if there were more people like Marlowe, "The world would be a very safe place to live in, and yet not too dull to be worth living in."

Comment: The other Marlowe novels are *Farewell, My Lovely* (1940), *The High Window* (1942), *The Lady in the Lake* (1943), *The Little Sister* (1949), *The Long Goodbye* (1953), and *Playback* (1958). The short story collections are *The Simple Art of Murder* (1950) and *The Smell of Fear* (1965).

In motion pictures, Dick Powell played the sleuth in *Murder My Sweet* (1944), which was based on *Farewell, My Lovely,* after which Humphrey Bogart took the part in *The Big Sleep* (1946), directed by Howard Hawks. Next up was Robert Montgomery in *Lady in the Lake* (1946), though the star was seen only in one shot, in a mirror, as the camera (and voiceover narration) told the story from his eyes. George Montgomery took over in *The Brasher Doubloon* (1947), after which the detective was dormant, cinematically, until James Garner starred in *Marlowe* (1969), an adaptation of *The Little Sister.* Elliot Gould played Marlowe in *The Long Goodbye* (1973), and Robert Mitchum starred in both *Farewell, My Lovely* (1975) and *The Big Sleep* (1978).

On radio, the character appeared on *The Adventures of Philip Marlowe,* which aired on CBS for several years, beginning in 1949. Van Heflin and Gerald Mohr played the part. On TV, Dick Powell starred in *The Long Goodbye* on *Climax!* in 1954, and Philip Carey played the sleuth on *Philip Marlowe,* 26 half-hour episodes of which aired on CBS from October 1959 to March 1960. Carey's interpretation was far more docile and gentlemanly than previous Marlowes.

PHILO VANCE (L, MP, R)

First Appearance: *The Benson Murder Case,* by S.S. Van Dine, 1926, Scribners.

Biography: When Alvin Benson is shot to death in his New York apartment, District Attorney John F.X. Markham asks his best friend, youthful aristocrat and amateur detective Philo Vance, to lend him a hand in tracking down the killer. Though Sergeant Ernest Heath of Homicide resents the snide and arrogant young man, he respects his intellect and lets him work on the case. After the killing is solved, Vance becomes involved in cases involving a murdered Broadway singer, the slaughter of an entire family, a killer who bases homicides on Mother Goose rhymes, and more.

A graduate of Harvard who also studied in Europe, Vance knows a great deal about art and also about psychology, the latter interest making it fun and challenging for him to investigate, capture, and, when necessary, kill criminals. He is also a student of the writings of Nietzsche.

Vance is nearly six feet tall, has gray eyes, thin lips, and a straight nose.

Comment: Van Dine (real name: Willard Huntington Wright) was inspired to write his tale by the 1920 slaying of Joseph Elwell. He wrote 12 Vance novels in all: *The Canary Murder Case* (1927), *The Greene Murder Case* (1928), *The Bishop Murder Case* (1928), *The Scarab Murder Case* (1930), *The Kennel Murder Case* (1931), *The Dragon Murder Case* (1933), *The Casino Murder Case* (1934), *The Kidnap Murder Case* (1936), *The Garden Murder Case* (1937), *The Gracie Allen Murder Case* (1938), and *The Winter Murder Case* (1939).

Vance appeared in 14 feature films: *Canary Murder Case* (1929), *The Greene Murder Case* (1929), and *Benson Murder Case* (1930), all starring William Powell; Basil Rathbone played the part in *Bishop Murder Case* (1930). Powell returned in *The Kennel Murder Case* (1933), Warren William starred in *The Dragon Murder Case* (1934), Paul Lukas took the part in *Casino Murder Case* (1935), Edmund Lowe was the sleuth in *The Garden Murder Case* (1936), and Wilfrid Hyde-White headlined *The Scarab Murder Case* (1936). The next outing, *Night of Mystery* (1937), starred Grant Richards. Warren William was back for *The Gracie Allen Murder Case* (1939) and James Stephenson played Philo in *Calling Philo Vance* (1940). Last, there were a trio of films in 1947: *Philo Vance Returns, Philo Vance's Gamble,* and *Philo Vance's Secret Mission,* which starred William Wright in the first, Alan Curtis in the last two.

On radio, from 1936 to 1940, the character was played by Jackson Beck, then by Jose Ferrer.

PHRA (L)

First Appearance: *The Wonderful Adventures of Phra the Phoenician* by Edwin Lester Arnold, 1890, *The Illustrated London News.*

Biography: The man known as Phra was born over 1,500 years ago: Each time he dies, he revives 300 to 500 years later for reasons unknown. Phra remembers little of his first 30 years of life. He recalls hearing sea captains' tales, which inspire him to become a seaman trading in wine and olives. Sailing to Egypt, he saves a slave girl named Blodwen who turns out to be a British princess, marries her, and they have a son. He helps to defend his people against the Roman invaders, but the machinations of a jealous rival lead to his beheading as a Druid sacrifice; much to Phra's shock, though, he awakens in "another space of existence upon the world." Four hundred years have passed, and now he's a Roman soldier involved with Lady Electra but in love with a Christian slave girl, Numidea. When Numidea drowns, Phra keels over and dies—only to awaken this time as a Saxon in the service of King Harold battling the Normans, falling in love with Editha, and starting a new family. Looking back, says Phra, that was the time of his "passion-tossed existence" he most enjoyed. (At one point he laughs about how his "Eastern-British-Roman body" looked in a "Danish-Saxon-English tunic!") Once again, though, he isn't killed but simply melts into oblivion, this time reappearing 300 years later in a church and finding that he has been named a saint! After purchasing armor and posing as a knight, he joins the army of King Edward and wages war against France, becoming a close friend of the knight Flamaucoeur and a favorite of the monarch, as well as enamored of Lady Isobel of Oswaldston. She follows him in Flamaucoeur's armor and dies saving Phra in battle, taking a lance meant for him; afterward he wanders off, enters a crypt he had known in his first life, and is trapped there. He dies again, waking now when the tomb is opened, this time during the reign of Queen Elizabeth, where he crosses paths with an unscrupulous Spaniard and falls in love with Elizabeth Faulkener, who perishes.

In the end, he craves nothing more than final peace—which he hopes he will be able to spend in the company of his beloved Blodwen, who has appeared to him from time to time as a ghost, encouraging him and giving him advice.

Phra has black hair, a beard, and a "dusky face."

Comment: The story was syndicated in 26 parts, from July to December, and was published in book form by Harper's at the end of the year. Arnold also wrote about the adventures of LT. GULLIVAR JONES, as well as a comical novel, *Lepidus the Centurion: A Roman of To-day* (1901), recounting the adventures of a Roman warrior revived in modern times.

PISTOL JIM (CS)

First Appearance: *Pistol Jim,* October 1945, *Gran Chicos* #1 (Spain).

Biography: Dressed entirely in black, save for a six-gun emblem over his heart, fast-shooting Pistol Jim roams the American West with his young, freckle-faced friend Nick Rolly, a martial artist, keeping the peace and helping those in need. His usual adversaries are bank robbers and kidnapers. Whenever time permits, he visits one of his two lady friends, wealthy rancher Nelly Cayo and saloon entertainer Belle Smith.

Comment: The strip was created by Carlos Freixas and carried its hero through five adventures; though well drawn and written, it offered nothing new and disappeared in October 1946. However, it was one of the first of the Spanish strips about the American West; years later the subject would become a staple of European comic books (see COMANCHE), spearheaded by the popular hero Gringo, who debuted in 1963 and was created by Carlos Gimenez. Gringo was actually Syd Viking, a ranch foreman who leaves the spread to keep peace on the plains.

PLANET TERRY (C)

First Appearance: *Planet Terry* #1, 1985, Marvel Comics.

Biography: Far in the future, young Terry is separated from his parents at birth. The white-haired boy has many adventures as he searches the universe for

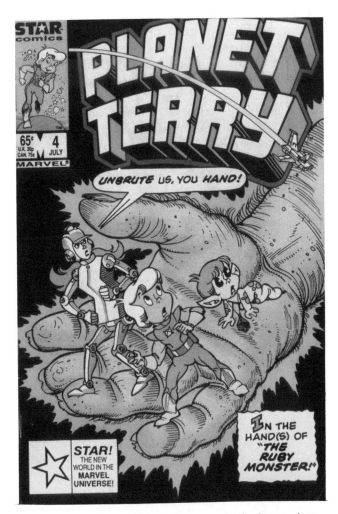

Robota, *Planet Terry*, and an alien named Elfin face a giant on Planetoid 172. © Marvel Comics.

them onboard his spaceship, accompanied by his brutish green alien friend Omnus, the robot Robota—who has a laser beam built into her forehead—and a small yellow alien who can say only "chippa." Terry wears a red body suit, with yellow boots and gloves and a yellow two-ringed symbol on his chest.

Comment: The character's magazine lasted for 12 issues and was one of the first children's titles in Marvel's Star Comics line. Another adventure character, who also starred in 12 issues of his own magazine, was Wally the Wizard, an apprentice to the medieval master wizard Marlin.

POLARIS SPANNER (C)

First Appearance: *Spanner's Galaxy* #1, 1984, DC Comics.

Biography: At some time in the future, the earth is part of the Milky Way Galaxy's Confederation of Free Worlds. Polaris is the son of Rigel and Cassie Spanner, farmers of jelly (giant amebae) on the planet Proxie. When he's 12, Polaris is allowed to train with the horselike Kaborians for five years to become a knight, a master of castling—a form of teleportation. Upon graduating, Polaris is also given a shek, a golden axlike device that also doubles as a shield and boomerang. Working on the freighter *Persius*, Polaris goes into partnership with bosun Cam and they begin trading gems, tools, and medicines on their own. However, a megalomaniac named Marcus Baka—who wants to obtain the special gem in Spanner's shek to build a weapon powered by a black hole—forges records that make Spanner the most wanted fugitive in the galaxy. With the help of his small, shrewlike mascot, Gadj, Spanner constantly outwits Commander Harris of the intergalactic police and the many pounders (bounty hunters) on his tail. His exploits earn him the admira-

Polaris Spanner eyes his new shek. © DC Comics.

tion of common folk everywhere, and he eventually proves his innocence—then sets out after Baka.

Spanner dresses in a red body suit with a white furlike collar and white front, blue boots, yellow headband, and orange sash for his shek.

Comment: The character starred in six issues of his own magazine.

POWERHOUSE PEPPER (C)

First Appearance: *Joker Comics* #1, 1942, Marvel Comics.

Biography: Endowed with great physical strength but a limited mind, Powerhouse Pepper goes from job to job (cowboy, boxer, laborer, motion picture extra) helping the defenseless or teaching lessons to bullies. Ironically, the tough, good-natured fellow is turned down for military service because there isn't a helmet big enough to accommodate his round, bald head. He is, however, a U.S. Marshal and thus authorized to capture bad guys. Powerhouse always wears a sweatshirt with horizontal stripes, sometimes red and black, sometimes yellow and black.

Comment: The character was created by the legendary comics/fantasy artist Basil Wolverton; he appeared in the first 31 issues of *Joker*, save #28, had five issues of his own title from 1943 to 1948, and also appeared as a backup feature in *Gay* and *Tessie the Typist*. For most of the strip's run, the characters often spoke in rhyme: "Ramjaw McClaw will perforate yore craw!" "Don't get your blood in a flood," and "Don't tan your man with that pan!" When the army can't fit him with a helmet, Powerhouse is informed, "A helmet teeters down over your cheaters, and there's no way to clap a strap under your map!"

POW-WOW SMITH (C)

First Appearance: *Detective Comics* #151, 1949, DC Comics.

Biography: In the 1880s, a Sioux Indian named Ohiyesa ("The Winner") decides to learn more about the encroaching white civilization. After leaving Red Deer Valley, he uses his talents at tracking and marksmanship with either a bow and arrow or a gun to land a position as a deputy sheriff. Dressed in buckskins and nicknamed Pow-Wow Smith by the white folk, he is later appointed sheriff of Elkhorn. His girlfriend is the Indian woman Fleetfoot, who often helps him on cases, as does his deputy, Hank Brown.

Comment: The character moved to *Western Comics* with #43; it ended, as did the title, with #85.

PRINCE CORUM (L)

First Appearance: *The Knight of Swords* by Michael Moorcock, 1971, Berkley Books.

Biography: At some time in the past, Prince Khlonskey of Castle Erorn is a leader of the Vadhagh Folk, a loosely knit people who live an average of 1,000 years and dwell in family castles scattered across a continent named Broan-Vadhagh. Their enemies of a million or more years have been the Nhadragh, but now both races are quickly being supplanted by Mabden—humans—a new breed that reproduces "prodigiously." Khlonskey's wife is named Colatalarna; he also has twin daughters, Illastru and Pholhinra, and a son, Corum Jhaelen Isrei (Corum, the Prince in the Scarlet Robe).

Corum is away when Mabden invade the land, killing his family and the rest of the Vadhagh. He returns in time to exact some revenge, but is captured and maimed, his right eye cut out and his left hand severed. Fortunately, he is rescued by the legendary Brown Man of Laahr. When he is healed, he makes a pact with the sorcerer Shool: Corum gives the wizard dibs on his soul in exchange for the Eye of Rhynn and the Hand of Kwll. Thus rearmed, he sets out to destroy the Sword Rulers, Lords of Chaos, the gods who have caused human beings to come about.

His first task: to defeat Arioch, Knight of Swords, master of five of the 15 planes of reality. His second: to defeat Xiombarg, the Queen of Swords. This time, though, he is accompanied by the beautiful Mabden Margravine Rhalina of the gentle Lwym-an-Esh; the devoted Jhary-a-Conel, who calls himself Companion to Champions; and the winged cat Whiskers. When he is victorious, he undertakes his third mission: To enter the city of Tamelorn and battle the Lost God Kwll, the King of Swords.

When this has been accomplished, Corum settles down to a peaceful life with Rhalina. They live together for some 70 years but, sadly, she has only a mortal life span. After her death at the age of 96, Corum remains in Lwym-an-Esh watching as the age of humans begins to flower. (His own people have descended into beings known as Elf-folk, but he has come to enjoy the company of pacifistic humans.) After a decade, however, a new problem arises in the form of new beings, the Fhoi Myore—also known as the Cold Folk—the brutal offspring of Chaos and Old Night. They control the seas, winds, and dark animals, and threaten all of civilization. After climbing back on his warhorse, Corum defeats the new gods, dying at last of a sword wound when "this world is free of all sorcery and all demigods."

In addition to his robe, Corum wears a conical silver helmet and carries a bow, lance, and war-ax.

Comment: The other novels in the series are *The Queen of Swords* (1971), *The King of Swords* (1971), *The Bull and the Spear* (1973), *The Oak and the Ram* (1973), and *The Sword and the Stallion* (1974).

Moorcock has written novels about other adventure heroes. Among these are his 1964 Mars trilogy (*Warriors of Mars, Blades of Mars,* and *Barbarians of Mars*), written as Edward Powys Bardbury, in which Earthman Michael Kane goes to Mars via a matter transmitter and fights barbaric races for the love of Queen Shizala (an homage to Edgar Rice Burroughs's JOHN CARTER); his 1967–76 Dorian Hawkmoon saga (*The Jewel in the Skull, Sorcerer's Amulet, Sword of the Dawn, The Secret of the Runestaff, Count Brass, The Champion of Garathorm,* and *The Quest for Tanelorn*), about the Duke of Koln (in Europe) and his adventures with the Runestaff, an artifact older than Time; the *Elric* tales from 1961 to 1984 (*Elric of Melnibone, The Sailor on the Seas of Fate, The Weird of the White Wolf, The Vanishing Tower, The Bane of the Black Sword, Stormbringer,* and *Elric at the End of Time*), the saga of the crimson-eyed albino, the last ruler of Melniborne, who wields the living sword Stormbringer against the forces of Chaos; and the John Daker tales, *The Eternal Champion* (1970) and *The Silver Warriors* (1973).

PRINCE DARGON (T, C)

First Appearance: *Sectaurs* toy line, February 1985, Coleco Industries.

Biography: "Somewhere in space, somewhen in time," the planet Symbion is home to insect humanoids. There are two kingdoms on the world: the Shining Realm and the Dark Domain. The latter is ruled by the Dread Empress Devora, who has made slaves of her people and has sent her Sting Troopers under General Spidrax and Commander Waspax to conquer the rest of Symbion. The Shining Realm is the home of peaceful city-states, ruled by lords; all answer to King Markor of Prosperon and his noble son, the Prince Royal Dargon. Other leaders in the king's circle are Dargon's mentor Mantys and his fellow warrior Zak.

Dressed in silver armor, Dargon gets about on the back of his airborne Dragonflyer and fights with a lance known as a Skallspear.

Comment: In addition to the toy line, Marvel Comics published ten issues of the *Sectaurs* comic book from 1985 to 1986.

Marvel also published a four-issue series called *Animax* from 1986 to 1987, based on a Kiscom toy line that failed to catch on. The characters live on future Earth, which is divided into a Liteside, inhabited by humans, and a Niteside, home of mutant animal

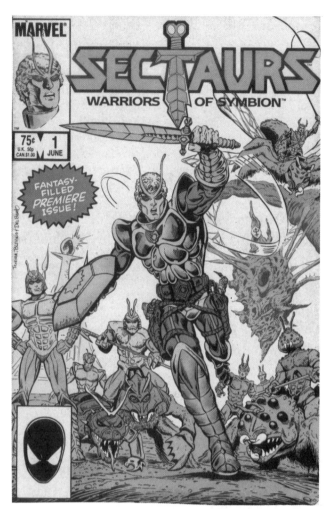

Prince Dargon of Symbion. © Seven Towns Ltd.

humanoids. The latter are led by the megalomaniacal X-Tinctor, the former by Max Action of Peoplopolis.

PRINCESS SARA (TV)

First Appearance: *Wildfire,* September 1986, CBS.

Biography: In order to conquer the world of Dar-Shan, the sorceress Diabolyn must first destroy the hereditary leader, Princess Sara. But the devoted talking horse Wildfire is too quick for the witch: He spirits Sara away, promising her father, John, that he will look after her. When she reaches adulthood, Sara mounts Wildfire and takes the battle to Diabolyn and her fumbling servant, Dweedle. At Sara's side are her devoted friends, the farmer Alvinar and young Dorin, who rides the accident-prone horse Brutus.

Comment: Hanna-Barbera produced 13 animated half-hour adventures. Georgi Irene was the voice of Sara and John Vernon was Wildfire; noted stars Rene

Auberjoinois was John, Jessica Walter was Diabolyn, and Billy Barty was Dweedle.

PRINCE VALIANT (CS, C, MP, L, TV)

First Appearance: *Prince Valiant,* February 13, 1937, King Features Syndicate.

Biography: Fleeing his enemies, the King of Thule and his loyal soldiers sail to the shores of Britain where, after a brief fight, the locals allow them to settle on an island "far out in the great fens." The king agrees, and his only son, young Prince Valiant, learns how to hunt with spear, net, and bow and arrow. He also learns how to face and defeat the marsh dragons that inhabit the region. An "inattentive" student, Valiant is determined to become a warrior—a dream he pursues relentlessly after his young mother dies of illness spawned by the fen. He learns swordplay, horsemanship, and eventually journeys to Camelot, where he becomes squire to Sir Gawain and learns to wear chain mail. Valiant becomes a peerless warrior himself, albeit headstrong in his defense of his Britain against the invading Huns and Saxons.

During the course of his adventures, Valiant travels the globe, visiting Africa, the Holy Land, and even the New World (in A.D. 600!). His love is Princess Aleta, Queen of the Misty Isles, whom he weds; they have four children, one of whom, Arn, becomes a great hero in his own right.

Comment: Hal Foster had created the strip in 1934 and shopped it around without success. *Prince Valiant* appeared only in a gorgeous color Sunday strip, never a daily. What was unique about the presentation—apart from its wonderfully detailed art—was the lack of word balloons. All of the text was presented in blocks, with quotes around the dialogue. Foster wrote and drew the strip from its inception until he turned it over to John Cullen Murphy in 1971. *Prince Valiant* continues to this day. Valiant and Aleta wed in 1946.

Prince Valiant appeared in over 100 issues of David McKay's *Ace Comics* from 1939 to the late 1940s, in seven issues of Dell's *4-Color,* and in sundry other titles. The character's best-remembered excursion outside the comic strip and comic books was in a 1953 motion picture starring Robert Wagner as Valiant (complete with Valiant's distinctive pageboy haircut) and Janet Leigh as Aleta. Hastings House published seven novels based on the strip, and a cartoon series debuted in the fall of 1991 on the Family Channel, featuring the voices of Robby Benson, Efrem Zimbalist, Jr., and Tim Curry.

PROFESSOR CHALLENGER (L, MP, C)

First Appearance: *The Lost World* by Sir Arthur Conan Doyle, 1912, Doran.

Biography: George Edward Challenger was born in Largs, on the Firth of Clyde in Scotland, in 1863. He was educated at the Largs Academy and then the University of Edinburgh, after which he worked as an assistant at the British Museum (1892) and Assistant Keeper of Comparative Anthropology (1893). He won the Crayston Medal of Zoological Research, has won countless foreign awards, and has been published extensively. Challenger is a man of unflinching devotion to his own opinions and quickly becomes violent with those who dare to argue with him. He makes his home at Enmore Park in Kensington, London, and enjoys walking and Alpine climbing. His wife is the long-suffering Jessie, and his devoted chauffeur and butler is Austin.

In his first and most famous adventure, he leads an expedition comprised of soldier Lord John Roxton, journalist Edward D. Malone, Professor Summerlee, and servants including Gomez and Zambo, to a South American plateau (Maple White Land, named after a previous explorer) where prehistoric animals still survive.

Challenger is a big man with a barrel chest, black mustache, and spade-shaped beard that reaches down over his chest, blue-gray eyes, and a "bellowing, roaring, rumbling voice."

Comment: The character's second adventure, *The Poison Belt,* was published in 1913, and had the hero rescuing Earth as it enters a cloud of poison gas. A collection of four stories, *The Maracot Deep,* was published in 1929. Challenger was inspired by the real-life Professor Rutherford, who taught Conan Doyle anatomy at the University of Edinburgh.

In motion pictures, Challenger was played by Wallace Beery in the 1925 version of *The Lost World* and by Claude Rains in the 1960 version.

In 1960 Dell published *The Lost World* comic book, based on the second film, as part of their *4-Color* series.

PROFESSOR QUATERMASS (TV, MP, C)

First Appearance: *The Quatermass Experiment,* July 1953, BBC.

Biography: When manned rocket Q-1 crashes outside of London, Professor Bernard Quatermass is summoned to investigate. When he helped launch the rocket, there were three crewmen inside; now there's just one. All that's left of the others are empty space-

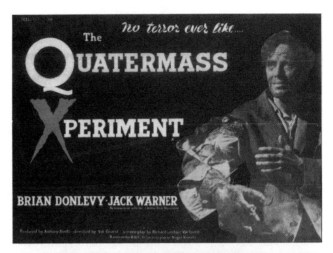

The British posters for the first two *Professor Quatermass* films. © Hammer Films.

suits. The survivor acts strangely, and, in time, he begins killing plants, animals, and people, the result of having been invaded by an alien life-form while in space. Ultimately, the astronaut becomes a monstrous, slimelike hybrid of all it is and has eaten (which includes his rocketmates), a mass that slithers into Westminster Abbey, where Quatermass confronts it. The scientist speaks to the minds of the three astronauts still lurking inside and convinces them to throw off the alien presence, which they do. They expire with it, of course. Undaunted, Quatermass makes plans to launch rocket Q-2.

Quatermass's second adventure has him trying to get a moon project going, only to be distracted when he learns, by accident, that for the past 18 months, hollow stones from space have been arriving, popping open, and releasing microscopic creatures that enter the human nervous system and take over the mind. Many members of the government and sciences have been taken over by the aliens. Quatermass also discovers that each "cell" is a member of a larger intelligence that is planning to rejoin in a huge dome its slaves are building, and take over the earth. With the help of nonpossessed humans, Quatermass destroys the alien base in space (an artificial asteroid) and sabotages the dome on Earth. The cells are forced to leave their hosts and, exposed to oxygen for too long a time, perish.

In his third adventure, Quatermass investigates a 5-year-old "missile" found by workers excavating a new subway tunnel. In time, Quatermass determines that it's a ship from Mars, sent here when the Martians were dying out. They operated on apes and turned them into proxy Martians, who became modern humans. However, Quatermass discovers that our ancestors were also imprinted with the Martian capacity for evil (the Martians, in silhouette, look like the devil), which the uncovered ship triggers in all who approach it. As Quatermass seeks to control the maddened masses, his colleague Dr. Roney uses a crane to "ground" the ship's energy.

In his last chronicled adventure *(The Quatermass Conclusion),* he investigates a beam from outer space that is killing Earth's young people.

Quatermass is an intense, brilliant man who can be curt and sarcastic. He tends to dress in suits and tweeds. Sometimes he wears a mustache, other times a full beard. Though he is a man who prefers thought to action, he can throw a punch or tackle an enemy when he has to.

Comment: The character was created by Nigel Kneale, who scripted his adventures. The original TV series was a six-part, four-hour serial starring Reginald Tate. The second four-hour TV miniseries, *Quatermass II,* aired two years later with John Robinson in the title role. A third, *Quatermass and the Pit,* starred Andre Morel and aired in 1958. All were turned into theatrical features: the first was retitled *The Quatermass Xperiment* (known as *The Creeping Unknown* in the U.S.) in 1956, with one major difference in the story—here the creature is electrocuted. The second was filmed in 1957 (titled *Enemy from Space* in the U.S.). Both star American actor Brian Donlevy as Quatermass. The third (*Five Million Years to Earth* in the U.S.) was filmed in 1968, starring Andrew Keir. A fourth film, *The Quatermass Conclusion,* was made for British TV and starred John Mills.

The character's first adventure was told in comic book form and serialized in *The House of Hammer* magazine #8 and #9 in 1977.

In 1979, Nigel Kneale published a novel based on the last film.

Q

Q.T. HUSH (TV)

First Appearance: *Q.T. Hush,* September 1960, syndicated.

Biography: The diminutive, round-faced private eye Q.T. Hush wears a trench coat and deerstalker cap and has two special assistants: a tall, thin, shadow named Quincy (Q.T.'s shadow), who wears a trench coat and can go off on his own; and a clever bloodhound named Shamus, who also wears a deerstalker cap.

Comment: Ten complete mysteries were produced by Animation Associates, each of which was comprised of ten segments. (Five aired per show).

R

RAMA (L)

First Appearance: *The Ramayana* by Valmiki, 500 B.C.

Biography: Rama is the eldest son of Dasa-ratha, King of the Kosalas, and his wife Kausalya. After Rama marries Sita, daughter of Janak, King of the Videhas—whom he won by bending her father's mighty bow—Dasa-ratha decides to abdicate in favor of his son. But Dasa-ratha's new wife Kaikeyi fears that Rama may hurt her son Bharat. Kaikeyi persuades her husband to name Bharat regent and to banish Rama for 14 years. Rama goes willingly, accompanied by his wife and his youngest brother, Lakshman. During his travels, Rama meets Valmiki, the poet who will one day record the saga.

Saddened by what he's done, the king dies and Bharat asks Rama to return. Rama says he cannot, for that was not what his father wished: He will return only when his exile is finished. Rama builds a home in the Forest of Panchaviti, on the banks of the Godavari. But he and his companions will not know contentment, for the Raksha (demon) princess Surpa-nakha covets him and attacks Sita. When Rama runs to protect her, Lakshman slashes Surpa-nakha's nose and ears. She complains to her brothers Maricha and Ravana, King of Ceylon, and while the former takes the form of a deer and lures the men away, Ravana becomes an eagle and carries Sita to the top of a mountain nestled in a vast sea. Rama and his brother set out after her and, after many years and numerous adventures, finally link up with Hanuman, the king of the monkeys. Hanuman becomes Rama's close aide, and it is he who finds Sita in the mountains of Lanka. Rallying the monkeys, Hanuman has them gather stones and trees and builds a causeway to the mountain. Ravana's own brothers, Bibhishan and Kumbha-karna, urge him to surrender, but he refuses; Bibhishan defects to Rama's side, and Ravana is defeated. Sita and Rama are reunited (after he first puts her through an ordeal of fire to determine if her virtue is intact). After boarding a swan-drawn cart, they fly home to Ayodhya, where Rama now becomes king. Alas, after many years, the people complain to their king that they cannot honor a woman who has lived among the Rakshas, and he reluctantly sends her away. She moves in with Valmiki and becomes the mother of his sons Kusa and Lava. In time, the boys visit Rama and recite the *Ramayana;* the hero is so moved that he asks Sita to return. She does, but is so sad that she perishes.

Rama is a muscular, handsome man who is regarded as the seventh avatar (incarnation) of Vishnu, one of the three gods of the Hindu Trinity.

Comment: The epic poem, whose title means "Relating to Rama," consists of 24,000 stanzas. Author Aubrey Menen rewrote the tale as a spoof, *The Ramayana,* in 1954.

RAMAR (TV, MP, C)

First Appearance: *Ramar of the Jungle,* October 1952, syndicated.

Biography: Ramar, or "White Medicine Man," is the name given by the Kenyan natives to Dr. Tom Reynolds. The son of missionaries, he studies to become a physician then returns to the jungle to help the natives, conduct medical research—and, of course, battle interlopers, poachers, despotic chieftains, and other ne'er-do-wells. He is assisted by Professor Howard Ogden.

Comment: Jon Hall starred in the half-hour series, 56 episodes of which aired through 1954. Ray Montgomery played Ogden. Hall's own Arrow Productions produced the series, shooting each episode in two days—three shows a week—for an average of $13,000. Several episodes were edited together into films and released theatrically.

Toby Press (#1), then Charlton Comics, published five issues of a Ramar comic book in 1954 to 1956.

Hall—a former action film star (*Ali Baba and the Forty Thieves,* 1944)—began working on another adventures series in 1957: *Malolo of the Seven Seas.* However, he quit after three episodes, weary of the weekly TV grind. The completed shows were edited into a feature film.

RANGE RIDER (TV, C)

First Appearance: *Range Rider,* September 1952, syndicated.

Biography: In the days following the Civil War, the heroic Range Rider (he has no other name) and his young friend Dick West roam the West from Mexico to Canada, from Missouri to California, helping those in need. Their only criterion is fair play: Whether it's an Indian, a U.S. Marshal, or a member of the Royal Canadian Mounted Police who needs them, they're there.

The Rider usually wears a black hat and white buckskins. His horse is Rawhide; Dick rides Lucky.

Comment: Seventy-eight half-hour adventures were produced; they remained in syndication through 1965. Future movie Tarzan, six-foot four-inch Jock Mahoney, starred as the Range Rider, with Dick Jones as Dick. The actors promoted the show with a live, ten-minute stunt-fight display that they took on tour with rodeos nationwide.

Dell published one issue of a *Range Rider* comic book as part of their *4-Color* series (#404) in 1952.

RANGER JACE PEARSON (R, C, TV)

First Appearance: *Tales of the Texas Rangers,* 1952, CBS.

Biography: Jace Pearson and Clay Morgan are Texas Rangers who symbolize the courage and determination of the breed. They appear in adventures that span the years from the late 1830s to the late 1950s, using the tools of those eras—from horses to high-speed automobiles—to fight outlaws, kidnapers, corrupt oil barons, rustlers, smugglers, spies, and the like.

Comment: Joel McCrea played Jace on the radio for its 3-year run. Dell published 20 issues of *Tales of the Texas Rangers* (later, *Jace Pearson's Tales of the Texas Rangers*) from 1952 to 1958; the characters also appeared in other Dell titles.

The series came to TV in September 1955; the half-hour episodes aired on CBS until May 1957, then were rerun on ABC in various times until May 1959. Willard Parker starred as Jace and Harry Lauter was Morgan.

These characters were unrelated to the heroes of the motion pictures *The Texas Rangers* (1936) or *Texas Rangers Ride Again* (1940).

RAVAGE (C)

First Appearance: *Ravage 2009,* 1992, Marvel Comics.

Biography: Early in the next century, Paul-Phillip Ravage works his way up from "highly-trained combat specialist" to the commander of Eco Central, the organization responsible for keeping the world free of pollution. When Ravage learns of murderous corruption in Alchemax, the industrial giant of which Eco Central is a part, its director-general, Anderthorp Henton, orders him framed (the charge is collusion with the monstrous Mutroids of the toxic island of Hellrock) and arrested. After defeating the agents that are sent to his office, the red-haired Ravage escapes. He sets up headquarters in a junkyard, where he attires himself in chains and discarded athletic equipment, makes a hubcap shield, uses a pipe and cogs for weapons—he tosses the latter like throwing stars—hot-wires an old garbage truck, lines his coat with stolen, "blasterproof" kevlar, and sets out to battle Alchemax and Dethstryk (leader of Hellrock).

Ravage's devoted assistants are Tiana, his former secretary, and young Dack, whose father was also framed and killed by Eco Central.

Comment: The character was created by veteran comics writer Stan Lee and artist Paul Ryan. The magazine is still being published.

RAWHIDE KID (C)

First Appearance: *Rawhide Kid* #1, 1955, Marvel Comics.

Biography: Originally, the man who "shares his saddle with danger" is an outlaw, a gunfighter who is "as tricky as a cornered rattler" and equally adept with a whip, which he uses for personal gain. However, the Rawhide Kid soon decides to uphold the law instead of breaking it: Assisted by his sidekick Kid Randy, he becomes a cattle rancher outside of Shotgun City, regularly using his talents to stop outlaws of all kinds.

The next version of the Kid is considerably different. This time he's John Clay, orphaned when his parents are killed by Cheyennes. (His brother Joe panics and flees, but later finds his courage and becomes a sheriff; brother Frank is taken prisoner, escapes, and becomes a gambler.) John is overlooked and is found by Ben Bart, a retired Texas Ranger, who ranches in Rawhide, Texas. Bart adopts the boy and teaches him marksmanship. When Ben is slain by an aspiring gunman, the 18-year-old John goes after his killers—wounding but not killing them. Unwilling to go back to the ranch, John decides to become a roving lawman, the Rawhide Kid. Astride "his famed stallion Nightwind," the Kid manages to thwart other outlaws and help folks in need, all the while staying out of the reach of the law. The Kid has had a number of unusual adventures, such as donning a pair of wings made by

Navajos so he can dogfight the airborne bandit the Raven.

In addition to his expertise with guns, the Kid is an excellent hand-to-hand fighter. He has a sixth sense about danger, feeling a tingling whenever it is near. The Kid dresses entirely in blue with a white hat and gloves and brown boots.

Comment: The Stan Lee creation ran 16 issues in its original incarnation. The character was conceived before the provisions of the watchdog Comics Code Authority had been put into effect, and by the second issue the character's cruelty was toned down and he became a rancher. This didn't do anything to help sales and the title was canceled. It was revived in 1960 with the new John Bart Kid, had a successful run through #151, then returned as a four-issue miniseries in 1985.

RED BARRY (CS, L, MP)

First Appearance: *Red Barry,* March 19, 1934, King Features Syndicate.

Biography: Red-headed Red Barry is an undercover operative for an unnamed big-city police department. Reporting to Inspector Scott, he spends a great deal of his time in Chinatown, where many Oriental and Eurasian villains operate. Occasionally assisted by the waif Ouchy Mugouchy and by kids known as the Terrific Three, Red has battled the likes of killer Judge Jekyll, gangleader Monk, forger Hans Bruno, and foreign smuggler/killer/temptress Flame.

Red's girlfriend is reporter Mississippi. His real first was never revealed.

Comment: The strip was created by Will Gould (unrelated to DICK TRACY's Chester Gould). Dark and nasty, it was pulled in 1939 and reintroduced the next year as an eight-page comic book insert—lighter, brighter, and gone within two months.

Red starred in a pair of Big Little Books: *Red Barry, Hero of the Hour* (1935) and *Red Barry, Undercover Man* (1939).

Buster Crabbe played the hero in the 13-chapter serial *Red Barry* (1938), in which the hero spends a great deal of time in Chinatown chasing down $2 million in stolen bonds. The serial was directed by Ford Beebe and Alan James and featured Frances Robinson as Mississippi and Wade Boteler as Scott.

RED RYDER (CS, L, C, MP, R)

First Appearance: *Red Ryder,* November 6, 1938, NEA Service.

Biography: Just before the turn of the century, young Red Ryder owns the modest Red Ryder Ranch outside the town of Rimrock, Colorado. Helping him run it are his aunt, Duchess, and Little Beaver, a Navajo orphan Red has adopted (and who tends to add the suffix "um" to words, like "think-um" and "yip-um"). However, when trouble threatens the region and the aging sheriff Newt can't handle it, Red is quick to leap onto his horse Thunder and ride into action, Little Beaver at his side, settling feuds among ranchers, miners, and Indians, hunting down rustlers or robbers, and battling such colorful villains as Donna Ringo and her train robbers, killer Banjo Bill, gambler/assassin Ace Hanlon, and many others.

Comment: The strip was created by Fred Harman, who stayed with *Red Ryder* until 1960. The strip struggled along for the better part of the decade without him, before riding off into the sunset.

The hero starred in ten Big Little Books: *Red Ryder and Little Beaver on Hoofs of Thunder* (1939), *Red Ryder, The Fighting Westerner* (1940), *Red Ryder and the Code of the West* (1941), *Red Ryder and the Western Border Guns* (1942), *Red Ryder and the Outlaw of Painted Valley* (1943), *Red Ryder in the War on the Range* (1945), *Red Ryder and the Squaw-Tooth Rustlers* (1946), *Red Ryder and the Rimrock Killer* (1948), *Red Ryder and the Secret Canyon* (1948), and *Red Ryder and Circus Luck* (1949).

In comic books, Hawley, then Dell (from #6) published 151 issues of *Red Ryder Comics* from 1940 to 1957.

The character was played by Don Barry in the 12-chapter serial *Adventures of Red Ryder* (1940), which pit him against Ace Hanlon and introduced Red's father, Colonel Tom Ryder, to the legend. The serial was directed by William Witney and John English; Tommy Cook was Little Beaver. On the 1940s radio series Reed Hadley, then Carlton KaDell and Brook Temple, played Red; Tommy Cook, then Henry Blair, was Little Beaver.

There was also a Red Rider, the hero of an eponymous movie serial in 1934. Buck Jones played the sheriff who releases a man from prison, then must prove he was innocent.

REID FLEMING (CS, C)

First Appearance: *Georgia Straight,* 1978.

Biography: The rye-guzzling, cigarette-smoking, two-fisted Reid Fleming works as a deliveryman for Milk, Inc., which is owned by Herbert O'Clock. Though he isn't a classic hero, Reid has guts to spare and believes in the dignity of the little guy, though he has what might be charitably called a short fuse. If customers tick him off, he'll pour their milk in their fishtank; if drivers tick him off, he'll chase their car and push his cigarette into their gas tank; if his supervisor

Mr. Crabbe ticks him off, he'll blackmail him in some underhanded way. Reid is a daredevil in his milk truck, and he's powerful enough to lift the truck on his back if need be. Reid's girlfriend is the "three-time divorcee" Lena, and his closest friend is 19-year delivery veteran Lowell Cooper. His favorite TV show is the action-packed *Dangers of Ivan*.

Comment: After the underground newspaper's demise in 1979, writer/artist David E. Boswell continued the hilarious and outrageous adventures of his hero in his own comic book. Boswell published the first one himself in 1980, called *Reid Fleming, World's Toughest Milkman;* Eclipse published the title from 1986 to 1990.

REMINGTON STEELE (TV)

First Appearance: *Remington Steele,* October 1982, NBC.

Biography: When ambitious, intelligent Laura Holt opens her own detective agency, she finds that business is flat because she's a woman. She creates a fictitious boss, "Remington Steele," and she suddenly has more work than she can handle. Unfortunately, clients want to meet the enigmatic Steele. Enter a young, polished Englishman (whose name is never revealed) who has no experience as a detective but certainly looks like a Remington Steele. Laura hires him to play the part, but the detective movie buff decides he wants in on the cases. They become a team, "Remington" fumbling a lot as he learns his trade (and uttering the inevitable "God, I'm good") as Laura tells him how to solve a case.

Comment: Pierce Brosnan starred as Steele and Stephanie Zimbalist was Holt in the hour-long series. Several episodes in the show's third season were filmed in locales ranging from Ireland to Malta.

Although the show had been canceled in 1986, interest in Pierce Brosnan grew when he was about to be named Roger Moore's successor as JAMES BOND. That caused the rerun ratings to climb; NBC still had contractual dibs on Brosnan and brought him and Zimbalist back for a pair of two-hour movies. Ironically, because Brosnan was tied up again with *Remington Steele,* the Bond producers went with Timothy Dalton for agent 007. The new shows were ratings flops.

RETIEF (L)

First Appearance: *Envoy to New Worlds* by Keith Laumer, 1963, Ace Books.

Biography: Jame Retief is a spacefaring, 27th-century second secretary and envoy-at-large in the Corps Diplomatique Terrestrienne, reporting to First Secretary Ben Magnan. Commonly finding himself on probation due to "undiplomatic behavior," he is nonetheless an effective ambassador and troubleshooter. Among his triumphs are helping to stop the tentacled Ree from expanding into human territory, mediating (and fighting) in a war between the outlaw gangs on Bloor and the invading, five-eyed Groaci, trying to make peace between the lobsterlike Haterakans and the Terran Defense League, and the like.

Retief is "tall, powerfully built" and carries a needle-pointed dagger in his boot. When going into hostile territory, he also wears an energy gun on his hip.

Comment: The first short story collection was followed by other Retief collections and novels: *Galactic Diplomat* (1965), *Retief's War (1966), Retief and the Warlords* (1968), *Retief: Ambassador to Space* (1969), *Retief of the CDT* (1971), *Retief's Ransom (1971), Retief: Emissary to the Stars* (1975), *Retief at Large* (1979), *Retief: Diplomat of Arms* (1982), *The Return of Retief* (1985), *Reward for Retief* (1989), *Retief to the Rescue* (1990), *Retief and the Pangalactic Pageant of Pulchritude* (1991), *Retief in the Ruins* (1992), and *Retief and the Rascals* (1993).

REX BAXTER (CS)

First Appearance: *Dime Comics* #1, 1942, Bell Features (Canada).

Biography: After serving with British forces in North Africa during World War II, Canadian soldier Rex Baxter is given leave. He takes a voyage on the SS *Luxor,* which is sunk by a U-boat; Baxter and his companion, Gail Abbott, manage to reach a small island where they meet Captain Zoltan and Tula. The men take the castaways into a metal globe and whisk them to the underground empire of Xalanta. There the benevolent Queen Riona has been deposed by the evil regend Lerzal, who intends to conquer the surface world via bacteriological warfare. Together Rex, Gail, the queen, and Zoltan work to battle Lerzal and save both the inner and outer worlds. Rex defeats Lerzal and other inner-earth foes, and, after World War II ends, he becomes a United Nations counterspy. His most famous mission is to find Adolf Hitler, who has managed to escape from Berlin and reach the underwater realm of Mu.

Comment: The strip was created by Edmond Good, who left after the 14th installment and was replaced by Adrian Dingle. Rex expired before the end of the decade. *Dime* also featured Major Domo and Jo-Jo; the latter was a legless midget who sat on the back of the former, an armless giant, who pretended to be a huge hunchback. Other Canadian heroes of this era included Dart Daring, Daredevil Master Swordsman;

Whiz Wallace, a pilot who is teleported to the Invisible Planet; and Active Jim, a superb athlete.

REX BENNETT (MP)

First Appearance: *G-men vs. the Black Dragon,* 1943, Republic Pictures.

Biography: Standing six foot four, the rugged Rex Bennett is a special agent for the U.S. government. In his first adventure, he's sent to Los Angeles to investigate and, it is hoped, smash the Black Dragon Society, a group of saboteurs led by the mysterious Haruchi. He is joined by British agent Vivian Marsh and Chinese Secret Service agent Chang Sing. Their first task is to destroy the Haruchi-run paint company that is making incendiary paint for U.S. ships. That done, they obtain a submarine locator, which Haruchi tries to steal; Haruchi steals microfilm plans that Rex and company struggle to retrieve; and finally, Haruchi is killed when he battles Rex on a speeding motorboat, which Rex abandons just before it crashes into a surfacing Japanese submarine.

After his first chronicled adventure, Rex is sent on a mission to besieged Stalingrad, about which little more is known. A German Gestapo captain there reportedly kills him and returns to Berlin; but Rex is actually alive and working undercover as agent G-27. In Berlin, the "captain"—our boy Rex—discovers a nefarious plot. To ensure victory in North Africa, the Nazis need the help of Sultan Abou Ben Ali and the many sheiks he controls. The sultan is leaning toward supporting the Allies (here called the United Nations). Thus, the Germans forge a long-lost sacred relic, the Dagger of Solomon, and a holy scroll to which it apparently led them—one that orders the Arabs to follow the sign of the swastika. To make certain the plan works, the evil Baron Von Rommler has the sultan imprisoned in Casablanca and takes his place at the meeting of the sheiks being held there. Though Rex is found out in Berlin, he manages to escape by plane and joins American reporter Janet Blake and Captain Pierre LaSalle of the French Diplomatic Headquarters in Casablanca, where they thwart the Nazi scheme.

In addition to being an ace pilot and a tough hand-to-hand fighter, Rex is a terrific swimmer, marksman, and swordsman.

Rex's assistant in L.A. is named Spencer. After defeating Haruchi, the American keeps his pet raven, renaming him Yankee.

Comment: *G-men vs. the Black Dragon* starred Rod Cameron as Rex, Constance Worth as Vivian, Roland Got as Chang, and Nino Pipitone as Haruchi. The 15-chapter serial was directed by William Witney and

was later edited into the feature film *The Black Dragon of Manzanar.*

Secret Service in Darkest Africa starred Cameron with Joan Marsh as Janet, Duncan Renaldo as LaSalle, and Lionel Royce as the sultan and the baron. The 15-chapter serial was released in 1943 and was directed by Spencer Bennet. It has been retitled *Manhunt in the African Jungles* for video release but is otherwise intact.

REX HAVOC (C)

First Appearance: *1984* magazine #8, 1978, Warren Publishing.

Biography: By 1985 monsters "had become so numerous" that the government was unable to deal with them. Moreover, they had learned how to use the courts to sue over abuses by law enforcement agencies, frowned on the term "monsters"—they preferred to be called "fantastics"—and campaigned for the passage of the Fantastic Rights Amendment. Rex Havoc has no stomach for them. Born on October 31, 1938—the same day as Orson Welles' infamous "War of the Worlds" radio broadcast—Havoc grew to monster-hating adulthood and founded the Asskickers of the Fantastic, whose motto is "We haul ours to kick theirs." The team is based in a storefront office in downtown Tarzana, California, and travels around in a van.

In addition to the six-foot-two inch Havoc, who is a man of "steel-hard muscle" but little brain, the Asskickers consist of monster expert and scientific genius Major Lars Wurlitzer, mechanic Springer, and buxom Bruno Zagwides.

Among their foes are Sebastian, King of the Vampires; the Spud from Another World (during their Arctic showdown, Rex builds a snowman and hides inside to surprise the potato monster); the immortal sorceress Ayesha (a.k.a. She-Who-Must-Be-Okay); and the giant lizard Humungus (which they tackle in Japan with the help of local Asskicker wannabes Kayo Komodo and the Strikers of Brutish Behinds).

Comment: The wonderfully clever parody appeared in *1984* numbers 4, 5, 6, and 9. To capitalize on the success of the film *Raiders of the Lost Ark* (see INDIANA JONES), the adventures were reprinted in *Warren Presents* #14—though the team name was changed to the kid-friendly Raiders of the Fantastic, and a great deal of writer Jim Stenstrum's marvelous dialogue was cleaned up. Abel Laxamana drew all of the adventures.

RICHARD BLADE (L)

First Appearance: *The Bronze Axe* by Jeffrey Lord, 1969, Macfadden-Bartell.

Biography: Englishman Richard Blade is an agent for MI6A, a "secret intelligence agency" run by the mysterious J. Recruited straight out of Oxford, Blade quickly becomes one of J's toughest and most successful agents. He is schooled in unarmed combat and excels at military strategy and psychological warfare. Meanwhile, scientist Lord Leighton has created a computer that, he hopes, when linked to a human brain, will download stores of information to create a race of supergeniuses. But something goes wrong. Helpless inside a telephone-booth-size glass case, Blade is hurled on a time/space journey into Dimension X, home to a seemingly endless supply of alternate Earths, each with a different history. In his first adventure, he rescues the beautiful Princess Taleen from the barbaric Albs. When Leighton manages to bring him back, Blade remembers nothing for a time—though his body is bronzed and scarred.

When Leighton figures out what has happened and Blade's mind has returned, the agent agrees to take further trips into Dimension X and ends up battling the batlike oranki; emerging in another dimension where women dominate and literally ride men; finding himself in a land populated by sleeping people; being transformed into a baby with a man's brain; and ending up in an England known as Englor that is at war with Russians called Red Flames. Blade brings new metals, new weapons, and new knowledge back from these journeys, which the government in our Home Dimension puts to good use.

It isn't possible for Blade to visit the same dimension twice. While he's gone, he remains in contact with the computer via a chip implanted in his skull.

Blade is swarthy, with thick black hair and bushy black eyebrows. His longtime girlfriend, Zoe Caldwell, was killed by the monster Ngaa, and he has never loved anyone else.

Comment: Lord is a house name for a variety of authors. Pinnacle Books picked up the line after Macfadden-Bartell went out of business and reprinted them all. In order of publication from 1969–1973, subsequent titles in the series are *The Jade Warrior, Jewel of Tharn, Slave of Sarma, Liberator of Jedd, Monster of the Maze, Pearl of Patmos, Undying World, Kingdom of Royth, Ice Dragon, Dimension of Dreams, King of Zunga, The Golden Steed, The Temples of Ayocan, The Towers of Melnon, The Crystal Seas, The Mountains of Brega, Warlords of Gaikon, Looters of Tharn, Guardians of the Coral Throne, Champion of the Gods, The Forests of Gleor, Empire of Blood, The Dragons of Englor, The Torian Pearls, City of the Living Dead, Master of Hashomi, Wizard of Rentoro, Treasure of the Stars, Dimension of Horror, Gladiators of Hapanu, Pirates of Gohar,* and *Killer Plants of Binaark.*

RICHARD DIAMOND   (R, TV)

First Appearance: *Richard Diamond, Private Detective,* 1949, NBC.

Biography: Richard Diamond is a New York police officer who leaves the force to become a private detective. With the help of his devoted ex-superior, Lieutenant Levinson, he is able to get information that would otherwise be inaccessible. Diamond's cases involve everything from homicide to messy divorces.

Comment: Dick Powell played Diamond on the radio series; Ed Begley was Levinson. The series ended in 1952 and moved to TV in July 1957, produced by Powell's own Four Star Productions. By that time, Powell felt he was too old to play the part and hired David Janssen as Diamond. In 1957–58, the show remained fairly faithful to its radio roots, with Lieutenant McGough (Regis Toomey) as Diamond's police contact/aide. But the producers felt a move to Hollywood would give Diamond some sex appeal, so he moved west, befriended Lieutenant Kile (Russ Conway), got a girlfriend named Karen Wells (Barbara Bain), and acquired a telephone answering service, whose sexy employee Sam frequently reached him on his car phone. Sam's legs were all that viewers ever got to see; she was played by Mary Tyler Moore for four months (February–May 1959), after which Roxanne Brooks filled her shoes.

The half-hour series went off the air in September 1960 and was syndicated under the title *Call Mr. D.*

RICHARD DRAGON   (C)

First Appearance: *Richard Dragon, Kung-Fu Fighter* #1, 1975, DC Comics.

Biography: Early in the 1960s, thief Richard Dragon was in Kyoto, Japan, to steal a jade Buddha. Caught by an old man, the O-Sensei, and his young, black martial arts student, Benjamin Turner, Dragon believes the O-Sensei's claim that he can become an important force for good. Dragon remains with these men and learns martial arts while building a strong moral code. When their studies are done, the two students open a martial arts school in New York City.

Shortly thereafter, the men are approached by Barney Ling, of the secret organization G.O.O.D., whom they help stop crooked industrialist Guano Cravat from plunging the world into war. The two like the hero business and continue to make themselves available to anyone in need; they are later joined in their exploits by the Kung-Fu master Lady Shiva. Ben is ultimately brainwashed by the evil Professor Ojo and becomes the criminal Bronze Tiger, whom Dragon bests and places in rehabilitation.

Dragon's sole weapon, besides his body, is the Dragon's Claw, a jade amulet that helps him (mystically, it seems) marshal his strength and energy.

Comment: There were 18 issues of Richard Dragon's comic book.

RICHARD SEATON (L)

First Appearance: *The Skylark of Space* by E.E. Smith, Aug–Oct. 1928, *Amazing Stories* magazine.

Biography: Richard Ballinger Seaton was raised in northern Idaho, the son of widower backwoodsman "Big Fred" Seaton. An avid reader and athlete, Seaton earns his Ph.D. as a "physical chemist" and goes to work for the Rare Metals Laboratory in Washington, D.C. There he discovers an antigravity material, Metal X, and sets up a corporation with multimillionaire friend Martin Reynolds Crane. Together they undertake the construction of a spaceship, the *Skylark.*

Meanwhile, jealous scientist Dr. Marc C. "Blackie" DuQuesne steals Richard's plans; builds his own ship, abducts Seaton's girlfriend, Dorothy Vaneman, and a secretary named Margaret Spencer; and takes off for space. Two days pass before Seaton and Crane can take off after them. DuQuesne's ship malfunctions and he, Dorothy, and Margaret (who becomes Crane's ladyfriend) are taken aboard the *Skylark.* Low on copper, which is the source of their power, Seaton's ship searches for it from "one solar system after another" until they reach an earthlike planet, encounter a shape-changing alien, and depart in terror. Upon reaching the world of Osnome with "seventeen great suns," they become involved in a war between the alien races before they're able to return to Earth on a redesigned *Skylark Two.*

Though Seaton warns DuQuesne, "I'll kill you like I would a snake" if he ever bothers the four of them again, he remains their nemesis on future adventures, which involve using the new *Skylark Three* to prevent the destruction of Earth by the Fenachrone (and to keep a new weapon out of the hands of DuQuesne), boarding the new *Skylark* of Valeron to battle disembodied four-dimensional beings, and ultimately teaming with DuQuesne to protect Earth from destruction.

Seaton stands "well over six feet" and stays in shape by "playing tennis, swimming and motorcycling." Eventually he and Dorothy marry and become the parents of Richard Junior.

Comment: The serialized story was revised and published in book form in 1946. Subsequent novels in the series are *Skylark Three* (1948), *Skylark of Valeron* (1949), and *Skylark DuQuesne* (1966). Smith wrote many important science fiction novels and series, which remain in print and continue to sell.

RICK O'SHAY (CS)

First Appearance: *Rick O'Shay,* April 27, 1958, Chicago Tribune-New York News Syndicate.

Biography: Young, clean-cut Rick O'Shay is a friend of the powerful gangster Deuces Wilde; when Deuces becomes mayor of the western town of Conniption, he appoints Rick as his "puppet" marshal. But, like Thomas à Becket, Rick takes the job seriously and maintains the law and order (with an occasional assist from General DeBillity's Fort Chaos).

As one might expect, Conniption is inhabited by a lively bunch of people, including the gunslinger Hipshot Percussion, who later becomes Rick's partner, and Horse's Neck of the Kyute Indians. Rick's girlfriend is saloon entertainer Gaye Abandon.

The strip was originally set in modern times, with Conniption as a ghost town; after 13 years, the strip was relocated to the 1890s.

Comment: Stan Lynde created the strip, which ran until 1977. He also created new adventures for book publication in 1992: *The New Adventures of Rick O'Shay and Hipshot.*

RIP HUNTER (C)

First Appearance: *Showcase* #20, 1959, DC Comics.

Biography: As a college student, Rip Hunter and his friend Jeff Smith devise a method of time travel and begin building the Time Sphere. By the time they finish it, they've earned their doctorate degrees and take on time-traveling partners: historian Bonnie Baxter—who quickly falls in love with Rip, despite the fact that he's "as romantic as a sack of potatoes"—and Corky, her little brother. The time travelers are based in a "secret mountain laboratory" (to make sure the Time Sphere doesn't fall into the wrong hands), and their services are free to any scholar who needs research done in the past or future. Occasionally they will take a scientist with them, such as Rip's old teacher Professor Hale.

Onboard the incredible sphere are "speech translation discs" that allow them to talk with people of any era and the Encyclo-matic, a computer full of historical data. The Sphere can fly like a helicopter, and, in case Rip is ever in danger, a small transmitter in his belt allows him to summon the Time Sphere via morse code. The time travelers wear green uniforms with red cuffs, collars, shoulders, boots, and belts.

More recently, Rip has teamed with the superheroes Animal Man, Dolphin, Congorilla, and Immortal Man, and the nonsuper, semiretired Rick Flagg (see SUICIDE SQUAD), CAVE CARSON, and Dane Dorrance (see

Rip Hunter, about to be turned into a robot, as a horrified Bonnie looks on. A quick SOS to the Time Sphere saves the day. © DC Comics.

SEA DEVILS) as the Forgotten Heroes, with whom he has had several adventures.

Comment: Rip and company appeared in four issues of *Showcase* before getting their own magazine; *Rip Hunter . . . Time Master* lasted 29 issues. The Forgotten Heroes first appeared in *Action Comics* #552 in 1985.

RIP KIRBY (CS, C)

First Appearance: *Rip Kirby,* March 4, 1946, King Features Syndicate.

Biography: A former Marine Corps major, Rip Kirby is a master criminologist who takes on seemingly routine cases—solve a theft, locate a missing person, uncover a blackmailer—which usually turn out to be more complex and seedier than they seemed at first. Though he will use fists or guns if he has to, he prefers to settle cases through nonviolent means. His assistant

is former thief Desmond; his girlfriends are blond model Honey Dorian and dark-haired Pagan Lee.

Kirby is a cultured but not effete man who wears glasses, is never without his pipe, and enjoys chess, golf, French brandy, and playing the piano. He stays in shape by boxing, though his cases often require him to climb ropes and run after foes.

Comment: The character was created by King Features editor Ward Greene and by legendary artist Alex Raymond. Upon his untimely death in 1956, the strip was taken over by John Prentice. Rip was also a backup feature in numerous comic books over the years.

ROB THE ROVER (CS)

First Appearance: *Rob the Rover,* May 1929, *Puck* (Great Britain).

Biography: Young Rob is found floating in the ocean by old Dan the Fisherman, who nurses him to health and becomes his close friend. Rob remembers little about his past, and begins a globe-girdling search to find out who he is and what he was doing in the sea. He journeys to a desert island, to the North Pole, to the jungle, to the Valley of the Kings, to India, and elsewhere; eventually he links up with Professor Seymour, with whom he travels about on the subplane *Flying Fish.* Rob's girlfriend in these later adventures is the brave Joan.

Comment: *Rob the Rover* was created by Walter Booth and was the first action comic strip in England. He continued in *Puck* until the nearly 36-year-old title was shut down in May 1940; he spent two weeks in *Sunbeam* before that title also folded.

ROCKET ROBIN HOOD (TV)

First Appearance: *Rocket Robin Hood and His Merry Spacemen,* September 1967, syndicated.

Biography: It's the year A.D. 3000 and, stationed on Sherwood Asteroid, the interplanetary peacekeeper Rocket Robin Hood rockets forth with the Merry Spacemen—Little John, Will Scarlet, Friar Tuck, Alan, and Jiles—to fight the wicked Sheriff of N.O.T.T. Other foes include robots, magicians, dinosaurs, and evil scientists.

Comment: There were 149 ten-minute animated episodes in all.

ROCKY JONES (TV, MP, C)

First Appearance: *Rocky Jones, Space Ranger,* February 1954, NBC.

Biography: The captain of the 21st century Space Rangers, Rocky Jones lives in an era when "each world does its share for the benefit of all." Garbed in a tight flight jacket, T-shirt, and baseball-style cap, Rocky pilots the pencil-thin *Orbit Jet,* keeping peace among the stars and battling natural disasters (such as the "atmosphere chain" between two gypsy moons that threatens to destroy space station OW 9). He is assisted by his copilot Winky, cadet Bobby, girlfriend Vena Ray, and Professor Newton—most of whom spend time on the space station, exchanging banter with Rocky or the numerous transport ship crews that dock there.

Comment: There were just 39 episodes of the half-hour series, though many of these were edited into a number of feature films released in various regions of the country in 1955–1956: *Beyond the Moon, Blast Off, The Cold Sun, Crash of Moons, Duel in Space, Forbidden Moon, Gypsy Moon, Inferno from Space, Magnetic Moon, Manhunt in Space, Menace from Outer Space, Out of This World, Robot of Regalio,* and *Silver Needle in the Sky.* Richard Crane was Rocky, Scotty Becket was Winky, Robert Lydon was Bobby, Sally Mansfield played Vena, and Maurice Cass was Newton.

The character starred in Charlton Comics *Space Adventures* #15–#18, 1955–56.

ROCKY KING   (TV)

First Appearance: *Rocky King, Inside Detective,* January 1950, DuMont Network.

Biography: A determined, unassuming detective on the New York City Homicide Squad, Rocky works diligently to uncover clues. He works closely with Sergeant Lane at the 24th Precinct; in later years, Rocky King has a younger, less jaded associate, Detective Hart.

Rocky is married to Mabel; they have a son, Junior.

Comment: The half-hour series aired through December, 1954 on the short-lived DuMont network. It was the first of the realistic police dramas. Had the series appeared on NBC or CBS, which had more affiliates—its life would have been considerably longer. Roscoe Karns starred as King, Grace Carney was Mabel, Earl Hammond played Lane, and Todd Karns (Roscoe's son) was Hart.

Neither Mabel nor Junior was ever seen on-camera. This started out as an economy measure (whatever actress was appearing on the show that week could be the voice of Mabel). Audiences enjoyed it, however, and even after Mabel got a permanent voice, she remained unseen. Conversations with Mabel over the dinner table or phone typically provided the hook for exposition.

ROD BROWN   (TV)

First Appearance: *Rod Brown of the Rocket Rangers,* April 1953, CBS.

Biography: Rod Brown is a Senior Ranger in the Rocket Rangers, an interplantary defense force of the 22nd century. Rod and his fellow rangers, Frank Boyle and Adjutant Wilbur "Wormsey" Wormser, fly through the galaxy on the *Beta,* exploring the surface of Venus or preventing Planet H from destroying the earth. Back at Omega Base, Brown reports to Commander Swift.

Comment: The Saturday morning series was broadcast live from New York and lasted until May 1954. It helped to launch some distinguished careers: Cliff Robertson starred as Rod Brown, Jack Weston was Wilbur, the series was produced by William Dozier (who went on to produce TV's *Batman*), and the floor manager was future director John Frankenheimer *(The Manchurian Candidate).* Bruce Hall was Boyle and John Boruff was Swift.

ROD CRAIG   (CS, R)

First Appearance: *Rod Craig,* November 1946, *Melbourne Herald* (Australia).

Biography: In his early years, burly Australian Rod Craig runs a charter boat throughout the Pacific islands. Later, however, he becomes more and more involved in mysteries set on the land and sea involving escaped Nazis, smugglers, kidnapers, revolutionaries, and the like. His assistant, for a while, is Cal Rourke, who is later replaced by ex-circus strongman Geelong. Craig's girlfriend is the lovely Leeanna (later, just Anna); Geelong's girlfriend is Lacey, who works for the wicked nightclub owner Cherub Bim.

Craig's most nefarious continuing foe is Carlina, a seductive villainess who is into any illegal activity that will turn a profit. He also battles regularly with Head, the dwarf who runs the One World Government group.

Comment: The strip was created by Syd Miller and, within months of its initial appearance, was being syndicated worldwide by the Herald and Weekly Times Ltd. It ran until November 1955 and spawned a short-lived radio show during the early 1950s.

ROJ BLAKE   (TV, C, L)

First Appearance: *Blake's 7,* January 1978, BBC.

Biography: In the aftermath of galaxywide nuclear wars, the evil Terran Federation becomes the foremost power in the known universe. Revolution is ruthlessly crushed, and rebels are brainwashed, imprisoned, or killed. In the third century of the second calendar (some 900 years from now), Roj Blake, an Alpha Grade engineer, becomes the leader of the outlawed Freedom Party, which is hunted down and destroyed by Space Commander Travis. Blake is captured, tried, and brainwashed. However, he is sought out by his former cronies and breaks through the reprogramming, only to be arrested once more. Placed on the spaceship *London,* he is sent to the prison world Cygnus Alpha. However, en route, Blake along with prisoners Kerr Avon (a computer expert) and Jenna Stannis (a crack pilot) are sent to investigate an abandoned spaceship, the *Liberator,* which they manage to steal by communicating with the master computer, Zen. After declaring war on the Federation and constantly bedeviling the Pursuit Ships sent to apprehend them—in particular, Travis—Blake and his crewmates are soon joined by the Auron guerilla and telepath Cally and by former prisoners Gan, a native of Zephron, and Vila Restal, a lockpicker, rounding out the original seven.

Gan is the first to die in battle, killed by Travis; Jenna loses her life running a blockade; and Cally perishes in an explosion. New members of the rebel crew include Dayna Mellanby, daughter of rebel leader Hal Mellanby of Sarran, and Del Tarrant, a Federation officer who defects.

Blake himself perishes in the final episode, apparently having given up the fight to become a ruthless bounty hunter. Fortunately, though, the onetime hero had been duplicated by Clonemaster Fen, and his other self is living with the former slave woman Rashel on an unnamed world, implicitly ready to lead the anti-Federation forces. (A second clone is also rumored to exist.)

Comment: The series was created by Terry Nation, 52 episodes airing on the BBC through December 1981. Gareth Thomas played Blake, Paul Darrow was Avon, Sally Knyvette was Jenna, Peter Tuddenham was Zen, Jan Chappell played Cally, David Jackson was Gan, Michael Keating played Vila, Josette Simon was Dayna, and Steven Pacey played Tarrant.

Three novels were written by Trevor Hoyle and published in England in 1979–1980: *Blake's 7, Project Avalon,* and *Scorpio Attack.*

Marvel Comics published a *Blake's 7* monthly magazine in England beginning in 1981, which featured articles as well as eight-page comic book and short stories featuring the characters.

THE ROOK (C)

First Appearance: *Eerie* #82, 1977, Warren Publishing.

Biography: A technophysicist, Restin Dane is the son of a career diplomat who was slain while posted in Cambodia. Restin lives in a secluded fortresslike estate in the desert outside of Cottonwood, Arizona. Inspired by the exploits of his paternal grandfather, Adam Dane—who invented a time machine and went into the future (inspiring his friend H.G. Wells to write his famous novel)—Restin constantly "experiments with . . . physics, computers, and advanced robotronics." Helped by other specialists as well as by his A-Series Compurob, Manners, and the robots Nuts and Bolts, he creates his own time machine in the shape of a chess piece—the Time Castle—and, as the Rook, uses it to travel through time to meet his ancestors. First stop: the Alamo, to try to rescue his great-great-great-grandfather, Parrish Dane. Restin fails but is able to save his great-great-grandfather, Bishop Dane, who is just a boy. They go their separate ways but meet again in 1874. Bishop comes to the present with Restin, after which they enjoy many time-traveling adventures. That year Restin and Bishop also meet their respective inamoratas, Kate McCall and January Boone, prostitutes who join them in the present.

In one adventure, Rook finds his grandfather stranded in the future described by H.G. Wells, and reunites him with his wife, Louise. In another, Kate goes back to 1874 and meets Castle Dane, Bishop's son

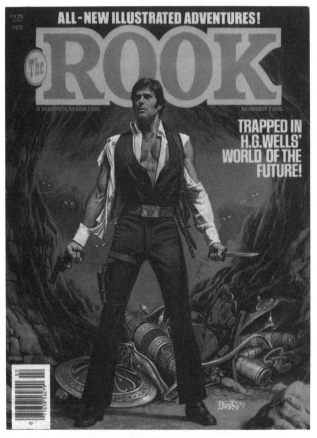

The Rook, interpreted by Bob Larkin. © Warren Publishing.

by Amelia Dane. She falls in love with him and becomes the mother of Adam Dane. In still another tale, we learn that in the early 21st century, Restin—by then a senator from Arizona—will fight and overthrow war hero Alexander Martinson Tavyl, who has become president, then dictator, of the United Nation-States. Battling at Restin's side will be his 19-year-old future-daughter Coral and his young ward William Dane.

Comment: The well-developed characters were created by writers Bill DuBay and Budd Lewis. After running in *Eerie* until issue #105, several adventures were reprinted in *Warren Presents* #2, and then the character was given its own magazine, *The Rook*, which lasted 14 issues. He returned to *Eerie* in #132 (with a tale inevitably titled "The Dane Curse"), though for just two more adventures.

DuBay also created and wrote *Time Force*, which appeared in the first issue of Pacific Comics *Bold Adventure* in 1983, chronicling the adventures of young men who attempted to save humankind from oblivion.

THE ROVER BOYS (L)

First Appearance: *The Rover Boys at School; or, The Cadets of Putnam Hall* by Arthur M. Winfield, 1899, Mershon.

Biography: The Rover Boys were brothers Dick, Tom, and Sam, cadets at Putnam Hall, a military school—and later, students at Brill College in the Midwest. These "lively, wide-awake American Boys" get into sundry adventures during vacation, ending up out west, on the Great Lakes, in the mountains, on the farm, in New York, in Alaska, or even in the jungle. With them on many of these adventures are their respective girlfriends, Dora Stanhope and Grace and Nellie Laning, and their good friends John "Songbird" Powell and William Philander Tubbs. In time, the boys graduate, wed their ladies, settle down as neighbors on Riverside Drive in New York City, open a business—the Rover Company—and allow their children to carry on the tradition of adventuring.

Comment: The characters were actually created by Edward L. Stratemeyer, who wrote the early stories himself. Nineteen novels in the series were published through 1916, ending with *The Rover Boys on a Tour; or, Last Days at Brill College.* Another ten novels were published in the Second Rover Boys Series for Young Americans, beginning with *The Rover Boys at Colby Hall; or, The Struggles of the Young Cadets* in 1917 and concluding with *The Rover Boys Winning a Fortune; or, Strenuous Days Afloat and Ashore* in 1926. From 1901 to 1911, "Winfield" also wrote six novels about other cadets at Putnam Hall.

In addition to *The Bobbsey Twins,* BOMBA, THE HARDY BOYS, NANCY DREW, and TOM SWIFT, the Stratemeyer Syndicate created many series for young readers, including several others with an adventure slant. These included the Dave Porter series, 15 novels published between 1905 and 1919 following the growth of a schoolboy through his service in France as an army engineer during the world war; the six Lakeport novels, published between 1908 and 1912, about different boys and their adventures in one town; and the four-novel Boy Hunters series published between 1906 and 1910. Other Stratemeyer series included the Motor Boys, the Radio Boys, Ralph of the Railroad, the Motion Picture Boys, and the Moving Picture Girls.

ROWDY YATES   (TV, C, L)

First Appearance: *Rawhide,* January 1959, CBS.

Biography: It's 1866. The Civil War is over, beef is scarce, and the nation is starving. To Gil Favor, trail boss, and his number-two man, Rowdy Yates, nothing matters more than getting the cattle from North Texas to Sedalia, Kansas. If Indians demand cattle as payment for passing through their land, the men will give them cattle—then steal them back in the night. If Favor is too hard on his men (as he is at one point) and they abandon him, he'll continue on alone.

Yates eventually breaks off and becomes boss of his own drive, assisted by Simon Blake. Other members of the drive include Wishbone, the cook, and scout Pete Nolan.

Comment: The hour-long series aired through January 1966. Clint Eastwood starred as Rowdy, Eric Fleming was Gil, Paul Brinegar was Wishbone, and Sheb Wooley was Pete. Raymond St. Jacques played Blake, the first black actor to costar in a western.

Dell published seven issues of a *Rawhide* comic book from 1959 to 1962, and Gold Key published two from 1963 to 1964.

Frank C. Robertson wrote a *Rawhide* novel in 1960.

RURIK   (C)

First Appearance: *Spitfire Comics* #1, 1941, Harvey Comics.

Biography: Rurik is a young Danish king who travels the North Atlantic in search of adventure onboard his black, serpent-headed vessel. In his second adventure, he journeys to the Antarctic, where he discovers a hidden kingdom and restores the rightful king to the throne. The brown-tressed Rurik wears a yellow tunic and a fur cape. His faithful, fumbling sidekick is Relth.

Comment: The hero appeared in both issues of *Spit-

fire Comics. The comic was also the home of Gary Morgan, foreign correspondent, who travels the world with his assistant Miss Watson; and the Buckskin Boys, two preteens who fight in America on behalf of the Revolutionary cause.

RUSTAM (F)

First Appearance: Persian folklore, circa A.D. 700 (see COMMENT).

Biography: Rustam is the son of the heaven-blessed Zal and the noble Rudabeh. He was born in an unusual manner: Instructed by a simurgh (an all-knowing bird), attendants open Rudabeh's side and draw the child through the incision. The child, Rustam, was an able horseman by three, ate man-size portions at five, and was the strongest warrior in the land by eight. He once slew a rampaging elephant with a single blow, captured and tamed the demonic foal Rakush (who became his mount), and on several occasions bested his lifelong rival Afrasiyab, the Prince of Turan.

His most famous exploit concerns the theft of his horse. He follows it to the small kingdom of Samengan, where he meets the beautiful Tahmineh, daughter of the ruler. She confesses that she had Rakush stolen so that she might bear Rustam's child. The two are soon wed, and Rustam stays but one night. A son, Sohrab, is born from the union. Fearing that her husband will want the boy sent to him, Tahmineh informs him that she has given birth to a daughter. Rakush had mated that night too, and the horse born from the union becomes Sohrab's mount. When he is a young man, Sohrab rides forth and encounters Afrasiyab, who knows the boy's true identity—though Sohrab does not. The prince convinces the young warrior to ride with him against Rustam, and word of his valor soon reaches his father. The two meet in single, mounted combat, a confrontation so fierce that their spears, swords, clubs, and bows and arrows are shattered in turn. They wrestle for a while, then break until the morrow.

The next day they wrestle again, Sohrab getting the better of Rustam but allowing him to live; on the third day, after a night of prayer, Rustam is victorious. He shows Sohrab no quarter, stabbing him in the side; as he lays dying, Sohrab tells the victor his name—and Rustam realizes who he is. The horrified warrior tries to kill himself, though Sohrab prevents it. Rustam places his son's remains on a bier, wanting to cut off his own hands and live out his life in darkness. But he lives for the sake of his people and goes on to defeat the treacherous Afrasiyab.

Comment: The poet Firdausi is credited with having written down early tales of Rustam in the seventh century, though the stories are much older than that, perhaps going back as far as the seventh century B.C.

RUSTY RILEY (CS)

First Appearance: *Rusty Riley*, January 1948, King Features Syndicate.

Biography: At the age of 13, Rusty Riley and his fox terrier, Flip, run away from the orphanage where the boy has lived since his parents were killed in an accident. Stopping at the spread of millionaire Mr. Miles, who breeds racehorses, Rusty catches sight of the animals and talks the stable managers into hiring him as a stable boy. Eventually he becomes a jockey and in one adventure wins the Kentucky Derby astride Bright Blaze.

When he isn't riding or romancing Miles's daughter Patti, Rusty (and Patti) are busy solving crimes, sniffing out gamblers and mobsters at the track, and finding missing horses. In one early adventure, he has to find out who's really killing the sheep on neighbor Woolly Smith's farm before local authorities destroy Flip.

Comment: The strip was created by the superlative Frank Godwin, who drew the adventures; Rod Reed and Frank's brother Harold wrote the scripts. *Rusty Riley* lasted until July 1959.

S

SABRE (C)

First Appearance: *Eclipse Graphic Album Series* #1, 1978, Eclipse Enterprises.

Biography: The year is A.D. 2020, and the world is in chaos. There's severe famine, an energy crisis, and a plague that leaked from a top secret laboratory. People carry laser pistols for protection. The U.S. government rules from a fortress, and rebellion is rampant—though the military is quick to put it down. Yet some people don't believe that the government has the right answers. One of these is Sabre, a black man and "a romantic idealist [who] is dedicated to evading and outwitting the power mandates of 2020." Armed with a knife, pistol, sword, and lightning reflexes, he and his companion, test-tube-born Melissa Siren, alternately look for peace and quiet, and help the rebels of the future try to set things right again.

Comment: Sabre got his own comic book in 1982, and it lasted 14 issues. The character was created by writer Don McGregor.

SADR AL-DIN MORALES (C)

First Appearance: *Shatter Special* #1, 1985, First Comics.

Biography: It's the middle of the 21st century. Puerto Rico and Hong Kong are U.S. states, and there's a move afoot to make Vietnam the 53rd. Daley City is fraught with crime, especially terrorism. Sadr al-din Morales—also known as Shatter—is a "temp" who works whatever difficult job comes his way, whether it's working as a police officer in a voice-activated flying car or as a bounty hunter.

Sadr lives in a modest apartment, typically wears a white shirt and trousers and black vest, and carries a variety of firearms. He got his name when his parents tried "to cosy up to their Arab employer."

Comment: After the *Special,* the character was seen as a backup feature in *Jon Sable, Freelance* numbers 25 to 30. His own magazine, *Shatter,* debuted in December 1985; 14 issues were published through 1988.

The character was created by writer Peter B. Gillis and artist Michael Saenz, who drew the comic book on an Apple Macintosh computer—a comics first.

THE SAINT (L, MP, R, C, TV)

First Appearance: *Meet the Tiger* by Leslie Charteris, 1928.

Biography: Simon Templar is a young man who becomes bored with the "miserable little mildewed things" that people busy themselves with—himself included—and decides to become an adventurer, living a life in which he can experience "battle, murder, sudden death," and women. Though he occasionally works outside the law, his aim is always to right wrongs and help the downtrodden—hence his nickname, the Saint (inspired by his initials, ST). Whether he is dealing with friend or foe, he invariably leaves behind his *carte de visite,* on which appears a stick figure with a halo above it.

When he lives in London, Templar occasionally helps (and more often thwarts) Scotland Yard's Chief Inspector Claud Eustace Teal; when Templar moves to New York, Inspector John Fernack is his occasional nemesis. Templar's girlfriend and occasional associate is Patricia Holm.

The Saint is a slender six foot two, with broad shoulders and blue eyes. His dark hair is slick and smooth, his skin well tanned, and he dresses expensively and immaculately. He is an expert at hand-to-hand combat, horseback riding, knife-throwing, fencing, and is also a pilot.

Comment: The Saint starred in 17 novels, 44 novelettes, and dozens of short stories.

There were nine films featuring the Saint: *The Saint in New York* (1938) starring Louis Hayward, *The Saint Strikes Back* (1939), *The Saint in London* (1939), *The Saint's Double Trouble* (1940), *The Saint Takes Over* (1940), and *The Saint in Palm Springs* (1941), all starring George Sanders (he departed to play THE FALCON); *The Saint's Vacation* (1941) and *The Saint Meets the Tiger* (1943), both starring Hugh Sinclair;

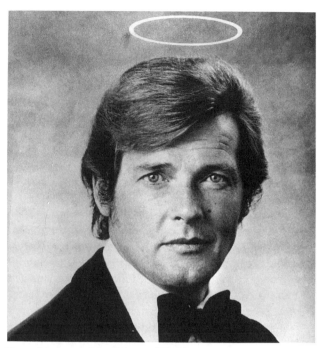

Roger Moore as *The Saint*. © ITC Entertainment.

and *The Saint's Girl Friday* (1954), which brought back Hayward.

On radio, *The Saint* debuted on NBC in 1944 and ran until the end of the decade. Templar was played, in turn, by Edgar Barrier, Brian Aherne, Vincent Price, Tom Conway, and Barry Sullivan.

In comics, the character has guest-starred in a handful of titles, but had his most significant run in his own magazine, which was published by Avon. Twelve issues appeared from 1947 to 1952.

The character is best known due to three TV series. The first hour-long show starred Roger Moore and aired from May 1967 to September 1969 on NBC. The second featured Ian Ogilvy, who starred in *The Return of the Saint* on CBS in 1978. The third starred Simon Dutton in a series of movie-length programs that aired during 1989–90.

SAM MCCLOUD (TV)

First Appearance: *McCloud: Who Killed Miss U.S.A.?* February 1970, ABC.

Biography: A deputy marshal from Taos, New Mexico, Sam McCloud heads to New York on the trail of a criminal—and, after nabbing him, remains in New York, assigned to the 27th Precinct, reporting to Chief Peter B. Clifford. Though McCloud is supposed to be learning big-city police methods, he invariably captures crooks his own way. His regular (and reluctant) partner on the force is Sergeant Joe Broadhurst.

McCloud is never without his walnut-handled six-shooter and his big Texas cowboy hat. His girlfriend is Chris Coughlin, a writer who is working on a book about the criminal who first brought McCloud to New York.

Comment: The pilot film spawned a series that, for the first season, rotated with four other series as part of *Four-In-One: The Psychiatrist, San Francisco International Airport,* and *Night Gallery.* The hour-long series starred Dennis Weaver as McCloud, J.D. Cannon as Clifford (Mark Richman played the part in the original TV movie), Terry Carter as Broadhurst, and Diana Muldaur as Chris. The second season, it joined the *NBC Sunday Mystery Movie* lineup, alternating with *Columbo* and *McMillan and Wife.* (See LT. COLUMBO and COMMISSIONER STEWART MCMILLAN.) It ended in August 1977. In the 1989 TV movie *The Return of Sam McCloud,* he's no longer a crimefighter by profession, but a U.S. senator who chases down a drug dealer in Europe.

The series was inspired (albeit, uncredited) by the 1968 Clint Eastwood film *Coogan's Bluff,* in which a lawman goes from Arizona to New York on the trail of a fugitive.

Weaver also starred as Detective Sergeant Daniel Stone in the short-lived police drama *Stone,* which aired on ABC from January to March 1980.

SAM SLADE (C)

First Appearance: *2000 A.D.,* August 1978, IPC Magazines.

Biography: Sam Slade is a denizen of future Earth, which he calls the "over-crowded cesspool of the galaxy." For 40 years, since 2100, he's made his living as a Robo-Hunter, tracking down and destroying rogue robots. When necessary, he also travels to other worlds to fight robots there. His motto is "When they get Slade, they stay Slade."

Slade packs a blaster that fires destructive bolts or limpets—pellets that send a 1,000-volt charge into a robot's neural banks, causing it pain. Slade can convert the blaster to a blowtorch to lobotomize renegade robots and turn them in to the government for bounty. Slade's companions are his robot aides Hoagy the cigar-shaped, Spanish-speaking stogie; robot house detective Hoskins; and his holsterlike robo-meter that warns him when a robot is near and determines what kind it is. At his office, the B.S.C. (Building Surveillance Computer) Carlton takes messages for him.

Slade has a suite in the Savoy Hotel, wears a baseball cap, boots, a T-shirt, and a vest loaded with projectiles, and smokes cigars.

Comment: The character's success in the weekly *2000 A.D.* also spawned a six-issue run in his own Eagle Comics title in 1984, followed by a nineteen issue run under the Quality Comics banner. The bulk of the character's adventures have been exquisitely drawn by Ian Gibson.

See also *Magnus, Robot Fighter.*

SAM SPADE (L, MP, R)

First Appearance: *The Maltese Falcon* by Dashiel Hammett, 1929, *Black Mask* Magazine.

Biography: Based in San Francisco, Samuel Spade agrees to take a case from gorgeous redhead Brigid O'Shaughnessy, and immediately thereafter his partner Miles Archer is murdered. Despite the fact that the two didn't get along (indeed, Spade was having an affair with Mrs. Archer), he feels obliged to hunt down Archer's killer. In the course of his quest, he encounters Brigid's boss, Fat Man Casper Gutman, and his odd assortment of coworkers—all of them looking for a black statue worth nearly $2 million.

Though Spade breaks the law on occasion, he does so in order to apprehend criminals. Fearless and single-minded when on a caper, he is equally undaunted by stunning women and guns pointed in his direction. He is on a first-name basis with most of the city's lawmen—and criminals.

Spade stands six feet tall, has rounded shoulders, a long and bony jaw, yellow-gray eyes, pale brown hair, a hooked nose, and a V-shaped mouth. He looks "rather pleasantly like a blond satan." His secretary ("sweetheart") is Effie Perine and his license number, for the record, is 137596.

Comment: The *Black Mask* serial was published in hardcover the following year and became a huge best-seller. Three other Spade tales were collected in *The Adventures of Sam Spade and Other Stories* (1944). Hammett has described his sleuth as "What most of the private detectives I've worked with would *like* to have been . . . able to take care of himself in any situation."

In the movies, Spade was played by Ricardo Cortez in the first version of *The Maltese Falcon* (1931), directed by Roy Del Ruth. In *Satan Met a Lady* (1936), Spade (called Ted Shayne) was played by Warren William. The most famous Spade, however, was Humphrey Bogart, who starred in the second, definitive *The Maltese Falcon* (1941), directed by John Huston. (It is also, without question, the definitive "hard-boiled" detective film.) Sydney Greenstreet was equally memorable as the Fat Man.

On the radio, Howard Duff, then Steve Dunne, played Spade on the CBS series that debuted in 1946.

It moved to ABC, then NBC, and after five years was replaced by the short-lived *Charlie Wild, Private Eye,* a result of Hammett's publicized Marxist leanings. (Both shows were sponsored by Wildroot Creme Oil, whose slogan was "Get Wildroot Creme Oil, Charlie"—hence, the sleuth's name.)

See also THE CONTINENTAL OP; NICK AND NORA CHARLES.

SARGE STEEL (C)

First Appearance: *Sarge Steel* #1, 1964, Charlton Comics.

Biography: The earliest record of Sargent Steel is when he's serving as a captain in the Special Forces in Vietnam. Thanks to his efforts, Communist agent Ivan Chong is imprisoned; through operatives, Chong has a hand grenade rigged to explode when Steel uses it. The blast costs Steel his left hand, which is replaced by a steel fist. Upon returning to the States, Steel becomes a hardbitten private eye, assisted by secretary Bess Forbes and tooling around in a sports car, license S1S. After several years working on private and government cases—fighting saboteurs and would-be dictators at the behest of the FBI and CIA—Steel closes down his shop and goes to work for an unspecified branch of government intelligence.

Sarge is a judo master and packs a Luger. Though he can't use his steel fingers in the traditional way, the fist proves useful breaking through walls, blocking sword thrusts, and felling enemies.

Comment: Editor/artist Dick Giordano created the character, whose stories were told in the first person. *Sarge Steel* lasted for ten issues, the last two of which

Sarge Steel imprisoned—but not for long! © Charlton Comics.

were called *Secret Agent.* After that, he appeared several times as a backup feature in the *Judomaster* comic book, beginning with #91.

Acquired by DC Comics, he became a CIA official, whose assistant is Fenwick and whose operatives include KING FARADAY.

SAVAGE (C)

First Appearance: *His Name Is . . . Savage,* 1968, Adventure House Press.

Biography: During World War II, teenage Savage compiles "an impressive combat record" as part of a special assault group lead by Brigadier General Simon Mace. After the war, Mace forms a crack mercenary force that works for the highest bidder, with Savage as an important member. Savage even falls in love with Mace's daughter Sheila—though Mace's increasing monomania eventually puts him at odds with his protege. Ultimately, Savage is forced to flee from the ruthless Mace, whom he disfigures with a hand grenade. Half man, half metal, Mace continues to lead the force while Savage goes to work for the Committee, a clandestine government group responsible for "high-level espionage." On at least one occasion, Savage has assassinated an unnamed world figure and been sentenced to death, only to be saved by "friends in high places."

In his first and only chronicled adventure, Savage must stop Mace's group from assassinating the President of the United States. Savage's weapons and tools include a .357 Magnum and a portable grapple.

Comment: Artist Gil Kane created the character in

Savage attacks a bogus Lyndon Johnson. © Gil Kane.

order to do something hard-edged away from the jurisdiction of the repressive Comics Code Authority. There was only one issue of the black-and-white title, which was reprinted by Fantagraphics Books in 1982. The adventure was written by Archie Goodwin.

THE SCALPHUNTER (C)

First Appearance: *Weird Western Tales* #39, 1977, DC Comics.

Biography: In 1839, in the Missouri hills, the ranch of Matthew and Laurie Savage is attacked by Kiowa Indians. They kill Laurie, leave Matthew for dead, and abduct their son, Brian, who is taken in by the tribe, given the name Ke-Woh-No-Tay ("He Who is Less Than Human"), and becomes a brave. In 1862, after a battle, he's captured by soldiers and taken to Fort Caroline, where Dr. Samuel Grey recognizes a star-shaped birthmark on the back of his neck. The soldiers take the young man to Matthew, who survived the Indian attack and has built "the biggest horse and cattle ranch west of the Pecos." (Doubtless, author Michael Fleisher meant "east.") Brian refuses to have anything to do with his father; but Brian realizes he isn't a Kiowa either and becomes an outcast. Matthew dies shortly thereafter of tuberculosis and wills Brian his lands, though Brian doesn't accept the bequest, insisting that "Only God may own the earth." He roams the land, fighting and scalping evil men of all races. Though he holds women in low regard, he will go out of his way to prevent one from being harmed. Years later he learns he has a young sister, Samantha, and goes to visit her in Atlanta—though without ever telling her who he is.

Comment: The character was a recurring feature in the magazine until its demise with #70.

SCARAMOUCHE (L, MP)

First Appearance: *Scaramouche* by Rafael Sabatini, 1921, Houghton Mifflin.

Biography: In the days before the French Revolution, Andre-Louis Moreau believes himself to be the illegitimate son of his godfather Quintin de Kercadiou, Lord of Gavrillac. At age 15, he goes to the Lycee of Louis Le Grand in Paris to study law, intending to practice with Rabouillet, the attorney who manages his affairs. However, when Andre-Louis is 26, his life and career are changed when his dear friend Philippe de Vilmorin, a divinity student and political activist, is provoked into a duel and slain by the master swordsman Gervais, the Marquis de La Tour D'Azyr. Andre-Louis vows to carry on Philippe's work, fighting for the freedom of the oppressed Third Estate and learning how to handle a sword. To make Andre-Louis's grief complete, his lady friend, Kercadiou's niece Aline, is promised to the marquis.

Becoming a fugitive by virtue of his mob-inciting activities, Andre-Louis joins a company of actors, playing the part of Scaramouche in their plays. In the meantime, he studies fencing with famed Bertrand des Amis. His skill increases to a point where the rebel Danton asks him to join the Assembly, where the nobles routinely provoke less skilled swordsmen from the lower classes into duels, killing them and strengthening their own political sway. Andre-Louis agrees to serve and quickly whittles down the arrogance, and ranks, of the "Privileged Classes." Then, two years after Philippe's death, Andre-Louis finally faces the marquis, only to learn that he was born of an adulterous liaison between the Countess Thérèse de Plougastel, whose husband was away at war, and the marquis. Andre-Louis's paternity is as much a shock to the marquis as it is to the young man, as the marquis had been told the child died at birth. Andre-Louis permits the marquis to leave France. Aline then is free to marry him.

Physically, Andre-Louis is just "above middle height," lean, with a prominent nose, high cheekbones, and black hair grown to his shoulders. As Scaramouche, he wears a close-fitting black costume, flat velvet cap, and rosetted shoes, with a white face and mustache glued to it.

Comment: Houghton Mifflin published Sabatini's inferior sequel, *Scaramouche the King-Maker,* in 1931. In it, Andre-Louis crosses swords with the power-hungry Comte de Provence. Sabatini is also the author of THE SEA HAWK and CAPTAIN BLOOD. A seriously underrated novelist, Sabatini opens *Scaramouche* with the classic, "He was born with a gift of laughter and a sense that the world was mad."

The novel was first brought to the screen as a silent film in 1923 starring Ramon Novarro as Andre. In the colorful 1952 version, Stewart Granger played the part. Both films are quite faithful to the novel, though the latter dropped "Louis" from Andre's name and changed Gervais to Noel, the Marquis de Maynes and Philippe to Gaston Binet. Moreover, the film turns the Marquis into Andre's brother. A French-Italian-Spanish coproduction, *The Adventures of Scaramouche* (1964), starred Gerard Barray.

SCORCHY SMITH (CS)

First Appearance: *Scorchy Smith,* March 1930, Associated Press Newsfeatures.

Biography: Initially a barnstormer whose adventures are aviation-related—such as helping pilots in distress or flying through a storm—Scorchy Smith soon becomes an adventurer who, dressed in riding breeches and wearing a gun, travels the world in his plane, battling kidnapers, revolutionaries in South America, smugglers, and other antagonists. During World War II, he flies missions in Europe and on the Russian front. In time, he makes the jump to astronaut and goes soaring through space onboard a rocket ship, having adventures in the jungles of Venus, on Mars, and elsewhere.

Comment: The character, inspired by Charles Lindbergh, was created by John Terry, who turned it over to the brilliant Noel Sickles after three years, with scripts ghosted by Milt Caniff. (See STEVE CANYON and TERRY LEE.) Bert Christman, Frank Robbins, Edmond Good, Rodlow Willard, Al Hollingsworth, and George Tuska succeeded Sickles from 1936. The strip was finally discontinued in 1961.

SEA DEVILS (C)

First Appearance: *Showcase* #27, 1960, DC Comics.

Biography: The Sea Devils are divers Dane Dor-

Ramon Novarro in costume for the silent version of *Scaramouche.*

rance—the group's pipe-smoking leader and the son of famed Navy frogman and, later, oceanographer John Payton (apparently Dane's mother changed their name when John became a villain)—strong but dull-witted Biff Bailey, beautiful actress Judy Walton, and her kid brother Nicky. The four meet when, individually, they go searching for the same sunken treasure. (Judy is actually there so she can become famous enough to land the lead part in the movie *Sea Devils,* for which the producer wants a well-known actress.) They team to bring it to the surface, and Judy suggests that they remain together as the Sea Devils—even though she doesn't get in the motion picture.

All wear skintight red scuba diving suits (later adorned with a yellow circle and fist holding a trident on the chest) with blue tanks and flippers, and prowl the seas in their "floating headquarters," the PT boat *Sea Witch,* which is armed with a lasso-gun.

While on salvage, search, or rescue missions for various museums, laboratories, oil companies, and other groups with interests in the seas, the skindivers face fantastic monsters such as the huge fish-man Horro, the lionlike Griffisaur, a giant talking ape, an enormous living magnet, and so on. Once in a rare while they get to tackle human menaces, most memorably the Sea Angels, "Beatle-looking" underwater bikers ("Hey, mates! Maybe we're playing too rough for big daddy!").

The divers can talk to each other underwater thanks to communicators in their face masks. They also carry knives, spear guns, gas pellets, concussion bombs, flares, multiple-lasso spear guns, and vibration signalers that they use to "buzz" for help if their communicators are out of range, and they occasionally ride underwater sea sleds. In early adventures, Judy was sometimes assisted by her pet sea lion Pappy.

The International Sea Devils are introduced in *Sea Devils* #22, comprised of "skindivers from every one of the seven seas," including Sikki from India and Molo from Africa. They meet inside a giant golden robotic statue of the "legendary" Neptimus, which can walk about "the sea's eternal floor." Also introduced in that issue is the team's sleek 100-mile-an-hour hydrofoil *Flying Fish,* which is equipped with a five-person vessel known as the *Crab,* able to walk the ocean floor; and Man-Fish, the former Marquis Juan VallamBrosa, who was transformed into a green-skinned, pointy-eared, shape-changing amphibian man due to radiation accidentally released by Dane's oceanographer father.

The heroes are multiple "Davy" Award winners. "The most coveted skin-diving prize in the world" is awarded for bravery during ceremonies held at the Moby Dick Theatre.

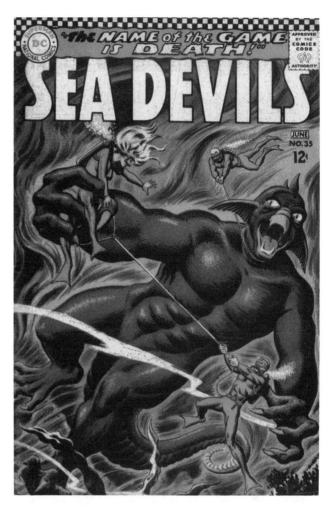

Sea Devils Biff (Bottom), Judy, and Nicky battle a monster as they search for the missing Dane. Art by Russ Heath. © DC Comics.

In 1985 Dane returns to action as a solo adventurer as one of the Forgotten Heroes (see RIP HUNTER,). The other Sea Devils work in or around the ocean in some capacity.

Comment: After three starring appearances in *Showcase,* the Sea Devils were given their own comic book, which ran for 35 issues. The magazine was distinguished by its painted covers.

THE SEA HAWK (L, MP)

First Appearance: *The Sea Hawk* by Rafael Sabatini, 1915, Houghton Mifflin.

Biography: Sir Oliver Tressilian of Penarrow estate is the son of Ralph Tressilian. When the latter died, seriously in debt, Sir Oliver sold some land, bought a ship, and preyed on Spanish shipping, becoming wealthy. A patriot, he has recently distinguished himself by his "harrying of the late Invincible Armada" of Spain and, at age 25, was knighted by the queen.

Sir Oliver is in love with 17-year-old Rosamund, whose self-righteous coguardian Peter Godolphin does not approve of the shrewd pirate. When Peter wounds Sir Oliver's half-brother Lionel, the 21-year-old kills him and Sir Oliver takes the blame. Fearful that a trial will clear Sir Oliver and implicate him, and seeing this as an ideal time to take over Penarrow, the treacherous Lionel has his brother abducted, to be carried by ship to Barbary and sold as a slave to the Moors. Though the kindly Captain Leigh plans to return Sir Oliver to England, his ship the *Swallow* is sunk by Spaniards and both men are carried off in chains. After being tried in Lisbon by the Court of the Holy Office, they are sent to work as galley slaves in the Mediterranean. Over the next six months, Sir Oliver becomes "a man of steel and iron, impervious to fatigue, superhuman almost in his endurance." When the vessel is attacked by the Muslim corsair Asad-ed-Din, Sir Oliver uses his chains to assault the Spaniards. His valor impresses the pirate, who takes him under his wing. He quickly becomes Asad's lieutenant and buys the freedom of any Englishmen he encounters; five years after his capture he becomes Sakr-el-Bahr, the Hawk of the Seas, who, with his Sea Hawks, is the scourge of Spain in the Mediterranean.

Upon learning that Rosamund is affianced to Lionel, the Sea Hawk sails forth and abducts her; when she finds out what really happened, which Lionel acknowledges, Rosamund becomes Sir Oliver's wife. Later the Sea Hawk and his crew board the rescue ship of Rosamund's coguardian Sir John Killigrew; during the attack Lionel is fatally wounded. However, Sir John was ready for them, threatening to blow up the ship unless the Sea Hawk surrenders. To save his crew, Sir Oliver hands himself over, is charged with kidnaping and is sentenced to be hanged. However, Rosamund says that she went willingly with her beloved and that if they hang him, she will charge Sir John with murder. Lionel corroborates the story of his own treachery before dying. A pardon from the queen is promised, and it is intimated that Sir Oliver and Rosamund will be returning home shortly.

The Sea Hawk is a man of "great height" and has a swarthy face, black brows, a large nose, and "brooding eyes with a gleam that was mocking, crafty, and almost wicked." Once he joins the Muslim crew, his head is shaved save for the forelock.

Comment: The first film version of the novel, made in 1924 and starring Milton Sills, was relatively faithful to Sabatini's story. The second was not. Made in 1940, when England stood virtually alone against Hitler's Germany, it is the sweeping saga of Captain Geoffrey

Thorpe (Errol Flynn) and his Sea Hawks, privateers who prey on the ships of the hated King Philip II of Spain and turn the booty over to Queen Elizabeth I. Captured on a mission to intercept Spanish plunder from Panama, Thorpe and his men are condemned by the Inquisition and made to row as galley slaves. But the heroes manage to steal a ship, return to England, and warn the queen—in time—of the armada with which Philip plans to invade England. The tale of Thorpe and his ship the *Albatross* has more in common with the historical Sir Francis Drake than with Sakr-el-Bahr, but it's still rousing entertainment.

THE SECRET SIX (C)

First Appearance: *Secret Six* #1, 1968, DC Comics.

Biography: At some point in the past, five people have been helped by a mysterious sixth known only as Mockingbird. Mike Tempest, a Vietnam veteran and boxer, refuses to take a dive, testifies against the mob, and is beaten nearly to death by thugs. Mockingbird gets him to a hospital and, when he recovers, he roams the world one step ahead of the vengeful mobsters until Mockingbird takes him in. Crimson Dawn, a.k.a. Kim Dawn, is a model who becomes an actress. She weds golddigger Johnny Bright who divorces her and leaves her broke; with no other means left to support herself, she becomes a prostitute. After killing a pimp, she is hustled to safety by Mockingbird. Dr. August Durant, a government scientist, is slipped a genetically engineered bacterium by Soviet agents; Mockingbird obtains an antidote from the Soviets, but it's a temporary cure. Durant must keep taking the medication to survive, and only Mockingbird can supply it. King Savage, a Vietnam pilot, is taken prisoner by the enemy and, under torture, tells them information that compromises U.S. forces. Mockingbird frees him from the North Vietnamese POW camp and he becomes a movie stunt actor—with Mockingbird keeping his "treason" a secret. Carlo di Rienzi is a magician whose house is bombed when he crosses the Mafia. His wife is killed and his son maimed, but Mockingbird sees to his rehabilitation—treatment the illusionist could never have afforded. Finally, Lili de Neuve, a French actress, is accused of a murder she didn't commit. Mockingbird helps by giving her an alibi. Lili goes on to become a successful filmmaker.

One of these people may be a fraud: According to hints in the chronicles, one of the members is Mockingbird. And for reasons known only to that person, the other five are brought together to operate outside the law, each using his or her particular talent to fight criminals, spies, and Communists: Mike's muscle;

Crimson's acting skills and beauty; Durrant's scientific skills; King's abilities as a flier/driver/daredevil; Carlo's illusions and tricks; and Lili's makeup ability. Though none of the six really wants to be part of the team, they have no choice; if they stop providing their talents to Mockingbird, he will cease protecting them from their shady pasts.

When the original team is killed in a plane crash, Mockingbird (either the original, or a new one) assembles a new Secret Six. This time the members are six people with disabilities: Olympic medalist Luke McKendrick, who lost his legs in a terrorist attack; Marine Vic Sommers, who was blinded in Vietnam; Dr. Maria Verdugo, a computer expert who suffers from epilepsy; reporter Anthony Mantegna, who was deafened by a blast while investigating a union; actress LaDonna Jameal, who was maimed and lost her voice when a fan doused her with acid; and special effects artist Mitch Hoberman, who is an arthritic. Mockingbird provides the six with accoutrements that overcome their handicaps; in return, they must serve in the Secret Six.

Comment: This exciting title lasted for seven issues, after which the heroes lay dormant for nearly 20 years. They were reintroduced, with the new—and frankly, less interesting—lineup, for a brief run in *Action Comics Weekly* #601.

SENORITA RIO (C)

First Appearance: *Fight Comics* #19, 1942, Fiction House.

Biography: Though actress Rita Farrar is the star of the hit film *Lady Dance No More,* she is distraught by the death of her young fiance at Pearl Harbor. Deciding that what she really wants to do is serve her country, she fakes her own suicide and, based in Rio de Janeiro, works as the "bewitching American secret agent." Her beat is Brazil and all of South America; as the "queen of spies," she sniffs out Nazis, destroys their airfields, and chases saboteurs. After the war, she hunts down the new enemies of America or would-be despots, terrorists, cults, and even lost civilizations up and down the Amazon.

Comment: *Fight Comics* usually featured one of its heroines on the cover, scantily clad and/or in jeopardy. Senorita Rio appeared through issue #65; by that time her luster (and cover appeal) had been dimmed by the sexy Tiger Girl, a jungle heroine introduced in #32, "a golden princess who ruled with singing whip [that] writes Congo law!" Having trained tigers for the Allies didn't hurt either.

Other adventure series featured in *Fight Comics* during its 86 issue run included Risks, Unlimited; Kayo Kirby; "sea adventurer" Captain Fight; Rip Carson, the "daredevil Jap-smasher 'chute trooper" who becomes the "sky-fighting ace" of Korea; Shark Brodie, "freelance of the South Seas"; and Hooks Devlin, "devil dog detective" and special agent.

SGT. CHIP SAUNDERS (TV)

First Appearance: *Combat,* October, 1962, ABC.

Biography: Rough, cynical, cigarette-smoking Sergeant Chip Saunders is in command of a platoon slogging its way toward Berlin after the D-Day landing. Reporting to the well-groomed, by-the-book Lieutenant Gil Hanley, Saunders doesn't lack courage, but he loathes battle and is very attached to his men, the weak as well as the strong. He is frequently sent on missions behind enemy lines and once spent some time in SS Captain Steiner's POW camp.

Other soldiers in the platoon are privates Paul "Caje" Lemay, William G. Kirby, Littlejohn, Billy Nelson, and Braddock. The medics are Doc Walton, followed by another called just Doc.

Comment: The hour-long series ran until August 1967. Vic Morrow starred as Saunders and Rick Jason was Hanley. Death was a commonplace occurrence on the show, making it the most realistic war drama on TV.

Dell Publishing's long-lived *Combat* comic book, which began in 1961, was unrelated to the series.

SERGEANT DEATH (C)

First Appearance: *Radical America Komiks,* 1969, Radical America.

Biography: A Vietnam soldier from Anytown, U.S., Sergeant Death believes in one thing and one thing only: "Death to Communism." With two cigars clenched in his teeth, his chest bare, USMC tattoo bulging on his thick arm, the hero battles North Vietnamese with the assistance of his Merciless Mayhem Patrol. The Patrol consists of Zeb Turnipseed, a seven-foot four-inch "fightin' hillbilly from Tennessee"; Brooklyn tough guy Iggy Schwartz; Tijuana's Manuel Lopez, who wields a revolver and a machete; Watermelon Jones, who finds riot-torn Watts too tame; Harvard Ph.D. (at 16) Algernon Truffle; and midget Michael O'Rafferty.

Comment: The underground comic book characters were created by Gilbert Shelton and were a parody of NICK FURY and his Howling Commandos. They appeared just this once.

SGT. JOE FRIDAY (R, TV, MP)

First Appearance: *Dragnet,* 1949, NBC.

Biography: A humorless, scrupulously moral officer

with the Los Angeles Police Department, Sergeant Joe Friday investigates everything from missing people, to robberies, to murder. Using gun and fists only when he absolutely has to, Friday appears to have had no life outside of police work (Ann Baker, his fiancee in the later days, is hardly ever seen) and virtually nothing makes him nervous—except, once, when he has to appear on TV. His badge number is 714, and his oft-used phrase is "Just the facts, ma'am." In narrating his adventures, the meticulous Friday frequently describes the dead ends he encounters and invariably mentions the time while describing police procedures—touches that give a sense of verisimilitude to the shows.

Friday tends to wear the same gray suit every day (so that location scenes for several episodes could be shot at once without worrying about costume changes) and has a habit of giving self-righteous lectures to hippies and anyone else who leans to the political left.

Friday's original partner is Mexican-American Sergeant Ben Romero; he's followed by Sergeant Ed Jacobs, then by Officer Frank Smith. These two stay together for many years, eventually making Lieutenant and Sergeant. By the time cynical, slightly neurotic Officer Bill Gannon replaces Smith, the Hippie movement is in full swing, and the show frequently features cults, drug dealers, dropouts, and runaway kids. Friday is also back to being a sergeant again, though just why is never revealed.

Comment: Jack Webb had first hit upon the idea for *Dragnet* while playing a police officer in the film *He Walked By Night* (1948). He first starred as Friday on the radio, with Barton Yarborough as the original Sergeant Ben Romero; Webb and Yarborough also starred on the *Chesterfield Sound Off Time* TV tryout show in 1951, though Yarborough died and Barney Phillips took his place as Jacobs when the series began its original NBC TV run, which lasted from January 1952 to September 1959; Jacobs was gone by the fall of 1952, replaced by Smith, played by Herb Ellis. Ellis left the following year, and Ben Alexander played Smith for the rest of the original run. The series was called *Badge 714* when the original shows were syndicated. Harry Morgan came aboard as Gannon when *Dragnet* was revived from January 1967 to September 1970. It was in this version that Ann Baker appeared, played by Dorothy Abbott.

In all its incarnations, the half-hour show used the famous Walter Schumann opening theme (dum-de-dum-dum . . . dum-de-dum-dum *dum*) and the disclaimer, "The story you have just heard is true. Only the names have been changed to protect the innocent."

Webb also starred in *Dragnet,* a feature film inspired by the series and released in 1954, costarring Ben Alexander; Webb and Morgan toplined in *Dragnet,* a 1969 made-for-TV movie. Dan Aykroyd played Friday's ultra-straight, thick-headed nephew in the 1987 sendup *Dragnet.*

A syndicated *Dragnet* lasted 52 episodes from 1989 to 1990, starring Jeff Osterhage and Bernard White as Vic Daniels and Carl Molina, plainclothes LAPD detectives reporting to Captains Boltz and Lussen (Thalmus Rasulala and Don Stroud).

As a producer, Webb was also responsible for the hit series *Adam 12,* in which Martin Milner and Kent McCord starred as LAPD officers Pete Malloy and Jim Reed. The series ran from 1968 to 1975. It was revived as a syndicated show from 1989 to 1990, starring Peter Parros and Ethan Wayne and officers Gus Grant and Matt Doyle. It, too, lasted 52 episodes.

Prior to playing Friday on the radio, Webb starred as adventurer *Jeff Regan* for CBS in the early 1940s, then moved to NBC, first as the eponymous sleuth in *Pat Novak for Hire* and then as a San Francisco waterfront detective in *Johnny Modero, Pier 23.*

SERGEANT PAT O'HARA   (CS, R, MP)

First Appearance: *Radio Patrol,* April 1934, King Features Syndicate (see COMMENT).

Biography: Handsome Pat O'Hara and Stutterin' Sam are a pair of police officers who patrol the streets in a then-new development: the radio car. The two men are able to respond instantly to crimes in progress, as well as to intercept hijackers, smugglers, kidnapers, robbers, racketeers, and other criminal types.

The duo is aided by young and ambitious Pinky Adams and his Irish setter named Irish, and by Officer Molly Day, who's in love with Pat.

Comment: The strip was originally launched, in a somewhat different form, as *Pinkerton Jr.* It was created for the *Boston Daily Record* by writer/editor Eddie Sullivan and artist Charles Schmidt, and debuted in August 1933. It proved so popular that King Features picked it up, had the creators rework it (young Pinkerton Jr. became Pinky in the new strip) and relaunched it as *Radio Patrol.* Later the strip was renamed *Sergeant Pat of the Radio Patrol.* It was discontinued in December 1950.

A *Radio Patrol* radio program aired in the middle 1930s, and in 1937 Grant Withers starred in the 12-chapter serial *Radio Patrol,* directed by Ford Beebe and Cliff Smith. In it, Pat must keep a formula for bulletproof steel out of the hands of criminals. Adrian Morris was Sam, Catherine Hughes played Molly, and Mickey Rentschler was Pinky.

SGT. PRESTON (R, TV, C)

First Appearance: *Challenge of the Yukon,* 1943, ABC.

Biography: Sergeant Preston is a highly regarded member of the Royal Canadian Mounted Police at the turn of the century. Based in the town of Dawson in the Yukon Territory, he reports to the inspector but patrols on his own, deputizing citizens as need-be "in the name of the Crown" to track down escaped criminals, missing persons, and gangs such as the Vipers that prey on miners and prospectors. Preston lives in a modest cabin in the woods, gets about on his horse Rex, and is never without his faithful husky Yukon King, the lead dog of his team, who has been known to surprise criminals by playing dead and then chomping on an arm or leg.

Comment: The character was created by George W. Trendle and Fran Striker, who also created the Lone Ranger and the Green Hornet. The radio series ran until 1947.

CBS launched a half-hour TV show *Sgt. Preston of the Yukon,* which lasted from September 1955 to September 1958. There were 104 episodes in all, the last season of them in color. Jay Michael, Paul Sutton, and Brace Beemer played the part on the radio; dashing Richard Simmons was Preston on TV. The exteriors for the series were shot in California and in Ashcroft, Colorado. The popular theme song for both the radio and TV shows was the overture to *Donna Diana* by Emil Von Reznicek.

The character's first name was William on the radio, though Simmons's Preston was named Frank.

Dell published 29 issues of a Sgt. Preston comic book, from 1951 to 1959.

Another popular Mountie was Inspector Douglas Renfrew, whose adventures were first heard on CBS radio's *Renfrew of the Mounted* in 1936. The popular character and his dog Lightning were created by Laurie York Erskine, and the series starred House Jameson; James Newill played Renfrew (now a sergeant) in a film and in a syndicated, half-hour TV series *Renfrew of the Royal Mounted,* in 1953.

Other Mountie heroes included Sergeant Tom Clancy in the 1933 serial *Clancy of the Mounted,* Sergeant King in the 1940 serial *King of the Royal Mounted* (based on a novel and comic strip created by Zane Grey), Sergeant MacLane in the 1942 serial *Perils of the Royal Mounted,* Captain Wayne Decker in the 1945 serial *The Royal Mounted Rides Again,* Captain Chris Royal in the 1948 serial *Dangers of the Canadian Mounted,* Sergeant Don Roberts in the 1953 serial *Canadian Mounties vs. Atomic Invaders,* and Corporal Jacques Gagnier in the syndicated, half-

hour series *Royal Canadian Mounted Police* in 1960.

SGT. ROCK (C)

First Appearance: *Our Army at War* #81, 1959, DC Comics.

Biography: Frank Rock is the oldest son of John Michael Rock, who died in World War I. He and his brothers—Larry, Mickey, and Eddie—and an unnamed sister are raised by a stepfather in Pennsylvania. When their stepfather dies in a mining accident, Frank quits school and becomes a boxer to help support the family. Though he's a formidable athlete, Frank doesn't fare well in the ring and goes to work in a steel mill; at the outbreak of World War II, he enlists and is assigned to Easy Company. He sees action for the first time during an air attack against the troop ship that's taking him to North Africa, where he and Easy will serve under General Patton. (Early stories report that

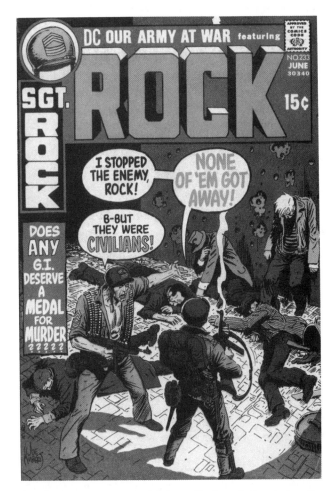

Sgt. Rock surveys some of Johnny Doe's unfortunate handiwork. This cover, by Joe Kubert, appeared in 1971, at the height of the Vietnam war protests, and earned a lot of publicity for DC Comics. © DC Comics.

Rock is still a private at D-Day, where he wins a medal, but this time frame is ignored in future tales.) During one battle—a reconaissance mission on a nameless hill—he quickly rises from private, to private first class, to corporal, to sergeant as men fall around him, though he turns down future commissions so he can remain with Easy on the battlefield. His brother Larry, a lieutenant, dies in the Pacific.

Many members of Easy Company come and go over the years, men such as chaplain Father Kelly; Green Apple, who gives the enemy indigestion; "Worry Wart," who expects to die at any given second; bazookamen "Long Round" and "Short Round," who replace wounded Zack Nolan; whistling "Canary"; the late, brave Clack-Clack and Bates; the fleet Dash, who dies racing toward the enemy; the giant, obese "Heavy" Horace Smith; Nick, Sid, Al, and Mack, the heroes of No-Return Hill; and the trigger-happy Johnny Doe, who mows down civilians. The permanent GIs are Ice Cream Soldier (under fire, he's "Cool—real cool"), the bearded Wild Man, the Apache Little Sure Shot, Bulldozer ("Bullets didn't bother this character as much as achin' bunions"), and former heavyweight boxing champ Jackie Johnson, with occasional appearances by Beanpole and Curly, sharpshooter Four-Eyes, and "Farmer Boy," the GI with a green thumb.

The team of "combat-happy Joes" sees action throughout the European theater of operations and has even done some fighting in the Pacific. When the need arises, the cigarette-smoking Rock—who has a sixth sense he calls his "combat antenna"—can operate as a frogman; he even gets to fight alongside Superman in one story (*DC Comics Presents* #10).

Comment: Rock quickly became the featured character in *Our Army at War*; the magazine's title was changed to *Sgt. Rock* with #302. The magazine was discontinued after #422 in 1988, though Rock continues to make guest appearances in other magazines and in special titles. Bob Kanigher created the characters and wrote the stories for many years, with stunning art by Joe Kubert. A Sergeant Rock film was announced in 1990, first to star Arnold Schwarzenegger, then with Bruce Willis. As of this writing, it's in limbo.

SGT. SAM TROY (TV, L, C)

First Appearance: *The Rat Patrol*, September 1966, ABC.

Biography: The members of the armored car outfit known as the Rat Patrol are a trio of Americans—hard-as-nails Sergeant Sam Troy, Ivy League Private Mark Hitchcock, and former moonshine runner Private Tully Pettigrew—and one Englishman, the brooding explosives expert Sergeant Jack Moffitt. The quartet spends World War II in North Africa, fighting Rommel and his Afrika Korps. Their usual mode of travel is a jeep that boasts a pair of mounted machine guns on either side.

Their regular foe is Hauptmann Hans Dietrich, though more than once the enemies teamed to battle Arabs who hated Allied and Axis intruders alike.

Comment: The half-hour series aired through September 1968. Christopher George starred as Troy, Gary Raymond played Moffitt, Lawrence Casey was Hitchcock, and Justin Tarr played Pettigrew. Hans Gudegast played Dietrich; the actor later changed his name to Eric Braeden.

The series was created by Tom Gries, who went on to become a distinguished feature film director (*Will Penny*, 1968). Gries based his series on the exploits of a British unit known as the Long Range Desert Group.

David King wrote six *Rat Patrol* novels in 1967–1968: *The Rat Patrol, Desert Danger, The Trojan Tank Affair, Two-Faced Enemy, Target for Tonight*, and *Desert Masquerade*.

Dell published six issues of a *Rat Patrol* comic book from 1967 to 1969.

SGT. STRYKER (C)

First Appearance: *Savage Combat Tales* #1, 1975, Seaboard Periodicals.

Biography: Ben Stryker, of Prairie Mission, Kansas, is the son of a doctor, who learns to shoot to put food on the table. At the outbreak of World War II, he's drafted and sent to Africa; he leaves behind his girlfriend, Laurie Kenton, whose kid brother Andrew enlists and fights alongside Stryker. When Andy is killed, Stryker blames himself; but Sergeant Bloom is killed as well, and Stryker—who is at heart a pacifist—has no choice but to become the leader of what is dubbed the Death Squad. Members include judo expert Lee Shigeta, acrobat Duke Ripley, wrestler Turk Ankrum, and convict Ice Marko. The men fight their way through Africa and Europe, stopping their own bickering only long enough to shoot at the Germans.

Comment: Stryker starred in all three issues of *Savage Combat Tales*. The character was created by writer Archie Goodwin and editor Larry Lieber. A fourth issue was drawn but never published. Seaboard also published another adventure title: *Western Action*, which lasted just one issue and featured Kid Cody—Tom Corbett, who becomes a gunfighter when his folks are murdered by outlaws in Cody, Wyoming—and the orphaned-pioneer-boy-raised-by-Indians saga of White Eagle, the Comanche Kid.

Sgt. Stryker in his first appearance. © Seaboard Periodicals.

SGT. SUZANNE ANDERSON (TV)

First Appearance: "The Gamble," *Police Story,* 1974, NBC (see COMMENT).

Biography: Sergeant Suzanne "Pepper" Anderson is an undercover officer who works for the Los Angeles Police Department's vice squad. Her job requires her to pose as a hooker, moll, junkie, porn actress, and the like, often giving her nowhere to hide her pistol. Once in a while she'll try to find out who killed a crusading reporter or priest. She reports to Lieutenant William Crowley and is ably assisted by Detectives Joe Styles and Pete Royster, who also wear "street" disguises.

Pepper has an autistic younger sister, Cheryl.

Comment: In the pilot episode, the character was called Lisa Beaumont. When it proved successful, an hour-long series, *Police Woman,* began airing on NBC in September 1974; it remained on the air through August 1978. Angie Dickinson was Lisa/Pepper, Earl Holliman played Crowley (replacing Bert Convy in

the pilot), Ed Bernard was Styles, and Charles Dierkop was Royster.

The series was created by Robert Collins, though author Joseph Wambaugh had input in the original *Police Story* episode.

SGT. ZEKE ANDERSON (TV)

First Appearance: *Tour of Duty,* September 1987, CBS.

Biography: In Vietnam 1967, Sergeant Zeke Anderson of B Company is serving his third tour of duty. A leader who runs as loose a ship as possible, his overriding concern is for the physical safety and psychological well-being of his men. He frequently butts heads with Second Lieutenant Myron Goldman, the green platoon leader who insists on doing things by the book. (They once agreed, though, to order an artillery strike on their own position in order to hit at the enemies in their midst.) His soldiers include: All-American Iowan Danny Percell; Kansas City-bred jungle fighter Marvin Johnson; pacifist, harmonica-playing Roger Horn; Bronx-reared Puerto Rican Alberto Ruiz; Southern California surfer boy Scott Baker; and others—some of whom die—including the medic, Doc Randy Matsuda, and Captain Rusty Wallace.

After a year the platoon is assigned to the airbase at Tan Son Nhut near Saigon, with reporter Alex Devlin following the fate of the platoon, Dr. Jennifer Seymour helping with their psychological problems (and having an affair with Sergeant Anderson), and Lieutenant Johnny McKay ferrying them into combat by helicopter. Also joining the team were the new medic, Dr. Francis "Doc Hock" Hockenbury, and Colonel Brewster.

Comment: The hour-long series aired through August 1990. Terence Knox starred as Anderson, with Stephen Caffrey as Goldman, Tony Becker as Percell, Stan Foster as Johnson, Joshua Maurer as Horn, Ramon Franco as Ruiz, Eric Bruskotter as Baker, Kim Delaney as Devlin, Betsy Brantley as Seymour, Dan Gauthier as McKay, John Dye as Doc, and Carl Weathers as Brewster.

SEXTON BLAKE (L, MP, CS, TV)

First Appearance: "The Missing Millionaire" by Hal Meredith, December 1893, *The Halfpenny Marvel #6.*

Biography: A London-based detective, Sexton Blake lives on Baker Street (home of SHERLOCK HOLMES) and solves crimes with the help of his young assistant, Tinker. His landlady is Mrs. Bardell, and his dog is Pedro, a bloodhound; Blake's former nemesis, later lover, is Mademoiselle Yvonne. His foes include Dr. Huxton Rymer, an insane surgeon; the Hooded Stranger, "the most dangerous crook in Europe"; and Prince Wu Ling, leader of the Brotherhood of the Yellow Beetle.

During World War II, Blake works as a secret agent in adventures that take him all around the world.

Comment: Meredith was a pseudonym for Harry Blyth. Blake is one of the most successful characters of all time, featured in over 4,000 stories that continued in publications such as *Detective Weekly, Union Jack,* and the hero's own *Sexton Blake Library.*

In motion pictures, the character was featured in a number of silent films, beginning in a 1909 short starring C. Douglas Carlile and continuing in the silent shorts and featurettes *Sexton Blake vs. Baron Kettler* (1912; credits unavailable), *The Further Exploits of Sexton Blake* (1919) starring Douglas Payne, and a series of shorts starring Langhorne Burton, including *The Great Office Mystery, The Clue of the Second Goblet,* and *The Mystery of the Silent Death.* Blake appeared in features as well: *Sexton Blake and the Bearded Doctor* (1935), *Sexton Blake and the Mademoiselle* (1935), and *Sexton Blake and the Hooded Terror* (1938), all starring George Curzon; and *Meet Sexton Blake* (1944) and *The Echo Murders* (1945), both starring David Farrar.

In comic strips, Blake first appeared in the weekly children's magazine *The Knockout* in March 1939. Various artists drew the strip until it was discontinued in 1960.

On TV, Laurence Payne played the hero in a British TV series in 1967. Concurrently, the strip reappeared in the weekly magazine *Knockout,* but lasted only as long as the series did, until 1968.

SHANG-CHI (C)

First Appearance: *Special Marvel Edition* #15, 1973, Marvel Comics.

Biography: The son of the fiendish villain Fu Manchu, Shang-Chi is raised on his father's estate in Honan, China, where he's trained and educated by scholars and masters of martial arts. At 19, he is sent out to kill an enemy of his father's—unaware that his father is a criminal mastermind. When he encounters his father's enemy, Sir Denis Nayland Smith, Shang-Chi learns the truth—and becomes the sworn enemy of his father, whom he describes as "the most insidiously evil man on earth." In addition to working with Smith and British Intelligence to destroy Fu Manchu, Shang-Chi fights other criminal figures. Eventually tiring of "deceit and death," he retires to become a fisherman in the Chinese village of Yang Yin.

Shang-Chi tackles members of the Leopard Cult in London. © Marvel Comics Group.

In his prime, not only can Shang-Chi beat just about any foe and duck a thrown knife, he can overturn a car with a kick.

Comment: Shang-Chi is not present in the original Fu Manchu tales, which author Sax Rohmer began writing in 1913. *Special Marvel Edition* became *Master of Kung Fu* with #17, featuring "The Hands of Shang-Chi." The character starred in the magazine until it ended with #125. He also starred in other Marvel titles, including the 33 issues of the black-and-white comics magazine *The Deadly Hands of Kung Fu.*

SHEP STONE (MP)

First Appearance: *Black Eye,* 1974, Warner Brothers.

Biography: A suspended Los Angeles police lieutenant, the hard-hitting Shep Stone becomes a private eye and undertakes investigations into pornographers, dope dealers, and religious freaks who operate in and around Venice, California.

Comment: Fred Williamson starred as Stone; the film was directed by veteran science fiction and action director Jack Arnold. Though this was the character's only appearance, Williamson played a number of other "blaxploitation" heroes including Jefferson Bolt in *That Man Bolt* (1973), a spy and martial arts expert who battles Japanese megalomaniacs holed up in an island fortress.

SHERIFF FRANK MORGAN (TV, C)

First Appearance: *The Sheriff of Cochise*, September 1956, syndicated.

Biography: Lantern-jawed Frank Morgan is the sheriff of modern-day Cochise County, Arizona, chasing criminals in a squad car instead of on horseback. He is later promoted to marshal, with the entire state as his bailiwick. Over the years, his deputies are Olson, Blake, and Ferguson.

Comment: The half-hour series aired through 1960, a total of 156 episodes being produced; reruns were syndicated under the title *U.S. Marshal.* John Bromfield starred. Mobil published a one-shot comic book giveaway in 1957.

SHERLOCK HOLMES (L, S, MP, R, C, TV, CS)

First Appearance: *A Study in Scarlet* by Sir Arthur Conan Doyle, 1887, *Beeton's Christmas Annual* (magazine).

Biography: Holmes was born on Friday, January 6, 1854, on the family farm of Mycroft in the North Riding of Yorkshire. He has an older brother, Mycroft (who is wiser and more sensible than Sherlock). In 1874, while attending Oxford, this young man with unparalleled observational and deductive skills solves his first case ("The 'Gloria Scott'"). Three years later he moves into rooms on Montague Street and becomes a consultant detective, in which profession he would be unparalleled for 23 years. In January 1881 he moves to 221B Baker Street. Seeking someone to share the place, he is introduced to Dr. John Hamish Watson, who becomes not only his roommate but his aide, confidant, and the chronicler of his escapades. (Watson, born in 1852, was graduated from the University of London Medical School, served in the Fifth Northumberland Fusiliers, and was wounded in India before returning to London to establish a practice.)

The deadliest of Holmes's foes is the "Napoleon of Crime" Professor Moriarty, a mathematics professor who is at the center of a network of criminals that spreads throughout London and beyond. The "clean-shaven, pale . . . reptilian" Moriarty crosses swords with Holmes on a number of occasions, most notably at the top of the Reichenbach Falls in Switzerland. During a struggle, the two plunge over the edge, Moriarty apparently perishing and Holmes surviving— though vanishing for three years, so his enemies (and even Watson) would think him dead. During this period, he takes the name Sigerson and, posing as a Danish explorer, heads to Tibet, where he learns many of the secrets of the mystics, including how to prolong one's life. (Reportedly, Holmes is still alive to this day.)

Holmes stands over six feet tall, is extremely thin, possesses "sharp and piercing" eyes, has a "hawk-like nose," a square and prominent chin, and his hands are "invariably blotted with ink and stained with chemicals." He is an expert fencer, pugilist, and singlestick player, and is much stronger than he appears. He is fond of taking target practice with his revolver indoors, and has been known to be rude to clients who waste his time or tax his patience.

Holmes tends to sleep late, unless he's been up all night, smokes a pipe with strong tobacco, and plays the violin. When faced with a shortage of cases, his mind grows bored and he injects himself with a 7 percent solution of cocaine. When he's out and about, his preferred attire is his trademark deerstalker hat and Inverness cape. Watson describes the detective's knowledge of literature, philosophy, and astronomy as "nil," of politics as "feeble," of botany as "variable," of geology as "practical, but limited," of chemistry as "profound," of anatomy as "accurate, but unsystematic," of sensational literature as "immense," and of British law as "good." As an author, Holmes's published works include *Practical Handbook of Bee Culture, With Some Observations Upon the Segregation of the Queen; Upon the Distinction Between the Ashes of Various Tobaccos; A Study of the Influence of a Trade Upon the Form of the Hand; A Study of the Chaldean Roots in the Ancient Cornish Language;* and *Upon the Polyphonic Motets of Lassus.*

Holmes's landlady is the long-suffering Mrs. Martha Hudson (Holmes is prone to "incredible untidiness"); his sometimes ally, often rival, is Scotland Yard's fumbling Inspector Lestrade; his occasional "butler" is Billy the Page Boy; and his frequent helpers are the famed street urchins, the Baker Street Irregulars who, under the leadership of Wiggins, are paid to hunt for clues. The great love of Holmes's life was American Irene Adler, born in 1858 in New Jersey. The wife of lawyer Godfrey Norton, she is the prima donna of the Imperial Opera in Warsaw. Reportedly, the two had a short affair and, rumor has it, a child was born of the relationship. Irene died in 1903. Upon her death, Holmes retires to the southern slopes of the Sussex Downs, raising bees and being looked after by Mrs. Hudson. He takes on his last known case shortly before World War I.

Watson is married to Mary Morstan, who dies after a few happy years, and he subsequently remarries.

The expression "Elementary, my dear Watson" was popularized by the movies and radio. In the stories, Holmes is most inclined to cry "Exactly!" with an occasional "Smart fellow!" "Excellent!" "Hum!" or "Ha!" Holmes typically uses "My Dear Watson" when writing to his associate.

Comment: Holmes was inspired by one of Doyle's professors at the University of Edinburgh, surgeon Joseph Bell. Doyle wrote 60 stories about Holmes, four of them novels: In addition to *A Study in Scarlet*, there were *The Sign of Four* (1890), *The Hound of the Baskervilles* (1902), and *The Valley of Fear* (1915). The 56 short stories—the first of which was "A Scandal in Bohemia," which was first published in *The Strand* in 1891—are collected in *The Adventures of Sherlock Holmes* (1892), *The Memoirs of Sherlock Holmes* (1894), *The Return of Sherlock Holmes* (1905), *His Last Bow* (1917), and *The Case Book of Sherlock Holmes* (1927). In collecting *A Treasury of Sherlock Holmes* in 1955, son Adrian Doyle drew upon his father's own stated preferences to select the best of the tales: "The Red-Headed League," "The Adventure of the Six Napoleons," "The Final Problem," "The Five Orange Pips," "The Adventure of the Dancing Men," "The Adventure of the Dying Detective," "The Adventure of the Blue Carbuncle," "The Naval Treaty," "The Adventure of the Beryl Coronet," "Silver Blaze," "The Musgrave Ritual," "The Adventure of the Speckled Band," "The Adventure of Black Peter," "The Reigate Puzzle," "The Adventure of Charles Augustus Milverton," "The Adventure of the Engineer's Thumb," "The Adventure of the Second Stain," "The Adventure of the Abbey Grange," "The Adventure of the Mazarin Stone," "The Problem of Thor Bridge," "The Adventure of Shoscombe Old Place," "The Adventure of the Devil's Foot," "The Greek Interpreter," "The 'Gloria Scott,' " "The Adventure of the Priory School," "The Adventure of the Empty House," and "His Last Bow."

On the stage, William Gillette wrote and starred in the first and best of the plays, *Sherlock Holmes,* which debuted in 1899 on Broadway. He continued to play Holmes for 36 years, on stage, in film, and on the radio. His last three-year tour with *Sherlock Holmes* began in 1929 when he was 76. It was Gillette who, with Doyle's permission, married Holmes to one Alice Faulkner. Doyle wrote his own adaptation of "The Speckled Bird," which was staged on Broadway in

1910, and a musical, *Baker Street,* starring Fritz Weaver, had a modest Broadway run in 1965. John Wood starred as Holmes in England's Royal Shakespeare Company's revival of the Gillette play, which came to Broadway in 1974. According to the star, he was the 109th actor to play the sleuth in film and stage. Paul Giovanni's 1978 play *Crucifer of Blood* was loosely based on *The Sign of Four,* and *Sherlock's Last Case,* written by Charles Marowitz, starred Frank Langella on Broadway in 1987. In 1989, Ron Moody played the part in composer Leslie Bricusse's West End musical.

It would take a separate book to catalog all of the films about Sherlock Holmes: England's Eille Norwood played the part in over 40 silent films made in 1921–22, and *The Hound of the Baskervilles* alone has been filmed ten times in the movies, the most famous starring Basil Rathbone in 1939, Peter Cushing in 1959, and (the most *in*famous) Peter Cook as Holmes and Dudley Moore as Watson in a 1977 comedy. Highlights of the Holmes movie catalog would have to be Gillette's film version in 1916, John Barrymore's interpretation in *Sherlock Holmes* (1922), Clive Brook's two turns in *The Return of Sherlock Holmes* (1929) and *Sherlock Holmes* (1932), Raymond Massey in *The Speckled Band* (1931), and Arthur Wontner in five films: *Sherlock Holmes' Fatal Hour* (1930) (known as *The Sleeping Cardinal* in England), *The Missing Rembrandt* (1932), *The Sign of Four* (1932), *The Triumph of Sherlock Holmes* (1935), and *Murder at the Baskervilles* (1937, known in England as *Silver Blaze*).

However, the most famous film Holmes is Basil Rathbone, who got the part after producer Darryl F. Zanuck spotted him at a party. Nigel Bruce was hired to play a humorous, bungling Watson (contradicting the literary character) in the series, which began with *The Hound of the Baskervilles* and *The Adventures of Sherlock Holmes* (1939). After that, Universal Pictures took over the series from Twentieth Century-Fox, making a dozen less elaborate, contemporary thrillers: *Sherlock Holmes and the Voice of Terror* (1942), *Sherlock Holmes and the Secret Weapon* (1942), *Sherlock Holmes in Washington* (1943), *Sherlock Holmes Faces Death* (1943), *Spider Woman* (1944), *The Scarlet Claw* (1944), *The Pearl of Death* (1944), *The House of Fear* (1945), *The Woman in Green* (1945), *Pursuit to Algiers* (1945), *Terror by Night* (1946), and *Dressed to Kill* (1946).

More recent films include *Sherlock Holmes and the Deadly Necklace* (1962) starring Christopher Lee; *A Study in Terror* (1965), pitting Holmes (John Neville) against Jack the Ripper; *The Private Life of Sherlock Holmes* (1970) starring Robert Stephens; *They*

Might Be Giants (1971) starring George C. Scott as a delusional man who believes he's Holmes, with a psychiatrist, Dr. Watson (Joanne Woodward) trying to help him (the film was remade for TV in 1976 as *The Return of the World's Greatest Detective,* with Larry Hagman in the part); *The Seven Percent Solution* (1976) starring Nicol Williamson as Holmes, based on the successful 1974 novel by Nicholas Meyer (Meyer wrote two follow-ups: *The West End Horror* [1976], *and The Canary Trainer* [1993]), *The Adventure of Sherlock Holmes' Smarter Brother* (1975), a comedy starring Gene Wilder as Sigerson Holmes; *Young Sherlock Holmes* (1985) starring Nicholas Rowe as a teenage Holmes undertaking his first case; *The Return of Sherlock Holmes* (1987) with Michael Pennington, in which Holmes's frozen body is revived in the modern day; and *Without a Clue* (1988), with Watson (Ben Kingsley) as the brains of the team and Holmes being "played" by an actor (Michael Caine).

On radio, Gillette starred in a dramatization of the play in 1930. That year a regular series, *Sherlock Holmes,* was first heard over NBC. Over the years a succession of actors played Holmes: Gillette, Richard Gordon, Louis Hector, Basil Rathbone, Tom Conway, Ben Wright, and John Stanley. Leslie Charteris *(The Saint)* was among the writers. After the show went off the air, the BBC launched its own 13-part series in the late 1950s, starring John Gielgud. Ralph Richardson played Watson and Orson Welles was Moriarty.

In comic books, *Classics Illustrated* adapted "The Sign of the Four" as part of *Three Famous Mysteries* (1944, #21), *The Hound of the Baskervilles* (1947, #33), and *A Study in Scarlet* (1953, #110). Charlton Comics was the first to do a regular series, transferring the detective to New York for *Sherlock Holmes,* with two issues published in 1955–56. Dell published two issues of *The New Adventures of Sherlock Holmes* as part of the *4-Color* series (1961), DC Comics published one issue of *Sherlock Holmes* in 1975, and the character appeared in numbers 5 and 6 of *Marvel Preview* the following year. Holmes has also appeared in numerous British comic books, beginning with *Super Detective Library* #65 in 1955.

On TV, Ronald Howard starred as Holmes in *Sherlock Holmes,* which was filmed in France and syndicated in 1954. Thirty-nine half-hour adventures were produced in all. More recently, Jeremy Brett starred as a remarkably authentic Holmes in the BBC series *Adventures of Sherlock Holmes* and *The Return of Sherlock Holmes,* which began airing in the U.S. on PBS in 1984 as part of the *Mystery!* series. David Burke played Watson and was later replaced by Edward Hardwicke. Thirty-five episodes have been produced to date. Many feature films have been made for television as well, most notably the 1972 adaptation of *The Hound of the Baskervilles* starring Stewart Granger, Roger Moore in the 1975 movie *Sherlock Holmes in New York,* and another *The Hound of the Baskervilles* starring Ian Richardson in 1983. Richardson also starred in *The Sign of the Four* in 1983. In 1984 Peter Cushing returned to the part in the British TV film *Sherlock Holmes and the Masks of Death,* while Christopher Lee starred in the syndicated *Sherlock Holmes and the Leading Lady* and *Sherlock Holmes at Victoria Falls,* both 1991. That same year Charlton Heston starred as Holmes in the cable version of *Crucifer of Blood.*

In comic strips, writer E. Meiser and artist Frank Giacoia handled *Sherlock Holmes* for the *New York Herald Tribune* in the 1950s.

Over the years there have been countless spoofs of Holmes in all media, beginning with Sherlaw Kombs in Robert Barr's "The Great Pegram Mystery" (1894), and the comic strip "The Adventures of Chubblock Homes" in the June 16, 1894, issue of *Comic Cuts* in England. In literature, the character has been parodied in R.C. Lehmann's *The Adventures of Picklock Holes* (1901), Bret Harte's Hemlock Jones ("The Stolen Cigar Case," 1902), John Kendricks's stories about Shylock Homes (beginning in 1903), O. Henry's Shamrock Jolnes (1911), Frederick Arnold Jummer and Basil Mitchell's tale of Sherlock's daughter Shirley Holmes in "The Adventure of the Queen Bee," 1933 (it went to Broadway in 1936 as *The Holmeses of Baker Street*), and many others. In comic strips, Sherlocko the Monk made its debut in the *Monks* strip in the U.S. in 1910, while Herlock Sholmes was a comic strip in Yugoslavia, Sherlock Lopez in Spain, and so on.

Other writers have written legitimate Holmes stories, the best of which were collected in *The Misadventures of Sherlock Holmes* (1944), edited by ELLERY QUEEN. In 1954, author John Dickson Carr, along with Sir Arthur's son Adrian Conan Doyle, published a short story collection called *The Exploits of Sherlock Holmes.*

Holmes also inspired many detectives, the best known and best loved of which may be August Derleth's Solar Pons. With Doyle's blessings, Derleth created a character that is virtually identical to Holmes, down to his deerstalker hat and Inverness cape; a sidekick/chronicler Dr. Lyndon Parker; a London base (Praed Street); and identical deductive methods. Pons goes to work in 1907, after it becomes plain that Holmes is determined to stay retired. The first of the tales, "Adventures of the Late Mr. Faversham," was published in 1929, and the first collection of short stories, *"In re: Sherlock Holmes": The Adventures of Solar Pons,* was published in 1945.

SIEGFRIED (F, O, L, MP, C)

First Appearance: *The Nibelungenlied,* circa A.D. 1200 (see COMMENT).

Biography: The son of the King of the Netherlands, Siegfried is a mighty warrior who slays a dragon, bathes in its blood, and becomes impervious to harm, save where a leaf fell on his back. After defeating the dragon, he bests the Nibelung (dwarf) kings, stealing their gold, weapons, and other belongings, including a cloak of invisibility. After learning of the legendary beauty Kriemhild, Siegfried heads for Worms (western Germany), determined to make her his bride. Her brothers, all kings, ask his assistance in fighting the Saxons, which he gladly gives. Afterward one of the brothers, Gunther, asks for his help in winning the hand of Brunhild, Queen of Iceland. Siegfried agrees, provided he can marry Kriemhild on their return.

The two journey to Iceland, where Brunhild has agreed to wed any man who can beat her in spear-throwing, hurling a stone, and leaping. Using the cloak of invisibility, Siegfried stands by Gunther's side and helps him win the contests and the queen's hand. There is a double wedding, though Brunhild harbors doubts about her husband's abilities and ties him up to see if her suspicions are true. Sure enough, an invisible figure comes in to rescue him and also steals the queen's ring and girdle. Later, when Brunhild sees Kriemhild wearing these items, she realizes the truth. Curiously, though, she doesn't act on it. Meanwhile, one of Gunther's retainers, Hagen, is unhappy at how Siegfried has become more famous than Gunther. After learning from Kriemhild of Siegried's one vulnerable spot, Hagen arranges a hunt, during which he kills the hero. He also steals the Nibelung treasure from Kriemhild and sinks it in the Rhine.

Not about to let these crimes go unpunished, grieving Kriemhild agrees to marry Attila the Hun if he will slay her brothers; this is accomplished with the help of his heroic warriors Hildebrand and Dietrich of Bern. Kriemhild herself kills Hagen.

Comment: The author of the German epic is unknown. The work draws heavily on the *Völsunga Saga,* which is several hundred years older. In this prose cycle of legends, the hero is named Sigurd, who is the son of Sigmund—himself the son of Volsung whose father was Odin, king of the Norse gods. After slaying the dragon Fafnir, Sigurd takes the treasure and the enchanted horse Grani (a gift from Odin) and stumbles on the sleeping Valkyrie Brunhild. They become engaged, after which he goes off adventuring, befriends the sons of a king of the Rhine, and is given a magic potion that makes him forget Brunhild. Sigurd is promised the hand of the king's daughter Gudrun

(Kriemhild) provided he'll help her brother Gunnar (Gunther) marry Brunhild, who has placed herself in a circle of fire that all prospective suitors must cross. Disguised as Gunnar, Sigurd plucks Brunhild from the flames and she agrees to marry him; when she later learns that it was actually Sigurd, she has him slain and then takes her own life. Gudrun marries Attila. This tale was wonderfully retold by William Morris in *Sigurd the Volsung* (1876).

Oral tales about the hero are older still, going back as far as A.D. 500 and 600.

The most famous contemporary version of the tale is the cycle of four operas by Richard Wagner, which draws from both the *Volsunga Saga* and *The Nibelungenlied.* The operas, and the dates of their first performances, are *Das Rheingold* (September 22, 1869), *Die Walkure* (June 26, 1870), *Siegfried* (August 16, 1876), and *Gotterdammerung* (August 17, 1876). In this version, Siegfried is the son of Siegmund and Sieglinde, brother and sister and the children of Odin. After he is murdered by Hagen, Brunhild (here Brunnhilde) rides into the flames of his funeral pyre.

In literature, the most celebrated version of the tale is Jean Giraudoux's novel *Siegfried et le Limousin* (1922); Giraudoux also wrote the play *Siegfried* (1928).

In motion pictures, the character first appeared in the 1912 Italian film *Sigfrido.* He was also featured in the Italian *Nibelungen Saga* (1913), in the 1957 Italian *Sigfrido,* and in the 1971 German/U.S. coproduction *The Long, Swift Sword of Siegfried,* an erotic version starring Lance Boyle (Ramond Harmstorf). However, his best-known and most satisfying screen appearance is in director Fritz Lang's epics *Siegfried* (1923) and *Kriemhild's Revenge* (1924), both of which starred Paul Richter.

In comic books, DC published a four issue adaptation of *The Ring of the Nibelung* in 1989–90.

THE SILENT KNIGHT (C)

First Appearance: *The Brave and the Bold* #1, 1955, DC Comics.

Biography: In a small kingdom in sixth-century England, in the time of King Arthur, sorcery, and dragons, the evil Sir Oswald Bane secretly slays coruler Sir Edwin Kent. Before Bane will allow Edwin's blond, 15-year-old son Brian to succeed his father, he insists that he become a knight. Brian squires with the elderly Sir Grot, a friend of the dead Edwin, who fears Bane will kill the lad if he ever becomes too strong a warrior. Thus, Grot teaches Brian the skills of knighthood in secret, while publicly making him out to be something of an oaf. Riding from Greystone Castle into the Forest

Perilous one day, Brian plunges through the soft ground into a deep pit, where he finds a trunk containing a magnificent suit of silver armor, a sword, and a red helmet and shield that had belonged to his father. After spotting travelers being accosted by Bane's brutish soldiers, Brian dons the armor and drives the bullies off—never speaking, lest his voice give away his identity, and thus becoming known as the Silent Knight.

Brian stores his armor in a secret glade in the forest and continues to fight for the rights of those whom Bane would oppress. Because of his "knightly vows," he will never take advantage of a foe—for example, by using a weapon with a greater reach than theirs. He is also incredibly strong, once diving to the bottom of a lake, recovering a necklace, and swimming up again—in full armor!

Though Brian is in love with the Lady Celia, her heart belongs to the Silent Knight—a tough pill for the lad to swallow.

The Silent Knight battles for possession of a necklace. © DC Comics.

Comment: The character appeared in *The Brave and the Bold* through #22; his origin was retold in *Secret Origins* #49.

SILVER EAGLE (R)

First Appearance: *Silver Eagle, Mountie,* July 5, 1951, ABC.

Biography: Silver Eagle, a.k.a. Jim West, is a member of the Canadian Northwest Mounted Police. According to the opening legend, he serves justice "with the swiftness of an arrow" and is "the most famous Mountie of them all." His superior is Inspector Argyle; his confidant is the crusty Doc.

Comment: The character was created by famed radio adventure producer James Jewell, a veteran of both *The Lone Ranger, The Green Hornet,* and *Jack Armstrong, the All-American Boy.* The series was broadcast from Chicago and starred Jim Ameche as West; John Barclay, then Jess Pugh, as Argyle; and Clarence Hartzell as Doc. The show went off the air on March 10, 1955. When it died, it was the last of the major action series to go, effectively marking the end of the era of radio adventures.

See also SGT. PRESTON.

SILVERHAWKS (TV, C, T)

First Appearance: *SilverHawks,* September 1986, syndicated.

Biography: Led by Commander Stargazer, the five SilverHawks are four humans and one alien of the future who have been transformed into superandroids to keep peace throughout the universe—in particular, to try to nab the intergalactic criminal Mon*Star. Headquartered in the space station Hawk-Haven, the SilverHawks are encased in silver skins and are comprised of leader Quicksilver and his faithful cyborg-bird Tally-Hawk; Bluegrass, who pilots their ship *Mirage;* the female Steelwill and Steelheart, mechanics; and the youthful Copper Kid from the Planet of Mimes, a computer expert. Mon*Star raids the universe from his squidlike vessel *Skyrunner,* aided by the equally nefarious Buzz-Saw, Hardware, Meoldia, Mo-Lec-U-Lar, Mumbo-Jump, Poker-Face, Time-Stopper, Windhammer, and Yes-Man.

Comment: There were 62 adventures, three of them an hour, the rest a half-hour. Marvel Comics published six issues of a *SilverHawks* comic book as part of their juvenile Star Comics line, in 1987–88, and there were various toys, coloring books, action figures, and the like. The series was Rankin-Bass Productions' failed attempt to capitalize on the success of their *ThunderCats* series. (See LION-O.)

SIMON and SIMON (TV)

First Appearance: *Simon & Simon,* November 1981, CBS.

Biography: Andrew Jackson Simon and Rick Simon are brothers and partners in a San Diego-based detective agency. The two are nothing alike: A.J. is hardworking and well groomed, drives a well-scrubbed convertible, and lives in a clean apartment. The older Rick is a swinger who is partial to cowboy attire, is singularly gruff, drives a battered pickup, lives in a dirty houseboat, and would rather play guitar than work.

The brothers have a way of mucking things up. Hired to help an accountant get a new identity, they discover he's actually a spy wanted by the FBI. Mistaking a smuggler for a client, they become embroiled in his operation. The two move in to bust a high-profile criminal and become the prime suspects. Witnessing a murder, they can't convince the local law whodunit. Though the siblings always come out on top, their bad luck (coupled with a knack for attracting low-paying clients) annoys their mother, Cecilia, greatly.

Over the years, the two have worked with an eclectic group of associates. Young Janet Fowler lends the lads a hand in the early years, despite the fact that she's the daughter of rival detective Myron Fowler. On the police force, they get cooperation from irreverent undercover police detective Marcel "Downtown" Brown and, later, much less help from Lieutenant Abigail Marsh.

Comment: The hour-long series aired through December 1988 and starred Jameson Parker as A.J. and Gerald McRaney as Rick. Mary Carver was Cecilia, Jeannie Wilson was Janet, Eddie Barth was Myron, Tim Reid was Downtown, and Joan McMurtrey was Abigail.

SINDBAD (F, L, MP, C)

First Appearance: Unknown (see COMMENT).

Biography: In the Bagdad of Caliph Harun al-Rashid, the jealous porter Hindbad complains aloud how unfair it is that he lives a harsh life while Sindbad lives in luxury. Overhearing him, Sindbad takes Hindbad aside and tells him his life story. As a child, Sindbad inherited a great deal of money from his merchant father. (No mention is made of Sindbad's mother.) After squandering most of it when he came of age, he used what little remained to buy goods and join a company of merchants.

On the first of his seven voyages, the sailors dropped anchor on an island that turned out to be a giant fish. Sindbad was thrown into the water and drifted to the realm of King Mihrjan, who appoints him harbormaster. Eventually he found a ship headed to Bagdad and booked passage.

On the second voyage, he shipped out with more merchants, who left him behind on an island when he walked off and fell asleep. After finding a nest of the giant eaglelike rukh (or roc), which feeds elephants to its young, Sindbad lashed himself to its leg and was borne to a high hill. There he found a stash of diamonds, survived the Valley of Serpents (dragons), and found merchants on the island who take him to Basra, then to Bagdad.

Though rich now, he longed to travel and undertook his third voyage in the company of more merchants. Blown off course, they came to the Mountain of the Zughb, apelike creatures who stole the ship and left the men stranded. A black giant came along and roasted two of the men on a spit ("like a Kabab-stick"); the others escaped by blinding him with heated pokers while he slept. After a brush with a giant snake who ate several more men, Sindbad made it to the shore and was picked up by a passing ship.

"Forgetting all my perils and hardships" and longing "for the society of the various races of manking," Sindbad headed out with another group of merchants on his fourth voyage. They landed on an isle of cannibals, and all but Sindbad were eaten. Fleeing, he encountered a civilized race of people and took one of them of "high pedigree" as his wife; only when she died did he learn that it is the custom of these folk for the living spouse to be entombed with the dead. Fortunately, a "wild beast" entered the sealed cave and Sindbad was able to follow it out. After waving down a passing ship, he returned to Bagdad.

Sindbad bought more goods and set out on his fifth voyage. The ship landed on an island where the sailors cracked a rukh's egg and killed the chick for meat; the parent birds arrived and dropped boulders on the fleeing ship. Sindbad alone survived and reached an island where he encountered an old man. The frail fellow asked Sindbad to carry him on his shoulders across a channel; Sindbad did so, unaware that the man was the Shaykh al-Bahr, the Old Man of the Sea. The Old Man rode men to their death, refusing to let go. For days Sindbad was unable to shake the man, who even slept and relieved himself on his shoulders. Finally the sailor got him drunk and crushed his head with a rock. A passing ship found Sindbad and, in due course, he returned to Bagdad.

"It must be a marvel to you how, after having five times met with shipwreck and unheard of perils, I could again tempt fortune and risk fresh trouble," Sindbad says. "I am even surprised myself." This sixth time, though, he journeyed by land to India and set sail with a captain there. Notwithstanding the change,

H.J. Ford's 1898 interpretation of the Old Man of the Sea and *Sindbad.*

the crew was shipwrecked on a mountainous island. Sindbad was the sole survivor and, after building a raft, he floated along an underground river until he was discovered by natives. They took him to their king in the city of Serendib, which lies in the shadow of the tallest mountain in the world. The monarch welcomed Sindbad, who climbed the mountain, found rubies and diamonds, and was thereafter given gifts for the caliph and a ship with which to return to Bagdad.

By then Sindbad had no desire to sail again. But the caliph bade him to return to the Serendib with gifts for the king, and he obliged. This time, pirates seized his vessel and sold him as a slave to a rich merchant. The merchant sent him out to hunt elephants for their tusks; he was so successful that after two months, the elephants themselves took him to their secret graveyard, that he may harvest what he needs without killing them. In gratitude for his discovery, the merchant granted Sindbad his freedom. He returned to Bagdad on an ivory ship.

His saga ended, Sindbad gives Hindbad enough money so that he can stop being a porter and do what he wants with his life.

Comment: The stories may date as far back as several centuries B.C. and, some scholars suggest, may even have been derived from tales of the voyages of *Odysseus,* to which they bear many similarities. They first appeared in Europe in translator Antoine Galland's 1704 opus *Mille et une nuits,* though Sir Richard Francis Burton's 15-volume *Arabian Nights' Entertainments, or The Thousand and One Nights* (1885–86) contains what is considered the complete, definitive version of the tale.

Burton and others use the spelling "Sindbad" in their tales. However, early 20th-century scholars saw the tales as an allegory for good and evil, and found the hero (and his name) to be a fitting reflection of this. Hence, the "d" was dropped, and the hero became Sinbad in various children's stories and in his motion picture incarnations. Also, in some versions of the tale, Hindbad is also named Sindbad, the two being described as Sindbad the Hammel (porter) and Sindbad the Sailor.

In films, the hero, played by Bluto, has battled Popeye in the spectacular animated featurette *Popeye the Sailor Meets Sinbad the Sailor* (1936). He has also been seen in *Sinbad the Sailor* (1947) starring Douglas Fairbanks, Jr., *The Son of Sinbad* (1955) starring Dale Robertson, *The 7th Voyage of Sinbad* (1958) starring Kerwin Mathews, *Captain Sinbad* (1963) starring Guy Williams (TV's Zorro), *The Golden Voyage of Sinbad* (1973) starring John Phillip Law, *Sinbad and the Eye of the Tiger* (1977) starring Patrick Wayne; *The Magic Voyage of Sinbad* (1961), which is actually not a Sinbad film but a dubbed verion of the 1952 Russian film *Sadko,* based on the Rimsky-

A pair of movie *Sindbads*: Kerwin Mathew (with Kathryn Grant) in *The 7th Voyage of Sinbad* . . .

. . . and John Phillip Law in *The Golden Voyage of Sinbad*.
© Columbia Pictures, courtesy Ray Harryhausen.

Korsakov opera and starring "Edward Stolar" (Serge Stolyarov); *The Lost World of Sinbad* (1965); which also is not a Sinbad film but the dubbed 1963 Japanese pirate film *Daitozoku* starring Toshiro Mifune; and *The Last Voyage of Sinbad* (also known as *Sinbad of the Seven Seas*) (1992) starring Lou Ferrigno. An animated film from Japan's Toei Studios, *The Adventures of Sinbad* (1962), had the young boy and his friend Ali as adventure-loving stowaways onboard the ship *Golda*.

The hero has also appeared in various comic book adventures, including Marvel Comics' adaptations of both *The 7th Voyage of Sinbad* and *The Golden Voyage of Sinbad,* and the British comic book adaptation of *Sinbad and the Eye of the Tiger* (General Book Distributors). For copyright reasons, Marvel called him the Arabian Knight when he fought in their *Contest of Champions* three-issue series in 1982. There have been other comic book stories as well, though perhaps none as bizarre as "The Last Voyage of Sinbad" in *Creepy* #129, in which author Budd Lewis hypothesized that Sinbad was "a simple man" and "mad."

Fawcett published Graham Diamond's novel *Captain Sinbad* in 1980, sending the hero on new and somewhat lusty voyages throughout the Middle East, Greece, Spain, and elsewhere.

SIR DENIS NAYLAND SMITH   (L, MP, R, TV)

First Appearance: *The Insidious Dr. Fu-Manchu* by Sax Rohmer, 1913 (U.K. title: *The Mystery of Fu-Manchu*, Methuen).
Biography: The Chinese villain Dr. Fu Manchu will stop at nothing to conquer the world, and Sir Denis Nayland Smith will stop at nothing to prevent this. He does so not "in the interests of the British Government merely," he says, "but in the interests of the entire white race." Working for Scotland Yard as an inspector, and then as a Criminal Investigation Department commissioner before becoming a freelance sleuth, Smith is luckier than he is smart, frequently escaping traps by chance rather than skill. His associate is Doctor Petrie, an Egyptian-born chemist who narrates the adventures and is married to the beautiful Karamaneh, a former slave of Fu Manchu's. In a change from the way these things normally work, Karamaneh regularly saves both Petrie and Smith from their enemy.

Smith has been knighted for his ongoing battle against Fu Manchu. He is "a tall, lean man," with a "square-cut, clean-shaven face sun-baked to the hue of coffee." His hair is "more grey than black," and there is fire in his eyes and constant "tense nervous vitality" about him.

Comment: The two archenemies crossed swords in most of the 13 Fu Manchu novels (the name was hyphenated only in the first three) and in a pair of short stories. In film, Fu Manchu was seen in 23 short subjects produced from 1923 to 1925 and in numerous features. The best-known of these were *The Mysterious Dr. Fu Manchu* (1929) starring Warner Oland as the fiend and O.P. Heggie as Smith; *The Mask of Fu Manchu* (1932) starring Boris Karloff as Fu Manchu and Lewis Stone as Smith; the 1940 serial *Drums of Fu Manchu* starring Henry Brandon as the villain and William Royle as Smith; *The Face of Fu Manchu* (1965), with Christopher Lee as Fu Manchu and Nigel Green as Smith; *The Brides of Fu Manchu* (1966) and *The Vengeance of Fu Manchu* (1967) starring Lee and Douglas Wilmer; *Kiss and Kill* (1970) and *The Castle of Fu Manchu* (1972) starring Lee and Richard Greene; and, in his last screen appearance, Peter Sellers playing both Smith and Fu Manchu in the critically panned *The Fiendish Plot of Dr. Fu Manchu* (1980).

On radio, Smith was played by Charles Warburton. The CBS series debuted in 1932 and ran for most of the decade. On TV, 39 episodes of the half-hour *Adventures of Fu Manchu* began airing in syndication in 1956. Glen Gordon starred, with Lester Matthews as Smith. Previously Cedric Hardwicke had played Smith with John Carradine as Fu Manchu in an unsold pilot (1952).

SIR JAMES BLAKE   (MP)

First Appearance: *Blake of Scotland Yard*, 1937, Victory Pictures (Sam Katzman).

Lobby card featuring *Sir James Blake,* on the right, as he tries to save Hope from the Scorpion's henchmen. © Victory Pictures.

Biography: A former inspector with Scotland Yard, the two-fisted Sir James Blake has teamed with his niece, Hope Mason, to develop a death ray to be used in the fight against crime. Count Basil Zegelloff, a munitions dealer, sees a demonstration of the weapon and hires a black-cloaked figure known as the Scorpion to steal it. But canny Blake has removed a radium tube, rendering it useless, and the Scorpion uses kidnaping, explosives, and other means in an effort to get the missing part. Eventually Blake arrests Zegelloff and lets the Scorpion steal the ray—which he's left in a safe, wired with a dose of electricity that knocks the Scorpion out cold.

Comment: Ralph Byrd (DICK TRACY) starred as Blake and Joan Barclay was Hope. The 15-chapter serial was directed by Bob Hill. Blake was an unusual hero: Typically, books, movies, and radio heroes from Scotland Yard are more from the reflective SHERLOCK HOLMES mold.

SISTERHOOD OF STEEL (C)

First Appearance: *Sisterhood of Steel* #1, 1984, Marvel Comics.

Biography: In another world on an island named Ildana, a race of warrior-women, the Sisterhood of Steel, has arisen in a time comparable to Earth's Hellenic age. Ildana is ruled by a Matrix consisting of the Queen of Swords, the Priestess of Swords, and the Princess of Swords, as well as two parliamentary Houses, the House of Gold and the House of Silver.

Only the best, brightest, and strongest women become warriors, trained from the age of four to 13 before they can become a Novice. Those who fail to make the grade become "menial" cooks, gardeners, seamstresses, and scribes. The major characters in the saga are Princess of Swords Vandalis, Priestess of Swords Greyan, Commander First Class Ambyre, a.k.a. "The Merry Widowmaker," Commander First Class

Gill, the one-armed Instructor First Class Lanna, Cadet First Class Mayal, Cadet Boronwe, and failed warrior, now administrator, Kelki.

All are devoted to protecting their island from invasion and upholding their bold traditions.

Comment: The characters were created by writer Christy Marx and artist Mike Vosburg. Eight issues of the comic book were published under Marvel's adult Epic imprint through 1986. The characters also starred in *Eclipse Graphic Album* #13 in 1987.

SKY COMMANDERS (T, TV)

First Appearance: *Sky Commanders,* 1987, Kenner Toys.

Biography: Toward the end of the 21st century, the wicked General Plague has devoted himself to world destruction. The only ones standing in the way of Plague and his evil aides Mordax, Raider Rath, and Kreeg are a group of soldiers known as the Sky Commanders: Cutter Kling, R.J. Scott, Books Baxter, Spider Reilly, Jim Stryker, Red McCullough, Kodiak Crane, and leader General Mike Summit.

Comment: In addition to the toy line, which was introduced in Feburary 1987, there were 13 animated adventures that aired as part of *The Funtastic World of Hanna-Barbera* beginning in July 1987. The series had a large number of well-known actors doing voices, including William Windom as Kling, Darryl Hickman as Scott, and Dorian Harewood as Stryker. Bob Ridgley was the voice of Summit.

SKYHAWKS (TV)

First Appearance: *Skyhawks,* September 1969, ABC.

Biography: Captain Mike Wilson, a retired U.S. Air Force pilot and widower, is the owner of the air cargo passenger service Skyhawks, Inc., based in San Marcos Field. Wilson is aided by his 17-year-old twins Caroline and Steve, who are both pilots; by World War I pilot Pappy Wilson, who prefers his Sopwitch Camel to modern planes; by chief mechanic Joe Conway, a military pal of Wilson's; and by Mike's two wards, 14-year-old Baron "Red" Hughes, a glider pilot, and nine-year-old Cynthia "Mugs" Hughes.

In addition to routine transport, the Skyhawks' diverse missions include aerial photography, crop dusting, flying for skydivers, rescue missions, and all-important top-secret work for the government transporting national security materials to a secret site. The latter work annoys Buck Devlin of the rival Buck Devlin's Air Service, who wants the government contract and Mike's other work for himself, and regularly sabotages Skyhawks aircraft in an effort to put them out of business.

Comment: The series aired through September 1971; 17 half-hour adventures were produced. Michael Rye was the voice of Mike, Casey Kasem was Steve and Joe, Iris Rainer voiced Caroline, Dick Curtis was Red and Pappy, Melinda Casey was Mugs, and Bob Arbogast was Buck.

SKY KING (R, TV)

First Appearance: *Sky King,* 1947, ABC.

Biography: Schuyler King is the owner of the Flying Crown Ranch. After serving as a naval aviator in World War II, he returns to his Flying Crown Ranch in Arizona (whose foreman is the devoted Jim Bell) only to find that his spread is being threatened by the frequently invisible Dr. Shade. After defeating Shade, King—along with his teenage niece Penny and nephew Clipper—partake in many adventures in the U.S. and abroad, fighting the occasional superscientific villain along with routine smugglers, rustlers, spies, kidnapers, and others. The heroes get about in their twin-engine Cessna *Songbird* or, for long hauls, the jet *Black Arrow.*

Comment: Broadcast from Chicago, the half-hour radio series starred Jack Lester, followed by Earl Nightingale and Roy Engel as King, Beryl Vaughn as Penny, and Jack Bivens as Clipper. It went off the air in 1954. The show came to ABC TV in September 1953 and lasted just one year—though reruns were seen regularly through 1966. The half-hour series starred Kirby Grant as Sky, Gloria Winters as Penny, and Ron Hagerthy as Clipper.

See also HOP HARRIGAN.

SKY WOLF (C)

First Appearance: *Air Fighters Comics* #2, 1942, Hillman Publications.

Biography: Sky Wolf is an "anti-Nazi prowler of the skies" who commands a crack team of fliers: the Turtle, a Polish fighter whose tongue has been sliced out by the Germans (he communicates from his cockpit by tapping out Morse Code on his head!); the Judge, who had been turned down by the RAF because of his age; and Cocky Roche, a scrappy Cockney kid. The squadron flies about in a plane that splits in two, giving the men a distinct element of surprise in dogfights.

In their first adventure, the heroes battle Colonel Von Tundra, whose left side is covered with metal, the result of an encounter with Sky Wolf. (Hitler describes his officer looking "like a half-open can of herring!") They also meet Frisco, a singer who is trusted by the

Germans but works for the Allies. In their second adventure the team meets the Heap, ace Baron Emmelmann who had crashed in a swamp during the last war, merged "with the . . . dreary vegetation," and became a blood-sucking humanoid covered with moss.

Initially, the character wears a purple body suit and white wolf's-head cowl. Later he turns in these threads for more traditional military attire with a flashy yellow scarf (though he keeps the wolf's-head).

Comment: *Air Fighters Comics* became *Airboy Comics* with #23, named for its featured character, a youthful superhero. It lasted 111 issues, Sky Wolf continuing in the title until 1947. He got his own title in 1988, when Eclipse revived the hero for three issues. The Heap became a comics superstar, tearing up bad guys, coming to the U.S., becoming the sidekick of young Rickie Wood, and remaining in *Airboy Comics* until the end. In 1971 he was briefly revived by Skywald Publishing (albeit updated), appearing in both his own one-shot title and in *Psycho* magazine. Other characters introduced along with Sky Wolf were the Bald Eagle, an ace who lost his hair while flying through a fire and pilots the remarkable *Flying Coffin;* the airborne ace the Flying Dutchman; the costumed superheroine the Black Angel; and THE IRON ACE.

Ironically, the first issue of *Air Fighters Comics* had been a sales disaster, featuring a slew of adventure heroes who were never heard from again: American ace and superspy Barry Haynes, a.k.a. the Black Commander; Tex Trainor, Test Pilot; Jack Dale, Flying Cadet; the Mosquito, a short but tenacious flier with the border patrol; test pilot Mach Duff; Navy ace Crash Davis; and the adventures of the Black Sheep Squadron.

SLAM BRADLEY (C)

First Appearance: *Detective Comics* #1, 1937, DC Comics.

Biography: A Cleveland native and high school dropout, Slam is a private eye who operates in New York, assisted by his "partner pal [and] runt," young "Shorty" Morgan. Bradley frequently goes undercover on investigations, pretending to be athletes, entertainers, and countless professionals. He travels the world, as cases demand, from Hollywood to the North Pole, and eventually has adventures in outer space and through time. Pipe-smoking Slam relies on his fists more than on firearms, and relaxes from "the tension of manhunting" by taking joyrides in his convertible and courting young women he meets on cases.

Comment: Slam was the product of Jerry Siegel and Joe Shuster, the team that created Superman. Slam was

Slam Bradley and Shorty (right) confer with the police chief after wrapping up a case. Art by Joe Shuster. © DC Comics.

still appearing in *Detective Comics* when Batman was introduced (#27); his adventures ended in #152, by which time other writers and artists had worked on the strip. *Detective Comics* also featured other adventure heroes, including Buck Marshall, Range Detective, who works with local sheriffs to solve crimes; sleuth Bruce Nelson; Speed Saunders, an erudite, natty, blond "ace investigator" who works alone and relies more on his wits than on his fists; detective Larry Steele; the crime-busting reporter and "young America's hero" Cliff Crosby; and no-nonsense D.A. Steve Malone.

SLASH MARAUD (C)

First Appearance: *Slash Maraud* #1, 1987, DC Comics.

Biography: Slash Maradovitch—a.k.a. Slash Maraud—is a Detroit-based bodyguard turned international mercenary when the alien "Shapers" invade at some point in the near future. Their home planet is polluted, overpopulated, and dying, so they take over the earth; world governments crumble as the aliens remake our world more to their liking with purple snow, see-through trees, dinosaurs, and other oddities. The Shapers are able to transform themselves from flylike humanoids to people, which makes it difficult for the human rebels, or Xenos, to sniff them out. The rest of humanity—99 percent of it—simply does what the aliens tell them.

Tooling around the nation on his radar-equipped motor-bike, Slash is not among the obedient ones. Though the loner prefers to stay away from Shapers they always cross paths—at which point he isn't averse to blowing them away with his handgun or miniature explosives.

Comment: The comic book ran six issues and was created by writer Doug Moench and artist Paul Gulacy.

SLATE SHANNON (R, TV)

First Appearance: *Bold Venture,* 1951, syndicated.

Biography: A cynical, two-fisted American who has moved to Trinidad, Slate Shannon is the owner of a hotel called Shannon's Place and a 60-foot sloop called *The Bold Venture.* Together with his ward—beautiful young Sailor Duval, who is in her early 20s and whose father was Slate's closest friend—he gets into trouble involving killers, kidnapers, smugglers, revolutionaries, and others who pass through Trinidad.

Comment: Humphrey Bogart and Lauren Bacall starred in the radio series, which lasted a year. Dane Clark and Joan Marshall starred in the syndicated series, which began airing in January 1952. Thirty-nine half-hour episodes were produced.

SLOCUM (L)

First Appearance: *Slocum* by Jake Logan, 1975, Jove Books.

Biography: John Slocum is in his middle 30s and roams the turn-of-the-century West from Kansas City, to Colorado, to Wyoming. Sometimes the marksman "with leather and steel in his bearing" works as a bounty hunter, sometimes as a sheriff, and sometimes he rides shotgun for Wells Fargo. He's also worked as a ranch hand and held other odd jobs. Regardless of the line of work, he always manages to find danger, whether it's Apaches, timber czars, stagecoach bandits, bank robbers, vigilantes, or even killers on the streets of New York City.

Slocum wears a pair of Colt .44s and rides a "tough little Appaloosa." When he's on horseback, Slocum and the animal are one.

Comment: There are 175 Slocum novels to date.

See also THE GUNSMITH; LONGARM.

SMILIN' JACK (CS, L, C, MP, R)

First Appearance: *On the Wing,* October 1, 1933, Chicago Tribune-New York News Syndicate.

Biography: A former Texas barnstormer, "Smilin'" Jack (originally Mack) Martin is an aviator for whom no job is too dangerous. Though he says with tongue-in-cheek that "it's swell" teaching students to fly, he prefers searching for missing persons, working with the Coast Guard, exploring uncharted territory, testing new aircraft, and chasing down criminals of all kinds. A Clark Gable look-alike, he grows a mustache as a disguise in an early case, and keeps it. (Earlier his nemesis, Dart Blackstone, was the one with the mustache—and a promotional piece describing the strip said you could tell he was "the villain of the piece" because of the hair on his lip.)

Jack—who once, when he was bound and left in the cockpit, flew using his teeth to steer and worked switches with his nose—flies a variety of planes over the years, from the *South Sea Scout* to a homemade glider when he has to escape from Death Rock. He is assisted by his youthful ward Pinfeathers; his cook and helper Fat Stuff (a former South Seas headhunter who tacks "um" onto words, as in "What can Fat Stuff do to help-um with weddum?"); former barnstormer Downwind Jackson/Jaxon (the spelling varies), whose face is always averted from the reader (usually to look at girls); and the grumpy Velvet Harry. After he dates temperamental Dixie Lee a number of years he's dumped for Dude Duncan; Jack makes Pinfeather's sister Mary Miller, his "co-pilot for life" on November 24, 1940, though he adamantly refuses her request to "get a nice safe job on the ground somewhere." (Indeed, if he weren't so brave, Mary and Dixie both would have died when they fought and knocked themselves out inside a giant wind tunnel and were sucked toward the whirring propeller.)

Unquestionably the most traumatic event of Jack's professional life is when he loses his pilot's license and takes a job flying cargo around Mexico—unaware that he's working for smugglers.

Toward the end of the strip's long run, rugged Smilin' Jack, Jr., takes over. At the very end, Jack, Jr., takes the appropriately named Sizzle to be his wife in a ceremony attended by most of the large cast.

Comment: The strip was created by Zack Mosley, who became an airplane buff when he was a kid and an army plane was forced to land on his father's land. The name of the strip was changed to *Smilin' Jack* on December 31, and it lasted until 1973.

Jack starred in seven Big Little Books: *Smilin' Jack and the Stratosphere Ascent* (1937), *Smilin' Jack and the Coral Princess* (1938), *Smilin' Jack in Wings Over the Pacific* (1939), *Smilin' Jack Speed Pilot* (1941), *Smilin' Jack Flying High With Downwind* (1942), *Smilin' Jack and the Jungle Pipe Line* (1946), and *Smilin' Jack and the Escape from Death Rock* (1947).

In comic books, the character appeared in 11 one-shots, costarred in various other titles, and headlined eight issues of Dell's *Smilin' Jack* (1940–49).

Jack was featured in the 13-chapter movie serial *Adventures of Smilin' Jack* (1943), starring Tom Brown as Jack (the only character retained from the strip) and pitting him against Axis agents in the remote land of Mandon. There, Jack tries to establish an overland route between Allied forces and China, thwarting the German and Japanese designs in the mountain kingdom. Fortunately, he is inadvertently assisted by the enemy, who spend as much time bickering among one another as they do fighting him.

Frank Readick played the character on the short-lived radio show.

SOJARR (L)

First Appearance: *Sojarr of Titan* by Manly Wade Wellman, March 1941, *Startling Stories.*

Biography: Ten centuries in the future, humans have colonized the planets as far out as Jupiter. A fortune in prize money is offered to the first person to go beyond, to Saturn. Heroic Pitt Rapidan takes up the challenge, but crashes in a jungle on Saturn's moon Titan. The sole survivor of the crash is Pitt's three-year-old son Stuart, who had been placed in a protective harness just before the crash. Before perishing, Pitt tells the child to be "a good soldier"; thinking his name is Sojarr, the boy grows up in the jungle, using a knife to protect himself from the alien monsters and learning to speak by listening to the radio in the wreckage of the spaceship. In the lesser gravity of Titan, he is also stronger and quicker than he would be on Earth. Upon reaching young adulthood, Sojarr falls in with a humanlike band under the leadership of Birok, who is at war with the Truags, four-armed apes led by Hekta. Sojarr becomes the greatest human warrior, excelling not only with a sword but with pistols that fire turo, an explosive ore.

Twenty years after Pitt's crash, a flight sets out under the command of his one-time rival, John Kaiser. The crew reaches Titan, where Kaiser is eventually killed and Sojarr rescues his niece, the lovely Ursula. Though members of the crew remain behind to start a colony, Ursula returns to Earth with samples of turo. Clearly, though, she will return one day.

Comment: The story was inspired by editor Mort Weisinger, who wanted Wellman to write a Tarzan in space story, with elements of JOHN CARTER thrown in. *Sojarr of Titan* wasn't published in book form until ten years later, issued under the Prize imprint. The prolific Wellman also wrote a series of stories about the Stone Age warrior Hok for *Amazing Stories.*

SPACE ANGEL (TV)

First Appearance: *Space Angel,* February 1962, syndicated.

Biography: One-eyed Scott McCloud is a space ma-rine, a member of the Earth Bureau of Investigation's top-secret Interplanetary Space Force. He travels throughout the solar system onboard the spaceship *Starduster,* investigating mysteries and keeping peace. With him are crew members Crystal, an electronics engineer and navigator; Taurus, a pilot and mechanic; and Professor Mace, who is also in charge of their headquarters, Evening Star.

Comment: The characters were created by Dik Darley and Dick Brown, though legendary comic book artist Alex Toth art directed the 52 half-hour adventures. Ned Lefebver was the voice of Scott.

The Cambria Productions series was created using the Synchro-Vox process. (See CLUTCH CARGO.)

SPACE FAMILY ROBINSON (C, TV, L)

First Appearance: *Space Family Robinson* #1, 1963, Western Publishing.

Tam Robinson struggles to save her father from a Golick. Just another day in the lives of the *Space Family Robinson.* © Gold Key Comics.

Ian Stannard, the *Space Man,* with Mary and Johnny. © Dell Publishing.

Biography: The Robinson family consists of Craig and June Robinson, ages 41 and 39, and their children Tim, 16, and Tam, 15, along with dog Clancy and parrot Yakker. After the Robinsons leave our world in the year 2001 to conduct research onboard a giant space station in Earth orbit, the station "[breaks] loose from its earth orbit" and casts the family "adrift in trackless space." Guiding the H-shaped space station through the stars, the family uses "endless spectrograph tests" in an effort to find our sun and return home. The station has a spacemobile, which allows the occupants to explore worlds they encounter—exotic, typically life-bearing planets, such as Orious, Kliklag, Norica, Zero, Altair, Kormat, Syltron, Raynoid, Zytrox, and Kregara.

The space station possesses a "time-shift mechanism" and can make "extra-dimensional space maneuvers," which allows the Robinsons to travel through time, for example, to ancient Mars and Earth of the past.

Comment: The title, published under the Gold Key imprint, became *Space Family Robinson Lost in Space* with #15, then simply *Lost in Space* with #37. It lasted 59 issues. Innovation revived the title in 1991, based on the TV characters, and it continues to be published, written by the TV costar Bill Mumy.

Irwin Allen produced the TV series, which aired from September 1965 to September 1968 and was different in several ways from the comic book. It starred Guy Williams as Professor John Robinson, June Lockhart as his wife, Maureen, Marta Kristen as eldest daughter Judy, Mumy as son Will, Angela Cartwright as daughter Penny, Mark Goddard as pilot Major Don West, and Jonathan Harris as stowaway Dr. Zachary Smith. In the series, the year is 1997 and the Robinsons are sick of the crowded, polluted earth. The spaceship *Jupiter II* is supposed to carry the family and West on a five-year journey to a planet circling the star Alpha Centauri. However, foreign agent Smith sabotages the ship and, though it doesn't blow up as he'd planned, it becomes lost in space with him still onboard. When the Robinsons emerge from suspended animation, they and the cowardly Smith establish a fragile truce for the duration of their journey. Clancy and Yakker were not featured on the show: Will's companion was the ambulatory Robot, with Bob May inside the costume and Dick Tufeld providing the voice.

Like their comic book counterparts, the Robinsons have adventures on different worlds each week. Though their saucer-shape ship can land on different worlds, they get about on the surface via the enclosed, vanlike "space chariot."

The TV series spawned a novel by Dave Van Arnam and Roy Archer, published in 1966.

SPACE MAN (C)

First Appearance: *4-Color* #1253, 1962, Dell Publishing.

Biography: A member of the first graduating class of the Space Academy, Ian Stannard is now a 12-year veteran of the astronaut corps (placing the series in the middle 1970s). In his first chronicled adventure, Ian and 14-year-old Space Academy graduate Johnny Mack—the son of famed astronaut Hugh Mack—head to a top-secret American base inside the moon. There they are told by commander Colonel Hooper that for 15 years, the U.S. has been a member of the Galactic Guard, which consists of soldiers from other worlds and whose primary foes are the evil Garrak-Axos from the Alpha Centauri galaxy. The aliens provided plans for a cyborg workforce and a mothership was constructed, capable of traveling faster than the speed of light. Ian is to be given command of the ship, with its atomic energy guns, and is also put in charge of training new cadets. He is assisted in all of his endeavors by the devoted cyborg Claud.

The men are allowed to return to Earth—Ian to his pilot fiancee, Mary Lansing, Johnny to his mother, Grace—before heading secretly to space for training. Later Mary is allowed to join Ian on his journeys throughout space.

Comment: Space Man got his own title, which ran for ten issues (the *4-Color* issue is considered #1), the last two of which were reprints. Even though the history it weaves turns out to have been faulty, the stories were entertaining and there was generally excellent interior art by Jack Sparling.

SPACE RANGER (C)

First Appearance: *Showcase* #15, 1958, DC Comics.

Biography: Based in New York of the 22nd century, Rick Starr is the son of cigar-chomping industrialist Thaddeus Starr, president of Allied Solar Enterprises. Rick pretends to be a lazy good-for-nothing so that no one will suspect him of secretly being the heroic Space Ranger; only his secretary, buxom, blond Myra Mason, knows the truth about her boss. When danger threatens anywhere in space, Rick leaves his office, boards his private spaceship, and races to a hollowed-out asteroid between Mars and Jupiter—his headquarters as Space Ranger, the Guardian of the Universe. (A much smaller base, located on Earth, is used for storing weapons.) Rick's secret identity is also known to his short, pink, elephant-nosed alien sidekick Cryll, whose life Starr saved when the creature was stranded "in the deeps of space beyond Pluto." Cryll lives in the asteroid and can change shape at will. Starr patrols the universe aboard the red (sometimes yellow and red) rocket *Solar King,* which boasts hyperspace drive (sometimes called overdrive) to carry him quickly to

Though Cryll and Myra are incapacitated, *Space Ranger* fights on against evil Illyrions. © DC Comics.

any region of space. His chief weapon is his "multi-ray" gun, which can fire ten-second-long antigravity blasts, paralyzer rays, destructive beams, a "force wall" that can repel enemy rays, a vacuumizer (to dig holes in rock), a thermoblaze to melt things, and numb rings that can knock out most life-forms. Other bizarre weapons in the arsenal of the planet-hopping hero include carboralyx pellets to whip up sandstorms, star-grenades that "sap the energy" of enemies, a dissolverizer, and much more.

Space Ranger wears a yellow body suit with red boots, gloves, shoulders, and a "weapons belt" that includes his ray gun holster. His transparent bubble helmet covers everything but his nose, mouth, and chin. One version of this costume is Special Uniform K-76, which contains "a concealed lining" loaded with additional weapons such as the thermo-liquid, which destroys everything but glass.

Comment: The character was created by editor Jack Schiff and writer Arnold Drake. After two appearances in *Showcase,* the character moved to *Tales of the Unexpected,* where he remained from #40 to #82 before moving to *Mystery in Space* from #92 to #103.

THE SPECIALIST (L)

First Appearance: *A Talent for Revenge* by John Cutter, 1983, New American Library.

Biography: Jack Sullivan is a Vietnam veteran turned international freelance troubleshooter who carries a mini-Uzi and a 9mm Beretta automatic and specializes in neutralizing terrorists and tyrants. A "killing machine" with muscles so well toned that he is "impervious to blows that would incapacitate the average man," he has never failed in any of his hundreds of missions, whether it's bringing down an African dictator, disbanding an urban gang called the Meat Hooks, hunting down a mad cult leader, destroying Neo-Nazis, tackling the Mafia, and the like.

Sullivan has a long scar on his right cheek and a girlfriend, Bonnie Roland, who lives in New York with ten-year-old Melinda, whom Sullivan rescued from a child pornography ring. Though Sullivan loves Bonnie, he does not avoid having sex with other women while he's on the road.

Comment: Ten other adventures of the Specialist were published through 1985: *Manhattan Revenge, Sullivan's Revenge, The Psycho Soldiers, The Maltese Vengeance, The Big One, The Vendetta, One-Man Army, Vengeance Mountain, Beirut Retaliation,* and *American Vengeance.*

SPECTRAL KNIGHTS (T, TV, C)

First Appearance: *Visionaries* toy line, February 1987, Hasbro.

Biography: It is the "final hour" of the age of science on Prysmos, heralded by a mystical alignment of the planet's three suns. Machines fail as the laws of science cease to function and the age of sorcery dawns. Wearing armor forged from the now-useless machines, knights protect their communities—though it appears as if no one will be able to stop the evil mage Darkstorm and his Darkling Lords from ruling the world. Fortunately, the magician Merklynn is able to lead one group of knights to a mystical pool; when they touch their staffs to the waters, they receive wisdom and strength in addition to special powers correlating to the animals that are their totems. The newly christened Spectral Knights are Leoric (the lion/leadership), Cryotek (the bear/strength), Ectar (the fox/cunning), Witterquick (the cheetah/speed), Feryl (the wolf/tracking), Galadria (the dolphin/wisdom), Cindarr (the gorilla/climbing), and Arzon (the eagle/flight).

Unfortunately, Darkstorm and the Darkling Lords make it there as well, though they don't carry staffs and have to settle for simply emulating the animals their natures personify: Darkstorm (the mollusk/scal-ing and sliminess), Cravex (the phylot/scavenger), Mortredd (the beetle/scampering), Lexor (the armadillo/cowardice), Reekon (the lizard/stealth and treachery), and Virulina (the shark/killing).

The heroes travel around in a Lancer Cycle, a "jousting vehicle" equipped with a battering ram, and in a Capture Chariot that has detachable pods for each warrior. The Dark Lords get about in their knifelike Sky Claw, which is armed with a laser cannon, and in the Dagger Assault land vehicle, equipped with battering rams, catapults, a prison cell, and a detachable Scout Flier.

Comment: Hasbro's line of action figures featured holograms in the chests of the characters and on the staffs of the Spectral Knights. In addition to the figures, Sunbow Productions produced 13 half-hour animated adventures that were syndicated in September 1987. Marvel Comics published six issues of *Visionaries* from 1987 to 1988.

That same year Hasbro also released a line called *Ninja Warriors, Enemies of Evil,* which consisted of the hero Oji San and his horse Windspirit, and the warriors Scorpio, Dojo Kan, Starcaster, Dragonmaster, Lord Taka, and Nunchuka-San.

SPEED RACER (TV, C)

First Appearance: *Speed Racer,* 1965, Japanese TV.

Biography: Speed Racer is a young race car buff who travels around the world pitting his remarkable Mark Five (some sources say Mach Five) car against other racers and any evildoers who cross his path. Inspector Detector frequently asks Speed for help in solving cases involving cars (smuggling, gambling, high-tech theft, etc.). Assisting him are his "Go Team," which consists of his girlfriend, Trixie; his kid brother, Spridle; their monkey, Chim Chim; mechanic Sparky; and Speed's parents. Speed's older brother, Racer X, often joins in the races behind the wheel of his Shooting Star #9.

Comment: The Tatsunoko Productions animated series was syndicated in the U.S. beginning in 1967. There were 28 separate adventures, ranging from a half hour, to an hour, to one 90-minute extravaganza. Jack Grimes was the voice of Speed Racer.

From 1987 to 1990, Now Comics published 38 issues of a *Speed Racer* comic book.

In 1973 Hanna-Barbera introduced a similar though less successful CBS series called *Speedy Buggy,* in which young Tinker, Debbie, and Mark travel the world in their souped-up flivver in search of adventure. Sixteen half-hour episodes were produced.

SPENSER   (L, TV)

First Appearance: *The Godwulf Manuscript* by Robert B. Parker, 1973, Houghton Mifflin.

Biography: An ex-Boston policeman and prize-fighter, Spenser is now a gourmand and a top-notch private eye who has worked routine cases, such as finding missing people, working as a bodyguard, and solving murders, to more unusual cases, such as helping a prostitute go straight and a senator's sex-and-drug-addicted wife clean up her act, and finding out if a baseball pitcher is on the take. His jobs often lead to slug-fests and gunplay. Spenser is assisted by steel-fisted freelance operator Hawk, who has worked for criminals as well as for law officers. He also works with Lieutenant Martin Quirk of the police department.

Spenser and Susan Silverman have been an item for many years, though she briefly left him (in *Valediction*).

Comment: The other Spenser novels are *God Save the Child* (1974), *Mortal Stakes* (1975), *Promised Land* (1976), *The Judas Goat* (1978), *Looking for Rachel Wallace* (1980), *Early Autumn* (1981), *A Savage Place* (1981), *Ceremony* (1982), *The Widening Gyre* (1983), *Valediction* (1984), *Pale Kings and Princes* (1987), *Crimson Joy* (1988), *Pastime* (1991), *Double Deuce* (1992), and *Paper Doll* (1993).

On TV, the character was played by Robert Urich in the popular hour-long TV series *Spenser: For Hire,* which aired on ABC from September 1985 to September 1988. In the series, he drives a Mustang and works closely with Lieutenant Martin Quirk of the Boston police. Avery Brooks costarred as Hawk, Richard Jaeckel was Quirk, and Barbara Stock was Susan.

The Lifetime cable service aired the made-for-TV movie *Spenser: Pale Kings and Princes* in January 1994, starring Urich and Brooks.

SPIN and MARTY   (TV, C)

First Appearance: "Spin and Marty," *The Mickey Mouse Club,* 1955, ABC.

Biography: Spin Evans and Marty Markham are two young boys who spend their summers at Mr. Logan's Triple R Ranch. Spin is a down-to-earth kid, but polo-playing Marty is rich and spoiled: He arrives with his chauffeur, Perkins, and immediately alienates his bunkmates, who include Ambitious, Speckle, Joe, and others—including, later, little Moochie. Only after Spin and Marty trade blows does the teenager get off his high horse and join the group. The boys are excellent riders, Spin on his horse Sailor and Marty on his horse Skyrocket, and help defeat rival North Fork Camp in a rodeo.

Throughout three summers at the ranch, there is danger (Spin, out alone one night, is thrown from his horse and knocked out), drama (Spin, obviously accident-prone, is struck by a toy boat during a swim meet and knocked unconscious yet again), fights and intrigue with the North Fork boys (and Circle H girls), and more.

Comment: Tim Considine was Spin and David Stollery was Marty in the original serial and its two sequels. Moochie, played by Kevin Corcoran, joined the lineup in the second serial, "The Further Adventures of Spin & Marty."

Dell published 11 *Spin and Marty* comic books from 1956 to 1960.

THE SPOOK   (C)

First Appearance: *Eerie* #57, 1974, Warren Publishing.

Biography: The Spook is a zombie, a black man who lives in a shack in a Louisiana swamp, circa 1835, and fights to protect the rights of local slaves against cruel whites, evil blacks, or power-mad practitioners of voodoo. It isn't known how he came back to life; however, it is known that he had a romance with the voodoo priestess Sarena and that she apparently took his life in order to restore her own youth. The dead man gets about by poling his small skiff through the waters. Nearly seven feet tall, the Spook possesses great strength, "devastating speed and supple agility." The Spook knows how to cast voodoo spells, but prefers to fight with the knife he carries—and throws, with deadly accuracy—the chain he wears slung around his neck, and a bow and arrow he keeps in the skiff. He usually leaves the spell-casting to his friend, freeman Andrew Jackson Tobias, a.k.a. Crackermeyer, who believes in using the power of voodoo for good. Spook continues to fight for human rights through the Civil War.

Comment: The character was created by writer Doug Moench; diverse hands wrote and drew the strip over the years. New Spook adventures appeared in *Eerie* through #65.

STAR HAWKINS   (C)

First Appearance: *Strange Adventures* #114, 1960, DC Comics.

Biography: A private eye in the 21st century—cases are covered from 2079 to 2092—Hawkins works out of New City in the United States, aided by his devoted robot secretary/housekeeper Ilda. Because he eventually becomes so successful at nabbing notorious zips ("twenty-first century slang for a crook!"), the law-keeping National Science Center makes him an agent. After earning 250 million credits for capturing Galactic Enemy Number One, Bio-Room, and rescuing the abducted Stella Sterling, Star established the Hawkins-Sterling Academy of Robot-Detection, which trains robots to become sleuths. (Quite a change from the early days, when Star repeatedly had to pawn Ilda at Mr. Krikee's shop to raise funds, redeeming her "when fortune smiled his way.")

Star wears a purple jacket and shoes, and a black shirt and trousers, and packs a ray gun; among the five-foot-tall Ilda's resources are X-ray vision, short-distance telepathy, an infra-red heat generator, electric stun bolts, and a can opener. Her yellow, "no-glare plasto-metal" body is impervious to ray guns and is covered with a red and white striped minidress; she has emotions that run from love for Star to fear that "makes my oil run cold."

Comment: The character appeared in 22 issues of *Strange Adventures* through #185.

STAR HAWKS (CS, L)

First Appearance: *Star Hawks,* October 5, 1977, Newspaper Enterprise Association Syndicate.

Biography: "A long way from here, a long time from now," the Star Hawks are agents of the Interplan Law Service, the central headquarters of which are on the planet Barnum. Dressed in red body suits with blue trim, the agents keep peace throughout the universe. Agents Rex Jaxan and the bald ladies' man Chavez are partners based on the Interplan satellite Hoosegow in orbit around the planet Esmeralda in the Barnum system. Little is known about the heroes' backgrounds. Daredevil Rex apprenticed with Gideon, a space explorer; Chavez was jump-rope champ of the space academy middle school. Their boss is Chief Agent Alice K. Benyon, who is also Rex's lover. Assisting them in their escapades is the Canine Robot Agent Sniffer, who not only has an extraordinary nose but fires debilitating beams from its eyes. Other agents are Doc Ajax, Tammany Coyne—a woman who puts chauvinist Chavez in his place—Norleans, and the late Anmar. The Hawks' arsenal consists of daggers; blasters; powerful thermite grenades; jetpacks known as skybelts, which enable them to fly through the air; and the skycar, which can travel in air and space and is equipped with a talking robot guidance system and a soundbeam that can eavesdrop on conversations aboard other ships or on the ground.

After two years, the strip changed direction; the Barnum system was destroyed by alien Vrylaks, and Jaxan and Chavez put together a crew to hunt the perpetrators down, rescue the abducted Alice (who is

killed in the process), and maintain peace from aboard their starship the *Stellar Cross.* Helping them are Operations Chief Lhassa McKade, Science Officer Z'Ard (a lizard-man), a Battle Mek robot, and ship's mascot Widget, a monkeylike reptile that once belonged to Gideon.

Comment: Though the success of *Star Wars* in 1977 (see HAN SOLO) helped to shape the strip (note opening line) and sell it to newspapers, Newspaper Enterprise Association executive Flash Fairfield had started putting together the art/writing team of Gil Kane and Ron Goulart during the summer of 1976. Writer Archie Goodwin replaced Goulart in 1979, at which time the strip warped into its "quest" mode; Roger McKenzie took over from Goodwin in December 1980. Though *Star Hawks* expired in 1981, the adventures were reprinted in the fan magazines *The Comic Reader* and *Amazing Heroes,* and were also collected in book form as *Star Hawks* and *Star Hawks II* from Ace Books. Ron Goulart's Star Hawks novel, *Empire 99*—which was based on the second comic strip adventure—was published by Playboy Press in 1980.

Doc, Chavez, and Rex of the *Star Hawks*. © United Feature Syndicate.

For its first two years, the comic strip had a two-tier layout—the equivalent of two daily strips piled one atop the other—that allowed Kane to draw spectacular scenes unique to daily comic strips. It went to a single-tier format in July 1979.

STARMAN JONES (L)

First Appearance: *Starman Jones* by Robert A. Heinlein, 1953, Charles Scribner's Sons.

Biography: Maximillian Jones is a boy from Clyde's Corners on Earth. Though he hasn't graduated from high school, he has an enormous aptitude for math, thanks to his late uncle Chester Arthur Jones, a mathematician and astrogator. When Max's father dies, his mother, Nellie, remarries and her new husband, Montgomery, sells the farm that has been in their family for four centuries. Distraught, Max runs away to Earthport, near Oklahoma City, intending to become an astrogator. With the help of a clever vagabond named Sam Anderson, Max gets aboard the starship *Asgard*, a liner/freighter, as a crewman; first stop, Garson's Planet circling Theta Centauri.

Max's abilities and his kinship with Chester earn him a quick promotion to Chartsman—despite the fact that he is on the ship illegally—and after several escapades on Garson's Planet the ship heads to Halcyon, a world circling Nu Pegasi. En route, astrogator Dr. Hendrix dies of overwork and the crew fills in, resulting in Max becoming an apprentice astrogator. Unfortunately, a hyperspace "transition" is incorrectly plotted and the ship emerges in unknown space. They land on an unexplored world they dub Charity, establish a colony called Charityville, and survive meteor showers, an encounter with a race of centaurs, and the death of several crew members, including Sam. Eventually Max becomes acting captain, and, thanks to his computations, the ship is able to make it to Halcyon.

Upon his return to Earth, Max is named assistant astrogator of the *Elizabeth Regina*; after returning to visit his former farm, he ships out for other adventures.

Comment: *Starman Jones* was one of the acclaimed author's many juveniles, books that helped to shape a generation's view of science fiction. Indeed, the characterizations clearly inspired *Star Wars* (see HAN SOLO) among other works.

THE STAR ROVERS (C)

First Appearance: *Mystery in Space* #66, 1961, DC Comics.

Biography: The Star Rovers are a 22nd century team consisting of "novelist-sportsman" Homer Gint, who has "hunted on hundreds of star-planets"; "solar system champion marksman . . . former Miss Solar System and girl adventuress" Karel Sorensen; and "playboy and athlete" Rick Purvis. The three are actually friendly rivals: When one of them stumbles onto a mystery, the others are summoned and they work to solve it separately, each on his or her own private "spacer." Rick wears a purple uniform, Homer a green one, and Karel a red one.

Comment: The characters appeared in seven issues of *Mystery in Space*, six issues of *Strange Adventures*, and in *From Beyond the Unknown* #18 to #22.

Another adventure strip that appeared in *Mystery in Space* (starting with #1) featured the Knights of the Galaxy, heroes based on the space station Gala in the 25th century. The large organization of humans and aliens is charged with exploring the universe and keeping peace.

STARSKY and HUTCH (TV)

First Appearance: *Starsky and Hutch*, April 1975, ABC.

Biography: Detectives Dave Starsky and Ken "Hutch" Hutchinson are hip, hard-hitting plainclothes/undercover police officers who mix it up with drug dealers, pimps, shakedown artists, mobsters, and other criminal types in an unnamed metropolis (implicitly, Los Angeles). Their even hipper informant is Huggy Bear.

The gum-chewing, junk food-eating Starsky is more aggressive, tightly wound, and street-smart than Hutch, who is considerably more laid back and is fond of organic foods. The two report to Captain Harold Dobey and race around in Starsky's red and white Ford Torino.

Starsky carries a .45 automatic, Hutch a .357 Magnum.

Comment: The original TV movie had the heroes investigating a double murder and learn that they were supposed to be the victims. The film spawned an hour-long series that aired from September 1975 through August 1979. David Soul was Hutch, Paul Michael Glaser was Starsky, Bernie Hamilton played Dobey (Richard Ward had the part in the TV movie), and Antonio Fargas was Huggy Bear. The extremely violent series was created by William Blinn.

A pilot for Huggy, *Huggy Bear and the Turkey*, aired as part of the show in 1977. Dale Ribinette was the Turkey.

STARSLAYER (C)

First Appearance: *Starslayer* #1, 1983, Pacific Comics.

Biography: Torin Mac Quillon is the son of a Scythian chieftain's daughter and a desert brigand who left home before Torin was born. The warrior grew up on the banks of the Volga and moved west to Britain. He hates the Roman invaders and kills them any chance he gets; when they begin arriving in great numbers, he takes his wife, Gwynyth, and son, Brann, from their village to live in the relative safety of the woods. However, as he attacks a party of invaders and is an instant away from death, he is whisked to the future by the scientist Tamara; his only wound is an injured left eye, which she repairs with a golden lens.

He's been brought to "the twenty-second year of the new millennium," far in the future, after the sun has become a red giant and human life on Earth is able to survive only in enclosed cities. The cooling of the sun has deprived colonies on the outer planets of heat, and the settlers have boarded spaceships to try to conquer habitable Earth. Tamara has scanned history and brought Torin to the future because he is not only a great warrior, but he was about to die and thus his disappearance would not change history.

Torin is given a uniform—black body suit and red boots—a spaceship, the *Jolly Roger,* which is powered by a solar sail, and weapons, including a mighty unbreakable sword and a Mark IX multifunction pistol. As Starslayer, Torin's constant companion/guide-to-the-future is the monkeylike computer SAM—a Simbionic Android Mindlink—with whom he's in constant contact via a special headband.

In a truly inspired touch (#3), after Torin has gone to space, he laments the names of the planets, remarking "Rome has cast its shadow even here among the stars." Ultimately, Torin perishes and, through numerous mystical and scientific means, the dying sun is reborn, spinning out new planets that will "bear new life of their own."

Comment: The character was created by artist/writer Mike Grell and, pictorially, appeared in a portfolio of drawings that predated the comic book. The character starred in 34 issues of his own title; it was published by First Comics from #7 on.

The comic book was particularly noteworthy for introducing the superhero the Rocketeer as its backup feature in #2 and #3.

STEVE CANYON   (CS, C, TV)

First Appearance: *Steve Canyon,* January 13, 1947, Field Newspaper Syndicate.

Biography: According to the strip, "Every take-off holds a promise of danger—and every landing is an invitation to adventure." During World War II, blond air force Captain Stevenson B. Canyon flies around the world as an air transport command pilot; after the war, he and a crew of ex-GIs open Horizons Unlimited, a global air taxi service that often requires Steve to "use his fists for more than just holding a throttle" as he faces Communists, ex-Nazis, smugglers, drug dealers, and every other kind of lowlife. His toughest foe is a woman, Copper Calhoun, the "she-wolf of Wall Street."

When war erupts in Korea, Canyon joins the air force as a colonel and fights throughout Asia; he returns to the region during the war in Vietnam. Eventually (April 1970), Canyon marries longtime girlfriend Summer Olson and becomes an undercover operative for the government—who spends a great deal of time looking for his wife after she vanishes (and falls into the clutches of Fingernail Fu, an arthritic torturer).

Comment: Milton Caniff created the strip after he left *Terry and the Pirates.* (See TERRY LEE.)

In comic books, Steve has appeared as a supporting feature in a number of titles; he also had his own six-issue run from Harvey Comics (1948) and a one-shot, *Steve Canyon in 3-D,* from Kitchen Sink Press in 1986.

On TV, NBC aired a half-hour series from September 1958 to September 1959; ABC aired reruns until September, 1960. Dean Fredericks starred as Lieutenant Colonel Canyon, who was based at Big Thunder Air Force Base but was usually traveling the world on air force business.

STICK-MAN THE BARBARIAN   (C)

First Appearance: *Stick-Man the Barbarian* #1, 1990, Fish Head Comics.

Biography: Nothing is known about the past of this scrawny, mustachioed hero, who wears fur boots and a fur loincloth and has one horn of his helmet downturned. He lives in a barbaric land of some unspecified time in which he yearns to do good—but doesn't quite have the smarts or strong sword-arm to pull it off.

In his first chronicled adventure, he crosses a lake by raft to prove his courage by fetching a crone's belongings from an island. En route, he's attacked by a bog monster who has an arrangement with the lady: She sends it food (human flesh) and it gives her the victim's gold. Stick-Man manages to slay the beast, then cuts off the old lady's head. In his second adventure, he decides to steal a dragon's treasure by slipping around the sleeping beast, only to have his behind toasted when the dragon wakes.

Comment: There was just one issue of *Stick-Man the Barbarian,* created, written, and drawn by Darrin LeBlanc.

Stick-Man the Barbarian vs. the bog beast. © Darrin LeBlanc.

STRAIGHT ARROW (R, C)

First Appearance: *Straight Arrow,* 1948, Mutual.

Biography: Steve Adams is the young, hardworking owner of the Broken Bow cattle ranch. However, whenever trouble strikes, be it rustlers, robbers, squatters, or people who are trying to steal land or treasure from the Indians, Steve—according to the legend—"disappeared and . . . in his place . . . came a mysterious, stalwart Indian wearing the dress and warpaint of a Comanche" and riding his "great golden palamino Fury." His weapon is the bow and arrow, which he uses with uncanny precision. He's also adept at rigging all kinds of traps.

Comment: Howard Culver played the hero throughout his six-year run.

The radio series spawned a successful comic book: Fifty-five issues of *Straight Arrow* were published by Magazine Enterprises from 1950 to 1956. The comics introduced his canine companion Blaze (#43) and also Sundown Valley (#4), which is located near the ranch. He chooses a cave therein to hide his equipment, a cave that glows with "light from an unknown source."

STUART BAILEY (TV, C)

First Appearance: 77 *Sunset Strip,* October 1958, ABC (see COMMENT).

Biography: A former OSS officer, Stuart is a judo expert and linguistics Ph.D. who planned to become a college professor. Instead, deciding he wanted more of a challenge, he becomes a private eye. His partner is Jeff Spencer, a lawyer who is also a judo expert and ex-government operative. The two open an office in Hollywood, where they take on gamblers, murderers, underworld thugs, and the like. Their office is next to Dino's Lodge, whose valet, a hipster named Gerald Lloyd Kookson III—a.k.a. Kookie—frequently teams with Stu and Jeff (and, even more frequently, is seen combing his lush blond hair). After three years, he joins the team officially.

Roscoe is a horse-betting contact man who frequently helps the sleuths, Suzanne Fabray operates the phones, and Lieutenant Gilmore of the LAPD regularly helps the detectives. For one year (1960–61), Rex Randolph was a third member of the team.

Eventually, Stu goes off on his own as a globe-trotting, JAMES BOND style investigator; in one epic (five-part) adventure, he pursues smugglers around the world. His new secretary is Hannah.

Comment: Efrem Zimbalist, Jr., played Bailey, a character who had been introduced as a solo operator on the anthology series *Conflict* in July 1957, in an adventure called "Anything for Money." The first two episodes of the new series were actually a feature film, *Girl on the Run,* which the studio made, then felt would work better as a TV series than as a theatrical feature. They were right; the hour-long series aired until September 1964. In addition to Zimbalist, Roger Smith was Jeff, Edd Byrnes was Kookie, Jacqueline Beer (Miss France, 1954) played Suzanne, Louis Quinn was Roscoe, Richard Long was Rex, Byron Keith was Gilmore, and Joan Staley was Hannah.

Dell published seven issues of 77 *Sunset Strip* as

part of its *4-Color* series between 1960 and 1962; Gold Key published two issues of a *77 Sunset Strip* comic book in 1962–63.

"SUICIDE" SMITH (C)

First Appearance: *Wings Comics* #1, 1940, Fiction House.

Biography: Known as "the blitzkrieg buster," Smith is initially a flier who leads a team known as the Air Commandos. Later he becomes more of a solo operator, the "Dare-devil of the Skyways," helped by young sidekick Chuck Hardy and a British spy named Hinda. Smith has some remarkable war-time adventures, following this with Cold War assignments and missions in Indochina.

Comment: Smith appeared in *Wings Comics* through its entire 124 issue run. Also appearing in the title were CAPTAIN WINGS; Jane Martin—War Nurse (who also worked as a spy); the Skull Squad (American Jimmy Jones, Englishman Kent Douglas, and Scotsman Sandy MacGregor); the Parachute Patrol; Calhoun of the Air Cadets; Clipper Kirk; Buzz Bennett of the navy; and F-4 of Air Intelligence.

SUICIDE SQUAD (C)

First Appearance: *The Brave and the Bold* #25, 1959, DC Comics.

Biography: The Suicide Squad is formed during World War II, made up of "the alienated, the disaffected, the border-line whackos" who were crazy enough to tackle dangerous missions—hence the name. Eventually, air force Captain Richard Montgomery Flag is brought in to whip the group into more of a fighting team. Flag eventually makes colonel and marries Karen Jace—the niece of JEB STUART. (Some accounts make her Sharon Race, a cousin of Stuart's.) Flag joins the Squad on missions in Korea though, in time, the Squad becomes an arm of the larger Task Force X. Flag and Karen have a son, Richard Rogers Flag; sadly, Richard is orphaned when his mother dies saving him from a skidding car and his father is killed battling a revived Nazi death machine, the giant War Wheel. Stuart raises the boy, who goes to West Point, becomes a test pilot, and joins the astronaut corps, where he becomes infatuated with nurse Karin Grace.

Both abandon their chosen careers to serve with Stuart's new Suicide Squad, along with astronomer Hugh Evans and physicist Jess Bright. Based on the SS-1—a large jet equipped with all kinds of scientific equipment and weapons—the team fights menaces from abroad, from space, and from other dimensions. During a mission to Cambodia, a Yeti kills Evans and

Bright; Karin goes into shock, and Flag becomes part of a team known as the Forgotten Heroes. (See RIP HUNTER.) Eventually he returns to command a new Suicide Squad, comprised of convicted supervillains Blockbuster, Bronze Tiger, Captain Boomerang, Enchantress, and Deadshot, who agree to work under Flag in lieu of rotting in prison. Over the years, other villains join the team, including Nemesis and Nightshade.

Comment: After three appearances in *The Brave and the Bold,* the team sat relatively dormant until getting their own title in 1987. The origins of each incarnation were told in full in *Secret Origins* #14.

SUN DEVILS (C)

First Appearance: *Sun Devils* #1, 1984, DC Comics.

Biography: At some time in the far future, the Triad

From the left: Scyla, Rik, Anomie, Pook (on her shoulder) and Shikon, a few of the *Sun Devils.* © DC Comics.

Confederacy is attempting to rule the galaxy. The planet Wolfholme (colonized two centuries before by Earthlings) is opposed to the Triad, and native navy man Rik Sunn resigns to join the Earth Diplomatic Corps and pursue a negotiated solution to the problem. Unfortunately, dictator and Confederacy cofounder the Sauroid Karvus Khun has no such interests, and he destroys Wolfholme. Among the dead is Kirk Sunn, Rik's brother. On Earth—which is surprisingly ambivalent to the conquerors—the distraught Sunn meets two women: smuggler Scyla of the Asteroid Belt and aspiring space navy pilot Anomie Zitar, a catlike humanoid of Mi's World. They steal a spaceship and head for Centauri, the last world actively opposed to the Confederacy. There they team with clone humans One, Two, and Three and help repel the invaders. Prime Speaker Temple of Centauri gives the world's saviors a special charter to function as a roving army; they are joined by the reptilian Shikon—a Sauroid who opposes Khun—and Myste, a sentient mist that used to be scientist Mi-Yin.

Anomi's "puff-ball pet," the shaggy Pook, dies saving her during the course of the Sun Devils' adventures.

Comment: The characters were created by writers Gerry Conway and Roy Thomas, and artist Dan Jurgens. The magazine lasted 12 issues.

THE SURVIVALIST (L, MP)

First Appearance: *Total War* by Jerry Ahern, 1981, Zebra Books.

Biography: John Thomas Rourke grows up with guns, hunting and camping, then goes to medical school. But he decides he likes the idea of keeping people from getting hurt rather than healing them after they are hurt, and becomes an operative with the CIA's Covert Operations Section. After being ambushed and shot up by anti-Communist partisans in Latin America, he trains himself to become a survival expert and earns his living as a freelance counterterrorist instructor. While he's working in Pakistan, the Soviet Union invades. He makes it back to his home, outside of Atlanta, to his wife, Sarah, and their children, Michael and Ann. As world tensions mount, he tells Sarah for the first time about "the piece of the mountain" he's bought, which he's turned into a fortified, nearly self-sufficient home. After Bourke goes to Canada to give a lecture, his return flight is diverted from Atlanta to Phoenix due to a Soviet missile strike against the U.S. En route, Rourke uses his medical knowledge—and the stripped wires of a hair dryer—to restart the heart of a woman who's suffered a heart attack. He also lands the plane outside Albuquerque when the pilot and copilot are blinded after witnessing an atomic blast in St. Louis.

The attack is brief and ends with Soviets landing in key cities and the midsection of the nation turned into a wasteland. Armed with his two Detonics .45s and other weapons he'd brought to Canada, Rourke destroys a gang of bikers who attack the plane and takes their Harleys. With fellow survivor, passenger Paul Rubenstein, Rourke heads east, hoping to find his family.

The cigar-smoking hero has dark brown hair, brown eyes, and a lean face.

Comment: Sequentially, other entries in the popular series—published two-a-year through 1988—are *The Nightmare Begins, The Quest, The Doomsayer, The Web, The Savage Horde, The Prophet, The End Is Coming, Earth Fire, The Awakening, The Reprisal, The Rebellion, Pursuit, The Terror,* and *Overload.* In motion pictures, Steve Railsback starred in *The Survivalist* (here called Jack Tillman) in 1987.

During the 1980s, there was a boom in the so-called men's adventure category, of which Zebra Books was at the forefront. *The Warlord* by Jason Frost is the saga of Erik Ravensmith, an Indian who becomes a marine and is well equipped to protect California when an earthquake and nuclear power plant explosions cut it off from the rest of the nation. There were six books in the series. Zebra published 15 novels in John Lansing's *The Black Eagles* series, set in Vietnam—with turbulent titles such as *Hanoi Hellground, Mekong Massacre,* and *Firestorm at Dong Nam*—and five novels in the John Sievert series *C.A.D.S.* (Computerized Attack/Defense System), in which Colonel Dean Sturgis and his team defends the U.S. after a nuclear first strike from the Soviets. In 1999, following World War III, American Ben Raines leads the resistance against a series of invaders in William W. Johnstone's five-title *Ashes* series, while from the cockpit of his fighter, Hawk Hunter protects the U.S. from postnuclear Soviet invaders in Mack Maloney's three-book *Wingman* series.

Jove Books also published several macho adventure series. Foremost among these were *The Guardians,* a 13-book series about soldiers who rally to protect the U.S. after a devastating nuclear exchange with the Soviet Union; the three-book *Freedom's Rangers* series, about time-traveling commandos who "fight the battles of the past to save America's future"; and the two-book *Steele* series, about a cyborg police officer named Donovan Steele.

T

TAILSPIN TOMMY (CS, MP, L, C)

First Appearance: *Tailspin Tommy,* April 1928, Bell Syndicate.

Biography: A barnstorming aviator, Tommy Tompkins, his girlfriend/aviatrix Betty Lou Barnes, and his young friend Skeeter found Three-Point Airlines. Together they carry passengers and cargo throughout the hemisphere, getting into adventures with smugglers, thieves, rival airlines, missing persons, lost treasure, and the elements.

Comment: The character was created by artist Hal Forrest and writer Glen Chaffin. The strip died in 1942, its action archaic compared to the real-life struggles in World War II.

In film, Tommy was featured in two serials. In the 12-chapter *Tailspin Tommy* (1934), he is an auto mechanic who is selected to fly with Three-Points Airline pilot Milt Howe in a mail-delivery race. His nemesis is Tiger Taggert, who wants to see Three-Points fail and the heroes dead. Maurice Murphy was Tommy, Patricia Farr played Betty Lou, and Noah Beery, Jr., was Skeeter. Louis Friedlander directed. In the 12-chapter *Tailspin Tommy in the Great Air Mystery* (1935), Tailspin and Skeeter try to prevent villains from stealing precious oil reserves. Clark Williams was Tommy, Jean Rogers played Betty Lou, and Beery, Jr., was Skeeter. Ray Taylor directed.

Tommy was the hero of nine Big Little Books: *Tailspin Tommy in the Famous Payroll Mystery* (1933), *Tailspin Tommy, The Dirigible Flight to the North Pole* (1934), *Tailspin Tommy Hunting for Pirate Gold* (1935), *Tailspin Tommy and the Island in the Sky* (1936), *Tailspin Tommy in the Great Air Mystery* (1936), *Tailspin Tommy and the Hooded Flyer* (1937), *Tailspin Tommy and the Sky Bandits* (1938), *Tailspin Tommy and the Lost Transport* (1939), and *Tailspin Tommy, The Weasel, and His Skywaymen* (1941).

Four one-shot Tailspin Tommy comic books were published by different companies from 1931 to 1946.

TARL CABOT (L)

First Appearance: *Tarnsman of Gor* by John Norman, 1966, Ballantine Books.

Biography: "Twenty-odd" years old, the red-headed Oxford graduate is an assistant professor of history at a small New Hampshire college. Hiking one day, he finds a letter from his father, Matthew Cabot, who had disappeared when he was an infant. Shortly thereafter a silver spaceship arrives, and Tarl boards, passes out, and awakes on the strange, barbaric world of Gor, also known as Counter-Earth, located on the opposite side of the sun from our world. Because it is slightly smaller than Earth, people from Earth have slightly greater strength and agility than natives. On Gor, Tarl meets his father, who teaches him the history, culture, and language of his new home, and also tells him of the Voyages of Acquisition that the sacred Priest-Kings occasionally order for reasons unknown and unknowable to mere mortals.

Tarl is taught how to ride the giant birds known as Tarns and is schooled by the best fencers and archers on Gor to become the protector of the city of Ko-ro-ba, of which his father is administrator. Tarl takes the beautiful Talena as his "companion" and has many adventures on Gor, beginning with a journey to the Mountains of Sardar to learn the true nature of the Priest-Kings, and followed by battles with assassins and adventures in Port Kar, "home to every outlaw and pirate on the planet." Ultimately Tarl becomes caught up in planetwide war and Cabot becomes the leader of the Delta Brigade, a force sworn to defeat the evil Cosian invaders.

Other Earth people who are brought to Gor during the course of the saga include Elinor Brinton of New York, a spoiled woman who must learn to survive on a male-dominated planet; Jason Marshall, who becomes a regular adventurer in the series; Tiffany Collins, who rises from slave-girl (kajira) to queen; and librarian and amateur belly dancer Doreen Williamson.

Comment: What began as an Edgar Rice Burroughs-style series became more and more oriented toward bondage and slavery, with such chapter titles as "Collar 708," "My Master Will Have His Girl Please Him," "I Am Chained Beneath the Moons of Gor," and "Bracelets and Shackles." The sequels to the original novel, published one-a-year, are *Outlaw of Gor, Priest-Kings of Gor, Nomads of Gor, Assassin of Gor, Raiders of Gor,* and *Captive of Gor* (all published by Ballantine). The series continued at DAW Books with *Hunters of Gor, Marauders of Gor, Tribesmen of Gor, Slave Girl of Gor, Beasts of Gor, Explorers of Gor, Fighting Slave of Gor, Rogue of Gor, Guardsman of Gor, Savages of Gor, Blood Brothers of Gor, Kajira of Gor, Players of Gor, Mercenaries of Gor, Dancer of Gor, Renegades of Gor, Vagabonds of Gor,* and *Magicians of Gor.*

TENSPEED TURNER (TV)

First Appearance: *Tenspeed and Brown Shoe,* January 1980, ABC.

Biography: When we first meet E.L. "Tenspeed" Turner—so-nicknamed because he's a master of disguise able to maneuver and shift gears as fast as a tenspeed bike—he is a con man and hustler who is granted parole—provided he find gainful employment. His solution is to team with naive, aspiring sleuth Lionel Whitney—a.k.a. Brown Shoe, a nickname for any straight, conservative fellow—and open a detective agency off Sunset Boulevard in Los Angeles. Since Brown Shoe's entire experience consists of reading Mark Savage Private Eye detective novels, it's up to Tenspeed to teach him the ropes.

After several years—presumably, when his parole requirements have been met—Tenspeed ends up in Texas. There he teams with Jerome Jeremiah Starbuck, a wacky billionaire who prefers detective work to managing his sprawling Marklee Industries.

Comment: The series aired through June 1980. Tenspeed returned on *J.J. Starbuck,* which was seen on NBC from September 1987 to August 1988. Ben Vereen played the character in both incarnations. Jeff Goldblum was Brown Shoe and Dale Robertson played Starbuck.

TERRY LEE (CS, R, C, MP, L, TV)

First Appearance: *Terry and the Pirates,* October 22, 1934, Chicago Tribune-New York News Syndicate.

Biography: The son of archaeologist Dr. Herbert Lee, "wide awake American boy" Terry is left a map of an abandoned mine in China by his grandfather, and teams with "two-fisted adventurer," pipe-smoking, automatic-packing Pat Ryan to find it. On the West River, they hire a steamboat owned by Dale Scott and her father Ol' Pop Scott, who join them on their journey along with ship's cook George Webster "Connie" Confucius. They are pursued by evil Poppy Joe, a half caste who intends to get the treasure. All meet in the mine, and, during an explosive showdown, the mine is flooded and Ol' Pop and Poppy die.

The survivors continue to travel China and the world in search of adventure, eventually meeting their most determined foe, the Dragon Lady, the leader of a band of pirates who operate along the coast of China. She falls in love with Pat, and, though he fails to reciprocate, she never stops trying to win his affection. Pat, in turn, falls in love with wealthy Normandie Drake, whose aunt, Augusta Drake, kidnaps her and takes her back to the U.S. By the time Pat and Normandie meet again, she's married. His next inamorata is the sultry Burma, a partner of the pirate Captain Judas, who refuses to give up her lifestyle for him. Terry himself had it bad for pretty young Southern belle April Kane. (His reaction after first seeing her in a hotel lobby was: "Ohboyohgeewhizhotdogohboyohboy.")

During World War II, Terry joins the Chinese Air Force as a pilot, reporting to Colonel Flip Corkin. After the war, he remains a pilot, becoming a U.S. Air Force major and battling Communists.

Comment: Arguably the greatest adventure strip of all, *Terry and the Pirates* was created, written, and drawn by Milton Caniff. George Wunder took over the strip in December 1946, when Caniff failed to come to contractual terms with the syndicate. Wunder remained until the strip's demise in February 1973—though it lost the visual and narrative flair Caniff had brought to it.

On radio, *Terry and the Pirates* was first broadcast by NBC in 1937, starring Jackie Kelk as Terry, followed by Cliff Carpenter and Owen Jordan. Agnes Moorehead was the first Dragon Lady. Clayton "Bud" Collyer was the first Pat.

In comic books, Terry costarred in numerous titles and also had his own magazines: from 1939 to 1953, Dell published 16 issues (many of which were premium giveaways and not newsstand magazines); from 1947 to 1955, Dell, then Charlton, published 26 issues.

There was only one *Terry and the Pirates* film: a 15-chapter serial released in 1940, directed by James W. Horne, and starring William Tracy as Terry and Sheila Darcy as the Dragon Lady.

There were seven Big Little Books starring Terry: *Terry and the Pirates* (1935), *Terry and the Pirates Shipwrecked on a Desert Island* (1938), *Terry and the Pirates and the Giant's Vengeance* (1939), *Terry and the Priates in the Mountain Stronghold* (1941), *Terry and the Pirates, the Plantation Mystery* (1942),

Terry Lee, Flight Officer U.S.A. (1944), and *Terry and War in the Jungle* (1946).

A syndicated, half-hour *Terry and the Pirates* live-action TV series aired in 1952, starring John Baer as Terry Lee and Gloria Saunders as the Dragon Lady.

See also DICKIE DARE; STEVE CANYON.

THESEUS (M, MP)

First Appearance: Greek mythology, circa 1300 B.C.

Biography: The son of King Aegeus and Queen Aethra of Athens, Theseus is born in Argolis, where his maternal grandfather Pittheus is King of Troezen. Aegeus leaves his sword and sandals under a massive boulder in Argolis, with instructions that his son is to come to Athens when he has retrieved these items. Theseus is raised and tutored by his grandfather and at age 16 is able to lift the boulder. Rather than sail to Athens straightaway, he decides to travel by land, defeating thieves and monsters and earning a reputation as a hero like his own idol, the demigod Heracles. Among those he waylays are the monster Periphates, who kills people with a club (said club becoming a part of Theseus's arsenal); Sinis, the robber-son of Poseidon; the wild sow Phaea; the murderous thief Sciron, who fed victims to a giant tortoise; the evil wrestler Cercyon; and the monster Procrustes.

Theseus is ritualistically cleansed of the blood he's spilled by the Phytalidae, after which he goes to Thebes, where his father has married the sorceress Medea. (See JASON.) Medea persuades Aegeus to kill the stranger, but the king recognizes him by the blade he carries and Medea flees.

Every year Athens is forced to pay a tribute to King Minos of Crete of seven maidens and seven men who are sacrificed to the Minotaur, a creature that is half man, half bull and lives in the Labyrinth maze on Crete. Theseus appoints himself as one of the seven men. On Crete, Minos's daughter Ariadne falls in love with him and provides him with a string that will enable him to retrace his steps through the maze. After sneaking up on the Minotaur as it sleeps, Theseus slays him with his bare hands, then flees Crete with the other Athenians and Ariadne. Unfortunately, Ariadne becomes seasick and has to be left on the island of Naxos; inexplicably, Theseus does not return for her. Theseus had set sail from Athens with black sails hoisted and had promised to raise white ones upon his return, thus signaling his father that he still lived. He forgets, and when the king sees the black sails, he flings himself into the sea, thereafter called the Aegean.

Theseus becomes king and, under his benevolent and democratic rule, Athens becomes a major power.

Still an adventurer at heart, he helps hunt the Calydonian Boar, joins the Argonauts on their search for the Golden Fleece, and journeys with Heracles to the land of the Amazons, where he weds Antiope, sister of Hippolyte, Queen of the Amazons. They have one son, Hippolytus. That relationship apparently doesn't work out, as Theseus also makes a failed play for Helen, a daughter of Zeus whose adulterous flight with the hero Paris would much later spark the Trojan War. Eventually he takes Ariadne's sister Phaedra as his wife, and they have two sons, Acamas and Demophoon. However, she lusts after Hippolytus, and when he spurns her, she tells Theseus that the young man tried to take her. Enraged, Theseus asks Poseidon to punish him, and the sea god sends a bull to frighten the youth's horses. In the process, however, Hippolytus is thrown from his chariot and dies; Phaedra takes her life in remorse.

These actions, along with the questionable behavior of Demophoon (among other things, his lateness for his own wedding causes his betrothed to commit suicide) ultimately cause Theseus to be exiled from Athens. He settles on the island of Scyros, where the envious King Lycomedes has him thrown into the sea, where he perishes. However, the dead warrior is later seen, in full armor, at the head of the Athenian army at the Battle of Marathon (490 B.C.). Fourteen years later, with the help of the Oracle at Delphi, his remains are found and reportedly brought to Athens, where they're buried in a temple called the Theseum.

Comment: In art, the character is portrayed as a powerful, beardless youth, armed with a sword. Works depicting his later years tend to show him with a club and a lion's skin cloak.

In motion pictures, the character was played by Olympic Decathlon champion Bob Mathias in the Italian-made *The Minotaur* (1961).

THOMAS BANACEK (TV)

First Appearance: *NBC Wednesday Mystery Movie,* September 1972, NBC.

Biography: Banacek is a wildly successful insurance investigator, a Polish-American who freelances for the Boston Casualty Company—getting a cut based on the value of whatever he recovers—lives in the city's ritzy Beacon Hill section, and has a chauffeur named Jay Drury. His occasional partner and girlfriend is agent Carlie Kirkland, and his best friend and sounding board is book and print shop owner Felix Mulholland.

Comment: *Banacek* starred George Peppard, with Ralph Manza as Jay, Christine Belford as Carlie, and Murray Matheson as Felix. The show alternated with two other series on this 90-minute anthology series:

Madigan and *Cool Million.* It was spun off on its own in January 1974, the 90-minute series airing until September.

Madigan starred Richard Widmark as a New York City police detective, a tough loner who lives for his work and to do what he can to help the victims of crime. The sergeant lives by himself in a one-room apartment. *Madigan* aired until August 1973.

Cool Million starred James Farentino as Jefferson Keyes, an ex-CIA agent turned very expensive private eye: His fee is $1 million for each case. A pilot, he gets around in his own jet aided by Elena and Tony Baylor, played by Adele Mara and Ed Bernard. The show aired through July 1973.

THOMAS HEWITT EDWARD CAT
(TV, C)

First Appearance: *T.H.E. Cat,* September 1966, NBC.

Biography: A onetime circus acrobat turned cat burglar, Cat has turned over a new leaf. Now he uses his skills as a bodyguard/private eye, his specialty being people who have received death threats. Cat not only protects them, but chases down whoever's after them. Dressed entirely in black, his only weapons are his hands and the ropes he uses for climbing.

When he's not working, the San Francisco-based hero frequents the Casa del Gato nightclub, which is owned by Pepe, whose life he once saved. Captain MacAllister of the police force provides Cat with whatever information he needs to do his job.

Comment: This superb half-hour show lasted until September 1967, and starred Robert Loggia as Cat, Robert Carricart as Pepe, and R.G. Armstrong as Mac-Allister.

Dell published four issues of a *T.H.E. Cat* comic book in 1967.

THOMAS MAGNUM (TV)

First Appearance: *Magnum, P.I.,* December 1980, CBS.

Biography: Thomas Sullivan Magnum is a veteran of naval intelligence, Vietnam, who settles down in Hawaii, where he lands a cushy job protecting the estate of rich writer Robin Masters. Masters is never seen and is frequently away; this gives Magnum a lot of free time to work as a private investigator, helping anyone who truly needs it. He frequently calls upon two navy pals for assistance: Theodore "T.C." Calvin, who runs the helicopter charter Island Hoppers; and Orville "Rick" (as in *Casablanca*) Wright, who runs a nightclub, then

gives it up to manage the King Kamehameha Beach Club. Rick's criminal contacts prove useful to Magnum. The detective's closest confidant is Jonathan Quayle Higgins III, Masters's effete manservant (who is ultimately revealed to be Masters—although some doubts remain). The rigid, disciplined Higgins and the easygoing, baseball-loving Magnum have nothing in common save a mutual respect.

Magnum lives in a beachfront home on Oahu (courtesy of Masters) and drives the boss's Ferrari. Ultimately he gives up private investigations and returns to the navy.

Comment: Tom Selleck starred as Magnum (the start date prevented him from accepting the role of INDIANA JONES in 1980), John Hillerman was Higgins, Roger E. Mosley was T.C., and Larry Manetti was Rick. The hour-long series aired through September 1988.

In what producers *thought* was going to be the last episode, Magnum was shot dead and went to heaven. However, the series was renewed, and Magnum's death was explained as a hallucination caused by his wound.

THONGOR (L, C)

First Appearance: *The Wizard of Lemuria* by Lin Carter, 1965, Ace Books.

Biography: Thongor the Mighty is the son of Thumithar of the Black Hawk people. Born at Valkarth in the Northlands of the lost Pacific continent of Lemuria in the year 6982—corresponding to 493,018 B.C.—he lives in a world where dinosaurs have not yet died out and wizardry is real. When he's 15, Thongor's people are wiped out by the mighty Snow Bear tribe; the sole survivor, he heads to the Southlands, a journey that takes him two years. From 6999 to 7002, he goes from city to city, earning his bread as a thief, assassin, and mercenary before ending up as a galley slave. After escaping during a mutiny when he's 20, Thongor spends the next four years sailing the seas as one of the feared Pirates of Tarakus. Exiled from Pirate City when he kills a pirate king in a duel, he meets the warrior Ald Thurmis and, together, they join the Mercenaries of Thurdis, serving in the Fourth Cohort for seven months. After leaving military service in 7007, he teams with the magician Sharajsha to foil the Dragon Kings, who plan to "summon the Lords of Chaos from their dark abode beyond the Universe, to trample all of Lemuria down." That accomplished, he tackles the vampire Xothun of Omm, meets and weds the Princess Sumia, and becomes Lord of the Three Cities, a.k.a. Patanga. In 7008 their son, Prince Tharth ko-Thongoru is born, and Thongor's descendants rule as kings for 250,000 years.

Ultimately Thongor is deified as Mahathongoyha: Thongoyha the Great.

Comment: The character was created by the late Lin Carter; the original novel (the first one by the prolific author to see print) was expanded and published as *Thongor and the Wizard of Lemuria* in 1969. The hero also appeared in *Thongor of Lemuria* (1966; expanded in 1970 as *Thongor and the Dragon City*), *Thongor Against the Gods* (1967), *Thongor in the City of Magicians* (1968), *Thongor Fights the Pirates of Tarakus* (1970), and *Thongor at the End of Time* (1970).

The character appeared in numbers 22 to 29 of Marvel Comics *Creatures on the Loose* in 1973.

See also JANDAR..

THUNDARR THE BARBARIAN   (TV)

First Appearance: *Thundarr the Barbarian,* October 1980, ABC.

Biography: A rogue planet passes between the earth and the moon, causing their obliteration. Yet, some 20 centuries later, a new planet accretes from the ashes of the devastated worlds. A new civilization arises as well, one in which cruel warlords use sorcery to enslave the rest of the human populace. Thundarr is a literate, perpetually angry slave of the sorcerer Sabian, whose stepdaughter Princess Ariel loathes the wizard's injustice. She frees Thundarr and also gives him the Sunsword, a blade of energy that can cut through virtually anything. Armed and free, he leads an ongoing revolt against Sabian aided by Princess Ariel, who possesses magic of her own, and Ookla the Mok, a powerful, apelike mutant.

Comment: Twenty-one half-hour animated adventures were produced by Ruby-Spears before the show went off the air in September 1982. Bob Ridgely was the voice of Thundarr and Nellie Bellflower was Ariel. The characters were created by writer Steve Gerber and coproducer Joe Ruby, and were designed by comic book greats Alex Toth and Jack Kirby.

TIM TYLER   (CS, L, MP, C)

First Appearance: *Tim Tyler's Luck,* August 13, 1928, King Features Syndicate.

Biography: An orphan who yearns to be out in the world and leading a life of adventure, Tim and his friend Spud Slavins decide to fulfill their dream. Upon making their way to Africa, they eventually join the Ivory Patrol, a police group dedicated to bringing civilization to the Dark Continent. After six years the boys return to the U.S. and join the Coast Guard (1940), battling spies and enemy agents during the

war. After that they return to the Ivory Patrol. Tim has also spent time as a cowboy. (See COMMENT.)

Comment: The strip was created by Lyman Young (brother of Chic, creator of *Blondie*), and ran through 1972.

The character was featured in a pair of Big Little Books with the mouth-filling titles *Tim Tyler's Luck, Adventures in the Ivory Patrol* (1937) and *Tim Tyler's Luck and the Plot of the Exiled King* (1939).

A 12-chapter serial, *Tim Tyler's Luck,* was released in 1937 starring Frankie Thomas as Tim, who journeyed to Africa to find his father, a scientist, and tangled with diamond-and-ivory thief Spider Webb.

In comic books, the character appeared in several one-shot titles and then in eight issues of *Tim Tyler Cowboy,* published by Standard Comics from 1948 to 1950.

TINTIN   (CS, C, MP, TV, L)

First Appearance: *Tintin aux Pays des Soviets (Tintin in the Land of the Soviets),* 1929, *Le Petit Vingtieme.*

Biography: Tintin is a teenage boy, a Brussels-based reporter for *Le Petit Vingtieme,* who travels throughout the world in search of stories. He invariably becomes a part of the story he is covering and ends up solving mysteries, helping others, and seeing that the lawless are punished. As he roams the world from Tibet to South America (and even leaves it, once, for a trip to the moon), he is accompanied by his devoted fox terrier Milou (Snowy in the English translations), who frequently complains to the reader ("How can a dog get a wink of sleep?"). Other allies include the twin, mustachioed detectives Dupont and Dupond (Thomson and Thompson in English); the powerful, rum-drinking seaman Captain Haddock; the deaf and dithery physicist Professor Tournesol (Cuthbert Calculus in English); and opera singer Bianca Castafiore. Thanks to the profitability of Tournesol's inventions, Tintin, Haddock, and Milou are able to move into a castle in Brussels that was owned by the evil brothers Loiseau. In their absence, it is looked after by butler Nestor.

Among Tintin's most memorable foes are the wicked Rastapopoulos and the cruel General Alcazar. On one occasion the young hero even faces Al Capone. Tintin stays in touch with friends and events around the world via shortwave radio.

Comment: The strip was created, written, and drawn by the late Hergé, the pseudonym of Belgian artist Georges Remi. (He took the initials and reversed them; the name is pronounced "Air-Zhay"). In 1926, when he was 19, Hergé created a Tintin prototype, Totor, a boy scout who appeared for three years in the pages of *Le Boy-Scout Belge.* His adventures tended toward the Rube Goldberg comical: fishing on a ship, he's yanked overboard, hitches a ride on a shark, and ends up on a U.S. submarine headed for New York, where he's hit by a car and clobbers a robber, collecting a $5,000 reward. Hergé created Tintin for the eight-page supplement that came with *Le Vingtieme Siecle* (*The Twentieth Century*—hence, *The Small Twentieth* for the children's supplement). The series was a hit, and adventures were reprinted in book form beginning the following year. After his initial anti-Communist escapade, Tintin appeared in *Tintin in the Congo, Tintin in America, Cigars of the Pharaoh, The Blue Lotus, The Broken Ear,* and many more; over 25 sprawling adventures have been collected to date in book form.

Tintin got his own magazine in September 1946, and the careers of many adventure heroes have been launched in its pages, including COMANCHE and KNIGHT ARDENT; "Blake et Mortimer"—Captain Francis Blake of British Intelligence who, with the erudite Professor Philip Mortimer, faces natural and human-made scientific dangers around the world; the world-trotting Luc Orient; the western heroes Lieutenant Burton and Buddy Longway; and private detective Ric Hochet, who frequently works with Commissaire Bourdon of the police force.

There have been two live-action Tintin films: *Tintin et le Mystere de la Toison d'Or (Tintin and the Mystery of the Golden Fleece)* (1961) and *Tintin et les Oranges Bleues (Tin-tin and the Blue Oranges)* (1965), both starring Jean Pierre Talbot. The animated features are *Tintin et le Temple du Soleil (Tintin and the Temple of the Sun)* (1969) and *Tintin et la Lac aux Requins (Tintin and the Lake of Sharks)* (1972).

On TV, Tintin starred in 26 half-hour animated adventures that aired on cable's HBO beginning in November 1992.

Author Frederic Tuten wrote several short stories about the character, which were published in Europe from 1972–1984; these were collected in book form in 1992 as *Tintin in the New World.* A U.S. edition was published the same year.

© HERGÉ

Tintin (center) with Milou at his feet. The other characters are, from the right, Dupond (or is it Dupont?), Bianca Castafiore, Dupont (or is it Dupond?), Captain Haddock, Professor Tournesol, and Nestor. © Hergé.

T.J. HOOKER (TV)

First Appearance: *T.J. Hooker,* March 1982, ABC.

Biography: After spending a number of years as a detective, Hooker decides to put on a uniform and go back to the street. His desire is to fight crime where it originates rather than clean up afterward. Sergeant Hooker is partnered with ambitious trainees, Officers Vince Romano and Stacy Sheridan; in time, Stacy joins forces with another experienced street warrior, Officer Jim Corrigan. All of the officers report to the strict Captain Dennis Sheridan, Stacy's father.

Hooker is divorced from Fran, but the breakup was amicable; they have two daughters, Cathy and Chrissie. Hooker must have bad karma: During the course of his police career, Fran is shot, his ex-lover is murdered, and so is one of his partners.

Comment: The hour-long series aired on ABC until September 1985, then moved to CBS, where it aired until September 1987 on late-night TV. William Shatner starred as Hooker, Adrian Zmed was Romano, James Darren was Corrigan, Heather Locklear played Stacy, Lee Bryant was Fran, and Richard Herd played Captain Sheridan. The character was inspired by the real-life police Sergeant Thomas Hooker.

Shatner's *Star Trek* (see CAPTAIN JAMES T. KIRK) costar, Leonard Nimoy, appeared in one episode as an officer teetering on the brink after his daughter is raped.

T-MAN (C)

First Appearance: *Police Comics* #103, 1950, Quality Comics.

Biography: The mustachioed Pete Trask is a "world wide trouble-shooter" for the treasury department, battling smugglers, counterfeiters, Communists, fiends from World War II ("The Return of Mussolini" and "Trouble in Bavaria—is it really Hitler? His death has never been proved!") and other criminal types. When abroad, Pete usually works in tandem with a native law officer, though, arguably, he oversteps the legitimate concerns of his government now and then—for example, when he destroys the radical xenophobic Anubis Party in Egypt. Pete is based in Washington.

Comment: T-Man got his own title in 1951, and it lasted 38 issues. His adventures were frequently illustrated by Reed Crandall. *Police Comics* changed over from being a superhero title with #103; other adventure heroes who appeared in its pages were Dan Leary, State Trooper; Inspector Denver; and Ken Shannon, "rough, tough, and rugged private eye" (who, with his assistant Dee Dee, was later given his own short-lived

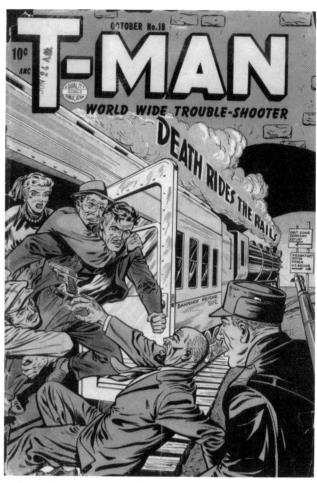

Captured by Communists, Pete Trask, the *T-Man,* makes a desperate bid to escape. © Quality Comics.

magazine with a mouthful of a title, *Private Detective Ken Shannon Crime-Busting Private Eye).*

The character is unrelated to the T-Man played on the radio by Dennis O'Keefe.

TOD STILES and BUZZ MURDOCK (TV)

First Appearance: *Route 66,* October 1960, CBS.

Biography: Gentlemanly Tod Stiles is the son of a millionaire, and rough, primitive Buzz Murdock is a product of New York's Hell's Kitchen, who used to work for the elder Stiles. When the old man dies, Tod learns that he hasn't been left any money. With no other prospects, he and Buzz decide to climb into Tod's white, 1960 Corvette convertible and drive Route 66 across the U.S., taking odd jobs and becoming involved in all kinds of adventures, romances, and natural disasters along the way. Eventually Buzz drops out and is replaced in the driver's seat in 1963 by Lincoln Case, a Houston-born veteran of the nascent Vietnam War, who is also searching for the meaning of life.

Comment: The hour-long series was created by writer Stirling Silliphant and aired through September 1964. Martin Milner was Tod and George Maharis was Buzz; when Maharis left the show (he and Milner reportedly didn't get along), he was replaced by Glen Corbett as Linc.

A new *Route 66* debuted in syndication in June 1993 and featured Nick Lewis (James Wilder) heading to the Midwest to pick up his red 1961 Corvette. En route, he picks up hitch-hiker Arthur Clark (Dan Cortese), who becomes his driving partner as he heads from Chicago to Los Angeles along the remnants of Route 66.

THE TOFF (L, MP)

First Appearance: "The Toff," 1933, *The Thriller* magazine.

Biography: Richard Rollinson, called the Toff by Scotland Yard (slang for a dandy), is a wealthy, "remarkably handsome" and athletic Mayfair playboy who works with Inspector Gryce to solve killings, kidnapings, robberies, insurance scams, and the like, and hunt down black marketeers, drug dealers, and spies in London and around the world. He is assisted by his devoted and wise valet, Jolly, and by his fun-loving aunt, Lady Gloria Hurst, who actually enjoys getting her hands dirty.

In one of his most famous cases (*Hunt the Toff,* 1955), he provides an alibi for a young woman who has been framed for murder. However, the frame is so airtight that the Toff is hunted as an accomplice to the killing! In one of his later adventures (*The Toff and the Fallen Angels,* 1970), he uses his niece Angela as bait to catch criminals preying on unwed mothers. One wall of his flat is a museum his adventures, containing weapons, poisons, a noose, bloody feathers, and other souvenirs.

Comment: The character was created by John Creasey. The first collection of Toff stories was *Introducing the Toff,* published in 1938; 54 other books followed, the most recent of which was *Toff and the Crooked Copper* (1975). In motion pictures, John Bentley played the Toff in two films released in 1952, *Salute the Toff* and *Hammer the Toff.*

TOMAHAWK (C)

First Appearance: *Star Spangled Comics* #69, 1947, DC Comics.

Biography: As a boy in pre-Revolutionary America, Tom Hawk goes west with a band of pioneers. Beyond the Allegheny Mountains, Hawk is nabbed by Indians; when he saves the powerful Black Thunder from a rampaging moose, Tom is taken in by the tribe and, over the year, is taught Indian skills. Because he is particularly good with the tomahawk, Tom takes that as his name; after returning to his own people, he becomes the guardian of an orphan boy, Dan Hunter. He also takes on a pet, his faithful dog Tracker.

During the Revolution Tomahawk—"woods-wise, hickory-tough, and heroic"—forms the Rangers, which are "about twenty-two" members strong. In addition to Hunter, who is now a young man, the team consists of powerful Maine blacksmith Big Anvil (real name unknown), an "amiable, power-packed giant"; Bill Howell; Brass Buttons (Private Jud Fuller) of Virginia; Cannonball (Sergeant Horace Calhoun) of Connecticut, a strong, rough Ranger who is Tomahawk's topkick; the beret-wearing "Frenchie" Duval, one of Lafayette's men; "Healer" Randolph, a black man who knows about medicine and herbal remedies; "Kaintuck" Jones, a pacifist and an expert shot who goes to war when the British murder his friend; "Long Rifle" Morgan, a Pennsylvania marksman; Matt Willis, who dies in the line of duty; "Stovepipe" (Leroy) Johnson, a general's son who spurns a comfortable job in headquarters and who stores various weapons in his spacious hat; "Suicide" Simms; and Wildcat (name unknown), a religious man from Pennsylvania who regards war as a necessary means to freedom.

Often, battle forces the Rangers to improvise anachronistically: In one adventure, they put kettles on their heads and use them as helmets, while in another, Tomahawk rigs wings and a tail and flies.

Tomahawk and Dan Hunter to the rescue! © DC Comics.

During the war, Tomahawk and his Rangers fight in some unusual forts: Fort Mystery, Fort Petticoat (all women, of course), and even the floating Fort Flotsam. After the war, they tackle more unusual foes, from the giant Frontier Frankenstein to the towering Gator-God, to the huge Gorilla-Ranger. Eventually Tomahawk hangs up his coonskin cap, marries the Indian Moon Fawn, daughter of Chief Grey Elk, settles in the Midwest's Echo Valley, and fathers Hawk and Small Eagle. Hawk—who is an expert with the tomahawk and gun—goes on to become a hero himself, protecting the rights of Indians and settlers alike.

Comment: Tomahawk was featured on the cover of *Star Spangled Comics* from #96 to #121. He went to *World's Finest Comics* from #65 to #101, and starred in his own title, which lasted 140 issues (1950–1972); from #131 on, the magazine featured the adventures of Hawk and was called *Son of Tomahawk.* The various Rangers were introduced at different points in the run of the series.

TOM CORBETT (TV, CS, C, R)

First Appearance: *Tom Corbett Space Cadet,* October 1950, CBS (see COMMENT).

Biography: In the early 2350s, war has been abolished, the nations of our world live in harmony as the Commonwealth of Earth, and Mars and Venus have joined to form the Solar Alliance. Teenager Tom Corbett is a cadet at the Space Academy, where the Solar Guards are trained for service on "distant planets." Along with Cadet Roger Manning, Cadet T.J. Thistle, Cadet Rattison, and the Venusian Astro, Tom trains in space, aboard the *Polaris.* Armed with weapons such as the Paralo-ray, they typically deal with natural catastrophes (asteroid swarms and the like), though occasional evil aliens or escaped prisoners are also on hand. In command is Captain Steve Strong; Tom's girlfriend, Dr. Joan Dale, also partakes in the crew's adventures.

The oath of the cadets is: "I solemnly swear to safeguard the freedom of space, protect the liberties of the planets and defend the cause of peace throughout the universe."

Comment: The 15-minute show had elaborate special effects and sets and aired three times a week for three months on CBS, then from January 1951 to September 1952 on ABC. Reruns were seen from July to September 1951 on NBC, from August 1953 to May 1954 on DuMont, then again on NBC from December 1954 to June 1955. Frankie Thomas starred as Corbett, Michael Harvey and then Edward Bryce were Strong, Jack Grims was T.J., Al Markim was Astro, Jan Merlin

played Roger, and Margaret Garland was Joan. Future *Gomer Pyle* costar Frank Sutton was Rattison.

A comic strip began in September 1951, drawn by Ray Bailey, and ran for two years. The popular show also spawned a short-lived radio series in 1952—rather different from the usual progression.

Prize Publications published three issues of *Tom Corbett Space Cadet* in 1955; it was also #102 of Western's *March of Comics* in 1953.

The series—whose working title was *Chris Colby, Space Cadet*—was inspired by but only loosely based on Robert A. Heinlein's 1948 novel *Space Cadet,* which is about the training and Venusian adventure of a new recruit in the Interplanetary Patrol.

Grosset & Dunlap published a series of novels using the house name Carey Rockwell: *Stand By for Mars* (1952), *Danger in Deep Space* (1953), *On the Trail of the Space Pirates* (1953), *Space Pioneers* (1953), *Revolt on Venus* (1954), *Treachery in Outer Space* (1954), *Sabotage in Space* (1955), and *Robot Rocket* (1956).

TOMMY TOMORROW (C)

First Appearance: *Real Fact Comics* #6, 1947, DC Comics.

Biography: Attending Spaceport in the middle 21st century (100 years ahead of the comic book's year of publication), Thomas Tomorrow graduates at the top of his class, becomes a colonel, and joins the Planeteers, reporting to Commander Jenkins. Tommy's assistant is Captain Brent Wood. Sometimes his work is exciting, pitting the Planeteers against thieves from the future; sometimes there's a mystery involved ("Great stars! A set of eyeglasses, which could only be worn by a three-eyed giant!"); at other times Tommy and Captain Wood end up working in the Space Lost and Found Department at Planeteer headquarters. It's all up to the commandant, to whom the Planeteers report. Tommy packs a ray gun and flies in a spaceship armed with atomic torpedoes and a one-passenger lifeship, and capable of reaching speeds of 10,000 miles per second; he also wears a wrist compass. The Planeteers dress in purple boots and shorts and a black shirt with purple sleeves. By the 22nd century, the police force will be known as the Super-Planeteers and wear blue uniforms and helmets.

Comment: In his original adventure, which was drawn by legendary science fiction artist Virgil Finlay, Tommy applied to Rocket College in 1954. He makes the first trip to Mars (solo) in just a few days and returns to Earth a hero. This history is ignored in subsequent adventures, when the Planeteers are introduced. Tommy Tomorrow was retroactively—and rather absurdly—tied to DC's future-earth hero KAMANDI . Tommy appeared in four issues of *Real Fact Comics* and also starred in *Action Comics* from #127 to #251, *World's Finest* numbers 102 to 124, and five issues of *Showcase* beginning with #41. *Real Fact Comics* #6 also published a letter by Harlan Ellison—the first time the soon-to-be-writer appeared in print.

TOM SAWYER (L, C, MP, TV, S)

First Appearance: *The Adventures of Tom Sawyer* by Mark Twain, 1876, Chatto and Windus.

Biography: A boy who's "full of the Old Scratch," Tom lives with his Aunt Polly, cousin Mary, and half brother Sid in St. Petersburgh, Illinois, on the Mississippi, circa 1840. His closest friends are Huckleberry Finn, son of the town drunk; a black youth, Jim; and Joe Harper, "a bosom friend." In their first adventure, the lads see no-good Injun Joe murder Dr. Robinson in a cemetery, settling an old score that had resulted in Joe being arrested. Injun Joe frames his companion, Muff Potter, for the deed, while the boys promise one another not to say anything about what they've witnessed for fear of what Joe might do to them.

After playing pirates on an island three miles from town, Tom, Huck, and Joe Harper are gone so long they're presumed dead—but return just in time for their funeral. Feeling conscience-stricken, Tom testifies at Muff Potter's trial, but Injun Joe escapes before he can be arrested. Meanwhile, Tom is presumed dead again when he and his girlfriend, Becky Thatcher, wander from a group and become lost in a maze of caves. Fortunately, Tom is able to find a way out, and in the wake of the near tragedy, a heavy door is attached to the cave. Ironically, Injun Joe is trapped inside, where he perishes. Shortly after Tom and Huck uncover a treasure chest in a "haunted" house and become wealthy young men. Huck's guardian, the Widow Douglas, invests the boy's money, and Becky's father, Judge Thatcher, does the same for Tom.

In their next chronicled adventure, Huck is kidnaped by his father and taken to a cabin on an island. Escaping, he falls in with Jim, a runaway slave. Their intention is to get to Cairo, Illinois, then head up the Ohio River to the North, where Jim will be free. Unfortunately, they end up going south, where a pair of ne'er-do-wells sell Jim back into slavery on the Pikesville, Arkansas, plantation of Tom's uncle and aunt, Silas and Sally Phelps. Huck is joined by Tom, and the two set out to rescue Jim. This is accomplished—though Tom takes a bullet in the calf—when Jim learns the good news: His previous owner, Miss Watson, has died and given him his freedom.

In their last adventures, Tom is "not quite fifteen" when he, Huck, and Jim climb into a "noble big balloon" headed for Europe but end up storm-tossed to Africa. (Huck and Jim seem to have *no* luck with direction). In the Sahara desert, they have adventures with a caravan, robbers, and a sandstorm before making their way to Mt. Sinai. There Tom sends Jim back to the U.S. for his pipe; when Aunt Polly catches him, she makes him get right back in the balloon and return for Tom. In their next adventure, the boys are visiting Silas's plantation and become embroiled in a case involving stolen diamonds, murder, and the arrest of Silas; Tom eventually uncovers the true perpetrators and Silas is exonerated.

Comment: The characters were based on people Twain had known in his youth. The first American edition was published by the American Publishing Company in December 1876. The English edition had been published in June. The sequel, *The Adventures of Huckleberry Finn (Tom Sawyer's Comrade)* was published in 1885. In need of money because of bad investments (in publishing, of all things), Twain wrote his last two Sawyer adventures, the novel *Tom Sawyer Abroad* (1894) and the novella *Tom Sawyer, Detective* (1896). Both were potboilers that lacked the texture and firm hand of the first two tales.

In comic books, Stoll and Edwards published *Tom Sawyer & Huck Finn* in 1925, *The Adventures of Tom Sawyer* was adapted by *Classics Illustrated* #50 (1948) and for *Dell Junior Treasury* #10 (1957).

Tom Sawyer and Huckleberry Finn have appeared in a number of films, the best and best-known being *Tom Sawyer* in 1930, starring Jackie Coogan as Tom, Mitzie Green as Becky, and Junior Durkin as Huck, and *The Adventures of Tom Sawyer* in 1938. *Tom Sawyer, Detective,* was also made that year. *Tom Sawyer* was the name of two versions made in 1973: one a musical starring Johnnie Whitaker, the other a TV movie. *The Adventures of Huckleberry Finn* has been filmed as *Huckleberry Finn* in 1931 (with the same cast as *Tom Sawyer*), 1939 (with Mickey Rooney), 1974 (as a musical), and 1975 (with Ron Howard), and by its original title in 1960, 1981, 1985, and 1993.

The Adventures of Huckleberry Finn was also adapted as the musical *Big River* in 1985, which played 1,005 performances on Broadway.

On TV, the character appeared in an animated series, *The New Adventures of Huckleberry Finn,* which aired on NBC from September 1968 to September 1969. Kevin Schultz provided the voice of Tom, Michael Shea was Huck. Twenty half-hour adventures were produced, all of which aired as part of *The Banana Splits and Friends.* The series spawned a Gold Key comic book, which lasted one issue in 1968. The 1982 TV movie *Rascals and Robbers: The Secret*

Adventures of Tom Sawyer and Huck Finn pits the duo against unscrupulous persons who are trying to cheat the town.

TOM SWIFT (L)

First Appearance: *Tom Swift and His Motor-Cycle or Fun and Adventure on the Road* by Victor Appleton, 1910, Grosset & Dunlap.

Biography: A precocious, superbright young man, Tom Swift is the only son of inventor Barton Swift. The two live with their "motherly" housekeeper Mrs. Baggert in a large house outside of Shopton, New York. Barton has made a great deal of money from his inventions, and Tom has already "followed in the footsteps of his parent and had already taken out several patents." He also becomes something of an adventurer, preventing sneaks from gaining control of his father's or his own inventions, whether it's a new form of turbine engine or more exotic devices such as a photo telephone. Tom's best friend and fellow adventurer is Ned Newton; they are occasionally assisted by a black handyman, Eradicate Sampson.

After years of adventuring, the adult Tom founds Swift Enterprises, which has research and development departments, a construction division, and more. He marries and settles in California and has a son, Tom, Jr., and a year-younger daughter, Sandra (a.k.a. Sandy). At 18, the tall blond Tom, Jr., continues in his father's footsteps. With his best friend Bud Barclay, they "invent, build, and test dozens of powerful atomic devices," including the flying lab, a giant robot, the "diving seacopter," the phantom satellite, and more. Tom Jr.'s girlfriend is Phyllis Newton, daughter of Tom Sr.'s longtime friend Ned.

Comment: Victor Appleton was a house name. Other titles in the original 38 book series include, in order, *Tom Swift and His Motor Cycle or the Rivals of Lake Carlopa, Tom Swift and His Airship or the Stirring Cruise of the Red Cloud, Tom Swift and His Submarine Boat or Under the Ocean for Sunken Treasure, Tom Swift and His Electric Runabout or the Speediest Car on the Road, Tom Swift and His Wireless Message or the Castaways of Earthquake Island, Tom Swift Among the Diamond Makers or the Secret of Phantom Mountain, Tom Swift in the Caves of Ice or the Wreck of An Airship, Tom Swift and His Sky Racer or the Quickest Flight on Record, Tom Swift and His Electric Rifle or Daring Adventures in Elephant Land, Tom Swift in the City of Gold or Marvellous Adventures Underground, Tom Swift and His Air Glider or Seeking the Platinum Treasure, Tom Swift in Captivity or a Daring Escape by Airship, Tom Swift and His Wizard Camera or the Perils of Moving Picture Taking, Tom Swift and His Great Searchlight or On the Border for Uncle Sam, Tom Swift and His Giant Cannon or the Longest Shots on Record, Tom Swift and His Photo Telephone or the Picture that Saved a Fortune, Tom Swift and His Aerial Warship or the Naval Terror of the Seas,* and *Tom Swift and His Big Tunnel or the Hidden City of the Andes.* The character was created by publisher/writer Edward L. Stratemeyer, and most of the adventures were written by H.R. Garis. The original novels were published between 1910 and 1938, while 36 Tom Swift, Jr., novels were published from 1954 to 1971, written by Victor Appleton II and beginning with *Tom Swift and His Flying Lab.* There were six novels in a third series by Victor Appleton, published from 1980 to 1981 and featuring Tom Swift in the far future, young again, flying throughout the universe with his friends Anita Thorwald and Benjamin Franklin Walking Eagle onboard their ship the *Exedra.* That series began with *The City in the Stars.* A fourth series by Appleton was launched in 1991, again featuring Tom, Jr., in the modern day, working with his father at Swift Enterprises, assisted by his two good friends Rick Cantwell and Mandy Coster. The series is ongoing with 13 titles to date, the first of which was *The Black Dragon.*

Grosset & Dunlap also published other Stratemeyer series including NANCY DREW, THE HARDY BOYS, and such lesser-known adventure series as the Outdoor Chums series about "four wide-awake lads, sons of wealthy men," who get into adventures in a small town; the Outdoor Girls series; the Moving Picture Boys series; the Moving Picture Girls series (the adventures of Ruth and Alice DeVere whose father, an actor, has "lost his voice [and] has taken up work for the movies"); the Boys of Columbia High series ("Never was there a cleaner, brighter, more manly boy than Frank Allen, the hero of this series"); and the Girls of Central High series ("There are many contested matches on track and field, and on the water, as well as doings in the classroom and on the school stage.").

TONY NEWMAN and DOUG PHILLIPS (TV, L, C)

First Appearance: *The Time Tunnel,* September 1966, ABC.

Biography: Based underground in the Arizona desert, Project Tic-Toc is a government-funded time travel research program that is in danger of having its budget eliminated. When Senator Clark comes to have a look at Tic-Toc and its laser-activated conical time tunnel, Dr. Tony Newman takes an unauthorized trip into the past to prove its worthiness—even though the tunnel hasn't been debugged. Tony lands on the deck of the *Titanic* while, back at the laboratory, Dr. Doug Phillips, Dr. Ann MacGregor, General Heywood Kirk, and Dr. Raymond Swain watch on a monitor, unable to bring him back; all the unfinished device can do is pluck him from where he is and, like a spin of the roulette wheel, deposit him somewhere else. But Doug is not quite willing to give up on the *Titanic.* He takes the Time Tunnel to the doomed vessel, armed with a newspaper report of the disaster; the captain refuses to believe that his ship will sink, and the scientists are snatched from the vessel right before it goes down. They land in the future, on a spaceship headed for Mars and, in subsequent weeks, end up in 1910, where Halley's Comet has a small town convinced the world is doomed; at Pearl Harbor before the attack (where Tony meets himself as a child and tries to convince his father an air raid is imminent); in the War of 1812; on Krakatoa just before the eruption; at the siege of Troy; at the Little Big Horn; and more. They never do get back to the present.

Comment: The hour-long series starred James Darren as Tony, Robert Colbert as Doug, Lee Meriwether as Ann, Whit Bissell as Heywood, and John Zaremba as Raymond. Thirty episodes aired through September 1967.

Pyramid published a pair of novels in 1967, *The Time Tunnel* (Tony tries to save lives in the Johnstown Flood) and *Timeslip!* (a nuclear bomb is headed toward the White House of a century before). In both of the books, which were written by noted science fiction author Murray Leinster, the heroes were brought back after each adventure.

Gold Key Comics published two issues of *The Time Tunnel* in 1967.

Joe Kubert's cover for *Tor.* © DC Comics.

TOR (C)

First Appearance: *1,000,000 Years Ago* #1, 1953, St. John Publishing Co.

Biography: A Cro-Magnon who coexists with dinosaurs, Tor is a "lone gladiator for justice" who works "to prevent the enslavement of his fellow man." In addition to his strong moral streak, Tor possesses "the strength of a mammoth" and an "insatiable curiosity to explore the unknown," and constantly ventures into new regions of the prehistoric world with his companion, the lemurlike Chee-Chee.

Comment: The character was created by artist Joe Kubert and writer Norman Maurer. The magazine became *Tor* and lasted to issue #5; #2 contained some of the first 3-D art created for the comics. *Tor* returned

in 1975, from DC Comics, and lasted for six issues, Epic brought it back in 1993 as *Joe Kubert's Tor.*

TRADER TOM (MP)

First Appearance: *Trader Tom of the China Seas,* 1954, Republic Pictures.

Biography: Tom Rogers is a trader who works the China Seas. During one voyage he learns that the evil spy Barent and his cohorts are planning a revolution in the small nation of Bumatra—a rebellion that they hope will spread to other countries in the region. Vivian Wells, the daughter of a United Nations agent, has been on Barent's trail and teams with the rugged Tom to stop arms from reaching the rebels and to find out where Barent is based. Eventually Vivian is kidnaped, Tom sneaks behind enemy lines to rescue her, and Barent is killed in a fiery blast.

Comment: Harry Lauter played Tom; the 12-chapter

serial was directed by Franklin Adreon and was one of the last movie serials ever made. Though this was Tom's only appearance, heroes with alliterative names continued to abound in adventure fiction; some examples include the Big Little Book hero Pilot Pete, syndicated TV hero Diver Dan, RED RYDER, radio hero Dick Daring, and many others.

TRAVIS MCGEE (L, MP, TV)

First Appearance: *The Deep Blue Good-By* by John D. MacDonald, 1964.

Biography: The six-foot four-inch McGee is a freelance operator who recovers ill-gotten gains, usually from criminals, and invariably works outside the law. Though his contracts stipulate that he keeps half of what he recovers, his motivation is not so much gain as righting wrongs. Based in Fort Lauderdale, Florida, on his boat *The Busted Flush,* he travels wherever he is needed, whether it's to New York to help the sister of a friend, Chicago to help a former girlfriend, Arizona to assist a woman whose husband owes her money (though she doesn't live to collect it), or Hawaii to help the daughter of a friend. Occasionally McGee gets involved with cases where there is no money involved, as when he's jailed by corrupt law officers or when he hunts down a religious cult responsible for the death of a girlfriend.

McGee's assistant, neighbor, and chess adversary is a financial wizard named Meyer.

Comment: The subsequent McGee novels are *Night-*

mare in Pink (1964), *A Purple Place for Dying* (1964), *The Quick Red Fox* (1964), *A Deadly Shade of Gold* (1965), *Bright Orange for the Shroud* (1965), *Darker Than Amber* (1966), *One Fearful Yellow Eye* (1966), *Pale Gray for Guilt* (1968), *The Girl in the Plain Brown Wrapper* (1968), *Dress Her in Indigo* (1969), *The Long Lavender Look* (1970), *A Tan and Sandy Silence* (1972), *The Scarlet Ruse* (1973), *The Turquoise Lament* (1973), *The Dreadful Lemon Sky* (1974), *The Empty Copper Sea* (1978), *The Green Ripper* (1979), *Cinnamon Skin* (1983), *The Lonely Silver Rain* (1985), *A Deadly Shade of Gold* (1987), and others.

Rod Taylor played McGee in the film *Darker than Amber* (1970), while Sam Elliott starred in the 1983 TV movie *Travis McGee,* based on *The Empty Copper Sea.*

THE TRIGGER TWINS (C)

First Appearance: *All-Star Western* #58, 1951, DC Comics.

Biography: Egon Treigar comes to the colonies shortly before the Revolution and fights bravely for independence. By the time his son heads west "to make his fortune," the family name has become Trigger. Twins Walter and Wayne are born to the pioneer and his wife in 1839. As they grow up, Walter is far more outgoing and adventurous; during the Civil War, he makes lieutenant while Wayne stays a private. However, the ironic truth is that Wayne is the braver

The Trigger Twins: Wayne helps Walt escape from quicksand. © DC Comics.

man and the much better shot. In fact, when Wayne slays five Rebel soldiers, he's wounded—and Walter takes the credit. After the war, Wayne takes over his father's general store in Rocky City, which is "built right over [an] old cave," while Walter becomes a drifter and gunfighter known as the Trigger Kid. Because of his war reputation and his gift of smooth talk, he rarely has to pull his gun—which is for the better, considering he isn't much of a shot. When he finally returns to Rocky City, he's appointed sheriff, counting on his infamy and sweet talk to make gunplay unnecessary. But that doesn't prove the case. Wayne, realizing that his brother is a "fumbler . . . a bungler," he frequently assists him; Wayne even keeps a duplicate of Walter's buckskin uniform and horse in the cave under the store. No one knows that he is secretly the "second" sheriff, the one who performs his brother's bravest acts.

So why doesn't Wayne just switch places with his brother for real? Because, for one thing, his girlfriend Linda doesn't want him risking his neck. For another, as Wayne puts it, their "secret . . . gives us an advantage against all the gangs in the territory."

Wayne shoots a gun "with the swiftness of lightning." Among their foes are the notorious Groton Gang, Doc Doom (before the Fantastic Four had a foe by the same name), the Cactus Gang, and the Flat Hat Gang.

Comment: The characters appeared in *All-Star Western* until #116. This incarnation of the magazine preceded its return. (See JONAH HEX.) The characters also costarred in *Secret Origins* #48 in 1990.

Other heroes who debuted in #58 are Strong Bow, who enforces peace in North America before Columbus arrived; Don Caballero, a fencing master who fights for justice in 19th-century Southern California; and the Roving Ranger, Captain Jeff Graham of the Texas Rangers.

TRON (MP, L, VG)

First Appearance: *Tron*, 1982, Walt Disney Productions.

Biography: When ENCOM Corporation bigwig Edward Dillinger steals programs created by Kevin Flynn and then fires him, the young programmer seeks to find incriminating evidence against his former boss. He is helped by programmer Alan Bradley and girlfriend, Lora. However, while Flynn works at the keyboard, Dillinger's bullying, computer-raiding Master Control Program (MCP) unleashes a beam that digitizes Flynn and brings him, alive and aglow, into the computer. There, in a city known as the System, he meets a captive program and superb game warrior,

Tron, a "User Champion" who is a dead ringer for Alan. Dressed in glowing, blue circuitlike armor and armed with a Frisbee-style Identity Disc that disintegrates enemy warriors, Tron is forced by the MCP and his Command Program Sark—who looks like Dillinger—to compete in the gladiatorial Game Grid. After a deadly Light Cycle race, Flynn, Tron, and the warrior Ram use the vehicles to escape. Ram "derezzes," but Flynn and Tron make it to the Factory Complex in the heart of the computer city. There they link up with Yori, who looks like Lora, and together the three hijack a Solar Sailer, fly over the Game Sea, and reach the huge Central Processing Unit, home of the MCP. Tron derezzes Sark with his Disc, after which he turns his weapon on the MCP, destroying it.

Flynn returns to the real world, where the liberated computer system begins dishing up all manner of incriminating evidence against Dillinger. Flynn is named the head of ENCOM, while Tron and Yori live happily in the newly liberated System.

Comment: Bruce Boxleitner starred as Tron/Alan, with Jeff Bridges as Flynn, Cindy Morgan as Yori/Lora, and David Warner as Sark/Dillinger. The film was directed by Steven Lisberger, who cowrote it with Bonnie MacBird. Brian Daley wrote the novelization of the film.

Tron was the first feature film to make extensive use of the kind of computer-generated graphics that would become commonplace a decade later in films such as *Terminator 2: Judgment Day* and *Jurassic Park*.

Not surprisingly, there were many *Tron* arcade and video games, including *Tron* and *Discs of Tron,* both from Bally Midway. The Intellivision system offered the *Deadly Discs* and *Solar Sailer* games, while their M Network (Atari-compatible) division produced *The Adventures of Tron.*

Fans of *Tron* are cultlike in their fervor, and, in 1983, an unauthorized, anonymous novelette/sequel was produced: *Warrior Tron,* in which the MCP takes over again when Alan leaves his keyboard to get popcorn. Tron must be transformed into the powerful Tron Invictus to battle MCP and a revitalized Sark.

TROOPER ROD BLAKE (TV)

First Appearance: *Star Stage,* February 1956, NBC.

Biography: As the chief criminal investigator for the Nevada State Police, tall, lean Rod Blake battles killers, kidnapers, mobsters, gamblers, and racketeers from Reno to Las Vegas and into the desert. He often works undercover to ferret out criminals.

Comment: Despite the fact that the character debuted on a network show, the proposed series was not bought by NBC. Thus, *State Trooper* debuted in syndication in January 1957. There were 104 episodes of the half-hour series, which aired first run through 1959. Rod Cameron played the part of Blake. The series was based on case histories involving Nevada state troopers, and many episodes were filmed on location.

Cameron also starred as New York police officer Lieutenant Bart Grant in 65 episodes of *City Detective*, a syndicated series that first aired in 1953.

TUGBOAT ANNIE (L, MP, TV)

First Appearance: "Tugboat Annie" by Norman Reilly Raine, 1927, *The Saturday Evening Post.*

Biography: Widow Annie Brennan runs the tugboat *Narcissus* in the Pacific Northwest, aided by her cook, Pinto, and enjoying a friendly rivalry with competing tug captain Horatio Bullwinkle. In addition to routine tug work, the big, tough-looking woman with the heart of gold becomes involved with capturing crooks and smugglers and helping people down on their luck or caught in storms.

Comment: The character is best known through a pair of motion pictures: *Tugboat Annie* (1933), starring Marie Dressler with Wallace Beery as her drunken husband, and *Tugboat Annie Sails Again* (1940), starring Marjorie Rambeau and costarring Ronald Reagan.

On TV, Minerva Urecal played Tugboat, once again a widow. The syndicated half-hour series began airing in 1958; there were 39 episodes. Walter Sande costarred as Bullwinkle. The series exteriors were shot in San Pedro Harbor.

TUROK, SON OF STONE (C)

First Appearance: *4-Color* #596, 1954, Dell Publishing.

Biography: At some point long before Europeans began settling in North America, Indians Turok and his teenage companion Andar are searching the desert for water somewhere north of the Rio Grande. They enter a cave, descend into a hole, wander for hours in the caverns, and become lost. They emerge in the subtropical Lost Valley, a.k.a. Lost Land, actually a series of valleys where dinosaurs still exist. As the men try to find a way out, they face dangers from the dinosaurs, which they call Honkers, and from the primitive peoples. (Somehow, Turok is able to speak their languages.)

Both men wear buckskin trousers with a red loincloth and sport a single feather in their hair. Turok usually wears a blue vest. The men are equally adept

Turok and Andar in a typical situation, being pursued by a (vegetarian) Honker. © Gold Key Comics.

with knives, spears, and the bow and arrow, the tips poisoned using special berries.

Comment: After two more *4-Color* appearances, Turok was given his own magazine. Western (Gold Key) took over from Dell with #30 (1962), and the title ran what was for then an extraordinary 130 issues. It returned with new adventures as *Turok, Dinosaur Hunter* in 1993, published by Valiant. In this incarnation, people from the far future also find the valley and raise an environmentally unsound civilization, "technologically enhancing" the dinosaurs and turning them into draft animals and killers. Turok battles the invaders, determined to slay their leader, Mon-Ark. Turok's inamorata in this new series is the native woman Serita.

TYNDALL (C)

First Appearance: *Marvel Super Action* Magazine #1, 1976, Marvel Comics.

Biography: An elf, Tyndall finds himself in Dwarf Haven, a village of Weirdworld; he knows nothing about his past, save that he comes from a place called Klarn. Leaving, armed with his crossbow and sword, he discovers a giant egg; it hatches and out walks the elf Velanna who, like Tyndall, has no knowledge of her past, other than that she comes from Klarn. In time, Tyndall learns that Klarn is a ringlike island that floats above Weirdworld. He gets to visit Klarn unwillingly when the evil wizard Grithstane sends him there, threatening to kill Velanna unless he returns with mystic dragon blood. Tyndall does so, after which he and Velanna have other adventures on Weirdworld. His origin has never been revealed, though he is clearly a pawn of the Higher Ones, godlike beings who dwell in the heavens.

Comment: The Weirdworld saga was created by writer Doug Moench and continued in *Marvel Premiere* #38, *Marvel Comics Super Special* #11–#13 (a saga entitled "Warriors of the Shadow Realm"), and then in *Epic Illustrated.*

U

UNDERSEA AGENT (C)

First Appearance: *Undersea Agent* #1, 1966, Tower Comics.

Biography: With orders direct from the White House, U.S. Navy jet pilot, Lieutenant Davy Jones, is sent to rendezvous with the submarine *Arotica* where he is taken to U.N.D.E.R.S.E.A.—the United Nations

From the left: Lt. Davy Jones, Skooby Doolittle, and Professor Weston, from the first issue of *Undersea Agent.* © Tower Comics.

Department of Experiment and Research Systems Established at Atlantis. U.N.D.E.R.S.E.A. is a city built on the bottom of the ocean, originally founded by Professor Weston to study the remains of the lost continent of Atlantis. Later it became an international effort "dedicated to the peaceful research of the problems of how man is to live under the ocean when the land areas become too populous." Meanwhile, however, evil Dr. Fang, underwritten by Red China, has been working to rule the world under the waves—and, eventually, the world above as well. Jones has been brought to U.N.D.E.R.S.E.A. to become Undersea Agent Number One. He is assisted by alliterative Junior Agent Scooby Doolittle ("Divin' Devilfish!," "Sailin' Sailfish," etc.), whom Weston once rescued from a sinking fishing boat; and by Dolph, the trained, freedom-loving dolphin.

The key item in Jones's arsenal is the diving suit "a single molecule thick" that works as gills, allowing him to breathe underwater. He is also equipped with a miniature energy cell, which turns sea water into electricity and allows him to swim "at incredible speeds," concussion bullets, and other weapons.

Comment: There were six issues of *Undersea Agent,* part of Tower Comics' ambitious (failed) program to launch a line of 25 cent comic books, using top talent, at a time when most comic books were 12 cents. The comic book was a clever and fairly literate variation of the popular JAMES BOND/Man from U.N.C.L.E. characters NAPOLEON SOLO AND ILLYA KURYAKIN.

THE UNKNOWN SOLDIER (C)

First Appearance: *Star Spangled War Stories* #151, 1970, DC Comics.

Biography: Little is known about the character's past. Along with his older brother Harry, he enlists to fight in World War II. The two serve in the same unit in the Philippines, Harry dying when he saves his brother from a Japanese grenade—though the blast destroys the survivor's face. When he recovers at a Washington, D.C., veteran's hospital, he trains to be-

The Unknown Soldier and a failed attempt to assassinate the Führer. © DC Comics.

U.S. ARCHER (T, C)

First Appearance: *U.S. 1* #1, 1983, Marvel Comics.

Biography: As a boy, Ulysses Solomon Archer and his older brother Jefferson Hercules used to stand by the highway and watch the big trucks pass. When their trucker-parents are killed in a wreck, the boys move in with family friends Ed and Annie Wheeler, owners of the Short Stop diner. Jeff goes to work as a trucker, and U.S. goes to college where he not only quarter-backs the football team but graduates magna cum laude, with degrees in computers and electronics. Upon graduating, he joins his brother as a trucker—until the evil Highwayman forces them off the road. Jeff is presumed dead and U.S. is seriously injured. The Wheelers agree to allow him to undergo revolutionary new surgery, in which his shattered cranium is replaced "with a new experimental metal alloy" that, rather unexpectedly, enables him to pick up CB com-

come an undercover operative, based in the Pentagon and working in both theaters of war. A master of makeup trained by actor Anton Vladchek, this soldier "of a thousand-and-one identities" (some of them female) keeps his face swathed in bandages when he is not in disguise.

Disguised as a German, he infiltrates Hitler's bunker during the fall of Berlin and helps kill the Führer. The Unknown Soldier himself apparently perishes in Berlin, saving a child from an explosion. However, either the Soldier or his ghost—the story never reveals which—shows up in Metropolis in 1982 to help Superman avert a nuclear holocaust.

Comment: *Star Spangled War Stories* became *The Unknown Soldier* with #205 and remained so until its demise with #268. The Superman team-up occurred in *DC Comics Presents* #42. The hero also starred in a special 12-issue run of *The Unknown Soldier* in 1988–89.

U.S. Archer, his customized rig, and the climactic journey through space! © Marvel Comics.

munications in his head. After customizing an 18-wheeler with radar and special weapons, such as an oil slick release, tire-shredding shrapnel, bombs, an ejection seat, and more, U.S. takes to the road to find the Highwayman. He discovers that it's actually Jeff who, as it turns out, wanted to get rid of his brother so that he, and not U.S., could accept an offer from aliens to be an agent in their Interplanetary Federation.

Ultimately, U.S., the Wheelers, young cook Mary McGrill, and the entire Short Stop are carried into space.

Comment: The vehicles were based on electric toys created by Tyco Toy Industries; the characters (and bizarre storyline) were created by writer Al Milgrom and Tyco staffers expressly for the comic book. The magazine lasted 12 issues.

V

VANTH DREADSTAR (C)

First Appearance: *Epic Illustrated* #15, 1982, Marvel Comics.

Biography: Vanth Dreadstar is a young man of 15 when his parents are killed by ice bears on the planet Byfrexia in a sector of the Milky Way that is distant from Earth. He survives starvation and exposure when he finds the mighty "sword of icy fire," which gives him the strength of 20 warriors, can suck up any energy directed against him, and prevent time and disease from affecting him. When the sword isn't needed, he can absorb it into his body for storage. He goes on to wield the blade on behalf of the Orsirosians, a noble race locked in a losing battle against the evil Zygoteans—the Orsirosian Lord Aknaton had left the sword on Byfrexia so it would be found by a worthy warrior. Ultimately preferring suicide to witnessing galaxywide genocide, the Orsirosians create and blow the Infinity Horn, a doomsday device that destroys the galaxy. Vanth survives in a mystical sphere created by the godlike Orsirosian Aknaton and drifts, for millions of years, in suspended animation. After 1,000 millennia, he awakens on the planet Caldor in the Empirical Galaxy. He's taken in by the "gentle cat people" who farm there, meets the human Delilah and marries her, becomes a farmer himself—then loses everything when war comes to Caldor, the two-century-old struggle between the Monarchy and the Lord High Papal and his evil Church of the Instrumentality. He uses his might to replace King Nellor of the Monarchy, who was responsible for the attack on Caldor, but when that fails to end the hostilities he takes to space, determined to snuff out "war madness" where he finds it.

Assisting him on his travels through space are his crew, which consists of his second-in-command, an old friend and former mystic and priest, Syzygy Darklock; Willow 327, a blind cybernetic telepath who sees through the eyes of her pet "monk" Rainbow; Oedi, a genetically engineered catman; Skeevo Phlatus, a brawny, purple-skinned smuggler; and Doctor Delphi, a healer.

Comment: The characters were created by artist/writer Jim Starlin. After the *Epic Illustrated* appearance, a *Dreadstar* comic book began publication in 1982; it moved to First Comics with #17. The character also starred in *Marvel Graphic Novel* #3 and in the six-issue Marvel reprint title *Dreadstar and Company.* All Marvel appearances were under their Epic Comics imprint.

VENGEANCE SQUAD (C)

First Appearance: *Vengeance Squad* #1, 1975, Charlton Comics.

The evil Marco Poleau vs. *The Vengeance Squad:* Candy and Tulsa below, Eric on the attack. © Charlton Comics.

275

Biography: "The most dangerous people in the world," the three members of the Vengeance Squad are ex-Treasury Agent Eric Redd, Tulsa Coyle, and Candy Orr. Bankrolled by people in Washington who "will spend any amount of money to wipe out big time crime," the international troubleshooters travel the world doing just that, helped by intelligence from Interpol and other agencies. The trio is armed with traditional weapons as well as various gadgets, such as antigas pills to allow them to survive poison gas.

When they're not on the job, the heroes live in a walled estate on the Hudson River.

Comment: The characters were created by writer Joe Gill and editor George Wildman, and boasted excellent art by PAM (Pete A. Morisi). The title lasted for six issues and also featured the comical adventures of Michael Mauser, Private Eye, and his secretary, Bambi Baxter.

VIKING COMMANDO (C)

First Appearance: *All-Out War* #1, 1979, DC Comics.

Biography: Toward the end of the fifth century, the Scandinavian warrior Valoric leads a group of tribesmen to rescue King Siggro and his daughter Thella, who have been carried off by Huns. Valoric is wounded in the attempt and is carried to Valhalla by the Valkyrie Fey. Unfortunately, Valoric isn't dead and cannot enter; instead, he's flung through time to Europe in 1944. He is found by Major Graham and, anxious to attack the German forces once he hears them referred to as "Huns," he becomes a valuable Allied asset. All the while, Fey hangs around, waiting for Valoric to die and visible only to the hero.

Valoric wears army-issue attire with a fur vest; he also carries a rifle, hand grenades, and his sturdy battle-ax Iron Fang.

Comment: Viking Commando appeared in the six issues of *All-Out War*.

THE VIKING PRINCE (1) (C)

First Appearance: *Brave and the Bold* #1, 1955, DC Comics.

Biography: This much is known about the legendary golden-tressed hero: His name is Jon, he lives in tenth-century Scandinavia, and he's a magnificent warrior. Apart from that, the chronicles are confused about his origin. In one tale, set in A.D. 964, he's an amnesiac young man found by Olaf, a Viking, taken to his village, and named after the ancient hero Jon the Shining. It turns out that Jon is the rightful heir to the throne—but in order to seize power from the evil Baron

The Viking Prince (1) gets set to tackle the fourth Task of Thor. © DC Comics.

Thorvald (a.k.a. Torgunn), he must undertake the 12 Tasks of Thor. The series expires before he can do so.

In another version—recounting events that may transpire before the encounter with Olaf—Jon is the princely son of King Rikk the Storm Cloud and is engaged to wed Princess Asa.

In a third tale, Jon's twin sister, Ailsa the Fair, is abducted by the evil Krogg the Red. When Krogg threatens to kill Ailsa unless Jon surrenders, the bold girl flings herself from a tower and perishes; Jon slays Krogg and, abandoning his lover Illan, becomes a wandering warrior intent on righting wrongs.

In a final tale—which may have sprung from any of the above—the wounded Jon is accidentally taken to Valhalla and falls in love with a Valkyrie. Since Jon isn't dead, Odin, the king of the gods, returns him to Earth, telling him he can return and wed his beloved *if* he perishes bravely in battle. The caveat: Odin makes Jon impervious to fire, water, wood, and metal. Jon finally succeeds in perishing during World War II, dying in an explosion while helping SERGEANT ROCK of Easy Company.

Jon's companion in his early adventures was the Mute Bard, who writes all his verse down. The hero is an expert navigator and skier, and though his wardrobe changes over the years—in some adventures, he's down to a loincloth and boots—he usually wears a winged helmet.

Comment: The character was brilliantly drawn by Joe Kubert and appeared in *The Brave and the Bold* through #24.

THE VIKING PRINCE (2) (C)

First Appearance: *The Rook* #5, 1980, Warren Publishing.

Biography: The kingdom of Thorwald is the Scandinavia of myth, a land of cyclopes, sea serpents, giant reptiles, and other fantastic creatures. Here, too, however, human treachery, is all too common, as the traitorous General Olaf slays King Torgest during a raid on Saxon lands. Returning to Thorwald, he plots to have his aide Baldr surreptitiously kidnap the king's baby son, Sigfrid, to slay him in the Dark Forest, another aide kill Baldr, and then comfort the grieving Queen Sybil himself. However, things don't quite go as Olaf planned. Baldr leaves the babe in the woods but does not slay it; Sigfrid is found by the woodsman Eric and his wife, who raise the child as their own. Eric also finds Baldr who, before dying, tells the woodsman the boy's true identity.

Olaf weds the queen and becomes a tyrannical king. Meanwhile, Sigfrid grows to manhood, and, when his mother dies and his father is slain by the king's raiders, he sets out with his sidekick, the powerful dwarf Sampson, to claim his rightful inheritance. His love is the woman Freyja—until he learns that she is the daughter of Olaf, and thus his half sister.

Comment: The character was created by writer/artist Jose Ortiz and appeared in two issues of *The Rook*—terminated, alas, before he could reclaim his throne!

VINNIE TERRANOVA (TV)

First Appearance: *Wiseguy,* September 1987, CBS.

Biography: An undercover operative for the Organized Crime Bureau (OCB), Vincent Michael Terranova, Agent 4587, serves 18 months in the Newark State Penitentiary to establish his reputation as a criminal, then sets about infiltrating the organizations of powerful mobsters in order to bring them down. Only Vinnie's brother Peter, a priest, his boss at the OCB Frank Xavier McPike (Agent 0129), and his OCB "Lifeguard" Daniel Benjamin Burroughs know that Vinnie isn't really crooked.

Vinnie's first task is to collect enough evidence to prosecute powerful Atlantic City mobster Dave Sonny Steelgrave—an effort that recently resulted in the death of Vinnie's mentor, Stan Dermot. Vinnie gets a job as his driver and is given a lavish penthouse apartment and a warning: "You mess up, you get

The Viking Prince (2) battles cyclopes while Sampson rides to his rescue. © Warren Publishing.

dropped in a hole near the turnpike." Naturally, it's Sonny who ends up behind bars, while Vinnie moves on to tackle mobsters who deal in drugs, munitions, and even has a run-in with crooked CIA operatives. The latter leaves Vinnie so disgusted that he leaves his job and goes to work at a gas station in his old Brooklyn stomping grounds. But being back on the streets reminds him how bad things are, and he returns to undercover work to try and clean them up.

Vinnie's mother, Carlotta, is married to Rudy Aiuppo, the top crime boss in New York: At one point, a murder attempt puts Rudy in the hospital and, ironically, leaves Vinnie in charge of the mob.

Ultimately, Vinnie gets fed up with his work and the seeming futility of it all and vanishes.

Comment: The show aired through December 1990; in all there were 70 hour-long episodes and one two-hour episode. The series was created by Stephen J. Cannell and Frank Lupo and starred Ken Wahl as Vinnie, Jim Byrnes as the "Lifeguard," Jonathan Banks as McPike, and Gerald Anthony as Fr. Peter Terranova. Ray Sharkey guest-starred as Sonny for the first few months of the show.

Vinnie "vanished" when Wahl left the show. He was replaced by Michael Santana (Steven Bauer), a Cuban-American ex-prosecutor who becomes an undercover operative.

VINT BONNER (TV, C)

First Appearance: *The Restless Gun,* September 1957, NBC.

Biography: Following the Civil War, Vint Bonner roams the Southwest; he works primarly as a cowboy, earning money and then moving on. He's torn by his love of pacifism and his hatred of bullies; as one of the fastest guns in the West, he's always challenged by hotshots, forcing him to kill them or stay on the move. Ironically, though he's often summoned to help local law officers keep the peace, he's sent away when it's all over, for ordinary citizens feel uneasy about having a gunman in their midst.

Comment: The half-hour series ran until September 1959, reruns airing until September 1960. John Payne starred.

Dell published five issues of *The Restless Gun* as part of their *4-Color* title, from 1958 to 1960.

VIRGIL TIBBS (L, MP, TV)

First Appearance: *In the Heat of the Night* by John Ball, 1965, Harper & Row.

Biography: Investigator Virgil Tibbs, a southern-born black man, worked in the college cafeteria to pay his way through school. Now a ten-year veteran of the Pasadena, California, police force, specializing in homicide and other "crimes against persons," he is inquisitive (he reads science books for leisure), intelligent, patient, and clever. In one of his most famous cases, he poses as a shoeshine boy and busts a drug ring, since the dealer thought nothing about doing business before a lowly bootblack.

In his most famous case, Tibbs is passing through the small southern town of Wells, waiting for a train to Washington after visiting his mother downstate. When musical conductor Enrico Mantoli is murdered, Officer Sam Wood arrests Tibbs and brings him to redneck Texas-native Chief Bill Gillespie, who reluctantly releases Tibbs when he learns who he is. The two form a tense professional relationship to solve the crime.

In other adventures, Tibbs tries to find out who committed a murder in a nudist camp and struggles to prevent a race riot by finding the white boy who killed a black man.

Tibbs has a karate black belt and has studied aikido.

Comment: Ball's other novels about Tibbs include *The Cool Cottontail* (1966), *Johnny Get Your Gun* (1969), and *Five Pieces of Jade* (1972).

In the motion picture *In the Heat of the Night* (1967), Tibbs works for the Philadelphia police force. Sidney Poitier is the detective, with Rod Steiger as Gillespie. In his other motion picture appearances, all starring Poitier, Tibbs moves to the San Francisco Police Department. He tries to prove that a minister wasn't responsible for killing a prostitute in *They Call Me Mister Tibbs!* (1970) and helps vigilantes steal heroin from a powerful drug cartel in *The Organization* (1971).

On TV, Howard Rollins played the part in the hour-long TV series, which debuted on NBC in March 1988 with a two-hour episode; it moved to CBS in the fall of 1992. This time redneck Sparta, Mississippi, police chief Gillespie is forced by Mayor Findley to hire Tibbs as chief of detectives so he can count on the black vote. Tibbs, who was raised in Sparta, learned police techniques in Philadelphia, and the two men clash over both racial issues and their very different big city/small-town sensibilites. Carroll O'Connor co-stars as Gillespie and Anne-Marie Johnson is Tibbs's wife Althea. The show remains on the air as of this writing, boasting more killers, drug dealers, robbers, and the like than any small town in American history.

THE VIRGINIAN (L, MP, C, TV)

First Appearance: "The Virginian" by Owen Wister, *Harper's,* 1902.

Biography: The Virginian is an otherwise unnamed hero who moves from Virginia to Medicine Bow, Wyoming, in the 1890s, where he works as a ranch foreman. In addition to this job, the taciturn hero manages cattle drives, thwarts rustlers, and helps those in need. One of his men, Trampas, resents being placed under the less experienced (but more responsiible) man, and the two become bitter enemies; during a poker game, Trampas not only accuses the Virginian of cheating but speaks ill of his ancestors—to which the Virginian makes the legendary response, "When you call me that, smile." Ultimately, the hero kills Trampas in a duel and weds New England schoolmarm Molly Wood, whom he saved from a stranded stagecoach.

Comment: The short stories that appeared in *Harper's* were collected in a book called *The Virginian,* which is frequently (and incorrectly) described as a novel. Ironically, author Wister never visited, and knew little about, the territory he was describing.

The stories were filmed as *The Virginian* in 1921 starring Dustin Farnum, in 1923 starring Kenneth Harlan, and, most famously, in 1929 starring Gary Cooper as the foreman of the Box H Ranch and Walter Huston as Trampas, with Mary Brian as Molly; in this first talking version of the stories, the hero's line was turned around somewhat to the equally legendary, "Smile when you say that." Victor Fleming directed. The hero came to the screen again in 1946 with Joel McCrea as the Virginian and Brian Donlevy as the villain.

Classics Illustrated published a comic book adaptation of the original tale in #150 (1959), and Gold Key published one issue of a TV-related *The Virginian* comic book in 1963.

On TV, James Drury played the part, with Doug McClure as Trampas. The 90-minute series aired on NBC from September 1962 to September 1971. This Virginian, who "forces his idea of law and order on a Wyoming Territory community," works on the Shiloh Ranch, which is owned in turn by Judge Henry Garth (Lee J. Cobb), John and Clay Grainger (Charles Bickford and John McIntire), and Colonel Alan MacKenzie (Stewart Granger). The series was renamed *The Men from Shiloh* in its last season.

VOLTAR (C)

First Appearance: "Voltar," July 1963, *Alcala Fight Komix.*

Biography: In some unspecified barbaric time, in a realm where mythological beasts are real, General Voltar leaves his father, Nicodor, his mother, Elsinor, his sister, Beth, and his beloved homeland, Elysium, to fight in "the wars of rich men and kings." When he returns, he finds his family dead and his homeland overrun with demons. After journeying to the citadel of King Antiochus, he learns that the warrior-kings of the nether realms, Gog and Magog, have made war on humans "so that their dark lord, the evil one, might rule these lands . . . for a thousand-thousand years." The warrior sets out through the Forest of Thorns to the pass that leads through the Impassable Mountains to the dark one's realm. Ultimately, he slays the ruler of the evil realm—none other than the king's son Taraval, who had mastered the black arts and been banished. Voltar dies while protecting the escape of Taraval's many human prisoners.

Comment: The character was created and drawn by Alfredo P. Alcala, in a style that borrowed from both Dore and Hal Foster. The strip came to the U.S. in *The Rook* magazine #2 in 1980, with new text written by Will Richardson (Bill DuBay). It appeared in every issue of *The Rook* through #9.

WAINAMOINEN (L)

First Appearance: *Kalevala,* author unknown, A.D. 800–1200.

Biography: The son of the sea and of Ilmater, the daughter of the air, Wainamoinen of Kalevala (Finland) is blessed with a beautiful singing voice. (His brother, Ilmarin, is a mighty smith.) When he wishes to marry the beautiful Aino, her brother Youkahainen forbids it; he relents when Wainamoinen sings so splendidly that the ground literally melts and Youkahainen finds himself neck deep in quicksand. But Aino herself doesn't wish to marry and takes her life; disconsolate, Wainamoinen heads north. The even more disconsolate Youkahainen fires a poison arrow at him. He misses, killing the singer's horse and leaving Wainamoinen adrift in the water for eight years, until a friendly eagle rescues him. The bird carries him to the land of Pohjola, where he is given shelter by Louhi, who agrees to give Wainamoinen the hand of his daughter, the Maid of the North, if he'll build her a mill; he says he can't do it, but his brother, Ilmarin, will. Louhi provides him with a horse and sledge and tells him his trip will be easy if he only looks ahead; naturally, he looks up when an image of the Maid appears in the sky, and he is set a series of challenging tasks to perform before he reaches Kalevala. His brother agrees to build the mill and, once in Pohjola, claims the Maid for his own. She refuses to go and he returns empty-handed—but not for long. After a friend, Lemminkainen, dies trying to win her hand (though the lad's mother brings him back to life with music), Ilmarin returns to Pohjola, woos the Maid and makes her his, and brings her home.

But the Maid is a heartless creature who angers everyone. Before long, a shepherd to whom she's fed bread laced with rock transforms his cattle into ferocious beasts that kill her. Feeling cheated by Louhi, Wainamoinen, Ilmarin, and Lemminkainen decide to go to Pohjola and annex it to Kalevala. En route, Wainamoinen slays a huge pike, makes a harp from its bones, and plays music so beautiful all who hear it weep, including himself. (His tears strike the sea and become the first pearls.) The harp allows them to conquer Pohjola bloodlessly, though the vengeful Louhi turns herself into an eagle and steals the sun, moon, and fire from Kalevala. This not only hurts the Finns, it annoys the supreme deity, Jumala Ukko, who sends lightning to Earth so he can see what's transpiring. Wainamoinen is able to capture a bolt and, though horribly burned, imprisons it in an elm tree for later use by humankind. Subsequently, the hero turns himself into a pike, swims to Louhi's hideout, kills her sons in battle, and rescues the sun and moon from a nest of vipers.

In his old age, Wainamoinen realizes he must pass the mantle to a younger adventurer. He looks around and sees the young maiden Marjatta, who had become pregnant from eating a cranberry. Her mother throws her from the house and she gives birth to a son in a stable. Wainamoinen senses the enormous power the child will one day have and, building himself a copper boat, sails westward, singing songs, never to return.

Comment: *Kalevala* is the Finnish national epic, the over 30,000 verses transmitted orally until Finnish philologist Elias Lonnrott published them in two volumes (1835 and 1849). Its unrhymed, alliterative, trochaic verse inspired the form for Henry Wadsworth Longfellow's later HIAWATHA.

WARLORD (C)

First Appearance: *First Issue Special* #8, 1976, DC Comics.

Biography: A native of Wyoming and a graduate of Thomas Jefferson Jr. High School, Travis Morgan becomes a lieutenant colonel in the U.S. Air Force. After losing his wife, childhood sweetheart Rachel, in a car accident, he sends his daughter, Jennifer, to live with her aunt Marie and goes to fight in Vietnam. Upon learning that a biological warfare facility may have been established over Soviet territory, air force intelligence sends him to investigate; his plane is damaged and, leaking fuel, Morgan bails out over the Yukon. There he passes through a dimensional barrier that brings him to the fantastic realm of Skartaris, an underground land of warriors, monsters, and wizardry. One of his first acts is to rescue Tara, princess of Shamballah, from a dinosaur, after which he learns swordsmanship and becomes a great hero known as the Warlord. Eventually he marries Tara and they have a son, Joshua.

Morgan returns, on occasion, to our world. During one such visit, he meets Professor George Lakely, who informs the now-teenage Jennifer that her father is alive. She joins a boat expedition to Skartaris, but she is the only one who survives a wreck. Her memory gone, she eventually falls in with the sorceress Ashiya, who teaches her the black arts. In time, after learning who she is, Jennifer turns on her tutor and becomes a benevolent witch who often assists her father.

The goateed, mustachioed hero is equally skilled with his broadsword and pistol.

Comment: Creator Mike Grell was originally going to call the series "Savage Empire." After the Warlord's appearance in *First Issue Special,* the Edgar Rice Burroughs/H. Rider Haggard-inspired character was given his own magazine. Despite its derivative nature, *The Warlord* lasted a remarkable 133 issues, in addition to various annuals and pocket-size specials. His origin was retold in *Secret Origins* #16.

THE WILD BUNCH (C)

First Appearance: *Hell Rider* #1, 1971, Skywald Publishing.

Biography: Based in Oakland, California, the Wild Bunch motorcycle gang lives outside the law until they meet Brick Reese. A lawyer and a black belt, Reese beats up their leader Animal at a bar and shows them the error of their ways. When Reese takes an experimental serum and becomes the superhero Hell Rider, the Wild Bunch help him in his war against drug dealers and other lowlife.

In addition to the powerful Animal, the Wild Bunch consists of Deke, an ex-college basketball star; small but cagy Slinker; pretty-boy mechanic Curly; and beautiful, two-fisted Ruby. The groups weapons are chains and switchblades. Ruby's boyfriend is police Lieutenant Ted Lawson, who works closely with the Bunch.

Comment: The adventures were written by Gary Friedrich and drawn by various artists. *Hell Rider* expired after the second issue; a third Wild Bunch story was drawn but never published.

WILLIAM TELL (F, S, O, C, TV)

First Appearance: Swiss folklore, circa A.D. 1390.
Biography: In the 14th century, Switzerland was

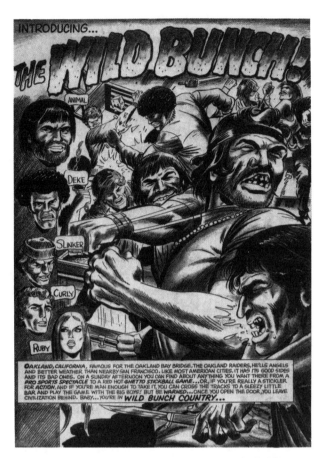

The *Wild Bunch* in a typical situation. © Skywald Publications.

comprised of 13 allied cantons (states) that were more or less in a state of perpetual war against invaders from Austria. According to legend, one of the most ruthless of the would-be conquerors was Gessler, appointed by Albert of Austria as governor of several of the eastern cantons.

William Tell, a hunter and legendary bowman, refuses to salute the visiting governor (or his cap, depending on the tale). For his impertinence, he's told to use his bow to shoot an apple from the head of his son Walter. He does so, and as he embraces his son an arrow falls from his robe. When Gessler asks what this is for, Tell answers, "To shoot you had I failed in the task imposed on me." Outraged, Gessler has Tell arrested and imprisoned in a snake-filled dungeon. But the peasants rally and rescue him; Tell delays his escape long enough to find and shoot Gessler, freeing Switzerland.

Comment: In truth, the Swiss defeated the Austrians not through the death of a governor, but in three great battles: Morgarten (1315), Sempach (1386), and Nafels (1388). It was these last two in which the historical Tell apparently took part. Though he probably did roughly what the legends say, nothing is known about his life.

On stage, the character was the hero of Friedrich von Schiller's play *Wilhelm Tell* (1804). Composer Gioacchino Rossini adapted the play—with librettists Victor Joseph Etienne de Jouy and Hippolyte Louis Florent Bis—as his last opera, *William Tell (Guillaume Tell),* composed for the Paris Opera and first performed in 1829. Both stories center around Tell's battle against Governor Gessler, whose son Arnold sides with Tell. (The famous, final section of the Overture was used as the theme music for the radio and TV series *The Lone Ranger.*)

In comic books, *Classics Illustrated* adapted the folk story in 1952, issue #101.

In 1953 Errol Flynn began shooting an epic based on the life of Tell, with himself in the title role. Roughly one-third of the film was completed before the money ran out.

On TV, the half-hour series *The Adventures of William Tell* was syndicated in 1958. Filmed in Switzerland, it starred Conrad Phillips as Tell, Jennifer Jayne as wife Hedda, Richard Rogers as Walter, and Willoughby Goddard as the vile Gessler.

THE WYOMING KID (C)

First Appearance: *Western Comics* #1, 1948, DC Comics.

Biography: When his father, a sheepherder, is murdered, young Bill Polk sets out to find the man who did it. His journey carries him to Texas where, to earn a living, he joins a rodeo, becomes an army scout, and turns to prospecting, all the while searching for his father's killer. When he nabs a trio of outlaws, he decides to work as a roving deputy, allying himself with whatever sheriff will have him, using the name Johnny Jones—or, more dramatically, the Wyoming Kid. For a while he settles down and becomes the sheriff of Saddlehorn. When railroad tycoon Randolph Hughes gives him a fortune to uphold the law, Polk picks up roots again and continues to fight crime as he seeks his father's killer.

He never finds him but, astride his steed Racer, he does manage to clean up the West single-handedly. His attire is a red shirt, yellow bandana, blue or tan trousers, and a big, yellow hat.

Comment: The Kid lasted as long as the title did, to #85.

X-9 (CS, L, MP)

First Appearance: *Secret Agent X-9,* January 22, 1934, King Features Syndicate.

Biography: X-9 is a G-Man whose specialty is infiltrating criminal organizations, sniffing out kidnapers, racketeers, extortionists, gamblers, and other lowlife types. After eight years, it's revealed that the character's name is Phil Corrigan; he marries Wilda in the 1940s and they have a daughter, Philda (though she's downplayed in later episodes).

Comment: The character was created by famed author Dashiel Hammett and drawn by artist Alex Raymond, both of whom left it in 1935. They were replaced by diverse hands over the years, most notably by artist Austin Briggs (1939–40) and artist Al Williamson and writer Archie Goodwin (1967–80), with the strip renamed *Secret Agent Corrigan.* The strip is still running, though the character now works on an international stage fighting spies as well as criminals.

Two Big Little Books were based on the comic strip: *Secret Agent X-9* (1936) and *Secret Agent X-9 and the Mad Assassin* (1938). The strip also inspired a pair of movie serials, both called *Secret Agent X-9.* In the first, a 12-chapter adventure released in 1937 and starring Scott Kolk, the agent must find stolen Belgravian crown jewels (Lon Chaney, Jr., had a small part). In the second, a 13-chapter adventure released in 1945 and starring Lloyd Bridges, the hero must prevent Japan's black Dragon Intelligence Service from obtaining a U.S. formula for synthetic fuel.

Y

YANCY DERRINGER (TV)

First Appearance: *Yancy Derringer,* October 1958, CBS.

Biography: Based in New Orleans after the Civil War, Yancy Derringer is a former Confederate officer, now an agent working for John Colton, the city's civil administrator. Dressed to kill (literally) with a small gun in his hat, the foppish Yancy works to keep the peace and capture crooks, smugglers, killers, and other lawbreakers. His constant companion is the Pawnee Pahoo Ka-Ta-Wah ("Wolf Who Stands in Water"), who carries a knife in *his* headdress. When Yancy isn't upholding the law, he's playing cards or courting the ladies.

Comment: The half-hour series aired until September 1959 and starred former movie stunt actor (and future movie Tarzan) Jock Mahoney. X. Brands co-starred as Pahoo and Kevin Hagen was Colton. *Yancy Derringer* was created by Mary Loos and Richard Sale.

YANG (C)

First Appearance: *Yang* #1, 1973, Charlton Comics.

Biography: In China of the 19th century, young Yang, a master of Kung Fu, swears an oath to his dying father—that he will live by the philosophy of Yin and Yang. "Yin is darkness and evil and cold," says the elderly man, "Yang is light and good and warmth! Be Yang to all men." Though Yang is taken to America on a slave ship, he gains his freedom on these shores, and, while making his way to San Francisco and his cousin Sun, he battles hostile Indians, religious fanatics, and other would-be oppressors, most notably the "Queen of Evil" Yin Li and her ferocious dragons, who dwell in the Valley of 1000 Deaths.

Yang wears blue trousers, brown boots, and a green robe with the Yin and Yang symbol over the heart.

Comment: There were 20 issues of *Yang* (the last three were reprints) and eight issues of *The House of Yang* (the last two were reprints).

THE YANKEE RANGERS (CS)

First Appearance: "The Yankee Rangers," June 1942, King Features.

Biography: The Yankee Rangers are based in England

Yang stops an enemy. Art by Warren Sattler. © Charlton Comics.

during the early days of America's involvement in World War II. The Rangers are trained hard by Colonel Force, who teaches them about guns and grenades as well as how to use "a razor-sharp trench knife against a ruthless enemy . . . employ jiu jitsu and guerrilla warfare—go for days without food or water and swim long distances with an 80-pound pack on your back." The Rangers' three main heroes are Chunky Tubbs, Rex Rand, and Riff Rafferty who, in their first chronicled mission, infiltrate the Nazi-held town of Dyuksen in the Netherlands. Though they're only supposed to draw a map to the munitions depot there, they end up destroying it.

Comment: The strip was drawn by Alfred Andriola and lasted just six weeks, one of the shortest runs in comic strip history. Nonetheless, it was a hearty war strip that helped to establish Andriola as one of the industry's up-and-coming new talents.

THE YOUNG MASTER (C)

First Appearance: *Young Master* #1, 1987, New Comics Group.

Biography: The Young Master has no name. Born to the Old Master on "a nameless mountain in an isolated range overlooking the Great Bodhisattva Pass," he studies the "family craft . . . the art of killing" from his father. Twice a year the two are visited by the Old Master's younger brothers: From his First Uncle he learns the art of the spear; his Second Uncle teaches him the throwing star; and his Third Uncle tutors him in the sword. At the age of 20—fast and strong enough to catch an arrow in flight—the Young Master is obliged to kill his uncles and father, take the latter's Murasama blade, and set out in service of the Great Lord—specifically, keeping in check the Lord's enemy, Old Man Yagyu and his ninjas. His companion is the blind Princess Yuki, whom he rescues from Yagyu's fortress.

Comment: The character was created by artist Val Mayerik and writer Larry Hama; the literate black-and-white title lasted for nine issues.

THE YOUNG REBELS (TV, L, C)

First Appearance: *The Young Rebels,* September 1970, ABC.

Biography: Based in Chester, Pennsylvania in 1777, the rebels are members of the Yankee Doodle Society. Their self-appointed task: to go behind British lines and sabotage enemy forces. The leader of the team is Jeremy Larkin, son of the mayor of Chester; working with him are his girlfriend, Elizabeth Coates, blacksmith and former slave Isak Poole, and chemist/scientist Henry Abington, who is constantly experimenting with new tactics and weapons. They are frequently aided by the Marquis de Lafayette and his soldiers.

From the left: Henry, Jeremy, Lafayette, and Isak, *The Young Rebels,* in their only comic book appearance. © Columbia Pictures Industries.

Comment: The show was designed to appeal to rebels of the modern day and aired until January 1971. Rick Ely starred as Jeremy, Lou Gossett was Isak, Alex Henteloff was Henry, Hilary Thompson was Elizabeth, and Philippe Forquet was Lafayette. Ace published two *Young Rebels* novels by William Johnston in 1970; Dell published one issue of a *Young Rebels* comic book the following year.

YOUNG WILD WEST (L)

First Appearance: "Young Wild West" by An Old Scout, 1902, *Wild West Weekly.*

Biography: As a baby, the future hero is found by a soldier named West, hidden in grasses beside a burned cabin. Actually named Young Wild West (though his friends just call him Wild), he grows up to be a "handsome, athletic boy" and, when still in his early 20s, strikes gold in the Black Hills. He uses his fortune to buy the Champion Ranch and, with that as his base, turns his attention to fighting outlaws, renegade Indians, blazing fires, mad hermits, and the like wherever he finds them in the post–Civil War West. He is accompanied by his good friends Cheyenne Charlie, a powerful man who is about ten years older than Wild, and Jim Dart, a teenager who can ride, rope, and shoot with aplomb. Charlie's wife, Anna, and Jim's girlfriend, Eloise Gardner, occasionally help out by rustling up grub or delivering messages or parcels. Wild's servant, Hop Wah, frequently helps out as well.

Wild's girlfriend is Arietta Murdock, a small blonde who is an equal partner in many of Wild's adventures, able to ride and shoot with the best of them.

Comment: The character appeared in countless adventures through 1927.

See also BILLY WEST.

Z

ZANGAR (C)

First Appearance: *Jungle Adventures* #1, 1971, Skywald Publishing.

Biography: Red-haired movie star Bob Gordon is in Africa shooting a movie—and communing with the big cats between takes—when the camp is attacked by white men who want to get at the oil located on the movie site. During the fray, the cats are released and Gordon is knocked unconscious. When he wakes, the lions are licking him awake and "saying something that sounds like—*Zangar!*" Deciding they've confused him with "a lion god of some kind," he decides to abandon civilization and live among the animals. After weeks of exercise, the loin-clothed hero arms himself with a knife and bow and arrow, and sets about protecting the weak, humans and animals alike, accompanied by his pet ocelots Dinga and Donga. Whenever he needs to return to civilization to get information, Zangar puts on clothes and poses as Bob Manning.

Comment: This rather unlikely character starred in all three issues of *Jungle Adventures.* The Skywald title also reprinted jungle tales from the 1950s, featuring Taanda, the White Princess of the Jungle, and her male ward Koru; and Jo-Jo, Congo King, a nondescript jungle hero from the late 1940s.

Zangar, his pets Dinga and Donga, and scenes from his life, in the jungle hero's first appearance. © Skywald Publications.

ZONE RIDERS (T, TV, C)

First Appearance: *Spiral Zone,* 1987, Tonka Toys.

Biography: In the year 2007, a renegade scientist named Dr. James Bent hijacks a space shuttle and uses it to drop Zone-producing generators in different sectors of the planet. The net they create is known as the Spiral Zone, an area that turns people into mindless, obedient creatures known as Zoners. Bent controls them all, in his new identity as the Overlord, and seeks to conquer the rest of the earth with the aid of the ruthless Black Widows—Reaper, Razorback, Duchess Dire, Bandit, Rawmeat and Crook.

To try to stop him, a quintet of bold warriors band together as the Zone Riders. Dirk Courage is their field commander, ably assisted by Lieutenant Hiro Taka, Second Lieutenant Max Jones, Sergeant Wolfgang "Tank" Schmidt, and Corporal Katerina Anastasia. (Later, First Lieutenant Benjamin Davis Franklin and Second Lieutenant Ned Tucker join the group.) The heroes are based in a heavily fortified Rocky Mountain headquarters known as Mission Command Central, which is run by General Steven Q. McFarland. From here the heroes travel around the world via fleet

Transport Crafts, which carry the vehicles and weapons they need for particular jobs.

Comment: In addition to the toy line, an animated series went into syndication in September 1987, with 65 half-hour adventures in all. In 1988 DC Comics published four issues of a *Spiral Zone* comic book.

ZUD KAMISH (C)

First Appearance: *Eerie* #119, 1981, Warren Publishing.

Biography: Jewish hero Zudkiel Kamish cuts his adventuring eye teeth as a member of the Cometeers, a unit of the Galactic Reserve and "the damnedest squadron of foolhardy dogooders that ever scorched spaceways." He fights in the Zombie War, rescues the daughter of the Orion Deathlord, thwarts space pirates, sends time vandals back to their own anti-universe, and battles the Hide Hunters of Yhaemo; his exploits earn him the title "Tamer of the Milky Way" as well as the Order of Burnt Flesh. After retiring from military service, he buys the star yacht *Galaxy Dancer* and, with an 18-woman crew and his butler Jeepers, begins flying around the dangerous Far Flung—the frontier of civilized space—escorting precious cargo, solving mysteries, working as a bodyguard, and the like. Despite his busy schedule, he finds time to go to the ten-year Cometeers reunion on Murray's Planet, where he ends up teaching manners to the terrorist robot Brassjacket the Unprogramable.

Zud has had his lungs laminated so he can indulge his fondness for Death Row Cigars; his other trademarks are his safari hat, his Star of David belt buckle, and his twin Star-Colt guns.

Despite his fame and riches, Zud has a lot of enemies: One is his ex-wife Domino, who is constantly after him for more alimony. Another is the assassin Shoka. After the hero throws acid in his face, he rigs a bomb in Zud's home on Saunder's Planet. The blast kills Zud's young son Raz, along with the hero's lover, Stella—who was a member of his crew—and his beloved robot-companion, Sparkgap. Zud is unharmed. After tracking Shoka to the planet Dakos, Zud kills him

Zud Kamish waits for his son at the spaceport. © Warren Publishing.

with a grenade that costs the hero his arms and legs. Unable to continue adventuring, he remains on Dakos and opens Zud's Adult Books.

Comment: The strip was created by writer Jim Stenstrum, who briefly threaded the storyline with that of MAC TAVISH. Art was handled by E.R. Cruz. *Zud Kamish* appeared in *Eerie* until #134.

FURTHER READING

Barbour, Alan J. *Cliffhanger.* Secaucus, N.J.: Citadel Press, 1977.

Battle, Kemp P. *Great American Folklore.* Garden City, N.Y.: Doubleday & Co., 1986.

Bell, John. *Canuck Comics.* England: Matrix Books, 1986.

Benet, William Rose. *The Reader's Encyclopedia, 2nd ed.* New York: Harper & Row, 1965.

Benson, Raymond. *The James Bond Bedside Companion.* New York: Dodd, Mead & Co., 1984.

Botto, Louis. *At This Theatre.* New York: Dodd Mead & Company, 1984.

Brombert, Victor. *The Hero in Literature.* New York: Fawcett Books, 1969.

Brooks, Tim, and Marsh, Earle. *The Complete Directory to Prime Time Network TV Shows 1946–Present, 5th ed.* New York: Ballantine Books, 1992.

Brosnan, John. *James Bond in the Cinema, 2nd ed.* Cranbury, N.J.: A.S. Barnes, 1981.

Bulfinch, Thomas. *Myths of Greece and Rome.* New York: Penguin Books, 1981.

Buston, Frank, and Owen, Bill. *The Big Broadcast 1920–1950.* New York: Avon Books, 1973.

Carpenter, Humphrey, and Prichard, Mari. *The Oxford Companion to Children's Literature.* New York: Oxford University Press, 1984.

Del Rey, Lester. *The World of Science Fiction 1926–1976.* New York: Ballantine Books, 1979.

Dille, Robert C., ed. *The Collected Works of Buck Rogers in the 25th Century.* New York: Chelsea House, 1969.

Drabble, Margaret. ed. *The Oxford Companion to English Literature.* New York: Oxford University Press, 1985.

Estren, Mark James. *A History of Underground Comics.* Berkeley, CAL.: Ronin Publishing Inc., 1987.

Foster, Harold. *Prince Valiant in the Days of King Arthur.* Franklin Square, N.Y.: Nostalgia Press, 1974.

Gould, Chester. *The Celebrated Cases of Dick Tracy, 1931–1951,* ed. Herb Galewitz. New York: Chelsea House, 1970.

Gerani, Gary. *Fantastic Television.* New York: Harmony Books, 1977.

Gerber, Ernst and Mary. *The Photo Journal Guide to Comic Books, Vols. 1 and 2.* : Gerber Publishing Company, 1989.

Gifford, Denis. *The International Book of Comics.* London: Hamlyn Publishing Group Ltd., 1984.

———. *Space Aces!* Green Wood Publishing Company, Ltd., 1992.

———. *Super Duper Supermen!* Westport, CT: Greenwood Publishing Company, Ltd., 1992.

Grossman, Gary. *Saturday Morning TV.* New York: Delacorte Press, 1981.

Hancer, Kevin. *The Paperback Price Guide.* New York: Harmony Books, 1980.

Harmon, Jim. *The Great Radio Heroes.* New York: Ace Books, 1967.

Horn, Maurice. *Comics of the American West.* : Stroeger Publishing, 1977.

———. *Women in the Comics.* New York: Chelsea House Publishers, 1977.

———. *The World Encyclopedia of Comics.* New York: Avon Books, 1976.

Kyle, David. *The Illustrated Book of Science Fiction Ideas & Dreams.* London: Hamlyn Publishing Group Ltd., 1977.

Lang, Andrew. ed. *The Arabian Nights Entertainments.* New York: Schocken Books, 1967.

Lee, Walt. *The Reference Guide to Fantastic Films, Vol. 1, 2, and 3.*

Lord, Glenn. *The Last Celt, A Bio-Bibliography of Robert E. Howard.* New York: Berkley Windhover, 1977.

Lupoff, Richard A. *Edgar Rice Burroughs: Master of Adventure.* New York: Ace Books, 1968.

Marill, Alvin H. *Movies Made for Television.* New York: Da Capo Press, 1980.

McNeil, Alex. *Total Television.* New York: Penguin Books, 1980.

Miller, Don. *The Hollywood Corral.* New York: Popular Library, 1976.

Nicholls, Peter, ed. *The Science Fiction Encyclopedia.* : Dolphin Books, 1979.

Okuda, Michael and Denise. *Star Trek Chronology.* New York: Pocket Books, 1993.

Overstreet, Robert M. *The Overstreet Comic Book Price Guide.* New York: Avon Books, 1993.

Peary, Danny. *Cult Movie Stars.* New York: Fireside Books, 1991.

Pickard, Roy. *Who Played Who in the Movies.* New York: Schocken Books, 1981.

Ransome, Arthur. *Old Peter's Russian Tales.* London: Puffin Books, 1974.

Raymond, Alex. *Flash Gordon in the Planet Mongo.* Franklin Square, N.Y.: Nostalgia Press, 1974.

Resnick, Michael. *Official Guide to the Fantastics.* Orlando, Fla.: House of Collectibles, 1976.

Robinson, Herbert Spencer and Wilson, Knox. *Myths and Legends of All Nations.* Totowa, N.J.: Littlefield, Adams and Co., 1976.

Robinson, Jerry. *The Comics.* New York: Berkley Windhhover, 1974.

Roseman, Mill. *Detectionary.* New York: Overlook Press, 1977.

Russell, Alan K., Selector. *The Rivals of Sherlock Holmes.* Secaucus, N.J.: Castle Books, 1978.

Sampson, Robert. *Yesterday's Faces Volume 1: Glory Figures.* Bowling Green, Ohio: Bowling Green University Popular Press, 1983.

Seymour-Smith, Martin. *Dictionary of Fictional Characters.* Boston: Plays, Inc., 1992.

Standring, Lesley. *The Doctor Who Illustrated A–Z.* London: W.H. Allen & Co., 1985.

Steinbrunner, Chris, and Penzler, Otto. *Encyclopedia of Mystery and Detection.* New York: McGraw-Hill, 1976.

Thomas, James Stuart. *The Big Little Book Price Guide.* Lombard, Ill.: Wallace-Homestead Book Co., 1983.

Weiss, Ken and Goodgold, Ed. *To Be Continued* . . . New York: Crown Publishers, 1972.

Wells III, Stuart W. *The Science Fiction and Heroic Fantasy Author Index.* Duluth, M.N.: Purple Unicorn Books, 1978.

Woolery, George W. *Children's Television: The First Thirty-Five Years, 1946–1981, Part 1: Animated Cartoon Series.* Metuchen, N.J.: Scarecrow Press, 1983.

INDEX

Entries are filed letter-by-letter. **Boldface** headings indicate extensive treatment of a topic. *Italic* locators indicate illustrations and captions.